TRAVELS
IN THE
HIMALAYAN PROVINCES OF HINDUSTAN
AND THE PANJAB;
IN
LADAKH AND KASHMIR;
IN PESHAWAR, KABUL, KUNDUZ,
AND
BOKHARA

FORT and VILLAGE of DANKAR in LADAKH.

TRAVELS

OF THE

HIMALAYAN PROVINCES OF HINDUSTAN AND THE PANJAB

IN

LADAKH AND KASHMIR; IN PESHAWAR, KABUL, KUNDUZ, AND BOKHARA;

BY

MR. WILLIAM MOORCROFT AND MR. GEORGE TREBECK,

FROM 1819 TO 1825

Prepared for the Press, from Original Journals and Correspondence.
By Horace Hayman Wilson, M.A., F.R.S.,

Member of the Royal Asiatic Society, and of the Asiatic Societies of Paris and Calcutta; of the Imperial Society of Naturalists of Moscow; of the Royal Academies of Berlin and Munich, etc. etc.; And Professor of Sanscrit in the University of Oxford.

Two Volumes
Vol. I

GYAN

Published by

GYAN

Gyan Publishing House
5, Ansari Road
Daryaganj, New Delhi-110002
Phone: 011-47034999, 9811692060
E-mail: books@gyanbooks.com

Distribution Network
gyanbooks.com
India, USA, Canada, UK, Australia, France

ISBN : 978-81-212-4144-1 (Set)
ISBN : 978-81-212-4723-8 (HB)
First Published, London, 1841

2nd Impression 2020

Printed at: Gyan Press, Delhi.

Travels in the Himalayan Provinces of Hindustan and the Panjab
in
Ladakh and Kashmir;
In Peshawar, Kabul, Kunduz, and Bokhara;
Author: Mr. William Moorcroft and Mr. George Trebeck

TO

SIR JAMES RIVETT CARNAC, BART.,

CHAIRMAN,

SIR JAMES LAW LUSHINGTON, K.C.B.,

DEPUTY CHAIRMAN,

AND

THE MEMBERS OF THE HONORABLE THE COURT OF DIRECTORS

OF

THE EAST INDIA COMPANY.

GENTLEMEN,

I TAKE the liberty of dedicating the following pages to you as the present representatives of a body to which I am under many and great obligations, and to which I am therefore glad of an opportunity to offer my public acknowledgments.

A like sense of obligation to the Court of Directors collectively, as well as to many of its individual members, was warmly cherished by the principal person engaged in the enterprise here described; and had Mr. Moorcroft survived to have been the narrator of his own travels, I doubt not that he would have availed himself of the same opportunity to have given utterance to similar feelings.

But I am further induced to inscribe these pages to your Honourable Court, by the persuasion, that at no period of its existence as a public body, did it comprise a larger proportion of members competent to take a sound and enlightened view of the true interests of British India and of the countries on its confines; and disposed to encourage every judicious effort of the Company's servants to acquire an accurate knowledge of the nations around them, to establish and maintain a friendly intercourse with whom will not only promote the commercial and political prosperity of Great Britain and her Indian possessions, but may effect the still more important end of teaching to yet semi-barbarous tribes the advantages of industry and civilization.

I have the honour to be,

GENTLEMEN,

Your obliged and obedient Servant,

H. H. WILSON.

London,
14*th September*, 1837.

CONTENTS OF VOL. I.

PART I.

CHAPTER IV.

CHAPTER V.

CHAPTER VI.

PART II.

CHAPTER I.

CHAPTER II.

CHAPTER III.

CHAPTER IV.

CHAPTER V.

CHAPTER VI.

CHAPTER VII.

PREFACE.

THE practical illustration of Geographical Science has at no period been prosecuted in this country with more unremitting diligence than in the present day. Travellers and tourists of all descriptions follow hard upon every change in the social condition or political relations of those countries with which we have long been familiar, whilst those of more adventurous spirit, or more ambitious pretensions, undertake to make known to us the character of man, and the features of nature, in the least frequented and least civilized parts of the earth.

Amidst all this bustle of curiosity and activity of science, it seems strange that Eastern Asia should be comparatively overlooked. Foremost in the march of civilization, and offering a wide and interesting field for investigation, there is no portion of this division of the globe which has been thoroughly explored, whilst there are very considerable tracts of it yet unvisited by any European traveller. Even the British possessions in the East, rich in objects of attraction for every observer, whether of man or nature, and, except in regard to distance, readily accessible to research, yet want a traveller, or a series of travellers, having the leisure as well as the ability to portray with truth and accuracy their natural wealth or social singularities: whilst of the countries upon their confines, to the east and to the north, we know less than we do of the central deserts of Africa. The whole of the intervening country between India and China is a blank; and of that which separates India from Russia, the knowledge which we possess is but in a very slight degree the result of modern European research, and is for the most part either unauthentic or obsolete. The statements of Chinese geographers, or the details to be gleaned from Persian historians and biographers, are calculated only to be a substitute for accuracy, and are preferable alone to utter ignorance; and the travels of Carpini, Rubruquis, Marco Polo, and the Jesuit Missionaries, even if they were more comprehensive and trustworthy than they are, were performed under circumstances not less different from the present in central Asia than in Europe. Such authorities, therefore, are wholly inadequate to the demands of the present age, and, except in a few of the great unalterable landmarks of their several routes, leave, as it were, yet undescribed some of the most interesting countries of the East:

countries which have been sometimes considered as the cradle of civilization, and which we know were, at no very remote date, the prolific source of the fierce and innumerable hordes that, under Jangez and Timur, devastated Asia and filled Europe with alarm.

Some attempts, it is true, have been made of late years to supply the deficiency, especially on the part of Russia, which has an obvious interest in acquiring a correct acquaintance with the districts along her southern frontier, whether for the extension of science, of commerce, of influence, or of power. The whole amount of her efforts we cannot well appreciate, from the very little conversancy that exists in this country with Russian literature. According to a competent authority *, articles relating to northern and central Asia are of daily appearance in the periodical journals of Russia; and we have in the more important travels of Mouravief, Meyendorff, and Timkowski, sufficient proofs of activity and intelligence at work upon either extremity of a long and important line. The commendable advance thus made by Russia from the north should be met by a corresponding movement from the south, and the government of British India, without being actuated by either illiberal jealousy or unworthy apprehensions, ought,

* J. Klaproth.—*Magasin Asiatique.* Prospectus.

both for the diffusion of knowledge and the promotion of its own commercial and political interests, to co-operate with its powerful neighbour for the purpose of dissipating the mist which still envelops the geography of central Asia.

The object, although not very adequately or connectedly pursued, has from time to time received encouragement. The embassy of Mr. Elphinstone to Kabul, in 1808, although for a special purpose, and limited to a particular locality, was the means of introducing us to much new knowledge of countries beyond the Indian Caucasus; and more recently, the travels of Lieut. Burnes, undertaken with the sanction of the Indian government, have completed the line of information from Kabul to Bokhara, and connected it with that obtained by Fraser and Connolly in Khorasan. Lieut. Burnes has also collected particulars of interest beyond the immediate direction of his course, and has furnished us with some insight into the state of the regions between the Hindu Kosh and the Oxus to the frontier posts of Chinese Turkistan.

The most enterprising, and, in a great measure, the most successful efforts to penetrate into central Asia from Hindustan, have, however, been made by, or have originated with, Mr. William Moorcroft; and these were undertaken not only without the encouragement of the government of India, but without their expressed approbation. A cold permission was Mr. Moorcroft's only incitement beyond the stimulus of a speculative mind and an enterprising disposition. His first attempt, which was made by way of Chinese Tartary, has been long the property of geographers, having been published in the twelfth volume of the Asiatic Researches*. In this journey he was the first European to cross the Himalaya, and make his way to the great plain between that and the Kuen-lun chain, the situation of the sources of the Indus and the Setlej, and of the two remarkable lakes of Rávan and Mánasa. Besides the natural difficulties of the way, he had to elude the vigilance of the Nepalese, then masters of the Himalaya, and who were on the eve of that war with the British which transferred the snowy mountains to the latter. Mr. Moorcroft had also to conciliate the Chinese authorities beyond the Himalaya, and in spite of all obstacles, and of sickness, induced by exposure and fatigue, he accomplished his purpose, ascertaining not only the valuable geographical facts alluded to (the situation of the sacred lakes of the Hindus, and the upper course of two important rivers), but the region, also, of the shawl-wool goat, and opening a way for the importation of the wool into Hindustan, and finally into Britain.

* A Journey to Lake Mánasarovara in Undes. *Asiatic Res.* vol. xii. Calcutta, 1816.

Mr. Moorcroft's ulterior object, however, was to penetrate to Turkistan, to the country of a breed of horses which it was his great ambition to domesticate in India. Although obliged to relinquish his purpose on the occasion of his first attempt, he very judiciously paved the way for a future enterprise, by sending, at his own expense, an intelligent native friend, Mir Izzet Ullah, to perform the journey. This gentleman left Delhi in 1812, and proceeded to Kashmir: from thence he went to Lé, in Ladakh, and, crossing that country, travelled to Yarkand, through which he was suffered by the Chinese to pass without question. From Yarkand he journeyed by way of Kashkar, Kokan, and Samarkand, to Bokhara, and returned to India from the last-named city by the route of Balkh, Khulm, Bamian, and Kabul. Of this journey, the most complete detour through the countries specified that is on record, Izzet Ullah kept a Persian journal, a copy of which falling into the hands of the Editor of the present work some years afterwards, was translated by him for one of the periodical journals of Calcutta *, whence it has been re-translated into French and German †. The observations of the Mir, though brief and unpretending, are intelligent, and in the dearth of more

* *Calcutta Quarterly Mag. and Review*, vols. iii. and iv. 1825.

† *Magasin Asiatique.* Juillet, 1826.—Ritter's Geography of Asia, ii.

ample and elaborate materials are of infinite value. The sketch which they afford it was the purpose of the travels now published to complete. That purpose, as will be seen, was but partially effected, and of what was accomplished the narration is imperfect. The unfortunate death of both the travellers, whilst it has delayed the publication of their labours, and thus defrauded them in some instances of that priority to which they have a rightful claim, has had the still more injurious effect of depriving their notes and journals of their own final revision, of that classification and arrangement which they were best qualified to devise, and of those additional developments and details which, like all travellers, they had been compelled to entrust to the tablets of their memory. The circumstances, however, under which the journey was undertaken, and under which an account of it is now offered to the public, will perhaps be best appreciated by connecting them with such imperfect notices as it has been found possible to collect of the travellers themselves.

Mr. William Moorcroft, who is to be regarded as the originator of the journey, and the principal of the enterprize, was a native of Lancashire, and was educated at Liverpool for the profession of a surgeon. Upon the completion of the usual course of study, however, his attention was diverted to a different pursuit, and he finally settled in London

b 2

as a practiser of veterinary surgery. His reasons for the change are thus detailed in a letter written from Kashmir to a friend in London.

"Whilst a pupil of Dr. Lyon, the colleague of Dr. Currie, at the Liverpool Infirmary, the attention of the physicians and surgeons of that institution was suddenly and strongly called to a formidable epidemic disease amongst the horned cattle of a particular district, and was thought to be extending. It was agreed to depute a pupil to examine the disease upon the spot. The choice fell upon me, and in company with a Mr. Wilson, the ablest farmer of the day, I performed my commission. As arising out of this occurrence, it is only necessary to remark, that two gentlemen, of whose judgment and patriotism I had the highest respect, took the trouble of endeavouring to show that if I were to devote myself to the improvement of a degraded profession, closely connected with the interests of agriculture, I might render myself much more useful to the country, than by continuing in one already cultivated by men of the most splendid talents. Convinced by their arguments, but opposed by other friends, and especially by my master, the matter was compromised by a reference to the celebrated John Hunter. After a long conversation with me, Mr. Hunter declared that if he were not advanced in years he himself would on the following day begin to study the profession in question. This declaration was decisive, and I followed the course of study which Mr. Hunter was pleased to indicate."

As there was no veterinary school in London at the time, Mr. Moorcroft went over to the continent and resided for some period in France. On his return he settled in London, where, in conjunction with Mr. Field, he carried on for some years a very prosperous and lucrative business. The nature of the profession, however, involved many occurrences unpleasant to a man of cultivated taste and warm temper, and amidst intercourse with persons of station and respectability, collision with individuals not always possessed of either. Mr. Moorcroft, therefore, became disgusted with his occupation, although he speedily realised a handsome property by it. A great portion of this, however, he lost in some injudicious project for manufacturing cast-iron horse-shoes, and he readily, therefore, accepted an offer from the Court of Directors of the East India Company to go out to Bengal as superintendent of their military stud. He left England in May, 1808, in the same fleet, though in a different ship, with the writer of this notice, who, when he occasionally saw Mr. Moorcroft, during the voyage, as the vessels spoke, or on their touching at Madeira, little anticipated that he should ever become his biographer.

The Company's stud was instituted for the purpose of improving the indifferent breed of horses indigenous in Hindustan, for the special service of their own cavalry. That the object had not been successfully prosecuted is to be inferred from the necessity of obtaining scientific superintendence from England. That it was attained in a very eminent degree within a reasonable period after Mr. Moorcroft's appointment, the observation of persons in India, however little conversant with the subject, could not fail to remark. In the letter above cited, Mr. Moorcroft observes, that at the time he left the stud on his present travels, there was not above one horse diseased for ten that he had found when he took charge of it. This amendment he attributes, amongst other things, to the use of oats as food, the cultivation of which grain he introduced into Hindustan. In order, however, to improve essentially and permanently the cavalry-horse of India, and especially in size and strength, Mr. Moorcroft strenuously urged the introduction of the Turkman, or English, in preference to the Arab horse. His representations were at one time so favourably considered by the authorities in India, that he was on the eve of being permitted to return to England to select a batch of suitable stallions; but the purpose was abandoned, and his thoughts were thenceforward fixed exclusively upon the neighbourhood of Balkh and Bokhara. This was the leading motive of his journey across the Himalaya, and this purpose prompted the second journey, which terminated fatally for his project and himself.

Coupled with the conviction that the native cavalry horse of India could be ameliorated only by an infusion of the bone and blood of the Turkman steed, was an equally strong belief in Mr. Moorcroft's mind of the possibility of establishing a commercial intercourse with the Trans-Himalayan districts, which should be highly advantageous to Great Britain. In some respects the belief was founded on sufficient premises. To the anticipation of an extensive demand for British fabrics, both of hardware and of woollen cloth, from the known absence of all manufacturing skill in the countries of Central Asia, and the necessity of warm clothing imposed by the climate, was added acquaintance with the fact that these very articles, some of continental, and some of British manufacture found their way from Russia across the whole of the intervening regions, even to Afghanistan and the Panjab. To secure a part, if not the whole of this commerce, was an object which Mr. Moorcroft entertained with the ardour and tenacity of his character, for, as he observes of himself, "his obstinacy was almost equal to his enthusiasm," in which, however, for obstinacy his friends would substitute perseverance. Accordingly, having wrung from the government of India a reluctant acquiescence in his journey to Bokhara, for the purpose of procuring horses, he also obtained its permission to carry with him such articles of merchandise as he thought likely to be most in demand, and, provided with this concession, he induced two of the mercantile firms of Calcutta (Messrs. Palmer and Co., and Messrs. Cruttenden and Co.) to entrust to his care a supply of goods to the value of about three thousand pounds. Some of these he sold or exchanged in Kashmir for shawls, and he subsequently added to his stock also about two thousand pounds' worth of coral and pearls. The ultimate proceeds of these articles were to be expended in the purchase of horses, which were, in the first instance, to be offered to the government for sale: such as they disapproved of were to be disposed of through other channels. The principle of the experiment was, no doubt, creditable to Mr. Moorcroft's patriotism, but many disasters, and much delay, eventually the cause, perhaps, of his death, may be ascribed to his incumbering himself with heavy packages, amidst impracticable routes, and amongst people who are little better than organised robbers, and who welcome the stranger merchant to their haunts merely that they may revel on his plunder.

Thus provided, Mr. Moorcroft set off on his journey some time at the end of 1819, accompanied as is described in the following account.

Of his only European companion, Mr. George Trebeck, I have not been able to learn many particulars, nor is it likely that much is to be told, as he was a young man, only on the threshold of the world. His father (Mr. Trebeck), who had been a solicitor in London, settled in the same capacity in Calcutta. He had some difficulties to contend with in his outset, but was gradually overcoming them, and acquiring a respectable business, when he died. One of his sons is still in Calcutta, following the profession of his father. The other, who had a turn for adventure, accompanied Mr. Moorcroft, and was a most invaluable companion. To him the geographical details were intrusted, and, as long as he was able to keep a regular field book, which he did until the party quitted the Panjab, the information he records is minute and accurate, and has been found of the greatest service in the preparation of the map which accompanies the present publication. In addition to his geographical notes he recorded various particulars, which show him to have been an intelligent and lively observer; and that he possessed talent for delineating the objects of art or nature which he encountered, the specimens which illustrate the following pages, and which are but a few out of many similar drawings, sufficiently evince. His share in the literary part of the following account, especially when he was on detached duty, is specified in its proper place. Amongst his many merits, however, there were some, not the least, for which other testimony may be found. Moorcroft always speaks of his young friend as alert, active, cheerful, sanguine, happy under every privation, enduring hardships with fortitude, and meeting peril with resolution; and Lieutenant Burnes remarks, when describing his burial-place at Mazar, "this young man has left a most favourable impression of his good qualities throughout the country which we passed."

The circumstances of the journey are narrated in the following pages up to the arrival of the party at Bokhara, and it is only necessary in this place to advert to some of Mr. Moorcroft's sentiments on occurrences which, in his opinion, materially influenced his movements. The government of India, in permitting him to undertake the journey, refused to grant him any accredited authority or political designation. He engaged in the enterprise at his own risk and expense, and the question of reporting his proceedings through any official channel was left to his own discretion. As he was permitted, however, to receive his allowances as superintendent of the stud, Mr. Moorcroft himself considered that the government had a right to the information which he might collect. In the letter above cited he writes, "If I fall or fail, the Company will receive for my salary only the compensation of such local knowledge as I may have acquired in countries wholly new to Europeans, and which will be found in my journals, deposited for transfer, in case of my death, with Captain Murray;" and, at a subsequent period, in reply to a request from Dr. Abel to possess and publish some of his papers, he writes from Kunduz: "My powers over the papers alluded to are more limited than they might appear and, in explanation, it is to be remarked that the official letters of public servants of the government become, through the act of transmission, the exclusive property of the latter, and it is only with the permission of the supreme authorities that the writers can publish their contents." At the same time he communicated unreservedly, and at great length, with a number of individuals, and addressed several papers to different public bodies, as the Asiatic and Agricultural Societies of Calcutta, and the Board of Agriculture in England, forwarding the latter communications, however, through the government of Bengal and the Court of Directors, and, consequently, with their implied sanction.

Certain it is, however, that the government of India never recognised Mr. Moorcroft in any diplomatic capacity, and his supposed assumption of it occasionally incurred their displeasure. Shortly after the commencement of his route he applied to the Governor General for a letter of introduction to the King of Bokhara, which it was not thought expedient to grant. A letter written on this occasion to a friend at Delhi is so characteristic of the writer, and explanatory of his feelings and his views, that its insertion here may not be thought irrelevant, observing, at the same time, that the tone of this epistle prevails throughout his correspondence during the entire period of his travels.

"*Mountains of Gurhwal, December 27th*, 1819.

"I HAD written to Lord Hastings under cover to you before your dispatch reached me.

"Relying upon your judgment, I conclude that you will have thought it improper to press further a subject on which the government have already decided.

"I am sorely disappointed, and would willingly say, as far as regards alone the public result of the enterprise touching Bockhara, but engaged as is my own reputation in the issue, I cannot but personally and poignantly feel the diminished probability of success arising from the want of the document prayed for.

"It appears that in due time I did not sufficiently appreciate the punctilious character of the King of Bokhara, nor the value of a complimentary letter from the Governor-General.

"So far, then, I have been in error, and may, perhaps, have dearly to pay for the oversight.

"It would be presumptuous to canvass the motives of the refusal, but will not, I trust, be considered disrespectful in me to observe, that whatever impression such event might have made on my mind previously to my journey, it now calls into all possible activity every energy I can employ to deserve success. The merits of the object of this expedition will stand unimpaired even by an unsuccessful result; but a successful result will give me a stronger claim to soundness of view, the more insulated shall have been my industry and perseverance.

"To you I beg to reiterate my grateful thanks for that friendly interest, which, to ensure my personal safety, would, even in this stage, approve the abandonment of the present enterprise.

"You may over-estimate, I may undervalue the personal dangers attending it, and thus we may not come to a similar conclusion; yet I see my course overhung with risks both numerous and formidable.

'It may be urged that the extension of British commerce was not within the scope of my mission, and that as much time as such extension may occupy is so much abstracted from its direct and special object.

"I will freely admit the first part of the position, but not the last, as the countries in which it is proposed to procure horses are not accessible to an European, except as a needy adventurer or as a merchant.

"The former character is absolutely useless in relation to the present object, whilst the latter may subserve the general interests of commerce, and the only mode by which horses are profitably procurable.

"Hence it follows, I presume, that the time employed in prosecuting that form of intercourse through which alone horses are profitably obtainable, is legitimately employed in promoting the special objects of my mission.

"And I hesitate not to acknowledge my satisfaction in finding these two objects so blended, and in being he instrument of attaining them.

"I shall not go further into stud affairs, than to state generally that our *matériel* has, in relation to its end, always been defective; and this deficiency has increased the expense and delayed the expected return of stud operations.

" The Honourable Court of Directors send a few horses of high value, annually, as stallions; the stud furnishes some, and others are purchased.

" Few persons will deny that these altogether are unequal to our wants, and this deficiency gives rise to expedients of supply, expensive and embarrassing to the two objects of improvement and extension.

" The Board, anxious to meet this deficiency, purchase as far as the Calcutta market will furnish such as they think suitable.

" But there is a great difference of opinion as to the kind of horses suitable for the purpose, and hence it sometimes happens that horses thus purchased are not approved when they arrive at the stud.

" For instance, since my leaving the Presidency, an English horse has been purchased and sent up to the stud, at the price of two thousand rupees, which I refused as unfit for our use, when tendered by the owner within a few miles of the stud.

" You must be aware that this state of things is awkward and embarrassing. If I expressed not my disapprobation of horses I considered unsuitable, I should obviously neglect my duty, and when I represent such unsuitableness after purchase, the opinion cannot fail to give umbrage to the party so purchasing.

" Whilst I remain at the stud, my opportunities of purchasing suitable horses is of course very limited.

" What is to be done?

" Is this uncomfortable condition to be continued, or is an effort to be made to place matters on a footing more cordial, co-operative, and efficient?

" The Government have agreed to allow me an opportunity of trying what I can do towards realizing the latter alternative, and my judgment in selection is amenable to public opinion.

" I know full well that the period in which I might have

made this attempt with greater probability of success, with less prospect of danger, has passed by; but I have not to reproach myself through inertness with having neglected the opportunity.

"If I succeed in reaching Ladakh it may be optional to push through the southern end of Chitral, to attempt crossing the Beloot Tagh range, and to reach Khoolm by the valley of Badakshan.

"But the Tibetian side of the pass across this chain may have been obstructed through fear of opening Tibet to the inroads of the Oosbeks. And if a passage were to be effected, I shall have to conciliate the good-will of several petty chiefs before I can reach the state of Meer Quleech Ulee Khan. If I abandon this pass and proceed to Pilpee Sooagh, at the northern extremity of Chitral, I shall find two roads, one leading to Badakshan, the other to Yarkand.

"Of the safety of these roads no sound calculation can be made here, although some of the inconveniences by that of Yarkand are known.

"But at Ladakh information can be had on this point from Yarkand and Kashmir merchants, and perhaps there may be an answer from Meer Quleech Ulee Khan to my letter of inquiry.

"Supposing the Badakshan road to Khoolm, and the Yarkand road to Bokhara, both shut, and these facts ascertained, at Ladakh I shall have to cross Kashmir to Peshawar, and to proceed by Bameean to Khoolm.

"The Khyber pass may be turned by going on the Karuppa road, which Hafiz Mohammed Fazil did, and the natives on this line of route are, comparatively with the Khyberees, quiet and reasonable.

"I shall not trouble you with speculations on political events in Kabul, but shall presume on the practicability of finding this road open in almost all contingencies, though I must pay for safe conduct, and perhaps largely, as the liberality of Mr.

Elphinstone has given the natives high notions of the wealth and munificence of Europeans.

"Disadvantageous as this may be, yet constituting only a question of private expense, I shall willingly meet it according to my limited means. I may be obliged to abandon the attempt by bodily disability, or by insuperable obstacles; but to desert the enterprise through any other cause, would be most culpably to sacrifice the interests of those individuals who, relying upon my judgment, have placed their property at my disposal, more in the hope of promoting the public, than of benefiting their private interest.

"I am bound to add, what I gratefully feel, that Messrs. Palmer and Mackillop were induced also, by private friendship, to risk this property, from it appearing to them the only mode by which could be accomplished that design on which I had been so long and so anxiously intent. And it is equally incumbent on me to observe, as it is creditable to these gentlemen, that when I urged them to accept a proportion of my salary as an insurance of their property against loss by my death or failure, they steadily rejected the pledge.

"If I had no other motives, this liberal conduct alone would compel me to spare no personal exertion or expenditure of my private funds to bring the enterprise to a successful issue.

"But to this must be added a decided conviction, that I shall hereby serve the object of my original mission more directly than in any other mode of employment, and a confident belief that I shall be able to open to British industry countries to which most of its manufactures are hitherto wholly unknown.

"And the distress of the Manchester and Liverpool manufacturers and merchants, brought on partly through stagnation of trade, and partly through investments to India disproportionately in excess to its consumption, would stimulate any man of common feeling to endeavour to relieve it by displaying a new channel, if such should seem within his reach.

"I have, however, heard it stated by men of great general knowledge in Calcutta, that little extension of commerce in the direction I have taken is reasonably to be expected, because the intercourse of the Cis and Trans-Himalayans, though of long standing, has never been so active as to countenance a supposition that there exists much reciprocal demand for the articles of their respective countries. And it is argued that if European merchandise were desirable to the Trans-Himalayans, it would, ere this, in some manner have made its way amongst them. I shall wait upon this opinion with the issue of the present expedition; but it may be not irrelevant, *en attendant*, to observe, that the scanty commerce hitherto carried on from British Hindustan across the Himaleh to Hither Tatary, from Lhassa up to Yarkand, is almost wholly in the hands of Kashmir, and of border traders, whose views, suited to their capitals, proceed in a regular routine, undisturbed by foreign competition, or by the influx of new articles of merchandise.

"These traders have effected a monopoly, and draw their profits from high prices upon a very limited import of foreign manufactures, and from comparatively low prices upon grain and raw materials.

"Favoured by local and political peculiarities, they have hitherto succeeded in keeping up a closed barrier against the extension of commerce except by their own channel.

"And it would seem that they would, even now, be satisfied with their usual trade, rather than let in a foreign trader, though he should tender to them increased profits. At least, I am most strongly impressed with this opinion by collating circumstances, which occurred in my former and present journeys, and the influence of which has had a share in my temporary disappointment. Under this impression I consider the measure most essentially conducive towards speedily establishing a free intercourse betwixt Hindustan and Hither Tatary, to consist in a British agent presenting himself at a trading town in the latter country, with an assortment of British merchandise, and attempting to effect so good an understanding with the ruling authorities, as to render it available as an entrepôt. With these views, I shall *by some route* reach Lé, the capital of Ladakh, and if I succeed in these objects, all other difficulties will gradually be overcome.

"My allowances will certainly be absorbed by my journey, but this loss, accompanied as it will be by privations, fatigues, and dangers, will, in my estimation, be as nothing, if I can accomplish my views.

"If I fall, my country will set a due value on my motives, and at least allow me a claim to disinterested perseverance.

"But to turn back would be voluntarily to invite the indications of scorn, and to load me with feelings which would hurry me to the grave.

"If I fail, I shall lose my time, my property, perchance my reputation, and probably my situation, for an individual in this country has thought proper to address the late Chairman of the Court of Directors, Mr. Reid, in regard to me; and within a few days a letter has reached me from England, from the tenor of which, it may be fairly inferred, that if my journey prove not successful, I may almost to a certainty look to be superseded. So that my private concerns are in a hopeful train, and in case of failure, my devotedness to the interests of my employers, and to the objects of my mission, is likely to be rewarded by loss and disgrace, because my views concerning a subject on *which I ought to be well informed*, differ from those of the persons who have a powerful influence on stud affairs.

"To return *re infectâ*, would even now be fatal to my fortunes, and I must push the adventure to its end.

"Not even the expression of the individual in question, that he does not expect any good from this journey, nor the impression he has given with the worst consequences thence resulting, can shake a resolve founded on principles of duty to my employers, and of justice to myself.

"Once more I fervently thank you for your friendly and honest solicitude for my safety and welfare.

"Pardon me for intruding upon you with an epistle of such

unconscionable length, which had not happened if I had not thought it necessary more particularly to explain the impracticability of my receding from my present engagements."

After traversing the mountains in the manner described in the following account, Mr. Moorcroft and his party arrived safely at Lé by a route on which no European had preceded them, and on his way he first determined the upper parts of the direction and the sources of two of the three great rivers of the Panjab,—the Beyah, Vipása, or Hyphasis, —and the Chandrabhága, or Chinab,—the Acesines, or Abi-sin. A very small portion of this tract, or the southern parts of the hill states of Kahalur, Sukhet, and Kotoch, were crossed by Forster, but in a condition of personal restraint and danger, which left him little leisure for observation. About two centuries earlier (1624) the Jesuit missionary, Andrada, appears to have made his way from Srinagar to the north of the Himalaya into either Ladakh or Rodokh, and in the beginning of the last century (1715) the missionary, Desideri, entered Kashmir by the Pir Panjal pass, and thence proceeded to Lh'assa through Ladakh. Very little useful information, however, was obtained from these journeys, as the accounts published of them are brief, and are chiefly occupied with the personal sufferings of the travellers from the ruggedness of the routes, the inclemency of the weather, and the inhospitality of the people. The journey of Mr. Moorcroft from Joshimath to Srinagar, and thence to Lahore, and his march by way of Kotoch, Kulu, and Lahoul to Lé, as well as the details relating to the principality of Ladakh, are entirely new in the annals of geographical research,—nor has he had any successors. Some excursions into Sukhet and Kulu have been made from the British stations in the Himalaya, and the late Mr. Gerard penetrated by much the same route into Ladakh. His course was there arrested by the local authorities, and he was compelled to return to the British frontier of Bisahar. The notices of his travels which have found their way into various publications are desultory and unconnected, and by no means supersede the labours of his predecessor. They are, however, satisfactory, as they confirm some of the most remarkable particulars in Moorcroft and Trebeck's descriptions of the hill states and Ladakh.

Mr. Moorcroft and his party reached Lé in September, 1820, and remained there for a period of two years, or until September, 1822. Part of this delay was attributable to the negotiations at Yarkand, which at last ended in the refusal of the Chinese authorities to permit his passage through that city, but it was perhaps more protracted than was avoidable, and so it appeared to the Bengal government, which ordered the suspension of his salary during the further prolongation of his absence. It was not in Mr. Moorcroft's nature to attach much value to pecuniary considerations, and the order exercised no influence on his movements. He writes to his friend, Mr. Palmer, on this subject: "Is it intended to punish me for the delay in my mission? I have too high an opinion of the government to suppose they can have been so influenced, and the check, however originating, shall not weigh upon my measures, although, on account of my children, I could wish to avoid encroaching on my past savings: yet even this shall not be exempt, if it be necessary to the completion of my objects. The accumulation of property can never afford such gratification to my mind as the reflection of having been, in some degree, accessary to the benefit of my country, and of this retrospect no human power can deprive me." He was much more sensible of the disapprobation expressed by the government of his interposition in political matters, his becoming the medium of the tender of the allegiance of Ladakh to British authority, and his writing to Ranjit Sinh to expostulate with that chief on his unjustifiable demand of tribute from Lé. He accordingly wrote repeatedly and earnestly to the government, disclaiming all assumption of a diplomatic character, and justifying his conduct upon principles of humanity, complaining, also, not only of the undeserved severity of the reprimand, but of the difficulties and dangers which the notoriety of his disgrace would entail upon his enterprise, its disheartening effects upon his followers, and the probability that it might lead indirectly to his personal destruction. His apprehensions were, perhaps, exaggerated; nor does Ranjit Sinh appear to have been offended by Mr. Moorcroft's interference. No doubt the wily Sikh was well pleased to find that no interposition more weighty than the remonstrances of an unofficial individual stood between him and his destined prey, but he continued, at least, the semblance of countenance to Moorcroft's projects, and at this very time supplied him with matchlocks and bayonets wherewith to arm his followers. The fear of giving offence to Ranjit Sinh no doubt induced the government to reprove Mr. Moorcroft, and to decline the proffered allegiance of Ladakh; but it is much to be regretted that any such needless apprehension should have persuaded them to relinquish so justifiable an opportunity of extending British influence. The grounds on which the allegiance was tendered are explained in the following pages, and, whatever may be thought of the plea which they afforded, it is evident that Ranjit Sinh had not the shadow of a right to claim Ladakh as his own. It was an independent principality, at liberty to seek protection where it chose, and the buckler of the British power might have been warrantably thrown over it, without injury to its own independence, or to the rights of its neighbours. Although the allegiance might have been declined, yet a friendly intercourse might have been established at a very easy rate, and access thus secured to a territory conterminous with our own districts, and conveniently situated between Kashmir and Tibet, as well as forming an advanced post towards the frontiers of Chinese Tartary. Without participating in all Mr. Moorcroft's sanguine views of commercial advantages, there can be no question that a friendly footing in Ladakh would be highly favourable for establishing a beneficial trade with Tartary and Turkistan. Ladakh is now little better than a Sikh province, and, although the rule to which it is subjected is not likely to be permanent, yet a sort of right has been set up by actual occupation, with which at the period of Moorcroft's residence at Lé the question would not have been embarrassed.

Part of the detention at Ladakh was, however, owing to pecuniary difficulties. Unable to dispose of his merchandise at a fair price, the expense of maintaining his party, consisting of forty persons, for so long a period, exhausted Mr. Moorcroft's finances, and he was obliged to negotiate bills upon his agents in Calcutta, through the Resident at Delhi, Sir David Ochterlony. That officer probably did not consider himself authorised to advance money on the bills, at least without reference to Calcutta; some, therefore, he hesitated, some he refused to pay, and considerable delay ensued, which, whilst it subjected Mr. Moorcroft to much anxiety, prevented his departure from Ladakh. This conduct of the chief authority at Delhi he deeply resented, and addressed him a letter, of which some extracts may serve to mark the warmth of his feelings, both of resentment and gratitude:—

"In what way I have merited such pointed contempt and abandonment I am yet to learn; but if I had become obnoxious to you, what had my party done to be involved in the punishment with which I was visited? Or, if you did not feel for them, why did you not bestow a thought on the reputation of the Honourable Company, compromised by not giving sustenance to their servants in a new and foreign country? Thanks be to Heaven it has not been compromised!

"When my days were racked with anxiety,—my nights passed in sleeplessness,—when I saw only a refuge from loss of character in the miserable expedient of selling merchandise at one-third of its value, from a general combination of Kashmiri interest against me,—Providence raised up a friend in a native of Khojand, a trader of Yarkand, whose feelings of respect for British merchants, impressed by accounts related to him in Russia, induced him to advance money to relieve my embarrassment.

"This individual, Mullah Partab Bai, a name

that should be dear to every true-born Briton, did not, with cautious prudence, send my bill to you previously, to ascertain its value (the fate experienced by my draft on Messrs. Palmer), but, with a liberality worthy of even a British merchant, advanced, on the instant, the money I required.

"Thus my embarrassments were relieved at that moment. A second merchant took my bill on you for another sum, and the sacrifice of some of my own property enabled me to furnish subsistence for my party until the money came from you, which did not arrive till November, 1821.

"With little money, and with injured, if not ruined credit, it would have been impracticable for me to have proceeded, and the expedition would have been at an end.

"To observe, in reply, that the twenty thousand rupees *were* forwarded to me is no alleviation of the act, or of the consequences of the dishonour of my bill, for the conclusion of my letter directed and necessitated the transmission of the bill, and the money never was transmitted by you through Murali Dhar, the banker.

"And the slightest reflection on the long time which had elapsed between the date of the draft, and the period when I announced that, up to that moment, no money had arrived, must have shown to you that the unbroken sum of twenty thousand rupees would not have been too much for the exigencies of my journey.

"Again the generous Toork interposed. His friendship would not allow me to drain my nearly exhausted treasury of almost its last rupee, but replaced the ingots of silver I had borrowed, along with the interest and expenses, and gave me cash amounting, in the whole, to above seven thousand rupees, for which he ventured to accept my bill, in the fullest confidence on my honesty and honour.

"Under what feelings, but such as are painfully humiliating to me as a Briton, can I contemplate the contrast between the conduct of my countryman, the Resident at Delhi, and that of a stranger, a Tooranee merchant, who never before had seen an Englishman?

"But his generosity stopped not at the mere point of accommodation; he hoped, by this proof of his own reliance on my integrity, to arrest the clamour of calumny raised against my character, and the effort has been completely successful. Thus, in this country the name and credit of a Briton have not yet been stained."

There is much more of the same tenor in this letter, which is dated from Lé in April, 1822. The high character of Sir D. Ochterlony must acquit him of all intention to throw difficulties in Moorcroft's way, but he, perhaps, did not sufficiently consider the predicament in which the travellers were placed, nor attach much importance to the failure of the enterprise. Moorcroft himself observes, on more than one occasion, that he was accused of pursuing shadows; and the prevailing opinion in India was, that he had embarked in an undertaking from which little, except the gratification of his own taste for a wandering life, was to be expected to result. The opinion was, in a great degree, unjust, and was probably provoked by Moorcroft's exaggerated representations of the benefits to be derived from his journey, not to the geography of the new regions which he was to traverse, but to the commerce of India, and even of Great Britain.

After quitting Lé our travellers proceeded to the capital of Kashmir, by the route which was, most probably, that of Desideri, and which was followed by Mir Izzet Ullah from Kashmir to Lé. The party resided at the city of Kashmir about ten months, and collected much additional information regarding the geography and statistics of the province, and particularly respecting the manufacture of shawls. It was not quite untrodden ground. Forster visited Kashmir in 1783, and Berniers' account of the country is well known. There are also many particulars recorded in the Ayin Akberi of Abulfazl, translated by Mr. Gladwin. Lalla Rookh has also contributed to make Kashmir known, somewhat too favourably, to English readers. There was, however, an abundant harvest left for observers, and a very fair crop was gleaned by Messrs. Moorcroft and Trebeck. Since their visit Kashmir has seen several Europeans. The letters of M. Jacquemont contain but few particulars; but his journals, publishing by the French government, will, no doubt, enter more into detail, especially with regard to the natural history of the country. Baron Hügel and M. Vigne have also travelled recently in Kashmir. The former has communicated some of his observations to the Royal Geographical Society, and is about to publish an account of his travels. M. Vigne has not, as far as I am aware, yet returned to Europe.

Mr. Moorcroft quitted Kashmir finally by the Pir Panjal mountains, and descended by a route new to European travellers to the Panjab. Following the direction to Peshawar and Kabul, he came upon the line pursued by Mr. Elphinstone and the embassy to Kabul. At Kabul he was entangled in the political contests which divided the ruling family to an extent that exceeded prudence, but which was, in some degree, unavoidable, as he had travelled under the especial protection of one of the parties. From the moment of his crossing the Indus his merchandise and other valuables, which had previously caused him some embarrassment, became a serious incumbrance. Exaggerated reports of its nature and value were scarcely necessary to excite the cupidity of the needy and unprincipled adventurers amongst whom he was now committed, and he was not suffered to part from them without having been obliged to pay for his protection. He was fleeced, however, without rudeness, and under the affectation of friendship, and the money extracted from him was acknowledged as a loan, although, in all probability, it has never been repaid. The full and authentic work of Mr. Elphinstone, and at a later date the visit of Lieutenant Burnes to Peshawar and Kabul, leave to this part of Mr. Moorcroft's journey comparatively little that is now novel.

The route from Kabul to Bokhara was, at the time when it was travelled by Mr. Moorcroft, new to European investigation. Goez, who travelled from Kabul to Kashgar, and thence to China, in 1603, passed over a portion of it, but it is difficult to identify all the places which he names, and his account is concise and imperfect. Mir Izzet Ullah, on his way back to India, came by the same road, and since Moorcroft's death it has been traversed and fully described by Lieutenant Burnes. Bokhara itself has also been ably illustrated by the same traveller, as well as by Baron Meyendorff. The chief interest of this portion of Moorcroft's travels now, therefore, arises from his personal adventures, his detention and plunder by the unprincipled chief of Kunduz, and his death and that of his companions on their return. The misfortunes which he encountered, and the final failure of the enterprise may, no doubt, be justly ascribed to the delay in the commencement of his journey; for had he visited Turkistan a year sooner he would have found the chief of Khulm, Mir Khalich Ali Khan, by whom he had been invited into the country, alive, and he would, no doubt, have given him the friendly reception which he promised, as Khalich Ali was one of the few Uzbek chiefs capable of rational views of his own interest and of that of his country, and disposed to protect and encourage the resort of merchants to his principality. His death, and the dissensions which ensued amongst his sons, transferred the ascendancy to Murad Beg, a Tartar of activity and ambition, but a barbarian and a robber.

Mr. Moorcroft remained at Bokhara nearly five months, but the notes which he has left of his residence are so very desultory and imperfect, and so much superseded by subsequent publications, that I have thought it advisable to close the account of the journey with his arrival at that city. He was received by the King with as much kindness as could be expected from Mir Hyder, a selfish, sensual, and narrow-minded bigot, and, after various difficulties, arising from the meanness and cupidity, chiefly, of the monarch himself, disposed of part of his goods, and effected the purchase of a number of valuable horses, with which he purposed to return to Hindustan. After crossing the Oxus on his way back, about the 4th or 5th of August, 1825, Mr. Moorcroft determined to deviate from the road, in order to go to Maimana, where he understood it was likely that he should be able to make important additions to his stock of horses. "Before I quit Turkistan," he writes from Bokhara, "I mean to penetrate into that tract which contains, probably, the best horses in Asia, but with which all intercourse has been suspended during the last five years. The experiment is full of hazard, but *le jeu vaut bien la chandelle.*" His life fell a sacrifice to his zeal. At Andhko, where he spent some days in effecting purchases, he was taken ill with fever, and died.

Of the particular circumstances of his death there is no satisfactory account, as he had quitted his party and was attended by a few servants only, and a son of Wazir Ahmed, a pirzada, or Mohammedan of a religious character, who had replaced Mir Izzet Ullah as his native secretary and interpreter. It was reported that he had been poisoned; but there is no reason to believe that this was the case, although he had fallen amongst robbers, who seized upon his property, and put his followers into confinement. Such was the luckless fate of an individual who, whatever may be thought of his prudence or judgment, must ever stand high amongst travellers for his irrepressible ardour, his cheerful endurance, his inflexible perseverance in the prosecution of his objects, and his disinterested zeal for the credit and prosperity of his country.

The liberation of Mr. Moorcroft's servants having been with some difficulty obtained by the efforts of the son of the pirzada, they conveyed their master's body to Balkh, where it was buried. Here another loss was sustained in Mr. Guthrie, a native of India, who had been attached to the expedition as a medical assistant, and who seems to have sustained his share of peril and fatigue with the same spirit that animated his superiors. Mr. Trebeck, now left alone, moved on to Mazar, but was there, after some interval, seized with fever, and, after a short illness, followed his companions to the grave.

Deprived of a leader, the other members of the party dispersed, and the property being left without a responsible owner, was seized upon by Ata Khan, the mutawali or manager of the holy shrine at Mazar. The son of Wazir Ahmed managed, however, to secure a few horses, some of the property, and most of the papers of Mr. Moorcroft, and with these effected his return to Kabul, where his arrival was announced to Mr. Charles Trebeck by Gurudas Sinh, a banker of Kabul, from whose report the circumstances attending the death of the travellers, as here particularised, are derived. The accounts collected by Lieut. Burnes on the spot are somewhat different.*

The difference is not very material; the parties evidently fell a sacrifice to the insalubrity of the

* "The caravan assembled outside the city, near to another melancholy spot, the grave of poor Moorcroft, which we were conducted to see. Mr. Guthrie lies by his side. It was a bright moonlight night, but we had some difficulty in finding the spot. At last, under a mud-wall which had been purposely thrown over, our eyes were directed to it. The bigoted people of Balkh refused permission to the travellers' being interred in their burial-ground, and only sanctioned it near the city, upon condition of its being concealed, lest any Mohammedan might mistake it for a tomb of one of the true believers, and offer up a blessing as he passed by it. The corpse of Moorcroft was brought from Andhkoh, where he perished at a distance from his party. He was attended by a few followers, all of whom were plundered by the people. If he died a natural death, I do not think he sunk without exciting suspicion; he was unaccompanied by any of his European associates, or confidential servants, and brought back lifeless on a camel, after a short absence of eight days. Mr. Trebeck's health did not admit of his examining the body."—*Burnes' Travels*, i. 243.

"Mazar is the place where Mr. Trebeck, the last of Moorcroft's unfortunate party, expired. One of our companions, a Hajee, attended him on his death-bed, and conducted us to the spot where he is laid, which is in a small burying-ground westward of the town, under a mulberry-tree. After burying his two European fellow-travellers, he sunk at an early age, after four months' suffering, in a far distant country, without a friend, without assistance, and without consolation. The whole of his property was either embezzled by a priest who accompanied the party, or confiscated by the *holy men* of the sanctuary, who yet retain it."—*Ibid.*, 234.

climate, exercising a particularly noxious influence on constitutions which had been exposed to extreme vicissitudes of temperature, and to extraordinary privation, anxiety, and fatigue. The fatality was not even limited to the three Christian principals, for Mir Izzet Ullah, who had quitted the party at Kunduz, died in the course of the following year at Kabul. They had all very probably imbibed the germ of death at Kunduz, the unhealthiness of which place is notorious, and thus fell ultimately victims to the rapacity of Murad Beg.

It now only remains to give some account of the circumstances under which, after so considerable an interval, the publication of the travels of Messrs. Moorcroft and Trebeck has taken place. As intimated in Mr. Moorcroft's letters already quoted, and in many other parts of his correspondence, to which it is unnecessary to refer, he himself always considered his papers to be the property of the Bengal government. Accordingly on his death, in addition to such letters and reports as he had previously addressed to the secretaries of the government, or through them to different public bodies in India or in England, a considerable mass of journals and letters was forwarded from Captain Murray, with whom, as mentioned above, they had been deposited. Some hesitation at first occurred as to their appropriation, the payment of Mr. Moorcroft's salary having been suspended; but as the government finally authorized its discharge, the papers became their property. They were handed over to the Asiatic Society of Calcutta, which had naturally been interested in Mr. Moorcroft's proceedings, and had been in occasional communication with him. This took place shortly before the Editor's quitting India. At the time of his departure he offered to take charge of the papers to England, where it was thought they might be put into the hands of some person competent to fit them for public perusal, and in consequence of this offer they were subsequently forwarded to him through Capt. Burnes, and conveyed by that officer to England. Upon inspection it was found that the documents brought home consisted of a dozen volumes of journals kept with some regularity, eight volumes of letter-books intermixed with miscellaneous notes and journals, Mr. Trebeck's field-books, and a variety of loose papers. The regular journals extended only to the arrival of the party at Lé, and the miscellaneous papers to the departure of the travellers from Kashmir. The materials were therefore incomplete, and they were, as Mr. Moorcroft himself terms them in one of his letters, *rudis indigestaque moles*. "My journal," he says in another place, "if exhibited to the public, will not appear in its present shape. If even digested by myself it will be cut down so as merely to represent facts and observations connected with my journey." To say the truth, Mr. Moorcroft's writings were so voluminous, so unmethodical, and so discursive, that the chance of meeting with any person willing to undergo the labour of examining them, and reducing them to a moderate compass and methodized order, was considered by persons most competent to judge, exceedingly remote. In order, therefore, to secure the publication, it was necessary for the present Editor to undertake the task, for the performance of which he had at least the advantage of some experience, having occasionally digested some of Mr. Moorcroft's rambling epistles for the public press of Calcutta, and the use of the Asiatic Society.

Still, however, a difficulty remained in the absence of all notices of the concluding portion of the journey, the want of which, it was thought, would give them an artificial value beyond their real worth, and consequently depreciate such portion as might be published. On the death of the late Mr. Fraser, of Delhi, however, it appeared that he had succeeded in recovering the missing documents, the journals, and notes of both travellers, up to the period of their departure from Bokhara. These were obtained from his executors, and sent home in the course of last year. Besides a volume of Mr. Trebeck's, they consisted of seven volumes of notes and journals thrown together without much regard to compression or arrangement, and of a variety of miscellaneous fragments. They probably still leave some deficiencies, but they enabled me to conduct the narrative to its legitimate close, and to select the additional points of interest which they afforded.

The specification I have thus given, and the peculiarities of style to which I have alluded, may convey some notion of the trouble I have taken. I have, in fact, been obliged to re-write almost the whole, and must therefore be held responsible for the greater part of the composition. I have been compelled to compress unmercifully; but I have endeavoured to leave out nothing that appeared useful or interesting, and have attempted to narrate with fidelity the views entertained, or the incidents recorded by my originals. It is possible, however, that some details which are of value may have escaped me, scattered as they are through so many sheets of paper; and it may be satisfactory, therefore, to know, that the manuscripts are available, as they are deposited in the library at the India-House. Of my own fitness for the task the public will best judge; but it has been with much satisfaction to myself that, since engaging in the work, I have learned the sentiments of the individual most interested in the question. I have referred above to a letter written by Mr. Moorcroft to Dr. Abel on the subject of publishing his papers, and it has been an adequate compensation for my trouble to find that he looked to my friendship and interest for the guardianship of his reputation, and enjoined his talented correspondent to submit to my examination and judgment whatever he might think fitting to be tendered to the public.

Mr. Moorcroft's character as a traveller will also be best elicited from the perusal of his journals. In many respects he was most eminently qualified, and was not to be surpassed in determination, hardihood, endurance, and spirit of enterprise. His scientific attainments were strictly professional, and he had neither the preparatory training, nor the means to investigate profoundly the mysteries of Nature. Neither was he an oriental scholar or an antiquarian, although he had a practical use of some of the dialects of the East, and took a ready interest in the remains of antiquity which he encountered. His chief objects were on all occasions rural economy and manufactures, as he entertained a notion that much was to be learned in both from the natives of the East, as well as to be communicated to them. So much was he impressed with the capabilities of the countries he visited, and the advantages to be derived from the cultivation of their products, that it was his serious intention to settle, upon his return, in the lower range of the Himalaya, and devote the rest of his life to the occupations of a farmer. With such views and impressions, therefore, much that recommends travels in the present day—liveliness of general description, moving incidents by flood or field, and good-humoured garrulous self-sufficiency are not to be looked for; but if the travels of Moorcroft and Trebeck are not quite so amusing as those of some more modern voyagers, it is to be hoped that they will more than compensate for the deficiency by merits of their own.

NOTE.—The materials of the Map are, first, the field-books of Mr. Trebeck, which I have Mr. John Arrowsmith's authority for stating are minute, careful, and accurate; the measurement is made in paces, but the bearings by compass are noted with great precision, and corrected or confirmed by repeated comparisons. The latitudes of Lé, of Kashmir, and of various intermediate points, were determined by observation, and the height of the barometer and thermometer at the principal elevations set down. Their reduction to feet has been calculated by the Editor upon a comparison with the monthly average heights of the barometer and thermometer at Calcutta. As, however, only one thermometer appears to have been employed, there is no correction for any difference between attached and detached, and the elevations are not to be regarded as more than within a few feet exact. In two or three instances they are confirmed by the measurements of Dr. Gerard.

2nd. Various routes collected with much pains and industry by Mr. Trebeck at Lé, Kashmir, Peshawar, and Kunduz.

3rd. Marches of different days' routes by Mr. Moorcroft when alone, or in company with Mr. Trebeck, especially in the latter part of the journey.

4th. A manuscript map of his own route to Kashmir, liberally placed in Mr. Arrowsmith's hands by Baron Hügel.

5th. A manuscript map, believed to be by Gerard, of his route to Ladakh, belonging to the East India Company.

These, with other manuscript and published authorities, have enabled Mr. Arrowsmith to make many important additions to the geography of the upper part of the Panjab and of the countries north of the Himalaya, on the western extremity of the chain. The principal of these only are inserted in the accompanying map, as the scale of its construction necessarily excludes minuteness of detail ; but they will find a place in a map of more ample dimensions, which Mr. Arrowsmith purposes to publish.

TRAVELS

IN

THE PANJAB, LADAKH, KASHMIR,

&c.

PART I.—JOURNEY TO LADAKH.

CHAPTER I.

Detention at Joshimath—Journey to Srinagar—Trout in the Alakananda—Gold dust—Jhula over the river—Use of horses in mountain journeys—Tiri—Scanty population—Raja Sudarsan Sah—Practice of Barat—Tiger trap—Wolves—Nalapani—Kalanga—Dehra—Cross the Jumna into Sirmor—Kárda dún—Márkanda river—Nahan—Sikh territory—Raipur—Bees—Pinjore—Enclosed garden—Hindur—Reascent of the mountains—Malaun—Kahalur—Bilaspur—Its capital—Mode of crossing the Setlej on skins—Sukhet valley—Raj of Mundi—Progress stopped by Sikh interference—Departure for Lahore.

THE preliminary arrangements for our journey across the Himalaya having been effected, I left Bareilly in the end of October, 1819. The principal persons of my party were Mr. George Trebeck, the son of an old friend, who had volunteered to accompany me, and to render whatever service he might, especially as draughtsman and surveyor; Mr. Guthrie, a native of India, attached to the medical service of the Company; Mir Izzet Ullah, a native gentleman of talent and information, who had preceded me a few years before on the route I purposed to follow; and Ghulam Hyder Khan, a native of Bareilly, a stout soldier, and faithful servant*. I had hoped to have been accompanied by a gentleman eminent as a geologist and mineralogist, and he joined us in the outset of our journey; but his conduct towards the natives was so exceptionable, that I was obliged, at a very early period, to decline his assistance.

Besides our personal baggage, I had with me a quantity of English goods, chiefly cottons, broadcloth, and hardware, to the value of between three and four thousand pounds, belonging, for the most part, to

* Mir Izzet Ullah was sent by Mr. Moorcroft, in 1812, to explore the route to Bokhara, *via* Yarkand. The most interesting part of his journal has been translated and published in the *Calcutta Quarterly Magazine* for 1824. Ghulam Hyder Khan, who accompanied the party to the last, and returned almost alone to India, also kept a journal, of which a considerable portion, translated by Major Hearsay, is published in the *London Asiatic Journal*, 1835.—Ed.

Messrs. Palmer & Co., and Mackillop & Co., of Calcutta, who had agreed to incur the risk, in the hope of creating a demand for British manufactures in the heart of Asia. For the conveyance of our somewhat numerous and bulky packages, a supply of the public elephants and camels was placed at my disposal as far as to the foot of the hills. Amongst the mountains the articles were conveyed chiefly by porters, in procuring whom every facility was afforded me that was within his power by Mr. Traill, the Commissioner of Kamaon. We here also added to our party an escort of twelve Gorkha Sipahis. The expense of the whole devolved upon myself.

It had been my purpose to have crossed the Himalaya by the Niti pass before it was closed by the snows of winter. Our journey was in the first instance commenced rather later than it should have been, owing to delays in the arrival of the goods, but there was still ample time before us. On our arrival at Almora, we were assured by the native Agent, who was charged with procuring porters and cattle for the conveyance of the baggage, that everything should be in readiness for us when we reached Joshimath. We arrived at that place on the 12th of December, but neither porters nor yaks in sufficient numbers were procured until it was announced that the Ghat was no longer passable. It was no doubt difficult to assemble the means of transport, and it was much to be regretted that we were not at least a fortnight earlier at Joshimath. Still, more alacrity, and a less grasping spirit in the persons employed, would probably have secured our passage, as several parties of Bhotiyas came down the pass whilst we were waiting for conveyance; and even as late as the 21st of December a body of Hiuniyas returned by it to their own country*. Knowing how essential it was that no time should be lost, I proposed to leave our baggage, and, with a few followers, attempt to make our way across the pass. The guides, however, refused to accompany me, urging the imminent peril to which we should be exposed, not only from

* Hiun dès, the snow country. In Mr. Moorcroft's journey to Lake Mánas Sarovara, it was termed U'n des, supposed to imply "wool" country; but Hiun, from hima, snow, is the correct denomination.—Ed.

the severity of the cold and the depth of the snow, but the furious whirlwinds which in the winter season prevail amongst the precipices of the Himalaya. It was therefore necessary to abandon the project, and either to remain where we were until the next summer, or adopt a different route for our journey to Ladakh.

I had been induced to prefer the Niti pass as the most direct and practicable line of road, as affording an opportunity of establishing commercial relations with the Hiuniyas and people of Lassa, and as connecting the route to Ladakh with the direction of my former journey to Ghertop. Upon considering, however, the great loss of time which our remaining at Joshimath would involve, I determined to endeavour to obtain the acquiescence of Raja Ranjit Sinh to my proceeding by way of Kulu, and with that intention removed our camp to Srinagar.

The town of Srinagar, the old capital of Garwal, is situated on the left bank of the Alakananda river. It had much declined since it was visited by Captain Hardwicke. The province was conquered by the Gorkhas in 1803, and the capital was about the same time visited by the natural calamities of an earthquake and an inundation. It had not recovered from these disasters at the time of our visit, and more than half the city was in ruins. The palace, a spacious and rather ornamental structure, was erected about three centuries ago, but, being built of a friable stone, had suffered from time as well as accident, and was dilapidated and unoccupied. There were two Hindu temples in the city; but the chief building, and that in best repair, was a Dharm-sálá, a place of accommodation for travellers and pilgrims. The only street in Srinagar was the bazar, about a quarter of a mile in length, broad, and paved. The houses were mostly of stone, with slated and sloping roofs, and were two stories high, the lower story serving for a shop. There seemed to be but little trade; and the only manufactures were of coarse linen and woollen cloths for domestic use*.

* The latest account specifies the number of houses, 562. (*Asiat. Researches*, xvi., 148.) In 1796, when visited by Captain Hardwicke, the bazar was three-fourths of a mile long, and the houses were everywhere else so crowded together, as scarcely to leave room for two persons to pass. (*Asiat. Researches*, vi., 336.)—ED.

The Alakananda produces a species of trout which differs from any variety known in Great Britain. The lines employed in catching it are made here of the fibres of a creeping plant called murwa (*Sanseviera zeylanica*), and are remarkable for fineness and strength. In fishing, a small yellow flower is attached to the loose end of the line, and several nooses of white horse-hair are fastened round it: a leaden weight is passed through the centre, by which the line is sunk. The trout, attracted by the new object thus presented to them, come swimming about it, and being entangled in the snares, are drawn to the surface with great dexterity by the Srinagar fishermen *.

Gold is found in some quantities in the sand of the river, particularly after a heavy fall of snow or rain in the neighbouring mountains. The men chiefly engaged in its extrication are from Nahan. Their apparatus consists of a wooden boat-shaped trough, two shallow trays of wood, a bamboo sieve,

* The fish commonly called by Europeans the mountain trout in these countries appears to belong to a different genus, if it does not constitute a new one. (*Journal of the Asiat. Society of Bengal, January*, 1835.)—Ed.

half a gourd, a little quicksilver, some pieces of skin, and scales and weights. The trough is four feet long, eighteen inches broad, and as many deep, with a hole near the bottom at one extremity. It is placed on the river edge, with the end in which the hole is, somewhat depressed. The sieve is formed of straight pieces of split bamboo, laid side by side, and is laid across the trough. One of the two persons employed in the operation spreads a trayful of sand upon the sieve, and the other, turning up its edge so as to prevent any of the sand from being carried off, pours upon it a gourd full of water. This he repeats until the water having the finer particles of the sand in suspension, filters through the interstices of the sieve, and leaves the stones and pebbles and coarser substances on the surface. As a sufficient quantity of these washings accumulates in the bottom of the trough, the water drains off through the hole in its lower extremity, and the mud which is left is then again washed for the gold. For this purpose it is taken up in the wooden trays and fresh water poured upon it: the trays are then turned round by the hand, and the coarser and lighter portions separated and removed from the heavier and finer, until the largest grains of gold become visible, and can be extracted, when they are wrapped up in the pieces of skin. In order to recover the finer particles of the metal, the remaining portion of the sand is triturated with the quicksilver, and that again is driven off by heat. The operation is not a source of great profit, as the washers gain, on an average, no more than four rupees a month. The gold, after fusion into a globule, is sold at the rate of six ratis weight for a Farokhabad rupee, or one tola of twelve mashas (about one hundred and seventy-three grains) for sixteen rupees. There were not above fifteen individuals engaged in this business when I was at Srinagar, but under proper encouragement it might afford a profitable occupation to hundreds*.

We left Srinagar on the 4th of February, a little before noon, and at some distance

* It probably afterwards ceased altogether, for Mr. Traill, in his statistical account of Kamaon (*Asiat. Res.* xvi. 157) states the only minerals found in the province are the coarse metals, iron, copper, and lead. Gold dust is brought from Hiundes (*Asiat. Res.* xvii. 43).—Ed.

from its western termination crossed the Alakananda by a jhúla, or swinging bridge, of considerable span, and of the construction common in these mountains. The ropes used in its formation are made of a variety of spartum or star-three grass *. The river ran between high rocky banks and was thirty-six feet deep in the middle. After heavy rain it rises as much more, and has been known to attain a total depth of eighty-six feet, rendering it necessary to carry the bridge higher up the face of the mountain. In the channel of the river are enormous blocks of stone, of an entirely different description from the adjacent rocks, and evidently rolled down by the current from a higher eminence amongst the mountains.

The road along the north or right bank of the Alakananda was nothing more than a narrow, rugged, and undulating footpath. At the distance of rather less than two miles it was crossed by the Dundu, a small and shallow rivulet, which rises at Dunsir, about ten

* According to Professor Royle the cordage of this part of the hills is made from a species of sedge (*Eriophorum comosum*), which is most probably here intended.—Ed.

miles distant, in a north-easterly direction. A mile and a half further, the road led through a small town, called Muletha, the lands of which between the town and the river, were industriously cultivated with wheat, sugar-cane, tobacco, and onions, arranged in terraces, and partly enclosed by dry wattled fences. The path then diverged from the river, and followed a more northerly direction along the left bank of the Takoli rivulet, descending to it and crossing it repeatedly until our arrival at Takoli. The whole distance was above twelve miles, and was accomplished by our loaded porters in six hours. The way was for the most part wild and desolate, without partaking of the majestic character of the scenery of the more elevated mountain districts.

Our cattle had started on the 3rd, swimming across the river at Rani-hath, a village on the right bank of the Alakananda, opposite the gate of the palace at Srinagar, in order that they might proceed by a safer though more circuitous route. In the more difficult portions of their journey, porters had been provided to relieve them of their loads, but the grooms, confiding in the experience which they imagined they had acquired, refused to avail themselves of this aid, and consequently a valuable mule perished; his load came in contact with a projecting rock, and he was forced over the edge of the precipice on the other side of him, and killed by the fall. This was the fourth animal I had lost. The horses were killed by accidents, with difficulty avoidable, but the mules perished chiefly through the carelessness of their attendants. If horses are employed in such journeys they should not exceed fourteen hands, and those bred in the hills should be preferred. The mule, however, is a much safer animal, but for the Himalaya, the beast that excels all in caution and security is the jabu, or mule from the Yak of Tartary, and the cow.

February 5.—We left Takoli at 10 A.M., and for some time followed the course of the rivulet, crossing it repeatedly until the path quitted it on the right, and wound up a steep acclivity. From the summit of the ascent there opened the well cultivated valley of Naraini, watered by the Kaonli rivulet, running towards the north-west. We were met by the principal farmer of this demesne, an active and intelligent old man, who in reply to my astonishment at the absence of habitations in a tract of such apparent productiveness, informed me that at no remote period villages were numerous in the neighbourhood, but that the exactions of the Gorkha government had driven the people from their homes, and they were only now beginning slowly to return and resume their agricultural labours. The descent to the village of Deul, near which we halted, was almost precipitous. We encamped on a rising ground, on the left bank of the Kaonli, about a mile from its confluence with the Bilangra, a respectable river that rises in the mountains of Kedar. Our next day's march lay along the course of this river to Tiri.

At Tiri, Sudarsan Sah, the son of the last Raja of Garwal, had taken up his residence. He had been driven from his patrimonial possessions by the Gorkhas, and had sought refuge in the British provinces. After the Nepal war a part of the district of Garwal was restored to the Raja, but Srinagar and the country to the east, were retained by the British Government, in order to preserve unbroken the line of frontier formed conveniently by the Alakananda and Bhagirathi. The retention of the ancient capital of his race is, however, evidently a source of much mortification to the Raja, and it may be doubted if the country would not derive more benefit from his residence there, by attracting population and promoting commerce, than from its continuing in our possession. Tiri is far removed from the principal line of road, and is recommended by no peculiar advantage. At present, indeed, it contains only the house of the Raja, a very humble mansion, and the dwellings of his followers: the assembling population are dispersed in tents over the plain. At the distance of about half a mile from the residence of the Raja, the Bilangra falls into the Bhagirathi.

The country ceded to the Raja of Tiri is bounded on the east by the Mandakini, a river which falls into the Alakananda near Rudraprayag, on the west by the Pergana of Negwa, on the south by the Tapoban mountain, and on the north by Nailang, extending about one hundred miles from east to west, and fifty or sixty from north to south. The whole revenue derivable from this extent is estimated at but sixty thousand rupees, which is wholly disproportionate to the extent of the Raj. A great portion of the territory, however, must ever be unproductive, and much of that which might be brought under cultivation is without inhabitants. The scarcity of population in the habitable parts, was ascribed by the Raja to the oppression of the Gorkha government, which not only compelled many of the people to desert their villages, but carried off vast numbers of individuals, especially women and children, to be sold as slaves. At the same time there is no doubt that the population was always kept down by the practice which has immemorially prevailed in many of the mountain districts, of the sale of children by their own parents, in times of scarcity and distress. In some places, I was credibly informed, persons married more wives than they had the means of maintaining, for the purpose of raising money by the sale of their offspring. And although this may not be strictly true, yet the story itself proves that the people of these countries are accustomed to look to the disposal of their children as means of subsistence.

On our approach to Tiri the Raja came to meet us, and accompanied us to our tent. I had several interviews with him during my stay, and found him an active, intelligent man, very desirous to improve the state of his country. According to his assertions an annual tribute was paid by Hiundes to Garwal a very few years back, and was suspended only by the Gorkha conquest. The Raja had, therefore, sent a mission to Choprang to claim its renewal, and had been informed that his demand would be referred to the Court of Pekin. As the Chinese authorities must be aware that the Raja of Garwal is, in some degree, dependent upon the Government of India, the circumstance is likely to inspire some suspicion of the real origin and object of this demand.

I received a visit also from the uncle of the Raja, Pritam Sah, who, at the period of the Gorkha invasion, was taken prisoner, and carried into Nepal. He had no great reason, however, to regret his captivity, as he was kindly treated, and obtained in marriage the daughter of Ram Sah, the uncle and minister of the Nepal prince.

Upon my march from Srinagar I had observed preparations making for the performance of the ceremony called Barat, the hero of which I learned lived at Tiri. On my arrival at that place I sent for him, and was visited by a man of about sixty years of age, named Banchu, accompanied by his two sons, one about thirty, the other about fifteen, both his pupils. Barat is sliding down a rope fastened at one end to a tree or post on some elevated point, and carried obliquely to some fixed object below, to which it is attached. It is intended as a propitiatory rite to Mahadeva, and is performed to avert some impending evil, or to procure the removal of any actual calamity. It was, accordingly, performed by Banchu when the cholera was raging at Almora, and was supposed to have obtained that immunity from the disease which this part of the country actually enjoyed. Banchu brought me the articles employed on these occasions: a rope made of grass, about three inches in diameter, a wooden saddle, and two short sticks. The length of the rope used in his last descent was twelve hundred cubits. The saddle is something like a shallow and short pack-saddle, without pads, and with a very sharp ridge. The ridge was a foot and four inches long, the sides or flaps were eight inches deep, spreading outwards, so that the breadth at the bottom was three inches and a quarter. The saddle was scooped out internally nearly to the ridge to let in the rope, which fitted it exactly The sticks are fastened transversely from flap to flap, so as to give support to the thighs. The performer, bestriding the saddle, throws his body as far back as possible, and descends the rope rapidly by the effect of his own weight, aided by heavy stones fastened to his legs. Persons are stationed underneath with transverse cords to endeavour to catch him should he fall, and others stationed at the foot of the rope seize him and carry him some way forward, so as gradually to diminish the momentum of his descent. The performer is nearly senseless when he reaches the ground, and is some time before he recovers; a collection is made for his benefit, and he derives no slender credit from his patriotic devotion. There does not seem to be much danger in the operation when there is adequate dexterity in the performer, as Banchu had achieved the feat sixteen times without encountering any serious mishap.

Trout are caught in the Bilangra with nooses, on the principle of those made use of at Srinagar, but somewhat differently arranged. The snares are set at night, and eight fish were brought me, as the produce of one set of lines. The fish thus caught are seldom above a pound in weight.

The vicinity of Tiri is infested with tigers, and a kind of trap is used to catch them. This is a small chamber of loose, heavy stones, with a sliding door at one end, and a loop hole at the other. The door is kept raised by a slight moveable projection, and from the upper part of it a rope passes over the roof of the hut, which, entering it by the loop-hole at the other extremity, is tied to the neck of a goat, who is slightly fastened within. The tiger, attracted by his prey, enters the hovel, and attempts to carry off the goat. In the struggle that ensues, the door, shaken by the rope in contact with it, frees itself of the slight impediment opposed to its descent, and, falling down by its own weight, secures the tiger. The animal is then shot through the loop-hole.

There is a road from Tiri to Hiundes across the Himalaya, by way of the Nailang pass, which is said to be practicable for loaded yaks and mules. To Daba it is about a month's journey.

On the 12th of February we resumed our journey, and crossed the Bhagirathi by a swinging bridge. Both banks of the river, as far as the eye could reach, presented the appearance of cultivation. The road, leaving it on the right, proceeded through a pass on the left, and followed the course of a considerable feeder of the Bhagirathi, called the Chakarwara. We crossed large rice grounds, separated by stone fences, and saw several villages under repair, and land breaking up for tillage. Cotton is extensively cultivated in this neighbourhood, and at the village of Manear, where we halted, cotton cloths are manufactured: coarse blankets are also made here, usually about seven feet and a half long, by three feet and a half broad; they sell for a rupee each. There is some traffic with the plains, consisting chiefly of the barter of grain for Lahore salt.

The early part of our next day's journey led us through many fields of young poppy plant, which is cultivated partly for its oil, and partly as a pot-herb. It is eaten both raw, and dressed with butter-milk, salt, and capsicums, and is, in neither form, unpalatable or deleterious. Its use is probably restricted to its young state. As the road ascended it presented a pleasing view of cultivated land, and at a considerable distance the not less gratifying prospect of the Gorkha fortress of Chamwa-gerh in ruins. The mountains are not very high, and consist, near the path at least, of a bluish slate, occasionally coloured with iron. The Banj oak (*Quercus incana?*) is the most common tree, mixed with the Kaiphal (*Myrica sapida*) and the Burans, or crimson Rhododendron. Firs clothe the more lofty summits. Descending the Chamwa pass, at the bottom and on the left, extending southward, is the Nagri Sirai, or valley, through which flows the Heül Ganga, a feeder of the Alakananda. After again ascending a long and steep acclivity, the road passes along a high ridge above the well cultivated vale of Bhomund, in which is the village of Jhuda. It then crosses the hills which confine the valley on the north, and continues through a forest of birch and pine. Amongst the underwood I noticed two varieties of the Sitbharua (*Daphne cannabina*), the creeper from the bark of which paper is made in these countries, one with white and one with purple flowers. Our resting-place was the village of Sukliana, on the right slope of a valley, through which runs the Sungh rivulet. This stream flows into the valley of the Dún, and, after a southerly course of about eighteen kos, falls into the Ganges a little below Rikhi kés.

After proceeding some distance along the Sungh, on the following day we left it, where it was joined by another small stream, the Jura Gadh, and crossed the steep pass of the Jháli Khal, directing our course to the south-west. Here Mir Izzet Ullah, who was in advance, disturbed a pack of wolves in the act of pulling down a large deer, or, to speak more correctly perhaps, a kind of goat, and, having put them to flight, gave the animal its *coup de grace* in the prescribed manner (by cutting its throat), and secured a seasonable supply of venison for the Mohammedans of our party. The wolves kept prowling about us, and were not finally dispersed until several shots had been fired at them. They were of a reddish colour, with long, lank bodies, and bushy tails. The natives call them "khoa," and assert that a pack of them will attack and kill an elephant. The animal, for which we were indebted to them, was a young female, three feet four inches tall at the shoulder, and five feet four inches in length, measured along the neck and sides. The fur of the head and upper part of the body was of a dark-brown colour; that of the belly and legs white. The head was handsome, and surmounted by two cylindrical horns, measuring from base to tip seven inches and a half; through two-thirds of their length they presented alternate rings and depressions, but then became smooth, and terminated in a sharp point. A mane of stiff black hair ran along the whole of the back from the head to the tail; upon the neck the hairs were seven inches long, but on the back not above three inches. Round the whole of the neck was a rough bristly tippet of black hair, about four inches long. The natives gave the animal the name of Saraon. The flesh was dark-coloured and high-flavoured, without being rank *.

Having been delayed by this adventure, my tents had gone forward, and left me and some of my party so much behind that we were unable to overtake them before it grew too dark to proceed. We therefore sought shelter for the night in a buffalo-shed rudely constructed of boughs of trees, which stood near the road, under a projecting point of rock. In the middle of the night we were startled from sleep by a tremendous peal of thunder, and a violent storm came on, which continued with little intermission till day-

* According to Mr. Hodgson (*Jour. Asiat. Society* of Bengal, Sept., 1835) the name Saraon is applied in the Himalaya to the animal which he denominates Antilope Thâr, and of which the description agrees nearly with that of the text.—Ed.

break. The rain soon found its way through the roof of our shed, and rendered our situation sufficiently uncomfortable; but Izzet Ullah and myself congratulated each other that we had escaped the more serious evil of an earthquake or an avalanche. The words were scarcely uttered, when a low, rumbling, and confused noise was heard, and presently the loud rushing and crashing of blocks of stone threatened immediate destruction. The slip, however, soon ceased, and was confined, as it afterwards appeared, to a distance of about fifty yards from us. Next morning at daybreak we set off in a severe shower of hail, and after a fatiguing march of five hours, came to our camp at the conflux of the Bundela and Sunga rivulets, distant only two kos from the new cantonment of Dehra in the Dún, or Gurudwára, as it is sometimes called.

Moving from hence, we proceeded along the ridge of Nala Páni, from which we had a beautiful view of the valley of the Dún. Advancing towards the cantonment, we left the height of Kalanga upon our right, a place rendered memorable by the death of General

Gillespie, and the repulse of two attempts, at different periods, to carry it by storm. Two obelisks mark the spot where so many gallant lives were lost in the attack upon a contemptible fort now rased to the ground. We remained two days at Dehra, and received every attention from Lieutenant Beveridge, who commanded the station in the absence of Captain Young; that officer having gone to Haridwar, to superintend arrangements making for the great mela, or fair, which was shortly to be held there *.

On the 18th we resumed our route, and proceeded on that and the two following days in a direction west by north, over a tract of even ground, with little cultivation and few villages. From the plain of Dehra the road descends to another level, about thirty feet lower, by the pass of Nathuwala, and continues of the same character to the banks of the Jumna. Along the middle of the valley runs a considerable rivulet, the Asan, which receives the waters of several mountain

* In 1827, Captain Mundy speaks of Dehra as an inconsiderable town, but much improved by the exertions of Mr. Shore, the political agent.—*Sketches in India*, i. 184.—Ed.

streams, and pours them into the Jumna. The latter river, at Ráj ghat, where we crossed it, is about a hundred feet broad.

After crossing the Jumna we entered the Raj of Sirmor. Near the left bank, at a place called Pahuta, are the ruins of a stone fort, and in the vicinity are some grass huts, tenanted by persons employed in cutting timber, chiefly sal and sisu, in the forest of Raj-ban which stretches to the foot of the northern hills. The route continued through the Dún or valley of Karda, to the town of the same name. Prior to the Gorkha conquest, the Karda Dún is said to have contained eighty-four populous villages: at present there are not above seven, and those of no great extent*. The valley, however, is considered unhealthy, even when fully cultivated.

From Karda we proceeded along the low ground, crossing a number of small streams, more or less dry, and for a considerable distance along the bed of the chief of them, the

* In 1815, the number of houses in the Karda Dún was 280, containing only 600 inhabitants: the valley was exceedingly unhealthy, especially in the rainy season.—Ed.

Bhata, which runs into the Jumna, below Pahuta. At Kolson we left the line of the river, and ascended an eminence leading to a forest, which forms the western boundary of the Karda Dún. The spot is remarkable for the defeat which the Rohilla prince, Gholam Kader, sustained here from Jagat Prakas, the Raja of Sirmor. The Rohilla had overrun Garwal with little resistance, and counted upon equal success in Sirmor. The Raja, abandoning the valley to the enemy, posted himself at this pass, and after an obstinate conflict, in which the impetuosity of the Rohillas at first nearly overpowered the steady valour of the mountaineers, completely repulsed the assailants, and compelled them to evacuate his territory. This occurred about two years before Gholam Kader made himself master of Delhi. The forest is full of small swamps and springs, the waters of which collect and form the river Markanda, said by some to fall into the Kosila, near Patiala, and by others to spread over the low grounds and disappear *. We encamped at

* In the map it unites with another stream from the mountains,

a ruined village, called Bakri ka bagh, and on the following day marched to Náhan.

The town of Náhan made a figure in the late Nepal campaign, having in front of it the forts of Jamta and Jaitak, which for some time gave employment to the British forces under General Martindell. They were only ceded upon the fall of Maloun to Sir David Ochterlony. A stone obelisk to the memory of Lieutenant Thackeray, killed at Jaitak, in December, 1814, has been erected here by Captain Wilson *. The town is situated in a straggling manner along some eminences: the houses are mostly of stone, and the place has a cleaner and handsomer appearance

and the united river forms the chief branch of the Sursooty, or Saraswati, about fifteen miles west from Tháneswar. The Saraswati was formerly represented in the maps, concurrently with Hindu tradition, as losing itself in the desert. In the map referred to it falls into the Gagar river, and to that stream apparently the disappearance of the waters is ascribed, as it is made to terminate abruptly. This change of name, although authorized by local use, is objectionable, as introducing a nomenclature at variance with ancient Hindu geography, in this instance correct.—ED.

* According to Captain Mundy, a lofty obelisk, on the bank of a spacious tank, in the centre of the town of Náhan, marked the tombs of four British officers, killed during the attack on Jaitak. —ED.

than the generality of Indian cities. It commands beautiful views of the neighbouring mountains and valleys, with a distant prospect of the plain, and the river Markanda winding through them. Náhan is the residence of the Raja of Sirmor, Fateh Prakas, a youth of about fourteen years of age, who has had a tract of territory restored to him, estimated to yield an annual revenue of 40,000 rupees.

On the morning of our departure from Náhan the young Raja brought me a leopard, that had been shot near the town on the preceding day. His attendants asserted that there were both lions and tigers in the adjacent hills, but that the former rarely came down to the lower ranges. We resumed our journey on the 1st of March, in a western and southerly direction, along a rugged and narrow descent. At various parts of the declivity, reservoirs of water for bathing and drinking have been constructed of stone, by charitable individuals. At the foot of the hill is the bed of the Sulani rivulet, a feeder of the Markanda; it was now dry. The road then led up by a short but steep ascent, through a wood and grass jangal to the cultivated lands which belong to the Sikh border village of Dera, a place of no great extent, but protected by a mud fort.

Our next day's march soon took us beyond the cultivated belt that encloses Dera, and passed through much low jangal, intersected by water-courses, now mostly dry. Several villages occurred on either hand. At one of these, named Laha, we saw the people pulling up the white stalks of the lotus (*Nymphæa nelumbo*), which they use as a vegetable. They are cut in pieces and boiled until tender, when they are taken out and squeezed, and put into boiling butter, with some salt, with which they are eaten. In this neighbourhood is much land cultivated for sugar-cane, enclosed by fences of a kind of strong grass, to protect the cane from the deer. We encamped at the village of Buriwala, in a Mango tope. On the following day we proceeded through a country of a similar character to the town of Raipur, the residence of Krishna Sinh, the uncle of the Náhan Raja, and on the next day marched through Ram-gerh, a moderately large town, with a good mud fort, belonging to Hari Sinh. Having preceded my party, I placed myself in a cool spot, under the shade of a large pipal tree, on the branches of which I counted ten swarms of bees, of the kind called Bhaónra. Knowing the irascible temper of this bee, I warned my followers as they came up not to approach the tree. Notwithstanding this injunction and my own vigilance, as I remained in the shade, the bees were disturbed by a boy belonging to my train, and we soon felt the consequences. A bee fixed itself upon my left eyelid, and I had scarcely pulled it off when I was assailed by several others, who all aimed their attacks at my face. I fled through a thick fence into a neighbouring field, where a peasant coming to my aid set fire to some straw, and directed me to sit to leeward of the smoke. The camp soon exhibited a scene of the greatest confusion, and men and beasts were flying in all directions. Some of the fugitives sought shelter in Raipur, but were followed by their unrelenting foes, and the whole town of Raipur was presently in commotion. The scene was irresistibly ludicrous, however much the probability of mischief checked occasionally the disposition to laugh. At length the fury of the bees relaxed, and they retired to their head-quarters, leaving us at peace only at the close of day.

We broke up our camp the next morning (5th March) early, for fear of a fresh inroad. I marched up the pebbly and almost dry but very broad channel of the Gagar, but Mr. Trebeck proceeded by another route, which lay through the town of Mani-majra. The road I followed, after leaving the bed of the river, continued along its left bank. On the end of a low range of clay hills, running from the west, and stopping on the right bank, stands the fort of Chandi, commanding the pass. A little farther onwards was a custom choki, belonging to the Raja of Patiala, where we saw a quantity of pomegranate husks, detained until they had paid duty. They are used here for tanning light hides and in dyeing. The path then crosses the Gagar, and leads to a narrow pass, beyond which Pinjor is situated. Pinjor is at present a small village, but the sculptured stones in the walls of the cottages, and the carving and painting on the walls and columns of a large baonli, or enclosed well, indicate a period of greater wealth and importance. There are also numerous fragments of Hindu sculpture and architecture scattered about. The fort was dismantled by a French officer, M. Bourquin, in the service of Daulat Rao Sindhia, but he left the inner wall standing, which still constitutes the enclosure of a series of six terraced gardens, covering above two hundred bigas, or above sixty acres, originally well supplied with water by stone conduits, leading from a reservoir in the highest part, and forming in their descent from terrace to terrace, cascades, fountains, and lakes. The effect of the whole when maintained in order must have been highly pleasing, and in the hot weather refreshing. In the first, or upper and northern garden, stands a house, the former residence probably of the Killadar; it is small in proportion to the extent of the grounds, but is neatly built, and commands a view of the whole of the enclosure. It is occupied by a Thannadar, on the part of the Raja of Patiala, to whom it belongs.

The garden contains mango, orange, apple, and pomegranate trees, which bear fruit, and some Lombardy poplars. Poppies and sugar-cane are also cultivated in some of the divisions, and in others roses, from which a small supply of atar is annually manufactured for the Raja's use. The fort of Pinjor has often changed masters.

On quitting Pinjor we proceeded through a jangal of the small variety of prickly bambu, called Káth Báns, abounding with game, pea-fowl, wild fowl, black and grey partridges, elephants, buffaloes, leopards, and tigers. Wild cats are met with in the lower grounds, and lions on the summits of the hills, as are several species of deer, as the chital or spotted axis, the pára or hog deer, the káka, which resembles the roebuck, and the barasinga or stag. On our way to Gorakhnath we crossed the new road from Pinjor to the British cantonment of Subathu. Much ground upon our way was clearing for cultivation, by burning and felling the jangal. Proceeding along the valley of Pinjor we passed through much wood, chiefly babul, Indian fig, and bambu. The river Báladn, coming from the north and east, forms the boundary between Patiala on the east, and Hindur on the west. Badia, a small village on the right bank, belongs to Hindur, and is distinguished by a well-defined and broad road, which begins here and goes to Nala-gerh. On the left the river Sarsa, rising in Pinjor, receives the Báladh, and, after a course of about twelve kos, falls into the Setlej at Kanoli. Villages were numerous, and cultivation was abundant throughout our journey on this and the ensuing day to Nala-gerh, a fort belonging to the Raja of Hindur, taken from him by the Gorkhas, but recovered and ceded to him by the British. The Raja is as often called the Palási as the Hindur Raja, from his residing at the former place. Whenever spoken of by his people he was mentioned in terms of affection.

On the 10th of March we departed from Nala-gerh, and recommenced our journey upwards, towards the Himálaya, of which, for some time, we had skirted only the foot of the southern ranges. We passed over many water-courses and successive eminences, from which we had extensive and beautiful prospects over the plains, with the Setlej meandering through them. The road continued, upon the whole, on the ascent, to the pass of Jaynagar, leading to the valley of that name. At the western extremity of the valley on the right is the village of Panjal, separated from the road by the Gambhar, a small river that rises here, and falls into the Setlej below Bilaspur. On the left is the village of Dopé. Further on the road crosses the Jún-ki-gádh, a stream that falls into the Gambhar, and divides the state of Hindur from Bagla. The population of the former is estimated at 20,000 persons. A considerable portion of the working classes is employed by the Raja, who pays them only in grain. The roads through his territory are broad and good, and made at little cost.

On the heights opposite the pass called Pushkar Ghat in Bagla, stands the fort of Malaun, which was taken by Sir David Ochterlony from the Gorkhas. A pile of stones upon an eminence marks the spot where Bhagti Thapa, one of the Gorkha commanders, was killed. The valley of the Gamrora, which this fortress protects, is populous and well cultivated. Along the courses of the different small streams by which it is intersected are rows of pear trees, which at the time we passed them were in full blossom. Villages occurred repeatedly on either side of the road. At one of these, called Kat'hepur, we were met by a horseman, who had been sent by the Raja of Kahlur with orders to attend us to Bilaspur, his present residence, where we arrived on the 12th of March.

Considering me, apparently, as an itinerant trader, little better than a pedlar, the Raja, at first, seemed disinclined to honour us with any particular notice. I had, however, throughout my march, continued to exercise my professional skill and administer medicines to the sick. I had also frequent opportunities of performing the operation for cataract, which is singularly common in the hills. At Bilaspur, during the three days of our stay, I operated for this complaint upon eighteen cases. The Raja hearing of this, and, being indisposed, condescended to visit me and request my assistance. He was very anxious that I should have remained with him until the effect of my treatment could be fully ascertained, but this was impossible, as it was necessary for me to secure my progress to Kulu whilst the passes were open. I was, therefore, obliged to decline compliance with his solicitations.

Bilaspur is not unpicturesquely situated upon the left bank of the Setlej, which is here a rapid stream. The Raja's dwelling, whitened and decorated with flowers in fresco, is neat, but not large. His garden, containing chiefly pear and apricot trees, rose bushes, and beds of narcissus, had been suffered to fall into neglect. The Bazar was in a ruinous state, more than half the shops being deserted. This was ascribed to the town having been twice plundered by the Gorkhas within a few years; but it appeared that the Raja devoted almost his whole time to his private pleasures, and left the management of public affairs entirely to his officers, by whom the people were pillaged and oppressed. This Raj was formerly of great political importance in the Western Himálaya, and enumerated twelve Thakurs, or feudal chieftains, as subject to its authority. These lordships have now, for the most part, either become independent, or have merged into more recent territorial sub-divisions.

On the 16th of March we proceeded up the left bank of the Setlej, opposite to the town of Dehr. Both banks of the river were lined with a succession of small villages the whole way. Dehr, which belongs to the Raj of Sukhet, on the right bank of the Setlej, is defended by a fort of masonry. The passage of the river was effected on deris, or inflated skins. My party consisted of about three hundred persons, sixteen horses and mules, and about two hundred maunds of merchandise and baggage. Thirty-one watermen, each managing a skin, conveyed the whole across in little more than an hour and a half. The Setlej was about one hundred and fifty feet in breadth, and was running at the rate of five miles an hour. The skins used for this purpose are those of bullocks, which are stripped off in this manner. An incision is made in the back part of a hind leg, almost the whole length, and the skin, being flayed off from the hock upwards, is turned forwards, the same management being observed as in the process technically termed casing a hare, except that the skin is cut through below and round the knees and hocks, the legs being left adhering to the body. The hide is then doubled up, and buried for a few days, in order to suffer so much decomposition as will favour the separation of the hair, which is rubbed off by the hand or a blunt wooden knife, without abrasion of the skin. The skin is then turned inside out, and the natural openings of the eyes, &c., stitched up; it is then turned back again, and the main incision sewed up with thongs of raw hide. The open ends of the limbs are tied, except one, which is left open, as a tube by which to inflate the skin. The thin tar procured from the deodar and other species of pine, is then poured into the skin, and shaken about in it until the flesh inside is well charged with it, and it is then tanned exteriorly, by steeping in an infusion of pomegranate husks. When required for use the waterman blows into it through the hind tube, and ties up the opening. A double thin cord is fastened round the inflated skin, across which the waterman places himself on his chest, holding the string with his left hand, whilst, with his right, he manages a short oar, assisting his passage with his hands and feet. Sometimes a piece of stick is tied in one of the legs, and left projecting from it for the waterman to hold instead of the string. The passenger, with as much baggage as he can carry, sits astride the ferryman's back, with his knees bent, and resting on the skin. When heavy and bulky articles are to be transported, two skins are brought together, the ferryman of each laying hold of one of the projecting legs of the other skin, and a frame or raft, supporting the burden, lies across the backs of both. A charpai, or Hindustani bedstead, forms the most convenient raft. Horses and mules are led over, the waterman holding them by a string in one hand, whilst he paddles himself and his human load across in the manner above described. When not inflated the skin is slung over the back, and carried about without any inconvenience. No expedient seems equally well adapted for the transport of large bodies of men and baggage over the most rapid rivers, or so likely to be serviceable as a wreck buoy or float, to be carried on board ship. The cost of a deri is usually a rupee and a half, and its weight is not above sixteen pounds. A couple of deri-men usually accompany persons of rank hunting in the hills, in order to carry them across the mountain streams, the rapidity and fury, if not the depth of which, render it impossible to ford them without such assistance.

From Dehr to Sukhet the road lay partly over cultivated ground, and partly over rugged paths obstructed by large blocks of limestone. As it approaches Sukhet several forts are seen on the mountains to the left, amongst which is Bagra, belonging to the Raj of Mundi. We encamped near a spring, which forms one of the sources of the Sukhet river.

On the arrival of the first of our party at the village a general panic prevailed, and many of the people prepared to make their escape into the neighbouring thickets. A report had spread that the Feringis, or Europeans, were approaching with a numerous host to occupy and devastate the country, and the villagers imagined those of my people who had been sent on in advance to be the precursors of the invading host. When they found, however, that our proceedings were wholly pacific, and that we paid for the supplies we required, their terrors were allayed, and gradually confidence succeeded to apprehension. They had never yet beheld a European, and curiosity brought crowd after crowd to look at the Sahib log until it was dark. Night set in with a thunder-storm, and in the darkness we were disturbed by the singular howling of the hyænas, who approached our encampment, and are said to be common here*.

The valley of Sukhet is not very extensive, and, except to the south, where it is bounded by the Setlej and part of Kahalur, the whole Raj is shut in by the mountains of Mundi. The land is well cultivated, and more productive than any tract of similar extent I have seen in the Himálaya. The western side is watered by the Sukheti, and the

* From this point until his return to the plains, Mr. Moorcroft's route proceeds through a tract of country which, belonging to Ranjit Sinh and his dependent Rajas, has not been surveyed, and has been but little traversed by Europeans. Forster went over part of it in his journey to Kashmir, but he had no opportunity of making any very careful observations.—Ed.

eastern by the Kams, which rivulets unite and fall into the Beyah or Byas river above Mundi. The division between Sukhet and Mundi is indicated by a narrow ditch called Mukhi.

Having resumed our route, and entered the Mundi territory, we were met by a body of men armed with matchlocks, bows and arrows, and swords, headed by the commandant of the fort of Ner, on the left of our path, who prohibited our further progress without positive orders from the Raja to sanction our proceeding. A letter was, therefore, dispatched, requesting the Raja's permission to traverse his district, and sent off by one of my people, who was acquainted with the country.

In the evening the messenger returned with information that some Sikhs, who were at Mundi, for the purpose of receiving tribute, had threatened the Raja with the displeasure of Ranjit Sinh, if he suffered us to pass through his country; and shortly afterwards came a letter from the Sikh Sirdars, desiring us to remain where we were until an answer from their master, to whom information of our coming had been communicated, could be received. To this I replied, that as I was simply a merchant, travelling to Lé, with goods for sale, on which I was willing to pay all customary duties, I knew of no reason they could have for detaining me, and that, if they persisted in their purpose, I would have recourse to their Chief, and repair myself to Lahore. After some discussion they were obliged to consent to this arrangement; and, accordingly, taking a few of my people with me, I left the rest and all the merchandise under charge of my young friend and companion, Mr. Trebeck, at Dhansi, the place at which we were encamped. The Raja of Mundi promised to watch over its security, and furnish every facility that might be desired for its conveyance and disposal, as well as provide supplies for the people. He repeatedly assured me of his regret at opposing any impediment in my way, and of his being compelled so to act against his wishes by fear of the Sikhs; he even offered to allow us to proceed if I would take all the responsibility upon myself, and assure him of the countenance of my government. As, however, I was travelling in a mercantile character alone, without pretending to any political authority, I declined making him this assurance, and, thanking him for his civility and friendly intentions, persevered in my determination to appeal in person to Ranjit Sinh. Accordingly, on the 23rd of March, I set off for Lahore.

CHAPTER II.

Resources of the hills—Paper from the sitabharua—Lichen for mucilage—Honey and wax—Fir and oak timber—Fruits—Madder—Hemp—Turpentine—Cattle—Birds—Fish—Fishing-line—Improvements dependant on European settlers.

Before quitting the Himálayan provinces, which are more or less subject to British authority, I shall briefly notice some of their natural and artificial productions, which, if made the subject of attention and improvement, might conduce materially to the prosperity of the mountain population, and enhance the value of an extensive region, which is now comparatively unproductive.

Of the articles which might be profitably exported, one of the principal is paper, which might be manufactured to almost any extent from the Sitabharua, a plant that is everywhere found in great abundance. The bark of the stem and branches is detached by bruising, and the cuticle taken off by scraping. The bark thus cleaned, is sometimes boiled to make it tender, and at others, simply steeped in cold water, when it is pounded into a paste and then strained through a cloth, by which the coarser fibres are separated. The finer paste is spread upon a cotton cloth stretched on a frame, and is dried in the sun, when it is raised from the frame and folded. The paper thus rudely manufactured, is of a dirty white colour, and is less fit for writing than for packing; but it is admirably adapted for the latter purpose, as well as for the manufacture of pasteboard and *papier machè*, by its great strength and toughness. Improved processes in its preparation might also improve its appearance. Owing to the want of any glutinous or mucilaginous admixture, the sitabharua paper becomes rough and downy by rubbing, but when, as is sometimes practised in Nepal, the milk of unripe wheat is mixed with the pulp, the paper retains a smooth, uniform, and somewhat lustrous surface.*

* For a description of the plant, (*Daphne cannabina,*) by Dr. Wallick, see *Asiatic Researches*, vol. xiii.; a full description of the

It would not be difficult to find in the hills, a mucilage which would give consistency to the pulp of the sitabharua paper, and which might be equally serviceable to calico printers and others. In the neighbourhood of Joshimath, and many other parts of the hills, there hangs from the branches of the oak, the yew, and the pine, a green lichen in long tresses, applicable to such a purpose. Without separating the cortical part in which the colouring matter resides, I boiled some of this lichen, and speedily obtained a greenish insipid thick mucilage, or size, which by evaporation was soon reduced to the consistency of gum. The supply of this lichen is co-extensive with the limit of forest in the Himalaya. In the vicinity of Joshimath, a man could collect in the course of a day, three times as much as he could carry, although it is very light.

In most of the villages of the northern ranges of the Himalaya, bees are kept; and

mode of making the paper by Mr. Hodgson, is given in the *Jour. of the Asiatic Society*, vol. i. p. 8. Some of the pulp in the shape of bricks was sent to Scotland, where the paper made from it was employed to take proof impressions of copper-plate engravings. The first trials did not appear to answer, and no others were instituted. *Edinburgh Jour. of Science*, for *April*, 1829.—ED.

honey, whether the produce of the wild or domesticated bee, is an article of sale. It is commonly sold in the bazars at four to six seers for a rupee, and although not much thicker than syrup, is of a flavour equal to Narbonne, and less cloying to the stomach. There is no great demand for wax, otherwise this might be also plentifully supplied ; at present, the comb, after the honey is compressed, is usually thrown away. The domestic bee is known by the name of mahru, mohri, and mari ; it is not much above half the size of that of Europe, but is very industrious and mild tempered. The wild bee is termed bhaonra, a name by which the people of the plains designate the humble-bee, but it is not half the bulk of that insect, though larger than the domestic bee of Europe. It is of a darker colour generally, and has longer and broader wings. Its temper is irascible, and sting venomous. It commonly builds its nest under projecting ledges of rock, overhanging steep mural precipices, in a situation almost inaccessible to bears and men. The hive contains a large quantity of both wax and honey. The latter, if gathered before the month of Bhadra, is fully equal to that of the domestic bee, but in that and the following month, it is said to produce intoxication, followed by stupefaction. This effect is, with some probability, ascribed to the bee's feeding on the flower of a species of aconite, which is in bloom in Bhadra and Asharh, and which growing high up the mountain, is beyond the flight of the domestic bee. There is little doubt that both the honey and wax might form valuable articles of export to the plains.

The fir timber of the hills has been considered inferior to that of the north of Europe, but it has scarcely yet been submitted to a fair trial. That which was sent to Calcutta was cut at the foot of the hills, or on the lower ranges, and in this situation it is notoriously much less compact and strong than at higher elevations; but leaving this for further investigation, there is another kind of timber which has not yet reached Calcutta, and which appears to possess qualities highly deserving of a trial. This is the live or ever-green oak, of which there are three varieties, called by the natives near Joshimath, banj, mohru, and khasru. The banj occupies the lower slopes of the mountains; the mohru, the middle and upper part; and the khasru, the higher elevations, as far as it meets with soil enough for its support.*

The wood of the banj is tolerably hard and durable, but the timber does not acquire any considerable size. That of the other two varieties is hard and very durable, and the trees attain vast dimensions in thickness and height and spread, before they fall. Their timber is employed in the hills for the shafts of ploughs, and is often carried to a considerable distance. It is procured chiefly by lopping the branches, for to cut down an entire tree exceeds the powers of the mountaineers; neither would large blocks be of any use to them, although tempted by the fall of a tree, they sometimes succeed in cutting it into logs of five or six feet in length. I saw, however, several noble trees lying on the ground, which had resisted all attempts at their mutilation. The great difficulty would be the transport;

* These oaks and other species in the Himalaya, have since been determined, and named by botanists, especially by Dr. Wallich and Prof. Royle. The three kinds mentioned in the text have been denominated *Quercus dealbata, Q. elastica, and Q. semicarpifolia.*—ED.

but I apprehend, that at the season when the mountain rivers are at their height, and the vast blocks of stone which obstruct their beds at other seasons, are either washed away or completely covered, trees or rafts of timber might be floated down them with little risk of injury or loss. Certain it is that at Srinagar, the fishermen annually collect a considerable quantity of drift timber, and even entire trees. Some of the former I had an opportunity of examining, and found that it had sustained but very little damage.

There is a considerable variety of fruit-trees in the Himalaya, but in general, their produce is such as might be expected from their uncultivated condition, and they may be regarded chiefly as the stocks from which superior kinds may be successfully developed. The cherry-tree grows plentifully in the vicinity of Joshimath; the fruit is about the size of the wild cherry in England, and, like it, is only fit for ratafia. The apricot and pear grow at a still higher elevation, but their produce is indifferent. The pear is a native, of the same height, and its fruit small, speckled, and most abundant, is austere and astringent beyond conception. The walnut and hazel are free bearers, and their fruit is well flavoured, although the shell is in large proportion to the kernel. The vine flourishes, and yields tolerably well-flavoured grapes. In Bisahar, they are made into raisins. The lime and lemon (gulgne) are grown to the south of Joshimath, and are equal to the best imported into England; at Srinagar, five dozen lemons were bought in the bazar for two anas and a half, (about fourpence,) and six of them taken indiscriminately from the basket, weighed two seers and three-quarters (above five lbs.). It is customary to pluck the fruit in the month of Kartiek, when it has attained its full growth but is not quite ripe. It is then buried in deep holes in the ground, lining the pits and covering the fruit with dry leaves. In this situation, it attains maturity, and if not bruised in packing, retains its form and freshness for a considerable period. I saw some disinterred after they had been buried for three months, and they were in most perfect preservation. The oranges which are found in the immediate neighbourhood of Joshimath, are bitter, and allied to the Seville variety; but the loose-skinned kind which is raised below Srinagar, is good, although not equal to that grown within the hills near Butwal, which is little inferior to the orange of Malta. Currants and gooseberries were first met with, eight days' journey nearer the northern frontier than Joshimath. They were each of two kinds, yellow and red. The yellow, or orange-coloured currant, was small, with little flavour. The red variety, almost black when fully ripe, was as large, both singly and in its clusters, as the largest English currant. The skin was thin, and the seeds were small; the juice was abundant but acid. The bushes were ten or twelve feet high; luxuriant in leaf and wood, and abundantly laden with fruit. The gooseberry bushes were large, and every branch was set with long sharp prickles. The fruit was abundant but small, with a thick skin; large seeds, and scanty pulp. The barberries yield most profusely, and the fruit of the red variety equals that of England both in size and flavour. The red raspberry is smaller than the English fruit, but scarcely inferior in fragrance or taste. There are other varieties; as a light and dark yellow, but they are not equal in flavour to the red. Pomegranates are plentiful and good ; and their juice, as well as that of the barberry and lemon, boiled with the fragrant capsicum, to the consistence of syrup, is much used by the inhabitants as sauce. The fruit of the kaiphal, of the drupe kind, is deficient in pulp, but has an exceedingly agreeable mixture of sweet and acid, and would probably be improved by cultivation. Sugar-cane of excellent quality is raised in some parts of the hills, and the cultivation might, perhaps, be extended with advantage.

Madder grows wild in the vicinity of Joshimath, at the foot of almost every bush, and its black berries overspread their tops in the greatest profusion. The root contains abundant colouring matter, and it is used by the Bhotias to dye the coarse woollen cloths manufactured in the mountains, previously employing a bath of alum, which is found abundantly as an exudation on the face of some of the cliffs. It could be raised in any quantity.

Hemp grows freely in the valleys, and on the slopes of the mountains. It affords a strong, fine, and long fibre, and is worked by the natives into a coarse canvas, and into thread and rope. The gum collected from its flowers during the warm part of the day, and called from its resemblance to wax, momia, and well known when adulterated, by the name of kshir ras, has strong narcotic powers. Tar, pitch, resin, turpentine, are all procurable in any quantity. The oil distilled from the turpentine extracted in the hills is lighter, more fluid, transparent and fragrant than any manufactured in Great Britain.

The neat cattle of the hills are not obtainable for food except by the violation of local prejudices; but the short-tailed sheep of Tartary, after it has been employed some years in carrying loads, furnishes, after fattening, a mutton rarely surpassed for fineness of fibre, juiciness, and flavour. The sheep may be procured in any number at a rupee a head. The goat-mutton is very indifferent. The mast of the oak and horse-chesnut support great numbers of wild hogs, which haunt the upper part of the hills until compelled by the snow to seek for food lower down.

They are then waylaid by the inhabitants, and when entangled in the snow-drifts, attacked and speared. The domestic poultry is small, but good if suitably prepared. Pheasants exist in considerable numbers and variety. The male of the mon al pheasant weighs usually above five pounds, and is a bird of most magnificent plumage. The chakor or Francoline partridge and black partridge are in great plenty; woodcocks are also met with. I have already alluded to the trout of the Alakananda, which, although in its general form, and the colour of its flesh it resembles trout, differs from it in many particulars, especially in the structure of its mouth, which is placed more backward, and it has no teeth in its lips; the nose projects farther; the lower lip is thick, leathery, and flat below, and convex above, and applies exactly to some moveable bones in the fore part of the palate, against which it squeezes its food. It has a single row of teeth in its throat, and two barbs on each side of the upper lip. The mode of catching it has also been adverted to, but I should think that anglers in England would find it an advantage to substitute the line made from the fibres of the murwa for any tackle that they at present employ.

There are many other topics connected with commerce and manufacture in these mountains which might be worth inquiry; but there is little prospect of any such inquiry being judiciously directed, or any actual improvements effected until European skill and enterprise be domesticated in the Himalaya. Whenever that shall be the case, the capabilities of these provinces will, I am confident, be found far to exceed the most favourable estimate that has yet been made of them, and they will become a source of strength and revenue to British India, and of no mean advantage to the manufactures and commerce of Great Britain.

CHAPTER III.

Defile of Alexander—The King's Camp—Confluence of the Sir and Lag—Mahal—View of Kamla-gerh—Nadaun—The Byas River—Visit to Jwálá-mukhí—Temple of the Goddess—Inflammable Gas—Saline Springs—Return to Nadaun; its Decay—Resumption of Route — Rajpura — Temporary Detention — Descent to the Plains—Detention at Hoshyarpur—Mir Izzet Ullah dispatched to Amritsar—Permission from Ranjit Sinh to proceed—Advance to the Panjab—Jelalabad—Bhyroval—Amritsar — Arrival at Lahore — Shahlimar — Baraderi—Visit from Aziz ad Din — Audience of Ranjit Sinh — The Raja's Horses—Other Interviews with the Raja—His Familiarity — Anecdotes of Himself—Audience of Leave—Permission to go to Bokhara, by way of Kulu, or Kashmir—Account of Lahore.

At about two kos and a half from Dhansi, the road leaves the valley of Sukhet, and a flight of stone steps leads up a steep bank into the district of Mundi. After passing over some cultivated eminences, it descends to the Dagi rivulet, and then again ascends the eastern face of Sekander Ghat or the defile of Alexander. Villages were numerous, and the land was admirably cultivated, being laid out in terraces, rising nearly to the summits of the hills. My curiosity being excited by the name of Alexander, I took particular pains to inquire if any traces or traditions of the Macedonian monarch were to be discovered, but could only learn that the name, with or without the adjunct of badshah or king, was familiar to the people of the country. I was told also that at Leda was to be seen what was called the badshah's camp, and on my arrival at that place I climbed a height about a mile above our tents, where a cut through a ridge of rock formed a portion of the ditch. On the summit was an open space of about an acre, or rather more, surrounded by a low wall of rough stones, and beneath this was a ditch cut in the rock, extending round three sides, the fourth being the edge of a precipice. Here and there were the ruins of small dwellings. The whole was evidently the remains of a fortified camp, but I found nothing to indicate a Grecian origin. Some foresters, indeed, informed me that although there was a tradition of its having been a station of the Badshah's army, yet that within their recollection it had been a fort belonging to

Mundi, and had been taken and dismantled by the Raja of Kotoch.

I did not reach the western extremity of the pass until the following day: on the right hand, upon a circular eminence, formerly stood a tower, and opposite to its remains was a heap of chiselled stones, on one of which a couple of feet and a trident were rudely sculptured, showing these relics to be Hindu. The summit of the hill commanded a beautiful view of portions of the territories of Mundi, Kahalur, and Kotoch, watered by the rivers Sir and Lag, and shut in on the north by the Chamba mountains tipped with snow. Below the hill on the right was the fort of Byrkoth, and higher and more to the east that of Sidhkoth, both belonging to Mundi. From hence the road descended rapidly, and led through a pine forest to the small village of Hatli, where we halted. In the evening the village poured out its sick and infirm, and formidable indeed was the quantity of disease met with in so apparently scanty a population. Besides lame and blind there were many affected with leprosy, ophthalmia, cataract, bronchocele, enlarged spleen, or asthma. Upon repeating my inquiries after Alexander, they brought me some old copper coins, said to have been found in the Ghat and its neighbourhood: the characters seemed to be Cufic.*

From Hatli the road, following a direction south and west, crosses the Bijauri, a feeder of the Sir. On the right was the village of Burdwara, at the end of the highly-cultivated valley of Túk, running east and west, and separated from that of Bathel, which crosses it at right angles, by the Kaltri rivulet. The Sir flows along the middle of the Bathel valley, and falls into the Setlej, about five kos below Bilaspur. It divides Mundi on the east from Kahalur and Kotoch. The two latter again are separated by the Lag, flowing obliquely into the Sir, and having the district of Mankoth in the angle between the streams. At the apex of the angle is another spot called the Badshah's

* These coins have not been found with Mr. Moorcroft's papers. They were not improbably specimens of that ancient coinage which has, within a very few years, been so extensively discovered in the Panjab, and which is considered of Indo-Greek and Indo-Scythian origin.—ED.

camp, enclosed on three sides by a rude wall of pebble-stones, broken down in some places by the peasants having removed the stones for the divisions of their fields. No vestiges of antiquity, it is said, have been ever discovered here. The road, after ascending the Lag for about five miles, to near its source, diverges more to the south, and leads to the village of Mahal, on the right bank of the Kanwa rivulet, a feeder of the Byas. The Raj of Kotoch, which is subject to Sansar Chand, commences about two miles above the confluence of the Lag with the Sir.

The Kanwa, which we crossed, runs between banks of sandstone, lying between strata of earth and rounded pebbles, a disposition first noticed in the hills which lie between Mahal and the Lag. Mahal, the palace or station, is so named because a court for receiving rents was formerly held here. The road crosses the valley of Raipur, and passes between numerous villages. At Amirpur it proceeds up a flight of steps cut in the rock, and then through the Bazar. From a height, some way onwards from hence, I commanded a distinct view of the range of strong-holds called Kamla-gerh, the farthest of which was about twenty-five kos distant. These are a chain of fortresses, partly of masonry, partly constructed out of the rock, surmounting a range of high and almost perpendicular mountains, which extend at right angles along the four sides of a valley of about four miles square. The extreme distance between the western and eastern forts is about twelve kos. These forts belong to the Raja of Mundi, and are considered impregnable. Sansar Chand, when in the height of his power, tried his strength against them, and failed, after suffering a severe loss. The people report that the place was captured by Alexander, and that it contains a marble throne which belonged to that conqueror, having an inscription in unknown characters. The Alexander or Sekander, who is the hero of this tale, seems, however, to have been Sekander Lodi of Delhi. The inhabitants of this fortified valley, it is said, are never suffered to leave it, nor are strangers ever admitted into it; and these prohibitions are easily enforced, as there is no access to the interior except at the north-east, where stands the great gate called Nurpur, strongly situated, and as strongly fortified. It was on this point that Sansar Chand directed his principal but fruitless efforts. On every other side the rugged and precipitous ramparts which nature has reared, effectually prevent the approach of man. The accumulated treasures of the Rajas of Mundi are said to be here deposited.

From Samruya, where I had halted for the night, the road proceeded north-west by west. From an eminence, on which stands a temple dedicated to Devi, the valley of Nadaun lies full in sight, running south-east and north-west, and extending from Danta Siddhadhán to Belear, it is said forty kos. It varies in breadth from four to six kos. In some parts it is cultivated, but in others broken into ravines, and overspread with jangal. The southern flank is formed by the ridges of the Raj of Jaswal; the northern by those of Samruya and Moru, and it is separated from Belear by the Byas river. Beyond the Jaswal hills lies another valley of similar dimensions, reaching to the Setlej opposite to Nala-gerh. The Kanwa skirts the northern range of mountains. The Raj of Jaswal was formerly independent, but it is now parcelled out amongst Sikh chiefs, and the Raja is a pensioner of Ranjit Sinh.

Having descended into the valley by a steep and rugged declivity, I advanced along the bed of the Kanwa, now about thirty feet broad, and mid-leg deep. The channel, however, is one hundred and fifty feet in breadth, and the water-mark eight feet. After following the river bed for some distance, with occasional deflexions, we crossed it, the road finally leaving it at the hamlet and garden of Fattehpur, belonging to the Raja's brother. The tract of country between this place and Nadaun is little cultivated.

On my way thither I was met by a servant of Sansar Chand, sent to invite me to his capital, or, in the event of my declining the invitation, to attend upon me whilst in the Raja's country. I deferred visiting his master until my return, and, hearing that Ranjit Sinh was at Multan, and not expected to be at Lahore for a fortnight, I determined to take the opportunity of paying a visit to Jwálámukhí.

From Nadaun a long flight of stone steps led to the left bank of the Byas river, just above the town. This stream, now called Beyah or Byas, is the Hyphasis of the ancients. Opposite to the town the bed is thrice the breadth of the Setlej at Bilaspur, but about a quarter of a mile higher up, where it may be said to enter the plains, it is not above a hundred feet broad. The left bank is of sandstone, lofty and abrupt; the right of mould, lower and shelving. The current had the rate of about five miles an hour. I crossed the river in a commodious ferry-boat, but deris, or inflated skins, are also used here, and are so cheap that one fit for use may be bought for a rupee.

Jwálá-mukhí is about five kos to the north-west of Nadaun *, and is situated upon an elevated nook immediately under the mountains of Changa. It is a place of great sanctity in the estimation of the Hindus, and pilgrims come hither from all parts of India.

* Hamilton (*Indian Gazetteer*, vol. i. p. 501) erroneously places Jwálá-mukhí close to Koth Kangra, and, indeed, identifies it with that place. Buchanan (*Account of Nepal*) gives a more correct but brief account of it on native authority.—Ed.

Its holiness is owing to the inflammable gas which issues from various apertures in a temple dedicated to Devi, the wife of Mahadeo, who, as identical with the mysterious fire, is also called Jwálá-mukhí, the goddess from whose mouth flame is exhaled *. The vents through which the ignited gas, that is always burning in the temple of Devi, issues, are several in a shallow trough excavated on the floor, one in the north-western angle, one in the wall on the northern face, and two others on the outside of the wall: there are also some in a well within a small detached building. Observing the water in this well apparently free from vapour, I applied a lighted wick to it, and the surface was immediately ignited, though but for a short period. The same test showed the exhalation of gas from several of the apertures which were seemingly

* From the Sanscrit Jwálá, flame, and mukha, mouth. According to a legend in Hindi, procured by Mr. M. on the spot, the flame proceeds from the fire which Sati, the bride of Siva, created at the sacrifice of her father Daksha, and in which she burnt herself in resentment of her father's contumelious treatment of her husband. After the parties were reconciled, Siva removed this fire, which threatened to consume the world, and buried it in the hollow of the mountain.—Ed.

quiescent. There was no smoke, and but little smell. The interior of the temple was, indeed, blackened by smoke, but this had been generated by the offerings of Devi's worshippers, who place butter, sugar, and incense near the flame from the apertures as burnt-offerings to the goddess. The attendant brahmans were very civil, and allowed me to make what experiments I pleased. When a flame proceeded from any aperture longer and brighter than usual, an exclamation of *Ai Jwálá* arose from the adoring multitude. The temple was about twenty feet square, not in any way remarkable for its architecture, except that the columns were without capitals, and were more massive than any I remember to have seen in Hindustan. The crowd that pressed round me out of curiosity, and the confined space, as well as the heat from the burning hydrogen, rendered the air in the interior of the temple so suffocatingly close, that I was compelled to leave it sooner than I had intended. The interior of the temple has been lately painted and embellished at the expense of the Raja of Hindur.

The town of Jwálá-mukhí is prettily situated, and commands a view of the valley of Belear from Nadaun to the mountains of Haripur-goli on the west, and of the heights of Jaswal and Changa, with the Byas flowing down the former. It is of no great extent, and, notwithstanding its sanctity, is dirty and neglected. The environs of the temple are exceedingly filthy, from dirty water and fragments of offerings scattered about, and the concourse of brahmans, mendicants, and cows, the latter being much in the best condition of the trio. Up the sides of the mountains to the west are many buildings for the accommodation of the pilgrims, who are lodged and fed for a day at the expense of the temple, the cost being defrayed from the rents of lands with which it is endowed for that purpose. Most of them are mere paupers, and beset the shops of the grain dealers and sweetmeat venders, almost the only description of shops which the place contains, for their daily dole. Since Sansar Chand's revenues have been diminished by the loss of so many of his estates, not only has his patronage of Jwálá-mukhí been, in a great degree, withdrawn, but he claims a share of the actual receipts of the establishment. Whatever money is offered to the goddess is the Raja's, and the brahmans are held to be entitled only to the donations given to themselves, which they represent to be little enough, and wholly inadequate to the maintenance of several hundred persons. Their appearance was quite in harmony with their assertions. In the evening after my visit, an old brahman brought me a book in which the names of visitors were inscribed, and requested me to insert mine as that of the first European who had visited Jwálá-mukhí.

I had understood from native report that hot springs existed in the neighbourhood of Jwálá-mukhí, the use of which was extremely beneficial in bronchocele or enlarged neck, and I was much disappointed to learn that no such baths were known. I was shown, however, some stone basins under the road to the temple, which received the salt water of a concealed spring in the mountain, that was used for the cure of goître. This water is both drank and applied externally, and it is carried in earthen jars to other places. I had some of it brought to my tent, and boiled it in iron caldrons procured from the confectioners. It had a slight smell of sulphuretted hydrogen, and after standing for some time was coated with a very thin pellicle of oily matter. A pint of the water left upon evaporation 287 grains* of a greyish coloured salt. When it had been suffered to stand for about three hours before boiling, it threw up a red scum which imparted a similar tint to the salt that was left by evaporation. This tint was removed when the salt was rapidly dried by heat in the iron caldron, but was permanent if the residuum was dried slowly in the air. This colour might perhaps have been derived from the red earth of the ill-baked pots in which the water had been brought. I had no means of determining the nature of the salt. It is customary in cases of goître to administer about half a pint of the water early in the morning whilst the patient is fasting, preceding the dose by half a dozen pepper-corns, and following it by brisk exercise for a short time. In three

* The Journal has 3 miskals and 1 masha, which is rather indeterminate. Estimating the miskal at a dram and a half, and the masha at 17 grains, the result is expressed in the text.—Ed.

weeks it is said the cure is effected in a recent case; but a further period is required in a complaint of longer standing. That the remedy does not always succeed, is admitted, but the failure is ascribed not so much to want of virtue in the medicine, as to want of faith in Jwálá-mukhí, to whose favour, and not to any inherent quality, the water owes its efficacy. The water is said to act sometimes, but not always, as an aperient, and to produce in persons in health a sense of heat and uneasiness if drank to the usual extent for a few days. The poor people in the neighbourhood, however, use it instead of salt with their food. As there is a considerable quantity of fossil salt in the hills of Mundi, from the sale of which the Raja derives part of his income, Sansar Chand thought the salt-springs of Jwálá-mukhí must owe their impregnation to some similar deposit in the Changa mountains whence they rise, the discovery of which would be advantageous to him: his search, however, has hitherto proved unavailing. If the reputation which these springs enjoy, and the great resort to them of diseased persons afford any evidence of their powers, they would seem to be better entitled to confidence in the treatment of goître than borax, soda, or burnt sponge, which have been recommended for its cure. I had also heard that the waters of Jwálá-mukhí were highly serviceable in cases of cutaneous affection; but this character was not possessed by them on the spot, either in the pretensions or practice of the inhabitants. I have seldom seen itch and ringworm so widely prevalent.

On the 29th of March I returned to Nadaun. This place was formerly one of great resort, being the chief mart of a rich province, and the favourite resting-place of merchants travelling betwixt Kashmir and Hindustan *. It was proverbially famed for its comforts and attractions; and "Who that goes to Nadaun will come away again?" (Jaega Nadaun aega kaun) is a phrase current in the plains, bearing unequivocal testimony to its reputation. The duties on merchandise passing

* It should have been in the way of Forster's journey, but he was prevented from visiting it. "The common road to Jumbo from hence (Bilaspur) lay through Nadone, the principal town in the Kangra country, and through the district of Haripur; but these places being overrun by the Sicques, we were obliged to deviate from the usual track, and proceed to the westward."—Ed.

through it were farmed at 27,000 rupees a-year. The whole district now scarcely yields a fourth of that income. The principal article was shawl-goods, which, to avoid the danger of being plundered on the lower road, were conveyed through the states of the several mountain chiefs to Nahan and Dera, and thence to Najibabad or Saharanpur. The heavy duties exacted in each petty principality checked, but did not crush the trade; but as these duties did not purchase security, and the pillage of a whole caravan by one needy and unprincipled Raja was a contingency to which the merchants were nevertheless exposed, they were at last obliged to discontinue the transmission of their merchandise to the low country by this route. The principal persons engaged in the traffic were the Gosains of Jwálá-mukhí, the seniors of whom remained at the principal stations, whilst their pupils or chelas traversed the whole of Hindustan with the most valuable commodities. The confusion that prevailed for some years in the politics of the hill states, and the consequent impoverishment of their rulers, combined with other causes, have almost annihilated this traffic, and thinned the community of the Gosains; and the few that reside at Jwálá-mukhí are contented to remain at home, subsisting in humble tranquillity upon the produce of those lands which they owe to the piety of former benefactors.

Nadaun also suffered severely from its occupation by the Gorkhas; and the insolence and tyranny of their soldiery, some of whom were always stationed here, drove away all the respectable part of the population. Since its restoration its former inhabitants have begun to return; but it still presents a melancholy contrast to its once prosperous condition. The bazar, which was formerly crowded by bustling traders, is now frequented only by a few fakirs and pilgrims; and of the shopkeepers I observed one-third asleep, a third playing at draughts, and the rest scantily and listlessly employed. The vicinity of the town abounds with mulberry-trees of every description; so that if the climate be not unfavourable, the silkworm may be bred here to any extent.

On the 31st I left Nadaun for Koloa, following the bed of the Byas on the left bank. Close to the town I crossed the nearly dry mouth of the Kuna *, and farther on that of the Masi, which runs parallel with the hills of Jaswal, and separates that district from Kotoch. The Byas, although now reduced to a breadth of less than 200 feet, must bear a considerable body of water in the rainy season, for the bed is here about a mile broad. The road, after running some way between the Jaswal hills and the river, nearly at an equal distance from each, ascended the former at a pass called Chula Ghat above the village of that name. The hills are bare, and little cultivated, although villages are frequent. That of Koloa, where I halted, is little else than a cluster of grain-sellers' shops in an angle of two glens. On the following day I proceeded towards Rajpura, crossing the Koloa Ghat, which separates the two districts. From this eminence the course of

* Moorcroft considers this to be the same with the Kanwa formerly met with, but there is great reason to conclude that it is a different stream, and that he was misled by the similarity of the name; for he formerly mentions (p. 68) that the road quitted the Kanwa after he had crossed it, and it must, therefore, have turned to the right. Baron Hügel followed the same route to Nadaun, and makes the Kanwa join the Byas north of that town.—Ed.

the Rajpura river may be traced along the mountains to the village of Amb, where it enters Jaswal. Skirting the Rajpura hills, it takes an easterly direction to the Soaon river, which falls into the Setlej some way above Palasi. The road, with occasional deviations, lies in the bed of the rivulet until it reaches Rajpura.

Rajpura formerly belonged to the Raja of Jaswal, but was taken by Ranjit Sinh, and was now occupied by a Sikh detachment. The commander thought fit to detain me, until orders could be obtained from his superior, Dewan Magar Mal, who was at a village about two kos distant; and in the mean time, I was surrounded by a body of men miserably equipped with swords and bows and arrows, and pistols of an antique fashion. My detention was not of long duration, and a civil message from the Dewan authorized my liberation, and gave the requisite permission to proceed. After entering the great valley of Jaswal, along with the Rajpura stream, the road leaves it on the left, and pursues a westerly course, over a sandy and stony plain, covered in patches with tufts of coarse grass, amidst which were numerous herds of cattle, buffaloes, sheep, and goats. I observed also some brood mares in excellent condition. The Soaon river runs along the centre of the valley. Leaving the valley, I came to Tittira, where I found two persons dispatched by Magar Mal, to provide accommodations and supplies for my party. At the distance of a kos, is a pass leading from the Tittira glen to a piece of table-land commanding an extensive prospect. The descent is by a path cut in the soft sandstone, the steps of which are sometimes of an ordinary man's height. As the road advances towards the west, the hills decrease rapidly in elevation; and at the village of Munhkala the plain commences, bounded for some short way, only by small elevations on the right and left. Our path thence led to the west, passing by the walled town of Bahadarpur to Hoshyarpur, where I encamped. On this day's route, I observed a line of sisu, pipal, and other trees, about a foot long, projecting from a thin stratum of vegetable mould, underneath strata of sandstone, at least sixty feet in depth from the surface. The face of the cliff was perpendicular, so there was no ledge on which the seeds could have fallen, and however difficult it may be to conceive such an occurrence, the only probable theory to account for the growth of the plants in such a position, is to suppose that the seeds existed in the mould when it first assumed its present situation, and sprang into life upon exposure to air and light, by the partial breaking down of the cliff. At Munhkala, the rivulet of the same name which had accompanied us through the descent from Tittira, is absorbed during the dry weather by its broad bed of white sand; similar beds, however, indicate its continuous course at other seasons, south-west across the plain.

The thannadar of Hoshyarpur refused to allow of our advance without a reference to Lala Seodayál, who was at Phúl, thirty kos distant, and we were obliged to await the result; after staying three days, an answer came from this person, stating that he could not permit us to proceed without orders from Ranjit Sinh, to whom he would write, and desired me to do the same. As this did not meet my views I declined compliance with it, and instead dispatched Mir Izzet Ullah to

Lala Seodayál, with a written statement of my objects and intentions. This mission was fruitless. Seodayál persisted in detaining us, without authority from the court, and the only arrangement to which he would consent was the dispatch of Mir Izzet Ullah to Amritsar, whilst I remained where I was. These difficulties seem to arise principally from the absurd reports to which our journey has given birth; representing us as a strong military force which had taken possession of Mundi and Jwálá-mukhí, and was about to bring the whole of the hill districts under the British power. It had also happened that the Sikh arms had recently sustained some signal reverses. The tribe of Pathans, called Kather, inhabiting the mountains between Kashmir, Atak, and Peshawer, had risen in rebellion; defeated the troops sent against them; captured the fortress of Derbend, and slain Ramdayal Sinh, the elder brother of Seodayál, and governor of the country between the Indus and Byas, under his father, Moti Ram, the Dewan of Kashmir. These events had created much alarm amongst the Sikh chiefs on our route, and aggravated the suspicions they entertained of our strength and designs. We arrived at Hoshyarpur on the 4th of March, and it was not until the 20th of April that I received news of Mir Izzet Ullah's proceedings. He had had an audience of Desa Sinh, the governor of Amritsar, who promised to send a confidential person with orders to Seodayál to oppose no impediment to my journey.

Hoshyarpur is a large and populous town, surrounded by a brick wall, separated from another town, Bahadarpur, by a few fields only; the latter, however, is nearly uninhabited. The population of Hoshyarpur consists chiefly of weavers, dyers, confectioners, grainsellers, and turners in wood. The weavers are almost all Mohammedans, and are an orderly and industrious set of people. They are employed extensively in the manufacture of cotton cloths and muslins, which are sent to distant markets in various directions; as, white cloths to Delhi; white and red to Jaypur and Bikaner; coarse cottons to the Panjab and Kabul, and the finer sorts to Herat, Balkh, Bokhara, and Yarkand. The water of Hoshyarpur is said to be of great efficacy in whitening cloths The cotton is raised abundantly at the foot of the neighbouring mountains, and commonly sells at from 16 to 20 sers for a Mahmud Shahi rupee.

Upon my first arrival at Hoshyarpur I pitched my tent under some tamarind-trees in a Mohammedan burying ground, but the Thannadar, Dilbagh Sinh, insisted upon my removing to a house in the town which was used as a hospice for Hindu mendicants. It was situated on the edge of a dry, sandy water-course, which was a receptacle for filth, and the stench was exceedingly offensive. I remonstrated against the change, but in vain, and was obliged to take up my residence on a terrace of this mansion, over which I raised a small tent. The heat during the day was intense, but the night was commonly refreshed by a thunder-storm. I preserved my health, however, by rigid abstemiousness, abstaining wholly from animal food, and allowing myself a dinner once only in three days; on the others I lived upon breakfast, sherbet, and tea. During the whole of my stay I devoted a considerable portion of my time to surgical practice, and was in no want of patients. The prevailing complaints were affections of the eyes, and I operated upon forty cases of cataract with very fair success. The operation is not unknown to native practitioners, and many of the barber-surgeons here are in the habit of couching. Their instruments are, however, clumsy, and their process rude, and success is very disproportionate to failure. I prevailed upon one of them to assist me in my cases, and left him conversant with the European method, and provided with a set of our instruments.

On the 25th of April Ghous Khan arrived from Desa Sinh, and informed me he was directed to pay every attention to my wishes until arrangements for my progress to Amritsar could be effected. On the following day he returned with Dilbagh Sinh and some other persons, and intimated his wish to inspect my packages, which were immediately shown him. I objected to their opening a box of presents intended for Ranjit Sinh, but a Sikh, who had been impertinently officious more than once, said that he had heard that Europeans had boxes which, when opened, discharged balls and killed those who stood near them, and intimated a suspicion that the box in question was designed for the Raja's destruction. It was, therefore, submitted to the inspection of the party, and dissipated these idle and absurd apprehensions.

There was still an evident indisposition to facilitate my departure, and it was even intimated to me that it would be preferable for me to return. Dilbagh Sinh then wished me to sign a paper expressive of my satisfaction with the treatment I had experienced from him, but this I refused to do, although I assured Ghous Khan that it was not my intention to make any complaint. At length, on the 29th, came letters from Desa Sinh, announcing the consent of Ranjit Sinh to my route back through the mountains or to Amritsar, as I should think best, and his commands that, in either case, I should be well taken care of. In the event of my travelling to Amritsar an escort of fifty men was placed at my disposal, and, accordingly, on the evening of the same day, I set out in that direction.

The country through which I travelled was

dry and sandy, with crops of tobacco, sugar-cane, and wheat. On the 30th I halted in a burial-ground outside of the town of Halalpur, to which, in the course of the day, a number of persons resorted to drink infusions of poppy heads and hemp. Some seemed exhilarated, and some stupified by the potion, but none were particularly talkative, or noisy, or riotous. In the night a townsman of Hoshyarpur arrived at my tent, charging four soldiers of my escort with having stopped and robbed him of property of some value. It was, however, evident that he had mistaken the persons, and that none of our party could have committed the theft. He was obliged to return, therefore, without redress. On the following day as we passed through the bazar of Kytapur we saw four Sikh horsemen whose appearance answered the description which the unfortunate silversmith (for such was his avocation) had given.

On the 2nd of May we started at half-past two in the morning, for the sun now became intensely fierce as the day advanced, and exposure to it on the preceding day had given me a severe headache. Our route for several miles ran across a plain to the left bank of the Byas, which we followed for some distance to the town of Gangrawal; there we took boat and dropped down to Byrawal, about three kos below, passing by Jelalabad, in which were the largest buildings I have seen in any town in the Panjab. It was formerly the capital of Adina Beg, when appointed by the Mahrattas, viceroy of Multan and Lahore. With their aid he kept for awhile the Abdali, Ahmed Shah, at bay, and it was not until after his death that the Afghan entered Hindustan for the last time, and, in alliance with the Mohammedan chiefs of that country, defeated the Mahrattas at Panipat. Byrawal is a moderately sized walled town, belonging to Fateh Sinh Aluwála, who sent me a present of money and refreshments, which I civilly refused, on the plea that Ranjit Sinh had already supplied me with everything that was necessary. I also declined going into the fort, of which I afterwards repented, as my tent did not come up, and I had to sit under a tree all day, exposed to a scorchingly hot wind.

We started on the 3rd at the same hour.

Miri Mal, Munshi, joined me at Byrawal, and stated he had the Raja's orders to attend upon me. In the evening Kuteb ad din Khan, with an escort of eighty horsemen, met me at Jindiala, and a Munshi came from the brother of the Hakim, Aziz ad din, to inform me that a tent was pitched for me in the garden of Karam Sinh. I set out from Jindiala on the following morning at three, and when I arrived at Amritsar at seven, found, as announced, a tent prepared for me in a garden of some extent, inclosed by a brick wall. In the evening the Killadar of Govind gerh, Imam ad din, with a couple of respectable looking Sikhs, paid me a visit. The Killadar brought me a present of some gold mohurs from Desa Sinh, and an apology for not coming himself, as he was on the eve of setting out for Lahore. I refused the money, except two hundred and seventeen rupees, which were offered in the name of the Raja, and those I could not, with propriety, reject. Nothing could exceed, at least in expressions, the kindness of the Killadar.

On the 5th I marched from Amritsar to Baniawal, through a flat country covered with low bushes, and little cultivated. At this place were stables containing one hundred and forty brood mares belonging to the Raja. With a few exceptions they were poor and dirty, and the stud was both expensive and unproductive.

May 6. I started at three, and at nine reached Shahlimar, the large garden laid out by order of Shah Jehan, where I took up my abode in a chamber erected by the Raja close to a well, and a reservoir which it supplies, and from which *jets d'eau* are made to play so near to the apartment as to cool the air at its entrance. Ranjit Sinh has, to a considerable extent, put the garden in repair. It is said to contain a hundred bigahs, the whole inclosed by a wall, in the course of which are several buildings. The grounds are intersected by canals, and the walks are formed of bricks laid edgeways. In the middle of the garden is a large square basin for holding water, furnished with copper tubes for fountains, and a white marble slope carved into a surface of leaves and shells, divided into compartments by lines of black marble. There are some open apartments of white marble of one story on a level with the basin, which present in front a square marble chamber with recesses on its sides for lamps, before which water may be made to fall in sheets from a ledge surrounding the room at top, whilst streams of water spout up through holes in the floor. This is called Sáwanbhadon, as imitative of the alternation of light and darkness with clouds and heavy showers in the season of the rains. The ground is laid out in platforms, and is covered with fruit trees. The water for its supply is brought by an aqueduct from Shahjehanpur, a distance of eighty kos. The gateways are lined with enamelled porcelain, and are in very tolerable repair. In the centre is a building of about one hundred feet long, consisting of three lines of arched apartments separated by the pillars from which the arches spring; the roof is painted in *fresco* with flowers. Scattered about the garden, sometimes even in the walks, are fragments of marble sculpture and beautiful mosaic taken from some splendid baths built by the Mohammedan ruler, and suffered by the Sikh prince to fall into decay.

On the day after my arrival, the brother of Hakim Aziz ad din came to conduct me to the Baraderi, another garden nearer the fort, in which was a small building of three stories. The middle apartment was principally of wood with panels of open work, divided by small compartments of flowers, birds, and human figures, the whole painted with great care and highly varnished. The cornice was wrought in ornaments that looked like scrolls of *lapis lazuli* on a gold ground, and the ceiling was a mosaic of flower-work embossed, interspersed with small mirrors, and divided by gilt lattices. The effect was, altogether, light and pleasing. A fountain played on one side of an open verandah that surrounded the apartment; the terraced roof inclosed by a latticed screen, served the purpose of a sleeping-room in the hot weather. In the course of the day Ranjit Sinh sent me sweetmeats and money, the latter of which I begged permission thankfully to decline. A reference was made to the Raja, who ordered me to keep what had been sent, but left me at liberty in future to accept or not, as I pleased, of such donations. In the evening came Hakim Aziz ad din, the wazir of Ranjit Sinh, and engaged in conversation with me for some time. He is a man of about thirty-five years of age, and of remarkably pleasing manners. He was originally a barber-surgeon, and was attached to Ranjit Sinh in that capacity when Mr. Metcalfe came to Lahore with propositions from the British government so unpalatable to the Sikh prince that he meditated an appeal to the sword. All his courtiers and counsellors supported him in this determination except the Hakim and another individual, named Purupteal, who strenuously dissuaded him from collision with the British power. The Raja, after some hesitation, recognized the wisdom of their advice, and ever afterwards gave these two persons his fullest confidence. Purupteal died, but Aziz ad din was made prime minister, in addition to his charge of physician. To his next brother, Nur ad din, was intrusted the command of Lahore and the superintendence of the artillery; and a third brother, Imam ad din, is the commandant of Govindgerh, a strong fortress constructed by Ranjit in the vicinity of

Amritsar. The three brothers are men of extreme urbanity and of remarkable intelligence.

On the evening of the 8th of May the Hakim came to conduct me to the presence of Ranjit Sinh. Having passed through one of the western gates of the fort, we crossed the garden, in which stands the Jama Masjid, or principal mosque. Thence a long flight of brick steps led to a second gateway and court, crossing which we came to a third gate that opened into a more spacious inclosure, in which stood a number of horses caparisoned. From this we entered a large court flagged with marble, and on the side opposite the entrance was an open apartment, in which the Maharaja was seated. Upon my approach he partly rose from his chair, which was of gold, and pointed to another, of silver, opposite to him, for me to sit down upon. His courtiers sat upon the carpet on either side, forming a lane from his chair to mine. The gateways were well guarded, but here were only two matchlockmen, sitting one on either hand of the Raja. After the ordinary inquiries I expressed my thanks to him for the attentions I had received since entering his territories, and requested leave to offer the few trifles I had brought for his acceptance. These were a pair of double-barrelled, and a pair of three-barrelled pistols, a sword, and the model of a cannon, with carriage and all appurtenances complete. This miniature piece of ordnance was made by Mr. Donnithorne, the mint master at Farokhabad, and was of singularly beautiful execution. To these I added some white chowri tails and bags of musk from the mountains. Ranjit was much pleased with the pistols, and still more with the cannon. Entering upon the main purpose of my travels, that of procuring horses, he ordered some of his to be exhibited, and about fifty were passed in review. They had all rich bridles, saddles, and housings, and were of the breeds of Dhani and Ghep, forest districts in the Panjab, the Lákhi Jangal, Rohtas, Atak, Kabul, and Bokhara. One which had cost 1700 rupees at Bokhara was beautifully made except in the legs below the knees and hocks, where he was too slight. For a grey Persian horse the Raja told me he had given 7000 rupees (700*l.*), but it struck me as inferior to most of those exhibited. After the horses had been fully inspected I took my leave.

Early on the following morning the Hakim came and took me to Ranjit, who wished me to see his horses exercised. I found him in a neighbouring garden seated on a chair under an awning without any guards, his courtiers sitting round him on carpets. When I was seated, fifty horses, different from those I had before seen, were brought forward. The space on which they were exercised was a garden-walk twelve feet broad. The rider (for one only was employed) mounted each horse in succession, and sometimes walked a few paces; but in general urged him at once into a short and high gallop, in which the fore action was very high, the hind low and quick. This was continued with great rapidity for a few yards, when the horse was suddenly turned on his haunches, and the same movements were repeated, or they were sometimes broken by rapid side movements in most perfect obedience to the action of the body and the hand. Not a single horse neighed, or was restive or vicious in the slightest degree, or was uneasy at mounting, or diverged from the path, although the Raja affirmed that they had not been ridden for some time past.

On the 10th I was present upon the Raja's invitation at the parade of two regiments which he had formed on the model of the Company's sipahis. The men were Sikhs, Hindustanis, and Gorkhas: the first were in general tall well-looking men; the second were of a mixed appearance; the last generally short but muscular. The Raja beheld their evolutions from the top of a low building at the palace, where I joined him. He seemed to take great interest in his regular battalions, but they are not popular amongst his officers. Desa Sinh told Izzet Ullah that all Ranjit's conquests had been won by the sword, and he had never known the infantry and artillery of any service. The Raja told me that these regiments had been first trained by a Naik, who had deserted from the Company's service. He was very communicative. After the review he showed me some more of his horses, chiefly from Bokhara; and then consulted me on the state of his health, complaining much that he could not bear such strong potations as he had been used to do formerly; he told me also that he had once sent an account of his ailments to General Ochterlony, that a European surgeon might prescribe for him, and that he had in consequence received some medicines, but had never taken any of them. These were afterwards sent to me, and finding one of them to be elixir of vitriol, I mixed a few drops with water, and drank it in the presence of the Hakim, in order to remove any suspicion that might lurk in a mind so constituted as that of Ranjit appears to be. After I left him I received a message that I was at liberty to visit any part of Lahore, whenever and in what way I pleased, and desiring me to name what breed of horse I preferred, that the Raja might give me one. I returned due thanks for the Raja's kindness, but declined accepting the horse, at least until I should return from Bokhara.

During the other days of my stay at Lahore, I had several interviews with the Raja, in all of which he conversed with the apparent absence of all reserve upon a variety of topics. One of his favourite themes was his stud. He told me that most of his horses were presents from his tributaries and zamindars, and that he not unfrequently requited the donor of a superior animal with a village or a jaghir; no wonder, therefore, that he obtained capital horses for his own use. He is not singular, however, in his passion. Every Sikh in the country keeps a horse and a brood mare, and rears colts for his own riding or for sale. The Raja monopolizes the best; for in the party which escorted me from Jindiala there was only one good horse. Ranjit proposed to me, through Mir Izzet Ullah, to purchase some horses for him at Bokhara, and I readily assented; but there was some difficulty as to the model, and the matter ended by my stating, that if he would be contented with but one, he should select it from the string I hoped to bring down.

The Raja consulted me also confidentially, regarding his health, which appeared to me to have suffered chiefly from intemperance and excess. On my departure I left a paper of remarks and instructions, which I heard was canvassed by a conclave of native doctors, and was honoured with their concurrence. In all probability it was but little attended to by Ranjit in practice.

Ranjit conversed also freely upon his military arrangements, and upon his past exploits. He told me that he lost 1900 men in a few hours, in an attempt to carry the city of Multan by escalade, owing to its having been made whilst he was absent. The gates had been blown open, but strong mounds of earth had been reared behind them. The garrison amounted to 3000 men, the besiegers to 25,000: but the former were all Pathans, and "fought with one hand." In answer to the question I put, how many survived the capture of the fort, he said 500, on which Himmel Sinh, a favourite courtier, guessing the drift of my inquiry, which was to ascertain the truth of the report that they had all been put to death immediately, remarked that not a man was killed after the fort surrendered. Speaking of the wealth of the city, the Raja said it was estimated at four crores, on which Himmel Sinh observed that the Sikh officers did not attempt to restrain the soldiers from plunder, on account of the opposition that had been offered, and the loss sustained ; and the Raja stated that very little of the booty had come to his share. Neither the Raja nor Himmel Sinh mentioned the severe captivity to which the gallant but unfortunate Nawab Sirafraz Khan* is now subjected at Lahore.

Early on the morning of the 13th I had my audience of leave. The Maharaja was peculiarly communicative and familiar. He told me that when Lord Lake entered the Panjab in pursuit of Holkar, he felt a strong desire to see the European general and his officers. His courtiers endeavoured to dissuade him, affirming that the very sight would be unlucky ; but he was determined to gratify himself, and for that purpose disguised himself as a common trooper, and accompanied by a party of his soldiers, repaired to the British camp. They went to Mr. Metcalfe's tent, and sent word that some Sikhs had come out of curiosity to see the Sahibs, and

* The Nawab Mozaffer Khan was killed in the storm with two of his sons. Sirafraz Khan was a third son. Although the troops plundered the city, they were compelled to relinquish their booty to the Raja, and the most valuable part came to the public treasury.—*Prinsep's Life of Banjit Sinh.* Ed.

begged he would indulge them. He immediately complied with their desire, but soon distinguished Ranjit Sinh amongst his visitors. After many assurances of kindness towards me, and of friendship for the Company, he dismissed me with an honorary dress of valuable shawls, and similar distinctions of less value to Mir Izzet Ullah, and his son and brother.

I had submitted to Ranjit Sinh a proposal to establish a fixed scale of duties for the admission of British merchandise into his territories, but he postponed the consideration of the arrangement until the return of his principal officers from the campaign in which they were now engaged, as he said he wished first to consult them upon the subject. This, however, I consider as an adjournment *sine die*. He readily consented to my proceeding through Mundi and Kulu to Ladakh, and in case of my being unable to reach Bokhara from Upper Tibet, I had his authority to pass through Kashmir with two hundred followers. He appointed Miri Mal to attend me to Kulu, and furnished me with written orders to his officers to afford every facility to my journey.

In the evening Nur ad din, the Governor, came to conduct me through the city. Lahore is surrounded by a brick wall about thirty feet high, which extends for about seven miles, and is continuous with the Fort. The latter, in which the Raja resides, is surrounded by a wall of no great strength, with loop-holes for musketry; a branch of the Ravi washes the foot of its northern face, but it has no moat on either of the remaining sides. The palace within this inclosure, called the Saman Burj, which is of many stories, is entirely faced with a kind of porcelain enamel, on which processions and combats of men and animals are depictured. Many of these are as perfect as when first placed in the wall. Several of the old buildings are in ruins, others are entire, and throw into shade the meaner structures of more recent date Ranjit Sinh has cleared away some of the rubbish, and has repaired or refitted some of the ruined buildings of Jehangir and Shah-jehan; but his alterations have not always been made with good feeling or taste. The great square and buildings of the principal mosque have been converted into a place of exercise for his Sipahi infantry, and he has stripped the dome of the mausoleum of Asof Jah, the brother of Nurjehan Begam, of its white marbles, to apply them to the erection of some insignificant apartments in the garden-court of the Mosque. The Diwan Am, or general hall of audience, is a long apartment supported by many pillars. The Diwan Khas, or private audience-hall, is a suite of small chambers offering nothing remarkable.

Lahore is said to have been twelve kos in circumference, and however this may have been, it is clear, from the ruins of buildings beyond the walls, that it was once much more extensive than it is at present. Such of it as still remains within the walls is apparently very populous. The streets were crowded to an extent beyond anything I have ever witnessed in an Indian city. The houses were in general of brick, and five stories high, but many were in a very crazy condition. The Bazar follows the direction of the city wall, and is not far distant from it. The street is narrow, and this inconvenience is aggravated by platforms in front of the shops, on which the goods are displayed under projecting pent-houses of straw to protect them from the sun and rain. Through the centre of the remaining contracted space runs a deep and dirty drain, the smell from which was very offensive. The population consists of Mohammedans, Hindus, and Sikhs, the former in the greatest number. I saw no building of any size or magnificence, except the mosque of the Nawab Wazir Khan. The wall of the city was still under repair, and 3000 men were said to be at work upon it and upon the moat which the Raja was about to add to the defences. The place, however, could oppose no effectual resistance to European assailants.

CHAPTER IV.

Shahdehra—Tomb of Jehangir Shah—Appa Sahib the ex-Raga of Nagpur—Phular Sinh Akáli—Manufacture of Shawls at Amritsar—Jindiala—Recall to Lahore—Indisposition of Ranjit Sinh—Second departure from Lahore—Stud of Fatteh Sinh Aluwala—Sikh religious Establishment—Cholera at Amb—Magar Mal the Collector of the Revenue—Assessment of Land—Robbery at Koloa—Thannadar of Rajpura—Dains or Witches—Sujanpur—Europeans in the Raja's employ—Raja Sansar Chand—His Family—His political Misfortunes—Gorkha Invasion—Blockade of Koth-Kangra—Its Cession to Ranjit Sinh—Paramount Authority of the Sikh—Detention of Mr. Trebeck and Party at Mundi—Reference to Ranjit—Dangerous Illness of the Raja's Brother—Native Treatment—His Recovery—Gratitude of the Family—Advance of the Party from Mundi—Mode of catching Quails—Departure from Sujanpur—Account of Kotoch and of its Raja—Frequency of Satis.

On the 15th of May I recommenced my journey towards the hills, accompanied by a Jamadar and Harkaras sent by the Raja to escort me to Shahdehra, a town on the left bank of the Ravi, about two kos from Lahore. The road is intersected by three different streams or branches of the Ravi, separated in the dry weather by intervals of half a mile; but in the rainy season the two most easterly branches are united, and form an expansive and rapid stream. The water is always thick and muddy, and abounds with fish, which had been taken under the Raja's protection. In some moment of whim he had issued an order prohibiting fishermen to ply their trade upon the Ravi. The two first branches are fordable, but the third, which is the principal one, has a ferry. The boats are the largest and best built I have seen in India.

There is nothing worthy of note at Shahdehra except the tomb of Jehangir Shah. The structure, which is built of a reddish freestone, stands in the centre of a spacious quadrangle, to which entrance is given by a handsome gateway of marble and enamel. It is surrounded by a long corridor with cells for fakirs. The corridor is paved with variegated marbles, and the walls are decorated with paintings. In the interior of the mausoleum is an elevated sarcophagus of white marble, enshrining the remains of the sovereign of Delhi, the sides of which are wrought with flowers of mosaic in the same style of elegance as the tombs in the Taj at Agra. The floor and walls of the chamber are of marble, and along the latter run passages of the Koran. The building was surmounted it is said by a dome, but it was taken off by Aurangzeb, that his grandfather's tomb might be exposed to the weather, as a mark of his reprobation of the loose notions and licentious practices of Jehanjir. Such is the story; but more probably the building was never completed. The roof is now square, presenting an open-work screen, with a lofty minaret at each angle. The edifice is of great extent, and of surpassing beauty.

On the 17th we halted in the suburbs of Amritsar, where I learned that the fugitive ex-Raja of Nagpur, Appa Sahib, was in honourable durance, nominally as the guest, but in reality as the prisoner of Ranjit Sinh. An attempt was made to involve me in an intrigue professing to have for its object the Raja's being delivered to the British, from whom he had made his escape: but I refused to have anything to do with the matter, referring a man who had volunteered the information to General Ochterlony. I had also a message from Phular Sinh, the Akali, who on a former occasion attacked the English envoy, Mr. Metcalfe, but was beaten off, expressing his contrition for his former misconduct, his dissatisfaction with Ranjit Sinh, his determination to attach himself to the English, and his readiness to carry fire and sword wherever I should bid him. I declined the interview which he solicited, and recommended him to entertain more prudent and loyal purposes. Desa Sinh, the Governor, again sent an apology for not paying me a visit, having, in fact, been expressly forbidden, as he informed Izzet Ullah, by his master, to hold any personal intercourse with me. Desa Sinh had incurred, indeed, the displeasure and distrust of Ranjit some time before, in consequence of some interchange of civilities between him and the officer in charge of the hill frontier, Captain Ross.

At Amritsar shawls are largely manufactured, but they are of an inferior quality. The manufacture seems to have been introduced by Kashmir families, who, before the Sikh conquest of that province, fled to the plains from the oppressive government of the Afghans. The yarn was formerly imported from Kashmir, but the Governor of that country has prohibited the export, at the request, he pretends, of the Kashmirian weavers, but, in reality, to discourage the foreign manufacture of shawls, the duty on which constitutes the chief source of his revenue. The yarn employed at Amritsar is therefore prepared there partly from the wool of Thibet, and partly from that of Bokhara. From the former a third of fine wool is usually obtained. The latter is of mixed colour and uncertain quality, and is, I suspect, adulterated with the down or fine wool of the yak. The Thibet wool, when picked, sells for six or eight Nanak Shahi rupees a ser. The latter from two to four.

The web yarn is employed double, as well as the weft, which latter is nearly four times as thick as the former. The twist of the thread is very loose, and this, I imagine, contributes essentially to the softness of the cloth.

Having experienced insurmountable difficulty in picking and cleaning a parcel of shawl wool I brought down from Bhot, I took advantage of my stay at Amritsar to ascertain how these operations were to be best effected. A family of Kashmiris lodged in the gateway of my residence, and the wife picked and cleaned about two ounces of Thibetan wool in my presence. Of this quantity nearly half was fine, nearly half consisted of coarse hair, and the rest was dust and refuse. It was picked by hand in about two hours. Some rice which had been steeped in clean water for two days was then taken out and drained, and before it was quite dry was bruised and ground to flour, in a wooden dish with a stone. Into this the wool was thrown, and it was rubbed and kneaded with the hand until every part of it was impregnated with the rice, when it was taken out and separated. This process was repeated, and after the second opening and drying it was ready for spinning. The spinning-wheel was the coarse implement in common use. A woman could spin about a rupee's weight (about one hundred and seventy-five grains) of fine yarn in a day, and her husband could earn about two anas and a half by weaving. The weavers are all miserably poor, and can scarcely procure subsistence. Many came to me and offered to accompany me wherever I pleased to take them.

Having remained at Amritsar, engaged in these and other inquiries, till the 23rd, I then moved to Jindiala, but I had no sooner arrived than messengers came from the Governor of Govindgerh with letters from Ranjit, stating that his son, Kharg Sinh, was seized with fever, and desiring me to send some medicine; reminding me, also, that I had promised to send the Raja some brandy from my stock at Mundi. Before I could prepare the medicines which I thought likely to be of use, two of the Raja's principal officers arrived with a letter, desiring me to return with all speed to Lahore. Although not very well pleased with this recall, nor wholly satisfied as to its motive, I had no choice but to express my readiness to comply. When I announced that I was prepared to depart, the Sirdars stated there was no need of immediate haste, as a subsequent express had been received, directing me, in order to save me the trouble of unnecessarily returning, to wait a couple of days for further orders. With this I was also obliged to comply.

After waiting till the 29th, exposed in a small tent to the hot winds, a letter arrived, desiring me to leave my tent and people at Jindiala, and return to Lahore. The former part of these instructions I did not hold it prudent to comply with, for the state of the atmosphere indicated the approach of the rains, when it would be difficult to move with baggage across the mountains. I therefore ordered my servants to proceed to Mundi, and wrote to my young friend, Mr. Trebeck, to march with them and the merchandise and luggage to Kulu, as he would there be nearly beyond the range of the monsoon. I then set off for Lahore, and, travelling all night, reached Shahlimar at eleven on the 30th, from which the Raja's own palankeen and bearers conveyed me in the evening to a house in the city. The Hakim came to me shortly after my arrival, and from his report I found that Ranjit was really labouring under a sharp attack of intermittent fever, which had been treated with little else than diluent and aperient sherbets, and for the cure of which the most effectual remedy devised was the lavish distribution of money and food to a parcel of idle fakirs.

Public business prevented the Raja from seeing me before the morning of the 2nd of June. I visited him at six o'clock, and found him seated under an awning in the open air. Some of his courtiers were on one side, and on the other were ten or twelve grave-looking personages, who he said were his physicians. Several were advanced in years, some had books in their hands, and some were employed in running their fingers over a string of beads. Amongst them I recognized Rahim Ullah, the tutor of my friend, Izzet Ullah, an intelligent and liberal-minded physician. Ranjit represented himself as feeling better, but he looked unwell, and required a more active mode of proceeding. He described to me his feelings, and I gave him my advice. I took my leave at noon. In the evening I had a visit from Nur ad din, to whom I fully explained my views, and the inconvenience to which any unnecessary delay exposed me, which he promised to represent to the Raja.

In the course of a few days the Raja's fever abated under the management of the native practitioners, and I was assured I should be allowed forthwith to resume my journey. I had been summoned to Lahore evidently in a fright by Ranjit Sinh, although he could not make up his mind to submit to my care, especially as the disease became less violent. Still, however, the fear of a relapse induced him to detain me within call, and it was only when he thought himself recovered that he consented to my departure. I set off on the evening of the 8th upon an elephant, and, after losing my way through the blundering of a harkara, arrived at Amritsar at two in the morning. I had been fifteen hours in a howdah, and felt more fatigue than I recollect to have experienced from any other mode of conveyance for a much longer interval. The sense of weariness and pain, and the extreme heat of the night, prevented my falling asleep. Whilst tossing about in a state little short of delirium, and having no servants, I was no less surprised than refreshed by the movements of a fan which a stranger was waving over my head. It proved to be a poor Kashmir weaver to whom I had given medicine, by which he had benefited, and, observing my restlessness, he had thus testified his grateful recollection of my aid; this was of essential value, for I slept and woke refreshed. On making preparations to resume my route I found that no orders had been given for any escort, and there was no small risk of my being intercepted by my Akali friend. Kutteb ad din, however, took upon himself the responsibility of sending with me some of his horsemen, and, under their protection, I arrived safely at Bhyrawal, where I learnt that my servants and baggage had been detained at Hoshyarpur instead of advancing to Mundi.

A stormy night prevented my crossing the Byas until the morning of the 10th. I was desirous to visit the stud of Fatteh Sinh Aluwala, and, therefore, went something out of my direct route to the town of Kapurtala. I found about forty young horses and colts, but understood that the mares were the property of the zemindars, none of whom can dispose of the colts they rear until they have first offered them to their chief. Should he approve of any he takes them at his own price, which is rarely more than a half or a third of their value.

At noon I reached Kartapur in an excessively hot day, and was hospitably received at the Dharmasálá of a set of Sikh fakirs termed Udasis *. An apartment was given me, the floor and walls of which had been deluged with water to cool them. One of the Udasis, an old man, entered into conversation with me. He inquired by what name we Englishmen designated the Being whom the Hindus term Ram and the Mohammedans Allah? When I had told him, he asked of what colour and form we represented God? To which I replied by asking him how it was possible to represent that Power who was everywhere present, and in whom all things existed, by any shape or colour? On which he expressed his satisfaction at finding that

* So denominated from their abandoning all hope of temporal advantage, even from their devotions.—Ed.

our notions were so conformable to the doctrines of the Sastras. In the evening the whole party engaged in prayer, in the course of which, after offering their good wishes for their ruler, the Sinh Sahib, they invoked the protection of the deity for the Firingi (European) Sahib and the other travellers then in their dwelling. I have seldom met with persons of more simple, unaffected, and pious manners than these Udasis.

After a hot march I arrived at Hoshyarpur on the following morning, and found that the people and baggage I had sent on from Jindiala under charge of Miri Mal, who had been deputed to attend me to Kulu, were one march in advance. I therefore procured a fresh supply of cattle, and moved on to Amb, where they were. Miri Mal's plea for the delay was the absence of Dilbagh Rai and Karm Rai, the two chief functionaries of Hoshyarpur, from that place, and consequent impossibility of procuring any conveyance. I was informed, however, that he had spent the interval at his own house, and had only moved when he heard of my quitting Lahore. The town of Amb was nearly deserted, the people having fled to the neighbouring thickets in hope to escape from the cholera, which had lately been making great ravages amongst them. It was asserted that a preventive of the disease had been discovered in the expressed juice of the onion; persons who took it to the extent of the juice of five onions at a dose, which proved strongly cathartic, not having been attacked. Their desertion of their town, however, indicated but little trust in the antidote.

I was met here by two persons from Raja Sansar Chand, and by a nephew of Magar Mal, the collector of the district. On the following day the latter met me at Rajpura. He is a remarkable man, upwards of seventy, but active and intelligent; he is of fair complexion and athletic make. He was formerly the chief financial minister of Ranjit, but incurred his master's displeasure by a violent quarrel in his presence with a favourite courtier, and, as a mark of disgrace, was appointed to the collection of the revenues of this district, amounting, it is said, to 140,000 rupees a year. He had lately introduced a new principle of rating the annual collections, which, without diminishing the amount, was likely to be satisfactory to the peasantry:—this was by a rough analysis of the soil. A given quantity of the earth was put into a fine muslin sieve, and washed with water until all the mould was carried through and nothing but the sand left, and, according to its proportion to the whole, a deduction was made from the assessment. Four rupees for two bigahs was the fixed rate for rich soil, three if it contained one-fourth of sand, two if it had a half, and one where the sand was three-fourths of the quantity. The general character of the soil of the Panjab, composed chiefly of mould and sand, renders this mode of appreciating its assessment more correct than might be supposed, and it was, at any rate, preferable to the old plan of assessing the land according to the estimated out-turn of the standing crops. The persons appointed to form this estimate made use of their power to oppress the cultivators, and to levy from them heavy exactions, in which the zemindars not unfrequently were sharers, defrauding the state without benefit to the peasantry. After our interview I moved on to Koloa, where I halted.

Before day-break on the 14th a servant came to me to report that a bag of money had been stolen from the tent of Izzet Ullah. Miri Mal sent word of the circumstance to the Thannadar of Rajpura, but he refused to interfere, saying it did not concern him. Several of the people of the place now came forward and declared that many robberies had been committed of late in this quarter, of which the Thannadar had not taken cognizance, and which could scarcely have been committed with impunity without his connivance. The same man had lately been implicated in an attempt to murder the collector, Magar Mal, but had hitherto remained at large from want of sufficient proof. A zemindar, who had refused to pay the money due upon his estate, had been seized by Magar Mal and put in confinement. His friends bribed the Thannadar, Radhan Sinh, and his assistant, Raju Sinh, to assist in liberating the prisoner and killing the collector. Magar Mal resided in a small fort called Basantpur, about two kos from Rajpura. Radhan Sinh corrupted some of his followers, and a night was appointed for their giving admittance to a hostile party into the fort. When the time arrived the conspirators of the garrison demanded payment of the stipulated reward before proceeding to action, with which the friends of the prisoner hesitated to comply. Several messages passed between the parties, and the repeated opening and shutting of the gate at an unusual hour at last awoke Magar Mal, who had retired to rest. On inquiring the cause, he was informed some of the garrison had been suddenly taken ill; but, his suspicions being awakened, he rose, and going to the window of his chamber, found a ladder placed against it. Throwing this down, he alarmed the garrison, and the plot was discovered. Miri Mal wrote to Ranjit Sinh an account of the robbery, and expressed his conviction that Ranjit will replace the money; but the theft, combined with the circumstances of neglect, delay, and obstruction which have taken place since I left Lahore, seems to me to have been authorisedly perpetrated, and to be part of a scheme intended to frustrate my journey, even whilst acquiescence in its performance is pretended.

On the 15th I marched to Nadaun, where an uncle of Sansar Chand met us. Miri Mal and the Lahore news-writer entertained us with some marvellous tales of the power of the Daïns, or witches of the mountains; and, amongst others, one of a zemindar, who, having lost his son and a favourite cow, accused an old woman of the village of having destroyed them by magically "eating their livers." The poor woman, after a severe whipping, pleaded guilty, and accused a number of other women in the village of being witches also: her head was cut off: but when it was found that her supposed sisterhood comprised the wives of all the principal farmers, the Malik of the village contented himself with fining them 300 rupees. I suspect the Malik was no other than Miri Mal, for he said he was bewitched himself for three years afterwards by an ague, which was cured only upon his giving fifty rupees and a suit of clothes to the old woman whom he considered the cause of his malady. These credulous people tell me they will convince me of the real existence of witches both at Shujanpur and Mundi.

From Nadaun we crossed the mountains to Shujanpur, nine kos. A violent thunder-storm and hurricane on our march ushered in the rains. After it had ceased, and we had resumed our progress, I was met by a Mr. O'Brien, an Irishman, in the service of the Raja, who conducted me to a bangalo, where I found refreshments prepared for me. O'Brien, who is a strong, stout man about forty, was a dragoon in the 8th, or Royal Irish. It is said that having come on guard without some of his accoutrements, he was reprimanded by the officer, and on his replying insolently the latter touched or struck him with his cane. O'Brien knocked him down with the butt end of his carbine, and then set spurs to his horse and galloped off. Not daring to return to his regiment, he wandered about the country for some time, and at last found service with Sansar Chand, for whom he has established a manufactory of small-arms, and has disciplined an infantry corps of 1400 men. There is also an Englishman of the name of James in the Raja's service. He has been a soldier, though he denies his having ever been engaged in the service of either King or Company in India. He is an illiterate, but an ingenious man, with some skill in practical gunnery. These men are of some service to the Raja, and might be of more, but their means are limited, and their habits not of the most regular or temperate description.

In the evening I waited upon the Raja at his desire, and found him with his son and grandson in an open building in a garden. Raja Sansar Chand is a tall, well-formed man, about sixty. His complexion is dark, but his features are fine and expressive. His son, Rai Anirudha Sinh, has a very handsome face and ruddy complexion, but is remarkably corpulent. He has two sons, one of twelve, the other of five years of age, both less fair than himself. Sansar Chand was formerly the most powerful Raja from the Setlej to the Indus. All the potentates from the former river to Kashmir were his tributaries or dependants, and he was extremely wealthy, possessing a revenue of thirty-five lacs of rupees. He is now poor, and in danger of being wholly subjected to Ranjit Sinh. His misfortunes are mainly owing to himself, and his decline presents a remarkable contrast to the rise of his neighbour, and now paramount lord, Ranjit Sinh.

When Ahmed Shah Abdali invaded Hindustan for the last time, Gomand Chand, the grandfather of Sansar Chand, was military governor of the Doab of Jalandhar, between the Setlej and the Byas. The Afghans conferred his government upon him in perpetuity, along with the royal fort of Kangra. To defend his possessions Gomand Chand raised a force of 4000 men, composed chiefly of Rohillas, Afghans, and Rajputs, drawn from the Delhi and Afghan forces, to whom he gave liberal pay, or five rupees a month for each footman, and twenty for each horseman.

Tegh Chand, the son of Gomand Chand, maintained the same kind of force, and even increased the pay. Sansar Chand, for some time after his accession, adopted the same policy, and was enabled thereby to extend his authority over the hill rajas, and repel an invasion of the Gorkhas. A treaty was concluded with the latter, by which the Setlej was established as a boundary which neither was to pass.

At this time Gholam Mohammed, the deposed Raja of Rampur, was living in the territories of Sansar Chand. Although finally defeated by the British at the battle of the Dojaura rivulet, yet he had gained an important advantage at first, and had nearly achieved a victory, and this circumstance had given him a high military reputation. Sansar Chand, therefore, readily deferred to his counsels, and was persuaded by him to break up his own force as needlessly expensive, and levy an army of Rohillas on cheaper terms: Gholam Mohammed engaging to raise them at four rupees a month for each foot soldier, and twelve for each horseman.

As soon as the Gorkhas heard of the dismissal of Sansar Chand's old troops, they broke their treaty, and repeated their invasion before his new levies had joined. Sansar Chand opposed them as well as he could, and Gholam Mohammed brought up his troops with very creditable expedition. Before they could join the Raja, however, the Gorkha general drew them on to an engagement, in which they were completely routed and dispersed. The Gorkhas then occupied the country, and the Raja's only remaining hope was in the strength of the fortress of Koth Kangra.

The command of the place was intrusted to his son, whilst he stationed himself at Tíra to harass the enemy, and facilitate the supply of stores and provisions to the garrison. The fortress had been supplied with grain for twelve years, but great negligence and waste exhausted it in a much shorter period, and, the Gorkhas having prevailed on the Haripur Raja to forego his alliance with Sansar Chand and join them, the chief source whence the latter had derived provisions was cut off. The Raja had previously thrown himself into the fortress, and he and his garrison were without food, subsisting for four months upon little else than the leaves of vegetables. In this state of things, after the struggle had subsisted for more than four years, Sansar Chand was obliged to apply to Ranjit Sinh for assistance. The Sikh chief gave him effectual succour, and the Gorkhas were driven out of the country; but the Raja paid dearly for his liberation, being obliged to cede his fort of Koth Kangra to his ally, and to acknowledge a sort of vassalage to him, as his liege lord. Ranjit has not exacted yet any tribute from him, but he claims military service, and put him foremost in his late attack upon the Kahalur Raja, whose forts were captured by the troops and artillery of Sansar Chand under James and O'Brien. Ranjit sends for Sansar Chand to his court once a year, and the latter expects on one of these occasions to be detained a prisoner; but the Sikh's purposes do not seem yet to be matured, and, satisfied that his prey is within his grasp, he forbears awhile to pounce upon it.

The loss of territory, and falling off of his dependencies, have so much reduced the revenues of Kotoch, that, as the Raja assured me, he has but 70,000 rupees a year for the expenses of himself and his family after paying his troops. His resources are, however, still respectable; his country is strong, his peasantry resolute and warmly attached to him, and he has a large property in jewels, which might be turned to better account. His pride, however, prevents his making the sacrifices necessary to the improvement of his means, and, whilst he spends large sums upon a numerous zenana and a parcel of hungry retainers, he allows the defences of the country to fall into ruin, and keeps his soldiers short of powder and ball. He is very anxious to be taken under the protection of the British government, and in the event of a rupture with the Sikhs, it would find in him a zealous and useful partisan.*

On the 20th and 22nd letters arrived from Mr. Trebeck, stating that Mohan Sinh, the Sikh governor of Koth Kangra, had been at Mundi, and, after stationing guards round our encampment, had refused to allow him to proceed as I had instructed him to do. I received also a letter from Mohammed Hafiz Fazil, detailing the particulars of a conversation between him and Mohan Sinh, in which the latter asserted he acted under the express orders of Ranjit Sinh, and that he

* Sansar Chand died in the end of 1823, and was succeeded by his son, Anirudh Chand, with the concurrence of Ranjit Sinh; but, in 1828, the Raja refusing to give his sister in marriage to the son of the Sikh, Dhyan Sinh, a *protegé* of Ranjit's, was obliged to fly his country, and place himself and family under British protection. The Raj of Kotoch then became part of the territories of Ranjit.—Ed.

should not attend to any addressed to other officers: that his instructions were to prevent by all means my going on to Ladakh: that he knew his master's ways, who had treated me with civility to gain my confidence, but who never intended to permit the prosecution of my journey. My only resource was to appeal to Ranjit Sinh himself, to whom I also forwarded a report of this conversation.

Whilst I awaited at Shujanpur a reply to my letter, the Raja and his son and brother treated me with the greatest attention, inviting me to spend part of every day with them, and sending me presents of sweetmeats and fruit,—when an occurrence took place which confirmed their regard, and established between us a close and curious connexion. On the night of the 30th of June, Fateh Chand, the Raja's brother, a stout man about fifty-four, was taken seriously ill. He grew worse on the following day, and in the evening was considered to be in a dangerous condition. At the Raja's desire I went to see him. He was tossing and tumbling about on a low bed, on which he was with difficulty retained by several attendants. Upon the floor on one side of his bed was a row of lamps, by which a naked ascetic, with matted hair and body smeared with ashes, was seated, gesticulating and muttering charms and prayers. Eight or ten Hindu and Mohammedan physicians sat or knelt round the bed, and in an adjoining room was the Raja with his family and attendants.

Fateh Chand was insensible, and breathed like a person in a fit of apoplexy. One leg was swathed with cloth from the toe to the hip, and bands of various-coloured cloth and thread were bound round his arms and ancles. As cholera was prevailing in the neighbourhood, I thought, at first, this was his complaint, but the symptoms were more of an apoplectic character, and I recommended bleeding freely, and the actual cautery to the stomach and breast. The Raja, however, could not be prevailed upon to employ these remedies. The Brahmans had pronounced that the prince was possessed by an evil spirit, and the Raja ordered them to drive it away. I wished to withdraw, but, at the Raja's entreaties, remained with him for about two hours, and witnessed the gesticulations and mummeries practised as exorcisms. After about an hour had passed, one Brahman asked another more actively busied in gesticulating with his hands, and muttering incantations, what answer the goddess, Debi, vouchsafed?—to which he honestly replied Debi was silent, and his charms had no power. As the Raja continued averse to suffering me to adopt a more rational course, I at last retired.

At seven on the following morning a message from the Raja summoned me again to his brother. He had been removed from the bangala in the garden to an outer building, was abandoned by Brahmans, Fakirs, and physicians, and was placed on the ground to die. Much of his personal property had been distributed amongst the Brahmans and the poor, but his cows had not yet been given away. An astrologer had ventured to predict that if he recovered, it could only be through my aid, and the possibility of his recovery thus implied preserved his cattle, the grant of which would be injurious to his consequence should he recover. In complying with the Raja's request to attempt his brother's restoration, of which there seemed but little hope, I demanded, in the first place, liberty to do what I pleased with the patient, without objection or interference, and, in the second, that he should not suffer it to be said, in the event of that failure which was so probable, that his brother's death was, in any degree, owing to my treatment. He said that he gave his brother entirely up to me, and that, as far as he was able, he would prevent any blame being ascribed to me should I be unable to save his life. With this authority and guarantee I set myself assiduously, though with but little confidence, to adopt such measures as I conceived calculated to save Fateh Chand from apparently inevitable death.

It would be out of place here to detail the plans I pursued: they were, of course, of an active character, and such as, under other circumstances, would scarcely be warrantable: after resolute perseverance, however, they were effectual. The state of torpor was exchanged for vital, though sluggish, action in the course of the night. On the next day consciousness, though imperfect, was restored, and on the 4th he was sensible. He continued to mend, though slowly, during the 5th and 6th, and on the 7th might be pronounced out of immediate danger: by the 10th he was convalescent.

Nothing could exceed the expression, and I believe the sentiment of gratitude on the part of the Raja and his son. Besides a valuable dress of honour, the former conferred upon me a grant of land, desiring me to appoint some one to manage it on my behalf. The whole country seemed to rejoice in Fateh Chand's recovery, for his courage and frankness made him a general favourite. He himself, when sufficiently restored, insisted on exchanging his turban for my hat, and making me his brother by adoption. He placed his turban on my head, and my hat on his; each waved his hand, holding a handful of rupees, round the other's head, and the rupees were distributed amongst the servants. He also gave me some green *dúb* grass, which I was desired to wear, and thus, notwithstanding the difference of caste and complexion, I became an honorary member of the family of Sansar

Chand. Whatever might be the value of such an association, it was a most unequivocal testimony of the sincerity of their gratitude.

During these proceedings letters from Ranjit Sinh arrived, in which he disclaimed all countenance of Mohan Sinh's conduct, and assured me that orders had been sent to that chief not only to desist from offering any obstruction to the advance of my baggage, but to provide facilities for its conveyance. He also alluded to the robbery, and promised me, if the money was not recovered from the plunderers, he would be responsible for its restitution; and he concluded by good-humouredly desiring me to place more reliance on the word of Khálsa Jí—a title properly belonging to the Sikh confederacy, but which Ranjit had adopted for himself. Advices also came from Mundi that Mohan Sinh had announced that parties were collecting for the transport of the baggage to the frontier. I wrote to Mr. Trebeck to send me word when he had crossed the Byas, as I would then join him from Shujanpur; but the rain had been so incessant, and the river was so much swollen, that at present it would not be safe to attempt the passage.

One evening late I heard a sound, apparently not far from my tent, that seemed to be the booming of the batér or quail, and sallying forth to ascertain the cause, I found some boys snaring those birds. One of them was engaged in blowing into a small earthen pot with a hole at the bottom, which was placed close to the ground, and thus making the sound I had heard. Two others were seated with a light near a pile of dry grass. They told me that the noise, which was kept up for an hour or two, attracted the birds to the spot in considerable numbers, on which the boys by the grass set fire to it. The sudden blaze had the effect of bewildering the quails, so that they did not, for some time, attempt to escape, and, in the interval, the fowlers knocked them down with sticks. In this manner they often killed a great many birds; but it was only practised in the rains, and succeeded with none but quails.

I left Shujanpur on the 22nd of July. The Raja came to my tent in the morning, and took leave of me with much kindness. His son met me on my way to the river, and bade me a friendly farewell. I quitted the town at nine o'clock, having now before me no further obstacles to my penetrating to Tibet than the natural difficulties of the country and the state of the weather.

The Raj of Kotoch, or Kangra, which is subject to Raja Sansar Chand, is about forty short kos in length from north to south, and varies in breadth from east to west from fifteen to forty kos. The greatest length is from Pathichar Mahal on the north-west, near the frontier of Chamba, to Bilaspur, on the south-east: the greatest breadth is from Baidyanath Maharaj, or Iswar Linga, a shrine of Siva, and place of religious resort on the north-east, adjacent to Kulu and Mundi, to Tulhati Mahal, to the south, on the borders of Jaswal. It is surrounded by Mundi and Sukhet on the east; by Kahalur and the Vale of Jaswa on the south; by part of Jaswa, Siba, and Gula on the west; and Kulu and Chamba on the north. It is separated from the Bist (or Byas and Setlej), Doab of Jalandhar, by the states of Jaswa, Siba, and Gula; and from the great snowy range of the Himalaya by those of Mundi, Sukhet, Chamba, and Kulu. It is, however, close to the mountains, and is of considerable elevation. In some parts of it there is ice on the ground in July.

The Raj is divided into three provinces, or Kotoch, Changa, and Palam. The latter is the more western and northern, bordering on Chamba. Three considerable rivers flow from the northern mountains, the Bánganǵá, Kurali, and Nayagul, which unite in Haripur, and, under the name of Trigadh, fall into the Byas at Siba fort. The Byas itself waters the eastern portion of the Raj, flowing through Shujanpur, Tira, and Nadaun.

The natural products of Kotoch are not many, nor, in their present state, of much value, but they might be much improved under an enlightened government, strong enough to protect its territory from foreign aggression. Iron has been found, but the ore has not been wrought. In the neighbouring Raj of Mundi there are valuable mines of this metal. I have not heard of any other mineral productions except salt, of which there is a deposit in Mundi, from which the consumption of the mountaineers in these districts is principally supplied.

Amongst the vegetable products may be enumerated rhubarb, which is procured in abundance on the farther hills of Kangra. All the pieces of the root which I have seen are, however, injured by decay of the central part, which makes it comparatively of little use. Opium is raised largely on the Kulu frontier, but the cultivation of the poppy and extraction of the juice are ill understood. There is a considerable demand both for opium and the poppy in the Panjab, as the Sikhs, whose religious creed forbids the use of tobacco, supply its place by opium and an infusion of poppy heads, to both of which they are much addicted, the former being used by the more wealthy, the latter by the poorer people. Cotton is reared on the skirts of the mountains at the head of the Doab, and furnishes the material from which the finer cloths of Hoshyarpur are manufactured, for the supply of the north-western parts of Asia to a very great extent. Agents from very remote places attend at Hoshyarpur, make advances to the weavers, and, taking the cloth in the rough from the loom, bleach, wash, and pack it each in his own fashion to suit the market of his country. The cloths of Hoshyarpur, however, are generally light and flimsy. The district of Palam and the country east of Shujanpur produce plentiful crops of wheat and rice of a superior description. No timber trees of any bulk occurred upon the road, but firs of large size are said to grow in some of the tracts along the Byas. At no great distance from that river, also, on a mountain range called Nag ki Dhar, is an extensive bambu forest, from which the whole country is supplied. One of the most abundant trees met with is the mulberry, and it might be possible, therefore, to introduce the silk-worm with advantage into the country. Bees, both large and small, are numerous, and are domesticated for their honey, which is of an excellent quality.

Since the loss of Kangra, the Raja has resided principally at Shujanpur, or rather Alempur, on the right bank of the Byas, in gardens in which some small buildings accommodate himself and his court, and a larger one is erected for his zenana. His earlier residence, and that of his predecessor, was at Tíra, where an extensive pile of buildings stands upon an eminence on the left bank of the river; the apartments are more spacious and commodious than is usual in Indian palaces, but they are now made no use of, except for the Raja's personal armoury, in which are some splendid swords, and for a small manufactory of carpets for his own use. Sansar Chand quitted this residence it is said in consequence of its being distant from water; but another reason is assigned by popular rumour. On one of the Raja's visits to Lahore, Ranjit Sinh remarked that he had heard much of the beauty of the palace at Tíra, and should like to see it. Sansar Chand replied he should have felt honoured by the visit, but that he had quitted Tíra, and the place had fallen into so much decay, that it was unfit to receive the Sikh chief, as he might satisfy himself by sending a person to inspect it. Ranjit accordingly dispatched an envoy for this purpose; but a messenger, sent off immediately by Sansar Chand, with orders to travel night and day, anticipated the Sikh envoy in sufficient time to give Tíra a dismantled and desolate appearance. The report made by the Sikh deterred Ranjit from his proposed visit, but the circumstance excluded Sansar Chand from his patrimonial mansion.

Raja Sansar Chand spends the early part of the day in the ceremonies of his religion; and from ten till noon in communication with his officers and courtiers. For several days prior to my departure he passed this period at a small bangala, which he had given up for my accommodation, on the outside of the garden. At noon the Raja retires for two or three hours; after which he ordinarily plays at chess for some time, and the evening is devoted to singing and naching, in which the performers recite most commonly Brij bhákha songs relating to Krishna. Sansar Chand is fond of drawing, and has many artists in his employ: he has a large collection of pictures, but the greater part represent the feats of Krishna and Balaram, the adventures of Arjuna, and subjects from the Mahabharat: it also includes portraits of many of the neighbouring Rajas, and of their predecessors. Amongst these latter were two profiles of Alexander the Great, of which Rai Anirudha gave me one. It represents him with prominent features, and auburn hair flowing over his shoulders; he wears a helmet on his head begirt with a string of pearls, but the rest of his costume is Asiatic. The Raja could not tell me whence the portrait came: he had become possessed of it by inheritance.

Sansar Chand deduces his descent from Mahadeo, and has a pedigree in which his ancestors are traced to their celestial progenitor, through many thousand years. I requested to have a copy of this document, and some Kashmir Pundits were ordered to transcribe it against my return. The pedigree is written in verse, and contains in general little more than the birth and death of each male individual of the family.

The practice of the horrible rite of Sati is frequent in these mountains: two widows were burnt during my stay, the elder of whom was not more than fourteen. The wives of Fateh Chand were in readiness to accompany his body to the pile, when the success of my endeavours rescued them, for a while at least, from so fearful a consummation.

CHAPTER V.

March from Shujanpur—Palace at Bijapur—Cultivation—the Binoa River—Baidyanathpur—Fertility of the Lands—Forts of Mundi—Stone Bridge over the Gugli—Hindu Temples—Sculptured Feet—Vegetable Tinder—Town of Gumha—Salt Mines—Buza Beer—Heavy Rain—Village of Hulhu—Annual conflict of Wizards and Witches—Uttar Sal River and Village—Pass of Tilakpur—Prospect—Syri—Bajaura—Hindu Temple—Sultanpur, the capital of Kulu—Raja's Palace—Meeting with Mr. Trebeck—His Journal—Mundi—Byas River—Raja of Mundi—Salt Mines—Iron—Tiri—Festival of Adi Brahma—Bajaura—Death of the Rani—People of Kulu—Parbati River—Hot Springs of Mani Karn—Legend of their origin—Raja of Kulu—Vazir Sobha Ram—Fruit Trees—Unhealthiness of the Climate—Dress and Diet of the People—Departure.

I QUITTED Shujanpur at nine on the 22nd of July. The morning was dry, but heavy masses of white clouds hanging on the mountains of Mundi, threatened rain. The road descended to the bed of the Byas, and proceeded along its right bank for about half a mile, when it ascended a ravine called Sakku Ghat, leading to a few straggling houses on the top, which constituted the village of Sakku, from which the white palace of Bijapur, which is about five kos north-north-east from Shujanpur, was in sight straight onward. Pears were in abundance of a small size. Wild grapes were also plentiful: they are ripe, it is said, in August. Three kos on the road was the village of Kangwen; and beyond it, flowing from the mountains on the left, was a considerable water-course which descended to the Byas. The district between the stream and the mountains forms the Jagir of Fateh Chand, whose residence at Palasi, a village on an eminence, was visible from the road. The Jagir is bounded by a stream which flows from the elevated plain of Jaysinhpur, the former residence of the Raja's ancestors. Kamla Gerh is here in sight, some distance to the east, and at about an equal distance beyond it, a small river called the Bakar khad, rising in the passes on the frontier of Mundi, falls into the Byas on its right, and with the Binoa, another feeder of the Byas, incloses an island covered with sisu trees, which is often a source of dispute between the Kotoch and Mundi Rajas. The rain came on heavily in the afternoon, and I took up my lodgings in a hut on the plain of Jaysinh, near a new palace which Anirudh Rai is building.

On the 23rd I moved at nine, and soon crossed the rivulet of Bijapur, which skirts the foot of the heights, on which stands the palace, formerly defended by a square fort between it and the river: towers were erected on eminences commanding the approach, and the ascent from the river led through a strong gateway. The road skirts the foot of the mountains for above a mile, crossing another nala, and then turns off from the right bank of the Byas, leading through Tumiana Ghat to a flat with a temple and grove of mango trees: the spot is called Amal Tappa, and is about a kos and a half from Bijapur.

The path led hence northward, up an ascent to Sidhchaori, taking an hour and twenty-five minutes; ten minutes more brought us to some heights from which the jangal had been cleared, and which were laid out in terraces for cultivation. Farm-houses were scattered about upon the summits and slopes, and the scene offered an agreeable contrast to the rough thicket from which we had just emerged. This district is called

Chadiari, and extends several kos in all directions. It is contiguous on the north with the pargana of Drug, divided by the Binoa river from that of Kargaran.

The Binoa river rises in Chamba, from Yara ki joth about fifteen kos north-east of Baidyanathpur, and passing that place to the south, falls into the Byas opposite Kamlagerh, insulating with the Bakar khad the tract already noticed, called Molag. Its whole course is about twenty-seven kos, and it receives the Loni and the Sansari rivers. Both these rise in Kulu; the former at Tatto-ani (hot spring), ten kos north-north-east from Baidyanathpur, and falls into the Binoa at Diwar, two kos from Baidyanathpur; the latter at a place distant from Baidyanathpur, six kos east by north, and falls into the Binoa about two kos from that place in the same direction. The Binoa varies much and suddenly at different seasons. In the cold weather it is fordable in many places; in the hot weather its depth is much increased by the melting of the snows; in the rains it is a deep and rapid stream. We crossed it on skins at Goldon Ghat, where it was sixty feet broad and eight deep. Fronting us was a bank of perpendicular rock forty feet high, over which the water from the rice grounds fell in two beautiful cascades. A sais or groom of Mir Izzet Ullah, who was a strong man and able swimmer, chose to swim across: he effected the passage, but again venturing into the current, was carried away and dashed against the rocks: he sank several times, but at last rising in face of a rock, he was laid hold of by the ferryman, and brought to shore exhausted and senseless. It was not without difficulty that he was restored.

The country north of the Binoa to Baidyanathpur slopes upwards, and consists entirely of rice grounds, watered partly by the rains, and partly by channels led down from the mountains: the soil is a reddish clay retentive of moisture, and extremely fertile, yielding the finest rice in the hills in the rainy season, and the finest wheat in the cold weather. The Raja keeps this tract in his own hands, giving two-thirds of the produce to the cultivators, on condition of their finding labour, tools, and seed; so that he has one-third clear of expense. We reached Baidyanathpur at six o'clock, after a complete drenching and a most toilsome journey, for the soil being so wet and heavy, our horses could scarcely drag their feet through it. Baidyanathpur is a most miserable place, containing only a few huts and grainsellers' shops. I had much difficulty in finding shelter from the rain. I did not go into the temple, but was informed that it presented nothing remarkable. On my way I received a letter from the Rani of Chamba, who was indisposed, stating her ailments, and inviting me to Chamba. I sent her what I thought likely to be of service, but excused myself from visiting her. The road hence is said to be very difficult, it being necessary in many places to drag men and baggage by ropes up the scarps of the rocks.

It was necessary to halt during the 24th to allow our baggage to dry, as the weather had cleared up: we should have been detained at any rate, for the Rani of Kulu had lately died, and all the provincial functionaries were at the capital. I therefore sent off to the son of the Vazir, who was the nearest to us, to request he would direct a supply of porters; and at the same time wrote to Sansar Chand, to request I might take on his people and soldiers to Kulu: this country forms an angle where the states of Kangra, Mundi and Kulu meet, and is much infested by robbers, from Mundi especially. I had received two letters from Sansar Chand, with some confectionary from the ladies of his zenana; and at Baidyanathpur an agent of Anirudh Rai brought me a present of two goats, and a large quantity of rice, sugar, and other supplies.

On the 25th orders arrived from Sansar Chand for one hundred porters to be furnished me, with an escort of thirty sipahis to attend me to Kulu, and supplies for ten days. A letter from the Rai also came, asking me if I had seen any lands on my march at Jaysinhpur or Baidyanathpur that I should prefer: heavy rain fell on this and the following day, and the Binoa rolled along with a blackened and rapid current. I wished to have crossed back to the west bank to examine the aspect of the country, and made an attempt, but the ferrymen were reluctant to persist, and the servants of the Raja most earnestly dissuaded me from the undertaking: I therefore relinquished it. The soil here is of the same description as that before noticed, and being well watered by canals, trenches, and rivulets from the hills, which everywhere cross it in their course to the Binoa, is extremely productive. An unusual drought prevailed last cold season, and the crops were scanty, amounting to what is here considered a scarcity; yet fine rice was selling at thirty-six paka or full sers, and coarse at forty-eight sers for a rupee. Wheat was forty sers for a rupee. The cattle are small, and sell for four to six rupees a head. Labour may be had at two rupees per month. Porterage to Lahore, one hundred and twenty kos, is at the rate of two and a half rupees per paka maund. The country is healthy, if any opinion may be formed from the looks of the inhabitants.

On the morning of the 27th a few porters arrived from the son of the Kulu Vazir, with intimation that others would meet us on the road: above eighty more had been assembled from the peasantry of the neighbourhood, and we therefore set off. The direction of the road was up a steep ascent north-east in the mountains of Mundi. We had not marched far when the rain poured down with a violence of which those unacquainted with tropical climates can form no conception; and constant torrents rushed across the road and embarrassed and retarded our progress. We met with no accident, however, and in an hour and a half reached the cultivated grounds of Aija. On the summit of a ridge on the right, about two hundred and fifty feet above the road, stood the most western fort of Mundi, which is visible from Shujanpur; a deep ravine separates the ridge from the main land, and is crossed by a wooden bridge. The rivulet which runs to the west from the heights of Aija empties itself into the Binoa just above Baidyanathpur: we had some trouble in fording it. On the sides of the road were abundance of barberry bushes covered with fruit; along with them grew a prickly shrub with a red berry of an agreeable sub-acid flavour. The hill people who had accompanied me from Nahan recognised it as a native of their country, where it is called Khai-an. Further on the road, but stretching to the east, are two other forts; these with the first we passed are called Shirpur, Shahpur, and Shujanpur; the middle one seems to be the strongest. The plain was crossed by several streams which unite into one large trunk, the Rani, that flows to the south-east, and falls into the Byas at Puna-ka-tir, near Mundi.

In front of our road to the north-east appeared the fort of Karnapur on an eminence; it was merely a cluster of bastions, united by walls, and of no strength. The road wound round the hills on which it stood, so as to bring it to bear on the north-west, and then proceeded easterly and north over the plain to the Gugli river, the most considerable of those which form the Rani, and at this season a broad and rapid torrent, but fordable. A stone bridge had been erected across it, but the arches being too small, the water had washed away the structure, though it was twelve feet thick. This district formerly belonged to the Raja of Bangore, but his more powerful neighbours the Rajas of Chamba and Mundi dispossessed him, and divided his country between them. We stopped at Hara bagh, or green garden, so called from a pine forest adjacent, eight kos from Baidyanath-pur: it had several temples and a house belonging to the Raja of Mundi, in which we took shelter along with the women and children of the families of the herdsmen, who pasture droves of buffaloes in this neighbourhood, subsisting on their produce.

The morning of the 28th saw us set off in a mizzling rain. We passed on our left a group of Hindu temples, decorated with sculpture. Before each of them that was of any size was a figure of Nandi, the bull of Siva, his face towards the door of the temple, and the figure of a herdsman laying hold of his tail. The road ran to the east, over a rough causeway, through a thick wood of pine trees covering the side of a steep hill. The summit of the ascent, about half a mile from the village, was called Garhwa Chelí. The path then descended rapidly, between a small temple on the left, and an altar or mound of masonry, with two feet sculptured on it. These altars are very common, and, perhaps, indicate the former prevalence in these parts of the religion of Buddha, which, more than any other Indian creed, employs this emblem. Going down the declivity one of the people plucked a leaf from a shrub growing out of the wall, the lower surface of which was covered with the cottony down that serves the mountaineers as tinder, catching fire readily from the sparks of a flint and steel, and burning slowly and without flame. The Nahan people call it kaphi, the Gorkhas, kapas or cotton*. Three mountain torrents, now swollen to rivers, were crossed on our way to the small town of Gumha, which is prettily situated half way up the face of a mountain. For nearly a mile the road leads up a steep flight of steps, and the whole distance from Baidyanathpur is paved irregularly with large stones. The town is of no extent, and the houses are arranged without any plan. They are two stories high, of stone, cemented by clay, and strengthened by fir timbers laid horizontally; thin planks of deal pierced with holes serve for windows; a band of yellow paint borders the doorway, and a low open verandah extends along the front; the roofs are constructed of fir spars

* It is noticed in Royle's Illustrations (p. 247) as the Chaptalia gossypina, and figured in plate 59. A kind of cloth is made from it.—ED.

covered with slates, but the slates are laid loose, and are of every shape and size, just as they come from the quarry: it is not wonderful, therefore, that they imperfectly keep out the rain. I showed some of the people how to fasten the slates with pegs, and, as they listened attentively, they may, perhaps, hereafter, be indebted to me for drier lodgings. The temple at Gumha was covered with carvings.

Gumha owes its erection in this spot to the vicinity of salt mines, into one of which I descended. A horizontal shaft, about four feet square, extended from the side of the hill about twenty yards, where pine trees cut into notches for steps led down a slope to a second, and thence to a third shaft; the latter was perpendicular, and was descended by a bambu ladder to the bed of salt. The sides of the passage were protected by hides, and a stream of water ran along the bottom. Torches of pine wood lighted us down, but I could see little except a large cavity, the roof of which was formed of salt, and the bottom covered with shallow water. The salt occurs in solid masses in a rock of grauwacke, crossed by veins of quartz. As the art of boring is unknown, the mineral is discovered by digging. A horizontal gallery is cut from the face of the hill, and as it advances is roofed with deal spars supported by sections of the stem of the fir tree. If this, after passing some way, does not come upon the salt deposit, wells are sunk until it is found, and then other shafts are constructed accordingly. When the face of the bed is laid bare, a stream of water is conducted to it by trenches from some hill spring along the bottom of the galleries, until it covers the surface of the bed. It lies there for one day. On the second the workmen cut grooves in the bed for the water to pass, and on the third day they break up the moistened salt, and carry it out of the pit. On the fourth it is conveyed to the public office, where it is sold to traders who come hither from all the neighbouring districts. The produce varies according to the season and the number of mines open. At this time two were worked, and yielded about two hundred maunds (about seven tons) every third day. In the winter about five hundred maunds are raised in the same period. The salt is the property of the Raja, and is sold at two paka or six kachha maunds * for a rupee. The average profit is about sixteen thousand rupees a year. The workmen are paid at the rate of two rupees a month, half in cash and half in salt. The occupation is hereditary. The salt is of a reddish colour, very compact and heavy. When any of a white colour is found it is reserved for the Raja's own use. When the water accumulates in the mine, and the latter is superficial, it is brought out in pans; but if the excavation is deep, a lower shaft is dug into the bottom of the mine, by which the water is run off, and the salt brought out. The lumps of salt are packed in wicker baskets, which are fastened to the shoulders of the porters with straps;—women are often employed in this capacity. The porters, when paid by the traders, receive four rupees annually, and two and a half kachha sers per day of wheat flour. There is another bed of salt at a place called Drung, which yields an income to the Raja of eight thousand rupees a year. A salt spring flows

* A kachha ser, it is mentioned in the Journal, consists of thirty-two rupees' weight.

from the Drung mountain, but none issues from the Gumha hills.

I had great difficulty in procuring a lodging at Gumha, not so much for myself as for the Mir and my Musselman followers, the people declaring that they could never again occupy a dwelling polluted by Mohammedans. At last, however, I obtained leave for my people to enter two empty houses, and to place my own bed in the verandah of a hut belonging to an old woman and her son. We were scarcely housed before the rain fell in torrents.

Having heard that a sort of beer called buza was made in this country, I desired some might be brought. It had the appearance of gruel, or water thickened with oatmeal, and a sour and spirituous smell. It is prepared from barley, the grain of which is parched and ground, and the flour is mixed with rice which has been softened by steeping in water. The powder of the root of some bitter and aromatic plant that grows higher up in the mountains is added to the mixture, and the whole is put into a press to squeeze out the water, and dried. When required for use a piece of the dry cake is thrown into a vessel of water, and in the course of three or four days fermentation takes place, and the liquor is ready for drinking. It is a favourite beverage with all classes, and intoxicates only if taken to excess.

Incessant rain continued throughout the night, and the weather moderated only about eleven on the 29th. We moved at noon, in a south-east direction, up a steep ascent. At about a kos we passed through a wood of stately cypress trees, some of which must have been eighty feet high: it extended for two miles to the little village of Rowara. Beyond this the road lay between lofty and rugged cliffs, and descended to a water-course. This part of the route is termed Sileswar. We then again ascended, and from the summit of the pass looked down upon a valley running right and left, along which several villages were visible. Just below it we came to the hamlet of Phuta Khad, where the villagers cleared some of their upper apartments for our accommodation;—to be sure the lower ones were occupied by cattle, and not kept in a very cleanly condition, and the air in our chambers was not of the purest. We were too glad, however, to obtain shelter from the heavy rain which had recommenced, to be fastidious. Barberry bushes, full of fruit of a blue colour, were numerous, and I found French beans in a garden.

Soon after starting on the following morning heavy rain encountered us, with a strong and piercingly cold wind, driving the clouds past us like thick smoke. It became difficult to see our way and keep our footing, and one of the party endeavouring to protect himself with a chattah (or umbrella), was blown off his horse; luckily he was not hurt. The storm lasted for above two hours, and when it cleared we were on the top of a height, from which a cleft in the mountain through which the Byas was said to flow was seen in a direction south-east, about three kos off. On our left, in the bottom to the north-east, ran the rapid stream of the Ao; and beyond it, about four kos in the same direction, perched upon the peak of a mountain, was the fort of Amir Gerh, belonging to Kulu. The road ran a little more to the north of east to the height of Khajauti; from hence we plainly distinguished the town of Mundi on the left bank of the Byas, about seven kos distant; and we saw also another face of Kamla Gerh bearing south-west, distant about fifteen kos.

After skirting the line of the right bank of the Byas at a distance of about four kos, the road suddenly turned to the south, and crossed the mountain of Gogar: at about two kos we came to the village of Hulhu or Hurhu, where Mia Zalim Sinh, the brother of the Raja of Mundi, had a house. Notwithstanding the rank of its owner, it was not equal to a good mud cottage in England. We took up our abode in it, as it was deserted; for Zalim Sinh having quarrelled with his brother, had been obliged to quit Mundi, and was now protected by Sansar Chand. The mountain of Gogar is famous for a fierce conflict which is said to take place in it annually, beginning on the 20th of Bhadon (August—September), between the Deotas or wizards, and Dains or witches, who assemble from far and near, even from Bengal and the Dekhin. About half a kos north-east of Hulhu is the salt mine of Drung: the town of Mundi is said to be four kos distant.

On the 31st we moved in light rain: our journey lay over a rugged path of ascent and descent, in a south-eastern direction, having the river Hulhu* on our left coming from the north. At a quarter before two we reached its bank, where the stream was about eighty feet broad, running with great rapidity, and foaming furiously over large blocks of stone. Finding a part free from these obstacles, our horses swam across with the assistance of our deri-men. Descending the bank, we came to a wooden bridge formed of overlying timbers and planks, upon the same principle as those which are common in Kamaon. The lower tier consisted of trees fastened at one end in a buttress of stone, and having the other end projecting over the river; above this another stage of timbers was secured, and jutted out beyond the lower; and a stage of planks resting upon the ends of this, completed the span of the river: the whole was bound together with loops of timber, and there was not a single piece of iron in the structure.

* The Ohl of Trebeck's journal.

After crossing the bridge we turned to the north-east, having on our left the Uttarsal rivulet, which falls into the Hulhu; and after crossing a hill, the ascent of which was by four hundred and sixteen stone steps, we again descended to the rivulet, and forded it to the village of Uttarsal. This consisted of a few mean huts, and the inhabitants were almost naked, and looked miserably poor. Two brick towers about twenty feet high, divided into two stories, were said to belong to the Raja.

The 1st of August was the first sunshiny day we had seen for a long time, and we started at eight o'clock. The road lay along the right bank of the Uttarsal for about two miles, but then crossing to the left, ascended a steep eminence. From hence we saw that the Uttarsal was formed of two considerable branches, which join a little below the village. Some hill forts in Kulu were also visible on the left; the nearest was said to be Amir-koth. Passing over a small plain, we again ascended to the village of Shuru, where a rivulet on our left, running into the Uttarsal, marked the boundary between Mundi and Kulu. We then proceeded north-east, and about one reached the pass of Tilakpur. Throughout the latter part of our march the appearance of the country was delightful : vast slopes of grass declined from the summits of the mountains in a uniform direction, but separated by clumps of the cedar, cypress, and fir: the rhododendron and the oak were growing upon our path ; the ground was literally enamelled with asters, anemones, and wild strawberries. In some places the tops of the hills near at hand were clearly defined against a rich blue sky, whilst in others they were lost amidst a mass of white clouds. Some of them presented gentle acclivities covered with verdure, whilst others offered bare precipitous cliffs, over which the water was rushing in noisy cascades. In the distance right before us rose the snowy peaks, as if to bar our further progress. Vast flocks of white goats were browsing on the lower hills, and every patch of table-land presented a village and cultivated fields : glittering rivulets were meandering through the valleys, and a black forest of pines frowned beneath our feet. We were not long allowed to contemplate the beautiful picture, for a strong south-west wind overspread it with vapour and cloud, and concealed all the more elevated portions from our sight, threatening us at the same time with a deluge of rain. We therefore quickened our steps and plunged into the forest. Many majestic trees, varieties of pine, including the cedar, embellished the precincts of the wood.

The road was now a continued descent, and was accompanied by many water-courses, which uniting at the foot of an eminence, on which stood the village of Syri, formed a considerable stream, the Rupareri. This river here divides Mundi from Kulu, and running under the walls of Bajaura, falls into the Byas on its right bank. Bajaura is a large square fort belonging to Kulu; it consists of square towers connected by a low curtain; the whole built of hewn stone strengthened with beams of fir. On the right bank of the Rupareri was a Hindu temple covered with sculptures in relief, in general well executed. A sort of chest with raised sides, and festooned with flowers, was an ornament frequently repeated; but the chief decoration was in the clustered pilasters at the doorways, tastefully entwined by richly-carved scrolls of creeping foliage. There were many images, most of which were in good preservation, except their noses, which were said to have been knocked off by the soldiers of the grandfather of Sansar Chand when he invaded Kulu. Mr. Trebeck informed me that the statues of the Rajas of Mundi have suffered a similar mutilation.

We encamped upon the right bank of the Byas. The river runs from hence south-east towards Mundi; its breadth opposite our station was one hundred yards, and its rate five miles an hour. On the 2nd of August we marched along its right bank over flat land, laid out in steps between the stream and the mountains on our left: the breadth of the river frequently varies, and it is often broken into channels by small islands overgrown with alders. The Serbari, at this season a considerable feeder of the Byas, crossed our path in two divisions: one was fordable; a wooden bridge was laid across the other: beyond this a high plain gave us a view of the town of Kulu.

Sultanpur, or Kulu, the capital of the Raj

of the same name, stands upon a triangular spur of table-land projecting from the foot of the mountains; the apex of the triangle is placed towards the conflux of the Serbari and the Byas. The part next the river, forming the southern or lower town, is occupied by the buildings in which the Raja resides with his family and attendants. The upper part of the town consists of the houses of traders, artificers, and shopkeepers, and is separated from the lower division by a small bazar. A few coarse chintzes, blankets, and cotton cloths, with opium and musk, are the chief articles of traffic, the three former being brought from the plains, and paid for with the two latter. The principal traffickers are wandering mendicants, of whom a vast number assemble here on their way to holy places in the mountains: there are also above two hundred supported by allowances from the Raja. Kulu is of no great population or extent.

Here I was joined by Mr. Trebeck and the party from Mundi with our merchandise. Mr. Trebeck's journal will furnish the chief particulars of their journey hither.

"After a detention of some weeks we quitted Mundi on the 11th of July. The town presents little worthy of notice, although it is of some extent, being fully thrice as large as Kulu. It is situated in the angle between the Byas and Sukheti rivers. The most conspicuous object is the palace of the Raja, which stands in the southern part of the town, and presents a number of tall white buildings, with roofs of blue slate, concave, like those of Chinese pagodas. The general appearance of the houses resembles that of the buildings at Almora. Close to the entrance of the town are several pilasters, and smaller blocks of stone bearing representations, in relief, of the Rajas of Mundi. One of these is set up on the death of each Raja, and sometimes on the demise of his relations. Each is sculptured, also, with the figures of his wives who have been burnt with him; a practice carried here to a frightful extent. On several occasions, I am told, the number of these victims of superstition has exceeded thirty. A very good ghat cut in the rock leads to the river, which is crossed by a crazy ferry-boat. Most of our baggage was carried across on skins.

The breadth of the river varies as the high rocky banks recede. In one place it was two hundred yards across, and opposite to where we encamped it was above one hundred and fifty yards. In some places where the bank is shelving the river beats up it with a considerable surf. The depth varies: it was two fathoms where we brought to, but in some parts along the bank it was much more shallow. It undergoes, however, a periodical rise and fall every day, owing to the melting of the snow on the mountains, where it rises as the heat of the sun increases. The effect of this is felt at Mundi in the evening. The river then begins to swell, and continues rising through the night. In the morning it declines, and through the day loses considerably, perhaps one-third of its body of water.

"Near Mundi, on the opposite side of the Sukheti river, is a large temple, dedicated to an image which, five generations, or above two centuries ago, was purchased by an ancestor of the Raja at Jagannath for seven hundred rupees, and was brought here at a great expense.

"The Raja of Mundi, Iswari Sen, is a

short stout man, about thirty-five, of limited understanding and extreme timidity. The latter he inherits from his father, of whom it is asserted that he passed an order that no gun should be fired off in his country. In his infancy he was either a ward or a prisoner to Sansar Chand, and he was indebted to the Gorkhas for restoration to his Raj. He assisted them in their invasion of Kangra, and also aided Ranjit in his operations against Kangra and Kulu. This has not preserved him from the fate of the other hill Rajas. He is tributary to the Sikh, and treated by him with contumely and oppression.

"On the 13th we crossed the river Hulhu, which is said to rise in Chamba. It falls into the Byas at Bilwara, two and a half kachha kos from Mundi. We crossed it by a spar bridge, above one hundred feet long between the buttresses. The Hulhu is joined not far from this by the Uttarsal river. We halted at Kamand, from whence a deep but not broad valley separated us from the mountains in which are the salt mines of Drung. They seem to be very productive. In April and May, whilst we were at Mundi, two hundred persons with heavy loads of it passed us daily. At the mine it costs about seven anas per paka maund. This and the iron mines form the chief sources of the Raja's revenue. The iron is farmed to different persons. There is a great quantity of it in the neighbourhood of Kamand. It is found in grains in a blue slaty stone. After bruising and washing the ore is put into an earthen vessel in a small clay furnace, to which a couple of bellows are attached, their nozzles being placed just above the vessel with the ore. The metal is run together by this process into lumps, but the fusion is very imperfect. It is sold in this state at about three and a half rupees per paka maund.

"On the 15th we entered Kulu. On our road, at a place called Tirí, a number of people were celebrating the festival of a deity, Adi Brahma. The god was personated by a villager seated on a high-backed chair, with a pole on each side for carrying it. It was covéred with some dirty striped silk, and in the back were eight heads or masks made of metal, silvered and gilt.

Tufts of barley grass and peacocks' feathers were stuck about the chair, and every peasant wore a bunch of young barley in his cap. The man who acted the god affected to reply prophetically to questions that were put to him by the bystanders, and seemed frequently to afford them much merriment. Amongst other things, he foretold a fierce war at hand. The ascent to Tirí was very fatiguing, though rather from its length than its abruptness. It brought us once more into the region of the rhododendron, the cedar, and the oak. From the ridge no fewer than thirteen forts in Kulu were visible in front of us, and although these are miserable as fortifications, they are picturesque in their outline and positions on commanding heights.

"We halted near Bajaura, not far from the Byas, where it was joined by a small winding rivulet, which we had repeatedly forded on our march. On our way we had heard of the death of the Rani, whose body had been lately burnt near the place where we had halted. We were told that eleven of her female attendants had burnt themselves with her corpse, and no reason was assigned for this, but that they did not wish to survive their protectress. We were detained here two days, as all business was suspended, and porters could not be procured.

"The people of Kulu are stouter and more active, and a finer race than any of the hill tribes we have yet seen, but they are savage and vindictive.

"We resumed our journey on the 19th, and arrived at the capital, halting opposite to the end of an island which divides the Byas into two channels a short distance below the town.

"A road from the vicinity of our tents, which runs first east by north for about two miles, and then diverges east by south for three or four more, leads to the place where the Parbati, or Parba, river, nearly as large as the Byas, falls into the latter. It is crossed by a wooden bridge, and the road continues for some distance up its left bank, where another sanga or bridge leads across it to a place called Mani Karn, where are some hot springs, about forty paces from the river. The water is hot enough to boil rice, and rushes out with much violence and noise. It has no particular taste or smell. Besides three principal springs the water oozes out in many places beneath the stones, and nearer the river there are some reservoirs, in which it is received, and in which, when sufficiently cool, people who come hither in pilgrimage bathe. A dharma sala, in which pilgrims are lodged and fed, is maintained at the expense of the Raja. According to the legend the goddess Parbati having laid her jewels upon the bank whilst bathing with Mahadeva in the river, her ear-rings (manikarnika) were stolen and carried off to Patala, the regions below the earth, by the serpent Sesha. At the probable consequences of Mahadeva's wrath, the gods discovered the thief, and urgently pressed the Naga to restore his plunder. Sesha refused, claiming the ear-rings as his own property, but, as he snorted with indignation, the subject of the dispute issued from his nostrils, in which it had been concealed, and flew back to the goddess. Through the openings made by its passage to the surface of the earth boiling water has ever since continued to flow.

"Little is known here of the course of the

Parbati further than Kanaonwa, a village on its right bank, twenty kacha kos north-east of Mani karn; its source is supposed to be a day's journey from Kanaonwa. It enters the Byas close to the village of Bhuind."

The Raja of Kulu, Ajit Sinh, is at present a boy of less than ten years of age, and the affairs of the Raj are administered by the Vazir Sobha Ram, who appears to be a plain, intelligent man. He complains bitterly of the tyranny and exactions of Ranjit, and in common with all the hill chiefs is desirous of being taken under British protection: he has paid rather dearly for his attachment to us. When the ex-king of Kabul, Suja al Mulk, fled from Multan, where, under the plea of protection, Ranjit kept him a close prisoner, and fleeced him of his most valuable jewels, he first sought refuge in Kulu. The Sikh demanded him back, but the political agent of the British government recommended the Kulu Vazir to facilitate the Shah's retreat to Ludiana. Ranjit made him pay a fine of eighty thousand rupees for his compliance with this counsel. Again, in the war with the Gorkhas he was called upon by the British for some co-operation, which he readily afforded, and for which a present of five thousand rupees were given to him. Ranjit fined him fifty thousand for accepting the remuneration, and for interfering at all. He does not complain of this, however, and hopes a time may come when he may be freed from such oppression. He was as civil to us as circumstances would permit, ordering porters to be furnished, and giving me letters to the authorities at Lahoul, which is within the limits of Kulu, and to the Raja of Ladakh.

The vicinity of Kulu abounds with walnut, quince, and apricot trees; the two former were not yet ripe, the crop of the latter was over: an oil is distilled from the kernels of the apricot, and is in general use. Bronchocele prevails amongst the people here to a frightful extent; at least every other person is affected by it. Leprosy is not uncommon, and the situation of the place seems generally unfavourable to health; several of our party suffered from its climate.

The clothing of the people thus far has

been for the most part of white and coloured cottons, but from hence woollen garments prevail, generally of the colour of the fleece, but sometimes dyed of two colours; where this is the case the pattern is always a kind of plaid. The common garb of the poorer classes is little else than a blanket, which is first wrapped round the waist; one end is brought over the shoulders, and fastened across the breast with skewers, and the other is passed round the thighs and secured to the waist; the legs and feet are bare. When the snow begins to fall, however, a double coating is assumed, and trousers and bootkins are added: persons of respectability wear a sort of jacket and trousers, the latter very full above and tight at the ancle. Both men and women wear woollen caps; those of the former are flat, of red, with an up-turned border of black, or wholly black; the caps of the women are commonly left undyed, but they have a fringe on the top which hangs as a tassel on one side, and their long black or dark-brown hair plaited into one tress, and lengthened with brown worsted, is turned up behind, and twisted round the cap, and has not an unpleasing appearance. The women are in general small, and many are pretty; but they are often disfigured by goitre: they wear heavy rings in their ears, and broad massive anclets of a metal of the appearance of pewter.

The people seem to be moderate in their diet, and live chiefly on wheat and barley flour. The satu of barley, or barley boiled, parched and ground to flour, mixed into a paste with a little water, is a common article of diet, especially when travelling. Various common grains, and buck-wheat, chenopodium, and poppy seeds, are ground and made into bread. Although orchards are common, no esculent vegetables are reared. I do not think that any spirituous liquor is known to the mountaineers, at least beyond the buza, which every one drinks. A narcotic preparation of the juice of hemp is also used, but it is said that few are guilty of excess either in the use of this, opium, or tobacco: the latter grows in most of the gardens, but it does not appear to be very luxuriant.

Having remained some days at Kulu to colleot grain and porters, we resumed our route on the 10th of August.

CHAPTER VI.

Valley of the Byas — Ancient Capital of Kulu — Mineralized Springs at Bashisht—Limit of Rice Cultivation—End of the Kulu Valley—Ralha river—Ascent of Ses dhàr—Source of the Byas—Image of Byas Rikhi—Pass of Ritanka joth—Chandrabhága, or Chandra River—Province of Lahoul—Village of Kuksar—Monumental Piles—Sculptured Stones—Currant and Gooseberry Bushes—Junction of the Suraj bhága—Course of the Chandrabhága to the Plains—Source and Course of the Ravi—Tandi—Grain Store of the Raja of Kulu—Dress of the People of Lahoul—Of the men—Of the women—Ornaments and Implements—Willows—Villages—Gardens—Apples—Tartarian Wheat—Flocks of Sheep—Dharm Sinh—Lahoul Carriers—Tatar Cookery—Gniungti river—Last Village in Lahoul—Sacred Trees—Falling Mountain—Chukam River and Lake—Baralacha Pass—Natural Drains—Yunam Lake and River—Shattered Rocks—Fragments of Stone—Conglomerate Columns—Boundary between Lahoul and Ladakh—Pass of Lacha-lung—Insulated Rocks—Fantastic Cliffs—Plain of Kiung—Parties of Tatars—Hares—Ladakh Visitants—Pass of Tung-lung—Snow Clouds—Village of Rum-chu—Flight of Villagers—Approach to the town of Giah.

We crossed the two branches of the Byas by spar bridges, and proceeded along the left bank of the river; on our right, above the village of Grahan, we passed a neat white house belonging to Mia Kaphur Singh, the uncle of the present Raja. The valley was in some places of considerable breadth, and well cultivated. The villages were surrounded by orchards of peach, apricot, and walnut trees; the hedge rows and woods abounded with wild pomegranates, pears, figs, and grapes, both green and black: grapes are cultivated in the gardens about Kulu, but in general they are only fit for sherbet.

The cultivation of the valley continued for a great extent, and villages were frequent; the houses were in general of stone, and some three stories high; the ground-floor was uniformly appropriated to the cattle: our track repeatedly lay along watercourses dug for irrigation.

On the 11th we passed a house belonging to the Raja on our right, situated on an eminence, at the foot of which stood the ancient capital of Kulu, called Makarsa: a few houses are all that remain of it, as the removal to Sultanpur took place about three centuries ago. I could not learn that any old monuments had been discovered, although it is said to be the most ancient city in these mountains. Just before entering the village of Jagat Sukh we crossed the Doangnu, a mountain torrent, rushing over large stones and rocks, and having in one place a fall of twenty feet. The spray thrown up by the cataract is said to be the breath of the nostrils of some local divinity, who is also named Doangnu.

The valley narrowed as we ascended to the north, and was crossed by the Phari Nala, which we forded, and then by the Raini, over which a sanga was constructed. This stream was rapid and deep: it is said to rise in Piti, in Ladakh, at ten days' distance, and it falls into the Byas near at hand. On our right, close to the road, was the village of Arrheo, which was deserted; and higher up the mountain, in the same direction, was the hamlet of Hamta, whence a road passes to Rodokh. We then descended to the Byas, and crossed it at Jaharan, where it was sixteen or seventeen yards broad. Following the bed of the river, we came to a gorge, where the valley was not above a musket-shot broad. The rocks which bordered it on the left, though steep, were rounded; those on the right rose perpendicularly, forming castellated parapets on their summits, which were surmounted by a pine forest. Several cascades rushed down the sides of the rocks, and the whole formed a scene worthy of an artist's pencil.

Leaving our baggage at the village of Gosala, Mr. Trebeck and myself crossed to the left bank of the Byas, and ascended to the height of Basht or Bashisht, to visit the hot springs there. There was one spring which flowed partly at once into a reservoir, and partly by a side channel into a second reservoir or bath. A strong smell of sulphuretted hydrogen escaped with the vapour, and the water had the taste of Harrowgate water: no medicinal properties are ascribed to it by the natives, and it is visited only by a few devotees.

On the 14th we resumed our course along the right bank of the Byas: we here left the limit of rice cultivation, for which buck-wheat, now in flower, was substituted. Cedars, cypresses, and various kinds of pines occupied the sides of the river and adjacent heights. About a kos and a half on this day's march, the Sarahi from the north-west fell into the Byas, rushing down with great rapidity and noise. A Sanga bridge was placed across the rocks which confined this torrent, and which was not more than twenty feet broad. In some places higher up the river was five times that breadth, and the sudden contraction of its channel produced the fury and velocity with which it descended: it is also said to rise at times considerably above its present level, and sweeping away the bridge, to be impassable. We crossed with some risk, and one of my followers was thrown into the current by a hill pony: he managed however to get out unharmed.

The Byas river, above its junction by the Sarahi, was called the Byas Rikhi: in some parts of its course it passed along a narrow and deep channel of rock, which could not be less than eighty feet deep, and not more than eight or ten yards broad: a Sanga was constructed across the chasm. The road hence ascended up some rugged crags at a place termed Bagu Suan: the summit afforded pasturage to some pony mares. In front the long valley of Kulu terminated in an angle, being shut up by a range of cliffs, down which numerous streams of water were trickling. At the eastern corner the Byas entered the valley through a gorge, studded with oaks, sycamores, and pines, and divided by islets into several channels. Through this gorge lay our road: it was intersected by several mountain torrents, and by one considerable rivulet, the Ralha, which is said to flow from the Serkund, a lake in the same range, but to the westward of the Ritanka joth, and a few hours north of us: this lake is formed by the melted snow, and has two issues; one of which is the Ralha on its southern face, and the other on its northern is a feeder of the Chandrabhága river. After crossing this stream on the rather insecure footing afforded by three pine stems and some large stones, we came to the ascent of Ses dhàr, leading to the pass of Ritanka joth. On the right was a winding path for cattle, on the left a steep stone causeway: it is a rude but useful work, and deserves a tribute to the name of the constructor, Killat Bhagt, the guru or religious head of an establishment of mendicants at Bonua, a small village between Gosala and Phulchan. We encamped about half way up the mountain, and had the satisfaction of beholding the clouds now drifting along the valleys under our feet. Snow rested upon the mountain about a mile in front of us, and the herbage about us was intermixed with the small shrubs and plants of European fields.

The ascent on the following day continued first towards the east and then turned to the north. The Byas, on our right, flowing down the mountain, was joined by the Sagu, a stream as large as itself, issuing from beds of snow to the east. The summits of the less elevated peaks about us were bare, but those of the loftier were capped with snow, and snow lay in the gorges which were on a level with our path. From beneath one of these beds, in an angle of the mountain, a stream dashed across the road. Beyond this the ascent proceeded in a more easterly direction for about a mile and a half, and on the right, at a short distance, was the source of the Byas, about a hundred feet below the top of the pass. A rill about three feet broad and a few inches deep trickled from underneath an insulated block of mica slate. The soil about the spring was soft and spongy, and intersected by many shallow channels: the ground inclined gently, and the spring ran in a south-westerly direction. A few feet in front of the rock a low wall of loose stones formed three sides of a quadrangle, the side next the stream being open, to leave the access to it free for its presiding genius, Byas Rishi*, of whom a small image, about a foot and a half high, stood against the wall nearest the rock. A smaller figure stood by its side. Although sculptured out of a hard stone, the images were much worn, apparently by time and exposure. Within the walls were strewed flowers, offered to the Rishi by Hindu pilgrims, with whom it is also customary to set up a stone on end in commemoration of their visit. Our people constructed a small pile, as a memorial of the first visit paid by a European to the source of the Byas.

The ghat or pass of Ritanka Joth†, which

* Byas, or Vyása, is the reputed arranger of the Védas, and compiler of the Puranas, the scriptural authorities of the Hindu religion. According to Hindu chronology he flourished about five thousand years ago.—ED.

† Dr. Gerard, who followed this route about ten years afterwards, calls the pass Rotang: his estimate of the height is thirteen thousand feet. *Asiat. Res.* vol. xviii. 275.—ED.

is above thirteen thousand three hundred feet high, forms a gap in the most northern and elevated mountains of Kulu, running with a tolerably level surface, about a quarter of a mile in breadth, for a short distance, between mountains of not much greater elevation. A clear sky displayed before us the lofty and still distant peaks of the mountains of Tartary, white with perpetual snow. Snow also tipped the crests of the inferior ranges, which were nearest to us, and although discoloured by rain and the debris of the mountains, it filled up the ravines and hollows, and fed numerous torrents, which sometimes flowed gently, sometimes dashed precipitously down the sides, and fell into the Chandrabhága, or rather the Chandra, the main branch of the river which is properly called by the former name only after it is joined by another considerable stream. This river, separating Kulu from Lahoul, was flowing along the bottom of the valley on the northern side of the pass, entering it at a narrow gorge on the east, and proceeding towards the west, and receiving also the waters that descended from the northern face of the chain of mountains on which we stood.

Just below the ghat were two pools sacred to the deity Gepan, the patron of Lahoul. The road then descended for about five miles to the left bank of the Chandra, across which a swing bridge led to the hamlet of Kuksar, formed of two villages, one to the east, the other to the north of the bridge, both surrounded by lands well cultivated with crops of barley and buck-wheat. The houses were of stone, cemented with mud, and with flat roofs. Here we found the red Alpine strawberry, with a very fine flavour, as well as the other tasteless or steril varieties which had previously been met with.

We were detained here for one day, owing to the difficulty of crossing our horses. In the attempt to help a hill pony across by a rope fastened to his neck, the animal was drowned. The others swam over loose, attended by a couple of deri men, who with much difficulty were prevailed upon to trust themselves to the current. The river was, indeed, rushing along with fearful rapidity, foaming in spray over the large stones and rocks that obstructed its course. Where crossed by the jhula it was ninety-six feet broad; but this place had been chosen for a bridge, as the narrowest in the vicinity. Near this place the river that flows from the Sar Kund, opposite to the Hulhu, falls into the Chandra. The bridge was made of ropes formed of birch twigs, and the flooring was of wicker work of the same material.

The road led us along the foot of the bare cliffs of Kuksar, between them on the right, and the river on the left. At upper Kuksar we noticed a pile of stones, on the top of which were laid slabs of various sizes and forms, having inscriptions cut upon them in two or three different characters, with which I was unacquainted. I saw many such piles in Hiundes, and there understood that they were erected by the Lama who had charge of the district, but here I learn that they are monuments to deceased individuals, bearing the name, age, and character of the person in honour of whom they are constructed, and being of an extent proportioned to his rank. Some of them were, at a distance, like small houses or towers, being twelve or fourteen feet high, tapering at the top, and occasionally whitewashed. On our way we fell in with two half-starved Hindu fakirs: one of them had come from Chapra, the other from Ougein: both were going on a pilgrimage to Tilaknáth.

Between the first and second village of Sisu we crossed the Sisu river, a narrow torrent rushing down with a force which must wear away the most compact rock. Growing near it was the variety of currant which I had observed at Niti. On the summit of the ascent from the water a flat stone, sculptured with figures and flowers, was set up on the right of the path. Further on the road passed through a stone door-way, sacred to Gepan, and stuck full of flowers on the sides, whilst the top of the wall was ornamented with pieces of white and coloured quartz. Another sculptured stone was erected at the end of the second village. Here I saw the first gooseberry bush that had occurred on our journey. We encamped at the third village or town of Sisu. These were mean-looking hamlets, but the crops of barley and wheat about them indicated both a good soil and industrious tillage.

On the succeeding day we passed many small villages on both banks of the river, and much land in cultivation with the same crops. Each village had a plantation of willows, they were all pollards: the twigs are used for baskets. The Francoline partridge was in plenty, but the young ones were but just beginning to fly. It rained in the night in the valley, but snow had fallen on the heights.

On the 21st of August the path lay along the slope of the mountains, and over crumbling fragments of rock, which threatened constantly a slip into the river, about two hundred feet below. After ascending and descending repeatedly, we again came to the bed of the river, and crossed it by a suspension bridge. A river coming from the east here fell into the Chandra, and the stream was thenceforward known properly by the name of Chandrabhága. The tributary, according to the Kanungo of Tandí, is called the Surajbhaga.

After receiving this accession the Chandrabhága was above two hundred feet broad, and flowed with a steady current towards the north. It proceeds hence to Kishtewar, one hundred and fifty kos; thence to Aknúr, fifty kos; and to Gujrat, sixty kos, from whence its course by Vazirabad is well known. It receives the appellation of Chin-ao, in Kishtewar, and Chiñ-ab in the plains, indicating a belief, apparently, of its rise in Chin, or China. May not the Greek name Ace-Sines have had some such allusion also? The only information we could obtain of its source was, that it was situated in Piti in Tartary, and that a man following the course of the river would reach the head of it in ten days according to some, in two according to others. From the muddy appearance of the water, and the proximity of the snowy mountains, towards the east and north, it seems likely that the latter report is nearest the truth, and that the distance does not exceed thirty miles at most.

Whilst on this subject I may mention what I learnt regarding the source of another of the Panjab rivers, the Ravi or Hydraotes, from two persons who came to me from the Rani of Chamba. There are two lakes in a mountain called Manmakes, about ten days from Tandí, in a westerly direction, named Dal Kund and Gauri Kund: a small stream from each of these unites with the Sib Kirotar, a rivulet that rises from a spring between them; and the three, forming a current large enough to turn a mill, runs to Harsar, one day's journey to the south-west. At this place the stream, increased by mountain torrents, is called the Raiva. It then flows past the city of Chamba, built on its right bank, opposite an angle formed by it and the Sawa, a river from the north-east, five kos in length. Leaving Chamba it flows to Ulans, seven days' journey, where it receives the Siang, from Bhaunso, also in the Chamba country, thirty kos from the capital. It is then called the Ravi. At Tirmu Patan it receives the Tavi, which rises in the mountains of Seoj, in the Raj of Badarwa, eighteen kos from Jamu, and which has been augmented on its course by the Uj from Koth Belota, thirty kos west from Jasrota. Thirty kos lower down, and fifteen or twenty from Lahore, the Ravi is crossed by the bridge of Shah Doula. Both the Ravi and the Byas rise to the south and west of the Chinab, although they run east of it in the plains, being included, as it were, within an arch or semicircular sweep made by the latter river. About three hundred paces north-west from the spot where the Surajbhaga and Chandrabhága unite is the village of Tandí, and opposite to it is that of Gosha: the latter is much the larger of the two. Tandí consists of but a few houses, but one of these of some extent is a store belonging to the Raja of Kulu, in which the grain paid by the peasantry as rent is deposited, and sold on the Raja's account. Two of his officers, the Hakim and Kanungo, or commissioner and accountant, reside here. The peasantry of Lahoul hold their lands of the Raja of Kulu, except at four villages, Barkalanak and three others, which we passed on our way to Tandí, and which, whilst they acknowledge military fealty to the Raj of Kulu, pay rent to the state of Ladakh.

The inhabitants of this part of the country are much employed as carriers between Chamba, Kulu, and Ladakh, transporting merchandise from the latter country, chiefly wool, on ponies about thirteen hands high, well made, strong, and well trained to the peculiarities of mountain carriage. Sheep are also used to carry grain and goods. The hire of a pony from Tandí to Lé was ordinarily eleven rupees, each carrying two paka maunds: we were made to pay thirteen rupees. Although the charge was high, yet, as supplies were not likely to be abundant on the road, and grain is ordinarily dear in Ladakh, I laid in a considerable quantity of wheat flour at Tandí, and engaged carriers and ponies for its transport.

In this part of the country both men and women dress in woollens, winter and summer. The cloth is worn as it comes from the loom, and is made by the peasantry. Wool is bought here at twelve kachha sers of twenty-seven rupees, or about eight pounds for the old Delhi rupee. Two pieces of woollen cloth, with a thick felt on one side and smooth on the other, soft and strong, and each measuring twenty-one feet long by ten inches broad, were purchased by us for three rupees, or less than six shillings. The dress of the men consists of a woollen cap, coat, trowsers, and a blanket, with grass sandals. The trowsers are made very long and loose above the middle of the leg, where they fit tight, and the upper part, falling over this, descends to the ancle, and answers the purpose of stockings. Some wear tippets and coats of sheepskin, cured by simply rubbing between the hands: the wool is clipped short, and worn next the person. The women, in general, go bareheaded, but sometimes wear a circular shallow plate or cup of silver on the crown, having a loop in the lower edge on each side, through which a lock of hair is passed, and plaited over the top. The ends of their long tresses falling down their backs are collected under a square or circular piece of mother-of-pearl shell, from the lower edge of which depends a braid of three or four rows of beads, to the bottom of each of which a small bell is fastened. Sometimes a band of leather stuck with turquoises passes round the head, or a similar fillet gives support to strings of mother-of-pearl beads, and coral, depending on the forehead and below the ears. Lappets of leather, also set with turquoises, sometimes depend from the crown of the head, as low as the waist behind. The stones are large, but ill shaped, and of a greenish hue, with many and deep flaws: they are brought, it is said, from the interior of Tartary. Amber beads, large, but of an inferior quality, form the favourite necklace: they are bought at Amritsar at so low a price that it is clear they cannot have come from Prussia. The women thus decorated are the wives of carriers, and as they march along with their sheep loaded with grain, they make almost as much jingle as the leader of the team of an English west country farmer. Both sexes carry little leather bags round their necks with amulets given them by the Lamas, and the women have large leather purses in which they carry needle-cases and other implements of female industry. The men are as fond of ornament as the women, and wear ear-rings, armlets, and necklaces. Every man carries a knife hanging from his girdle, and a chakmak, or steel for striking a light, fastened to his girdle also, by a chain, along with a leather pouch containing some vegetable tinder and a few pieces of quartz. The chakmak is of a peculiar and ornamental construction, and is an article of foreign import, selling for a rupee, or if much decorated a rupee and a half. It might be supplied advantageously, I should think, from Britain, as might the knives and needles: as the latter are needed for coarse woollens only, they should be of a substantial size.*

On the 28th of August we departed from Tandí, and proceeded along the right bank of the Surajbhaga in a north-easterly direction. The road was stony and irregular. In general the interval between the bases of the mountains was almost wholly occupied by the bed of the river; but a small expanse near Beling, where we halted, afforded ground for cultivation, and for a grove of willows: one of these near my tent was sixteen feet in circumference. This tree is planted for the large head of croppings which it affords, and which are made up into faggots, and piled round the roofs of the houses as fire wood for the winter. Several of the

* Drawings and specimens of the chakmak were forwarded by Mr. Moorcroft to several of his friends in this country. Whether any manufacture or export of them was ever attempted is not known. They might, probably, be advantageously sent by the newly opened commercial channel of the Indus to the Panjab, and thence to Kulu and Ladakh.—ED.

trees were hollow; for when it is discovered that decay has affected the wood, the interior is scooped out till little but the bark is left. In this state it not only throws out its branches at top, but I noticed in some of them branches descending from the head inside the tree, and taking root in the earth at its base. The people are careful to keep up these plantations.

Above Beling we crossed the Jo, a rivulet descending to the Surajbhaga, by a Sanga. On the left of our path we observed a sepulchral urn, larger than several we had previously noticed on the side of the mountain, above the place of our last encampment. The whole of this day's journey passed through a succession of villages, each containing from ten to twenty houses. The houses were of stone, two and three stories high, with flat roofs, well stored with faggots of willow and fir. Some had open virandas, others had them inclosed with wattles plastered with clay; the ascent from story to story was by moveable ladders of the notched stem of a pine; the lower story was left open for cattle, and an open space was appropriated to the accumulation of manure. The disposition of the houses row above row on the steep sides of the mountains gave them the appearance of a broad flight of stairs, each lower row serving as a stepping-stone to the next above it. Near Sitigiri, where we halted, there was little herbage except stinking hyssop, abrotanum, artemisia, pimpernel, chenopodium, and sorrel. The dog rose was abundant, with a rich crop of scarlet hips. Gooseberry bushes of large size grew by the side of our road, covered with fruit little larger than grapes, and very acid, even when ripe. The orange-coloured currant was rather less common, but the fruit was not more palatable. In a farm I met with some apple trees bearing fruit, about the size of a pullet's egg; the apples were unripe and as sour, though not so austere as those of the wilding crab. The wheat, called here Tro, was mostly ripe; but the chief cultivation was that of the Awa Jao, or Siberian barley, here called Né, one ear of which was as heavy as two or three of the wheat. Buck-wheat, also, was in course of being gathered, which is done by pulling it up by the root. Although the crop of this when standing appeared to cover the ground, yet after exposure for a few days the produce was scanty. The wheat crop would not be fit for cutting for three weeks.

A steep and broken path led from hence up the sides of the mountain for some way, and near the summit was a small flat called Silsila, which served as a resting place for the carriers. Rolls of sheep's wool, and bags of borax and satu from Ladakh, were piled up here in the form of a wall. Opposite to Silsila, on the left bank of the river, was the small town of Cherzoban; further on we passed through the village of Karung, opposite to which was Tinun, the largest town we had passed for some time. In front of it stood a conspicuously large and white sepulchre, and near it, at the foot of the mountain, was a flock of several thousand sheep and goats, which were returning to Kangra, after six months' pasturage in Lahoul. Hearing that the Sanga over the river which lay in our direct route to Ko-lang was broken, we descended to the Surajbhaga by an almost precipitous path, and crossed it by another plank bridge, where it was about thirty feet broad, deep and rapid, but full of blocks of stone. We then ascended the left bank of the river, and encamped on a small plain near the fort of Ko-lang, belonging to Thakur Dharm Sinh, who is considered as the head man of the district. Strongholds were formerly necessary to check the predatory incursions of the Bhotias, but these have been for some time exchanged for peaceable and commercial intercourse.

On the morning of the 31st, when we were preparing to start, intimation was brought to me that the Thakur, Dharm Sinh, had been in bad health for some time, and wished me to prescribe for him: as the only way of doing this satisfactorily was to see the patient, I consented to wait until he could come to me, and accordingly remained till two o'clock, when he arrived. Notwithstanding his Hindu name he spoke not a word of Hindustani, and in figure and countenance was much more of a Tartar; his dress was in the usual style, but of better quality, and he wore a cap of black velvet faced with brocade, in the crown of which were stuck five or six large needles, two of them were of brass. Great deference was paid him by the Lahoul carriers, who addressed him with the terms of Thakur and Raja. Whilst waiting for Dharm Sinh, numerous flocks of sheep and goats passed us on their way to Kangra and Chamba. The goats were generally white, the sheep were white, black, pied, and dun; they were in general well shaped, but the fleeces were less fine than I expected to have found them. Izzet Ullah purchased three wethers selected by him from the flock for four rupees, and I bought two for the same sum.

After prescribing for Dharm Sinh, who was labouring under inflammation of the chest, we resumed our journey, ascending and descending over rough and precipitous paths which would have been deemed impracticable by persons unaccustomed to mountain travelling. At the villages of Bugnad and Jisba, in the district of the latter name, the valley opened and presented a considerable tract of cultivation. On the right bank of the river opposite to Jisba we forded a rapid stream which escaped from a bed of snow upon our right, and rushed down its stony channel with such impetuosity as threatened peril to our cattle at least. They waded through it, however, cautiously and securely. Many foals six months old traversed the torrent by the side of their dams. We encamped on a small plain where there was pasturage for our cattle.

We were detained all the 1st of September in discussing arrangements for the hire of our cattle, the carriers requiring to be here paid in full of their charge to Lé, on the plea that they were about to be called on for contributions to defray the expense of presents to the Brahmans in honour of the last Raja of Kulu, who died four years ago. Nama, the kanungo of Tandí, who had been directed to attend me to Ladakh, here joined us, and becoming responsible for the delivery of the property at Lé, I acceded to the demands of the carriers. We had an opportunity here of witnessing Tartar cookery on a more sumptuous scale than usual, but it was not of a character to invite a participation in the meal. A sheep belonging to some of the carriers having died in the night, the carcase was skinned and cut up, and boiled in a large cauldron, together with all the viscera both of the chest and belly. Into the water also they threw cakes made of flour, mixed with the blood and small lumps of flesh.

Near our encampment grew abundance of the deep red variety of currant in full bearing, with large bunches of acid fruit full of stones, and thick skinned ; the juice stained the fingers purple : juniper bushes and dwarf tamarisks were also numerous. During the last few days the red-billed and red-footed crow has been seen, and at this place the large Tartar raven made his appearance close to our tents.

Our march on the 2nd of September led down to a rough stony plain, bordering the left bank of the river. From a valley to the south descended the Gniun-thi Chu*, a deep and rapid river, said to rise from the northern face of the mountain above Koksar, which notwithstanding the distance we have come by the detour we have been obliged to make, is said to be not more than eight or nine

* Chu, or Chhu, is the Tibetan for river or water, and may therefore be dispensed with in the names of rivers. It occurs also in the names of places and districts, from their comprising some piece of water.—Ed.

kos off in a direct line. Several villages are situated near the debouche of the Gniun-thi. We encamped on the face of a mountain beyond one of those called Labrang, in the district of Dar-cha, having marched only a kos and a half, in consequence of the ruggedness of the road.

About a mile from the point where the Gniun-thi falls into the Suraj-bhaga, the latter divides into two branches, or to speak more accurately, is formed by two rivers. The one on our right, along which lies our road, is the Dar-cha Sum-do, coming from the north*. The other on our left, which is something larger, flows from the west of north, rising, it is said, in the Zanskar mountains, about three days' journey distant.

The village of Labrang† is the last in the Raj of Kulu, and the last that occurs on the

* Sum-do implies a conflux or the three points of land round the meeting of two rivers.—Ed.

† According to information subsequently received by Mr. Trebeck, this village should be rather named Dar-cha as well as the district. Labrang he places more to the north-west. Mr. Gerard also calls the last village of Lahoul, Dar-cha; according to him it has an elevation of eleven thousand feet.—*Asiat. Journ.* N. S. vol. v. p. 90. Gholam Hyder also calls this place Darsah.—*Asiat. Journ.* N. S. vol. xviii. p. 174.

road for several days' journey. Near it were a number of cypresses much decayed, and many quite dead. Some of my people had begun to strip them of their dry branches for fuel, when one of the conductors of our caravan came to me in great agitation, and implored me to command them to desist. The trees he said were sacred to the deities of the elements, who would be sure to revenge any injury done to them by visiting the neighbourhood with heavy and untimely snow. He promised that fire-wood should be supplied if the trees were spared, and this condition was fulfilled. On the tops of some of the houses I observed piles of horns looking like chimneys, decorated with branches of cypress. Although these also were dedicated to local divinities I purchased a pair; they seemed to me to be the horns of the ibex.

The road to Ladakh formerly followed the southern bank of the Zanskar river for some way, and then crossing it by a sanga, proceeded along the Dar-cha river. This route has been obstructed for some years by the gradual subsidence of a mountain, which was still in progress, and which we had therefore an opportunity of witnessing. About two-thirds up the acclivity of a mountain, about half a mile distant, a little dust was from time to time seen to arise; this presently increased, until an immense cloud spread over and concealed the summit, whilst from underneath it huge blocks of stone were seen rolling and tumbling down the steep. Some of these buried themselves in the ground at the foot of the perpendicular face of the cliff; some slid along the rubbish of previous debris, grinding it to powder, and marking their descent by a line of dust; some bounded along with great velocity and plunged into the river, scattering its waters about in spray. A noise like the pealing of artillery accompanied every considerable fall. In the intervals of a slip, and when the dust was dispersed, the face of the descent was seen broken into ravines, or scored with deep channels, and blackened as if with moisture. About half a mile beyond, and considerably higher than the crumbling mountain, was another whose top was tufted with snow. It was surrounded by others lower and of a more friable nature. It appeared to me that the melting of the snows on the principal mountain, and the want of a sufficient vent for the water, was the cause of the rapid decay of the mountains which surrounded it; for the water which in the summer lodges in the fissures and clefts of the latter, becomes frozen again in winter, and in its expansion tears to pieces the surrounding and superincumbent rock. Again, melting in the summer it percolates through the loosened soil, and undermining projecting portions of the rock, precipitates them into the valley. As, however, rubbish accumulates on the face and at the foot of the mountain, a fresh barrier and buttress are formed, and the work of destruction is arrested for a season.

A sanga across the Dar-cha river placed us on its left bank, along which the road lay. The lower and middle parts of the rocks were clothed with a scanty vegetation, but the summits were bare, or were covered with snow. Occasionally the path lay over beds of snow; occasionally small plains of herbage occurred, the usual halting-places of the shepherds. Many small streams, some stealing from beneath the snow, and some bursting out of the sides of the mountains, supplied the river; and in one place a mass of snow which had fallen into the river occupied its bed, and afforded us a bridge by which we crossed to the right bank, to the old road to Ladakh. This again descended to the river; further on were some planks laid from projections in the rocks, which afforded us the means of repassing to the left bank. On the 4th we passed the junction of the two rivers which form the Dar-cha river; one of these, the Chukam, we followed, the other, the Kakthi, is said to come from the snows, about two kos to the north-west. Our path lay over vast slips of rock along a narrow valley, shut in by high and barren mountains, and offering no vestige of villages or cultivation. On the night of the 4th it froze hard where we were encamped.

Soon after starting on the 5th, we forded the Chukam, and continued to ascend the valley, in which the only signs of life were now and then a tailless rat, the red-tailed lark, and a species of hoopoo. At a distance of about four miles the river was formed of two branches, the one on the right hand rising from snow about one thousand paces south. Although now the most considerable of the two it is said to be dry in winter. Following the other branch we soon came to a place where it issued from the middle of a natural dike, which filled up the space at the foot of two mountains, ascending to the summit of which we beheld a basin of clear water of a deep green hue about a mile in circumference. This small lake, also called the Chukam, collects the water from the surrounding heights, and may be regarded as the source of the Suraj-bhaga portion of the Chinab*. From the lake we ascended a steep pass that led over the rounded back of a part of the Bara Lacha ridge†. According to barometrical measurement we had attained here

* Mr. Gerard also regards this as the source of the Suraj-bhaga, and makes its elevation sixteen thousand two hundred feet.—Ed.

† Mr. Gerard calls this the Paralassa chain, and makes its elevation also sixteen thousand five hundred feet: the range which he calls Lachha, he estimates at more than seventeen thousand feet. The proper denomination, if it has any, of this pass, is probably given by neither traveller; for La-tsa or La-sa, means any pass in a mountain, or the foot of a pass, and Ba-ra, between. Bara-la-tsa is therefore a mountain ridge or pass 'between' two districts. According to Gholam Hyder, many of the party experienced severe headaches in crossing this elevation.—Ed.

an elevation of sixteen thousand five hundred feet. Some of the peaks about us were apparently one thousand feet higher. On all the great slopes and crests of the chain the snow lay in vast undisturbed masses. The summit of the pass was tolerably level. Immediately on crossing it we came to a pile of loose stones, formed by the contributions of travellers, and decorated with bits of wool and rags, and a piece of cloth with an inscription in printed letters. On the right of the road was a plain of at least two miles in extent, skirted by a rivulet, which appeared to rise at no great distance to the south-east. The soil on and near the pass was swampy and soft, and strewed with fragments of rock or small stones, which although dry on the upper surface were immersed in water, and gave way when stepped upon. In some places long flat stones were deposited for a considerable extent, and, until terminated by a declivity, in a direction perfectly parallel, forming a gutter or drain as regular as if it had been constructed by the hand of man, a very unlikely thing, however, in such a situation, and originating, no doubt, in the direction taken by snow streams from the mountain.

After crossing the plain we followed the left bank of the stream by a rugged path, crossing ruins of rock covered with a saline efflorescence. The river opened suddenly upon its left into a lake about three miles round, called the Yu-nam. Not a weed deformed nor a wave ruffled its pellucid and tranquil waters: there seemed to be no fish in it, nor was any bird or even a fly in its vicinity. I was told that it had been more extensive, but had been contracted by the falling into it of masses of rock: except on its edge no stones were visible. The river that had fallen into the lake re-issued from it, and was thence called the Yu-nam river. Where it first quitted the lake it worked its way through mounds of cream-coloured clay at the foot of perpendicular cliffs: the clay was of great purity.

Rising from the river the road wound through large masses of micaceous schistus, which had fallen from the rocks on our left, whilst a tract of several acres upon our right was strewn with large irregular fragments of a reddish coloured sandstone, of a variety of shape and disposition of which it is impossible to convey an idea. I was informed that these wrecks were the effect of an earthquake, and nothing short of some mighty throe, which had upheaved and shattered a whole mountain, could account for such a scene of fantastic ruin. We again descended to the river, and, having forded it, remained a day on its banks to rest our people and cattle. Many of the former had suffered much from exposure and fatigue. The sun for a few hours was intensely hot, whilst the wind blew piercingly cold from the snow-clad peaks of the Bara Lacha mountains. I braved the blast in the same habiliments I had been accustomed to wear, but I had some pain in my head, my face was almost stripped of skin, and my lips were shrivelled and cracked. Many of the people were in the same state, and some were attacked with fever. Fuel was scarce, but a halt was desirable at this spot, as there was some pasturage for the cattle in the vicinity.

The road at starting on the 7th led over an ascent to a plain, scattered over which were many large mounds of sandstone and fragments of rock: they were mostly from thirty to fifty feet high, and were so distant from the mountains on either side that it was impossible to suppose that they had rolled so far. They were, in general, oval or rounded at their summits, and sloped gradually down to a broad base, and might in any other position have been thought artificial tumuli. It seems more probable that they are the harder fragments of a mass from which the softer portions, the clay and sand, have been removed by gradual decomposition. Several plains occurred in this day's march, covered, it seemed, on first approach, with herbage, but this proved to be a kind of furze common in Tibet. On the left bank of the river were many columnar projections of pebbles conglomerated by sand and clay, resting on bases of sand projecting into the river. In the river bed pebbles were found agglutinated by a calcareous earth; and the water was hard. Since we descended from the ghat the mountains have much diminished in height, and their texture is less compact. Some of them still present bold and perpendicular faces, which are stratified, and are diversified in tint as well as outline; but from the rough and jagged brows of others descend sandy slopes in a plane gently inclined to their bases. The general character of the rocks in this neighbourhood I should conceive to be sandstone tinted yellowish by iron, and veined by some harder mineral. The plains are almost barren, and have very little water, as the snow runs off fast into the river: such scanty pasturage as they afford, however, is very grateful to the sheep, and is apparently wholesome. A high, square, and insulated rock in the middle of one of these plains divided into two portions by the river, constituted the boundary mark between the states of Kulu and Ladakh. It is called Ling-tí by the people of Kulu, and by those of Ladakh Fa-lung-dinda. Other landmarks of a similar kind were observable across the river. Beyond this a river from the west, said to rise in the district of Zanskar, almost as large as the Yu-nam, joined the latter. We were told that at this season the plains are generally covered with flocks, but that our approach had excited so much alarm that the cattle had been withdrawn: we met with some sheep, however, on their way from Bhot, laden principally with borax.

On the 8th we forded the Tserab river, which comes from the mountains east by south, and falls into the Yu-nam, which then takes the name of Sar, or Ling-tí. The source of the Tserab is not likely to be more than twenty miles remote. The bed and banks are formed of pebbles united by clay and sand and some stalactitic matter, and on the banks rise pillars like those formerly observed. On the bank of a watercourse farther on, two such insulated columns of pebbly conglomerate were met with, on the summit of one of which rested a block of stone many tons in weight, and upon the top of the other stood a smaller block nearly on a point.

We were detained on the 9th by our horses having strayed in quest of pasture, and resumed our route only late on the 10th, proceeding along the right bank of the Ling-tí until it diverged to the westward, proceeding towards the Zanskar river. The road then led by zig-zag paths up the steep ascent of the Lacha or Lacha-lung* pass, and after crossing it continued over rough undulating ground intersected by rivulets and water-courses. On our way we met with a party of Lahouli Tartars, with about a hundred horses, returning from Lé, whither they had carried the goods of a Kashmiri trader. Most of the cattle had been overloaded, and were bruised and wounded in the withers. Part of the road lay along the left bank of a rivulet coming from the north and running east: this was occasionally obstructed by falls from the mountain. On the left, at a few hundred feet from it, stood an insulated sugar-loaf mass of rock above three hundred feet high, the base of which was loose and pebbly, and in a state of decomposition which threatened to bring down the whole superincumbent heap at no distant period. In another place the road ran for about ten yards between a detached pillar on the edge of the stream and the solid rock, and was not wider than sufficed for the passage of a man on horse-back. A tortuous and difficult tract then led to an eminence where, although neither

* La-tsa as before, a pass, and Lung-or Lung-pa a valley.—ED.

water nor fuel was procurable, we were obliged to halt. We had been nine hours on the road, the sun was about to set, the wind was piercingly cold, and some of the party were still considerably behind, not joining us indeed until ten.

On the following day we proceeded along the left bank of the rivulet. The cliffs forming its right bank were apparently at their summits of compact sand, but their faces were decorated with projections more or less irregular and grotesque, resembling towers, columns, and spires, and repeatedly mistaken by us at a distance for a temple or a castle. Caverns apparently of great capacity, high up in the rock, penetrated into its interior, and from the mouths of some of them streams of fine sand were trickling like water. The rock was in some places of a black colour, veined apparently with quartz: in others it was stratified, and consisted chiefly of clay slate. Proceeding along the rivulet, after crossing to its right bank, the road came to a plain, along the borders of which two streams meeting with that which we have accompanied formed the Sum-ghi-el, or Three

Spring river. Following its right bank we came upon a party of men, women, and children, some from Chamba, some from Kangra, and some from Lassa, carrying borax from Ladakh. A couple of rugged ascents brought us to the extensive plain of Kiung, which is about two miles in breadth, but considerably longer, forming a valley bounded by low mountains, with sloping sides and flattish summits. We halted in a small cavity, after a march of about four miles over the plain, and our tents were scarcely pitched when a piercing wind and heavy fall of snow came on.

The march of the 12th continued along the plain; there was some pasture upon it, but very little water. In one place were two or three pools, surrounded by an extensive bed of sand, from the upper part of which issued a mirage resembling waves. The valley is said to be frequented by wild sheep, and some of their horns of immense size, but injured by exposure, bore evidence of the fact. Shortly after reaching Ruk-chu, a shepherd's station, near the end of the valley, where we halted, a small party of Ladakhis came to my tent, one of whom saluted me in the Mohammedan fashion, and said he was there upon the Raja's business, but that he was going to a village three kos off, where he would wait for us. We remained at Ruk-chu for two days, during which Mr. Trebeck and myself shot a few hares; they were of a bluish-white colour, and were not much larger than English rabbits.

We moved along the rest of the valley on the 15th, and on the 16th crossed the ghat of Tung-lung. The pass was about seven hundred feet above the plain; from its top the horizon was beheld everywhere skirted with sharp-peaked mountains capped with snow; the snow-clouds were distinctly observable, travelling from peak to peak, or throwing out processes towards them, as attracted by each, and showering down a portion of their contents: lightened by the discharge, they then rose and floated in the air, until they again accumulated, and were again attracted within the sphere of the crest of the mountain. From the ghat the road descended rapidly, and was marked by a rivulet, which rose on the northern slope of the pass, and in the bed of which we noticed blocks of green granite, a stone not found in the mountains we had passed. We halted in the evening at a shepherd's station, not far from the village of Rumchu, in advance, the first abode of man we had seen for fourteen days: our first intercourse with our kind was not of very favourable augury. The villagers refused to supply some people I sent to purchase it with firewood, and when I repeated my application I was informed they had deserted their houses. We were therefore obliged to be contented with the scanty stock we had on hand.

On the morning of the 17th of September we passed the village, which consisted of a few stone houses, and was surrounded by fields of Siberian barley, laid out in patches, enclosed by low stone walls, and well watered by means of stone channels conducted from rivulets at some distance. The village belonged to priests, some of whom I saw in the fields, and beckoned to them to approach. An old man advanced, and presented me with a handful of ears of corn. The road, crossing a rivulet of clear water, came to two large white sepulchral buildings:

they were about twenty-five feet high: a square turret stood upon a base of several steps, and terminated in a similar series of steps, on the summit of which was a large urn, ornamented with sculpture: the upper part was rounded, and a pole, above six feet long, projected from the top. Along the road, in several parts, extended stone walls, intended, apparently, as defences. As we advanced, the water of the rivulet was discoloured by red earth. At a short distance from its left bank, at a sharp turn in the road, the town of Giah came in view. At the suggestion of the chief carrier, I consented to pitch my tents here, until a communication with the officers of the Ladakh government, who I understood were in Giah, could be effected, and arrangements made for my advance to the capital.

PART II.

RESIDENCE IN LADAKH.

CHAPTER I.

Meeting with Abdul Latif—Visit of Mir Izzet Ullah to the authorities—Audience of the Raja and Khaga Tan-zin—Buttered and salted Tea—Visit of the Raja—Journey resumed—Praying Cylinder—Letter from the Khalun prohibiting advance—Rocks—Action of the Weather—Sinh Kha bab, or Indus—Village of Marsilla—Head Lama—Cardinal's Hat—Old Telescope—Villages of Changa—Thik-se—Gompha—Meeting with Khaja Shah Nyas—His History—His friendly interposition—Valley of Chu-shut—Entrance into Lé—Monuments—Apprehensions of the Khalun—Public Audience—Audience Chamber—Europeans on the Frontier—Caravans from Lassa and Yarkand—Communications with Shah Nyas and Izzet Ullah—Proposed Commercial Treaty—Delays—Reference to Gardokh—To Lassa—Treaty concluded.

On the evening of the 17th of September the person whom we had met at Rum-chu again made his appearance, and, in conversation with Mir Izzet Ullah, informed him that his name was Abdul Latif, a pupil of a celebrated

Pirzada, or holy man, Shah Nyas Khan, who was a friend of Izzet Ullah's, and was now residing in Lé. Abdul Latif availed himself of this connexion to inquire confidentially of the Mir, what were our real character and purposes, and being satisfied on these points, engaged to conduct him on the following day to the Raja of Giah, and the Khaga Tan-zin, the brother-in-law of the Khalun, or chief Vazir of Ladakh. Accordingly, on the morning of the 18th, Mir Izzet Ullah went to the city, and had an interview with those officers. They seemed to be tolerably well informed of the extent of the British power, and of our relations with the Sikh ruler, and very suspicious of the real object of my journey. Satisfied, however, apparently, by the strenuous declarations of my representative, and by the letters from the Raja of Kangra, and Vazir of Kulu, as well as those to the governor of Kashmir from Najib Sinh, that my purposes were strictly mercantile, and that no harm was likely to accrue to Ladakh from my presence, they promised to write a favourable report to Lé, and appointed the following morning to receive my visit.

On the morning of the 19th, accompanied by Mr. Trebeck, Mir Izzet Ullah, and his son, I rode to the Raja's dwelling ; it was situated at the end of the town, and the access to it was along a stony and narrow path, between low flat-roofed houses on the right hand, and a walled enclosure for cattle on the left. The town was of small extent, and thinly peopled. After entering a court-yard, we passed through a dark doorway, and ascended a steep stone staircase, feeling, not seeing our way to an open gallery, on one side of which were several doors. In one of the apartments to which they led, we found the Raja, sitting on one of two chairs which I had sent for the occasion, and the Khaga Tan-zin on a camp-stool: on the side of the room opposite to the Raja was placed the chair intended for me. When I had taken my seat, the Raja made some civil inquiries in Tibetan, through Abdul Latif, who explained them in Kashmir Persian to Izzet Ullah, who interpreted to me, regarding our journey, and he expressed his hope that we had not suffered any inconvenience from the weather, or the ruggedness of the way. A moderately-large tea-pot, of gilt copper, and of beautiful workmanship, was brought in, and salted and buttered tea, without milk, handed to the company. The Raja took out of a breast-pocket, or pouch, his own tea-cup of yellow china. The Khaga Tan-zin also produced his, of chestnut-wood, mounted with silver. We had come provided with our own cups. The tea was not very strong, and tasted like weak broth. After some conversation on indifferent topics I took leave, and invited my hosts to my tent in the course of the day, which invitation they accepted.

The chamber in which the interview took place was sufficiently spacious but low; it contained little furniture; the principal article was a small wooden temple with two figures, one wholly covered, the other having the face exposed. The wall near where the Raja sat was covered with pictures of figures in attitudes of devotion.

About an hour after our return, the Raja and the Khaga Tan-zin arrived at our tents, and were received with suitable attention. Tea was served, with the accompaniments of milk and sugar; the chiefs partook of the former, but declined the latter. A glass of noyau was then offered them: the Khaga Tan-zin only ventured to sip his; the Raja emptied half the glass, and would probably have taken the whole, had he not been deterred by the temperance of his companion. The attendants requested the residue of the two glasses, which pleased them so well that they solicited a little more, and drank it out of the palms of their hands, expressing their satisfaction by gestures and smacking their lips. I made some presents of red and blue cloth to the two principals, who departed, to all appearance, in a very friendly mood towards me. The Raja sent a supply of satu with a sheep and a goat. In the evening some persons were deputed by the Raja to inspect our merchandise, that the frontier duties might be levied; and some difference of estimate as to the quantity occurring, he declared that he would forego the duties at present, as means for verifying the weight of the bales were not at hand, and would be satisfied with what it might prove to be when we arrived at the capital. The Raja, whose name was Tsimma Panchik, was a short stout man, about fifty.

Tan-zin was of similar person, but some years younger.

On the 20th we proceeded along the left bank of the Giah rivulet. Opposite to the town, on a lofty ridge of rocks, was a large pile of houses, formerly inhabited by the Raja; and lower down, one belonging to the Lama. On a stream, falling into the rivulet, was a small stone building, which at first view appeared to be a water-mill, but which proved to be a religious cylinder, carved and painted, and turned round by the current. Close to the road were several monumental urns, with figures and flowers sculptured on their pedestals. The banks of the river, on each side, were high and rugged, and consisted of a kind of pudding-stone; in its compact state, the prevailing colour was red, but when detached, it consisted of pebbles and of soil of a great variety of hues. We passed a small hamlet on our left, called La-tu, and then entered a finely-cultivated valley, in which stood the town of Mi-ru. We encamped near it in a plantation of poplars. Here the Khaga Tan-zin informed me he had received a letter from the Vazir, desiring us to take another road to Yarkand, through Nobra, as the small-pox, he said, was in some of the villages on our route to Lé, and we might, by passing through them, bring the infection with us to the capital. This intimation was equally unexpected and unpalatable. The Khaga Tan-zin, however, and Abdul Latif, recommended us to address the Khalun, and urge him to reconsider the matter, and the former promised to write to him to the same effect, recommending us, in the mean time, to press forward. Mir Izzet Ullah wrote to Shah Nyas to urge him to use his influence in our favour, and Abdul Latif took our dispatches, and engaged to exert himself personally in procuring us a favourable reception.

We therefore continued our journey on the 21st, still following the course of the rivulet. Great labour and ingenuity had been bestowed upon the road, which crossed the river repeatedly, whenever the path along the bank became dangerous or difficult. The character of the rocks continued the same; but in the first part of the road they were much intersected with veins of quartz, and studded with glittering and transparent points of rock crystal. Farther on they were scooped out into deep furrows, divided by parallel projections, looking like low walls, running from the level of the water to the summit of the rock, and forming, as it were, avenues artificially constructed, descending to the brink of the river. These, of course, are the harder parts of the rock, from betwixt which the softer portions have been washed down by the snow. Even the harder parts, however, seem to be readily affected by the weather; for, although on blocks recently detached, or on surfaces sheltered from snow, the pebbly matter was left projecting, offering a rugged and uneven face, yet blocks that had been long separated had their exposed superficies, when it was either perpendicular or sloping, so as to afford no lodgment to wet, as smooth and uniform as if it had been polished by a mason. At the town of Uk-shi, the rivulet of Giah fell into a deep river, about fifty yards in breadth. This was the river of Lé, the Yuma, or Sinh Kha bab, which may be considered as the main branch of the Indus, flowing from the province of Gardokh. Ukshi consists of not more than ten or a dozen houses, tolerably well built, and having walled gardens.

We were on horseback at an early hour that we might approach as near to Lé as possible before replies to our application for permission to advance could be received. The road lay along the left bank of the Yuma, over a high and uncultivated plain, enclosed on every side by mountains, the tops of which were covered with snow, now falling in long dark pillars upon many of the peaks. After proceeding along the plain for some distance, the road descended to the bed of the river, at the foot of a ridge of high cliffs, the usual conglomerate resting on compact sandstone. On again ascending, the eye was delighted by the sight of an enclosure of poplar trees, which at the distance of two miles looked like the belt of a park: on a nearer approach several of these belts were seen connected with villages and with corn fields interspersed. After crossing a watercourse which led to the left bank of the river, and from which different trunks carried water for irrigation over the adjacent grounds, I was met by a servant of the Khaga Tan-zin, and conducted to an enclosure, where we were directed to pitch our tents: no answer had yet arrived, and appearances were unpromising. The chief of Marsilla, the neighbouring village, was a Lama, and the spiritual guide of the Khalun, and principal municipal officer in this part of the country. I thought it advisable therefore to pay him a visit, and propitiate him by a suitable present. Before we set out the Lama rode past the tents, attended by two servants on horseback: he was of a portly presence, about forty, and was clad in a crimson cloth dress, with a low-crowned, broad-brimmed hat, like a cardinal's, covered with red cloth, tied under the chin, and bound with a band of broad riband, the ends of which floated loose behind; it was also decorated with two white cords and tassels of white silk: his attendants wore similar hats, but plain. On repairing to his habitation we were received by a Gelum, and conducted to the apartment of the Lama: he received us very courteously, gave us salted tea, and placed before us a quantity of apples, rice, and flour. Our intercourse was rather imperfect, but it seemed to have the effect of securing his favourable opinion of us, and of our intentions. We found in his possession an old telescope, made by Pyefinch, London. The Lama said it had belonged to the great Lama, by whom it was given to one of his predecessors. It may have found its way to Lassa perhaps on the occasion of the mission sent by Warren Hastings to Tibet. The village of Marsilla consisted of some very good houses, the exterior of which was very neat and clean : the cultivated lands round it were very extensive, and were well supplied with water. Opposite to Marsilla, on the right bank of the river, stood the village of Chumri, amidst lands equally well laid out and cultivated. Upon our return to our tents we were joined by Abdul Latif, who brought letters from the Vazir, which permitted our advance, and dispelled all doubts of the reception which awaited us at Lé.

Our road next day proceeded over the cultivated lands of the village of Changa, which were irrigated by a watercourse from the rivulet which divides the grounds of Marsilla. As the fields of Changa have a considerably lower level than the aqueduct, it becomes necessary to adopt some contrivance for retarding the current; and this is done by the interposition of corn mills worked by the stream. Between Marsilla and Changa we passed two temples, with houses of the Gelums adjoining; one on the right bank of the river, and one on the left, but farther off, and near the foot of the mountains. Beyond Changa we crossed a plain, and then came to the lands of other villages, the chief of which were Takna and Mashu. On an eminence stood a building that was considered as a sort of fortress, and several houses extended from it to the west; over the plain beneath, other houses were erected, rather in a straggling position. The Yuma river separated these lands on the left bank from the small towns of Thik-se and Gompha on its right; the houses of the latter rose in stages up the face of a height: it was inhabited, it was said, by great numbers of Gelums, and of the relations of the Raja. Opposite to the eastern end of Thik-se began the extensive valley of Chu-shut, covered with villages and farmhouses; the dwellings with their roofs, covered with a thick pile of firewood, and dry lucerne, whitewashed walls, and balconies attached, presented a neat and comfortable appearance. We were here met by a servant of Khaja Shah Nyas, who resided at Sheh, a town on the right bank of the river, and who expressed a wish to see us. We crossed two branches of the stream, and on an island between the second and a third branch we found the Khaja in a tent, which he had had pitched for our meeting.

The grandfather of Khaja Shah Nyas, Khaja Mohammed Yusef, who was descended from a branch of the same family as the Emperor Baber, was the hereditary ruler of Tashkend: his son Khaja Abd-ur-rahim went during his father's lifetime on a pilgrimage to Mecca, and extended his travels to Constantinople, returning by way of Hindustan: he was received with kindness by Kamar-ud-din Khan, the celebrated Vazir of Mohammed Shah, and by Mir Manu, the governor of Lahore; the latter persuaded him to remain in his district, and gave him the town of Imad-abad for his support.

When the invasions of Ahmed Shah, the

Afghan, had thrown the Panjab into confusion, Khaja Abd-ur-rahim repaired to his native country, where his father had died, and the principality was occupied by Unas Khaja, his sister's son. Unwilling, or perhaps unable, to raise a party in his favour, he withdrew to Kashmir, and died there at a very advanced age, in high esteem for his learning and piety. His son, Khaja Shah Nyas, succeeded to his reputation, and obtained from the Afghan governors of Kashmir very extensive and valuable grants of land, the revenues of which were chiefly appropriated by him to acts of charity and benevolence. Upon the conquest of Kashmir by Ranjit Sinh, the jagirs of the Khaja were confiscated, and his personal safety was endangered, so that he held it expedient to seek an asylum in some neighbouring region. He has, for the present, established himself in Ladakh, but the Mohammedans of Yarkand are desirous of his taking up his abode with them, and Mohammed Yar Khan has offered him a considerable jagir in Kabul.

We found the Khaja a man of about sixty years of age, short and stout, with a pleasing expression of countenance, although his features were Uzbek. He had a large turban on his head, and was dressed in a wrapper of brown cloth lined with chintz. Soon after we were seated a repast was placed before us of salted tea, wheaten cakes, Yarkand biscuits, apples and apricots of Ladakh, and grapes from Kashmir. He told us that the persons most adverse to our reception were the Kashmir traders, who apprehended we should interfere with their shawl wool traffic, and would, therefore, oppose every possible impediment to our journey: he had incurred great disgrace with them, he said, on our account, as they accused him of having invited us to Ladakh: he had been consulted by the Khalun, he informed us, as to what measures should be adopted when our approach was first heard of, and had told him that if we were really coming as foes, opposition would be fruitless, and if as friends, it would be discreditable to the government, and unjust towards us: that a refusal to allow us to proceed should have been intimated before we crossed the frontier; and that the best plan now would be, not only to permit our advance, but to treat us civilly; and that the minister might feel assured we were what we professed to be, inoffensive travellers and merchants. I was much pleased with the earnestness with which our new friend recapitulated the heads of this discussion, and with the apparent frankness and cordiality of his manners. After a short time I took leave of our host. Mir Izzet Ullah remained with his ancient friend.

Our route lay along the Valley of Chu-shut, the crops in which were cut, and the straw was piled in cones: the chief labourers in the fields were women: the men, when not busy at the thrashing-floor, were smoking and lounging about. We crossed the river by a bridge, and encamped on its right bank.

On the 24th the Mir and Abdul Latif set off early to prepare our lodgings in the city, and Mr. Trebeck and myself followed at noon. The road led over a sandy ascent wholly destitute of vegetation, between two low ranges of barren rock. On turning a narrow defile, by the side of a pile of stones, it came to two large sepulchral towers, connected by a pile of stones a thousand paces long. We next came to a second pile, still longer, uniting two smaller towers, on the square sides of which was sculptured, in relief, the figure of an enormous quadruped of mythological invention, the head and breast of which something resembled those of a lion, except that the mouth was armed with tusks. Some of the monuments we have seen have been surmounted by a large urn, something resembling an earthen oil jar; others by a conical pillar of burnt brick. The urns had always a pole projecting above them: the pillars were crowned by double coronets of gilt copper. The upper coronet was the smallest, and had its largest circumference upwards, whilst the reverse was the case with that below. In the bowl of the upper one rose a crescent, in the concave part of which was a circle with flat sides like a cheese on its edge, with a figure like a pear having its stalk upwards, on its upper edge: these ornaments were of copper or brass, gilt. At Marsilla a piece of rock crystal was stuck into the centre of the flattened sphere, and wires projected from the horns of the crescent and stalk of the pear. These lines of wall were the avenues to the town, in the streets of which we found ourselves presently after passing the second pile. The streets were crowded with people to see the entrance of the Firingis, and in the groups were mingled the good-humoured faces of the Ladakhis, and the sullen and designing countenances of the Kashmiris, the high bonnets of Yarkand, and the bare heads of the Lamas, with the long lappets and astonished looks of the women. The Khalun had ordered a house of his own to be prepared for us, which was sufficiently spacious to accommodate our whole party and our baggage, and which, although of rude fabric, was a palace to persons who had been so long exposed in tents, and those the worse for wear, to every blast of wind, and frequent visitations of snow and rain.

On the second day after our arrival Mir Izzet Ullah waited upon the Khalun, and, according to the Mir's report, the conference afforded a curious picture of the feelings and opinions prevalent in this part of the world regarding the British power in India: it was evident that the mind of the Khalun was preoccupied with distrust of our professions and apprehensions of injury, either political or commercial, to the interests of Ladakh: indeed he confessed as much, and remarked that he had been told it was the practice of the English to appear at first in the guise of merchants, merely to gain a footing in the country, and that, having effected this, they speedily brought it under their authority. The Mir laboured especially to remove the impression that the British government entertained any designs against the independence of Ladakh, and we were fortunately able to produce some evidence to this effect which seemed to have great weight with the Khalun; a letter from Mohammed Azim to Mir Izzet Ullah, intimating a tender of allegiance for Kashmir, which he wished the Mir to convey to the Resident at Delhi: he had, however, under my directions, declined becoming a party to the negotiation. If any secret purpose against Ladakh had been within our views this would have been the readiest mode of accomplishing it, as the occupation of Ladakh would at once have followed the possession of Kashmir.

Leaving the Khalun to consider the question maturely, we remained quiet in our mansion until the 1st of October, when we were summoned to an interview. The streets were, as before, lined with spectators, and both Ladakhis and Kashmiris saluted us civilly as we passed. After threading some narrow passages we entered a court-yard, where we dismounted. A band of music struck up as we entered. We then ascended two flights of stairs to an ante-chamber full of attendants, where the Khaga Tan-zin met me, and taking my right hand led me into the audience chamber. The Khalun was seated on some cushions at the further end of the room, on the left of a window; and on his left sat two other persons, one of whom was the Núna, or deputy Khalun. As I advanced to him he put out his hands, took mine between them, and slightly bowed. I then took my place on a chair placed opposite to him, and a conversation chiefly complimentary ensued. He inquired after our health, hoped we had not suffered from the cold, asked our ages, our country, its situation and distance, the name of the king, whether we were on terms of friendship with the Vrús (Russians), Katháís (Chinese), and Ranjit Sinh, whether we had ever visited Rúm (Constantinople). Speaking of the small-pox, which had been lately prevalent, I endeavoured to explain to him the advantages of vaccination, and recommended its introduction. The Khalun replied at great length, and with much animation. The interpreter evidently compressed his reply, but the purport seemed to have been a reluctance to change old customs for new. We were then served with salted tea, which was distributed to every person present, and after making our presents took our leave. The Khalun and his two friends shook hands with us, and the former expressed a hope that he should soon see us again.

The Khalun, or chief minister of Ladakh, whose name is Tsiva Tandu, appeared to be about sixty. He had lost most of his teeth, was thin, and of middle stature, with a countenance expressive of shrewdness; he was plainly dressed, in a loose brown wrapper and velvet cap, without any ornament. During the interview he smoked a hukka, small, but richly decorated. The other two persons were much more splendidly apparelled. The audience-chamber was a long, low-roofed apartment; the roof was carved and painted green and vermilion, and was supported by two rows of wooden pillars, painted red and varnished, and having capitals carved with flowers and foliage of green and gold; round the shafts letters were suspended by cords; a deep cornice of foliage, intermixed with grotesque figures, extended round the room; and below this the walls were hung with Tatar bows and arrows, shields, swords, and matchlocks. The walls were panelled, and each panel was painted in the Chinese style. One side of the room was chiefly filled by a large window, without glass, but partly screened by a curtain of pink brocade. Over the head of the Khalun, a small canopy, covered with a kind of stuff, in which the Dragon of China was conspicuous, was suspended from the ceiling. On the wall, above and behind him, was a large square of patchwork, like a chequer-board, and on each square was worked a letter or word in Tibetan characters. On his right hung a picture of a female divinity, with a green face and red eyes, sitting cross-legged on the cup of a flower. In front of the Khalun and his companions stood a low table or stool on a carved stand. In front of this a narrow Persian carpet, of great beauty, extended nearly the whole length of the room, on which sat the Khaga Tan-zin, and felts and long cushions were distributed about for the attendants. We had chairs placed upon felts. Where the floor was seen, it was of plaster of a chocolate colour, and appeared to have been lately polished. A few painted Chinese chests were arranged along the left side of the room. Small red perfumed tapers were burning on the bench in front of the Khalun, and in various parts of the chamber.

The absence of the Khalun for three days delayed the repetition of our intercourse, and in the interval we heard of the arrival of an express from the Garpan of Gardokh, with information that a European, who had attempted to enter that district, had been compelled to retire. Advices were also received from Undela, that a European had arrived there, with an intention of entering into Ladakh, but had been stopped until orders could be received from the superior authorities. These accounts probably related to the movements of Mr. Gerard, who had some time before apprised me of his intention to follow the Setlej, if permitted, to its source, and then return and join me in Ladakh. On the 5th, the Khalun returned, and sent for Mir Izzet Ullah, with whom he entered into friendly and confidential communication. He confessed that the Kashmiris had endeavoured to prejudice him against us, and prevail on him to prevent our coming to Lé; but, he added, he was very well pleased he had not listened to their suggestions.

For some days after this nothing of any interest occurred. We were occupied in our domestic and mercantile arrangements, and making inquiries necessary for our onward journey to Yarkand. In the course of October, a caravan of Chabbas, as they are termed, traders from Lassa, arrived, with many yaks laden with tea, also a caravan from Yarkand, of twenty-five horses, with shawl-wool, felts, tea, and silks. The latter was the first arrival from Yarkand for many months, and its unusual delay had excited great anxiety amongst the Kashmiris. Some disputes, it was known, had arisen between Omar Khan, the ruler of Ferghana and the Chinese authorities at Yarkand, and it was feared that the chief merchants, who are mostly from Indejan, and subject to Ferghana, had left that city. Although this was true, yet the delay had rather arisen from the depressed state of the market at Yarkand, in consequence of which the caravans had proceeded to Bokhara. The horses were small, low, but of great depth of chest and strength in the fore-legs; they were of two breeds, Kirghiz and Kozak, and the whole were purchased for fifty rupees a head, by a native dealer, for exportation to the Panjab.

Khaja Shah Nyas having come to the vicinity of Lé, was visited on the 21st by the Khalun, the Nuna Khalun, the Khaga Tan-zin, one or two other officers of Ladakh, Mohsin Baba, a merchant of Turan, and Abdul Latif, and a conference ensued, in which our character and objects were again canvassed. The Khalun said that he had received cautionary letters from Gardokh, and that an officer from Lassa had come there to inquire what was meant by the visit of Europeans to the frontier. That the governor of Kashmir had intimated to him that Ranjit Sinh would take offence if he gave us encouragement; that Ahmed Shah, the malik of Balti, had written to him to know who and what we were; and that advices came from the Bisahar frontier of the approach of a European party. These circumstances, he said, had very much shaken his confidence in us, and he was at a loss what to decide. The Khaja repeated the arguments he had formerly used in our favour, and appealed to the Khalun's knowledge of his friendship for Ladakh in proof of his not being likely to give advice detrimental to the interests of the country. He reminded the Khalun that Ladakh was not dependent either upon Lassa or Lahore; that the English, a much more mighty power than any other, were, by the possession of Bisahar, quite as much his neighbours, and still more to be conciliated; and that the establishment of a commercial intercourse especially must be highly beneficial to Ladakh. Mir Izzet Ullah was then summoned, and desired to state explicitly what we wished or expected, and as he was instructed, he replied, that all we sought for was, 1. liberty to trade with Ladakh, and through it to other countries; 2. moderate duties; 3. a permanent factory at Lé; and 4. the good offices of the government, with that of Gardokh, to induce the latter to open the Niti Ghat to British commerce. The three first, after some discussion, were promised, but the Khalun expressed his doubt whether the Gardokh authorities themselves could permit access to the district: however, he promised that a confidential person should accompany me to Gardokh whenever I wished it. It was only further necessary, he stated, that these articles should be confirmed by the Raja to become the basis of a formal engagement.

As the administration of affairs was wholly in the hands of the Khalun, the Raja being little more than a cipher in the state, we now imagined that all difficulties were at an end. In this, however, we were disappointed. The Kashmiris having failed to influence the Khalun against us, had recourse to the Lompa, the governor of Lé, and engaged him to counsel the Raja not to accede to any treaty, but to send us off with all dispatch. Our old friend the Khaja here again assisted us, and gradually prevailed upon the Lom-pa to withdraw his opposition. We exchanged visits, and upon his falling sick he applied to me for medical advice, which proved of service to him; and he became also friendly towards us. Still there was a delay, for the Khalun stated it was necessary, at least, as an act of courtesy towards the authorities of Gardokh, who were the ancient friends and connexions of Ladakh, to communicate with them before coming to any decision. A letter was accordingly written, and in a few weeks an answer arrived which disapproved strongly of the Khalun's conduct, and recommended our immediate dismissal. The Khalun was rather offended at the tone of this remonstrance, and determined to refer the matter to Lassa, requesting me to remain patiently at Lé, a measure to which I the more readily consented, as the prospect of effecting a passage by Yarkand was yet a subject of uncertainty. Owing to these interruptions the business was not brought to a close until the beginning of May, when, although no reply had been received from Lassa, engagements were exchanged between the Raja and chief officers of Ladakh on the one part, and myself on behalf of the British merchants of Calcutta on the other, calculated to throw open to the enterprise of the latter, and through them to the manufactures of Great Britain, the whole of central Asia from China to the Caspian Sea.

The interval that elapsed between my arrival at Lé, and the signing of this treaty, was occupied with frequent communications with the authorities, with medical practice, with arrangements preparatory to the continuation of my journey, with correspondence public or private, and with the collection of information on various points relating to Ladakh and the neighbouring countries: my time was therefore fully engaged, and I found it impossible to keep a regular journal of our proceedings, or to digest and arrange the materials which I collected. Some of the principal features of this country, however, one hitherto unvisited by Europeans, will be found in the following account.

CHAPTER II.

Description of Ladakh—Limits—Extent—Surface—Rivers—Indus—Sinh-kha-bab—Its tributaries—Feeders of the Setlej—Soil—Climate—Agriculture—Grains—Wheat—Barley—Varieties of both—Grasses—Prangos—Vegetables—Fruits—Apricots—Apples—Willows—Poplars—Animals—Minerals.

LADAKH is bounded on the north-east by the mountains which divide it from the Chinese province of Khoten, and on the east and south-east by Rodokh and Chan-than, dependencies of Lassa: on the south by the British province of Bisahar, and by the hill states of Kulu and Chamba. The latter also extends along the south-west till it is met by Kashmir, which with part of Balti, Kartakshe, and Khafalun, complete the boundary on the west and north-west. The north is bounded by the Karakoram mountains and Yarkand.

The precise extent of Ladakh can scarcely be stated without an actual survey; but our different excursions, and the information we collected, enabled us to form an estimate, which is, probably, not far wide of the truth. From north to south, or from the foot of the Karakoram mountains to the fort of Trankar in Piti, the distance is rather more than two hundred miles; and from east to west, or from the La Ganskiel pass to that of Zoje La, it cannot be less than two hundred and fifty. The outline, however, is irregular, being contracted on the north-west and south-west, and the whole area may not much exceed thirty thousand square miles.

Although the country of Ladakh lies at a lower elevation than the mountain ranges, which serve as ramparts to its northern and southern frontier, yet its general character is that of its gigantic neighbours, and its lowest levels are in the vicinity of perpetual snow. It is, in fact, a series of narrow valleys, situated between mountains not of very great altitude as compared with the land at their feet, but ordinarily towering to a height above the sea, which surpasses that of the pinnacles of the Alps. The elevation of Lé itself is more than eleven thousand feet above the sea, and some parts of the northern pergana of Nobra are two thousand feet above that level. The passes that lead into Ladakh on its southern frontier are above sixteen thousand feet high, and there are several mountains within the country which are crossed in travelling from one valley to another, as the Kandu La, Chang La, and Parang La, which are of still greater altitude.

The principal valley in Ladakh is that which follows the course of the Indus, and extends from south-east to north-west through the greater part of the country. It may be said, indeed, to be continued throughout, or along the course of the Dras river to the frontiers of Kashmir. Another considerable valley runs nearly parallel to it, a short way to the north, from the frontier of Rodokh to the valley of Digar, and this, like the preceding, may be considered as continuing with interruptions through Ladakh, forming the bed of the Shayuk branch of the Indus. The general direction of the valleys is, however, at an oblique angle to these main lines, giving passage to the rivers that supply the Indus or its principal branches. These valleys vary in extent; they are sometimes little better than deep ravines or defiles, and even at their greatest expanse they do not exceed a few hundred yards in breadth: occasionally a small plain is left by the receding hills of a mile or two in diameter, but such spots are very rarely met with. The general character of the surface is, extreme inequality, consisting of steep and bare mountains capped with snow, and close and rocky dells, with rapid torrents or deep rivers rushing along their hollows.

The river that may be regarded as the most striking and important feature in the geography of Ladakh, is the great eastern branch of the Indus, or, as termed in the country, the Sinh-kha-bab, the river that rises from the lion's mouth, in reference to the Tibetan notion, borrowed perhaps from the Hindus, of the origin of four great rivers from the mouths of as many animals; as the Indus from the lion's mouth; the Ganges, Mab-cha-kha-bab, from that of the peacock; the Setlej, Lang-chin-kha-bab, from that of the elephant; and the Ster-chuk-kha-bab, or river of Tibet, from the mouth of the horse.

The Sinh-kha-bab rises in the Kan-re, Kangri or Kantesi mountains, the Kailasa of the Hindus, and after traversing the country of Chan-than in a direction from south-east to north-west, enters Ladakh on its eastern, and follows the same course to its western frontier; at Khalets, about thirty miles east of Lé, it takes a turn more to the north, and passes through Kartakshe to Sagarkhoad, or Skardu, the capital of Balti, from whence it flows for a considerable distance in a north-westerly direction, and then turns to the south, in its course towards the plains of Hindustan: during its progress through Ladakh it is joined by several large streams.

The Shayuk is the principal river that joins the Indus on the north. Rising from the foot of the Karakoram mountains, it flows several days' journey to the south, till within two days' journey to the north-east of the village of Ahkam. There it receives the Duryukh, a river that collects the waters from the eastern portions of the northern valley, and it then turns, at almost a right angle, to the west. From Hundur, the capital of the district of Nobra, it flows in a direction north-west out of Ladakh, and passes nearly to the extremity of the small state of Khafalun, within two or three days' march of Sagarkhoad, where it is incorporated with the Sinh-kha-bab, forming the Aba Sind, or Indus Proper. Near Hundur, the Shayuk receives a stream of some size, the Churasa, which also rises from the southern foot of the Karakoram ridge; passing some way to the east, it turns off to the south, and flowing nearly parallel with the Shayuk on its east, it joins that river a short way to the east of Hundur.

Several streams, of lesser extent and size, flow to the Sinh-kha-bab, on either bank, but they are mostly of the character of mountain-torrents and watercourses. A more important tributary is the Zanskar river, which, coming from the south, joins it opposite to Niemo. This rises near Labrang, on the southern frontier, and is soon joined by the Ling-ti. It follows a direction nearly due north, receiving on its way the Sum-giel and Marka rivers.

At four days' march west from Khalets, another river, flowing from the south-east, crosses the road, and is met by a stream from the south-west. These are denominated, from the places by which they pass, the Pushkyum and Kartse rivers: flowing to the north, their united stream is joined by another from the south-west, the Dras river, rising in the mountains separating Ladakh from Kashmir, and furnishing a body of water as considerable as the Sinh-kha-bab itself at Lé. The Dras river again is joined on the west by the river of Shingo flowing from the steppe of Deosoe, in the principality of Balti. These different rivers combining, pour into the Sinh-kha-bab the collected waters of the western highlands, as the Shayuk brings those of the northern, and the Zanskar, Pushkyum, and Kartse, those of the southern elevation; thus constituting the Sinh-kha-bab the great drain by which the snows upon the lofty ridges of Tibet are the means of fertilizing the plains of the Panjab. These different rivers, however, varying in size and extent, are affected by the same influences of site and climate, and present the same attributes. Except where arrested by the hand of winter, they hurry along with rapidity and force, and are frequently unfordable, rather from the impetuosity of their currents than their depth. The latter is, however, often considerable, especially in the summer months, when the snow is abundantly melted. They are liable, from the same cause, to extreme and sudden vicissitudes, and the stream that was scarcely knee-deep in the morning acquires a depth of several fathoms in the afternoon, when the rays of the sun have acted sufficiently upon the sides and summits of the neighbouring mountains.

Ladakh, although chiefly the reservoir of the Indus, contributes largely to another of the principal Indian rivers, and from Piti, its southernmost district, sends off a large stream that may be considered as the western branch of the Setlej. The Piti river, or, as it is termed in the valley, the Losar, rises in two chief branches, the smaller from the mountains towards the Bara Lacha pass, and the larger and more southerly, from the eastern face of the Kulzam La, on the frontier of Kulu. Opposite to the fort of Trankar it is joined by the Pin river, from the south-west; and beyond the Ladakh boundary it is said to meet with the Tsurip river from the north. The united stream enters the British dependency of Bisahar, and joins the eastern branch of the Setlej, near the village of Namja.

As the surface of Ladakh is thus broken by steep mountains, deep rivers, and the ravines or valleys in which they run, it may easily be supposed that there is little space left for the labours of agriculture. These are confined to the levels along the borders of the streams, and the easier slopes of the lower hills, or the bases of the higher. The proportion of such available surface is comparatively small, and does not probably exceed one-fifth of the whole. The soil consists almost entirely of the disintegrated rocks, torn to pieces and crumbled by the successive congelation and thaw of water in their crevices and chasms, and by the action of snow and torrents upon their surfaces. The mountains being for the most part primitive, the decomposition of the granite and felspar clothes the levels with a coating of clay, sand, gravel, and pebbles, which is only rendered productive by human industry and skill. The general aspect of the country, when not under cultivation, is one of extreme sterility and barrenness, in which a few willows and poplars are the only timber-trees, and the chief verdure is that of Tartaric furze, with a few tufts of wormwood, hyssop, dog-rose, and other plants of the desert, and the rock, exposing, rather than concealing, the barrenness of the soil.

Nor would the climate be expected to prove more auspicious than the soil to the labours of the husbandman. Frost with snow and sleet commences early in September, and continues with little intermission to the beginning of May. From the middle of December to the beginning of February we found the thermometer out of doors at night seldom above fifteen degrees, and on the 1st of February it was as low as nine degrees and a half. In an inner apartment of our dwelling it ranged from twenty-three to thirty-two, but did not rise above the freezing point till the 8th of February. In May the days become warm, although early in the morning the rivulets not unfrequently present a coat of ice, and this may be observed in some spots even in June, whilst on the loftiest mountains snow falls occasionally in every month of the year. During the summer months the sun shines with great power, and for a short part of the day his rays are intensely hot. At Lé, on the 4th of July, the thermometer in the sun rose at noon to one hundred and thirty-four, and on the march to Piti it stood ten degrees higher: at night the temperature was seventy-four degrees. Even in the depth of winter the heat of the sun is very considerable for an hour or two, and the variation of temperature is consequently extreme. On the 30th of January the thermometer showed a temperature of eighty-three at noon, when it was only twelve and a half at night. The great heat of the sun in summer compensates for the short duration of the season, and brings the grain to rapid maturity. Barley that was sown in the neighbourhood of Lé on the 10th of May, was cut on the 12th of September; and at Pituk, five miles from Lé, and about eight hundred feet lower, in a sheltered angle of the valley, the same grain is ready for the sickle in two months from the time of sowing.

The atmosphere of Ladakh is, in general, dry, the moisture being converted into snow in the winter, and speedily evaporated by the scorching suns of summer; there is consequently very little rain. During our stay in the country rain fell but on ten days, and then in very small quantities, between the end of April and the middle of September, and this we were informed much exceeded the average fall.

Notwithstanding these unpromising conditions the harvests of Ladakh are by no means unproductive, and they present also the peculiarity of yielding equally abundant crops year after year from the same land, without its ever being suffered to lie fallow, and without any attempt being made to cultivate a succession or alternation of produce. There are some other peculiarities in the agricultural economy of Ladakh, arising from the character of the country and the climate, which may afford not unserviceable lessons to the inhabitants of Alpine regions in other parts of the world.

The first step in the process of tillage is to clear the ground of its incumbrances, and, as far as possible, equalize the surface. The larger blocks of stone are left undisturbed, but the smaller fragments are collected and arranged in longitudinal piles or walls, traversing the face of the declivity, which every field more or less presents, forming a series of parallels, the space between which is made as level as possible by conveying materials from the upper to the lower edge of the slope. In this manner a succession of terraces is constructed, each supported by a stone breast-work, and down which stone channels communicating with some spring or natural reservoir on the higher ground conduct a plentiful supply of water. This is the disposition of the grounds in the vicinity of the villages and towns which are situated in the different valleys forming the inhabited and cultivable portion of Ladakh; but even in solitary spots, remote from human habitations, stone dikes may be observed crossing the sloping sides of mountains near their base: these are constructed by the peasants to assist the deposit of soil and gravel by the melting snows, and they are thus left for many years, perhaps for some generations, for the operation of natural agency to prepare for the labour of man, and the more ready conversion of an abrupt and steril declivity into an accessible flight of terraces of cultivation.

Upon the field thus gained from the mountain soil has to be, in the first instance, supplied, and afterwards enriched by manure. As there is great scarcity of wood the dung of cattle is mostly consumed as fuel, and the means of ameliorating the ground must, therefore, be sought in the habitations of man. The houses are well provided with apartments for this purpose: the floors of these are strewed with a coating of gravel three or four inches in thickness, which is removed from time to time, and with the ashes of the burnt fuel forms the pabulum that sustains the nutritive properties of the soil. In some villages public receptacles are constructed for the people, and the accumulation of soil for general use.

According to the dryness of the ground water is let in, either previous or subsequent to the first ploughing. After the land has been once ploughed, the manure, brought in sacks upon asses to the field, is spread over it, and a second ploughing takes place, in the furrows of which the seed is sown. The grain is sometimes sown broad-cast, at others in the furrow, and is also put in by the dibble. In the neighbourhood of Lé the plant was suffered to acquire a height of five or six inches before it was watered, but after this it was refreshed by a thin coat of water almost every day. The water is, in general, clear and pure, but is subject to many variations in colour and quality, and is often discoloured by earth, and impregnated with soda and alum. In general it is unwholesome to strangers, and at some seasons even to the natives.

Oxen of the common kind are not used for ploughing, the zho ox, or hybrid male between the yak, or bos grunniens, and the common cow, or the humped variety called zebu, being greatly preferred, as is its sister, the zhomo, for the dairy. Ploughing is performed by a pair of zhos, driven by the ploughman without reins, but guided, when well broken in, with the utmost precision, by the voice or by a willow wand.

The plough is entirely of wood, generally willow, save the point, which is formed by a small piece of iron. The whole structure is simple, unexpensive, and the instrument is little liable to be out of repair, excepting the point, which, from the softness of the metal, requires to be frequently sharpened. The furrow made is superficial in mellow lands, even not exceeding four or five inches from the top of the ridge to the bottom angle, but the clods are broken, and the earth is made almost as fine as for garden culture, and the seed is covered with especial care.

The necessity of taking advantage of every available article for the food of the cattle leads to a regular and effective mode of weeding the corn fields, and when the corn has been sown for about three weeks, women and children are turned into the field every morning to collect the grass and weeds springing up with the grain. No harm results from this process, and although the stems are for a little time disturbed by the footsteps of the weeders, they are never trodden down, and recover their erect position in a few hours after the field has been watered. The regular removal of the weeds gives the corn the benefit of the whole power of the soil, and admits the access of light and air to the roots of the plants.

The kinds of grain cultivated in Ladakh are wheat, barley, and buck-wheat, of various descriptions. The generic name of the first in Tibetan is To, of the second Nas, and of the third Do, in the eastern, and Bro in the western parts of Ladakh.

The wheat indigenous in Tibet is of three kinds. To Chand, red wheat; To Karmo, early wheat; and To Surutze. There is also another species, termed To Mondhu, or beardless wheat, or from the country whence it comes, Hasora wheat.

The whole of the wheat of Tibet has the merit of being hardy, but the To Karmo is the most productive, and yields the finest flour. Wheat is in general sown in spring, from March to May, and reaped in summer, from July to September, according to the temperature of different localities. The straw is in general less luxuriant than in Europe, but the crops are beautifully regular and clean. There is very rarely any disease amongst the crops, although after a fall of rain heavier than ordinary, a few ears may sometimes be affected with ergot, or speckled with mildew.

The Hasora wheat, which is cultivated in some of the western districts of Ladakh, is characterised by a peculiar structure of the ear, which may be described as formed of two sides and two pillars. The sides are nearly flat, and the stem of supporting straw runs perpendicularly between two pillars of grain. The ear is much shorter than in the other varieties of wheat, but it is broader, and each ear contains from forty to seventy grains. The straw, though not differing in diameter materially, is much more solid than usual, so that a broken or bent stem is rarely seen. It is of a bright colour, and from its lustre, strength, and flexibility, would make a valuable material for platting. It is occasionally worked by the women of Ladakh into small stars, with which they decorate their caps, or their hair. The grain of the Hasora wheat is of a yellowish white colour, whilst that of the Ladakh wheat is more or less tinged with red; it is also shorter and more rounded. The ear is distinguished from that of the other varieties in Ladakh, by exhibiting no trace of a beard, whence it derives its appellation. The other kinds are all furnished with this appendage, and even the Hasora wheat, after some years' cultivation in the province, puts forth a few bristly straws from the summit. The Hasora wheat I was informed bears cold better than any other kind. On poor lands it is said to give a scanty return, but largely to repay the expense of manure.

The barley of Tibet is of two kinds, distinguished by the peculiarity of retaining or parting from the rough exterior capsule, after the grain has quitted the ear. The first, called Nas Swa, is not different from the common barley of Europe. To the second sort, the term Sherokh* is applied, and this is distinguished into six varieties. 1. Chu

* It would appear that Marco Polo met with a species of the Sherokh, or naked barley, in Badakhshan, as he says, " good

Nas, slow, or late barley. 2. Giok Nas, quick, or early barley. 3. Nas Yan Karmo, which also signifies early. 4. Nak Nas, black barley. 5. Tughzut Nas, or six-sided; and 6, Mendokh Nas, or flower barley.

The husked barley, or that of Europe, is of necessity raised in those localities which are the warmest, for although the seeds of the Sherokh may be sown in such situations, the produce will be rough barley. The latter again yields naked barley in elevated and cold sites, as in the lands of Lé. The Chu Nas, or late barley, is cultivated on those spots where, although the temperature is not the most severe, yet the summer heat is not sufficient to raise two crops a year, or one of barley, and one of buck-wheat. Giok Nas is employed in very high situations which have short summers with very hot days, the nights at the same time being cold: this is the principal cultivation of the valley of Dras. Nas Yan Karmo, or, as sometimes denominated, Sarmo, is cultivated in all places, vary-

wheat is grown there, and a species of barley without a husk." This, according to Marsden, is the *hordeum nudum, h. glabrum,* or *h. vulgare seminibus decorticatis* of European botanists.—MOORCROFT.

ing from temperate to warm. It is preferred to all the other kinds of barley, as its produce is great, and its flour is little inferior to that of wheat. Nak Nas, or black barley, is the hardiest of all the varieties of Sherokh, and grows at the extremest altitude at which grain can be raised. It flourishes at Wakka, where, partly from its elevation, and partly from being surrounded by snowy mountains, the climate is excessively severe; and rain in summer is of more frequent occurrence than in other parts of the country: it gives a good yield, but its flour is objected to, even by the Tibetans, who are not fastidious on account of its black colour. The six-sided barley, or Tughzut Nas, is also grown at Wakka, but is considered inferior to the Yan Karmo, both in produce and quality. Mendokh, or flower-barley, is said to have been recently introduced from the neighbourhood of Lassa, and was cultivated to a very limited extent. It was likely, however, to become a favourite crop, as it was said to produce abundantly, to thrive equally well with or without rain, and to yield a flour little inferior to wheat.

The return of grain at Dras is said to be about twenty for one. At Sankho it varies so much, according to the varying condition of the soil, that an average could not be procured; and after much exertion I was obliged to abandon my attempts at obtaining an averaged estimate of produce. If the land be very poor, the seed gives only a single stem, but if in good heart, it yields several; and in Wakka, it is said to be no uncommon occurrence for one plant of the Yan Karmo to consist of from twelve to fifteen ears, but the filling is almost always proportioned to the liberality with which the field has been dunged. I have not seen so rich an average yield as that just mentioned, although I have counted eighteen ears produced by a single seed, on a spot enriched by horses having been kept stationary, and well fed upon it during the preceding winter. But this richness may be carried to a mischievous excess; ample manuring so permanently sustaining the vegetating powers of the plant, as to prevent the grain ripening in short summers, a circumstance I have more than once witnessed in this country. And though giving much straw, a green head with small grains justifies only a considerable use of manure, which, if not expensive in money price, is not collected without much labour. Whilst at Korbo seeking for Mendokh Nas, my eye was caught by the regularity of the plants of a field of Yan Karmo, which was almost as great as if the whole seed had been disposed in small squares of equal size, but I could not learn that more than common care had been employed in sowing it. And a similar evenness was observed in the height and strength of the straw, in the length of the ears, and in their equality of approach to ripeness. It was the finest crop I ever beheld; and a spirited English farmer would have thought himself sufficiently repaid for a ride of many miles by a sight of it. From being close to the house of the farmer, it had probably obtained a larger share of manure than other fields more distant; and this might account for the crop being somewhat backward, and for the equal size of the plant, but not for its regularity as to distance, which must have been produced by good ploughing, and even hand in sowing broadcast, as drilling is not used in Purik, though practised in Nobra.

The husk of the Sherokh varieties, whether bearded or beardless, breaks when the grain is ripe, and discloses the latter apparently naked. The axilla is double, the outer having a tinge of green, blue, purple, yellow, or white, according to the specific variety, influenced apparently by the locality.

A short time before the grain of Sherokh barley becomes ripe, it is particularly large and plump, and seems to expand the husk so as to cause it to burst; when quite ripe it begins to shrink, and when hard it actually loses so much of its former dimensions, whilst the husk retains those it acquired in its greatest state of dilatation, that the grains standing in the cup or husk on its end become too small for the latter, as seen but partially covered by its former coats, and so loosely attached, as to be capable of being dislodged by a slight shake. If the crop be left standing after it is fully ripe, the grain is more disposed to shed than common barley; and this circumstance justifies the Tibet practice of reaping before it be perfectly matured. Through this premature gathering, the grain shrivels and becomes smaller than if it had been allowed to become fully ripe, but no injury is sustained in respect to the quality of the flour, or the power of vegetating, at least as far as could be made out by a casual observer. The latter remark, however, must be taken as relative only to the crops of Tibet in general, as there are certain localities of this country, of which the summer begins too late to afford heat enough for ripening the grain so fully as to admit of its vegetating, and these districts procure their seed corn from others more happily situated; yet in the former good flour is obtained from grain cut whilst green, and which of course yields a smaller proportion than that which is matured.

Instead of the crop being bound in sheaves in Ladakh, it is laid on the ground in flat unbound bundles, so piled, that the ears are concealed by the butts of the stems for a few days in fine weather to ripen more completely; but if it is cloudy, or rainy, it is exposed in shocks, with the ears uppermost, on large stones on the sides of rocks, where, by a few showers, the straw loses its white or cream-like colour, and speedily contracts a tint bordering on that of sulphur, without injury to its quality, unless there be an excess of rain, which seldom happens. When the soil is very dry, the grain is pulled up by the roots; when moist, it is cut by means of a greatly-curved, but short-bladed sickle, which, perhaps, is quite as well adapted to the purpose as that of Europe. Every inch of straw is of value to the farmer for feeding his cattle in the long winter of Tibet; and this value suggesting the pulling up of the straw by the roots, where it can be extracted without bringing up soil along with it, indicates also the expediency of cutting the stem as near to the ground as possible, in situations so moist as not to admit of the former method being employed; and to prevent the fingers of the reaper being hurt by scraping along the surface of the gravelly soil, either the handle of the sickle has at its lower surface a projecting guard of wood, or there is a niche in which the fingers are lodged, the plan differing in different provinces. This handle is made of willow or of poplar. As the clods are broken with the most scrupulous care, the straw is cut almost within two inches of the surface of the soil. Near large towns scarcely any weeds remain, they having formed a valuable resource for stall feeding, so that the butts of the straw become dry nearly as soon as the heads; but in single farms or villages, where the labourers have a larger surface of land under cultivation compared with their numbers, the practice of drawing the crop is adopted, and the weeds are either left to be eaten off as they stand, provided the winter be near, or turned into the soil as manure for a crop of buck-wheat, which ripens in six weeks or two months, if there be enough of the warm season left after the corn crop is got in.

Tibet offers many peculiarities likely to influence the constitution of the barley. In an unclouded sky, the solar rays passing through a thin atmosphere, are finer, and they are vigorously reflected from the rocks, and in many parts from sand, or from a light-coloured stony soil; but the nights, as before observed, are cool, and frequently cold. The roots of the plants are moistened by irrigation with very cold water, whilst the stem and the ears, in by far the greatest proportion of localities, are kept almost continually in a state of dryness. Whether the sudden expansion of the grain, and its subsequent contraction, would take place in an equal degree in the less cold, and also less hot, but more humid climate of Britain, it is impossible to determine, except by actual experiment. In no other country have I seen an equal surface in barley as regularly covered with plant, and never plants with better heads. Although the degree of influence of sudden alternations of exposure to heat and to cold, to dryness of atmosphere and moisture of soil, the latter by irrigation with cold water cannot be precisely determined; yet the influence of a continual high temperature, and of a dry atmosphere with a moist condition of root, produced by irrigation with water rather tepid, is known to convert the barley now alluded to into common barley. This has happened in the Panjab, and at Peshawer, if I may trust to the reports of merchants, who stated, that they had actually witnessed the fact in the third year on the produce of seed taken from Ladakh to those countries. The individuals in question having noticed that I was engaged in making inquiries and observations in respect to this barley, separately, and from friendly motives, advertised me that I should be disappointed by sending it to Hindustan, as it would quickly degenerate into common barley. Even at Pituk, in the very heart of Ladakh, the same effect takes place.

Sherokh barley is preferred in Ladakh to the common, or husked barley, for all uses; but especially for the preparation of the fermented liquor called Chang. It would probably, therefore, be valuable to the maltster, whilst from its hardihood, the quickness of its growth, and the abundance of its crop, it might be cultivated with advantage in some of the cold countries in the north of Europe and America. I considered it, therefore, worth while to collect the grains, and sent a considerable supply to my friends in India and in Europe.

Of buck-wheat there are said to be three varieties, but it is unnecessary to particularise any of the peculiarities of this grain, as it is well known under the name of Phaphar throughout the hill districts subject to British authority.

The natural sward of the unimproved glebe is composed chiefly of a starveling low grass, and dwarf sow-thistle, the spring shoots of which are dug up for a potherb. In bogs the surface is covered by a short rush and bent-grass, with some varieties of crowfoot (*ranunculus*), and dwarf equisetum. The islands and banks of the rivers in some places naked, are in others fringed or concealed by bushes of a new kind of thorn, bearing an abundance of small red acid berries, affording winter food to the birds. In some places on the plains natural springs keep the surface in a perpetual state of humidity during the warm weather, and are surrounded by beds of low rush and aquatic grass, offering wholesome pasturage to the cattle during the spring and summer. If, however, the stock be allowed to graze upon these lands in August and September, the sheep and goats are sure to be affected by the rot, from the abundance of the liver fluke (*fasciola hepatica*), which either in the egg or in the young worm is then eaten with the herbage. Lucerne, called Olh while green, and Champu when cut and dry, is both wild and cultivated: it grows with great luxuriance in some parts of the province, and is collected and piled on the parapets of the houses as winter fodder for the cattle: there are said to be two varieties of it, one which quickly comes to perfection, but dies in three years; the other of slower growth, but of much longer duration, the roots living and bearing for fifty or sixty years. A species of sainfoin grows wild in some parts of the mountains, and is much sought after by wild goats and sheep: the inner bark of its root affords the only material employed for paper.

One of the most valuable sources of fodder of Ladakh, and perhaps of any country whatever, is a plant known by the name of Prangos, and which grows only in the western parts of the country at Imbal or Dras. This occurs of various sizes according to its age, from a single leaf covering not more than an inch of surface, to a cluster of leaves and flowers spreading to a circumference of twelve and eighteen feet. This bush consists of long feathering leaves of a dark green colour, crowned, when in blossom, by a profusion of large tufts of yellow flowers; the leaves when of full size are two feet in length, and the bush is circular with a rounded top. The flower-stalks rise from two to five, or even six feet, in old plants. The leaves emit a strong odour, which at first is disagreeable, but becomes less so when a person is familiar with it; they have also when fresh a pungent, bitter, and slightly aromatic taste, but these properties disappear in the dry state. The flowers are slightly odorous, and when first opened are covered by a glistening, viscid, and sub-saccharine exudation, which attracts the ants in such numbers, that the flowers are sometimes blackened by them. Some copper-coloured beetles, and some small wild bees, are also busied in gathering this substance. The root is perennial: the leaves and flower stems are in life for about four months. The plant flowers in June, and at the end of August the seeds fall and spontaneously sow themselves; they lie in the ground till the snow begins to melt, or in April, and the plant then makes its reappearance. It is not, however, till the third year that the root is fully developed and begins to spread; thenceforward it continues to put forth fresh shoots for an indeterminate period, so that, in the belief of the peasantry, a plant scarcely ever dies.

The head of the Prangos, including leaves, flowers, stems, and seeds, is converted into hay, as winter forage for goats, sheep, and cows. Late in August, or early in September, the plants are cut to within two or three inches of the ground, and laid on it in bundles, kept down by heavy stones. These bundles are sufficiently dry in three or four days, to be gathered and piled in thick layers on the housetops, where stones are placed upon them to prevent their being blown away: they require no shelter. In the winter months about a hundred weight is considered sufficient for twenty sheep or thirty lambs for twenty-four hours. Healthy sheep fed upon Prangos hay are said to become fat in twenty days, and that if fully fed with it for two months, their fatness approaches to suffocation. It is said also to be of a heating quality, but not to a greater degree than is desirable in such a climate. It displays its nutritive properties in cows as well as in sheep and goats, but it is said that it does not increase the quantity of milk; and as beef is not an article of food in Ladakh, there is no advantage in feeding neat cattle upon it. Horses thrive upon it, but they are not readily reconciled to it; and it is remarkable, that whilst growing, no animal will browze upon the leaves of the Prangos, although they will feed upon its flowers. It is only as hay that the foliage is an acceptable article of food. Prangos has not been raised in any other of the districts of Ladakh, rather, it would appear, from no pains having been taken to transplant it, than from any difficulty in localizing it elsewhere, as one or two experiments had been made, I was informed, many years since, and the plants had flourished. Considering the value of this plant as fodder, its growing in a poor sterile soil, in every variety of site, except actual swamp, and in a bleak, cold climate, and its flourishing wholly in independence upon the care and industry of man, it would seem probable that it might be introduced with national advantage into many parts of Britain, and would convert her heaths, and downs, and highlands, into storehouses for the supply of innumerable flocks*.

It is no small advantage of the Prangos that it does not prevent the contiguous growth of common grass or different kinds of lucerne, which spread round its stem, underneath its bushy head, or even run over its summit. The yellow lucerne is often found in this situation, as well as growing wild in many of the mountains. It is also cultivated in some districts, and when duly supplied with water yields a luxuriant and useful crop. The leaves of this lucerne are smaller than those of the blue and purple varieties of Europe, and the stems are less strong and erect, but the heads are more fully covered with tufts of flowers. There is also another

* The Prangos has been placed by Mr. Lindley amongst the Umbelliferæ as a new genus: the Ladakh kind he denominates Prangos pabularia.—*Asiatic Journal*, vol. xix., p. 798. Mr. Royle considers it likely to be the Silphium of the ancients.—*Illustrations of the Botany of Himalaya*, p. 230. The seeds sent home by Mr. Moorcroft in 1822, had, unfortunately, lost their vegetating power, and it does not appear that any subsequent supply has been received.—Ed.

variety of lucerne called Yarkandi, a biennial, which has a larger stem than the ordinary kinds, growing to a height of four or five feet. The appearance of the straggling and thinly covered stems of this grass gives it a rather unprepossessing appearance, but the stalks are eaten by the cattle with great avidity. At Lé this is sown along with the perennial variety, and by its greater yield the first and second year supplies the defectiveness of the latter.

A very valuable herbage occurs in the Long-ma, or sand grass of Ladakh, which, growing on loose, sandy soil, and forming an intricate net-work both on the surface and beneath it, protects the slender covering of the primitive substratum from being blown away by the strong winds that sweep the valleys, and the whole country from being converted into a succession of bare rocks and mounds of sand. The Long-ma rarely reaches more than a height of ten or twelve inches, and frequently not more than five or six, a considerable portion of the blade being always buried in the sand. The length of the root is much more considerable, and strikes so deep that it cannot be extracted entire. At a depth of five feet it was found little diminished in circumference, throwing off numerous lateral fibres through its whole course. The grass on the surface does not extend uniformly, but affects the form of patches, by which it more effectively arrests the driving sand. Cattle will not eat it whilst it is green, or while other pasturage is procurable; but it is sufficiently hardy to outlive other herbage, and in November, when there is nothing else on the ground, it is eaten by horses and yaks. It is then of a yellow tint, but when the leaves and crown are eaten off, the brown stems are left almost level with the ground, their interstices filled with sand, and the appearance of each patch resembling that of an oakum door-mat. The plant emits a pleasant smell, and has a sweet and agreeable taste, but the leaf is stiff and harsh, with sharp edges. Although cattle do not fatten upon it, it is said to be very invigorating, and, perhaps, the extremely rich quality of the milk of the yak in winter may be due to this grass. The stories related by the carriers of its effects in restoring vigour to over-worked horses border on the marvellous. It furnishes almost the whole of the winter food of the unstabled brood mares and colts of the Raja of Ladakh, of the kiang, or wild horse, of the yak, and of all cattle which are left unhoused at that season.

There is no great variety of vegetable produce in Ladakh, but onions, carrots, turnips, and cabbages are reared in some places during the spring and summer. For winter use the leaves of the cabbages and turnip tops, or sliced turnips, are dried : carraway, mustard, and tobacco are grown in a few gardens.

The only fruits cultivated are apricots and apples, standards of which are reared abundantly in the orchards of every farm-house. Of apricots there are said to be ten varieties, and they certainly present much difference in size, shape, flavour, colour, and surface. They are all standards, and are raised from the stone with one exception, which is multiplied by inoculation. This is a small fruit not much larger than a walnut, somewhat flattened at top and bottom, of a glossy skin, and pale yellow colour, inclining to white, which changes to a reddish brown where it faces the sun. The pulp is of the usual consistence next the skin, but becomes softer as it recedes, and next the stone is little thicker than honey in the comb. The whole fruit partakes of the lusciousness of honey, combined with a slight and agreeable bitter, and the flavour is unsurpassed by any variety of apricot I have ever met with. The stone is of a light yellow colour, approaching to white. The trees grow in the Pargana of Ladakh proper, and especially at Saspula, not far from Lé, on the bank of the river.

There are two other kinds of apricot, which might, perhaps, be advantageously introduced into European horticulture. One has a smooth shining surface, without down, is round, and of the size of a greengage, and holds, both in appearance and taste, a middle station between an apricot and a plum. The third is a little larger than the preceding, with a short down on the skin, which is of a redder colour. The stones of both these kinds are of a dark brown, bordering on black. The other varieties are deficient in juice and flavour, acid, or mealy and are fit only for drying and preserving.

The trees blossom in April and May. Much fruit is gathered in August, but the season is not over before the end of September. The greater part of the fruit is dried in the sun, in which state it remains good for many years, and is stored for home consumption, or exported to Lassa and Tartary. About six hundred maunds are annually exported, and ten or twelve pounds are sold for about a rupee. The dried fruit has a mixture of sweetness and sub-acidity, and is a wholesome and palatable article of diet. An oil, used as a perfume, is extracted from the apricot kernels.

The apple-trees are also numerous, and of several varieties: some of them are engrafted, but the greater number are wildings: they bear freely, endure great cold and intense heat, require little rain, and are very rarely attacked by disease. The ordinary fruit is of the middle size, rather oval than round, of very regular shape, and of great beauty and variety of colour: it is very juicy, and of an agreeable, though not very decided flavour, and the pulp is light, without being at all woolly. They are ripe in September, and are kept in very good preservation through the winter.

The Sarsinh is a tree which yields a fragrant flower and agreeable fruit. It grows no farther eastward in Ladakh than at Ayu, a village about four miles from Lé, but it is constantly found in the vicinity of the villages of the western districts, and is said to extend northwards to the foot of the Muz Tagh mountains. It is a tall slender tree, rising sometimes to the height of forty feet, and not exceeding a foot in diameter. The leaves are something similar to the myrtle, and are either dark-green, or are covered with a short white down, so that when agitated by the wind the foliage bears some affinity to that of the Protea. It bears a minute yellow flower, which in the season emits a diffusive and most delicious fragrance, and is highly prized as a perfume by the natives. The fruit when ripe is of the size and shape of a French olive, of a cream colour, or yellow, or orange, according as it has been exposed to the sun. The skin is thin and shining, the stone long and narrow, and the space between it and the rind filled by a sweetish and mealy pulp. In Ladakh the produce is scanty, and is at once consumed. In Yarkand, where the tree is termed Igdi, the fruit is abundant, and is variously employed. When reduced to powder it is eaten either dry, or mixed with water into a paste, or still further diluted it forms a sherbet. Its principal application, however, is to the still, as upon fermentation it yields a brandy which it is said both Mohammedans and Chinese prefer to brandy distilled from the grape. The flavour of the potation is sometimes heightened by an admixture of the flowers. The sediment after distillation is given beneficially to cattle. The wood is also occasionally employed as fuel, and is said to burn with an agreeable odour*.

These are the only fruits cultivated in Ladakh, but pears, of a kind not unlike the Cressanne, are imported from Balti, grapes from Kashmir, and melons from Yarkand. The only wild fruit I observed was a small round orange-coloured berry, which was produced in great abundance by a prickly shrub

* It appears to be the *Elæagnus Moorcroftii* of Dr. Wallich's MS. catalogue in the library of the E. I. Company.—Ed.

called Chírma, or Chasta Ruru. The fruit is too acid to be eaten, although the flavour is agreeable, but the plant flourishes through the winter, and the berries are a great resource to the smaller birds.

A vegetable product of much interest, both in a scientific and commercial view, and which is met with in great abundance in Ladakh, is Rhubarb. It is found, indeed, in various places on the southern, as well as the northern face of the Himalaya, but nowhere in greater quantity or luxuriance than in this part of Tibet, where it approaches the line of country from which all Europe is supplied. It has been asserted that all the rhubarb of commerce comes from the frontiers of China, and there is no doubt that such is the principal source of its supply, part finding its way through Russia, and part through Turkestan, by Bokhara to the Caspian, and into Persia and the Turkish provinces of Asia Minor, whence it is conveyed to the ports on the Mediterranean. Its growth, however, is by no means confined to the districts under Chinese authority, as it is found in Gerhwal, near Joshimath, and occurred on various places on the road from Niti to Gardokh, on a former journey. On the present occasion it was procured at Kangra, near Shujanpur, on the Ritanka pass, at Tandi, at Darcha, and almost everywhere in Ladakh. It grows in some spots in such quantities, that two men may dig up in a couple of hours more than three men can carry. It is said to be also produced in great abundance on the northern face of the mountains which separate Khoten from Chan-than.

Botanists have distinguished three kinds of rhubarb according to the shape of the leaves, as palmated, undulated, and compact. The plants which occur in Ladakh present undoubtedly varieties of this nature; the leaves being sometimes deeply indented at the edges with sharp points, others being scalloped, or wavy, rather than indented, and others being nearly smoothly circular. It seems not improbable, however, that these varieties are not permanent, and that the same plant may present all the differences of leaf according to circumstances. There is no apparent difference in the condition or properties of the root; nor is there reason to think that the plant is not the true rhubarb, although Mr. Sievers, who was directed by Catharine II. to search for the drug on the confines of Siberia and China, pronounced the plant which he met with in that locality to be spurious*.

Of the rhubarb which is brought by the caravans from China, there are said to be three kinds, distinguished and named from a fancied similitude to certain forms; the first and most esteemed is termed *Amrudi*, or pear-shaped, the next *At toyághi*, horse-hoof shaped, and the third *Zardiki*, or carrot-shaped. The price varies, but the best kind, or amrudi, is ordinarily purchased at the rate of a jing and a half, or one Delhi ser (something less than two pounds avoirdupois), for one rupee four anas, or about two shillings and sixpence. The second sort sells for about one-fifth, and the third for

* Dr. Royle observes, of one kind of rhubarb of which a specimen was forwarded by Mr. Moorcroft, that it was probably *R. spiciforme*, or a new species distinct from *R. emodi*. *Illustrations*, p. 36. And in another place he remarks, 'Some of the finest rhubarb I have ever seen was sent by Mr. Moorcroft from Ladakh.' p. 39.—Ed.

two-fifths less. Every piece of rhubarb has a hole in it, through which a string has been passed whilst the root has been hung up to dry; but the larger perforations are probably the relics of a rottenness, to which the roots of this plant seem to be invariably subject. And of one kind said to be imported into Europe from Canton in long flat-sided pieces, it is likely that the roots have been longitudinally slit, so as to avoid the decayed portion, and afterwards compressed. The Chinese are said to pack the rhubarb in hempen sacks, and to cover these with raw hides, which in drying contract upon the bale, and effectually defend it from moisture if the seams have been properly contrived.

Almost all the roots that have come under my inspection have been found either completely rotten in the middle, or in a state more or less approaching to decay. Yet even from roots which present little more than a crust of bark, the crown throws out leaves and flower stems of such luxuriance as to indicate no sign of rottenness at the root. Indeed the defect of the principal root is more than compensated by the fibres which it throws out annually, and which supply its place until they in their turn become large and diseased. In some localities roots which can scarcely be regarded as a year old are affected in this manner. In one situation, that of Neril Lá, nature had apparently devised means to arrest the extension of the decay, the rotten part being inclosed in a thin membranous case, formed apparently of a resinous exudation from the sound portion. Long cores of rotten and dried substance, as well as insulated nodules, might thus, on slitting the roots longitudinally, be turned out from the sound part entire, like kernels from a nut, or like diminutive mummies from their cerecloths. Sometimes the investing membrane occurs double, the plates being separated by a brown fibrous substance. In no other situation did the rhubarb roots present the same appearances, and the peculiarity was only to be explained by the more than usually dry situation of Neril Lá: for although it seems likely that rhubarb will flourish only on a soil seldom saturated with water, as is the case in the greater part both of Ladakh and

Chan-than, yet it seems to affect moist places, growing especially in ravines and dells, and sheltered and damp spots, or on the slopes of mountains, down which water is constantly trickling from springs or melted snow. This moisture, however favourable to the development of the foliage, is probably the cause of the rottenness of the root, and if it could be counteracted by diminishing the absorbing powers of the root, or by cutting off the superabundant supply of water, its occurrence might be prevented.

The medicinal virtues of the root do not seem to be impaired by the disease, and in various trials which we instituted, the Ladakh rhubarb was found to be fully as efficacious as that from China, with a much less nauseous flavour.

The facility which is thus offered to the supply of rhubarb, either from the British Himalayan provinces, or from Tibet, would probably very soon transfer the trade in this article to British enterprise, if it were once directed to the subject. If inferior in quality to the China, or the so-called Turkey rhubarb, inferiority which is by no means established, might very possibly be remedied by care in the cultivation, in the preparation, and in the packing. The transport by way of Calcutta being chiefly by water-carriage should be much cheaper than by St. Petersburgh or the Levant, and the merchants of British India could consequently undersell those of Russia or Turkey. It can scarcely be thought that the trade is not of sufficient value to merit attention, as even if the limited use of rhubarb as a drug were considered as rendering a trade in it of little importance, yet there seems a probability that it might be used extensively as a dye, if it could be brought to market cheap enough for such a purpose.

The only timber trees found in Ladakh are the willow and poplar, and chiefly the former. In order to render it more productive of branches, required for fuel, for roofing, for baskets, and other wicker-work, the natives adopt a method of treating the tree which renders its growth singularly luxuriant. Willow staves from pollard heads about two inches in diameter and ten feet long, from which the leading and side shoots have been cut, have their butt ends immersed in water until they throw out root-fibres: three of them are put into the ground on the edge of a natural or artificial water-course, bound together with grass. After three years a broad strip of bark is torn off from each, from about a man's height down to the ground, and notches are cut in the bark and wood, commonly on the opposite side, to form a ladder by which a man may climb up the tree. As the wood which has been laid bare dries, it is chipped off, and this operation is repeated until the tree is little more than a hollow cylinder of bark, lined with a thin layer of wood. The tree thus contributes from its substance a supply of fuel, and at the same time the branches from its head are multiplied. The first formed or oldest branches being but feebly supported, bend outwards, and sometimes in a slight degree downwards, and from their upper surface springs a crop of perpendicular shoots, greatly exceeding that of the heads of common pollards. The principle on which this occurs may be analogous to that which seems to prevail in espalier fruit trees, the branches of which, being horizontally disposed, throw out a greater number of upright shoots than they would do if suffered to grow in their own natural direction.

The poplars which, along with willows, are planted about every village in Ladakh, are sometimes the Lombardy, but more frequently the black poplar. They are in very insufficient numbers for the wants of ordinary consumption, as the plantations are not allowed to encroach upon the cultivation of corn. The supposed deficiency of surface for timber, without trespassing upon land appropriated to tillage, has suggested an expedient for the multiplication of the produce of wood, which is ingenious and successful. When a poplar, at about five feet from the ground, has attained a diameter of five or six inches, it is headed down. The summit of the stool, just below the cut surface, is girded by a willow withe four or five times, so tightly as to become slightly imbedded in the bark, and the top is covered with a thick lump of clay. Shortly after this a crop of shoots rises from the whole circumference of the bark of the tree, which is thinned to the number that it is supposed will thrive. These also, as they reach a sufficient growth, are removed, and repeated crops of poplar staves are in this manner obtained.

The animals of Ladakh of the domestic species are horses, asses, yaks, cows, the Zho or Yak-mule, sheep, goats, dogs, &c. Of these the horses are small, but active and hardy; they are not numerous nor much used. The yak is found only on high lands, and is inferior in appearance and strength to that of Chan-than. The males are applied almost solely to the transport of burdens. The neat cattle are kept entirely for milk and butter, the consumption of which latter, especially with tea, is very considerable.

The Zho is a hybrid, between the male yak and the cow: the male is employed as a gelding for carrying loads and for ploughing, in which latter occupation he is remarkable for docility and endurance. The female Zho is not strictly speaking a mule, but her progeny degenerates.

The native breeds of sheep, though larger than those of India, are much smaller than the sheep of Chan-than. There is one species, however, the **Purik**, which is very diminutive, and is remarkable for its complete domestication. This, when of full growth, has scarcely attained the size of a South-down lamb of five or six months; the bone is small, and carcase large in respect to its bulk, and its mutton most excellent. It gives two lambs within twelve months, and is twice shorn within that period. The clip may afford three pounds in the annual aggregate, and the first yield is fine enough for tolerably good shawls: the whole of the wool is worked up into narrow cloth for home consumption. The dog is scarcely more perfectly domesticated than this little animal. During the day in the summer months it is pastured amongst the mountains, but at night, and throughout the winter, it finds shelter in a walled yard, or under the roof of its master. In this state it seeks with incessant assiduity, grass, straw, chaff, grain, peelings of esculent vegetables, and always attends the meals of the family for morsels of flour-cake, barley meal, tea buttered and salted, or exhausted tea leaves, and will sometimes even nibble a bone. It would be an invaluable appendage to the cottage of the British peasant, as it could be maintained at scarcely any cost*.

The common breed of goat in this and the neighbouring countries of Lassa, Chanthan, and Chinese Turkistan, is the shawl-wool goat, the fleece of which in Ladakh is much finer. The fleece is cut once a year; the wool picked out is sent to Kashmir, but the hair is made into ropes, coarse sacks, and blankets for home consumption. The dogs are large, with a shaggy coat of a dark colour, and are in general of a fierce, but intelligent disposition.

The wild animals are not numerous; they are principally of the goat kind, which are much larger than the domestic goat, and yield a finer wool. The Ibex frequents the loftiest and most inaccessible crags; the male is called Skin, and the female L'Danmo. The wild sheep (ovis ammon) is also met with, and is much larger than the domestic

* A letter on the Purik sheep, and other topics relating to Ladakh, from Mr. Moorcroft to J. Fleming, Esq., is published in the first volume of the *Transactions of the Royal Asiatic Society*, p. 49.—ED.

one. In the eastern parts of the country is a nondescript wild variety of horse, which I may call Equus Kiang. It is, perhaps, more of an ass than a horse, but its ears are shorter, and it is certainly not the Gur-khor, or wild ass of Sindh. Its activity and strength render its capture difficult. A mouse nearly three times the size of the English mouse, with a thick coat of gray fur, and a tail one-third of an inch long, is met with. Hares in some parts of Ladakh are found in considerable numbers, as has been noticed already; and I obtained skins of the squirrel, fox, ounce, bear, lynx, and leopard, although I did not meet with them alive. The natives assert that there is a kind of tiger, or jaguar in the mountains, though rarely visiting the valleys. The marmot was seen in considerable numbers on some of the mountain-passes in summer, but in winter it had vanished, slumbering amidst the snow. The birds are not numerous, nor in general remarkable. One of the largest is the raven, which is a fierce and powerful bird, of a lofty and active flight in summer, but sullen and dull in winter. Another large bird is the gigantic chakor, which is much larger than the common partridge. Sparrows, linnets, and robin redbreasts, are numerous and mischievous at seed time and harvest. The crested skylark sings as sweetly as in England, and the gelinok or snow-lark frequents the higher regions. Water-birds of various descriptions haunt the pools and lakes which are dispersed through Ladakh. Fish abound in all the streams, but the chariness of life which is taught by the religion of Buddha, prevents their being caught, notwithstanding they would form so important an accession to the means of subsistence available in such a region.

Of the mineral productions of Ladakh little information was procured. There are a few mines of sulphur in some parts, but in Chan-than it is abundant. Soda is found in great plenty along the banks of the eastern branch of the Indus, and in the district of Nobra. Lead and iron are found in pits, and other mountain districts remote from Lé, and copper mines are said to have been discovered towards Kashmir. Scantiness of fuel, and the unenterprising character of the people, however, prevent their being worked. Gold is frequently found in the rivers of Chan-than, and it was also discovered in the sands of the Shayuk. The government, however, stopped the search, lest its collection should be followed by a bad grain harvest, as some Lama had formerly, either from policy or superstition, predicted. In some parts of Chan-than a superstitious belief prevails, that lumps of native gold, occasionally found in the mountains, belong to the Genii of the spot, who would severely punish the human appropriation of their treasures.

CHAPTER III.

Divisions—Lé, the Capital—Construction of Houses—Palace of the Raja — Population — Revenue — Domestic Institutions—Dress—Ornaments—Diet—Government—Raja—Chief Officers—Historical Notices—Religion—Lamas—Religious Assemblies—Figures of Chenresi — Chamba—Dramatic Representation—Masks —Amusements—Mohammedanism —Commerce —Wool Trade—Shawl Wool—Sheep's Wool—Asli Tus—Tea—Teas of Bisahar—Miscellaneous Articles —General Character of the Trade—Whether to be in the possession of Britain or Russia.

THE principal perganas or divisions of Ladakh are, Nobra on the north, Zanskar on the south, and Spiti or Piti on the south-east. Ladakh Proper occupies the centre, extending along both banks of the river. Lé, the capital of Ladakh, is situated in a narrow valley, formed by the course of the Sinh-khabab, and bounded on the northern and southern sides by a double chain of mountains running east and west, the highest of which are from eighteen hundred to two thousand feet above the plain. It is built at the foot and on the slope of some low hills, forming the northern boundary of the valley, and separated by a sandy plain about two miles broad from the river. It is enclosed by a wall, furnished at intervals with conical and square towers, and extending on either side to the summit of the hills. It is approached by a double line of the sacred structures or manis, frequently noticed in the journal, and houses are scattered over the plain without the walls on either hand. The streets are disposed without any order, and form a most intricate labyrinth, and the houses are built contiguously, and run into each other so strangely, that from without it is difficult to determine the extent of each mansion. The number, it is said, is about a thousand; but I should think they scarcely exceeded five hundred. They vary from one to two or three stories in height, and some are loftier. The walls are in a few instances wholly, or in part of stone, but in general they are built with large unburnt bricks: they are whitened outside with lime, but remain of their original colour inside. They are usually furnished with light wooden balconies; the roofs are flat, and are formed of small trunks of poplar trees, above which a layer of willow shoots is laid, which is covered by a coating of straw, and that again by a bed of earth. In rainy weather this is a very insufficient defence, as the water soon softens the earth, and pours down into the apartment: the stairs are formed of rough stones. The rooms, though frequently of good size, are low, rarely above seven or eight feet high; and the ceilings are made like the roof, of poplar beams, supporting slender willow sticks or laths, sometimes peeled and laid quite close together, and covered with earth. In the houses of the poorest classes the roofs are commonly made of branches of poplar, with the leaves on. In those of persons of rank, as the Raja and Khalun, the ceiling is of wood, arranged in squares or lozenges, stained and painted. The main rafters are supported by cylindrical or square pillars of wood, the top of which under the truss, is in the houses of the peasantry encircled by a band of straw and ears of wheat, forming a primitive sort of capital. It is the custom, I was told, to consecrate the two or three first handsful of each year's crop to a spirit who presides over agriculture, and these bands are thus deposited: sometimes rams' horns are added to this decoration. The top of the pillar is everywhere carved into the form of hatters' blocks, one inverted on the other, and separated by a circular ridge; and in the houses of persons of distinction, carved, painted, and gilded, as are the trusses between the capital of the pillar and the beam. The most considerable building in Lé is the palace of the Raja, which has a front of two hundred and fifty feet, and is of several stories in height, forming a conspicuous object on the approach to the city. This, as well as the houses in general, diminishes in extent as it rises, and the whole town at a distance has much the appearance of a cluster of houses of cards. The temples are built of the same materials as the houses, and pillars of timber, like those in private dwellings, support the beams, being little more, in fact, than the stems of the willow or poplar stripped of their bark and painted. None of the houses have any mode of excluding the weather, except by curtains suspended before large open windows in the balconies, or shutters closing small slits or loop-holes in the walls; nor are the rooms provided with chimneys, and the smoke from the wood fires is not only offensive and suffocating, but often productive of lasting mischief to the eyesight. In the kitchen there is sometimes a square hole which acts as an imperfect ventilator. The doors are made of planks of poplar mortised together: iron nails are rarely used, as they are too costly, for although there is plenty of the metal, it cannot be wrought for lack of fuel, and such iron implements and utensils as are used are of foreign importation. A few felts and sheep-skins, and a bench or two with a large box, constitute the principal articles of furniture. The floor serves for chair, table, and bed, and is not unfrequently shared with sheep and goats, and swarms with more exceptionable tenants.

The population of Lé, as of the country at large, is of the Tibetan stock, but a very considerable number of Kashmirians are domesticated at Lé, and a mixed race has originated from them and the women of the country, termed Argands. The Kashmiris and their descendants are engaged in commerce, and the lower orders follow the business of butchers, cooks, and petty retailers. There are also some Turani merchants, and in the lands of Chushut a colony of Balti Mohammedans is established. According to such information as could be obtained, the whole population of Ladakh may be between one hundred and fifty thousand and one hundred and eighty thousand, of which two-thirds, at least, are females.

There is not much wealth in the country, but what there is is equally diffused, and the great body of the people are in easy and comfortable circumstances, owing chiefly to the valuable fleeces of their goats. They pay no money-taxes to the state, but are bound to suit and service, both domestic and military, and furnish contributions in kind for the support of the Raja and the governors of districts. Thus the inhabitants of the country about Lé supply the Raja with fuel, milk, butter, tea, grass for his cattle, servants for his person, and labourers in his fields. These contributions press very heavily upon the industry of the people, particularly where their rulers are avaricious and rapacious, a character unluckily too common.

The Ladakhis are, in general, a mild and timid people, frank, honest, and moral when not corrupted by communication with the dissolute Kashmiris, but they are indolent, exceedingly dirty, and too apt to be addicted to intoxication. The Kashmirians here, as well as everywhere else, are notorious for every kind of profligacy, and where they abound the people of the country are tainted by similar vices.

They have some singular domestic institutions. When an eldest son marries, the property of his father descends to him, and he is charged with the maintenance of his parents. They may continue to live with him if he and his wife please, if not, he provides them with a separate dwelling. A younger son is usually made a Lama. Should there be more brothers, and they agree to the arrangement, the juniors become inferior husbands to the wife of the elder: all the children, however, are considered as belonging to the head of the family. The younger brothers have no authority, they wait upon the elder as his servants, and can be turned out of doors at his pleasure, without its being incumbent upon him to provide for them. On the death of the eldest brother his property, authority, and widow devolve upon his next brother.

The women of Ladakh, in consequence of their great proportionate number, find it difficult to obtain subsistence, and besides domestic occupations and wool-picking, in which they are very expert, they are the principal labourers in the fields. They are a very lively good-humoured race, and scolding and railing are almost unknown amongst them.

The severity of the climate renders the use of warm clothing indispensable, and woollen cloths are worn by all orders and both sexes. The men wear close dresses of cloth made in the country, next their body, over which those who can afford it throw a full mantle or gown of European broadcloth lined with lambswool, or in summer of flowered chintz. The inferior classes wear mantles of sheepskins with the wool inwards: both wear broad girdles or kammerbands of some kind of cloth, in which they stick daggers, sometimes richly ornamented, knives, and chakmaks, or flints. The cloth worn by people of property is dyed of an imperfect black, or dark-brown colour. The Lamas wear red or yellow, according to their order. The dress of the Grand Lama at Lassa is yellow, but that of the chief Lamas in Ladakh is red. Many of the religious persons, male and female, or Gelums and Anis, dress in the former colour. The poorer classes wear the cloth as it comes from the loom. The woollen cloth manufactured in the country, although thick and strong, is soft, and of a regular thread and fabric. It is very cheap, —a piece a foot broad, fifteen yards long, and weighing five pounds and a quarter, may be purchased for about three rupees. The men wear caps of the same general shape for all ranks, and differing in the material only. That of the Khalun, as of the other chief officers, was made of velvet—silk velvet of Russian fabric. It was lined with cotton cloth starched, to give the cap firmness: the lower half of the lining was formed of China brocade, which when the cap was put on was doubled up, and constituted an outer bordering: to render this the more easy a perpendicular slit was made in the back part of the rim. The caps of the lower classes are generally made of black cloth: they are shorter, and the tops fall over on one side or other, whilst those of persons of rank are erect.

The dress of the women consists of a jacket, with sleeves fitting, though loosely, to the shape, with a collar half way up the neck. Continuous from the jacket fall bands forming the frame-work of a petticoat, the spaces between being filled up with narrow stripes of various colours, about two inches broad at the bottom, and narrowing to a point at top, making the lower edge of the petticoat of much greater extent than at the waist: as many as eighty or one hundred of these stripes may be comprised in the whole circumference. Over the shoulders, and fastened with a loop and button on the right shoulder, is worn a mantle of sheepskin with the wool inwards, and covered exteriorly with coloured cotton or woollen cloth, with

China satin or Benares brocade, according to the means of the wearer. Both sexes wear stockings—they are of three kinds: of sheep's wool felted, of sheep's wool knit, and of goat's wool knit. The former is the most common. They are in various shapes, as long stockings reaching above the knee sown into shape, the same cut out of felt, and joined behind, and simple leggings, reaching from below the knee to the ancle. The second sort is that most in use. The foot part is made by wearing, being very imperfectly shaped in the original. The stockings are bound at top, and sometimes decorated on the legs with a fillet of coloured silk. The leggings are fastened with a long coloured band of cross gartering. One kind of stocking, made of shawl wool, is fancifully decorated, and is very showy. For summer wear half stockings of cotton are imported from Kashmir and Kabul. Both sexes also wear boots, the soles of which are of thick leather, like those of the Chinese, whilst the leg part is either of leather or of strong stiff cloth. This is an article of dress in which the Ladakhis take much pride, and the commonest boots are dyed of some bright colour, and have the seams embroidered. Some of the wealthiest have boots of Russian or Chinese leather, or of goat or sheepskin dyed red, and glazed, the seams and welts of which arc of gold cord, or are decorated with embroidery in silk, or gold and silver twist. Instead of thick soles, green slippers, iron shod, with high heels, are used. Some of the most ordinary kinds are made in Ladakh, but the more ornamented boots come from Lassa and from Kashmir.

The men do not wear many ornaments,—the principal consisting of large ear-rings and a small cista, or box of gold, decorated with turquoises, or of less costly materials, and containing some sacred text, by way of amulet, which is suspended from the neck. The women are more gaily decorated, but their chief ornaments are the head lappet, a stiff necklace or collar, and ear-rings or oreillettes. The first is like that we noticed in Lahoul, consisting of a piece of cloth lying flat on the top of the head, and descending to the waist, or lower, bearing turquoises, carnelians, and amber beads in transverse rows. The hair, tressed in narrow plaits, is assembled in a queue, which is lengthened by tassels of coloured worsted, intermixed with shells, bells, and coins, until it nearly touches the ground. On either side of the lappet on the top of the head festoons of small pearl descend to a little below the ears, and are united and knotted above and below with an ornament of jewellery, and persons of rank have strings of coral hanging over either shoulder. The most costly ornament is the collar, a stiff band of silver or gold, more or less wrought, bound with strings of coral, pearls, or silver beads, and studded with turquoises in flowers, encasing the neck: below this a necklace of several tier of large gold and silver beads, intermixed with turquoises, descends low on the bosom. Some notion may be formed of the composition of this collar from the price, which is about forty pounds. Its effect is rather heavy than rich, and amongst the women of the Mohammedan Ladakhis is discarded for a more simple necklace. At Lé a curious appendage to the head-dress is worn, which might be termed an oreillette. It is an oval piece of seal-skin, which, confined under the side tresses, covers and conceals the ear, the edge projecting beyond which is fringed with fur, whilst the outer part is covered by brocade. In general the head has no other cover than the lappet, but on gala days a flat circular hat of seal-skin rises like a fan from the crown. The face on such occasions is smeared with the pulp of the fruit of a kind of bella-donna, which has the effect of glazing, and detains, by its viscidity, a number of small flat seeds, which are thought still farther to improve the beauty of the countenance. A Ladakhi female in full costume would cause no small sensation amongst the fashionable dames of a European capital.

The diet of the Ladakhis, and of the Tibetans generally, is nutritious and wholesome, and is remarkable for the prominent share which is taken in it by tea. All classes of Tibetans eat three meals a day. The first consists of tea, the second of tea, or of meal porridge if that cannot be afforded; the third of meat, rice, vegetables, and bread by the upper, and soup, porridge, and bread by the lower classes. For a breakfast of ten persons this would be the preparation: about an ounce of black tea, called here zancha, and a like quantity of soda, are boiled in a quart of water for an hour, or until the leaves of the tea are sufficiently steeped. It is then strained, and mixed with ten quarts of boiling water, in which an ounce and a half of fossil salt has been previously dissolved. The whole is then put into a narrow cylindrical churn, along with the butter, and well stirred with a churning stick till it becomes a smooth, oily, and brown liquid, of the colour and consistence of chocolate, in which form it is transferred to a tea-pot of silver, or silvered copper, or brass, for the richer classes, ornamented with flowers and foliage, and grotesque figures of leopards, crocodiles, dragons, or heads of elephants, and the like, in embossed or fillagree work. The poorer people use plain brass or tinned copper tea-pots. Each man has his own cup, either of China porcelain, or, which is more common, made out of the knot of the horse chestnut, edged or lined with silver, or plain. About five thousand of these, in the rough, are annually exported from Bisahar to Gardokh, and sold at the rate of six for a rupee: they are finished and ornamented in China. The latter kind of cup contains about a third of a pint, the China cup something less. Each person drinks from five to ten cups of tea, and when the last is half finished he mixes with the remainder as much barley meal as makes a paste with it, which he eats. At the mid-day meal those who can afford tea take it again, with their wheaten cakes, accompanied with a paste of wheat flour, butter, and sugar, served hot. The poorer people, instead of tea, boil two parts of barley flour with one of water, or meat broth seasoned with salt until it becomes of the thickness of porridge. The evening meal of the upper classes is formed of some preparation of the flesh of sheep, goats, or yaks, and eaten with rice, vegetables, and wheaten cakes, leavened or unleavened. The poorer classes eat at night the same barley porridge as at noon, or a soup made of fresh vegetables, if procurable, or of dried turnips, radishes, and cabbages, boiled with salt and pepper in water, along with pieces of stiff dough of wheat flour.

The use of tea has been common amongst the wealthier Tibetans for some centuries, but it has been universal only within the last sixty years. It has extended itself within the same period to Bokhara and Kashmir, and is becoming general in the Panjab and Kabul.

The Tibetans never drink plain water if they can avoid it. The wealthier drink grape juice and water, or sherbets; the poorer a beverage called Buza by the Kashmiris, and Chang by the Tibetans, which is made from barley. The grain is boiled until it is soft, and then dried; to about ten pounds of this softened grain, three ounces of the dough used for wheat cakes, but dried and pounded, are added, and the mixture is put into a bag, and kept in a warm place until it ferments, which it does usually in two or three days. Equal measures of the prepared barley and cold water are put together in an earthen vessel, and after standing for two days the fluid is strained off; a similar quantity of water is again added, and treated in the same manner, and the beverage is the liquor called Chang. This is sub-acid, somewhat resembling palm juice when it begins to ferment, but neither so palatable, nor so potent, although it is said to be inebriating if drunk immoderately. The grains remaining after infusion are dried and ground into flour*.

The government of Ladakh is a simple despotism, but it is curiously modified by the circumstances of the people and the influence of the hierarchy, so that unless a person of more than common talent and energy, the Raja is an individual of little real power, and may be deposed or elevated at pleasure; his successor in the former case being a member of the reigning family. During the early part of my residence at Lé, a revolution of this kind had nearly taken place. At a solemn festival, at which the Raja presided, a Lama of great celebrity as an astrologer was interrogated by the former, publicly, as to the events of the coming year: an abundant harvest was the reply to the

* Many other particulars characteristic of the people of Ladakh may be found in the journals of Mir Izzet Ullah (*Calcutta Quarterly*, March, 1825), and of Gholam Hyder (*Asiatic Journal, N. S.* vol. xviii.)—ED.

first interrogation. The second was, What consequences would result from the novel visit of Europeans? Nothing but good, was the answer; but the Lama becoming the interrogator, demanded of the Raja what he dared to expect? and then, turning to the people, he declared to them, that the Raja by his tyranny had become unworthy to reign, and called upon them to depose him, and seat his son upon the throne. The proposal was received with acclamations. The Lama professed to be unconscious of what he had uttered, and the intimation was received as the voice of Heaven. The Raja was confused and frightened, and announced his readiness to abdicate in favour of his son. His Rani, a Mohammedan by birth, was less accessible to the terrors of superstition, and easily detected in the Lama's pretended inspiration an intrigue instigated by the Lompa, who had been affronted by the Raja, and whose wife was the nurse of the heir apparent. Assisted by the Khalun, a strong party was made by the Rani in her husband's favour; and when the assembly was convened, at which his renunciation of his rights was to have taken place, he declared his resolution to maintain them, and threatened his enemies with punishment. There the business terminated. The Raja retained his authority, the Lompa his office, and the Lama his reputation and immunity.

The present Raja of Ladakh was a Lama, but on the demise of his elder brother was called from his convent to the sovereignty. He is said to be rapacious, but his prevailing qualities are extreme timidity and indolence, and he relinquishes the management of affairs entirely to the Khalun, passing his time in personal indulgence at different mansions in the country suited to the change of seasons. In the winter he resides at Lé.

The young Raja, his son, is said to be a youth of talent and activity, but his education in Tibetan legendary lore, and his close confinement to the walls of the palace are not favourable either to intellectual or physical energy.

The business of the government is administered by the Khalun, or prime minister, assisted by the Nuna Khalun, or deputy, the Lom-pa, or chief municipal and military officer and governor of Lé, the Chug-zut, or treasurer, who is a Lama, and the Banka, or master of the horse. The administration of the districts and towns is entrusted to inferior Khaluns, or Tan-zins, or Rajas. A second Chug-zut is the superintendent of customs, and the business of the magistracy is discharged by officers called Nar-pas, and by the head men of the villages. Most of these are paid by assignments of land, and by claims on the people for contributions of articles of daily use. The Raja, the Khalun, and the Lom-pa also divide between them the produce of the imposts on merchandise in transit, and they all carry on a trade in shawl wool and tea, from which their principal income is derived. The present Khalun, though advanced in years, has a shrewd apprehension and sound judgment, but, being of a pliable and timid disposition, he is easily influenced by the persons about him, and is sometimes led to adopt measures of which his deliberate consideration disapproves. He is accused by foreign traders of rapacity, but I saw no reason to credit the justice of the charge.

The military force of the country consists merely of the peasantry, who are called upon to serve occasionally in disputes with the neighbouring states. These are generally adjusted without any very sanguinary appeal to arms, as may be supposed from the cowardice of the soldiery, and the inefficiency of their equipment. In a late contest with Balti, although the cavalry were tolerably well furnished with bows and arrows, the infantry had but one matchlock for ten men, and one sword for six.

The earlier history of Ladakh is that of Tibet in general, as it originally formed one of the provinces of that kingdom, governed as to temporal matters by an independent prince, and in spiritual affairs by the Guru Lama, or chief pontiff of Lassa. Subsequently the Chinese extended their authority over Tibet, and appointed the temporal ruler, but Ladakh seems to have retained its own princes. About a century and a half ago, the Kalmak Tartars invaded Ladakh, and occupied Lé, and the Raja flew to Kashmir, and implored the aid of Ibrahim Khan, the governor of that province in the reign of Aurangzeb. With the permission of the emperor, and on condition that the Raja became a Musselman, Ibrahim Khan led a body of troops into Ladakh, expelled the

Tartars, and replaced the Raja on the throne, by the title of Akabal Mahmud, conformably to his new faith. A mosque was erected in Lé, which is still kept up. The son and successor of the Raja reverted to the national creed, and the apostacy was overlooked at Delhi in consideration of the encouragement given to Mohammedanism in the country, and a small annual present or tribute paid to the governor of Kashmir as the representative of the emperor. When the Afghans became masters of Kashmir they exacted the continuance of this tribute, and now that Ranjit Sinh has conquered that province, he demands the like annual payment. At the same time the ruler of Ladakh pays a tribute, disguised under the name of a present, to the authorities of Gardokh, on behalf of the government of Lassa, and there can be no doubt that the principality would soon become wholly dependent upon some of its more powerful neighbours if it were not for their mutual jealousies and fears*.

Of the language and literature of the coun-

* Late advices from India represent Ladakh to have been taken possession of by the Sikh.—Ed.

try I must confess myself incompetent to offer any account. On my journey to Dras I was met by Alexander Csoma de Körös, a European in the garb of an Armenian, who had travelled over land from Hungary to Tibet. He remained with me some time, and after I had quitted Ladakh I obtained permission from the Khalun for him to reside in the monastery of Yangla in Zanskar, for the purpose of acquiring a knowledge of the Tibetan language, and from his erudition and acquirements accurate information on these points may be expected *. The Lamas are

* An account of this enterprising traveller and scholar, furnished by himself to the political agent at Sabathu, in January, 1825, has been published in the *Journal of the Royal Asiatic Society*. Mr. Csoma Körösi afterwards proceeded to Calcutta, and continued to reside there, engaged in communicating to the public, under the patronage of the Bengal government and the Asiatic Society of Calcutta, the results of his acquaintance with the language and literature of Tibet, of which he is the first European who has attained a critical knowledge. In the beginning of 1834 he published, at Calcutta, a Tibetan and English dictionary, and at the end of the same year a grammar of the Tibetan language. Before the appearance of these useful publications he had communicated to the Asiatic Society of Bengal notices of the contents of the two great collections in which the principal works of the literature and religion of Tibet are comprehended, the Kah-gyur, a collection of one hundred large volumes, and the Stan-gyur of two hundred and twenty-five. Of the former Mr. Csoma also prepared a detailed analysis, part of

the repositories of all the literature of Tibet, and have a number of printed books in use, relating chiefly to religious subjects.

To the same authority I must refer for an authentic view of the religion of Ladakh, which, like that of Tibet and China, is the worship of Buddha, under a peculiar hierarchy. Every family in which there is more than one son furnishes a Lama or Gelum, who is at once a cænobite and a family priest, attached to a monastic institution under a Lama, or abbot, and ordinarily living amongst the people, and conducting the rites of their daily worship in their own houses, in which a chamber is usually appropriated to an image and an attendant priest. The chief Lamas are appointed from Lassa, and continue to acknowledge the su-

which is printed in the twentieth volume of the *Asiatic Researches*. A summary account of both these works, compiled from his information, is printed in the *Calcutta Gleanings of Science*, vol. iii., and an abridgment of his analytical view of the whole of the Kah-gyur, in the first volume of the *Journal of the Asiatic Society* of Bengal. He has also furnished to the same periodical several interesting papers on subjects connected with Tibetan literature and the religion of Buddha in that country. Late advices mention his having left Calcutta on a journey to the north-eastern frontier of the British possessions.—Ed.

premacy of the pontiff of that city. They all profess poverty and celibacy, but a man who has been married is admissible into their order. There are also establishments of religious females, called Chumas or Anis. The Lamas, Gelums, and Anis, or priests, monks, and nuns, are divided into two sects—the red, or old, and new, or yellow priesthood, and both possess numerous monastic and conventual establishments. They by no means confine themselves to strictly religious duties, but take an active share in the cultivation of the lands, the rearing of sheep, and goats, and the fiscal and political administration of the country.

With regard to their religious belief and practice it seems to be a strange mixture of metaphysics, mysticism, morality, fortune-telling, juggling, and idolatry. The doctrine of the metempsychosis is curiously blended with tenets and precepts very similar to those of Christianity, and with the worship of grotesque divinities. The Lamas recognize a sort of trinity, or a triad consisting of a paramount deity, a prophet, and a book, and the people are exhorted to truth, chastity, resignation, and mutual forbearance, and good will. A number of images are observed in their temples and chambers, to whom incense, fruit, and meal are offered, and hymns and prayers are addressed: yet these images are not considered as the representation of the highest order of beings, of Buddha himself, or of his manifestations. In the audience chamber of the Khalun we observed the representation of a female divinity, with a green face and red eyes, sitting cross-legged upon a lotus. Portraits and figures of Sakyamuni are also frequent. On a wall in one of the temples I noticed a fresco painting representing the world, and the various conditions of its inhabitants, as well as their trial after death, in which some were ascending to heaven, some were going down to Tartarus, and others were passing through various transmigrations by creeping through a vessel shaped like a dice box,.at one end of which, for instance, was seen the head of a fish, and at the other the legs of the man who was undergoing the metamorphosis.

I was present on more than one occasion at their religious ceremonies, to which they made no hesitation in admitting me. In the temple of Chenresi I witnessed the consecration of food for the use of the souls of those condemned to hell, where it seems they would otherwise starve. The Kashuk Lama presided, and was seated above the other priests. I was placed close to him, and the other assistants were ranged in cushions along the wall. The Lama consecrated barley and water, and poured them from a silver saucer into a brass basin, occasionally striking two brass cymbals together, reciting or chanting prayers, to which an inferior Lama from time to time uttered responses aloud, accompanied by the rest in an under tone. After the ceremony, tea was served round. Chenresi, the god of the dead, is a male figure of the middle size, in a sitting attitude, having four arms, the two outermost elevated, and the two inner raised and joined as if in prayer. The features were mild, and the expression agreeable; the whole person was coated with gold. The head was encircled by a tiara of thick plates of gold, resembling large leaves, which were studded with turquoises, and his breast was covered by a net-work of the stones, intermixed with small rubies and emeralds of no great value.

One of the principal temples at Lé is dedicated to the god Chamba, in the figures of which, although the person is male, the countenance is female, and the whole appears to be an androgynous type of the powers of nature. Chamba has also four arms, of which the upper one on the right holds a rosary, and the lower is open, with the palm turned forwards; the upper one on the left has some flowers, and the lower holds a water-jug: the figure is seated, and is naked except at the waist, from which a short petticoat depends; but the lower limbs are very commonly concealed by passing through the floor into a lower chamber. Chamba is decorated with bracelets and a necklace, and the head is surmounted by a tiara; the hair is raised in front, but flows down the sides and back in matted tresses. The ears are long, as if elongated by the weight of their heavy ear-rings. The eyes are small, with the lids drooping in the centre, indicative, it is said, of contemplation: the character of the countenance in this, as in all the figures in the temples of Tibet, is Tartar; but a colossal representation of Chamba, cut out of the rocks near Molbi, had the features of a Hindu, with the peculiarity of wearing the Janu or sacred cord of the Brahmins.

The religious service of the Lama, which is performed daily at the Gom-pas, or temples attached to monasteries, consists chiefly of prayers and chanting, in which the formula, "Om manipadme hum," is frequently repeated, and the whole is accompanied with the music of wind instruments, chiefly harmonizing with tabrets and drums. Amongst the former is a sliding trumpet of large size, which is upheld by one man whilst blown by another, and has a very deep and majestic intonation; a hautboy, the reed of which is surrounded by a circular plate covering the mouth, and the conch shell with a copper mouth-piece: metallic cymbals, much more mellow and sonorous than others, complete the band. These musical accompaniments are not confined to temples, but form part of the state of the higher secular dignitaries, and the Raja is always preceded by minstrels and musicians when he leaves his palace.

On religious festivals part of the ceremony consists in rude dramatic representations by the Lamas, of animals, of human persons, or supernatural beings, and the masks which are worn on these occasions surpass in ingenuity and grotesqueness those of all ancient or modern times. They are not unfrequently modelled after nature, and I witnessed the representation of a Darby and Joan by two Lamas, the features of which were exaggerated portraits of an old couple in the city. The persons so disguised perform dances, which are said sometimes to have a mystical or symbolical import.

Dancing is a favourite amusement of the Ladakhis, with both men and women, but the performances are in separate bodies. Singing is also one of their recreations, and is remarkable rather for vociferation than melody. A very favourite diversion is that of Polo, the Chaugan of the Persians, in which two parties on horseback, furnished with long light rackets, attempt to drive a ball beyond certain boundaries, the one that first effects it being the victor.

In the western provinces, and those bordering on Balti and Kashmir, the Mohammedan religion is spreading rapidly, and effecting a material change in the habits and character of the people. One good effect is its promotion of temperance by the prohibition of chang and fermented drinks, but on the other hand it has introduced much more dissoluteness, dishonesty, and disregard for truth, than prevails in those places where Lamaism still predominates.

The commerce of Ladakh is of no great value or interest as affects the produce or consumption of the country itself, although both may be taken into account in the general result. Its chief consideration, however, arises from its centrical situation, by which it becomes the great thoroughfare for an active commercial intercourse between Tibet, Turkistan, China, and even Russia on one hand, and Kashmir, the Panjab, and the plains of Hindustan on the other.

One of the most important articles of the trade of Ladakh is shawl wool, of which it forms, in some degree, the source, but in a still greater, the entrepôt between the countries whence the wool is chiefly supplied, Rodokh and Chan-than, and that in which it is consumed, Kashmir. The wool is that of a domesticated goat, and consists of the under fleece, or that next the skin beneath the outer coat of hair; the breed is the same in Ladakh as in Lassa, Great Tibet, and Chinese Turkistan, but the wool is not so fine as in the breeds of the districts on its eastern and northern frontier. The fleece is cut once a year, and the wool, coarsely picked either in the place from whence it comes, or at Lé, is sold by the importers to the merchants at that city, by whom it is sent on to Kashmir. The Raja and Khalun deal extensively in this trade, but it is also shared by merchants, both from Kashmir and Turan. About eight hundred loads are annually exported to Kashmir, to which country, by ancient custom and engagements, the export is exclusively confined, and all attempts to convey it to other countries are punished by confiscation. In like manner it is considered in Rodokh and Chan-than as illegal to allow a trade in shawl wool except through Ladakh; and in the latter country considerable impediments are opposed to the traffic in wool from Yarkand, although it is of superior quality and cheapness. The hair of the goat after it is separated from the wool is made into ropes, blankets, and bags for home use, and as wrappers for bales of merchandise.

Although the fleece of the sheep affords a material similar to that of the goat, it is not in sufficient proportion, nor of adequate length, to be considered fit for the manufacture of shawls. It is, therefore, either worked up into woollen cloth, the greater portion of which is reserved for domestic consumption, and a small part is exported, or it is exported for a like manufacture to Kotoch, Chamba, and Kulu, and even to Kashmir. Some of this cloth shorn and singed into an imitation of long piled velvet, is not without merit as a fabric. The sheep of Chan-than are also articles of trade, as they are larger and stronger than the breeds to the westward, and being imported from thence, are re-exported to the hill states, where they are largely purchased as beasts of burden, carrying from twenty-five to thirty pounds weight.

Besides the fleece of the domesticated goat, that of the wild goat, under the denomination of Asali Tus, is exported in smaller quantities to Kashmir. It is of a light brown colour, and exceeding fineness, and is worked into shawls, a species of soft cloth called Tusi, and linings for shawl wool stockings; very few shawls, however, are made from this material. I purchased a small quantity of it at eight rupees the manwati: when picked, for which an additional charge of seven rupees was made, I received about five ounces, or one-eighth of the original quantity back in very fine shawl wool: another parcel yielded a fifth. In general the pickers of shawl wool are paid by the hair, but in this case the hair was considered unfit for making into ropes, &c. Shawls made from this material would be much softer, lighter, and warmer, than those of ordinary fabric. When without being picked the Asali Tus is worked into Tusi, it forms a warm, soft cloth, of a drab or gray colour, which is much worn in the hills. It is manufactured at various places in the Panjab. A piece bought at Amritsar for ninety rupees was sold at Delhi for two hundred and fifty, but the Tusi cloth which comes to Hindustan is made from a mixture of the Asali Tus with other wool. This article must be always high priced from the difficulty of procuring the animal that produces it, the wild goat rarely venturing within gun-shot during the day, and being obtained only by snares at night, when they come down from the mountains to browse in the valleys.

The next article of importance in the trade of Ladakh is tea, the consumption of which in the country is very considerable, but which is also exported in large quantities to Kashmir and the Panjab. The teas of China are chiefly brought through Lassa, but some of the finer kinds are also imported by way of Yarkand. They are brought in square masses or lumps, consisting of the leaves firmly compacted as if they had been wetted, and in that state forcibly compressed: they are covered with coarse yellow paper, stamped with a seal in Chinese characters, and packed in the raw skins of yaks, the hair inwards, and the joints neatly secured by a sewing of thongs. The package, however, is an addition provided at Lassa, as the teas come thither in a package of grass. The consolidation of the tea in square blocks or bricks, renders it more easy of transport by reducing its bulk, and obviating the necessity of wooden boxes; whether anything is used to give firmness to these masses, or for any other object, as to improve their flavour or colour is questionable, but an intelligent merchant at Lé informed me he had detected small pieces of kheir (gum catechu) amongst the tea. A strong infusion, however, failed to precipitate gelatine, and therefore the admixture was not confirmed. A Yarkandi asserted that an infusion of poppy-heads was employed to render the leaves of the tea adhesive, but the authority was not a very good one, and moisture and pressure are in all probability the only means resorted to for moulding the tea into this shape. Each block, called Dom by the Kashmiris, and Ponkah by the Lassans, weighs about four Delhi sers, or less than eight pounds avoirdupoise. The green is sold usually at the wholesale price of three rupees per ser, and the black at less than two rupees, and the retail price is nearly double.

A discovery of much interest occurred in

the course of my inquiries into the tea trade of Ladakh, and it appeared that a considerable importation of a vegetable product, used as tea, took place from the British dependency of Bisahar. According to information obtained from two intelligent natives of that province, the tea of Bisahar is of two kinds, green and black. The green tea is the produce of a shrub which is an evergreen, seldom exceeding four feet and a half in height. It grows in both Bisahar and Kulu on a dry soil, especially near the banks of the Setlej, and in greatest abundance about Jhagul, between Rampur and Sarai. New leaves appear at the end of April and the beginning of May, and are gathered from July to November: the peasants cut the smaller branches into pieces, and mix them with the leaves, selling the whole to traders at a maund for a rupee. The latter infuse this tea in hot water for some time, until it has imparted much of a reddish colour to the water, and then throwing the infusion away, squeeze and rub the leaves between their hands, and dry them in the sun. They say that if the first infusion were used it would heat the body, and occasion pains in the limbs; but I drank some tea prepared from leaves which had not undergone this process, and experienced no ill effects. At Lé this is called Maun tea, Maun being one of their names for Bisahar, and sells at three paka sers for a rupee. It is not much in request.

The black tea of Bisahar is produced by a deciduous shrub found near the village of Asrang and Lipi, about seven days' journey from Rampur, and eight from Piti, in a situation more elevated than Jhagul. The leaves are put forth in April, and fall about October and November: they are plucked in July and August, and are sold to traders at the same price as the green. They are prepared in the same manner, but a colouring extract is in the first instance mixed with them, of which, after the first infusion, enough remains to tinge the water in which the tea is boiled. The leaves are dried and rolled in imitation of the China teas. This tea sells at fifteen Mohammed-shahi rupees per paka maund, and not less than a hundred maunds are annually imported into Lé. It is not much used by those who can afford to purchase the tea of China, but it is very often mixed with the latter by the poorer people. I have drank of it freely unmixed, and found no inconvenience from its use. The infusion of the green tea of Bisahar is of a yellowish-green colour, with less aromatic flavour than that of China. The black yields an infusion of a dark red colour, but of little flavour. It was the opinion of Mohsin Ali, a wholesale dealer in tea to a large extent, that the teas of Bisahar differed from the coarser teas of China only in the mode of preparing them for the market.

That the tea plant grows more extensively through the hill tracts than has been hitherto imagined, is probable from various circumstances. At Shujanpur Tira a Mohammedan brought me the leaves of a shrub, which he stated the Gorkhas had pointed out as the tea plant, and an infusion of them was of the colour and flavour of green tea of inferior quality, or spoiled by long keeping in India; and it is said that the Chinese troops returning from Nepal were observed to gather the leaves of some shrubs near Zigachi, which they used as tea, disposing of their own country tea in exchange for tobacco. These statements were communicated to the Bengal government in 1821. However this may be, the subject is of national interest, and well entitled to the fullest investigation*.

Besides shawl wool and tea the imports from the adjacent provinces of Tibet comprehend various articles of raw and manufactured produce, the latter principally from China. One of the chief articles of the former class is borax, which is brought through Ladakh from Bhot, sometimes by the Bhotias themselves, but more commonly by the people of Lahoul, who convey it to Kulu and Chamba, where it is refined, and whence it is conveyed to the Panjab and Hindustan, for the use of silversmiths and braziers. It is bought in Bhot at thirty-two battís, or one maund and twenty-four sers, Delhi weight, for a rupee. By refining it loses half its weight, but the thirty-two sers sell for five or six rupees. There is also a kind of smuggling trade carried on. The shepherds of

* The genuine tea plant has been recently discovered in the eastern districts of Asam, subject to British authority, and measures are in progress for its cultivation.—Ed.

these provinces receive a gratuity for pasturing the flocks of Kotoch, Chamba, &c., on the borders of Lahoul, but they sometimes take half the flocks with them to Bhot for borax, instead of leaving them to graze on the mountains, and are thus enabled to sell it at a lower price.

Another article of the trade is salt, which comes from the lakes and springs of Chan-than, partly for consumption in Ladakh, and partly for re-export to the hill states.

The manufactured articles are some plated and silver vessels, but they are chiefly materials of dress from China, as silks, velvets, and brocades. Silver is also imported in boat-shaped lumps, called yambos, stamped with Chinese characters, each lump weighing about one hundred and sixty rupees, and passing in the market for one hundred and eighty.

From Yarkand the chief imports are felts made from lambswool, a sort of camlet fabricated from the hair of the camel, dried sheepskins for cloaks, a small quantity of shawl-wool, and fine tea, yambo silver, steel for the formation of chakmaks, boots, Russian leather and brocades, velvets and broadcloth of Russian manufacture, horses and drugs. The greater part of these imports are destined for the Panjab.

From Balti, or Little Tibet, come vessels of grit-stone for cooking, and water-pots, and dried fruits, especially apricots, which are considered superior to those of Ladakh. About three hundred maunds are annually imported, partly for consumption in the country, and partly for export along with those of native growth: they are ordinarily bartered for wool. Of the Balti apricots two sers purchase a ser of goats' wool, and one ser is exchanged for two and a half of sheep's wool. The Ladakh apricots are much cheaper, and are commonly sold in ass loads, each load weighing about sixty sers, or a maund and a half paka.

The chief articles of import from Kashmir and the Panjab are shawls, chintzes, copper tinned vessels for culinary purposes, as cauldrons, chang pots, dishes, plates, tea-pots, spoons, and the like, and grain, intended chiefly for the consumption of Ladakh and the provinces of Tibet.

From the provinces south of the Himalaya various articles of domestic use are imported, as ghee, or butter, honey, raisins, and grain, for which they receive salt, borax, sheep's-wool, and gold dust. From Bisahar, also, tea-cups of wood are imported in considerable numbers, as has already been noticed, and a quantity of iron and iron utensils, the produce or manufacture of Hindustan, is also imported from that direction into Ladakh.

The general relations of the commerce with Ladakh, and through it with Tibet and Turkistan, are sufficiently obvious. They have their flocks and herds in abundance, provided with wool of peculiar properties, and admirably adapted for the finest manufactures. They have also some natural products of value, salt, borax, natron, and gold. They have no manufactures, and rear an inadequate supply of food. The latter can be plentifully supplied from the British provinces of India. Whether they shall be clothed with the broadcloth of Russia or of England—whether they shall be provided with domestic utensils of copper, iron, or of pewter, with implements of iron and steel, with hardware of every description, from Petersburgh or Birmingham,—is entirely in the decision of the government of British India. At present there is little doubt to which the prize will be awarded, for enterprise and vigour mark the measures of Russia towards the nations of Central Asia, whilst ours are characterised by misplaced squeamishness and unnecessary timidity.

CHAPTER IV.

Notices of adjacent Countries—Chan-than—Rodokh—Gardokh—Yarkand—Khoten.

THE jealousies and fears of the neighbouring governments opposing our passage through the territories adjacent to Ladakh, prevented us from acquiring a personal acquaintance with them, but we were enabled to collect some details respecting their site and condition from intelligent natives, with whom we were in habits of intercourse, and upon whose reports every reasonable reliance might be placed. At present it will be sufficient to notice those immediately to the east and north, reserving those on the north-west for a future opportunity.

Along the eastern frontier of Ladakh, in an almost semicircular line, is the province of Chan-than *. The more northerly portion forms a separate province, called Rodokh, which lies along the northern border of the lake of Pangkak, and continues by the valley of Chushul, from which the capital or fort of Rodokh is distant between three and four days' journey. The road passes by a small lake, called Tsurul (bitter), from the bitterness of its waters, and lies over sandy grass plains, which afford pasture to its sheep and goats. The fort itself is situated on a hill in the midst of an extensive plain, about twenty miles south-east from the extremity of the Pang-kak lake. The country is thinly inhabited, and the people are chiefly shepherds, who subsist by the sale of their wool to the merchants at Lé. It has a chief of its own, but he is subject to the authority of the Garphan of Chan-than. From Rodokh a road is said to cross the mountains to Khoten, and the journey is one of three or four days only. All attempts, however, to reach Khoten by this route are rigidly repressed by the Chinese.

* Or snow country,—known to the Bhotias as Hiun-des, and to the Tibetans as Nari. *Asiat. Res.*, vol. xvii. p. 45. *Jour. Asiat. Soc.*, vol. i. p. 124.—Ed.

South of the Sinh-kha-bab river the districts of Sumgiel and Tholing are immediately contiguous to Piti in Ladakh, and to the British dependencies of Bisahar and Kanawar. The chief town of the latter is situated on the left or southern bank of the Setlej, and is a place of considerable note. It is said to contain one hundred and eight temples, attached to most of which are a number of Gelums: the head Lama resides there during the summer, but in winter lives at Tashigon, near the left bank of the Indus, on the road from Ladakh to Gardokh. Further to the eastward, and along the Setlej river, is the district of Chaprang.

The larger division of Chan-than, called Garo, is in contact with Ladakh, on the line of the Sinh-kba-bab river. That river, at three days' journey from Kuk-jung, makes a short turn to the south, round the La Ganskil mountain, and then resumes its southeasterly direction. The road follows the course of the river, and is, in general, tolerably level, proceeding along sandy valleys, thinly coated with coarse pasturage, lying between bare and rugged hills. Within a kos and a half of Gardokh, also called Gartokh, Ghertope, or Garo, the chief station, which is said to be distant six days' journey from the frontier, the Sinh-kha-bab is crossed, and followed along its right bank. The chief halting places on the route are merely shepherds' shelters, except in the case of Tashigon, which is a place of some extent. Gardokh itself, which I visited in 1812, in my journey to the Manasarovara Lake *, is little else than an encampment, consisting of a number of small blanket tents, with a few houses of unburnt bricks, of a similar description as the houses of Ladakh : it is, in fact, little more than a trading station, or mart, where in the summer months the natural productions of Tibet and China are exchanged for those of Hindustan and Kashmir. In the winter months it is almost deserted. The Sinh-kha-bab rises from the Kangri, or Kan-tisi, Tisi, or Kailas range, a short way to the south-east of Ghertope.

Chan-than is the chief resort of the shawl wool goat, and is also the pasturage of numerous flocks of sheep, whose wool is an article

* *Asiatic Researches*, vol. xii.

of trade. In the plain adjacent to Ghertope we saw at least 40,000 head of cattle, goats, sheep, and yaks, principally the two former. The number had been much reduced at the period of our arrival by an epidemic disease, which had spread throughout Tibet, and in many instances almost annihilated the flocks. In Ladakh four or five were very commonly all that remained out of as many hundred. The wool of Chan-than is sold to the Ladakhis alone, by virtue of an ancient agreement. The province also produces gold in considerable quantities, but the search after it is discouraged by local superstition, and by the Chinese authorities.

Chan-than was formerly subject to independent princes, but their authority gradually merged into the supremacy of the chief pontiff at Lhassa. It is still nominally under his government, but in 1792, the Gorkhas having invaded the southern provinces, the Dulai Lama called the Chinese to his succour. The Chinese drove back the Gorkhas, but took the opportunity of establishing their own power in Tibet, and two Ambans, sent from Pekin, now permanently resident at

Lhassa, engross the political administration of the state. From Lhassa, two officers, natives of the country, are sent to Gardokh as Garphans, who are relieved every three years. The subordinate management of the districts is intrusted to two officers, commonly called the Deba and Vazir, the former appointed from Lhassa, the latter a native of the place: with these the chief Lama of each village forms a sort of local council, dependent upon the authorities at Gardokh, who again are obliged to refer for instructions on all matters out of the common course of events to Lhassa.

On the north Ladakh is bounded by the Pamer or Karakoram mountains, a very rugged and difficult road through which leads to the province and town of Yarkand, or Yar-kiang. This is situated on a river, and is a town of considerable importance, being the great emporium of the commerce between Turkistan, China, and Tibet, and the seat also of an active traffic with Russia. The population is said to be between fifty and sixty thousand, almost entirely Mohammedan, Tajiks, Turks, and Uzbeks. About sixty years before our visit to Ladakh the government of Yarkand was in the hands of the Uzbeks, but the chiefs quarrelling amongst themselves, one party invited the Chinese to their aid, and they seized the opportunity of establishing their power. Yarkand is now in the possession of China, and the political and military authorities of the city are Chinese. They allow the Mohammedans, however, to appoint a head man, or Hakim, from amongst themselves, by whom the civil administration is superintended. Besides the revenue derived from the customs, a poll tax is levied on all adult males. Yarkand is inclosed by a mud wall, and defended by a citadel, but it is a place of no strength. The Chinese are very jealous of the approach of strangers, and, as will hereafter appear, ultimately prohibited our paying it a visit *.

* It was visited, however, by Mir Izzet Ullah in his former journey, and many particulars relating to it are recorded in his *Journal*. Some further details were also collected by Lieutenant Burnes (*Travels*, vol. ii. p. 227) and by Timkowski (vol. i. p. 393). These accounts, however, in addition to the information derived from Marco Polo, the Jesuits, and the Chinese (Marsden's Marco Polo, p. 151), leave us with a very imperfect knowledge of Yarkand.—ED.

Eastward from Yarkand, and separated by lofty mountains on the south, a continuation of the Karakoram chain, is the district of Khoten, which extends about twelve days' journey from east to west, and is not more than two days' journey from north to south. It has the country of Aksu on the north, and China proper on the east. The present cities are six in number, Karakash, Elchi, Yurung Kash, Chíra, Karia, and Yangi Kishlak *, of which, and of the country in general, the following particulars were collected from a respectable Turani merchant, who had often visited it, and from other creditable information.

Karakash, or city of the black river, is the first met with on the road from Yarkand, at the distance of one hundred and twelve kos,

* Mr. Moorcroft doubts the existence of the city of Khoten, although referred to by Marco Polo. In this he can scarcely be correct, for its position has been laid down not only by Chinese geographers but by the Jesuits, in lat. 37°, and long. 78° 15′ 30″. Klaproth, *J. Asiatique*, No. xvii., *Histoire de la Ville de Khoten.* Remusat. *Quarterly Oriental Magazine*, Calcutta, Sept. 1834. The probability is that one of the cities named in the text is the city of Khoten under a new appellation. Elchi, or, as it occurs in the maps, Ilitsi, is identified by them with the city called by older travellers Khoten.—Ed.

or, according to other accounts, at seven days' journey: it contains three thousand houses *.

Elchi, on the same road, ten or twelve kos from the preceding, contains about six thousand houses. It is the residence of two Chinese Ambans, with a detachment of five hundred soldiers, and of the chief of the Mohammedan population.

The third city is that of Yurung Kash, little more than a mile and a half from Elchi, containing a thousand houses.

Chíra, the fourth city, is situated three days' journey south from Yurung Kash, and contains two thousand houses. Karía is twice as large, and lies four days' journey south-south-east, and Yangi Kishlak is four days' distant from Karía in the same bearing, and contains about one thousand houses.

* The stages from Yarkand to Karakash are thus enumerated:—

To Kargbalik	20 kos.
„ Chaulak	5 „
„ Guma	20 „
„ Muji	15 „
„ Psalma	20 „
„ Zawa	20 „
„ Karakash	12 „
	112

but these stages are, no doubt, in general much too long.

At the rate of six persons to a house, which is rather below the average of the houses of Ladakh, this would give one hundred and two thousand persons as the population of Khoten: perhaps ten thousand more may be added for its nomadic population.

The climate of Khoten is dry and salubrious: the winters are colder and the summers hotter than in Ladakh. The soil, though sandy, is productive, as water is abundant, and every house in the town is provided with a well. The greater part of the population is Mohammedan, and is said to be remarkable for personal beauty. The women are not subjected to out-door labour, as in Tibet, but are occupied principally in the rearing of silk-worms and spinning the thread. The men are engaged in agriculture, manufactures, and commerce.

The grains cultivated are wheat, barley, and maize. Pease and carrots are the chief vegetables. Fruit is reared in every garden, and of great variety, as pomegranates, plums, peaches, apricots, pears, apples, and melons: the vine is exceedingly productive. The timber trees, like those of Ladakh, scarcely deserve the name, and are restricted to willows and poplars, but the mulberry abounds everywhere, and furnishes sustenance for the silk-worm, which is very generally reared.

The domestic animals are horses in great numbers, of a hardy breed, though small size. Yaks are bred on the mountains, and common neat cattle on the plains. Sheep of the Dumba, or large-tailed variety, are reared in vast numbers, but their tails are smaller than those of the Kozak sheep: their wool is fine, but short, being shorn twice a year. Shawl-wool goats are not less numerous than sheep, and their fleeces are reported to be equal, at least, to those of Ladakh.

Wild animals of various kinds are abundant. The camels are generally brown, sometimes white, and have two humps: they are large, and swift of foot, and are hunted for their flesh, which is eaten, and much relished by the natives, and for their wool, from which a kind of cloth is fabricated. The Gor-khar, or wild ass, is common, as are many kinds of deer, including the musk deer, the produce of which in Khoten has been always highly celebrated throughout the East. From a description of the stripes on the skin it would appear that the royal tiger roams on the mountains of Khoten. Leopards, wolves, and bears are numerous,—none of the latter are black. Foxes, hares, and smaller quadrupeds are in abundance. The large variety of Francolin, which I believe has never been described, frequents the summits of the mountains, and the lesser kind, with other varieties of partridges and feathered game, are found in great numbers lower down and near the plains.

The manufactures of Khoten consist principally of woollens, camlets, cottons, and silks. The woollens got up in the loom are either of a thick and coarse texture, or thin and flimsy, and none of them approach the nature of European broadcloth. The felted cloths are large, fine, and well got up. Cotton cloths of a coarse kind are made in vast quantities, both for home use and exportation, and may be considered as the staple of the trade, although Khoten is more celebrated for its fabrics of silk. Various kinds of silk goods are fabricated, but they are coarse and inelegant: from their cheapness, however, they are in general use through Turkistan and Tibet.

The commerce of Khoten is of some value and interest. From Russia it receives broad-cloths, a fine cloth manufactured at Astrakhan from the wool of the camel foal of the first year, seal-skins, furs, green velvet, gold and silver thread for embroidery, Bulgar leather, hardware, amongst which are spades or hoes, logwood, loaf-sugar, and castor, which is used in medicine. The returns made through Turani merchants are silk cloths, raw silk, and cotton thread.

Raw silk, both white and yellow, is first taken to Bokhara, where it is dyed: it is then purchased by Nogai traders, and carried across the great Kirghiz steppe to various parts of Russia. Of cotton thread a thousand camel-loads annually are said to be furnished by Khoten to Russia.

The principal import from Bokhara is horses, of which about five hundred are brought yearly, and paid for by silks, raw silk, coarse cottons, and felts.

Similar articles are sent to Yarkand, Indejan, Aksu, and Ila. To the first, also, large quantities of sheep's-wool, which is there wrought into felts, are supplied in exchange for rice and cast-iron culinary vessels. From Ila and Aksu, Khoten receives droves of horses, bred by the Kalmaks. To the former it sends yearly from two to three hundred thousand bales of a coarse cotton cloth like Bengal gazi. The length of each piece is from seven to eight gaz, or yards, the breadth about twelve girehs (from twelve to fifteen inches), and the money price is a rupee. They are also exchanged for the cattle of the Kalmaks, at the rate of one piece for a sheep, three for a cow, and six for a horse.

There was formerly an extensive trade between Khoten and Hindustan, but political changes have completely destroyed all but a very limited traffic, carried on through Yarkand and Ladakh with the Panjab. It is said that there was formerly a royal road from Najibabad to Sarikia, a place half way between Yarkand and Khoten, and that it led through Gardokh and Rodokh. In that case it must have crossed the Niti Ghat, but no traces of it are now visible in that line. On my return from Manasarovara, however, I diverged from the common track, and came upon a fragment of road a few hundred yards in length, and about six feet broad, regularly and substantially paved with pebbles in some parts, and in others formed out of the levelled rock, which had every appearance of having been the work of a liberal and spirited government. According to the reports of the villagers, also, this was the rai, or badshah ki rah, the king's highway, on which, in ancient days, goods had been transported across the mountains.

The revenue which is drawn from Khoten by China is derived from two sources, the alban or capitation tax, commuted to a certain quantity of cotton cloths from every house, and a proportion, in some instances a tenth, of all produce, except garden fruits and silk. The currency of Khoten is of Chinese fabric, both silver and copper, or the usual lumps of the former, and the round flat coin, with a square centrical hole, of the latter. Uncoined gold, in grains and lumps, is also a medium of exchange.

The chief rivers of Khoten are the Karakash, or black river, also termed Kara-darya, and the Yurung Kash, or rapid river. The former rises in the mountains of Khoten, and runs from east to west for twenty-four kos to Shahid Ullah Khajeh, and then north for twelve kos, where it receives the Toghri su, or straight water, which rises in the Karlik Dawan, or ice mountains. It then runs north-east to Karakash, which is situated on its left bank. The distance from its source to the city is about nine days' journey. Pursuing its course in the same direction past the city of Yurung Kash on its right bank, it unites with the Yurung Kash river.

This latter stream, the Yurung Kash, rises in the Haringa Togh, or blind mountain, at three days' journey east from the source of the Karakash. It flows in a straight line to the city of Yurung Kash. The beds of this river and of the Karakash abound with the Yashm stones, or jasper agate, which are highly prized by Asiatics for various ideal virtues. Vessels made of them are supposed to fly to pieces if poison be put into them, fragments of them about the person are imagined to protect the wearer against lightning, and liquor from an agate cup is thought to allay irregular palpitations of the heart. The stones which are most free from specks and stains are considered the exclusive property of the Emperor of China, and the workmen employed to search for them are obliged to take the fruit of their labours daily to officers appointed to receive and inspect them. Guards are stationed along the banks to prevent their appropriating any to their own use, and to prohibit private individuals from engaging in the search.

The united stream of the Karakash and Yurung Kash flows into the river of Yarkand*. This river rises in the northern face of the Karakoram chain, and after running to the north-west some way is joined on the west by the Serakol river, a large branch from the Karakol Lake in the Pamer mountains, and then takes a bend to the east, past the city of Yarkand. From thence it pursues an easterly course through a distance

* This account omits some of the details given in the notice printed in the *Transactions of the Royal Geographical Society*, which were not confirmed by subsequent and, apparently, more accurate information.—ED.

said to be of ten days' journey, and after passing the latitude of the city of Yurung Kash, receives the waters of the two chief streams of Khoten.

At three days' further journey, the river, the appellation of which I could not learn, is joined by a stream from the north, the river of Aksu: this is said to rise by several streams, some of which come from the high mountains to the north of Turfan. One is said to rise near Ila, and another in the country of the Kirghiz, each about twelve days' journey in length. These two unite with the others at the city of Turfan, or Yengi Turfan (New Turfan), and thence proceeding in one channel to Aksu, three days' journey south, and thence for five days' journey in the same direction, fall into the river of Khoten. The trunk continues eastward for six days' journey to Bai, a small town, and thence, in the same direction, successively to Sairam, at a distance of one or two days' journey, Kucha, of five days', Karashehr, the black city, of ten or twelve days', Urumchu, of ten or twelve days', and Uchi, or Old Turfan, of twelve days' more.

From thence it flows in the same direction, for a distance of forty days' journey, through an uninhabited tract of desert and mountain to Kamul, a large city in China.

The person from whom I received this information had been no farther than Aksu himself, but he had received the account of the course of the river onwards from a friend who had accompanied the Hakim of Yarkand to Pekin and back. According to this authority the river continues its course east from Kamul for twenty days' journey through a sandy desert to Lanju, the Lanchu of Marco Polo, a city containing fifty thousand houses: hence for a journey of ten or twelve days to Siampur, a large city, inhabited chiefly by Mohammedans, or, as they are there called, Tunganis. From hence in twenty days more it reaches another large city, Suju, the Sochu of M. Polo. Its farther course through China was not known by the informant, but he had always understood that it took a large sweep to the westward, and quitting China, fell into the Irtish. If the sources of the Irtish are really to be found in the country of Yarkand, that river may rank with some of the longest in the world; but the accuracy of the account is very questionable. The retrograde course of such a river for such a vast distance seems, in itself, little probable; and although this might not be conclusive against respectable testimony, yet there are evident errors in the description, which tend to shake confidence in the whole: the relative position of Lanchu and Luju, for instance, is inverted, the former being the more easterly of the two. If the stream really reaches Lanchu, the probability is that it disembogues into the Hoang-ho *.

Eight days' journey from Yangi Kishlak, the last city of Khoten in the direction of south-south-east, is a district which abounds

* According to all the maps the Yarkand river, shortly after the junction of the river of Aksu, terminates in the small lake of Lop. Some Chinese geographers assert that it re-issues from the lake, and, crossing the smaller desert, or rather steppe, of Cobi, becomes the Hoang-ho, or Yellow River, of China. However this may be, it seems scarcely probable that the lake of Lop absorbs the waters of a trunk which must be so considerable as that of the river of Yarkand, after it has received the waters of the northern face of the Kuen-lun chain, of the southern face of the Thian Chan range, and of the eastern face of the Bolor-tagh, all mountains of great elevation, covered, more or less, with snow, and having no other vent for their waters.—Ed.

in gold, in grains and masses; in collecting which, five hundred to a thousand men are employed on the part of the Emperor of China. Khoten is supposed to possess this and other metals, but the knowledge of them is not divulged by the natives, lest they should be compelled to work them for the benefit of the Chinese government. At Aksu, it is said there is a mine of rubies which is not worked. A vein of silver was lately discovered near Ila, the chief station of the Chinese in this direction; but after the Amban had extracted from it a quantity for his own use, he ordered it to be closed. Intelligence of this being received at Pekin, the Amban was put to death, in the manner said to be commonly practised by the court; he was poisoned, by order of the Emperor, with a cup of medicated tea*.

* Mr. Moorcroft states the prevalence of a belief, which, though probably ill founded, shows the opinion entertained by the Turanis of their rulers. They assert that the Chinese government is in the habit of removing by means of poison, administered usually in a cup of tea, not only their own officers, but the chiefs of the Kalmaks, and thus preventing them becoming too powerful. It is said, that when the son of a chief attains the age of from ten to fifteen, the father is invited to Pekin, and after being treated with every mark of distinction, is sent back to his tribe. On the

A considerable portion of the population of Khoten consisted formerly of Kalmak Tatars, but it is said that when the Chinese subjugated the province, they deported the Kalmaks to the cities which collectively constitute the modern city of Ila, on the river of the same name, and to the adjacent districts. Their numbers, within a circuit of six miles from Ila in every direction, are computed at two hundred thousand families. Their chief employment is the breeding of cattle, camels, horses, cows, sheep, and goats; and for every hundred head they raise they pay a tax of one to the Chinese government. They bring annually from ten to twenty thousand three-year-old geldings to Ila for sale. These are ordinarily from thirteen and a half to fourteen hands high, and are sold in droves at about twelve for a yambo, or about fifteen rupees per horse. These horses are taken to Aksu, Yarkand, Kashgar, In-

route some Chinese functionary, in the course of the usual interchange of civilities, in which tea forms a prominent part, takes an opportunity of giving him a medicated draught: his son, whose youth and inexperience render him harmless, is raised to his father's dignity, to be removed by a similar method in his turn, before he becomes dangerous.

dejan, Khoten, and even to Bokhara, and are sold principally for carrying loads of merchandise. The Kalmaks are also employed as cavalry in the armies of China, and form part of the large garrison or standing army at Ila.

CHAPTER V.

Proceedings at Lé—Account of Aga Mehdi, the Russian Envoy—Excursions—Visit to Nobra—Sabu—Digar—Pass—Shayuk River—Churasa—Lokjun—Tazar—Rustic Hospitality—Hot Springs—Return by Undar—Tinder—Combing of shawl-wool Goats—Imitated by Wild Animals—Arrival at Lè—Mr. Trebeck fired at—Excursion to Knarung—Pithul—Sinh-kha-bab crossed—Pass of Kandu Lá—Marka River—Temple—Medicinal Spring of Knarung—Return—Confluence of the Sinh-kha-bab and Zanskar Rivers.

Soon after we were domesticated at Lé, and our intercourse with the Khalun had become more unreserved, the minister communicated to me a letter from the Emperor of Russia to the ruler of Ladakh, which had been brought to the latter by a person named Aga Mehdi, about six years before, professedly charged with the duty of opening a commercial intercourse with Ladakh: he had been the bearer of a similar letter to Ranjit Sinh, as he was instructed to extend his negotiations to the Panjab. This person, I learnt, was now on his return to these countries, and was shortly expected to arrive at Lé.

Although I had reason to expect a shrewd and able competitor in Aga Mehdi, yet I was anxious to see him, from the interest which was naturally excited by the rencontre of two European agents, from such opposite directions, in the mountains of Tibet, and from the hope that I might be able better to ascertain his real designs, as well as those of the ambitious power under whose patronage and authority he was employed, and whose views, which were no doubt political as much as commercial, he was to promote; our meeting, however, was prevented by his death, which occurred in the mountains of Karakoram, of a sudden and violent disorder.

In the middle of April, a person who represented himself as the partner of Aga Mehdi, Mohammed Zahur, arrived at Lé with a small kafilah, laden, as was pretended, with the effects of his principal, but which there was good reason to believe was public property. The chief articles imported proved to be dyeing drugs, as cochineal, indigo, woad, &c., both crude and prepared, intended to be employed in Kashmir in dyeing shawl goods, according to specimens of colour on flannel, furnished by a British artist at St. Petersburgh. There were no labels nor instructions; Aga Mehdi, it appeared, had spent a twelvemonth with an English dyer in Russia, in order to learn the use of these materials; but as Mohammed Zahur was ignorant of their nature and application, he was obliged to have recourse to me for advice. I was thus enabled to learn many interesting particulars relating to the Aga and his mission.

Aga Mehdi was the son of a Jew originally from Persia, who had settled in Kashmir, and a Kishtwar bondwoman. Left an orphan at an early age, he was for a time supported by his father's friends, and when old enough to shift for himself, he was first a menial servant, and then a sort of pedlar: he then traded on a larger scale as a shawl merchant, and in that character established himself in Russia. Brought up as a Shia Mohammedan, he became a convert to Christianity according to the ritual of the Greek church; and this circumstance, combined with his mercantile reputation, attracted the notice and patronage of some of the magnates of St. Petersburgh, by whom he was introduced to the sovereign. His knowledge of the people and language of Turkistan, Kashmir, and the Panjab, as well as his intelligence and enterprise, recommended him as a fit agent to be employed to extend the influence of Russia to the confines of British India, as well as to acquire information regarding the geographical and political circumstances of the intervening countries. His first attempt seems to have given satisfaction, as he was honoured, I was informed, with a gold chain and medal from the Emperor, and was soon encouraged to repeat his visit. On this, as on the former occasion, he brought letters from the Emperor of Russia to the rulers of Ladakh and the Panjab. Most of his papers were lost or destroyed upon his death, but a copy of the letter to Ranjit Sinh was brought to me. The original had been opened at Yarkand by Aga Mehdi himself, for the purpose of having a Persian translation made, and both the original and translation had been seen by many persons. I felt no scruple, therefore, about possessing myself of the document. The letter is signed by Count Nesselrode, and written by order of the Emperor Alexander. The bearer is styled Aga Mehdi Rafael, merchant and aulic councillor, and is recommended to Ranjit Sinh as a respectable trader, for whom free access to the Sikh territories for commercial purposes is solicited, assurance being given that equal facilities will be afforded to merchants from the Panjab. The motives of the Emperor, it is added, in opening this friendly correspondence with the Raja, are his exceeding benevolence towards the innumerable nations over whom he rules, and the deep interest he takes in the people of remote countries, and especially in the subjects of Ranjit Sinh. The letter to the Raja of Ladakh, which was subsequently communicated to me by the Khalun, differed from this only in the address.

Besides the drugs, Mohammed Zahur had with him a quantity of rubies and emeralds, the latter of which, although not perfect, were of considerable size and value. I understood from a Turani merchant that the Aga on his former visit had brought emeralds with him, for which there was no demand; and his repeating this investment was therefore apparently ill-advised. The size and setting of some of them also made them much too costly for the markets of Tibet and Lahore, and it seemed probable that they were designed for presents rather than for sale. There were other articles of a similar character, and some Russian telescopes, English cutlery, phosphorus boxes, and other trifles, were not likely to be employed as merchandise. Aga Mehdi had also a considerable sum, I was informed, in gold ducats, sixteen hundred of which were paid at Lé to a merchant of Yarkand, in acquittal of an ancient claim upon the Aga. Mohammed Zuhur had also in his possession above eleven thousand rupees*.

* Baron Meyendorf in his *Voyage d'Orenbourg à Boukhara* inserts a Persian paper on the commercial road from Semi-Palatynsk to Kashmir, with a translatiou and notes by Professor Senkowsly. In the latter (p. 340) reference is repeatedly made to a memoir by Mehdi Raphail, Juif Natif de Kaboul, who died a year before in Tibet, and who is the same, therefore, with Mr. Moor-

The inferences to be drawn from the means with which Aga Mehdi was thus provided were confirmed by the tenor of the information procured by Mir Izzet Ullah at Yarkand. It was there asserted, that the Aga had assured the Mohammedans of Kashgar of support from Russia, in any attempt to shake off the yoke of the Chinese, and had even invited the heir of the principality to St. Petersburgh, with a promise that he should be sent back with an army to recover the dominions of his ancestors. It was also generally reported that Aga Mehdi was to endeavour to prevail upon the Raja of Ladakh and Ranjit Sinh to send envoys to the Russian capital, the expense of whose journey he was authorized to defray. How far these assertions were well founded it is difficult to say; but their circulation indicated an ex-

croft's Aga Mehdi. His account of political events in Afghanistan shows him to have been a man of more observation than Asiatic traders usually are. This is not the only authority for details of this route possessed by the Russians, for the Baron cites (p. 122), *La Relation d'un Voyage aux Indes*, by Raphael Daniberg, a Georgian gentleman; printed at St. Petersburgh in 1815. He travelled from Kashmir to Semi-Palatynsk by way of Kashgar.—Ed.

tending disposition amongst the Mohammedans of Turkistan to anticipate the effectual interposition of Russia in their political as well as commercial condition. In respect to the latter, a kind of commercial treaty had not long since been entered into between that power and the ruler of Kokan, by which it had been agreed that the latter should give a safe convoy to the Russian-Chinese caravan through his dominions, from the Russian frontier to Kashgar, on receiving a rate of duty equal to that levied by Russia from the caravans from China and Turkistan.

From Shamei on the Irtish, Aga Mehdi had been escorted to Turfan Yangi, on the border of Chinese Turkistan, by a troop of cavalry, and had, nevertheless, been more than once in some danger from the attacks of the Kirghiz, provoked, it was probable, by depredations committed by his followers on the flocks and horses of the steppe. At Turfan he dismissed his escort, dividing amongst them, it was said, a number of horses carried off on their progress through the deserts, retaining only sufficient for the prosecution of his journey. At Yarkand he deserted his newly-adopted creed, and became a Musselman of the Suni persuasion.

After a short delay at Lé, Mohammed Zahur disposed of all the articles in his possession, and sending two confidential servants to Kashmir to lay out the money in shawls, repaired himself to Bokhara, there to wait for his people and goods. Whether it was his purpose to return to Russia, where his father was settled as a dealer in shawls, was somewhat doubtful. Under an impression that the articles in his possession were public property, I endeavoured strenuously to dissuade him from the sale of them, and strongly recommended to him to proceed to the court of Ranjit Sinh with the Emperor's letter: my counsels were, however, disregarded, for reasons best known to himself, but which it was not difficult to conjecture.

The death of Aga Mehdi was productive of some inconvenience to my movements. In reply to a letter from Mir Izzet Ullah, Kissak Shah, the principal judge at Yarkand, whilst he gave him a personal invitation, referred to the Russian envoy for a communication regarding my visit to that place. His death, and the absence of any written information, rendered me uncertain what measures to adopt, until a Turani merchant offered to act as my agent, and negotiate my passage by way of Yarkand. In the mean time some persons arrived at Lé from Yarkand, who, I was informed, were sent by the Kashmiri merchants of that place to ascertain the character and objects of our party. With these persons I had several interviews, and they departed in March, professedly convinced of my mercantile pursuits, and favourably disposed towards them. They intimated, however, the probability of the governor of Yarkand making application to Pekin for orders, in which case an answer could not be received for several months. The caravan then departed, but the roads were blocked up by the snow, and it was obliged to return. A week afterwards it again set out, and effected its passage, but with the loss of its chief. Mullah Nyas, the Kafila bashi, had fallen about twenty yards behind the rest of the party: just as they entered the gorge of the pass of Sha-skin-gomo, a sudden gust of wind brought on such a cloud of snow, as to conceal the Mullah and a little girl riding on a couple of yaks, from the mountaineer who attended them as their guide. The latter threw himself on the ground, that he might not be blown off his feet, and upon getting up when the blast had ceased, saw the yaks without their riders: they had been blown off their seats apparently, and were buried beneath the snow. After some delay the bodies were found: the girl recovered, but the old man was dead: he was a man of property and character. His companions deemed it expedient to carry the corpse with them to Yarkand, nearly forty days' journey at this season, in order to satisfy the Chinese authorities of his fate.

Pending the result of this reference, and of my despatches to Kokand, Kashmir, and Khulm, I took advantage of the interval to visit different parts of the country, the jealousy of the court having been overcome, and permission granted me to travel wherever I pleased. The first opportunity of this kind was obtained through the intervention of the Rani. Having good reason to believe that the execution of the commercial engagement with Ladakh had been accelerated by her good offices, I sent her a small present, and, after a few days, received a message from her through the Khaga Tan-zin, to know if there was anything in which she could promote my views. I availed myself of the opportunity to state my desire of visiting the hot springs at Nobra, for the benefit of my health, which had suffered from close confinement to the house during the winter. Leave was accordingly granted, and at the same time it was intimated to me that I might have an audience of the young Raja, a measure which had hitherto been delayed on various pretexts. We had been introduced to the Raja, his father, in the month of December, the ceremony on which occasion differed in no essential respect from that which had been observed when we visited the Khalun. In the present instance the audience took place in the garden of the palace, in a tent enclosed by a long wall of canvass on either side, forming an avenue, at the upper end of which, under the tent, which was open in front, sat the young Raja.

He was seated on a bench covered with cushions, with a covered table before him. In front of him sat two boys, his foster-brothers, and below them on either hand stood the Khalun and the Raja of Giah. The courtiers were seated on felts, which extended nearly the whole length of the enclosure. The young Raja was about ten or eleven years of age. He was so wrapped up in shawls that his person was quite concealed: he had a white turban on his head, with a small jewel in front. On our approach he seemed alarmed; but his fear subsided, and he laughed and talked to those near him. Through a side door I noticed some women anxiously watching the proceedings, amongst whom, as I afterwards learned, was the Rani.

The shorter road to Nobra was still closed by the snow, but the more circuitous one had the advantage of being the Yarkand road also, and would afford me, therefore, an opportunity of familiarising myself with the route which it was our purpose, if not disappointed, ultimately to follow. The first village was Sabu, to which we proceeded from Lé on the 28th of May, along the southern foot of the ridge of mountains forming the northern boundary of the valley of Lé, until we turned its angle, and proceeded towards the east, up a narrow valley, bounded by a transverse mountain elevation. Passing over this we descended into another small valley, in which the village was situated. The distance is about four miles from Lé, and Sabu lies about east from that place. The lands of Sabu, like those of Lé, slope to the river, but are separated from it by a long reach of barren soil, strewn with fragments of stone. On the other sides the valley is shut in by mountains, which at the north-east corner meet in an acute angle. It contains several small hamlets besides the principal one, in which latter the Raja has a dwelling. The lands were laid out, as usual, in terraces, and appeared to be of better quality, and more neatly and industriously tilled than those of Lé. The crops covered the ground, and were about two inches high. The trees and vegetation were of the same character as in the vicinity of the capital, but looked more flourishing.

From Sabu the road proceeded along the foot of the hills to the east, to the entrance of a narrow pass leading due north, and terminating in an ascent, on the face of which we halted, after a journey of about six miles. The only accommodation it afforded was a rude chamber, constructed of loose stones. We met a party of men from Balti, laden with stone cooking pots and rolls of wool. They were stout able-bodied men, with very wrinkled countenances from exposure to the cold. They had been fourteen days on the road. At night snow fell, and was four inches thick in the morning. As a pass which we had to traverse was blocked up by snow, I sent my servants back to Sabu, and remained in my tent with one man, very indifferently supplied with food, and without any fuel. Snow continued to fall until the 2nd of June, but it did not much accumulate, as that which fell in the night was mostly melted during the day. On the night of the 2nd there was no snow, but it froze hard. The pass, however, was open, but I was detained in expectation of a message from Lé. During the 3rd the daughter-in-law of

Khaga Tan-zin came down the pass, on her road to Lé. She was about twenty, a tall well-looking brunette, with an oval face, red cheeks, and fine teeth. Her head was covered with a rich brocade cap, and her neck loaded with gold and silver ornaments, turquoises, and coral beads. She rode a yak, and had a fine ruddy boy, about three years old, on her lap. She was accompanied by her brother, and about fifty attendants, with as many yaks, and the appearance of the whole party denoted considerable affluence.

On the morning of the 4th of June the thermometer in the tent was at 27°, but as the yak people were willing to move we resumed our journey. The direction was east of north, and then east, and the path was formed of snow trodden down by the feet of passengers, and uneven with alternate thawing and freezing, rendering it very rugged for men, and dangerous for horses. Being on a steep ascent, it was also very fatiguing, and the difficulty of breathing was more troublesome and painful than I had before experienced: this extended to the animals, particularly the horses; but the yaks were not wholly exempt, and we were obliged to halt repeatedly to give the cattle relief. I had no means of estimating the elevation of the summit of the pass, but imagine it cannot have been less than one thousand two hundred feet above the beginning of the ascent. From the top of the pass the country to the north and east appeared equally mountainous with that which we had passed, and which was shut in to the south and west by snow-topped ridges at no great distance. The descent to the west of north was less abrupt and laborious; but as the sun became powerful the snow softened, and the cattle, if they diverged from the path, sometimes plunged up to their shoulders in a snow bed: even on the track they were occasionally knee deep in snow. The effect of snow and sunshine together is in these countries distressing, and often injurious to the eyes, and the inhabitants either wear a kind of goggles made at Lé, or twist a loose braid of yak's hair round their head, so as to form a kind of veil to the upper part of the face. After some distance, generally descending, we came to the village of Digar, in a valley not above a quarter of a mile in breadth, stretching north-east. The place contains about sixteen houses. It lies very high and lofty, and considerably above Lé. The only grains cultivated are barley and buckwheat. The people, who are very poor, subsist partly by keeping yaks for the hire of travellers.

The mountains, at the base of which Digar is situated, were rugged, and bare of vegetation, and consisted chiefly of a clay slate bearing vegetable impressions. From a break in the summit of the ridge above the village, over which the path ascended, a broad sandy valley, running north by east, was seen, down which flowed the Shayuk river. At the closed extremity of the Digar valley it was joined at a right angle by the Duryukh, a river which rises in the mountains south-east of the village of Digar, and then continued its course in the same straight direction. The valley of the Shayuk was shut in by snow-topped mountains of a similar elevation with those around them, or one thousand, or one thousand two hundred feet above the river. The bed of the river was at least half a mile broad, but the stream occupied a small portion only of this extent. I was told by some inhabitants of Agham, a village I passed on my right, that the quantity of water brought down by the Shayuk was much greater than of late years, and that rain had formerly fallen with more frequency and abundance. After skirting the left bank of the river for some miles we crossed it by a sanga of willow planks, to the estate or farm of Roundo. This, occupied by one family, comprised a wood of tamarisk, willow, and poplar trees, and about forty acres of land, cultivated in terraces. It was bounded to the north by mountains, from a gap in which on the north-east a beautiful trout stream fell into the Shayuk, just above the bridge. The trout were larger and rounder than any I had ever seen. The fields were green with barley, and the verdure, contrasting with the white stone faces of the terraces, the streams of clear water that surrounded them, the belts of apricot trees, interspersed with bushes of the dog rose, now in full bloom, with willows, and here and there a walnut tree, the banks of the watercourses, fringed with the dwarf iris and large tufts of lucerne, the neatness of the houses, and the cordial welcome of the inhabitants, made Roundo more agreeable to me than any place I had seen since I left Joshimath.

On the following morning we proceeded along the valley, in a north-westerly direction. About five miles on our left was a gap in the mountains, near which the village of Yon-chu was situated, from whence a road proceeds to Lé, by Kondon, which is taken when that by Digar is obstructed by snow, or by the rise of the Shayuk. About three o'clock we arrived at a jangal, which is called the head of Nobra, and were received at a house, at Tirit, belonging to a son of the Khaga Tan-zin. On the next day we quitted the bed of the Shayuk, and turned up a valley a little to the west of north, watered by the Charasa, a river from the Karakoram range, which flows round the Lha Skarmo mountain, and falls, at nearly a right angle, into the Shayuk, about seven miles west from Lok-jun. At the latter village we stopped at the house of an old lady, named Amma Bunzun, who had consulted me at Lé for a liver complaint, and to whom my advice had been of advantage. Her gratitude was extreme, and she insisted on our dining with her. The houses here were more spacious and better kept than at Lé. A column of red stone stood near each, to avert, it was said, the effects of the "evil eye." The grounds of Lok-jun were surrounded by a plain of white sand, in many places blown into ridges. In the evening we reached the town of Tagar, the residence of the Khaga Tan-zin's youngest son.

On the next morning the old lady followed me with several pounds of butter, and two servants loaded with wheat cakes. My medical fame soon attracted a numerous attendance of sick, who here, as at Lé, and other places, paid me fees in kind, flour, bread, butter, tea, vegetables, and the like, so that had any stranger, unacquainted with the circumstance, seen me thus surrounded by my patients and their presents, he would have thought me a retail dealer of farm produce in the midst of customers. After leaving Tagar and skirting its grounds for a mile in a direction north by west, we descended into a level plain, the soil of which was moist in some parts, where it was overspread with short grass, and drier in others, where it was covered with soda. On the left hand of the valley, at the foot of the mountain, was the village of Charasa, looking like a fortress. On the right of the road lay another village, Cham-shed, and we passed, about two miles farther on, between two other villages, beyond which we came to the Charasa river, and crossed where it was about thirty-five feet broad and waist deep. At the village of Teresha, on our right, my guide was persuaded to stop and partake of the hospitality of his friends, in which I was invited to share. I was ushered into the best room in the house, and a felt carpet was placed on a bench for my seat. The host, a jolly-looking farmer, congratulated us on our arrival, and the hostess, a comely woman, with one child in her arms, and three clinging to her skirts, introduced a vessel made out of the hollowed stem of the willow, and furnished with a handle and a spout, and filled with chang. Several neighbours came in, and seated themselves round the room, each man with his wooden cup, in which chang or tea was incessantly supplied. I observed it was a point of hospitality never to suffer a cup to be emptied. As soon as the host or hostess saw one half empty it was replenished until the guest positively declined any more: satu and cakes were also distributed, and butter was placed before me and the guide. Five pots of chang were quickly despatched, and the purple nose of my guide took a deeper hue. None of the party were intoxicated, nor did this befall my conductor, although on leaving this mansion he stopped at a second to allay his thirst. In about an hour's walk from the second visit we arrived at Chusan, and stopped at a house belonging to the Khaga Tan-zin, where we were hospitably entertained, having come about twelve miles from Tagar.

In the vicinity of this house were situated the hot springs, which, in the evening, I visited. They issued from the face of part of the mountain ridge which we had seen on our right all the way from Tagar. The openings were small, and the water flowed gently and equably: it was quite clear, and of the same temperature, of 167°, at mouths distant two hundred yards from each other: each vent was surrounded by a bed of tufa, lined with a yellow crust. A leathery conferva grew in the currents where not above 110°, the upper leaves of which were covered with a yellow deposit: the water was wholly without taste or smell. Close to the hot springs issued small streams of cold water, the course of which was free from any earthy or stalactitic matter. Some rudely-constructed baths, consisting merely of a loose pile of stones round the edge of a natural cavity, had been made for the use of persons who resorted to them, chiefly for rheumatic affections. The edges of most of the streams were fringed with grass or moss, which, where subjected to the action of the water, was covered with a stony crust, and in every case, at about half a yard distance, was a bed of soda, following the course of the current. This is called, by the Tibetans, Phúl, and is used by them as soap, and mixed with tea. The soil about this spot abounds with soda. I tried a bath for rheumatic pains in my shoulder, which had distressed me during the winter, but derived more harm than benefit from bathing in so exposed a situation, that, although I had secured my clothes by placing large stones upon them, they were quickly sent after me into the bath by a violent gust of wind from the mountains. The appearance of the soil and of the detached blocks indicates the action of heat, but there are no traces of volcanoes in any part of the country. The water is collected in a reservoir at the foot of the mountain, and thence led over lands which are said to yield excellent crops of barley and lucerne. The country abounds with hares and chakors, and the view of the villages on the edges of the valley, in the midst of cultivated lands, bordered by the sandy plain through which the Charasa was flowing, was picturesque and pleasing.

Sending my baggage to Undar, along the left bank of the Charasa, I retraced my steps to the hospitable mansion of Amma Bunzan at Lok-jun, and thence proceeded to Undar, which lies in a recess of the mountains, nearly west from the former. The road lay through a forest of black thorn, and was constantly intersected by small streams, some flowing into the Shayuk, and others into the Charasa. The breadth of the Shayuk where we forded it, within forty yards of the junction, was not more than as many feet. The united river was called the Chu Dhumsa. Hares and hyænas abounded in the thorn forest, and the ibex and ovis ammon on the mountains.

At Undar, which is also called Shak-than Ring-mo (the Valley of Stones), was the residence of Dur-je Tan-zin, the eldest son of the Khaga Tan-zin. The place consisted of a village, and several estates detached. The soil, though stony, was productive, and the fruit trees were very flourishing: some of the apple trees were forty feet high. At this place I witnessed the preparation of a peculiar kind of tinder. A small shrub, not above an inch and a half high when in flower, was gathered, and placed on the bottom of a dry iron vessel over a fire: as the hairy heads expanded they were plucked off and thrown away. The plants were repeatedly turned over to prevent their being burnt: when considered sufficiently dry the pan was inverted, and the leaves, placed on its blackened under-surface, were beaten upon it with a small stick until well impregnated with the soot, any loose dust being carefully blown off. In this state the slightest spark was sufficient to ignite the preparation. This substance, wrapped up in a thin roll of paper, is also used as moxa, or as actual cautery, pieces about three-fourths of an inch thick being laid upon the skin, and set fire to. This is a favourite application for pain in the stomach.

We returned on the 17th to Tirit. The bulk of the Charasa and Shayuk had much diminished since we passed them, owing, probably, to the greater cold which had prevailed, and the days being overcast. The next day brought us back to Roundo. On the 19th I started before the porters, and, following the course of a narrow valley to the left, I came to a town of some extent, which was also named Taghar. Here I found that I was on the wrong road, or that proceeding to Chan-than, and had, consequently, to retrace my steps. At the end of three miles an ascent, by a narrow and steep path, brought me in sight of Digar. On my way I had an opportunity of witnessing the manner in which the shawl-wool was extracted from the fleece. After the hair of the goat had been cut short with a knife in the direction of its growth, or from the head towards the tail, a sort of comb was passed in the reversed direction, and brought away the finer wool almost unmixed with the coarse hair. The comb consisted of seven pegs of willow tied side by side, like Pan's pipes, and secured by cross bars: the pegs were cut away at the points to the thickness of quills, and were made slightly to diverge from each other. The operation was roughly performed, and brought away scales of the cuticle along with the wool. The wool, however, was, at this time, easily detached, for it is a curious provision of nature that, with the setting in of warmer weather, the delicate woolly clothing nearest the skin of the mountain animals, being no longer needed, becomes loosened in its attachment, and is removed, if not by man, by the animals themselves. I noticed the yaks at the end of April very busy rubbing themselves with their horns, and bringing off the finer hairs in considerable quantities. In sheep and dogs the wool rose to the end of the hair, and either fell off, or was got rid of by the animals rolling on the ground, or rubbing themselves against trees, and the like; and I was told that the wild goats and sheep relieve themselves in the same manner of a vesture indispensable to their comfort in winter, but unnecessary and inconvenient in the heat of summer.

On the 20th we were able only to reach the northern foot of the pass, which we crossed on the 21st. There was much snow on the northern face, the surface of which was mostly frozen over, but the crust was in many places very thin, and gave way beneath the weight of the cattle; they were constantly sinking deep into the bed of uncongealed snow, and delayed our progress, so that we were five hours in reaching the top of the pass. The descent was still more difficult and dangerous. The snow had been mostly melted, but a frost, as recently as on the preceding night, had glazed the water of such as had been thawed during the day; and the mixture of ice in sheets, or in powder, with fragments of rock and loose stones, rendered the footing insecure both for men and animals. An Arab horse of mine, having missed his footing, slid down a sheet of ice for some distance, and recovered himself only by a vigorous effort, just on the brink of a precipice several hundred feet high. We arrived at Lé on the same day. The Khalun and Khaga Tan-zin were absent, having gone with some troops to retaliate upon the territory of Balti an inroad committed by the Raja of that country upon Ladakh. The quarrel was not likely to lead to any serious results, for the people on both sides took little interest in the dispute, and their propensities were at no time of a very warlike description.

Notwithstanding the generally inoffensive character of the people, however, it appeared that some amongst them were capable of deeds of atrocity, for, about two o'clock on the morning of the 27th of June, Mr. Trebeck, who had sat up late preparing for an excursion on that day, was fired at from the street. The shot passed through the window, and struck the side of the room, in the direction of a light upon a table at which my young friend had been writing. He had, fortunately, quitted his chair a few minutes before, or he might have been killed. As our inquiries furnished no clue to the perpetrator of this attempt, and as it had luckily failed, we thought it unnecessary to suspend our purposed journey, and set off, accordingly, to Pittuk.

Pittuk is a village situated on the northern face of a hill on the right bank of the Sinh-kha-bad, south-west from Lé about four miles, and on a much lower elevation. The houses rise one above another to the top of the hill, which is of no great height. From the sheltered situation of the lands of Pittuk, which follow the course of the river, and have a slight fall towards it, as well as from the goodness of its soil, the crops come to maturity sooner than about Lé, as has been noticed.

Crossing the river, we proceeded along its left bank until we were opposite to the village of Phi, beyond and above which, on the top of an easy slope, was that of Phiang, about two miles in a horizontal line: the hills close to it are said to be frequented by the wild sheep and goat. At some distance beyond this we turned off to the south, leaving the river to the right, and after passing the night at a farm, ascended the pass of Kandu La, which we estimated by barometrical measurement at 16,600 feet high. The mountains near at hand were not much more elevated than the ghat, except one at some distance to the west, the peak of which was lost in clouds. A deep bed of snow lay on the left of the pass, and all the high ridges in sight were topped with snow. Some lower, intervening, and rounded mountains were bare, except that on their sides were patches of wormwood and furze, and occasionally a plant of rhubarb. On the top of the pass was the usual votive pile of stones, decorated with rags and bits of cloth. The descent led to a single farm-house and estate called Shingo, and was accompanied by a rivulet, which, passing the house, flowed into another small stream, called, from the villages situated upon it, the Marka or Skio rivulet: the latter stood at the junction, the former three miles higher up the stream to the east, on its right bank. The Marka flows from the mountains of Zanskar, and the road to that district lies along its course. Skio is situated on the northern bank of the Marka; but opposite to its confluence with the Shingo were the ruins of a number of houses, some of considerable size, and extending up the slope of a mountain. The buildings, it was said, had been overwhelmed by a fall of stones from the top of the mountain. There was an ascent to the summit, on which stood a sacred cairn, by a rude and fearful series of steps, formed of slates resting on wooden pegs driven into the face of the rock.

At the angle of the rocks, upon the right hand of the Shingo, where the ridge terminated, was a small temple, in which was a statue of the god Chamba. The image was erect, about twelve feet high, and naked, except round the waist, which was encircled by a narrow band of drapery. The walls were painted with figures of men, women, and animals, singly or grouped, and apparently in processions. The temple had been recently repaired, but the paintings were said to be very ancient.

From Skio the road continues due east for a mile, and then turns north for about the same distance up a narrow rivulet to the spring of Knarung, to which our visit was designed. We found the water trickling from the mountain into a natural reservoir, from which it is drunk. It was scarcely tepid, and of a mawkish taste, but without any decided flavour: along its sides were incrustations of soda. It is taken as an emetic, and is of considerable repute amongst the natives; but neither Mr. Trebeck nor myself discovered any medicinal property. The branches of a tamarisk near the spring were hung with scraps of cloth, some plain, some printed, as offerings to the divinity of the place.

In the course of the next two days we retraced our path to the main river, and, crossing it, proceeded to Phi, from whence we set off in a westerly direction to the confluence of the Lé and Zanskar rivers. Passing over barren plains for some distance, the road then followed a gentle ascent, from the summit of which it descended to Nimo, on the left bank of the trunk of the united rivers. The river of Lé, flowing from east by south, was a clear and placid stream: that of Zanskar, from west by south, came rushing with great rapidity, and dashed its turbid waters into the Sinh-kha-bad with so much vehemence as to cause a reflux current for several yards. The height at which the union of the two rivers takes place is nearly twelve thousand feet. The road to Kashmir takes this direction, and the village of Bazgo, which is the second stage from Lé, was visible at the distance of about four miles. From hence we returned to Lé, and arrived there in the forenoon of the 4th of July.

CHAPTER VI.

Political Relations of Ladakh with Ranjit Sinh—Tender of Allegiance to the British Government of India—Communicated through Mr. Moorcroft—Displeasure of the Government—Mir Izzet Ullah dispatched to Yarkand—Journey to Kag-jung—Chushut—Marsilla—Sakti—Lamas at Chumri—Hospitality of the Banka—Hares not eaten—Mode of preserving Plants—Chakors—Pass of Chang La—People and Baggage benighted on the descent—Intense cold, and want of Fuel and Provisions—Lake of Las Marma—Gigantic Chakor—Durgukh Village and River—Muglib—Tswar Lake—Extensive Lake of Pang-kung—Chushul—Haunts of the Kiang, or Wild Horse—Messenger from Rodokh—Letters from Lé—Mr. Moorcroft's Return—Journey continued by Mr. Trebeck.

BEFORE I set out on my journey to the hot springs of Nobra some conversation had occurred with the Khalun and Khaga Tan-zin, on the political relations of Ladakh with the ruler of the Panjab. It appeared that in the reign of Aurangzeb the country of Ladakh was invaded by the Kalmaks, and the government, unable to repel them, applied for aid to the Mogul governor of Kashmir. The assistance was granted on condition of Ladakh becoming tributary to the Mogul empire, and from this period, down to the reign of Mohammed Shah, Ladakh had paid, through Kashmir, a small annual tribute to the court of Delhi. On the invasion of Hindustan by Ahmed Shah Abdali the tribute was transferred to the Durani government of Kabul, and had been paid to their officers in Kashmir, until that province was invaded and subdued by the Sikhs. Ranjit Sinh having become possessed of Kashmir, had recently intimated some purpose of instituting the claim on Ladakh, and demanding the continuance of the tribute from his weaker neighbour. The Khalun, therefore, consulted Mir Izzet Ullah as to the policy that should be adopted on such an occurrence, and showed a disposition to tender a proffer of allegiance to the government of British India, as the legitimate representative of the dynasty of Timúr. The advice given to him was to follow this course at once, and not to await the demands of the Sikh, which would certainly be made, and which it would be then too late to refuse.

The timid indecision of the Ladakh rulers delayed, however, the offer of allegiance to the British until a message had been received from Kashmir, inquiring why the tribute had not been paid as usual, and threatening a forcible levy if it was not speedily dispatched. On my return to Lé, therefore, I found the Khalun most anxious to apply for protection to the British government, as to the paramount sovereign of Ladakh, and on his appeal to me I readily consented to be the medium of forwarding the tender of allegiance to Bengal, addressing a letter to the Sikh chief, at the same time, to apprise him of what had occurred. My motives, I conceived, fully justified my interposition. On the one hand I averted from an amiable and harmless people the oppressive weight of Sikh exaction and insolence, and, on the other, I secured for my country an influence over a state, which, lying on the British frontier, offered a central mart for the extension of her commerce to Turkistan and China, and a strong outwork against an enemy from the north, should such a foe ever occur in the autocrat of the Russias. That Russia was not insensible to the importance, commercial and political, of Ladakh, was evinced by the recent repeated efforts made to get a footing in the country, and I held it to be an act of provident self-defence to anticipate her ambitious designs. In every light, therefore, whether of humanity, of commercial benefit, or of political security, I conceived the allegiance of Ladakh, voluntarily proffered, and imposing no obligation from which the slightest inconvenience could result, could not fail to be acceptable to my government, and I forwarded the memorial and tender to Calcutta. From motives which I am unable to appreciate, and unwilling to scrutinise, my conduct was wholly disapproved of, and I was severely censured for taking unauthorisedly a part in political arrangements. The allegiance of Ladakh was declined, and, as Ranjit Sinh was informed I had acted without the sanction of the government, that state was placed at his mercy. To have been visited with censure where I must still think I merited commendation was a sufficient disappointment; but the consequences were still worse, and the difficulties and dangers which subsequently beset my progress were mainly owing to the harsh, peremptory, and public manner in which discredit was affixed to my proceedings by the Resident of Delhi and the government of Bengal.

Immediately after the adjustment of this affair I dispatched Mir Izzet Ullah to Yarkand to further the negotiations going on there for permission for us to proceed, and, pending the result, continued my investigations in the neighbourhood. Understanding that the Kiang, or wild horse, chiefly abounded in the eastern districts, I proceeded thither with the hope of procuring either a living or dead specimen of this animal. As the direction of this journey was towards Chan-than the Khalun was, at first, apprehensive of its compromising him with the authorities of that province, and some delay occurred before his permission was obtained. On the removal of this difficulty by my assurances that I would not cross the frontier, a further detention ensued by the setting in of frost and snow early in October, and it was not until the 21st of that month that we were able to start. We then crossed the river to the opposite suburb of Chushut, the scattered houses and grounds of which extend for some distance along the left bank. We encamped at the house of Mohsin Ali, a Kashmiri merchant, whom I had appointed the British factor at Lé. We were advised to be on our guard against hyænas, who sometimes descend from the mountains at night, and to whom our baggage asses would be an acceptable prey. We were not disturbed, however, by these visitants, and, resuming our route the next day, passed through the contiguous lands of Stakna, watered by a canal cut from the river, and arrived at our former halting-place, Marsilla. Our old friend, the Lama, was absent, having been obliged to meet the Raja at a village in his jurisdiction: he had taken care, however, to order a quantity of rice and a fat sheep to be dressed for our dinner.

We were detained two days at Marsilla for supplies, but on the 25th crossed the river by a sanga, where it is divided by an island into two channels, and proceeded up a narrow valley, leading to the village of Sakti. The sides of the valley, which was not above half a mile broad, and which was watered by a rivulet flowing into the Lé river, were disposed in terraces for cultivation. The crops were gathered, and the people were employed in treading out and winnowing the corn, enlivening their labours by a song more monotonous than musical. On the north-west side of the valley we passed the town of Chumri, containing about two hundred houses and a temple, said to be richly endowed: above five hundred Lamas reside here. The Raja was at this time on a visit to their principal. We moved on to a house belonging to the Banka, called Piu, where, although he was absent, a dinner had been provided for us by his orders. On the preceding day I had sent to him a present of game for the Raja, and it was fortunate I did so, for it is the etiquette in Ladakh to send such articles to the Raja in a dressed state only. The Banka took the game, and said he would have it cooked. The present did not include some hares which I had shot, as they are not eaten by the Tibetans, for no other reason, as far as I could learn, than that the length of their ears assimilated them to asses.

The Banka, who to his office of master of the horse adds the government of this district, prevailed upon us to remain in the vicinity of his dwelling until it could be ascertained that the pass of Chang-la was free from snow, and, although I thought we might determine this for ourselves, yet, as he was earnest in his expressions, and was, apparently, prompted by friendly motives, I was prevailed upon to delay our further advance until the 30th. During this interval I observed the gardener, who was here, as elsewhere in Tibet, a female, preserving some rose bushes and other plants of a less hardy description by pressing them on the ground, and covering them a foot thick with chaff, a precaution which she assured me would keep them alive through the winter. The district under the Banka comprises seventy villages. His office is hereditary, and is held by the condition of bringing seven hundred armed men into the field when required. On the top of his house was a large chapel, in which were a number of small images on shelves, and a large cylindrical drum upon a stand. In this neighbourhood the chakors are numerous, and are frequently taken alive, being at an early hour in the morning so stiffened with cold that they are unable to escape from the men and boys who have watched the place where they have roosted. A brace of them was sent me by the Banka, tied by the legs, and wholly uninjured. It was not easy to bring them down with a gun, although we saw several coveys; but they kept up on the highest parts of the rock, where we could not follow them. In the course of our chase we caught a glimpse of a small animal called wat-se. It was rather smaller, though like in shape to a fox, and of a light orange colour.

Moving on the 30th, we soon came to the straggling houses which constituted the village of Sakti. On the face of the mountain, forming part of the eastern limit of the valley, stood the fort of Sakti, a pile of buildings, surrounded by a wall and towers, the whole built of granite blocks cemented with clay: the houses were unroofed, but the walls were mostly standing. This fortress was evidently intended to command the northern entrance of the valley, but it was taken and dismantled by the Kalmaks nearly two centuries ago, and has never been repaired. Beyond this a road up an apparently easy ascent, going to the north, led to Nobra. Our route turned up a valley to the east, in which was situated the village of Tongur, on the left. Above the village stood a large temple, with two plates of brass suspended from the pediment in front. Beyond this the valley narrows and ascends, and at about a mile above the village cultivation terminates. The ground is then broken, and strewed with fragments of rocks, leaving only a channel for a mountain torrent, which runs into the Sakti rivulet. We here met two flocks of sheep and goats laden with wool.

Having rested on a sheltered platform during the night, we commenced the ascent of the Chang-la pass early on the 31st. A line of snow commenced about a mile and a half above our encampment, and our sheep charged with our baggage trod it, as they preceded us, into a path sufficiently firm to bear the yaks and horses. On the top of the pass, which was a level three hundred yards broad, stood the usual accumulation of stones and rags, to which the Banka had entreated I would contribute, as the omission, in the belief of the people, would offend the genii of the mountain, and would be punished by some awful catastrophe. I accordingly propitiated the spirits of the pass with the leg of a pair of worn-out nankin trousers, and gratified my people by ordering a sheep to be killed for their entertainment when we had reached the foot of the ghat. By the barometer the Chang-la pass was the highest we had crossed: it stood at 15° 52′, the thermometer being at 25°, and, consequently, it could not be much less than seventeen thousand eight hundred feet high. As far as could be estimated by the eye, the line of elevation of the loftiest ridges rarely exceeded this, with the exception of the mountain descried from the pass of Kandu-la.

The sun having softened the snow on the slope of the descent, rendered our path very laborious: the horses were sometimes neck deep, and we were occasionally obliged to wade through it up to our waists. It was not until the approach of evening that the persons of our party in advance reached a valley at the foot of the pass, running north-west and south-east, the upper part of which was free from snow, and presented some patches of vegetation. It was nearly night before my people arrived, and then they came without the asses, who had our tent and bedding, and three men had dropped behind. It appeared that after passing the pile the animals had proved unable to make their way with their burthens. The men who last arrived assisted to unload them, and then recommended their companions, two washermen and the cook, to abandon them and the baggage, and save their own lives. Half benumbed with cold, and bewildered with affright, the three individuals in question gave themselves up as lost, and, throwing themselves on the snow, declared they would rather die than proceed. Deeply concerned as I necessarily was at their probable fate, it was now impossible to devise a remedy. It was night, the cold was intense, and to have sent back aid would have involved the almost certain loss of other lives. The men who were missing had with them the sheep-skin cloaks of the whole party, Mr. Trebeck's bedding, and two tents:—if they had their senses about them, they had the means, therefore, of guarding against the cold better, indeed, than we ourselves. We had one tent and some fuel, but the latter was barely sufficient to heat some water, and we were ill provided with warm clothing. The sheep with our provisions had gone on, and there was no chance of finding them in the dark, so that a little barley porridge was the only sustenance that could be provided for our followers. My companion and myself remained without food. Mr. Trebeck doubled himself up in a felt carpet, and I endeavoured to sleep in my clothes and bedding on the ground: cold and anxiety, however, permitted neither of us to repose. The condition of the servants was less unenviable, and with such clothing as they could collect they crept into holes and hollows, screened from the wind by overhanging rocks or blocks, and rude walls of stone.

Some of them said that the shelter thus obtained, as contrasted with the open air, was like a hamam, or warm bath. The syces, or grooms, stripped the horses, and covered themselves with their felts and saddles. The poor animals, without clothing or food, were left exposed to the air.

In the morning the people were all well, and, having refreshed them with some warm tea, I set off in quest of those we had left behind, and my satisfaction may be better imagined than described when I saw two of the missing men on their feet endeavouring to reload the asses. The cook was lying on the ground, alive, and unharmed, though scarcely sensible. A short time longer would have been fatal; but, by dint of rubbing his limbs, and compelling him to make an effort, he was able, with the assistance of another man, to walk. They had not used the tents, it appeared, but they had covered themselves well with the sheep-skins, and had thus been able to weather out the night. Before mid-day the whole party was assembled at De-mo-chu, as the foot of the pass was called. I then rode on to look after the sheep and their conductors, and found that they had stopped on a plain about two miles ahead, much lower and warmer than where we had halted, and near the small lake of Las Marma*. This lake, about three-fourths of a mile in circumference, collecting the waters of the mountains bounding the valley of De-mo-chu, gives rise to a small stream, which runs into the river of Durgukh near the village of that name. It was now nearly frozen over. In the evening my people feasted on the sheep I had ordered to be killed for them, and enjoyed themselves the more for the peril and fatigue they had undergone.

Whilst halting here for the day, we observed the large variety of the chakor, a species never before seen by Europeans. It differs in nothing essential except size from the common kind; but one of them, after being plucked and drawn, was found to weigh nearly five pounds. We saw them in coveys of thirty or forty on the edge of the snow, particularly in the morning and evening, and their flight was always accompanied

* Mr. Trebeck calls it the Tsol-tak, or High Lake.—Ed.

with a clamorous screaming and chattering, like that of the sea-gull. Having wrapped myself up in a lamb-skin vest I experienced this night no inconvenience from the cold, but in the morning I found my breath had frozen and glued the coverlet of the bed to the pillow. The thermometer was at 3° above zero *.

On the ensuing day we proceeded along the valley to the village of Durgukh; the path was intersected by a decayed wall, which it was said was erected as a defence—an unavailing one—against the Kalmaks. Durgu, Duryukh, or Durgukh, is a village of about forty houses, on either bank of a river, called by the same name. After receiving the Changla rivulet it runs westerly and joins the Shayuk at Lama-yul, on the road to Yarkand. Our journey, during the two next days, ascended its course along narrow valleys in which scarcely any trees were seen, and the lands fit for cultivation were of small extent. Beyond the village of Muglib the river descended in two small streams from the mountains on

* Mr. Moorcroft's Journal of this Excursion here terminates, and the following particulars are collected from that of Mr. Trebeck.—Ed.

either hand, which must be the seat of its source. We halted on the 6th, on the bank of a small lake called Tswar, which was frozen. The hills forming the valleys, or rather defiles, along which we were passing, were of much lower elevation than those we had left behind, and their skirts were bordered with grass. Near Muglib were some brood mares belonging to the Banka, which were at pasture here, and were in good condition.

After passing over a sandy valley we came to a gorge formed, in part, by limestone cliffs, and after clearing this, the lake of Pangkung came in view, with a river flowing into it from the north-east, above a mile distant. The road then came upon the edge of the latter, and we encamped close to the water, after having skirted it for between four and five miles. The hills approached us on our right; those on the other side of the lake, rising abruptly from it, were about two miles distant. Onwards the water extended to the horizon, contrasting agreeably with the bounded and tortuous torrents to which we had so long been accustomed. The water was perfectly clear, and, for the most part, still, and there was no appearance of fish. The water was extremely salt. On the 8th we continued the same kind of route, having the lake upon our left and hills upon our right, which were about one thousand feet higher than the surface of the water. Snow lay down three-fourths of the slope, and some light falls occurred on our level. We halted at the village of Man, and remained there throughout the 9th to rest and refresh the cattle. The road of the 10th, and part of the 11th, continued along the shore of the lake. The lake then took a direction more to the north, and was visible for about ten miles in a horizontal direction; beyond that its course was not discernible. Where we quitted it, it was nearly three miles broad, and continued, apparently, of much the same breadth, contracted at intervals by projections of rock or sand. It is said that there is no path along its northern bank.

The village and river of Pangkung are in Ladakh, and was the route we traversed; but the country on the other side of the lake belongs to Rodokh. We were here met by reports, that an armed force had been stationed on the Gardokh frontier to oppose our entrance into that country, and that a party from Rodokh were at Chushul to arrest our Kashmiri interpreter, Maksúd, and Lagrukh, a servant of the Banka, who had been sent with us as guide.

On the 12th we proceeded, over better roads than usual, to the village of Chushul. On our way we passed a hot-spring, which is reputed to possess medicinal properties; it was of the temperature of 96°, without taste or smell—no enemies made their appearance. From thence we advanced, on the 13th, along the valley of Chushul, over a surface mostly of sand and gravel, partially covered with grass and furze: in many places a quantity of soda was spread over the soil: the valley was watered by several small rivulets. We were now in the haunts of the Kiang, and encountered a drove of sixteen, besides individuals, but they were very wild, and kept too far aloof for our guns to reach them. At our halting-ground we were visited by the men who had been at Chushul on the part of the Zongspun of Rodokh; the principal was a Lama; his three attendants were shepherds: they were merry, good-humoured fellows, and a little explanation made them our friends. Further to tranquillize the apprehensions of their governor, the Goba of Mirak, who happened to be at hand, undertook to transcribe a Tibetan letter which had been prepared by Mr. Moorcroft. The Goba was no great scribe, but he at length accomplished the task. The direction of Rodokh from this was east by south, and the road to it was by an opening in the valley, about a mile and a half from our camp.

For the three next days our route lay along the valley of Chushul, or rather a succession of valleys, separated by low hills of a similar character with that of Chushul. On the 16th we were overtaken by a letter from Mr. Guthrie, apprizing us that some persons had arrived at Lé from Yarkand, who had been sent by the Chinese government to ascertain if the representation given of us by Mir Izzet Ullah was correct. On the receipt of this advice, Mr. Moorcroft thought it advisable to return with all possible expedition to Lé, leaving me to prosecute alone the object of our excursion.

CHAPTER VII.

Pass of Tsaka La—Plain of Kag-jung, near the Sinh-kha-bah—Boundary of Ladakh—La Ganskiel pass—Messengers from Rodokh and Gardokh—Herds of Kiangs—Speed—Colour—Size—Return—Man-bar pass—Plain of Long Kong-ma—Cattle—Shepherds — Tank-tse—Merry-making—Pony-race—Durgukh—Chang-la pass—Severe Cold—Man frozen to death—Negotiations at Yarkand—Arrival of Messengers from Kashgar—Reply of the Khalun—Misrepresented by the Kashmirians—Other Letters prepared—Mir Izzet Ullah dismissed from Yarkand—First Dispatch sent by Abdul Latif—Proceedings at Lé—Disputes with Kulu and Balti—Seditious Placard.

After the departure of Mr. Moorcroft, I continued the day's route to the termination of the valley, and crossed by an easy ascent the pass of Tsaka La; its elevation, however, could not be less than fifteen thousand feet. On descending from it we came to the valley of Kongs-kok. Having loitered to watch some animals, which appeared like wild goats, I was overtaken by darkness, and whilst endeavouring to pick my way, was surprised by the tread and snorting of a considerable body of cattle; they fled, however, as I approached, and when I returned to the camp, I was told by the servants that a large herd, a hundred perhaps, of Kiangs had been seen by them.

Near our encampment, which was at a place called Ralmang, was a large house, the residence of a Lama, who was a kind of deputy to the Banka. He paid me a visit and was very civil. A rivulet on our right ran towards the Sinh-kha-bah, which was not above four miles in a horizontal distance to the south-east.

The hills on our left were low and rounded, and consisted apparently of clay-slate, although fragments of granite, quartz, and sandstone were strewn upon their sides; along their base grew a streak of furze and coarse grass, and patches of soda were visible. The path was over a gravel slope, which continued to the great river, being separated from it by a bed of sand bearing grass, but no wood. A strip of the same description extends along its left bank, and is bounded by steep hills.

On the 18th we encamped at Kag-jung, within one thousand five hundred paces of the

Sinh-kha-bah on our right. The tract along its borders consisted of a loose sand, with thin tufts of the Long-ma, or sand-grass, not sufficient to protect it from being raised in large clouds by the wind. Yet bare and desolate as the scene appeared, it was less so than other parts of Ladakh; and from December to February the flocks of Rup-shu are pastured in these plains, being sheltered at night by stone enclosures; these are chiefly on the other side of the river, and are further screened from the prevailing winds by the hills to their south.

On the 19th and 20th we continued to ascend the valley of the river, at various but inconsiderable distances, on our right. It was in general nearly sixty yards across, and appeared deep, but it was in most parts completely, or partly frozen over: the valley was about three miles broad. We halted near a stone-fold, called Chibra, and determined, after two or three days' rest, to return, as the boundary of Ladakh was pointed out to us as extending from the angle of a hill about five miles to the east, to the low pass of La Ganskiel, on the road to Gardokh, about fourteen miles distant to the southward.

The course of the river was visible for several miles, skirting the base of a line of hills rounded by the Gardokh road. The plain on which we were encamped was studded with small ponds or lakes, one of which was one thousand six hundred paces in circumference, and round the margin of each was a broad bed of soda. There were a great number of small pits, as if the soil had been removed for the extraction of the salt. A rivulet crossed the plain to the river, which was here divided by an island. In the winter the Gardokh traders, with their laden sheep, cross the Sinh-kha-bah on the ice. In the summer men and yaks ford it, either below Kag-jung, or near the Ganskiel pass.

On the morning of the 21st, we were visited by the Lama of Rodokh, who brought us a letter and a present of tea from his master. Although apparently well disposed, he was urgent with us to return, as, if snow should fall, the cold, he said, would be intense. To say the truth, we had reason to believe in his report, for though the day was beautifully clear, the north-west wind was benumbingly keen. I should think snow rarely falls in this plain; but storms of it were hovering on the tops of the hills, and the snow on some of them seemed to have withstood the summer's heat.

The Rodokh Lama had scarcely departed, when a person from Gardokh arrived to learn our intended movements; he had come from Gun-la, which was not above three days' journey. We regaled him with tea, and sent him back with a present and a civil message to his chief.

We saw many large herds of the Kiang, and I made numerous attempts to bring one down, but with invariably bad success. Some were wounded, but not sufficiently to check their speed, and they quickly bounded up the rocks, where it was impossible to follow. They would afford excellent sport to four or five men well mounted, but a single individual has no chance. The Kiang allows his pursuer to approach no nearer than five or six hundred yards; he then trots off, turns, looks, and waits until you are almost within distance, when he is off again. If fired at he is frightened and scampers off altogether. The Chan-than people sometimes catch them by snares, sometimes shoot them. From all I have seen of the animal, I should pronounce him to be neither a horse nor an ass. His shape is as much like that of the one as the other; but his cry is more like braying than neighing. The prevailing colour is a light reddish-chesnut; but the nose, the under-part of the lower-jaw and neck, the belly and legs, are white; the mane is dun and erect; the ears are moderately long; the tail bare and reaching a little below the hock; the height is about fourteen hands. The form, from the fore to the hind-leg and feet, to a level with the back, is more square than that of an ass, his back is less straight, and there is a dip behind the withers, and rounding of the crupper, which is more like the shape of the horse; his neck is also more erect and arched than that of the ass. He is, perhaps, more allied to the Quagha, but is without stripes, except a reported one along each side of the back to the tail. These were distinctly seen on a foal, but were not distinguished in the adults. Whilst engaged in the pursuit of the Kiang I came occasionally upon wild goats; they were rather higher than the sheep, long in leg, and spare in body, with a light head and neck, and curved horns of a moderate size. They bounded off as I approached exactly like deer.

On the morning of the 23rd we commenced our return march to Lé. At Chibra we were joined by five men and a boy, servants of the Khalun, with one hundred and fifty-six sheep loads of shawl-wool, and three or four of coarse wool; each load being about thirty pounds, and the value of each pack eight or nine rupees. They had been eleven months absent from Lé.

On the 26th we halted at Ralmang again, and I promised a reward of eight rupees for a kiang, and four for a wild goat: a shikari was sent us by the Lama, whom I sent out accompanied by a servant: they were absent the whole day, and reported on their return that one animal had been wounded, so that he must die in a few hours, and might be brought in next morning. On the following morning, however, the shikari did not make his appearance, and although I went out to look for the kiang he said he had wounded, no traces of any such animal were discovered. The Lama paid me several visits; he had been a great traveller, having been in China, and he was with the Lama at Kanre when Mr. Moorcroft visited the Lake of Mapang. In the house he inhabited, and another in its vicinity, were six Lamas, four other men, and fourteen women and children. On the 27th we recrossed the pass of Tsaka La; kiangs had been numerous all the way to the pass, but few were met with beyond it. Hares were in immense numbers, and partridges were frequent. At our encampment of the 28th the Gardokh messenger again appeared, bringing back the present I had sent the Garphan, who, he said, was highly incensed with him for having accepted it. On the 29th we reached Chushul, and from thence determined to proceed by the shorter road, that of Long Kong-ma to Lé. At Chushul a man brought me the head and feet, and part of the skin of a kiang, which he had killed some days before we first passed the village.

The road from Chushul to the foot of the Man-bar pass, occupied the whole of the 1st of December, and we crossed it on the following day; the ascent was not very difficult, though the elevation of the pass could not be less than sixteen thousand five hundred feet. From this we descended to the plain of Long Kong-ma, which was thinly covered with snow; a rivulet along its south-west edge was frozen, but was skirted by grass, on which above two hundred yaks were pasturing, the property, as well as five hundred sheep, of the Goba of Chushul, who with twenty attendants had halted in the vicinity. From Long Kong-ma, he was going to Kag-jung, where he purposed remaining with his cattle for two months. The Gobas of Pangkung and Rup-shu repair thither at the same time with their flocks and herds. On the 3rd the road continued along a series of narrow valleys, stopping in that of Long Yukma. On the whole road we were accompanied or encountered by droves of sheep and yaks, pastured during the winter in these valleys, or about to move to the more productive plains of Kag-jung; the cattle and their attendants, and the black blanket tents of the latter, surrounded by wild and snow-tipped mountains, presented many interesting pictures of the life of the Tartar shepherds: notwithstanding the exposure and privation they undergo, the shepherds are a merry race, and their tents at night resounded with laughter and jollity.

At about two miles on the road, on our march of the 4th December, a large body of water gushing from the foot of the rock crossed the road, and formed a pond on the right of it, from whence it flowed to the river of Durgukh; a few miles beyond this the pastures of Chushul terminated, and the district of Tanktse commenced. We halted at the town of the same name.

Having left the sheep and other cattle to refresh themselves in the Long Yukma valley, I awaited their overtaking me at Tanktse. From hence to Tagar are two roads, one over the Chang-la, and the other by the Ski-la pass; the latter was the shorter but more laborious, and had not been travelled lately, so that its state was uncertain, and I determined, therefore, to prefer the more circuitous route. At Tanktse I obtained a lodging in one of the houses; it was not very commodious or cleanly, but my host and his family were good-humoured, and very hospitable. On the evening of the 5th my people joined me, but our provisions were exhausted, and

I applied, therefore, for assistance to the Karphun. I found him in the midst of revelry, in a court-yard converted into a room by spreading a blanket over it; he was seated on a cushion close to the wall, with the Lamas and head men of his own and the neighbouring villages on either hand of him; in front of him sat the other people in rows, whilst the women in their gala dresses stood on piles of earth round the low walls of the court. The mirth was vociferous, but the only ingredients of the feast were cakes of barley-meal, kneaded with water into bricks, of which a large heap stood before the Karphun, and chang, from an immense cauldron-shaped vessel: both were unsparingly distributed, and simple as was the fare, the enjoyment was more genuine than at many a much more sumptuous banquet in a civilized country. The assistance I required was immediately given, and I was pressed to join the revel; this, however, I civilly declined.

On the afternoon of the 6th at Tanktse, the speed of the ponies of the neighbourhood was tried on a small strip of land about four hundred yards long. The cavalcade was headed by the nephew of the Karphun, and was preceded by a party of females gaily dressed, carrying jars of chang, which were placed at the goal, for which the horsemen started without any regularity. At Lé a similar race takes place at this time, with the addition of a mark to be shot at with the bow and arrow. This, however, is at so short a distance that it cannot well be missed. In the evening there was another feast of chang and barley-cakes: in the course of it the Karphun addressed a long speech to a man and woman seated near him, who were distinguished by a number of white crape and silk scarfs round their necks. It was said that they were the host and hostess; both of them wept violently before the conclusion of the speech.

On the 7th we set off and reached Durgukh without any material occurrence; on the next day we encamped at the pond of Tsaltak, which was now completely frozen; all around wore the aspect of winter, and the faint gleams of sunshine on the snowy pinnacles of the mountains, served only to light up their dreariness. On the morning of the

9th, at an early hour when we started, the thermometer was 6° below zero. The nose-rings of the yaks were frozen to the gristle, and the human breath turned to ice on the collars of the sheep-skin mantles; this lasted till some time after the sun had risen: it was noon before we had completed the ascent of the pass. Several of the people complained of pain in the head and chest, and one or two would have stopped in despair, if threats and entreaties had not been liberally administered: yet women and girls were traversing the path without fear or apparent fatigue. We were somewhat delayed by large flocks of sheep on their way to Durgukh, but at sunset we were safe again at Taghar, with exception of one man, who was unfortunately lost in the snow. This was a Hindu, a native of Tirhut, of the name of Sibu, who had remained behind with the sheep that carried our loads. An excellent Ladakh dog that was attending the flock had run away from it, and followed us to Taghar. Sibu missing the dog, imagined he had been left behind, and returned to Tank-tse to seek him. Finding that he was not there, he set off, contrary to the remonstrances of the Karphun, to cross the Chang-la by himself. He was seen by two of the Khalun's men on the ascent of the pass late in the afternoon, and was strongly advised to go no farther. He persisted, however, and the next traveller that went that way found his lifeless corpse. He had been benighted, had sat down on the road, and had been frozen to death. It was not until some days after our return to Lé that we learned his fate.

---

* Upon receiving intelligence of the arrival of a mission from Yarkand at Lé, I immediately returned with all speed to the capital, leaving tents and baggage, and trusting to the hospitality of the peasantry for food and shelter at night. A few days brought me back, but before I returned the couriers had departed. It appeared that Mir Izzet Ullah, supported by the Mohammedans of Turkistan at Yarkand, had prevailed upon the authorities to consent to my visit, and a day was appointed for signing the passport; when the Kashmir merchants, trembling for the loss of their

* Mr. Moorcroft's journal is here resumed.—Ed.

monopoly of the shawl-wool trade through European interference, so wrought upon the jealous and timid disposition of the Chinese governor, that he thought it necessary to make a reference to the superior functionaries at Kashgar. From Kashgar a deputation was sent to Yarkand, and a council held, before which the Mir and one Nakaju, a Kashmirian, who was our chief opponent, were examined. The commissioners evinced gross ignorance, but upon the whole, a disposition to be just, and the chief objection was the want of a precedent; all merchants on the custom records being arranged in two classes, Indejanis and Kashmiris, to neither of which we belonged. The result was another reference to Kashgar, from which came an order that no passport should be granted. The Hakim of Yarkand, however, willing apparently to keep open a chance of our success, directed the chief Kashmiri merchants at Yarkand to write to their friends at Lé, to ascertain precise information concerning us, and these were the letters which had arrived, and been so precipitately replied to before my return.

Upon expressing a desire to see the letter which the Khalun had written in reply, and which had been intrusted to a Kashmiri merchant, a paper was produced, which was said to contain the purport, though not the precise terms of the letter, the original draft having been lost. As this was rather a suspicious circumstance, and induced me to conclude that the Kashmirians, presuming on the Khalun's unacquaintance with Persian, in which language the letter had been written, had misrepresented his expressions, I had a copy made of the document which was produced, and had it attested by the Khalun. I also assembled the Kashmiri merchants, and persuaded them, as they pretended to be my friends, to draw up and sign a true account of our proceedings, and a testimonial to our mercantile character, which might satisfy the Chinese governor of Yarkand of our intentions. These papers I purposed forwarding to Yarkand by a person in whom I could confide.

In the meantime Mir Izzet Ullah had been ordered to quit Yarkand: meeting, on his way, with the couriers from that city, and learning what had passed, he suspected some foul play, and partly by persuasion, and partly by menace, succeeded in getting possession of their despatches, and inducing them to return with him to Lé. As soon as he arrived and apprized me of what had passed, I requested the Khalun to call a meeting of the Kashmiris, and in his presence, restoring to each man from whom a letter had gone, his epistle unopened, I called upon him to communicate its contents, if they were such as he dared avouch, leaving him to keep silence if the purport was at variance with his professions. There was a general silence, and each man seemed well pleased that his secret was not betrayed: this, however, availed them but little, for the Khalun unhesitatingly placed that which he had signed in my hand, and it soon appeared that it differed essentially not only in terms but in tenor from that which had been shown to me as the draft of it. Upon this I addressed the Kashmiris, and reproached them for their duplicity, their ingratitude, the attempts which I attributed to them against the life of Mr. Trebeck and myself, and their undoubted activity in frustrating my projects; and I announced to them that instead of forbearing to interfere with their trade, as I had hitherto scrupulously done, I would enter into the market as a purchaser of wool and tea, which, as they well knew, would be ruinous to their interests, unless they came forward to remedy the evil they had caused. At the close of my address, which they admitted they fully understood, they requested leave to consult together for a day or two, when they would give a reply. The result was a letter from them conjointly, of a very different tenor, no doubt, from that of their first despatches, and a favourable letter from the Khalun, both of which were despatched by a servant of the latter, accompanied by Abdul Latif, as my agent. These measures were necessary for our vindication, but their success with the short-sighted and prejudiced Chinese was more than doubtful.

Along with Mir Izzet Ullah, the physician of Omár Khan, the ruler of Fergana, had come to Lé, and, having taken an interest in my surgical operations, wrote a letter to his master in my favour, requesting him to interfere on my behalf at Yarkand. Omar

Khan's support would have been much more effective than the letters from Ladakh, as he had on several occasions treated the Chinese with a spirit and firmness that compelled them to treat him with deference. A Turani merchant of Yarkand undertook to convey a letter and a small present from me to the king at Indejan, and I would have gone thither myself, but the road by Serik-kol was shut up by snow, and the only route open was that by Yarkand.

The severity of the winter now confined us to Lé, and very much to the house, in which my time and thoughts were chiefly engaged in administering medicines and performing surgical operations, especially for cataracts, of which the cases were numerous. Notwithstanding, however, I sedulously disclaimed all pretensions to a political character, I could not decline compliance with the urgent application of the court to interfere in a dispute between Ladakh and Kulu, as far as a friendly remonstrance with Sobha Ram, the Vazir of Kulu, was calculated to have any effect. Some traders of Kulu had been detected in an illicit trade in shawl-wool on the frontier, and their goods had been seized: they had complained to the Vazir, and he had retaliated by sending an armed party into Ladakh, which had carried off a large number of horses and other cattle, and violated the sanctity of the temple by mutilating the images. The immediate consequence of this was the interruption of the trade, for the Lahoul carriers were afraid of reprisals if they ventured into Ladakh, and a considerable quantity of merchandise for Turkistan was detained on the frontier. The traders at Lé to whom it belonged, and the Chugzuts, conceiving a representation from me might remove the difficulty, by effecting a reconciliation, obtained a letter from me, but the bearers perished in the snow, and no adjustment was effected. The object of the Kulu Vazir, whatever might be pretended, was, no doubt, to raise means for paying the exactions of Ranjit Sinh.

Again, a person in the confidence of the Balti Raja, offered, on his part, to submit to my decision the matters in dispute between him and the government of Ladakh, but in this I declined to interfere, at least, without written credentials, when I was willing to interpose my good offices, as a friend to both parties.

A circumstance of a more serious nature, and likely to have compromised me with the government, had they not possessed full confidence in me, was the appearance of a seditious placard, which was affixed by night at one of the gates of the city. This paper contrasted the beneficent and able rule of the late Raja with that of the present, charged the latter with many acts of tyranny, and warned him that, if he did not alter his conduct, the most respectable of his subjects, according to a resolution already adopted, would depose him, and request the principal European now at Lé to assume the government. Whether this was seriously intended, or was meant only to render me an object of suspicion, was doubtful. It completely failed if the latter was its object, for I heard nothing of it for several days after it had been taken down, and no change occurred in my familiar and confidential intercourse with the ministers.

The interruption of all communication for

some months accounted for the non-arrival of information from Yarkand in reply to our despatches, during the winter. When the passes were opened, however, they were still delayed, and it was evident that it would be of no avail to expect them much longer. Unwilling, however, to relinquish the hope of penetrating by this route until all prospect of it must positively be resigned, I protracted my residence at Lé into the summer of 1822. In the middle of that year two excursions were performed, one by myself to Dras, on the road to Kashmir, the other by my companion to Piti, the province bordering on Bisahar.

END OF VOLUME I.

TRAVELS
IN THE
HIMALAYAN PROVINCES OF HINDUSTAN
AND THE PANJAB;
IN
LADAKH AND KASHMIR;
IN PESHAWAR, KABUL, KUNDUZ,
AND
BOKHARA

FORT and VILLAGE of DANKAR in LADAKH.

TRAVELS

IN THE

HIMALAYAN PROVINCES OF HINDUSTAN AND THE PANJAB;

IN

LADAKH AND KASHMIR; IN PESHAWAR, KABUL, KUNDUZ, AND BOKHARA;

BY

MR. WILLIAM MOORCROFT AND MR. GEORGE TREBECK,

FROM 1819 TO 1825

Prepared for the Press, from Original Journals and Correspondence.

By Horace Hayman Wilson, M.A., F.R.S.,

Member of the Royal Asiatic Society, and of the Asiatic Societies of Paris and Calcutta; of the Imperial Society of Naturalists of Moscow; of the Royal Academies of Berlin and Munich, etc. etc.; And Professor of Sanscrit in the University of Oxford.

Two Volumes

Vol. II

GYAN

Published by

Gyan Publishing House
5, Ansari Road
Daryaganj, New Delhi-110002
Phone: 011-47034999, 9811692060
E-mail: books@gyanbooks.com

Distribution Network
gyanbooks.com
India, USA, Canada, UK, Australia, France

ISBN : 978-81-212-4144-1 (Set)
ISBN : 978-81-212-4724-5 (HB)
First Published, London, 1841

2nd Impression 2020

Printed at: Gyan Press, Delhi.

Travels in the Himalayan Provinces of Hindustan and the Panjab
in
Ladakh and Kashmir;
In Peshawar, Kabul, Kunduz, and Bokhara;
Author: Mr. William Moorcroft and Mr. George Trebeck

CONTENTS OF VOL. II.

PART II.

CHAPTER VIII.

CHAPTER IX.

PART III.

CHAPTER I.

CHAPTER II.

CHAPTER III.

CHAPTER IV.

CHAPTER V.

CHAPTER VI.

CHAPTER VII.

PART IV.

CHAPTER I.

CHAPTER II.

CHAPTER III.

CHAPTER IV.

CHAPTER V.

TRAVELS

IN

THE PANJAB, LADAKH, KASHMIR,

&c.

PART II.—RESIDENCE IN LADAKH.

CHAPTER VIII.

Mr. Moorcroft's Journey to Dras—Lucerne—Flowering Plants—Nimo—Bagzo—Saspula Orchards — Lime-pounding — Village Pestle— Himis — Native Physician—Sneurla—Khalets—Chumas or Nuns—Sanga across the river—Northward course of the Sinh-kha-bab—Lama Yuru—Temples and Lamas—Religious Ceremonies—Musical Instruments—Pass of Phatu La—Kanji River — Hiunaskoth — Kherbo — Laghan — Nam-chu Pass — Zakut River—Figure of Chamba sculptured in the rock—Molbi—Nurse of the Nuna Khalun—Lotzun—Physicians—Gratitude of the People—Game of Polo—Interview with the Raja—Old Bible—Pushkyum—Course of the Pushkyum and Dras Rivers—Kartse River—Village of Gonh — Prevalence of Goître—Kartse Cheles — Neat Cattle — Butter—Sheep—Schoolmasters—Mohammedanism—Altered Costume—Deviation to Pharol—Nakpo River—Sankho—Omba Lá Pass—Marmots—Pass of Zwaje La—View of the Valley of Himbab, or Dras—Visit to the Nuna Khalun—Bed lost in the river—Native Attendants—Valley of Dras—Climate—Population—Character of the People—Prangos.

At the same time that my young friend was dispatched to Piti I undertook an excursion to Dras, and left Lé for that purpose on the

10th of June. The sowing of wheat had been finished at the end of May, and the most forward plants were now five inches high. Pease and beans were also above the ground. Lucerne was only just bushing where the soil was dry, but where it was well watered it was full and high. In Ladakh this grass is almost an aquatic; though in India it perishes if long under water in the rainy season. It is also worthy of remark, that in this country pure gravel, without mould or clay, will rear lucerne if it be plentifully watered. The plants now in flower were varieties of the iris, dog-rose, butter-cup, shepherd's-purse, and clematis. The ordinary birds of the country were flying about, except the geese and ducks, which had deserted the river and had gone to breed in the mountains. Flies were not numerous, but there were musquitoes on the low grounds. Our camp was pitched in a willow-garden, near the Phiang rivulet, where I remained next day, to acknowledge letters I had received in the night from Hindustan by way of Kashmir.

Part of the road from Nimo to Bagzo lies through the cultivated fields of the former,

now under barley and wheat, of which the former was in ear, and part over a sandy barren, bounded on the left by the river, and on the right by low alluvial mountains, formed from the ruins of the nearest primary range. The lands of Bagzo lie in a slope, beginning narrow from the north-west, and widening to the east, and consist of a reddish clay. The crops were good, but neither so rich nor forward as at Nimo. The town was perched upon the face of a rock, and was formerly defended by works to the east and west, which were now in ruins. This is the case with all similar structures in Ladakh, and argues either a feeling of security or the poverty of the state.

The road beyond Bagzo leads along a narrow water-way, flanked by pebble and clay walls, and ascends to a line of the structures called Mani-panis: it then divides; the right path going by Ling to Himis, and the left by Saspula; the former, though the more circuitous, is that taken with loaded cattle, as the latter, leading over the pass of Lagang Kuje, in the hills which from Nimo intervene between the road and the river, is more difficult. Saspula, on the right bank of the

river, is celebrated for its apricots. Amongst its orchards I noticed several of the trees with rams' horns let into the bark, and so covered by it as to be at first undistinguishable. They were in general inserted in the angle formed between a branch and the stem. Upon inquiring the meaning of this addition, it was stated that the horns were thus engrafted as a propitiatory offering at the time of an eclipse, and that trees so honoured bore ever afterwards an unfailing crop of the choicest fruit. At Saspula the Lompa had a house: his wife, who was a daughter of the Giah Raja, and apparently twice as old as her husband, sent me some flour, dried apricots, and apples, and turnip-tops as greens, with her regret that her husband was not at home to show me suitable attention. At this place I observed some women engaged in pounding lime. The mortar was a hole cut in a block of stone, and the pestle a heavy oblong stone rounded at the end. This apparatus is usually public property; one sometimes serves for a village, but, in general, one is found at each extremity of it. When the lime was pounded it was burnt and mixed with water, to form a white-wash

for the exterior of the houses. These public mortars are applied to various uses, as to the bruising of rape and mustard-seed, which are then kneaded and squeezed with warm water for the extraction of their oil. Apricot kernels are treated in the same way, and the fragrant oil expressed from them is used by the women for their hair. The mortar is also employed for bruising the wild madder-root, which, mixed with aluminous earth and pyrites, forms a brown dye for the woollen dresses of the men, and the trousers of women. The most frequent employment of the mortar, however, is the reduction of dried goats' dung to a fine powder, which thickly laid upon a sheep-skin with the wool outwards, forms the only bedding provided for infants until they are more than a twelvemonth old. The advantage of the powder is, that any part of it which is incidentally moistened can be readily removed and replaced.

From Saspula we proceeded along the skirts of the clay-hills on our right, and ascended to a single house, surrounded by cultivation, where the two roads from Bagzo to Himis reunite. From thence we continued our route over un-

dulating ground, the main line of hills which ran east and west being frequently interrupted by small glens and valleys, crossing it from north to south, and giving passage to rivulets flowing towards the Sinh-kha-bab. After crossing one of these by a sanga, we came to the village of Himis, consisting of a number of houses scattered irregularly over the sides of a green hill, and down a valley leading to the main river. The lofty mountains on the opposite side of the river were discernible from the high ground, and were tipped with snow.

When I was setting off from Himis, on the 15th of June, the physician of the lower village arrived in breathless haste, bringing me a present of some wheaten cakes, and a copper tea-pot, beautifully ornamented with fretwork of brass. It was of the manufacture of Chi Ling, opposite to Saspula, and had cost ten rupees. On expressing my regret at his having taken such unnecessary trouble, he replied that it was the duty of the hakim (the doctor) of any place visited by the sirdar or chief of hakims, to show their respect, and he was only sorry that he was so late.

He had been present, it appeared, at an operation I had successfuly performed on the eyes of Tsangre Sundar, of Chuchut. I of course acknowledged his civility, and made him a present of a gum lancet in return; an instrument not essentially differing in form, but infinitely superior in finish and sharpness, to the stakpo, or lancet used in Ladakh for venesection.

The road from Himis to Sneurla, after continuing some way on high ground, crosses what may be considered a pass; and then, for the most part, descends towards the village. On the way it approaches close to the right bank of the Indus, and meets a lower road, used by foot passengers, along the river, from Saspula. Sneurla, or, as the Kashmirians call it, Nur-ullah, is near the river, and is lower and warmer than the country we have yet passed. Trees were in consequence more numerous, and, in addition to the usual fruit-trees, willows and poplars abounded, and the fragrant sirsing was plentiful. I observed also, besides the single rose, the double rose, or maiden's blush, and the blue sweet-scented columbine, called by a native name signify-

ing asses' sugar (bombo khaira); why, I could not learn. Here I first noticed the appearance of any unhealthiness amongst the apple-trees, which may arise from the thinness of the soil.

From Sneurla the road passed along the right bank of the Sinh-kha-bab, which was about thirty yards broad, and rolled along with great rapidity and high broken waves. High-peaked mountains approached close to the left bank, but left a narrow slip of land, along which huts, orchards, and cultivated fields were occasionally visible. The hills on the right bank also approached, at times, near to the river; but they were neither precipitous nor lofty, and consisted of schistus and red clay. After crossing a deep water-course we came to the village of Khalets, or Khaletse, one of the largest in Ladakh. It has more orchard-trees than Sneurla, and amongst them the walnut, which produces very fine fruit. The river flows near it, but considerably below its level: at first sight, the situation appears unfavourable, presenting to southward a line of towering rocks, and encircled, nearly from east to west, by a ridge of brown and barren

hills. The cultivated ground is, however, of good quality, though rather incommodiously laid out in terraces. The grain sown here ripens in three months, and a second crop of buck-wheat or of turnips is obtained from the same soil.

A kind of sherbet is common here, made by mixing water with dried apples or apricots pounded. A number of chumas, or Buddhist nuns, were met with, who were very curious about my objects, my dress, habits, &c., apologising at the same time, with unaffected civility, for being so inquisitive. When we started early in the morning of the 17th, the women of the village were abroad, some watering the corn-fields, some collecting grass for their flocks, and some preparing the web for their woollen cloth. The cattle of the village had escaped the epidemic better than most, and formed a flock of eight hundred sheep and goats, chiefly the latter.

Immediately beyond Khalets we came to a wall and door-way leading to a sanga across the river. The bridge was substantially constructed, resting on two scarped rocks, and was about thirty yards long. The river was not

more than twenty yards broad, and was rolling black and impetuously about twelve feet below it*. On the left bank the path led under an arched passage through a tall Manipani.

After following the left bank of the Sinhkha-bab for a short distance, we took our final leave of it, as it turned off towards the north. Its course could be discerned for some way to west, half north, and then again more northerly still, between low gravelly hills, along the summit of which, on its right bank, was a good road, going, it was said, to Balti. At the point where we quitted it it was joined by the Yunga-chu, a considerable rivulet coming from the west, and repeatedly intersecting the road. It was crossed by rough sangas. As we ascended the road was contracted by the advancing rocks on either hand, to a narrow defile, scarcely leaving a path sometimes

* It is worthy of notice, that when Mr. Trebeck crossed the same bridge on the following November, he observed it was "forty-five or fifty feet above the water." Admitting that neither statement may be quite correct, the error cannot exceed a few feet, and the two accounts afford satisfactory evidence of the great rise of the river in the summer months, occasioned by the melting of the snow on the adjacent mountains.—ED.

along the edge of the stream. On quitting the course of the main rivulet, the path continued along much the same sort of dell, until we approached the monastery and village of Lama Yuru, where it widened into a valley about two hundred paces broad.

Lama Yuru is the site of a very large establishment of Gelums and Chumas, amounting, according to some accounts, to five hundred. They do not all reside together, but are dispersed amongst the people, as in every house there is a chamber appropriated to the Deity, and to a Gelum, whose business it is to place food and lights before the image, repeating prayers and beating a drum. They are all subject to one chief, who is a native of Lassa, and whose authority extends over the whole country west of Lé. He divides his time between Phiang and this place, living a year at each alternately. There were three temples at Lama Yuru; the principal one was situated on the top of a low hill, on the sides and along the base of which were the houses of the village, about a hundred in number. These were built, as usual, of brick and wood, and were painted red and white, denoting their

dependence upon the monastery. The situation was elevated and cold, and fruit-trees were rare; cultivation was late, and there was rather a deficiency of water for irrigation.

One of my horses having slipped into the rivulet on our march, and, although extricated, much bruised and cut by his fall, I deemed it advisable to halt a day (June 18) at this place, and availed myself of the opportunity to witness the religious service of the Lamas. They were summoned to prayers about eight o'clock by the beat of a drum. Each, as he entered the temple, raised his joined hands above his head, then opened, and again closed them before his breast. Next he placed them on the ground, so as to rest upon them whilst touching the floor with his forehead, in prostration before the images of Sakya Muni and his sanctified disciples and successors. The Lamas then sat down in rows from east to west, from the door to the shrine, upon cushions of felt, or low wooden benches. One of them had a sort of reading-desk before him, with the leaves of a book, from which he read, and was followed by the rest in the recita-

tion. They then began a performance of instrumental music, almost each man being provided with some instrument. The majority had small flat drums, but I noticed also two horns or cornets of copper, two large cymbals, two hautboys, two trumpets, and a bell. The hautboys were made of wood, with silver mouth-pieces, and shifting reeds. The trumpets were of copper, eight or ten feet long, and made with three joints, like those of a telescope. The open end was about five inches in diameter, the mouthpiece small. The tone was clear and deep, and might be heard to a great distance, but it requires long practice to blow the instrument properly. Nothing could be harsher than the sounds emitted by unpractised players,. In the temple the trumpet rested on the ground: when used in processions a young Lama assists in carrying it. The drum was not above five inches deep, and about twenty in breadth. It was suspended by a ring on one side to a cord stretched across the chamber, and, being steadied by the player with his left hand, was beaten by him with a crooked metallic rod, capped with

leather on the striking end. The recitations or chants alternated with the music, which, though monotonous, was not unpleasing, and the strength and spirit of the singers and players were kept up by copious libations of tea and chang.

The monastery of Lama Yuru is invested with the privileges of a sanctuary, which they assert have been confirmed to it by edicts from the Emperors of Delhi and their governors of Kashmir. Documents which they showed me, with the seals of Aurungzeb, Fidai Khan, and Shir Khan, were, however, only to the purpose of directing that the Gelums should not be disturbed in their religious usages, and that their lands should not be encroached upon. A similar injunction has lately been obtained by them from Ahmed Shah, the Shiah Raja of Balti, drawn up in more explicit language, and a still more liberal spirit. At the request of the acting superior I left with him a paper expressing my acknowledgments of his hospitality.

The neighbourhood of Lama Yuru abounds with wild goats, but the Lamas objected to

our shooting any, as animal, as well as human life,.should be sacred within the precincts of their sanctuary. Mr. Guthrie, however, brought one down amongst the rocks at some distance. He was too much injured by falling from a height to admit of very particular description, but the general character was allied both to the sheep and the deer. From Lama Yuru a road goes to Zanskar, which is said to be a journey of six days.

The road from Lama Yuru continued rough and ascending, until it crossed the crest of the Phatu La, a lofty pass, of the elevation of nearly fourteen thousand feet, in the ravines and recesses, adjoining which beds of snow were observable. After descending we proceeded along the right bank of the Kanji, a mountain stream coming from the southward at no great distance, and fed by different watercourses which crossed our path. Beyond the village or town of Eunasko *, a place consisting of about twenty-five houses and an old fort, the river was crossed by a sanga where it was about thirty feet broad, rapid, but not deep. Farther on at Kherbo,

* Hiunaskoth. Trebeck.

on its left bank, it expanded to a breadth of one hundred and fifty feet. The village of Kherbo was one of several which were situated on the skirts of a long, narrow valley, which was terraced and cultivated. It seemed to be in a state of decay, many of the houses were in ruins, and the people declared they were unable to furnish us with supplies. The poverty and dilapidation of the place were ascribed partly to a snow slip, which had destroyed many dwellings, and partly to the great havoc made by the late epidemic amongst the sheep. A third, and more mischievous cause, was the rapacity of the chief man, or Garpun. In the vicinity of Kherbo were several fortified enclosures, strongly situated on rugged rocks, but more or less in ruins. On this day's march we encountered several showers of rain, and twice we heard thunder, low and distant. The mountains on our right were not lofty, and presented somewhat gentle slopes; those on our left were steeper, but not more elevated. Corn is raised abundantly in this neighbourhood, and the surplus crop is sent, after the harvest, to Lé, where it is exchanged chiefly for salt brought from Chan-than. As there

was no obtaining fuel or fodder at Kherbo we advanced beyond it a short distance to Laghan, a small village on the right bank of the Kanji, in the same valley.

Crossing the river we advanced along its left bank to the village of Kanre, whence the Kanji runs off to the northward and falls into the Indus*. From hence the road ascended to the pass of Namikar, from which an extensive view presented itself of the valley of Molbi, and of a lofty chain of mountains beyond Kartse, one in particular towering high above the rest, and capped with snow. The descent lay over lower hills of clay soil, covered with a dwarf grass, on which large flocks of goats and Purik sheep were browsing, to a valley watered by a considerable stream, the Zakut, coming from the south-east. This river rises, it is said, about three days' journey off, and, flowing by Molbi and Pushkyum, receives the Kanji, and falls into the Indus. Near the end of this day's journey (20th June) the road

* According to information given to Mr. Moorcroft, the Kanji joins the Pushkyum river before it meets the Indus: from Mr. Trebeck's inquiries, however, it proceeds to the latter direct.—ED.

passed between the foot of the mountains on the right of the valley and an insulated pillar of rock, about fifty feet high. On the face of this was sculptured the figure of one of the Tibetan divinities, named Chamba. It differed from the same representation in the temples in being decorated with the Brahminical cord hanging from the left shoulder and over the right hip. The figure was naked except round the waist, and was about twenty-four feet high, but the lower part was concealed by a low wall in front: the upper had been protected by a screen projecting over it from the rock; but this was gone, leaving only the holes in which the pins that had fastened it had been inserted.

The valley of Molbi is of considerable extent, and several straggling villages occur along the northern bank of the river. On the south the mountains come close to the stream, and are of considerable height. The Nuna Khalun has a residence at Molbi, but he was absent at Dras. His youngest son was in the village, and, during my absence, had come to the enclosure in which my tent was pitched, but had shown no inclination to

give my people any assistance in procuring supplies. I, therefore, determined not to trouble him by any application, and we managed, though indifferently, to dispense with his aid. The nurse of the young man, however, on whom, some time before, I had successfully operated for cataract, brought me a pile of wheat cakes, with some butter, milk, and flowers. The house of the Khalun stood upon the side of a hill, and was of considerable size, though indifferently constructed. Crowning a high rock above it was a building which answered the purpose of a fort. A small toll is levied at Molbi on merchandise, especially on shawl-wool. The next day we marched to the village of Lotzun, along the right bank of the river, and over such rugged ground that our horses were much more distressed and exhausted than on many much longer journeys. I had intended to have gone on to Pushkyum, but at Lotzun I was entreated to stop, and give surgical assistance to several blind persons. The hakim, or physician of the village, cleared a couple of rooms in his house for

the accommodation of my party, and my bed was placed in the viranda of a small mosque, the pillars of which were festooned with wreaths of flowers and ears of corn, presenting a curious mixture of Lamaism and Mohammedanism, the bulk of the people from hence to Kashmir being Mohammedans of the Shiah sect. Every village has its physician, who is called Aba, or father. The physician of Lotzun brought me several patients, including his own son, and before I started on the 22nd I operated on three individuals for cataract. The gratitude of the people was expressed by abundant fees of wheat cakes and butter, which I was obliged to accept, that I might not wound their feelings, as a refusal would have indicated to them my dissatisfaction or disdain.

On the 22nd I resumed the march to Pushkyum, continuing to follow the course of the river. When we arrived near the village we crossed the latter to the left bank by a sanga. At the foot of the bridge a young man ran to my horse, and, after making sundry obeisances, took hold of the flap of

my coat, and put it to his forehead, and, whilst so engaged, was joined by an old man, who went through the same ceremony. They then pressed me to pitch my tent in the shade of some willow trees, where they said I should soon see the Raja. I thought, at first, they were his messengers, but I found that the old man had recovered his sight by an operation I had performed the year before at Lé, and the other was his son. When I had complied with their request they disappeared, but presently returned with provender for our horses, and firewood for ourselves, some flour, and a sheep; and no persuasion could prevail upon them to take back the articles, or receive their value in return. This was the only way, they said, in which they could show their gratitude for the blessing I had conferred upon the old man, and they prayed me not to reject such an expression of their thanks. I, therefore, accepted their presents, and was well pleased, though not at all surprised, to find so lively a sense of obligation entertained by these simple people.

My tent was pitched on a narrow stripe of stony land, between the river and a flat

about two hundred yards long by thirty broad. This, it appeared, was the playground of the village for the game of polo, for presently the Raja arrived on horseback with about forty persons, all mounted, and armed with rackets, who, dividing into two sets, commenced playing with great spirit. On the cessation of the diversion the Raja sent me a pot of tea and a plate of satu, and intimated his wish to see me the next day, when he should return to the Mall. Accordingly on the day following, about noon, he arrived at a sort of summer house, near the playground, where I was invited to meet him. The interview was merely an exchange of civilities, and then he set off again to his sport, in which he received a severe blow from the bat of one of his followers: he bore it with great good humour. It appears he has only of late become a convert to Islam. His wife, who is a daughter of the Nuna Khalun, professes the Buddhist faith. A Sayid, who seemed to act as his ghostly adviser, produced a book which had descended from his grandfather to the Raja, and which proved to be an edition of the Old and New Testament from the Papal press,

dated in the year 1598. It was bound in Morocco, with the initials I. H. S., surmounted by a cross, stamped on each side of the cover. How it had come there no person could inform me, but it might possibly have been given to the former Raja by Desideri, who visited Ladakh, although it is very doubtful if he reached Lé. The Khalun and Khaga Tan-zin made, at my request, very particular inquiry regarding any evidence of a European having been at Lé before us, and no proof nor tradition of such an occurrence could be traced.

Pushkyum consists of a number of houses scattered along two valleys; the eastern is narrow, the western may be half a mile broad, disposed in terraces, and well cultivated with wheat and barley. Lucern was growing in profusion, being cultivated and raised from the seed of the wild mountain lucern. Pushkyum is the principal place between Lé and Kashmir, and although it has no regular bazar, it contains a few shops where flour, butter, rice, and other provisions are to be purchased. The inhabitants are all Mohammedans, and a number of mosques have been erected; but,

in general, they are mean and dirty hovels. Shortly after leaving Pushkyum the river diverged from the road, proceeding more to the north of west. At Kargil, about two kos distant, it meets with the Kartse river coming from the south-west. The united stream shortly afterwards meets another trunk, formed by the union of the rivers of Dras and Shingo, and the whole then flow in one main stream, called the Chudresa, which joins the Sinh-kha-bab at Moral, in Balti, which is said to be four days' journey on foot from Pushkyum. The passage by water, in winter, may be accomplished in a day *. We soon encountered the Kartse river, running with a considerable body of water, and being in some places a hundred feet broad. It is said to rise from the snows of Pinji La, in Zanskar, about six or seven days' journey distant. We crossed

* On the 18th of November Mr. Trebeck, following a rather more northern route, came to the junction of the Dras and Kartse rivers, on the road between Pushkyum and Chenagan: he followed the course of the former, and on the 19th came to the two branches, forming the Kinon Wei from Shingo in Balti, above twenty miles to the north-west, and the Sin Wei, or Dras river. The road then proceeded along the banks of the latter river by Shimsha and Gindial, and leaving the Ombta La on the left, arrived at the end of the valley on the 21st.—Ed.

it by a substantial sanga to the village of Gonh. This village was situated in a close valley, of about three miles long and half a mile broad, divided by the Kartse into two lateral portions. It was flanked by steep and high mountains, the summit of which presented an almost unbroken ridge. The valley sloped gently, and bore a variety of herbage; the houses were scattered along the foot of the rocks. It is said to be cold in winter, and in summer, when there is no wind, it is intensely hot. In these characteristics, however, it partakes with very many of the villages in this part of Ladakh, and they afford no explanation of the great prevalence of goitre here, such indeed as to have given a name to the place, Gonh, meaning enlarged neck. Still less do they explain why the complaint is almost confined to the women, scarcely a woman being free from it, whilst it was rare amongst the men. The latter are like the rest of their countrymen; but the women, when young, have handsome features, and a complexion little darker than brunette. Whatever local cause affects the one sex must equally, it is to be supposed, affect the other, and this case

is only one out of many in which the occurrence of this complaint, so common in the mountain districts, varies in places, and amongst people, to all appearance, similarly circumstanced as to site, climate, water, food, and every presumable predisposing or exciting cause. From Gonh we proceeded along a similar valley to Kartse Cheles, a village in a bottom, with abundance of land in cultivation, the wheat and barley crops on which promised to be fit for the sickle in three weeks. The valley might have been a continuation of that of Gonh, except for the strangulated portion intervening where the rocks left barely space for the passage of the river. Goitre was also common, but it prevailed as much amongst the men as the women, though it was something larger in the latter. The cows of this district were more numerous, and in better condition than any I had seen since leaving the southern hills. They were small, but well shaped, with small horns; the prevailing colour was black, but it varied to pure red, and mixed with white. They are pastured on the hills, during the day, on lucern and white clover, and at night are fed with the

wild oat, gathered from amongst the corn for this purpose. Before being taken to their sheds they browsed upon some common pasture-grass, which was flooded an hour before their return. Two cows were fastened together by a rope attached to willow rings passed through their noses, and children were employed to prevent their straying.

The butter looked well, and as I had not tasted any in its natural state for two years, I promised myself a treat. I was disappointed, for it retained too much of the musty flavour of the old and unwashed skin in which it had been churned to be palatable. The yak, it is said, cannot live here, but the female thoma, from the male yak and the common cow, was numerous and handsome. It was said to give more milk than the cow. The sheep were small but of pretty good fleece. The lucern-fields of both kinds were good, and the general character of the country was fertility and abundance. The cottages were numerous, scattered along both sides of the river, in so straggling a manner, that it was not very easy to determine the limits of the villages. In each of these was an akhund, or village school-

master, and one or two individuals who could speak Persian or Hindustani. Every village had its mosque, and not a single Lama's house, or sculptured pile, made its appearance. Islamism is evidently making rapid strides, and there is every reason to expect that before long Ladakh will be entirely a Mohammedan state.

The Balti chief had agents in Pushkyum and the vicinity, who were detaching the affections of the peasantry from the government at Lé, and it was whispered that the chiefs of Pushkyum and of Soth meditated throwing off their allegiance, under the protection of the Balti Raja. Soth is but a few hours' journey from Pushkyum, on the right bank of the river, and consists of a village and a fort, the latter on a high and commanding elevation. With the change from Lamaism to Islamism an alteration has taken place in the costume of the women. Instead of the argus jacket and patchwork petticoat, a loose brown or black woollen tunic with sleeves, open in front to below the bosom, hangs from the shoulders nearly to the feet. It is sometimes tied round the waist with a girdle, but is com-

monly left loose in warm weather; underneath it the common dark woollen trowser was retained, but no boots were seen at this season. On the head the Tibetan lappet was displaced by a brown woollen cap; the hair was bound in a tress, and near the end was fastened a flat ornament, round or square, of coloured worsted-work, from which the usual tassels depended. Necklaces of coral or glass beads were worn, and amulets, of a piece of silk, with a verse from the Koran, were bound round the arm. The men had not deviated so much from the national garb, but wore fewer ornaments.

I had promised the Chugzat Lama of Himis that when I reached Kartse I would pay a visit to his brother, the head man, or Chuchu of Tamis, on the opposite bank of the river. The river was, however, now unfordable, and the sanga was high up; it was therefore arranged that I should meet him at Pharol, where he had a residence; and we left Kartse for that place on the 26th. The valley in which it is situated runs nearly north and south, and is divided into two parts by the Kartse Chu. The mountains enclosing it

were lofty, and those on the south were thickly covered with snow. In the day the sun was distressingly hot, whilst at night warm covering was indispensable. Goitre was here very common: the water was soft; whilst at Gonh it was too hard to mix with soap; but so it was at Lé, where goitre does not prevail: at all three it is derived chiefly from melted snow. On the 27th the Chuchu, with his son and several attendants, arrived, and were entertained at my tent.

Hearing from the Chuchu that the sheep, of which I was desirous of collecting a small flock, were likely to be procured more advantageously at some village higher up the river than at Pharol, I set off in that direction. Passing through the cultivated lands of that village, we descended by an easy slope to those of Sankho, on the left bank of the Nakpo chu, or black water. This stream comes from the west, and falls into the Kartse on its left bank. It is formed of two streams, the Mazadi and the Omba, from mountains so named. The water of the former is clear, of the latter dirty black; the latter flowing over the face of some soft black rocks, and

washing down a great quantity of the soil. It discolours the Kartse, along its left bank, for some distance after entering it. Two miles higher up the Kartse receives a considerable accession, on its right bank, from the Pulumba chu, coming from the east in the direction of Zamkar. Part of the road lay through narrow stony lanes, on each side of which the wild rose formed a beautiful and fragrant hedge. At one place a height commanded a view of the lands and villages of Sankho, lying in an amphitheatre bounded by mountains, on the tops of which snow was yet unmelted. The only timber consisted of pollard willows, and some fruit-trees; but the slopes of the hills were diversified by patches of verdure, and numerous flocks of goats and sheep, giving me a more favourable view of the produce of shawl-wool in Ladakh than I had been accustomed to entertain.

On my arrival at Sankho I found that a report of my purpose had preceded me, and so raised the price of the sheep that it was impossible to effect the purchase. I therefore left a commission with the Chuchu to procure for me the requisite number under more favour-

able circumstances, and resumed my journey towards Dras. Goitre was not common at Sankho, but it is said to be much more frequent on the lands on the eastern or right bank of the river in the same valley.

From Sankho we ascended the Nakpo chu along its right bank, a little more than a mile, to the village and lands of Stak-pa, where the sward reminded me of the pastures of Britain, consisting of a poa grass, white clover, plantain, dandelion, dock, bugloss, &c. The cattle were numerous and in good condition. The tilled lands were extensive, and laid out in slopes, but not supported by walls, and in general the cultivation was unusually slovenly for Tibet.

On the 30th of June we commenced the ascent of the steep and difficult pass of the Omba mountain. On the way we crossed the Mizadi, coming from the south-west, and pouring its waters with impetuosity into the Nakpo chu. It was forded with some difficulty, and we had then to ford the Nakpo chu, which was rushing along a broad and stony bed with much foam and fury. On an extensive level, interrupting the ascent, stood the village of

Omba, consisting of three clusters of houses, on the right bank of a rivulet, the Omba-chu coming from the mountain on the north, and joining the Nakpo-chu just below the village. The latter flows from the Braknak mountain, about a mile off, in a direction to the south-west. The situation of Omba was high and the winter had been severe. There were still immense masses of unmelted snow in the bed of the river, and I was told that, during the preceding winter, snow had fallen in the village to the depth of twelve feet, cutting off all communication with the neighbouring village, and sometimes blocking up the people in their houses for a week together. On our way up the ascent, between a village called Undih and Omba, I first met with the Prangos.

On the 1st of July we continued our upward path, and with much labour and difficulty reached the crest of the Omba La. The view from the crest presented a majestic line of snow-covered mountain-tops, very little above the level of the pass, extending round a circle of at least twenty miles in diameter. The uniformity of the ridges was very remarkable, for, although broken with peak and

gorge, yet there were no single mountains or mountain-chains that towered ambitiously above their fellows. The descent was abrupt, but not very difficult, passing occasionally over firm beds of snow, on the edge of which numerous marmots were playing about. Soon after leaving Omba we lost the prangos, but on the descent we met with the rhubarb plant just about to flower, and with a species of garlic, and of chive, the latter with yellow flowers, which are cropped by the marmot and the sheep. The marmots we met with on the ascent were sitting on their hinder legs on stones near their burrows, and on our approach made the rocks echo with their loud and shrill cries. There was no getting within gun-shot of them, as, approach in whatever direction we might, and with whatever precaution, we were sure to be detected by one or other, who immediately shrieked an alarm. I succeeded, however, in hitting one, who, more curious than the rest, repeatedly issued from his hole to look at us, and, although he escaped for the time, we found him next morning dead in his burrow.

At Twaje Chu, where we encamped, we

found a small plain and some walled enclosures, intended as shelters for travellers. The night was excessively cold, and in the morning I found my tent stiff with frozen dew: a sharp wind was blowing, and my people were shivering in spite of sheep-skins and fires. I expected to find the plants of the plain nipped by the sudden and violent transition from a scorching sun to a sharp frost, but I was mistaken, for soon after the rays of the sun had reached them the flowers were open, and as fresh and blooming as if the night had been temperate. On the sides of the mountains to the north-west of the pass, which were moderately clothed with verdure, close to the snow, were several droves of mares and geldings at pasture; they were in general about fourteen hands high, active and strong, in good condition and well-shaped, although rather too long in the back. They belonged to the carriers of Dras, carrying occasionally loads and travellers to Kashmir and Lé.

On the 2nd of July, a road of frequently alternating descent and ascent led us over the summit of a lofty mountain, from whence we had a full view of the valley of Him-bab

(snow-source), or Dras, a long narrow dale, stretching from north-west to east, with a fillet of river running down its centre from end to end, and fed by numerous rills rushing from the rocks on either hand. It was bounded to the west and south by lofty ranges of mountains, forming the eastern limits of Kashmir, and giving rise on one face to the Behut or Jelum, and on the other to the stream which was flowing beneath us. The valley appeared fertile, though not to the extent I had expected from accounts previously received; and, although there were many cottages, they were scattered about in an irregular and straggling manner, forming no village of considerable size. The fields were yellow with crops of wheat and barley, and the slopes of the hills presented patches of verdure. We descended the pass, and encamped in a field of prangos and lucerne.

On the following morning I paid a visit to the Nuna Khalun, who was encamped on the opposite bank of the Om-chu, a rapid and unfordable rivulet, flowing into the Dras river, crossed by a sanga. The Khalun was at breakfast with ten or twelve followers, and

we joined them in a repast of buttered tea. Mr. Guthrie and myself had left the people to follow with our tents and baggage, and a message was brought to me that one of the horses had stumbled in fording the Om-chu; and that his load had been thrown into the water. This proved most unfortunately to consist of my writing-box and bed; the former was broken, but recovered; all its contents, including one of my journals, being wetted: the bed, which was of brass, and so contrived as to fold up in a conveniently small compass, was carried down by the stream, and had disappeared. The Pushkyum Aba, who had accompanied me to learn the operation for cataract, threw himself into the stream to save the horse, but was carried under the water by the animal, and narrowly escaped drowning. A Yarkandi following his example, succeeded in bringing the horse to the bank, but the bed was not to be seen. It was in vain that I set people to search for it, as no traces of it were discovered; the rapidity of the current, and the diurnal increase of its waters from the melting of the snows at this season, rendering it dangerous to explore

its bed. The Khalun promised that it should be carefully searched for whenever opportunity permitted, but I had no expectation of recovering it, and I never saw it again. The accident was the more vexatious, as it proceeded entirely from the carelessness of the Hindustani Sais. If any European follow my track, I should strongly recommend him not to bring with him any Hindustani servants. In the winter they are benumbed by cold, and in summer careless and home-sick: with exception of a Khansaman and a writer, who may be natives of the plains, the servants for a journey in central Asia should be Persians, Tibetans, or Turanis. The first are objectionable when amongst the Uzbeks, on account of their Shiah faith, the second are apt to indulge in inebriety, the last are unquestionably the most useful.

The valley of Dras is situated in the district of the same name. If computed by the course of the river from its junction with the Kartse Chu to near its sources, it will be about fifteen miles long; but the part to which the name of Dras especially applies is a valley about two miles in length: in either case the breadth is

rarely more than a mile. The small valley is nearly closed at either extremity by the contraction of the mountains, and is everywhere much broken by projections from their base, or by torrents rushing down their sides, and crossing the slope to the river which runs along it, dividing it into two unequal portions, the northern being the most considerable. The mountains which bound it are lofty ranges of clay slate, backed by others of limestone of greater height, and of very rugged outline when the summit is not levelled by snow. Upon the former, below the line of snow, a thin vegetation of dwarf willow, stunted birch, rhubarb, and other alpine plants, commences; and lower still is the region of the prangos, and other hardy plants, including the great yellow orchis, the roots of which furnish salep. This the peasants collect and eat roasted, but they have not learned to make its nutritious infusion, nor do they cultivate the plant.

The climate of Dras is, like that of Ladakh in general, severely cold for half the year, and during the other half varying from intense heat in the day to cold almost freezing

in the night. Several showers fell during the month I remained in the valley, but at the same time dense clouds to the westward, and the information of travellers, established the fall of heavy rain in Kashmir. The crops cultivated are Sherokh barley, wheat, and buck-wheat; the first ripening in about three months, the second in five or six, and the last in six weeks or two months. The cattle are horses, cows, the hybrid between the yak and cow, and sheep and goats. The former, though small, are hardy, active, and tolerably well shaped: the price of a good five-year old gelding is eight or nine pounds sterling. The neat cattle are generally black, small, short horned, and well shaped, with rather a larger dewlap than is consistent with European notions of beauty. I could not ascertain the quantity of milk given by a cow, but I understood it to be tolerably large: the price of a cow in full milk after her second calf was to me two pounds, but this was more than the average price. The zho-mo, or female progeny of the yak and cow, was more valued for the dairy than the latter, and sold for a larger sum. In general the cattle

of this district were in much better condition than in any other part of Ladakh, owing to the abundant supply of prangos in summer, and its hay in winter, for their provender.

The population of Dras is small, and in poverty, being much exposed to predatory incursions from Little Tibet, the government taking no means for their protection, and the natural defences, which would seem, to an ordinary observer, to be impenetrable, being traversed with ease in winter, over the frozen snow, by the borderers of Tibet and Kashmir. The lands of Dras are the joint property of the Raja of Ladakh and the Malik, or chief landholder, of the neighbouring part of Kashmir, in consequence of a grant, in perpetuity, made by an ancestor of the Raja to a progenitor of the Malik *. The occupant of a house pays a rupee a-year and a small quantity of grain to each of these chiefs. This would be no great tax upon industry if it were the whole, but the people are subjected to various arbitrary exactions on the

* Baron Hügel says, the Maliks were officers in hereditary charge of the passes into Kashmir, appointed by Akber, who gave them villages to be held by this tenure. *J. R. Geog. Soc.*, vol. vi. p. 346.—Ed.

part of the local authorities. The Nuna Khalun was at Dras when I arrived for the purpose of raising contributions towards the expense of building a fort, and, whilst in the district, had exacted fifty sheep, besides a large quantity of butter, milk, and firewood, for the use of himself and attendants. The visits of the Malik are equally costly, and the people are further liable to be pressed as porters and labourers for either landlord, not only for their personal service, but that of all travellers and merchants, for the pecuniary profit of the superior. In a year of brisk traffic this has been known to amount to about fifteen thousand pounds, of which the Chamal, or head farmer, and the Karpun, or local governor, manage to pocket about one-third, transmitting the remainder, in equal portions, to the Raja and the Malik; the poor peasants receiving no compensation whatever for their labour, loss of time, and injury to their own lands. This system of oppression has not only impoverished the people; it has demoralized them, and they are the most dishonest race in Ladakh. They dared not plunder openly, but they lost

no opportunity of pilfering, and were most exorbitant in their charges, whilst professing extreme anxiety to serve me. I could not obtain a single fagot, nor half a pint of milk, for less than a piece of silver, in value seven pence. The disposition to purloin was incessantly manifested. A ewe, presented to me over night, was carried off before the morning. Whilst operating on a patient for cataract, my case of pocket instruments, which lay open beside me, was nearly emptied of its contents. A tent, which had got wetted, being hung out to dry, was shorn of one-fifth of its canvas. In short, we were obliged to be continually on the alert to preserve any part of our property that was profitable. This is not the character of the Tibetans in general, especially of those who follow the faith of Buddha. The people of Dras are Mohammedans, and my intercourse with the Shiah Mohammedans has found the upper classes intolerant, and the lower dissolute and unprincipled. The people of the western provinces, in particular, and of Ladakh generally, have suffered much moral detriment from association with the Kash-

mirians, the most profligate race, perhaps, in the world. The inhabitants of Dras are rather under the middle stature, though taller than those of the eastern districts, and have coarse and unattractive features. Their houses are built of pebbles, cemented with earth, and with terraced roofs, and are most inartificial fabrics. As usual they are built without chimneys, and the smoke with which they are commonly filled accounts for the frequency of complaints of the eyes. In the course of two months I operated on fifty cataracts, and the patients who applied for relief in inflammatory affections of those organs were exceedingly numerous.

The most valuable produce of the valley of Dras is the prangos, which grows in great luxuriance upon the slopes of the hills, and supplies an invaluable fodder, both in summer and winter, for the cattle. The inspection of it in its native seats was my chief inducement for the visit, and I had an opportunity of observing it in full flower. The result of my inquiries is recorded in another place: as soon as they were completed I quitted Dras, and returned to Lé.

CHAPTER IX.

Excursion of Mr. Trebeck to Piti—Tung-lung Pass—Plain of Rupshu—Religious Structures—Tents of Shepherds—Whirlwinds—Lake of Thog-ji Chenmo—Pass of Nak-po-gonding—Tsumereri Lake—Parang La Rivulet and Pass—a Horse lost—Country improved—River of Losar—Report of an English Traveller—Halt at Rerik—Captain Mercer on his way to Sujanpur—Valley of the Losar, or Piti River—Fort of Trankar—Frontier of Bisahar—Figure of Sakya—Radokh Goat—Orders for a Levy of the People—Cause of Dispute with Kulu—Subterraneous Watercourses—Description of Piti—Village—Population—Village Councils—Revenue—Trade—Harvest Festivities—Return—Storm at the Parang Pass—Kiangs.

MR. TREBECK'S EXCURSION TO PITI.

LEAVING Lé on the 8th of June, I proceeded by our former route through Stakna, Marsilla, and Giah, to the site of our encampment on the 15th of September, on the southern side of the Tung-lung pass. The chief difference observable was in the state of the rivers, which were now swollen by the melting of the snow. The Sinh-kha-bad was thrice its size, and petty rills, which were

scarcely noticed when we last traversed them, had grown to respectable and almost unfordable streams. Although, however, the heat of the sun during the day was intense, the nights were cold, and we descended the pass in a shower of snow.

On the 12th of June we proceeded along the valley or plain of Rupshu in a south-easterly direction. The valley varied in breadth, and occasionally expanded into a broad plain, but, in general, it was not more than from five hundred to seven hundred paces in breadth. The hills on either side were covered with the winter's snow, and we had occasional falls of hail and snow in the plain. The soil of the latter was at first loose clay, and afterwards consisted chiefly of micaceous sand, scattered over with stones, and thinly patched with stunted furze: several rivulets crossed it, and in their beds and on their banks a small quantity of grass was growing, which affords pasturage in winter to the flocks of the shepherds of the more exposed districts. Along the plain were a number of the structures called "Manis," the precise purpose of which we

were never able to ascertain. The most common are of the form of a parallelopiped, and roughly built of stones, the upper ones bearing inscriptions, chiefly of the sacred sentence, "Om mani padma hom." Another kind, often erected at the ends of the first, though not unfrequently detached, is built in the form of a cube, surmounted by a truncated pyramid, supporting the lower part of a cone reversed. Above all is placed a stick or pole, but the better kinds are ornamented by a pinnacle of well-burnt red brick, terminated by a crown or crescent of brass, or painted wood. Near the end of our day's journey we passed, at some distance, the large pond or lake of Thog-ji Chenmo. Near our encampment a Champa, or shepherd and his family, had encamped, and several other tents were near. One party had arrived from Kag-jung, only a few hours before us. They reported the destruction of a large number of cattle, in consequence of the severity of the winter and difficulty of procuring provender. The tents of the Champas are of ragged black blanket, about four feet high, and open along the top. Their

interior is furnished usually with abundance of dirty sheep and goat skins, some sewed into coats, two or three iron pots, and one or two of brass or copper, some iron spoons, a churn for tea, not for butter, which is made by rolling or shaking milk in a leather bag, and some wooden milk-pails, which are seldom, if ever, washed. The rest of the shepherd's equipment is carried about his person, as his tea cup, pipe, tobacco pouch, chakmak, or flint, and tinder, knives, a small spoon, and several needles; a small wooden flageolet is also sometimes stuck in the girdle. These articles, with their cattle, constitute the property, and are sufficient for the comfort, of a Ladakh shepherd and his family. The head ornaments of the women are of the fashion of Chan-than, not of Lé, the lappet being widest on the forehead, and falling in a narrow slip down the back. It is similarly decorated with turquoises and cornelians. The costume of the men is the same, except in the cap, which, by the shepherds of Gardokh and Rodokh, is worn of a yellow cloth, with a border of gimp or fox skin, and a top-knot of scarlet twist or

shreds of red silk. Amongst these people when an individual of property dies the body is burnt, as usual, but that of a poor person is left on the spot where he expired, the face only being covered. The party near us had with them about twenty yaks, nearly all of them black, and of form and size very superior to those of Chushul.

I had never seen the phenomenon of the whirlwind more common than on this plain: it was, perhaps, like that of the Arabian desert on a smaller scale, raising a column of sand suddenly to a great height at one particular spot, whilst all around the air was perfectly calm. In general these sudden gusts are not at all dangerous, but strange stories are told of their occasional violence in particular spots, and they are said to be sufficiently strong at Digar to carry horse and man off their feet, being accompanied by reports like those of artillery. I can confirm the truth of these last stories to a less exaggerated extent, having heard on the Digar pass the wind howling through the crags at a very considerable distance with a noise occasionally like that of a falling stone. Very pos-

sibly an exposed portion of rock had been blown down.

The greater part of the road of the 13th skirted the edge of the lake. The number of wild geese was prodigious. On a bank within it, about two hundred yards long, and twenty broad, there were at least three hundred; several chakwas, or Brahmani geese, were observed amongst them. After leaving the lake we ascended a narrow defile to a Latoh, where we halted. In the morning we encountered a bleak wind and snow; in the afternoon the thermometer rose to 89°, and the sun was very hot: at night again there was frost. In this neighbourhood are some sulphur mines, which are worked: the sulphur is cleaned by pounding, and then melting with a small quantity of suet over a slow fire.

The journey of the 14th led us over various ascents and descents of the usual barren and desolate character, unfitted, apparently, alike for vegetable and animal life. The principal pass traversed was that of Nakpo Gonding, which had an elevation of above seventeen thousand feet, and in surmounting which the whole party suffered much inconvenience

from difficulty of breathing. This sensation, in mountainous countries, is not, perhaps, exactly what is understood by similar difficulty in the plains, it may be best defined a frequent inclination, and, at the same time, a sense of inability, to sigh. The descent was comparatively easy, and led to the district of Chakshang. Early on the following day we arrived at the most northern point of the Tsumureri Lake, and continued, during that and the ensuing day, along its western bank. Steep mountains rise abruptly from the lake on either side of it. Those on the opposite side were about two thousand feet high, but those on our right were not so lofty. The general breadth of the lake may have been about a mile and a half, including the broken ground on its edges formed by ravines and watercourses, and it appeared to be deeper and less clear than the Lake of Pang-kung. It contained no fish, and was not much frequented by wild-fowl: the taste of the water was brackish*. A river of some size, formed of a number of watercourses and streams,

* Mr. Gerard afterwards visited this lake which he calls Chuinonenil: he places it at an elevation above the sea of fifteen thou-

which crossed the road, and turned the angle of the lake, flowed into it on the opposite side. In the middle of May the lake was frozen over sufficiently to be crossed by a man.

On the 17th we crossed a platform, chiefly of gravelly soil, in some places swampy, and intersected by the Parang La river, which we forded, and afterwards ascended through a long, narrow defile, between steep rocks, which sometimes approached so close as to leave no path except the river itself. The day's journey terminated on a small platform termed Pha-lung Palrak, or "stones where wool is clipped." The people of Piti and Rupshu annually meet here to barter, the former grain and provisions for the wool of the latter, and they find shelter in the lee of huge blocks of chert which are lying about. Appearances here announced a more difficult road than we had for some time traversed, the rocks being rugged and precipitous, dreary, and topped with snow. Near the summit of one in our vicinity there was an

sand feet, and observes, that whilst it is fed by several considerable streams it has no efflux, and is kept at its level entirely by evaporation.—*Asiat. Res.*, vol. xviii. p. 259.—ED.

accumulated mass of snow, at least fifty feet deep.

The same defile continued more or less filled by the river, to which frequent supplies were brought by rivulets and rills from the rocks on either hand, originating in the snow-beds with which every nook and recess was filled. In one part of the defile a mass of snow formed a complete bridge across the stream. Loose fragments of rock, piles of gravel, and mouldering clay and sand, were the principal substitutes for a path in the river's bed. At Nishing-long the defile opened into a valley, which was crossed, and another defile, that of Tratang Kongma, entered. The rocks that bounded it consisted of a flinty stone, of a dark grey colour, intricately veined with white quartz. Their surface was bleached to the straw-colour of limestone, and they rose in sharp craggy peaks ; one opposite to where we encamped, shot up in the form of a cone, to the height of one thousand five hundred feet, with sides too precipitous to be scaled. Here the gigantic chakor, called, in Piti, Komo, was numerous.

On the 19th of June we crossed the pass of Parang La. The ascent, though not of the

most abrupt description, occupied us from day-break till noon. In the lower part the snow lay in lines, with edges sufficiently frozen to bear our weight, and we stepped along as if we had been walking upon boards placed on their edges. Higher up it was softened by the sun, and we had the agreeable variety of sinking into it knee-deep. My horse was so utterly incapable of proceeding, long before reaching the summit, that it was necessary to dismount and leave him to his fate. I should have put an end to his sufferings, but was persuaded that some men might be sent back for him with food from Kiwar, though I had little expectation of this being effected in time. The height of the pass above the sea was not less than nineteen thousand feet*. To the south and south-west a confused succession of snowy peaks presented itself, none of which were much higher than the Parang La, though some loftier peaks appeared to the south-west. The Bara Lacha pass was pointed out to the south-west. The crest of the Parang La, and the descent on the southern face,

* This pass was also crossed by Mr. Gerard, who states it to have an elevation of more than eighteen thousand feet.—Ed.

were free from snow. The mountain on each side of the pass was not more than one hundred and fifty feet above us; the descent was very steep. The pass was, upon the whole, one of the most difficult we had encountered: we encamped in a gorge not exceeding twenty-five paces in breadth.

The road on the 20th commenced in the defile through which, as usual, flowed a rivulet intersecting the path, but we crossed upon natural bridges of snow. This opened into a valley where the villages of Kikiem and Kiwar and their cultivated lands were met with. Short grass and furze covered the less abrupt slopes of the mountains, and a few stunted willows adorned the edges of the rivulets. Although much less fertile than Lahoul, the country surpassed that to the north of the Parang La.

On the 21st it continued to improve, and we again saw our old acquaintances—sweet-briar, wild roses, and currant-bushes in abundance. A platform, extending from the foot of the mountain we had crossed, was skirted by the river of Losar. This is formed by two rivulets, one coming from this side of the Bara Lacha pass, said to be not more than one

day's journey from Kikiem, and the other from the Kulzum La, on the way to Kulu. There are roads to these places along the streams. Across the Losar are several villages, at one of which, Rerik, we encamped.

At Kiwar a report had reached us that an English gentleman, attended by four men, was on his way to Bara Lacha and Kulu, and this was confirmed at Rerik, which place the person in question had quitted only the day before. As there could be no doubt of the fact, therefore, I dispatched two men on horseback with a note to him, to ascertain who he was, and offer him assistance should he need it. I waited at Rerik the return of my messengers, and, on the 23rd, they brought me a reply. The gentleman was a Captain Mercer, on his way to Sultanpur. As he was pressed for time, he regretted he could not return to meet me. He was accompanied by four men, and his baggage was carried by them and two loaded asses, with which alone he would find it a serious task to cross the Kulzum La. I regretted not having been a day earlier, that I might have seen him and given him some information that might have been of service. It was now too late, and I

could only wish him the success which his enterprising spirit deserved. From Rerik I sent letters to Lieut. Gerard, at Kothgerh, to inform him of my approach to the frontier of Bisahar.

We left Rerik on the 24th, and proceeded along the platform, the average breadth of which, above the river, was seven hundred paces. The soil was clayey, and the greater portion of its surface cultivated. The river was joined, in the valley, by a number of small rivulets, deep though fordable. A sanga was thrown across the main stream, which rolled in a bed of gravel, and was fringed with willows, and some varieties of thorn. At some distance we passed through the village of Kaj, the cultivated lands of which were on the right; on the platform, to the left, at some distance ahead, were two temples, Tangiut and Gingul, with villages and lands attached. The level surface of the valley was here about five hundred yards broad, and branches of the river were running in every part of it. The day's journey terminated at the small village of Lara, where the breadth of the valley was about nine hundred

paces. The rocks on the left appeared to support a table-land; those on the right were connected with snowy ridges. The road on the 25th continued of much the same character along the Losar, which was joined by the Pin, a river of equal size, coming from the south-west. Towards its termination the road ascended the side of a steep and crumbling mountain to the fortress of Dankar, or, as more correctly called by the Tibetans, Trankar. This is built upon an irregular ridge of rock, running out to the south of the general line of the mountain. It presents a precipitous face to the river, and on the west, also, is almost inaccessible. The path to it, scarcely more than a foot broad, might easily be rendered impassable, by a few stones being rolled down. On the south-east the path is exposed, but, eight hundred feet above it, the mountains slope so gently that they afford pasture-lands to the cattle of the village. A pond is situated on this part of the rock, from the bottom of which two rills percolate the soil, and furnish water for irrigation. The hither one also supplies the fort with water, though inconveniently, as it lies far below.

A rough stair of bricks leads to it, defended at the bottom by a sort of bastion. The fort itself is of an irregular narrow figure, and does not differ essentially in shape or strength from a common house; some of the defences are whimsically placed, particularly a small enclosure with loop-holes, large enough to contain ten or twelve men, which is perched on the top of an isolated pile of gravel, rising like a column from the rill at the base. The rest of the houses are built on the lower portion of the eminence, and are constructed as usual of stone and large unburnt bricks. On the opposite side of the river, distant about three miles, was the village of Mane, and the crest of the pass, leading to Rubak in Bisachar, was not more than six miles horizontally distant, in the direction of south-east. The upper part of the defile leading to it had a considerable quantity of snow in it, but it did not appear more difficult than that of Parang.

As a principal object of my visit to Trankar was to communicate more readily with Lieut. Gerard, at Subathu, and to facilitate, if he continued to desire it, his journey to Lé, I

established myself in a house in the village to await replies to my letters. The house belonged to the Taoche, or head of the carriers, and he with Khaga Khan, the manager of the district, and the Pa-on or scribe, paid me every civility in the absence of the chief of Piti, Sultan Begh, whom I had left at Lé.

The Pa-on, in addition to his literary attainments, proved to be a skilful carver and gilder, and had executed in wood-work a representation of Sakya Muni, which with reference to the state of the arts in this country, and the coarseness and imperfectness of the tools, was an extraordinary performance. Sakya was represented seated cross-legged, as usual, upon a lotus, resting on a platform, supported by two white lions with bushy tails, like those of the yak. The body of Sakya was gilt, and the drapery about his person painted red: he was surrounded by foliage, amidst which were the figures of a white elephant, a lion, a horse and horseman, two parrots, one over each shoulder, and above them two heads of cherubs, surmounted by three-headed snakes. The whole was topped by a winged and horned nondescript figure, having the head

of an eagle, the body of a man, and the tail of a fish. The whole was grotesque enough, and not a little out of proportion, yet the effect was striking, and the workmanship curious and elaborate.

During my residence the chief Lama of the district departed on a trading trip to Tashi-gong; he was accompanied out of the village by forty Gelums, who walked after him in procession, and a few women with pots of butter milk. At the foot of the descent the party sat down and partook of the provisions they had with them, after which the Lama made them a speech, and gave them his blessing, holding out his hands over them, and putting them on the heads of those who were near him, in a truly patriarchal fashion.

On the 13th of August two Shikaris brought me a young goat, of the variety called Radokh: it appeared to be about two years old. The hair was of a light grey colour, slightly tinged with yellow. It was four feet two inches in length, from the tip of the nose to the end of the tail, and two feet five inches high at the shoulder. The huntsmen say

it seldom grows above five inches taller. If so, it must be a different variety from the wild goat in the neighbourhood of Lé, as that is considerably larger; but there are a number of species, no doubt, in these mountains, of a character between the goat and the deer, which are new to naturalists.

On the 15th orders were received from Lé, stating, that it was the purpose of the Khalun to levy an armed force for the purpose of retaliating upon Kulu, for the foray lately committed by that state on Ladakh, and ordering the people of Piti to prepare to meet him near Koksar, on the north side of the Ratanka pass. He threatens death to any who shall run away, should any fresh attack be attempted before his arrival; but this is only intended to give confidence to the people, for he knows very well, should they ever be persuaded to take the field, the first shot from a Kulu matchlock would put the whole Ladakhi force to flight. They do, however, sometimes grow pugnacious, and Khaga Khan was actually busied in adjusting a dispute between the two villages of Kiwar and Kikiem, in which an affray had taken place, and a few

heads had been broken. The circumstances of the dispute with Kulu were the following.

About six years ago, when Khaga Rabghi was the governor of the district, attempts were made by the Gadhes, or shepherds of Chamba, Kulu, and its neighbourhood, to export shawl-wool to the southern hills, by way of the Parang pass. As this was a contraband trade, an order was received from Lé to have it seized, and in obedience six or eight flocks, amounting, perhaps, in the whole to fifteen hundred sheep, partly laden with coarse wool, were stopped and possession was taken of the whole of the forbidden article, but nothing more: none of the animals were injured, nor was any violence offered to the shepherds. This deterred the traders from speculating again in the same way, and the authorities of Ladakh had no application made to them by the Raja of Kulu for the restitution of the property confiscated. Indeed, the occurrence seems to have remained unnoticed for more than four years, as both the Rajas were on friendly terms, and an agent from Kulu was residing at Lé when we arrived at that city. But somewhat

more than a year since, a large armed body of the Kulu peasantry, headed by a near connexion of Sobha Ram, entered Piti by the Losar pass, and meeting with no resistance, took possession of everything which was worth carrying away, and had not been concealed. They advanced no further than Rerik, and destroyed several houses by lighting large fires in the rooms. The Gonpa of Kih was much injured. The property taken off consisted chiefly of yaks, horses, and other live stock, but an estimate cannot be made of the amount of the loss. The conduct of the invaded was amusingly characteristic. Every family subject to taxes possesses a matchlock, a sword, and a bow and arrows; but instead of employing these in defence as would have been supposed, no sooner was information of the attack given, than most of them were buried in the nearest piece of land convenient for the purpose, and the owners fled precipitately to the least accessible part of the hills, dragging after them as much of their household furniture as possible. The Kaj sanga, and that across the Gingul river were broken down, and the

flight was general, even at Dankar. Khaga Khan shut himself up in the fort, and the Pa-on, after having in vain requested him to make an offer of a present of grain to such of the villagers as were willing to resist the enemy, saddled his tattoo, took refuge amongst the crags above, and remained three days concealed there. At the end of this period several of the people assembled, a drum was beat, a few matchlocks were discharged, and a report was spread that a force had arrived from Lé by the Burgiok road to their assistance. This had the desired effect, and the foragers immediately retreated. The list of killed on both sides might amount to about sixteen, but these fell in a very unusual way; six or seven of the attacked lost their lives by slipping from the cliffs, over which they were trying to escape, and the deaths of the remainder (of the offensive party) were caused [illegible]y overcharged stomachs, with the exce[illegible] of one only, who was drowned in the [illegible]. Sobha Ram's accusation is little lik[illegible] be true, not merely because the disp[illegible]n of the people is at variance with the commission of an act, such as the one as-

cribed to them, but because three or four of the Kulu men, who were afterwards taken prisoners, were permitted to escape without injury, even when the irritation excited by the inroad was at its height. The quarrel was, however, ultimately adjusted, without a farther recourse to arms.

I have noticed above the two subterraneous watercourses from the pond on the mountains. On the afternoon of the 15th the one that supplied the village was choked: after some interval its liberation was announced by a loud rattling noise, and presently an immense mass of mud, earth, and stones, came rushing through the gutter in such quantities, that the villagers were alarmed for their crops, and sought to arrest the fall, or turn it aside. Fortunately it ceased after a short time, but the effect was extraordinary, especially compared with the apparent insignificance of the rill. The stream seemed scarcely adequate to stir a stone of half a pound weight, but the slime brought down extended for several yards of the depth of three and four feet, and imbedded blocks of stone that could not have weighed less than

a ton. The most liquid portion of the mass had been in the centre, and had run off, leaving a large drain between heaps of rubbish on either side. I had often before noticed similar accumulations rising in ridges along the slopes of the hills, and had been at a loss to account for their origin.

The Lassan government, at least that of Chan-than, claims a jurisdiction over the south-eastern part of Piti, and a Lama, on the part of that province, resides at Kih Gonpa, a day's journey from Trankar. The larger part of the district is, however, subject to Ladakh, and perhaps its political authority is extended to the whole, the charge of the Lama being religious rather than secular. It is said to have been formerly included in Bisahar, subsequent to the Lassan conquest of Chan-than, since when Lassa has subjugated no part of Ladakh. The district contains a number of small villages, or thirty in Piti so called, and thirteen in the adjacent district of Pin, averaging rather less than ten houses in each. The male population was stated to be one thousand and seventy-eight, including children; and if the same propor-

tion prevailed as at Trankar, where it was to a house, men, one-seventh, women, one-ninth, and children, one-third, or nearly five altogether, the total population of the district would be about two thousand.

The people of Piti are completely of Tartar appearance in form and face; the men are less robust and better grown than those more to the north, and the women are far from good looking. The men are much less industrious also than those about Lé, and are of a worse character, being quarrelsome, dishonest, and still more addicted to chang, being rarely quite sober. Their dress consists of the usual black woollen cap, with a long coat and trowsers of the same material, and the common boots. The Lamas of Pin differ from their brethren, in allowing their hair to grow and to become matted, and in wearing black. The female tunic is also chiefly of that colour, but the trowsers are red. The hair is nicely platted into a number of small braids which hang down the back, and are collected into a point, which is decorated with pieces of amber and coral. The mantle which is used in winter is plain,

and either of sheep-skin or of coarse home-manufactured cloth.

The authority of the Raja of Ladakh, or rather that of the Khalun, is absolute, and is exercised through a chief, who seldom visits Piti, except at harvest time, to collect the revenue. This office is therefore discharged by a deputy, who is rarely a person of much influence, and whose measures are completely controlled by the Gatpos, corresponding with the Sianas of Gerhwal, and Mukhyas of Bisahar; householders acting for a month in turn as elders of the villages. These should meet five or six times a year to discuss the interests of the district; but unless some matter which they consider important is under agitation, those most distant from the place of rendezvous rarely attend: when they meet, these delegates of the Piti commons display more vehemence than wisdom: they seldom proceed to business before their faculties are whetted by copious draughts of chang, and the cup circulates freely during the debate. They sit down on the ground without any order, and one man may be seen resolving some grave question whilst he twirls a roll of

yarn, and another contemplating views of policy through a mist of tobacco smoke. An orator rarely makes much progress in a lengthy harangue, and the lungs of the whole assembly are generally in full play throughout the discussion, each being more anxious to be heard than to hear. If a dispute arises between individuals, the parliament of Gatpos must settle it; if a robbery is committed, they must inquire into it; and if the thief be discovered, award his punishment. The consequence is that thefts are constantly perpetrated with impunity. A knotty question with them was the provision of porters for my baggage, as how could they spare me half a dozen men, when they were all under military requisition for the warlike purposes of the Khalun. The conclusion they came to was, that the men could not be supplied, but that I might hire or buy ponies, or asses; or if I preferred it, I might have the women, as many as I pleased.

The whole revenue of Piti is collected in grain, by a measure called a khal, equal to eight pakka sers, and of the value of thirteen anas. The highest tax paid by any one is

fifteen khals, and the lowest seven; but as one-third of the population must be deducted as untaxable, having no landed property, the revenue is levied upon but two hundred and sixty-seven houses, and the average amount paid by each being estimated at eleven khals, the total will be two thousand nine hundred and thirty-seven khals, or in value two thousand three hundred and eighty-six rupees. Traffic is also carried on chiefly by barter, and money is almost useless. Salt, wool, tea, turquoises, sheep, and goats, are imported from Chan-than, and are paid for with grain, woollen cloth, and a few horses. From Bisahar and Kulu come iron, cooking utensils, brass, copper, tobacco, rice, dried fruits, tea-cups, timber, amber, and glass beads, &c., which are paid for with the grain, and horses, and woollen cloths of the district, and with the salt and wool of Chan-than, although the latter is an illicit export. The iron and metal vessels of the south are sent to Lé in exchange for tea, coarse cloth, coral, and dyeing drugs, &c. A lead mine exists at Po, but it is worked only on account of the Raja. The district is famous for its manufacture of

woollen cloth: several varieties are fabricated, some thick and heavy, with a long nap, others fine. All the wool made use of is of a coarse kind, and in consequence the finer cloths have a hardness, something similar to that of camelot or plaid, to which they are little inferior. They are much superior in strength to those of Lé, but are less soft and pliant: this is owing to the different methods which obtain in the construction. To the northward a coarse loom is in use, little unlike in its parts to the one common in Europe. Here the two ends of the warp are fastened together, and it is then stretched upon two rods, one fixed to the body of the weaver (who is invariably a woman) by a cord, which admits of the work being loosened or tightened at pleasure, and the other well fastened to some stones at a distance, equal to half the length of the cloth. The whole is close to the ground, on which the workwoman sits, but the portion close to her is slightly elevated by a third rod. Loops, each including a thread, and received upon a small stick like a rattan, supply the place of a heddle: of these there are three sets, which draw up

parts of the warp alternately as required. A large heavy mesh, into which a thin bar of iron is inserted, is a substitute for the reed, and three or more heavy strokes are made with its armed edge upon every thread of the woof. The last instrument must be taken out after the insertion of each piece of yarn, and when placed perpendicularly, with its two edges separating the warp, abundance of room is given for the passage of the balls of worsted made use of, without the covering of a shuttle. This part of the process is tedious, but the warp is prepared in a quick and simple way: several pegs are driven into the ground so near each other, that the whole may be reached without any material movement of the body: the yarn is fastened to one of them, and carried on round the others till a sufficient quantity has been wound: all are then taken out except three, which have their places supplied by rods, and the warp only requires spreading. Every woman knows how to weave, but only half their number may be considered as employed in the manufacture; for if a house contains two, one is usually busy in the management of domestic

affairs. It may be estimated that two thousand seven hundred and fifty-two pieces of cloth are annually fabricated in the district. Each piece is about seventeen inches broad, and the average length may be stated at seven and a half yards; so that the whole will amount to twenty thousand six hundred and forty yards, of which the annual consumption in Piti may be about one thousand six hundred pieces, and the remainder is exported, to the extent of as much as thirteen thousand one hundred and forty yards. Very good sacking is also made of the hair and wool taken from the yak.

The same grains grow here as are common in the northern parts of Ladakh, but it would seem that the sherokh in no part of the district changes to the common barley in a higher temperature. The buck-wheat is likewise produced, but the climate does not admit of its being successfully sown after another crop, as customary in Purik.

The cattle are also generally the same. The sheep are almost all imported from Chanthan, as well as the goats, the kids of which degenerate, both in size and quantity of wool.

The horses, or rather ponies, are extremely small; they seldom exceed in height twelve hands, and for the most part their forms are imperfect, though usually they are active and hardy.

On the 15th of August the approach of harvest was celebrated by a public festival, and at the invitation of Khaga Khan I joined the party at his residence early in the forenoon. I found his room crowded by the men of the village, and the whole party was engaged in emptying some large earthen vessels of chang, the contents of which diminished as briskly as might well be imagined. There was also abundance of smoking, abundance of noise, and better than all, abundance of good humour. I had not been long seated before three of the company rose to dance, to a tune played by the blacksmith, who had exchanged his anvil for a couple of drums. The performance precisely resembled what we often witnessed at Lé: the motion of the feet was extremely slow and spiritless, but was accompanied by various movements of the hands and arms, and the waving of a woollen cloth in the form of a shawl, which

latter is always used for the purpose by the more wealthy people to the north. At twelve o'clock the liquor was well-nigh exhausted, and every one went home to saddle his horse, and put on his smartest dress. After this had been done, the whole again assembled in the hollow below the village, where a piece of ground about one hundred yards long had been smoothed for the occasion. On one side of this a small mark was set up, and every one galloped his pony past it, in general throwing at it with a stone, though one of the riders made use of a bow and arrow, and two others had their matchlocks. The last were admirable caricatures: both rode about as fast as an active person might hop, and fired with the muzzle of their guns within a few inches of the mark, which it is but justice to observe they always hit. Amusement was now suspended till near four in the afternoon, when every inhabitant of the village, both male and female, met in a yard close to the fort. A second and larger batch of chang was in readiness, and the dancing was incessant, and much more varied and entertaining than any I had seen at Lé. The

most pleasing part of it was performed by the women, who joined hands, and moved in a circle, with a regular step and much vivacity, singing at the same time. A *pas-seul* of an old shepherd was also amusing, as it had more of humour than vulgarity, and would have done credit to a clown on an English stage. Notwithstanding the rain which was falling the greatest part of the evening, the general mirth continued till dark unabated. On the following day eating superseded other occupations; though, quite contrary to European custom, the men regaled in one house, and their companions of the other sex in another. The former killed two sheep, the whole of which they devoured; but the latter seem to have fared much worse, and to have had little more to feast upon than parched barley, flour, and butter, perhaps with the addition of a small quantity of tea. Forming an opinion from the apparent pleasure with which they partook of this, their ordinary food must be of a greatly inferior quality.

After exchanging several communications with Lieut. Gerard at Kotgerh, the delivery of which was much interrupted and delayed

by the carelessness and irregularity of our messengers, I learned from him that he was unable to obtain leave of absence, and was therefore unable to join us in Ladakh. As some articles of value, including a packet of pearls, were on their way from Calcutta, I dispatched a confidential servant, Gholam Hyder, to Subathu, to wait for them, and bring them after me, and set off to return to Lé on the 22nd of August. On our way to Kaj we met with a large party of Pin people proceeding towards Lara, on the road to Chan-than, and forming the third kafila that had gone thither within a few days, for tea, wool, salt, &c.

The ascent to Kiwar was a work of labour, and we were obliged to procure the aid of the villagers to relieve the asses of their burthens. The situation of this village is perhaps the loftiest in Ladakh at which crops of corn are raised; the elevation is at least thirteen thousand feet, and the snowy peaks are not much above it. There is abundance of pasture on the swells of land to the north-east and east, and the stock of neat cattle belonging to the village is unusually large. At Kiwar I first

learned that dahi, or curdled milk, is churned into butter, and found a pail employed as a churn, the churning-stick being supported by two arms fastened to a post, and turned by a rope as in Hindustan. The natives affirm that butter made from milk in the first instance disagrees with them.

On the night of the 27th, on our approach to the Parang pass, we were visited by a violent storm of sleet and rain, from which we were imperfectly sheltered, and during which we were kept in a state of perpetual alarm by the constant falling of small fragments of rock swept down by the torrents; luckily none of them came near us, or, although they were not of great extent, they must have done mischief. The weather continued unsettled on the following day, but we succeeded in making our way to the top of the pass. There we were stopped. The snow rose like a wall on its northern face, and was found much too soft to bear loaded cattle. We were therefore obliged to stay for the night where we were, taking shelter in a latoh, or enclosure for travellers.

Appearances on the following morning were

not more favourable, but it was necessary to move onwards, and we attempted to descend. The loads, however, were soon thrown off, for the asses were frequently so deep in the snow, even without their burthens, that they could not extricate themselves without assistance. It was past noon before we had reached a platform, beyond which the pass was clear; and here we were obliged to remain until the baggage could be brought down, and this was not accomplished till the next day. As my tent was amongst the things left for the night, I was obliged to construct a shelter by piling some stones in front of a fragment of rock, and throwing a blanket over the top. My people crept into holes and crevices in the face of the mountain. The night was clear though cold. The snow terminated on our left, about three miles from the top of the pass, in a bluff point nearly fifty feet high; several rills trickled from its base, to supply the stream which we were thence to follow. Early in the afternoon we arrived at the place of our former encampments at Trattang, and thence proceeded without much more difficulty or fatigue to Lé. The only occurrence worthy

of notice was the appearance of several kiangs near the Nakpo gonding pass. Not having a gun with me, I missed a good opportunity of bringing one down, as they approached nearer than on any former occasion. I had, however, a good view of the animal, and am inclined to pronounce him to be an ass with some affinity to a mule.

PART III.

JOURNEY TO KASHMIR AND PESHAWAR.

CHAPTER I.

Relinquishment of the route by Yarkand—Departure from Lé—Friendly sentiments of the Authorities; and of the People—Wife of the Nuna Khalun—Upper road—Parties met on the way—Fall of a horse—Pass—Valley of Dras—Inroad from Hasora—Precipitate retreat—Mischief inflicted—Causes of the aggression—Continuation of the route—Phandas—Matayan—Boundary between Ladakh and Kashmir—Entrance into Kashmir—Zwaje La Valley—Pine Forests—Sona-murg—Sindh River—Station of Gagan-gir—Met by Surat Sing and escort—Villages—Anchal Lake—Entrance into the capital of Kashmir—Permission to winter in the city.

In the month of September Abdul Latif returned from Yarkand, and brought information that all attempts to procure the sanction of the Chinese authorities to our journey to that city were unavailing. The design was therefore abandoned, and I determined to proceed to Bokhara by way of Kashmir and Kabul. As soon as this was known, the

Khalun and Banka expressed their regret at our departure, and at the disappointment we had experienced; they declared themselves entirely satisfied with our conduct during our stay, and requested us to leave testimonials of our opinion of their behaviour towards us, promising to forward to me, at any time, anything I might wish to have from the country, and to give a welcome reception to any European who might hereafter visit Ladakh. The Khalun also expressed his hope that the state of Ladakh would be looked upon with favour by the British government. The Lonpa concurred in these sentiments, and the Raja and his son stated that they prayed every possible good might attend us. Presents of china, silks, tea, and a horse, were then made me, and on the 20th of September I made my first march finally for Lé.

The Imam and all the principal merchants accompanied us the first stage to Skarra, and many quitted us only on the third morning, when we started for Ling. At Phiang the deputy of the monastery entertained us in the absence of his principal, and sent us a supply of flour and butter for our journey; and on

our arrival at Ling, we were met by many persons for whom I had prescribed in my former visit, and who evinced their gratitude by bringing supplies of meal, butter, and apples. At Himis I collected a quantity of the seed of the flower or beardless barley, and at various places on my route provided a supply of apple-pips, apricot-kernels, and the seeds of grain, for transmission to India and to England. At Molbi I was appealed to by the wife of the Nuna Khalun, who was absent at Zanskar, on account of the refusal of my carriers to pay certain fees customary at this place. Going to her to discuss the subject, she received me with much graciousness, taking my offered hand between both hers and carrying it to her forehead. A seat was given me, and, at my request, she sat down beside me and entered, with great fluency and animation, upon the subject in dispute. The Cho-cho, as she was called, was rather good-looking, and of juvenile appearance, although the mother of twelve children. She was a complete woman of business, and commanded great influence in the district.

Upon arriving at Pushkyum the carriers,

who had at first proposed to follow the high road leading over Omba La, now recommended the lower one along the Dras river; but to this I objected, unless they engaged to make good any loss that might arise from the falling of the baggage with the stream. As they would not agree to this condition, we took the upper road by Minji. Between Minji and Lang Kartse we met the son of the Nuna Khalun, with three or four females of his family, on horseback, the women riding astride; they were dressed in brocade with mantles of broad-cloth, and seal-skin boots. As I was in advance of the party, and without an interpreter, our greeting was brief. The Khalun was preceded by a large flock of sheep, goats, cows, and horses, too probably the produce of exaction or compulsory gifts. This young man imitates his father's example, and, although scarcely twenty, is detested for his rapacity. This seems to be the season for visiting, for on the following day we met the son of the Raja of Soth and his wife, who were going to Lé. They were accompanied by a band of music. Music and dancing have followed the introduction of Mohammedanism

in the western parts of Tibet, and have, in a great measure, excluded the use of intoxicating liquors. Chang is little known to the west of Molbi.

From Lang Kartse we proceeded by a different route from that formerly followed by Sankho, and ascended the bank of the Zakut river, running from west by south, and falling into the Kartse chu. The path was narrow, rugged, and steep. At the distance of a mile and a half we came to a small village, from the lands of which the crops had been lately reaped. A large patch of ground was thickly covered with prangos plants. As we ascended we experienced the keenness of the wintry wind, and round the stems of a species of dock thin bands or ribands of ice had formed. The road then descended, but soon again took an ascending direction, skirting the right bank of a stream at a considerable height above it, which was carrying a supply of water to the Kartse chu. Here, on stepping over a block of jasper which crossed the road, my horse fell, and rolled with me a considerable way down the slope before I could get loose. The softness of the snow prevented my receiving any seri-

ous injury, and the horse was brought up by a block of stone just upon the edge of a precipitous rock.

We encamped on the 15th of October on the banks of the Twaji rivulet: snow fell during the night. On the following day we ascended and crossed the pass: we reached the verge of the descent without difficulty, but there we found the snow from three to four feet deep, completely concealing the path, which ran along the edge of a cliff, in many places precipitous. We were obliged to unload the horses, and carry their burthens by men over the dangerous parts, an operation which delayed our progress. Below us the valley of Dras was at times concealed from our view by the clouds rolling under our feet, or by the snow storms which they discharged. On my arrival at the first house, called Sugatial, I was informed that Dras had been plundered on the preceding night by the Raja of Hasora, with eight hundred men, of all the cattle and every thing of value. Three hundred men, it was said, occupied the plain where I had pitched my tent in July, and several parties were pointed out to

me. Snow fell in large flakes, and we were surrounded by a number of half-naked and frightened people, who were unable to give us any assistance. As night was coming on, all we could do was to make the best possible arrangements against an attack, and I ordered the Sipahis of my escort to fire several rounds, for the double purpose of intimating our presence, and of getting their pieces in order, should they be required.

On the morning of the 17th we were joined by the Chamal, the principal landholder and receiver of the customs, and a party of people well armed, with whom we descended together to the villages on the left bank of the Dras river. The Hasoras had retired, alarmed at the approach of my party, against whose muskets their matchlocks were of no avail at such a season, when the snow rendered it impossible to keep the matches alight, and further deceived, perhaps, by our apparent strength, for it was ascertained that our march had been descried at a considerable distance; and as we were in all seventy persons, forming with our horses and sheep a long straggling line, we made a more formid-

able appearance amongst the mountains than our real strength would have presented. From whatever motive, however, it was, they withdrew before they had time to carry off the grain, or to finish a game of Polo, for which they had marked out the ground: the cattle and other property they carried off, along with the Karpun of the district. Two men, badly wounded, came to me to be dressed; and in one of the houses was found the body of Mohammed Malik, the younger brother of Rasul Malik, who had been shot in his apartment. Another man who had been killed was a Kashmirian. A party of seven men had been sent to seize or slay the Chamal, and had come to his house for that purpose. Rushing up stairs, but not knowing his person, they asked the first man they found, who was the Chamal himself, where he was; he had presence of mind to direct them to a lower apartment, on which six descended, and finding the Kashmirian, put him to death: the Chamal knocking down the man left to guard him, leapt from the top of the house, and escaped to the mountains. On inquiring into the amount of the plunder,

it appeared that about five hundred horses, eight hundred head of neat cattle, and ten thousand sheep had been driven off, and that most of the domestic utensils, and all the best wearing apparel had been taken away, reducing the villagers from a state of relative affluence to absolute misery.

On the 18th the Karpun returned, to the great joy of the people, with whom he was popular. He had been liberated by order of Sultan Shah, the Hasora chief, upon his disclaiming any knowledge of indignities offered at Dras to Wali Ju, a Kashmirian envoy from Sultan Shah to Lé. In the disputes between Balti and Ladakh, the latter power had intercepted the supply of salt to Balti, and a messenger had been sent from Hasora to represent the inconvenience suffered by that state from this privation, and to pray for its removal. Wali Ju arrived at Dras on this mission. Some time before this, some horses belonging to Rasul Malik had been stolen from Matayan, on the Tibet frontier, and had been traced to the Raja of Hasora, and when the envoy of the latter appeared at Dras, he was threatened with detention until the horses

should be restored. The character of the Raja was also rather uncourteously handled. The Karpun and Chamal declared that Wali Ju had never been in actual durance, and that he laid no claim to the character of an accredited envoy; he appeared as a trader, and was suspected by them as a spy: however this might be, he reported to the Raja that he had been confined, and not allowed to proceed on his journey, and that the functionaries of Dras had used insulting language towards his employer. It was to revenge these indignities that the foray had taken place. Amongst the rest I was a sufferer, for I lost sixty-seven sheep I had formerly purchased, which had been left in the charge of the Chamal. The difficulty of procuring fresh horses and grain, and the alarm and indecision of our carriers, detained us ten days at Dras, during which all the males, with the Karpun at their head, set off for Lé to make their complaints to the Raja. Finding there was no chance of procuring carriage, Mir Izzet Ullah took five horses and made the best of his way to Sona-murg; there he met an agent of the Malik with fifty men and

as many horses, which had been dispatched to meet us, in anticipation of the embarrassments we were likely to experience. They joined us on the 28th of October, and on the following day we resumed our journey.

After crossing a rivulet running into the Dras river on its right bank, our road skirted the latter, proceeding along the Himbab valley: at two miles and a half from the last village, a considerable stream* falls into the Dras river on its left bank: the course of the latter is much broken by rocks, over which it rushed with great rapidity, and the water though clear was of so deep a blue, that it looked as if it held some salt of copper in solution. At about four miles from Dras, in a narrow valley, we passed the small hamlet of Pandras, or Phandas†, the lands of which were mostly in grass. The Prangos had accompanied our march, and at this place its hay was piled up on blocks of stone. A little beyond Pandras

* Mr. Trebeck considered this to be one of the heads of the Dras river; and he understood it to rise about eight miles off. The last, and according to some, the chief village of Dras stood on its left bank, not far from the junction.—Ed.

† Gholam Hyder calls it, and probably correctly, Pain-dras, or lower Dras.—Ed.

the river flowed from the southward, and continued in this direction till we reached Matayan, where we halted.

Matayan was a miserable hamlet of half a dozen mean houses of rubble building, and the inhabitants seemed to be wretchedly poor. The flocks and herds, however, were numerous and in good condition. On the 30th we followed the course of the river, marching occasionally on either bank, until we lost sight of it at the end of a defile, one part of it coming from a recess in the rocks about a mile off to the north of west, and the rest from beneath a bed of snow, along which we passed. About a thousand paces further on, we came to a large stone which marked the boundary of Ladakh, and we thence ascended a steep and rugged acclivity, which led to the summit of a lofty pass. Soon after quitting the source of the Dras river we came to a small rivulet, taking an opposite direction, or south-west. This was soon joined by a large stream from the south, coming from under a bed of snow on the face of the Waga Sugan mountain, the pyramidal peak of which, visible at no great distance on our left, is said to be never free

from snow. The stream then crossed our path, and continued its course between perpendicular rocks on its southern, and a steep ascent on its northern side, forming a ravine which, in the winter months, is entirely blocked up by ice and snow. A rather steep acclivity led up the side of a hill, on turning which to the left, a valley, forming the entrance into Kashmir, came in view, and, as if by magic, presented a striking contrast in its brown mountains and dark forests of tall pines to the bare rocks and few stunted willows, to which we had so long been accustomed. It is this part of the pass to which the name of Zwaje La is applied, and which seems to be the same as the Baltal Kotal of Desideri. It is considered as the principal pass by the Kashmirians, but is less elevated than the one first crossed.

As the ascent from Matayan had been gradual and tolerably easy, we were not prepared for so abrupt a descent as the western face of the pass presented. The path was planned in zigzag, but it was so narrow, steep, and slippery, that we had great difficulty in keeping our footing, and still more in effecting the safe passage

of the horses. The mountains below were clothed to their summits with pines, and generally skirted at the bases with birch-trees. Another large feeder from the south joined the river, which is here called the Kana patri.

Although the sides of the mountains were deep in snow, and such vegetable surface as appeared was brown and withered, yet the air felt mild and even warm, compared with that to which we had been lately exposed. We encamped in a forest, and one very important change occurred in the no longer scanty supply of fuel. We indulged ourselves with such luxurious fires as Tibet had never witnessed. To my great alarm, however, the passage of the sheep over the ghât was delayed till after nightfall, and several men on horseback were sent to their aid. They reached the tents at midnight.

On the 31st we continued our march along the valley, running nearly east and west. It was not above a quarter of a mile broad: on the southern side, the steep acclivities of the mountains were covered with fir-forests; those on the north were less abrupt, but more thinly wooded, the pine evidently affecting a north-

ern aspect. The ground was abundantly carpeted with grass. In a convenient part of the forest, on the plain, were two log-houses, built for the accommodation of travellers. The river ran along our left, and was joined by another considerable stream from the south, coming from the neighbouring mountain. In one place, on its left bank, an extensive tract was covered by the ruins of trees, which had been felled, apparently, by a storm, as they were all lying in one direction, with their tops towards the north. At an early hour we reached the village of Sona-murgh, said to be so named from the golden bird, or pheasant, found in the vicinity. It consisted of five or six houses on the right bank of the river, which here takes the name of Sindh.

The first appearance of the people of Kashmir was anything but prepossessing. The dress of both men and women consisted of a long loose wrapper and a low woollen cap, both sufficiently dirty. The legs and feet were bare, or wooden clogs were bound to the latter by straps of leather or straw. Poverty and discontent were the prevailing characteristics. The chief article of food was a kind of

greenish-coloured bread made from the tromba, or buck-wheat.

On our advance from Sona-murgh, we were met by letters from the Malik, from Khaja Shah Nyas Khan, and from Surat Sinh, the latter of whom announced himself as deputed by the Subahdar of Kashmir, Dewan Moti Ram, to attend upon, and conduct me to the capital. On the preceding day I had received a letter from Raja Ranjit Sinh, apprising me that at my intercession he had granted Khajah Shah Nyas a pension of five thousand six hundred rupees. This proved to be little better than a nominal allowance; but it showed that I had not incurred the serious displeasure of the Sikh by my interference in the affairs of the Khaja and of Ladakh. For some way beyond Sona-murgh the road was little else than a narrow path along the right bank of the Sindh, which received several small streams on its way. In one place it ran between a narrow gap in the mountain, at a place called Hang, over which we had to proceed by a very difficult and scabrous ascent, obstructed by blocks and fragments of stone, and dangerous from frequent slips.

From hence the road runs through a forest, in which I recognised the walnut, horse-chesnut, sycamore, ash, apricot, and other varieties. On clearing the forest, we came to a cultivated slope with a few houses, called Gagangir, where a thana for the levy of customs had been established, to prevent the smuggling of shawl-wool, which was formerly conveyed across the mountains to the garden of Shahlimar, and thence privily introduced into the city.

We were met at this place by the son of the Malik, a boy of about ten years old, and by a pandit, who offered us a present of money and refreshments on the part of Jawahir Mal. As we advanced the valley expanded, and much land was in cultivation, and many villages appeared; at one of which, named Gondh, the residence of Rasul Malik, we were met by Surat Sinh, and several Sirdars, on horseback, and an escort of light infantry, armed with matchlocks, swords, and shields. He welcomed me on the part of the Dewan, and insisted on my taking one rupee out of a number which he presented. He

was accompanied by the Malik, who seemed much affected at his brother's death. We were conducted to his house, and ushered into a matted apartment with a hearth, on which blazed a cheerful fire of pine-logs. We were regaled with tea, and afterwards with roasted chickens and venison, accompanied with wheaten cakes. We were then again served with buttered and salted tea, and shortly afterwards, in spite of our remonstrances, with pilao. The Malik stated that letters had been received from the Raja of Balti, disavowing all concern in the late inroads from Hasora, and that as soon as the weather permitted a force would proceed from Kashmir to exact retribution from the aggressors.

On the 1st of November we crossed the Sindh, about two miles from Gondh, by a bridge; but we still continued to follow its course to the west. The land was only partially cultivated, and was much intersected with forest, chiefly of fruit-trees, or walnuts, apricots, and apples growing wild. We passed several villages, some of considerable size. Kangan, on the right bank, which was one of

the largest, had a large building, used as a mosque. Along the river we observed planks and timber floating down to the city. We halted at Mamar, a small village about half a mile from the river. From thence, on the following day, we proceeded to Nunar, about eight kos. A pandit, and some other persons, brought a present of fruit from the Dewan.

On the 3rd we quitted the Sindh and its valley, and turning the southern range of mountains, now degenerated to low hills, passed the village and guzar, or custom-house, of Gandarbal, and came in sight of the small lake of Anchal in front of us, and the Kohi maran, the fortress that defends the eastern extremity of the city, situated upon a small hill on our left. At the guzar we met the physician of Omar Khan, about to proceed to Indejan by Balkh and Hissar, and Mir Ali Baksh, a relation of Mir Izzet Ullah. About two miles from the capital, a party of horse, and a detachment of the regiment of infantry disciplined in the European fashion, under the son of Nand Ram, awaited our approach, and escorted us past the remains of the Nazim bagh

into the city. The streets and houses were lined with spectators, and we proceeded through them to a neglected garden, once that of Dilawar Khan, in a building in which some apartments had been prepared for our accommodation. As we advanced Surat Sinh was assailed by many clamorous appeals from the crowd, and hands were stretched out, and cries addressed to us, praying for our interference to save the inhabitants from starvation. An order, it appeared, had recently emanated from Raja Ranjit Sinh, prohibiting the sale of any of this year's crop of rice until a deficit of five lakhs in the revenue of the preceding year had been discharged.

During the first day subsequent to our arrival we were beset by crowds of people, who not only filled the garden, but came in boats along a lake adjoining, on the border of which stood a sort of summer-house, in which I had taken up my quarters. The Hurkaras of the Dewan would have prohibited the people from approaching me, but I desired them to be admitted, hoping that in a few days the public curiosity would be satisfied. This, however, was far from the case, and the mul-

titude rather increased: amongst the crowd were men who had served as sipahis in India, and merchants from Delhi and Benares: the latter, as well as the Banias of Kashmir, tendered their services to advance whatever cash I might require for my bills on Hindustan. There was one man who had been at Calcutta, and not a little mystified his countrymen by stories, for the veracity of which he appealed to me. He had come to Kashmir to purchase shawls, and his remarks on those of English manufacture may be worth recording. At the first glance, he said, they looked like those of Kashmir; but upon inspection were found less soft in texture, and less brilliant in colour; and the weaving of the flowers, when examined on the wrong side, looked more like the disposition of threads left by the needle of the embroiderer, than by the bobbin of the weaver. It was his belief that if a thread or two were unravelled, the whole flower would come out. He was satisfied, he said, that if we had the materials we should have the manufacture, and that it was our own fault if we had not the former.

The Dewan Moti Ram had fixed the second day after my arrival for giving me audience, but indisposition obliged him to defer this for several days longer, and in the mean time a reference to Ranjit Sinh became necessary. The Raja had stated in his instructions to Moti Ram that we purposed staying eight or ten days at Kashmir, a period that by no means suited my convenience. I had left Mr. Trebeck in Ladakh, to wait for a servant who was bringing me a valuable packet of pearls and coral from Delhi, and I could scarcely expect he would join me in less than a month. It also required some time for us to re-establish our marching equipage, exhausted and disfurnished at it was by our long sojourn in Tibet. It was therefore necessary to apply for permission to remain for a further period in Kashmir; and this being readily conceded, we quartered ourselves in Kashmir for the winter months, resuming our movements only in May, 1823.

The garden-house, belonging formerly to a nobleman named Dilawar Khan, situated on the Biari nam bal, a small lake, or rather an

expanse of one of the chief canals of the city, was assigned for our residence, and here, as at Lé, my time was spent in medical practice, collecting information, and occasional excursions.

CHAPTER II.

Description of Kashmir—Succession of Valleys and Mountains—Richness of Vegetation—Moisture of Climate—Vitastha or Behut river—Its feeders—Wular lake—Dal lake—Extent of the valley of the Behut—Breadth of Kashmir—Divisions—Situation of city—Canals—Houses—Public Edifices—Great Mosque—Bridges—Population—Distress—Disease—Revenues—Character of the people—Literature—Dress—Food—Agricultural and other products—Grains—Rice—Sinhara, or Water-nut—Lotus-stem—Floating gardens—Fruit—Vines—Walnut-trees—Forest-trees—Animals, &c.—Winter fodder—Cotton—Silk—Costus—Bees—Minerals.

KASHMIR has been often described, but it may be doubted if any of the descriptions yet published have conveyed an accurate notion of the country; and the designation of 'valley,' which is ordinarily applied to it, is by no means an appropriate term. The course of the Vitastha, or Behut, does, indeed, form one principal valley, extending from the eastern to the western limits of the province; but the greater part of the country is made up of a similar disposition of vale and mountain, as is observable in all these alpine regions, and consists of a series of mountain ranges, running mostly in parallel lines from south-west

to north and east, separated by glens, which are in general of no great breadth.

The chief peculiarity by which Kashmir is distinguished from the mountain countries on its confines is the richness of its vegetation. The mountains, although for a considerable part of the year capped in many parts with snow, are coated with rich forests, and at their bases is a productive alluvial soil abounding with verdure, or, where cultivated, with plentiful harvests, especially of rice. The cause of this is, no doubt, to be found in the humidity of its climate, which formed to our feelings a very disagreeable contrast to the dryness of the atmosphere of Ladakh.

The year in Kashmir may be divided into summer and winter seasons, of nearly equal duration, the former being in general somewhat the longest. Snow usually begins to fall in December, and disappears from the warmer valleys in March. In the passes on the frontiers it remains of considerable depth till the middle of April, and lies throughout the year on the crests of some of the loftiest of the chains which surround the province. The total annual quantity is so great, that it bends the branches of the wild apple-trees, on which

it rests for months, into a right angle with their trunks, giving them the appearance of cypresses.

The end of March and beginning of April are distinguished by the popular term of dirty spring, or mud season; and these appellations, in regard to the mire of the surface, and the rapid succession of gusts of wind and hail, with short gleams of sunshine, are well deserved. In April, 1823, there were but four days of sunshine, and the waters of the neighbouring lakes rose three feet, by the accession of large quantities of rain and of melted snow poured into them by mountain-torrents. In May, of the same year, scarcely a day passed without a shower, and dense clouds constantly rested upon the summits of the mountains, exhibiting an atmosphere surcharged with moisture. The remaining summer months are hot, and bring the fruits and grain to rapid maturity. The abundant supply of water from snow and rain is collected into numerous streams and lakes, the overflowing of which, with the evaporation from them, preserve both soil and atmosphere in a humid condition, more propitious to vegetable than to animal life.

The traditions of the country assert, that the whole of Kashmir, intending thereby the principal line of valley, was originally one large lake, and the aspect of the province confirms the truth of the legend, the subsidence of the waters being distinctly defined by horizontal lines on the face of the mountains: it is also not at all unlikely to have been the scene of some great convulsion of nature, as indications of volcanic action are not unfrequent: hot springs are numerous: at particular seasons the ground in various places is sensibly hotter than the atmosphere, and earthquakes are of common occurrence. What the central and more elevated parts of the mountains may consist of, we did not ascertain; but their sides and bases consist of clay, whilst in the valley the soil is a rich vegetable mould, often more or less extensively inundated, from the numerous streams and watercourses by which the surface is traversed. When neglected after cultivation, it throws up a thickly-matted sod of fiorin, or dúb-grass, little mixed with rank herbage, except in the immediate vicinity of unreclaimed forests.

The chief river of Kashmir is the Vitastha, Vehut or Behut, the Hydaspes of the ancients. This rises at an angle of the mountains, chiefly from the springs of Viranag, in the south-east extremity of Kashmir. It is immediately joined by a stream from the south, the Kaimu river, and another from the north, the river of Brang. This latter rises by two heads in the district of the same name, to the east of Islamabad, at eight kos distance. It again divides into two branches, the more northerly of which is joined by a small stream from Kotonhara, and the more southerly by the stream from Vir Nag: the two main trunks again meet near Islamabad and form the Behut, which, as it proceeds, receives other streams, as the Lambodari or the Lidder from the north-east, on the road to Amaranath, and the Shupien or Shuingulu river, which is formed by various rivulets from the north of the Pir Panchal mountains. The Sindh, which takes its source from the Zwaje La pass, forms its own valley, and passing round the city falls into the Behut on the northern bank, about seven kos above it, and the Dudh Ganga comes from the south, rising,

it is said, thirty kos off from the Sáng-safed, and joins the Behut just above the capital. The Behut passes through the city, receiving waters from its various canals. Besides the Dudh Ganga, it is joined from the south by the Haratirtha river, and then flows through an angle of the Wular lake. It is then joined by the Lalakoal river from the north, after which it proceeds to the pass of Baramula, where it leaves the province. It then turns southward to Muzeffarabad, where it is joined by the Muzeffarabad river, and then proceeds to the Panjab, where it is known as the Jhelum. During the whole of its course in Kashmir it is navigable, although it varies much in its depth. In December, in its course through the city, it was seventy yards broad, from one to two fathoms deep, and ran at the rate of eight hundred yards an hour. In May it rose twenty-five feet, and it was said that it sometimes attained an elevation of thirty.

The Wular, or Ular Lake, is of an elliptical form, and may be nearly forty miles in circumference*: it lies about twelve kos north-

* Baron Hügel says that it extends thirty miles from east to

west of the city. Adjoining to the latter on the east is the Dal, a less extensive piece of water, supplied by some small streams flowing down a confined valley, interposed between the valleys of the Behut and Sindh, and sending off its superfluous waters by different canals, flowing through the city to the Behut. There are several other small lakes within the province, as the Anchar, Manas, and others.

The whole length of the valley of the Behut, constituting the greatest extent of Kashmir from south-east to north-west, may be about fifty miles; the greatest breadth of the valley, immediately to the west of the city, is not above fifteen miles; and in many parts it is much less, or not more than five or six. The whole breadth of Kashmir may be about forty or fifty miles, the greatest portion of which, to the north of the Behut, consists of lofty mountains and narrow valleys, thinly

west, which is much beyond the truth. Forster says the Wuller lake is only seven or eight miles in circumference. According to Abulfazl, the circumference was twenty-eight kos, but of what kind of kos he does not mention, although he probably meant the Ilahi, which would make the extent of the lake about sixty miles. It may, perhaps, have somewhat filled up since his time—ED.

inhabited. The province is divided into thirty-six perganas, the names of which, with their principal places respectively, are the following:—

On the left bank of the Behut.

	Pergana.	Town.
1	Bannahal	Shahabad.
2	Deosar	Kolagam.
3	Batu	Shupien.
4	Suprasaman	——
5	Adwaind	Mohanpur.
6	Shukaruh	——
7	Mohammedabad	Mohammedabad.
8	Megam	Muran.
9	Yecha	Yechagam.
10	Dainsok	Wampura.
11	Manchamun	Suibok.
12	Birus	Wanigam.
13	Baladak	Khushipur.
14	Tahirabad	——
15	Parispur	Gondi Khaja Kasim
16	Tilagam	Patan
17	Bainjil	Uttamagam
18	Anderkoth	Sumbhelpur
19	Krohin	Wagur
20	Kamraj, including Kahol, Hamal Machipura, Durbed, and Karnao.	

On the right bank.

	Pergana.	Town.
1	Brang	Sagam.
2	Kotohar	Chatar.
3	Martand	——
4	Dakshinpara	Kanyalwan.
5	Kaharwapara	——
6	Islamabad	Islamabad.
7	Sair-ul Mawaza, upper	Several places.
8	Wular	Tral.
9	Vehu	Pamper.
10	Phak	Panjgam.
11	Lar	Lar.
12	Atsan	Atsan.
13	Sair-ul Mawaza, lower	Safapur and others.
14	Kuhiama	Alusa.
15	Zein-nagar	——
16	Lolab	Sogam *.

* Ritter has compiled from various sources a list of thirty-four perganas, the names of several of which agree with those of the text. It is also to be remarked that several names, both of districts and principal villages or towns, occur in the notes of the excursions made in the country by both our travellers, which are not included in the above list.—Ed.

Several of these districts are very small, and few even of their chief places are more than villages. The mountainous tracts have the general name of Narwao, and the valleys Nal or Nala. The principal passes into the country are, to the south the Shupien, leading over the Pir Panchal mountains, and others crossing the mountains of Prunch; on the west that of Baramula; Zwaje La on the east, and the Kamri-bal on the north. The elevation of Zwaje La is nearly twelve thousand feet; that of the valley in general about five thousand*.

The city of Kashmir, or as it was formerly called, Srinagar, lies on either bank of the Behut, extending about four miles: the principal part, the north-west, lies mostly to the north of the river; on the south-east and south of the river is the suburb of Sher Gerh, attached to a fortress of no great strength or extent: at the same end, the eastern extremity of the city, is situated the hill called the Hari-parbat or Kohi-maran, at the southern

* Baron Hügel names twelve passes, five of which are of recent use. *Journ. Geog. Soc.*, vol. vi. p. 347. M. Jacquemont calls the elevation of the city five thousand two hundred and forty-six feet. —Ed.

foot of which is the Lake or Dal, and immediately to the south of that rises the eminence called the Takhti Suliman, or Throne of Solomon. The Kohi-maran is surmounted by a long narrow fort, beneath the bastions of which, on the edge of the rock, two or three large guns are mounted, which command the city. It may be doubted if the fortress itself could be furnished with cannon, as it is entirely roofed over, and presents no appearance of embrasures. The slope of the hill is covered with houses.

The Dal or Lake is nearly circular, but the number of floating gardens it contains prevents its outline from being distinctly made out: it may be about nine miles in circumference. It is supplied chiefly by the waters of the valley, to the east of the garden of Shahlimar, the principal part of which flows through the canal of Tej-bal into the lake, and the rest, after supplying the cascades of the garden, also enters the lake. Towards the Hari Parbat the Dal breaks into several small canals, the principal of which is the Raini-war, and which flowing to the west, and receiving several smaller canals, divides above the bridge

of Naupura into two branches; one of these turning more to the south, joins another considerable canal from the lake, and the united stream flows into the Behut, at the water-gate of the city opposite to Sher Gerh. The other branch passes under the bridge, and turning to the north-west, expands into the Beari Nam-bal, on the western edge of which lay the garden of Dilawar Khan, in which we were quartered. From the northern edge of this expanse, the canal now called the Nala Mar proceeds through the town, passing underneath several bridges, and being the most serviceable of any of the canals, although not kept in very good order: it has water sufficient to admit of boats of considerable burden, and grain is brought by this means into the heart of the city. Between the bridges called Saraf-kadal and Kazi-kadal, and on each side of the canal, is the part of the town called Sheikh Mahal, in which are situated the best houses in Kashmir, occupied by merchants and bankers: to the east lies the principal mosque. From hence the canal follows a semicircular course, and issues from the town within a few paces

of the Eid Gah. It then flows to the small lake of Anchar, and again issuing from it, proceeds in a curved direction towards the Behut, which it joins near the debouche of the Sindh.

The Raini-war canal receives at its commencement, where it is called also the water of Khaja-yar-bal, a small supply from the northward. The contents of the canal by which it is brought are furnished by the Sindh, near the village of Kanja; passing over a platform, it skirts the base of the hills past Gandarbal, and sends off a main branch into the city, to fulfil one of the main objects of its construction, the provision of a supply of water to the Jama Masjid, to which it was led in as direct a line as the surface permitted. It is called the Lakhi canal, having cost a lakh of rupees, and was the work of Zein-ul-abaddin. The mosque has been thrice destroyed by fire, and it and the canal were last repaired by Aurangzeb. The latter is now choked, but was open till recently, and supplied several houses close even to the Biari Nambal. Another branch of the canal goes off to the Tej-bal, on the east of the lake, and the rest of its water passes towards the

foot of the old wall of Nagar, where it forms a broad ditch, and then continuing its course along the base of the Kohi Maran on the north-east, unites with the Raini-war, as above noticed. These canals are in general faced with stone, derived frequently from the ruins of Hindu temples, the sculpture on which is turned inwards. They are crossed in various parts by wooden bridges, and upon the whole afford evidence of the munificence and public spirit of the ancient princes of Kashmir. When properly taken care of, and filled with running water, they no doubt contribute to the salubrity, as well as to the cleanliness of the city; but their general condition is now that of decay, and they render the town neither cleanly nor salubrious.

The general character of the city of Kashmir is that of a confused mass of ill-favoured buildings, forming a complicated labyrinth of narrow and dirty lanes, scarcely broad enough for a single cart to pass, badly paved, and having a small gutter in the centre full of filth, banked up on each side by a border of mire. The houses are in general two or three stories high; they are built of unburnt bricks and timber, the former serving for little else

than to fill up the interstices of the latter; they are not plastered, are badly constructed, and are mostly in a neglected and ruinous condition, with broken doors, or no doors at all, with shattered lattices, windows stopped up with boards, paper, or rags, walls out of the perpendicular, and pitched roofs threatening to fall. The roofs are formed of layers of birch bark covered by a coating of earth, in which seeds dropped by birds, or wafted by the wind, have vegetated, and they are constantly overrun with grass, flowers, and seeds. The houses of the better class are commonly detached, and surrounded by a wall and gardens, the latter of which often communicate with a canal: the condition of the gardens is no better than that of the building, and the whole presents a striking picture of wretchedness and decay.

There are no public buildings in the city of Kashmir entitled to notice for their architectural or antiquarian merits. The oldest building is the tomb of the mother of Zein-ul-ab-addin, who reigned in the middle of the fifteenth century, and who is said to have made use of a more ancient Hindu temple for the

purpose. It is an octagonal building of brick, surmounted by a dome of great solidity and strength, the walls being seven or eight feet thick, but of no beauty. The shrine of Sayid Ali Hamadani is constructed chiefly of the wood of the Deodar pine, and is equipped with a pyramidal steeple of timber, capped with brass. The most celebrated structure, however, is the Jama Masjid, or great mosque, which is capable of containing, it is said, sixty thousand persons. After having been four times destroyed by fire, it was last re-built in the time of Aurangzeb: it had been shut up at the time of our visit by order of Ranjit Sinh, lest the plea it afforded for the assemblage of large bodies of Mohammedans should afford opportunities of plotting against his rule. The Jama Masjid consists in great part of wood, a dome and spire of timber of rude construction, resting partly upon wooden pillars, and partly on side walls, of which the foundation and lower portion consist of roughly hewn stones, and the upper of brick and mortar. The number of pillars is three hundred and eighty-four; the intervals are usually considerable. The columns are

formed of an assemblage of square blocks of Deodar, about a foot in diameter, laid at right angles to each other, so that each face presents a succession of butts and sides, or to speak more technically, a bond of alternate headers and leaders: the blocks are probably secured together by pins, but those are not seen exteriorly. The columns are in general about ten feet high, but some are taller than others. The peculiarity of their construction was, no doubt, suggested by the occurrence of earthquakes, which are frequent in Kashmir, though not very violent. Certain it is, that although the roof and walls have been rent and shattered in various places, not one of the pillars appears to have been seriously injured, or to have deviated from its original perpendicular. Such also is the durability of the timber of the Deodar, that in none of the columns was any vestige of decay from exposure or insects to be discovered, although they have been erected above a century and a half, and have received for some time past very little care or attention.

The same valuable material is employed in the formation of bridges over the canals and

rivers of the country. Very commonly the breadth of these requires merely a platform resting upon haunches; but in many places it is necessary to support the road-way by piers in the stream. In this case the piers are formed of four pieces of the trunk of the Deodar, laid at right angles over each other, and leaving in the centre a hollow square of about two feet. Each pier consists of a shaft, a basement, and a capital: the shaft is usually from twenty to twenty-five feet in breadth, the height varies with the depth of the stream. The foundation is constructed on the same principle, but extends beyond the shaft, and presents to the current a pointed extremity: it is also filled with heavy stones to prevent its being carried away. The capital consists of five graduated tiers of beams, crossing the water line, and forming the support of the platform, connecting them at top, which is formed of layers of Deodar timbers, crossed and fastened together by pins. This construction is so solid, that upon one of the bridges, the Zein-al-kadal, a line of shops, the best in the city, is situated. The shops are built of wood, each with a work-room and

show-room, and the concourse of buyers is very considerable. Other bridges over the Vitastha, as the Hab-alkadal, Fatteh-kadal, Ali-kadal, and Amir-kadal, the latter close to the fort of Sher Gerh, are all built in the same manner: the foundations and piers of most of them were in a ruinous condition, but less from decay in the timbers, than the action of the current, the displacement of the stones or blocks of wood, and neglect in giving them occasional repair.

The population of the City of Kashmir, although much diminished, must be numerous. One hundred and twenty thousand persons, it is said, are employed in the shawl manufacture alone; and, although this is the chief employment of the population, yet the other trades and occupations, essential to the support of a large city, must, at least, double the amount: the population of the province is estimated at eight hundred thousand*. Everywhere, however, the people are in the most abject condition; exorbitantly taxed by the Sikh government, and subjected to every

* Baron Hügel states it to have declined to one-fourth, or two hundred thousand. *Journ. Geog. Soc.*, vol. vi. p. 348.—ED.

kind of extortion and oppression by its officers. The consequences of this system are, the gradual depopulation of the country: not more than about one-sixteenth of the cultivable surface is in cultivation, and the inhabitants starving at home, are driven in great numbers to the Plains of Hindustan. In like manner the people of the city are rapidly thinning, though less from emigration, than poverty and disease: the prevalence of the latter in its most aggravated forms was fearfully extensive. I devoted every Friday to the reception of visits from the sick, and a greater number and cases of greater inveteracy crowded round my door than ever presented themselves at the Hotel de Dieu. I had at one time no fewer than six thousand eight hundred patients on my list, a large proportion of whom were suffering from the most loathsome diseases, brought on by scant and unwholesome food, dark, damp, and ill-ventilated lodgings, excessive dirtiness, and gross immorality.

According to the prevailing notions on the subject the whole of the land in Kashmir is considered to have been, time out of mind,

the property of the ruler. Of some portions of the Khalsa lands the sovereigns divested themselves by grants in Jagir for various periods, but when the country came into the hands of the Sikhs, Ranjit Sinh made a general resumption, and ousted the possessors of grants of land of every class, thus summarily reducing thousands who had long lived in comfort to a state of absolute destitution.

The Khalsa lands are now, as heretofore, let out for cultivation. Those near the city are termed Sar-Kishti, those more remote Pai-Kishti; or head and foot, upper and lower cultivation. When the grain has been trodden out, a division takes place between the farmer and the government: this was formerly an equal division, but the government has advanced in its demands until it has appropriated about seven-eighths of the Sar-Kishti, and three-fourths of the Pai-Kishti crop. The straw falls to the share of the cultivator, but his case would be desperate if it were not practicable to bribe the overseer or watchman to let him steal a portion of his own produce. He has also a

house to live in; he can keep his cattle on the mountains during summer, can cut wood and bring it to the city for sale, can sell wild greens and butter-milk, and can support himself and family upon the wild fruits of the forest. Still the cultivators of Kashmir are in a condition of extreme wretchedness, and, as if the disproportionate demand of the government was not sufficiently oppressive, the evil is aggravated by the mode adopted of disposing of the government share. It is sent into the market at a high price, and no individual is allowed to offer the produce of his farm at a lower rate, or sometimes to dispose of it at all, until the public corn has been sold.

A much larger revenue than that which is obtained from the land is realised from the shawl manufacture, every shawl being stamped, and the stamp-duty being twenty-six per cent. upon the estimated value. Besides this a considerable sum is raised by duties upon the import of wool, and a charge upon every shop or workman connected with the manufacture. Nor are these imposts restricted to the artisans employed in the

shawl fabric, every trade is taxed, butchers, bakers, boatmen, venders of fuel, public notaries, scavengers, prostitutes, all pay a sort of corporation tax, and even the Kotwal, or chief officer of justice, pays a large gratuity of thirty thousand rupees a year for his appointment, being left to reimburse himself as he may. A portion of the Sinhara crop, to the extent annually of a lac of rupees it is said, is claimed by the government. The revenue is farmed, and the farmer is independent of the military governor. At the time of our visit the sum paid by the farmer was thirty-eight lakhs of Panjab rupees, equal to twenty-nine lakhs of Sicca rupees, or about two hundred and ninety thousand pounds; but a much larger sum than this was extorted from the people, although it was only to be realised by the greatest rigour and oppression *.

* Late advices from India report the necessary consequences of this system. In 1835 scarcely any revenue could be collected. In 1836 twenty-three lakhs were demanded, but, according to Baron Hügel, it was not likely to be raised. Papers of the beginning of this year state that Ranjit had reduced the demand to eighteen lakhs, but that it was not possible to enforce even this collection.—ED.

The natives of Kashmir have been always considered as amongst the most lively and ingenious people of Asia, and deservedly so. With a liberal and wise government they might assume an equally high scale as a moral and intellectual people, but at present a more degraded race does not exist. The complexion of the Kashmirians varies from dark to olive, and is sometimes ruddy and transparent: the eyes are large and full, the nose is well defined, and commonly of an aquiline form. The stature varies, but the Hindus who have least intermixed with foreign races are, in general, tall and symmetrically made. The inhabitants of the city are rather slight, but amongst the peasantry, both Hindu and Mohammedan, are to be found figures of robust and muscular make, such as might have served for models of the Farnesan Hercules. In character the Kashmirian is selfish, superstitious, ignorant, supple, intriguing, dishonest, and false: he has great ingenuity as a mechanic, and a decided genius for manufactures and commerce, but his transactions are always conducted in a fraudulent spirit, equalled only

by the effrontery with which he faces detection. The vices of the Kashmirian I cannot help considering, however, as the effects of his political condition, rather than his nature, and conceive that it would not be difficult to transform him into a very different being. Religious bigotry forms no part of his character, and the teachers of either faith, Mullas or Pundits, are exceedingly ignorant, and possess little influence. Since the establishment of the Sikh authority Hinduism predominates, and the country is infested by numerous and audacious bands of mendicants. They are patronized rather by the Government than the people, and the latter would gladly get rid of their presence. There seems, indeed, to be little attachment of either the Mohammedans or Hindus of Kashmir to their respective creeds, and I am convinced there is no part of India where the pure religion of the Gospel might be introduced with a fairer prospect of success.

Literature of any description is almost unknown in Kashmir, and it is not easy to discover any relics of those celebrated Sanscrit compositions which originated in the

patronage of the princes of the country whilst it was a Hindu principality. Our attention was especially directed to this subject by a communication from the Secretary of the Asiatic Society, who was desirous of procuring copies of the Chronicles of Kashmir, the Raja Tarangini, of a local legend called the Níla Purána, and a collection of tales, entitled the Vrihat Kathá. The most particular inquiry was set on foot for these works, and, after much delay, we heard of two copies of the Chronicles, written on birch-bark, and one of the Vrihat Kathá, on a similar material. They were shown to us, and appeared to be antient. Nothing could induce the owners to part with them, but they had no objection to copies being taken. A copy of the Raja Tarangini was accordingly transcribed during our stay, and one of the Vrihat Kathá was put in hand, under the superintendence of a native friend, who promised to forward it when finished to Calcutta. The Níla Purána was less scarce, and a copy was purchased, and sent down *.

* The copy of the Raja Tarangini is in the possession of the Asiatic Society of Bengal, to whom it was presented by Mr.

These were the only Sanscrit works of the existence of which we obtained any information.

The dress of the people, both male and female, commonly consists of a long loose wrapper and trowsers, the former of woollen cloth. As a further protection against the cold in winter the Kashmirians usually carry under their tunic an earthen pot with a small quantity of live charcoal, a practice that invariably discolours and sears the skin, and not unfrequently occasions palsy. The Hindu women never go veiled, and never affect concealment, either at home or abroad. They had long been exempted from the cruel obligation of burning with their husbands, the custom of which, according to tradition, was never very popular in Kashmir, having been suppressed by an edict of Aurangzeb in 1669, and never subsequently revived.

Moorcroft. That of the Vrihat Kathá was never received. The Níla Purána was sent to me, and is in my possession, but I doubt its authenticity. The text of the Raja Tarangini has been printed at Calcutta, and an edition, with a translation by Captain Troyer, is about to appear at Paris. An edition of the Vrihat Kathá is also in course of preparation in Germany by Mr. Brockhaus, with either a complete or partial translation.—Ed.

The food of those who can afford it is partly of meat, mutton of goats or sheep, which sells at about threepence per pound. Beef is not procurable, as the Sikh ruler punishes the death of a cow capitally. The chief food of the people is vegetable; turnips, cabbages, and radishes, the Sinhara, or water-nut, and rice. The turnips are purple, or reddish, and speedily become woolly: the radishes are mostly white and strong: the cabbages do not head, but the leaves are frequently stripped. Besides these, lettuces, spinach, and other common vegetables are in extensive use, boiled into a sort of soup, with a little salt, or even the leaves of the dandelion, dock, plantain, and mallow; and the catkins of the walnut are employed as food, seasoned with a little salt, mustard, and walnut oil.

Although wheat, barley, buck-wheat, millet, maize, pulse, and amaranthus are grown in Kashmir, yet the staple of cultivation is rice. This is sown in the beginning of May, and is fit to cut about the end of August. The grain is either sown broadcast in the place where it is intended to

stand till ripe, or thickly in beds, from which it is transplanted when the blade is about a foot high. As soon as the season will admit after the 21st of March, the land is opened by one or more ploughings, according to its strength, and the clods are broken down by blows with wooden mattocks, managed in general by women, with great regularity and address, after which water is let upon the soil, which, for the most part, of a reddish clay, or foxy earth, is converted into a smooth soft mud. The seed grain, put into a sack of woven grass, is submerged in a running stream until it begins to sprout, which happens sooner or later, according to the temperature of the water and of the atmosphere, but ordinarily takes place in three or four days. This precaution is adopted for the purpose of getting the young shoot as quickly as possible out of the way of a small snail, which abounds in some of the watered lands of Kashmir, but sometimes proves insufficient to defend it against the activity of this diminutive enemy. When the farmer suspects, by the scanty appearance of the plants above the water in which

the grain has been sown, and by the presence of the snail drawn up in the mud, that his hopes of a crop are likely to be disappointed, he repeats the sowing, throwing into the water some fresh leaves of the Prangos, called Krangos, which either poison the snails, or cause them to descend out of the reach of its influence. The seed is, for the most part, thrown broadcast into about four or five inches of water, which depth is endeavoured to be maintained. Difference of practice exists as to watering, but it seems generally agreed that rice can scarcely have too much water, provided it be not submerged except for a few days before it ripens, when a drier state is supposed to hasten and to perfect the maturity, whilst it improves the quality of the grain. In general the culture of rice is little expensive, though more so in Kashmir than in Hindustan, from its being customary in the former country to manure the rice lands, which is never done in the latter. This manure, for the most part, consists of rice straw, rejected by the cattle, and mixed with cowdung. It is conveyed from the home-

stead to the fields by women in small wicker baskets, and is set on the land with more liberality than might have been expected from the distance it is carried. Many of the rice lands are situated much higher than might be thought convenient in Hindustan, and are rather pressed into this species of culture than naturally inviting, but still yield good crops, through the facility with which water is brought upon them from the streams which fall down the face of the neighbouring hills. In common seasons the return of grain is from thirty to forty for one, on an average, besides the straw.

In the time of Zein ul abaddin the annual produce of the rice crop is said to have been seventy-seven lakhs of ass-loads, of which the sovereign received one-half. At present the quantity does not exceed twenty lakhs of loads. The price of rice at the period of our residence was from two rupees and a half to three and a half, or between four and five shillings a load. A kharwar, or ass-load, is not an indefinite term, but a measure of sixteen taraks. This, which is the standard of Kashmir, is equal to six sers, a ser

is equal to twenty pals, and a pal ought to be equal to three Mohammed Shahi rupees, and a third. At this rate the ser should weigh nearly two pounds (the rupee being 173·3 grains). The actual ser, however, is not above one pound avoirdupois, and an ass load is, therefore, about ninety-six pounds. A horse-load consists of twenty-two taraks.

Another principal article of the food of the common people, the Sinhara, or water-nut, grows abundantly in the different lakes in the vicinity of the capital, and especially in the Wular lake, which yields an average return of ninety-six to a hundred and twenty thousand ass-loads a-year. It is fished up from the bottom in small nets, and affords employment to the fishermen for several months. It constitutes the almost only food of at least thirty thousand persons for five months in the year. After being extracted from the shell the nuts are eaten, raw, boiled, roasted, fried, or dressed in various ways, after being reduced to flour. The most common preparation is boiling one ser of the flour with two quarts of water, so as to form a sort

of gruel, which, though insipid, is nutritive. The Sinhara, in the shell, is sold at about a rupee per load.

Another article of food derived from the lakes is the stem of the Nymphæa Lotus. In the autumn, after the plate of the leaf has begun to decay, this has acquired maturity, and, being boiled till tender, furnishes a wholesome and nutritious article, which supports, perhaps, five thousand persons in the city for nearly eight months.

Another, and an important use, made of the abundant water surface of Kashmir, is the formation of floating gardens. Various aquatic plants spring from the bottom of the lakes, as water lilies, confervæ, sedges, reeds, &c., and as the boats which traverse these waters take, generally, the shortest lines they can pursue to the place of their destination, the lakes are, in some parts, cut, as it were, in avenues amongst the plants, which, in shallows, are separated by beds of sedges and of reeds. In the latter places the neighbouring farmer attempts to establish his cucumber and melon floats, by cutting off the roots of the aquatic plants just men-

tioned, about two feet under the water, so that they completely lose all connexion with the bottom of the lake, but retain their former situation in respect to each other. When thus detached from the soil they are pressed into somewhat closer contact, and formed into beds of about two yards in breadth, and of an indefinite length. The heads of the sedges, reeds, and other plants of the float, are now cut off, and laid upon its surface, and covered with a thin coat of mud, which, at first intercepted in its descent, gradually sinks into the mass of matted roots. The bed floats, but is kept in its place by a stake of willow driven through it at each end, which admits of its rising or falling in accommodation to the rise or fall of the water. By means of a long pole thrust amongst the weeds at the bottom of the lake from the side of a boat, and turned round several times in the same direction, a quantity of confervæ and of other plants is torn off from the bottom, and carried in the boat to the platform, where the weeds are twisted into conical mounds about two feet in diameter at their base, and of the same height, terminating at

the top in a hollow, which is filled with fresh soft mud, drawn from the bottom of the lake, to which sometimes wood ashes are added, though much more frequently omitted. The farmer has in preparation a large number of cucumber and melon plants, which have been raised under mats, and of these, when they have four leaves, he places three plants in the basin of every cone or mound, of which a double row runs along the edge of every bed, at about two feet distance from each other. No further care is necessary, except that of collecting the fruit, and the expense of preparing the platforms and cones is confined to the value of the labour, which altogether is trifling, as the work is very soon done. Perhaps a more economical method of raising cucumbers cannot be devised, and though the narrow beds are ordinarily almost in contact by their sides, yet, by their flexible nature, they are so separable that a small boat may be readily pushed between the lines without injuring their structure, and, for the most part, they will bear a man's weight, but, generally, the fruit is picked off from the boat. I traversed a tract of about

fifty acres of these floating gardens of cucumbers and melons, and saw not above half a dozen unhealthy plants ; nor have I seen in the cucumber and melon grounds in the vicinity of very populous cities in Europe, or in Asia, so large an expanse of plant in a state equally healthy, though it must be observed, without running into luxuriance of growth. This condition indicated the situation to be congenial to the constitution of the cucumber, of which, however, a more substantial proof was found in the very large number of young fruit set near the crown, which certainly exceeded what I have before witnessed in the usual modes of cultivating this vegetable. It has been noticed that the top of each mound is formed into a cup or hollow, which is surrounded by a circle or belt of weed. This prevents the male dust from being dissipated, and causes the fecundating process to be as complete as can be wished.

Finding that the floating gardens were most heavily taxed, that a very large quantity of cucumbers was daily brought from them into the market, and that these were

readily digested, and, when eaten largely, produced no disease, I was induced to pay the gardens a second visit a little more than a fortnight after the first, and at the end of June. The plants had thrown out vines, but these, though thick and well set with flowers, and with large healthy leaves, had not acquired great length. The fruiting was still confined, in great measure, to the crown, in each of which, notwithstanding the continued cropping, there were generally from one to three fruit, the largest from five to seven inches in length, and from one and a half to two inches in diameter. The number of flowers was great, and young fruit were thickly set. It was observed that the stems of many plants had been newly earthed up by about two handfuls of black mud brought from the bottom of the lake. At this visit I saw not any weakly plant save one, before remarked, and this, greatly recovered, was now full of flower. The general depth of the floating beds, or mats of weeds and of earth, taken together, was about two feet, and I now observed that some of the beds were about seven feet broad. The general

arrangement was a line of cucumber cones, bordering each edge, and one of water, or of musk melons, along the middle. The melon plants had become strong, and their cones were now wound round with a fresh addition of confervæ and of other weeds, so as to give to each about five feet in diameter.

The gardeners reported the utmost yield to be about twenty-five large fruit from each cone, which seemed to be but a small return in proportion to the large surface of flower, the length of the season of crop, and the rapidity of the growth of the fruit. The season lasts for three months and a half, beginning in June. The fruit is seldom or ever pulled in the small or girkin state, and differs in weight, when of a proper age for the market, from about eight or ten ounces to a pound and a quarter, or a pound and a half. From the first setting of the fruit to the time of pulling, seven or eight days are the ordinary period. Having been much acquainted with the unwillingness of the farmers of the East to make a true report of the produce of their farms, I employed a servant of mine, who lived amongst the water gardeners, to

obtain an accurate account of the yield of a cone. He stated that, in answer to his inquiries, the gardeners acknowledged that thirty full-sized fruit for every plant, or from ninety to one hundred, were the average crop of one cone in the season. In the early part the cucumbers of full size sell at the rate of about three for a piece of coin of about the value of a halfpenny, but as the weather becomes hotter, and the plants get into full bearing, ten, fifteen, and even twenty, are purchaseable for this price. It is calculated that every cone yields a money return of about eighteen pence, or each plant about six tunga of two pice each. Allowing sixpence for labour of every description, and including also the tax, the clear profit is a shilling for every two square yards. The yield of the melon and water-melon is numerically less, but the return of profit is at least equal, in consequence of the fruit being sold at from a halfpenny to twopence each. The seed of the melon is brought annually from Baltistan, or Little Tibet, and the first year yields fruit of from four to nine and ten pounds each in weight; but if the seed of this

melon be re-sown, the produce of the second year exceeds not from two to three pounds. On a more minute inquiry it would seem that the melons are sweet and well flavoured, whilst the water-melons are of the common quality of this fruit. Unless when eaten to great excess the melon produces not any derangement in the intestines, but in the latter instance sometimes causes purging. It is remarked that healthy persons, who live upon this fruit almost wholly during the season, become speedily fat, and the same effect is reported in regard to horses fed upon this fruit at Bokhara. Although water-mint grows spontaneously upon the floats, and the return is so profitable in cucumbers, no other vegetables are raised upon the spaces between the cones.

Thefts of whole floats are sometimes committed by persons joining in two or three boats, to tow them off to distant parts of the lake in the night, and the property thus stolen is difficult to be identified. To prevent such depredation, as well as night robbery of the cones, two persons generally sleep in a boat, which is pushed under the shelter of a roof

of mats. The floating gardens are generally cut off from the body of the lake by a belt of floating reeds, which also serve, in some degree, to protect the cones against the winds. The boatways through the fences are closed by twisted withes of willow twigs, which, passing through the ends of the beds, join them closely together.

Abundance of fruit grows wild in Kashmir, and many thousands of acres, skirting the foot of the hills, are covered with apple and pear trees, and vines in full bearing; they are also cultivated, as are apricots, peaches, cherries, and plums. An article of horticultural cultivation is the walnut, of which there are four varieties; one called khanak, is wild, the other three, termed wantu, dunu, and kaghazi, are cultivated. The forest walnut is diminutive, with a thick shell and scanty kernel. The wantu has a larger nut, but the shell is thick and very hard, and the kernel deficient. The nut of the dunu is somewhat larger still, its shell thick, but in a less degree, and the kernel, large and good, is easily extracted. The kaghazi is so called from its shell being nearly as thin as paper (kághaz),

so that it may be readily broken by the hand; it is the largest of the whole, and its kernel is large and easily extracted. Its superiority is said to be attributable to its having been originally engrafted: however this may be, it is now raised from seed alone, and does not degenerate. The nuts steeped in water for eight days are planted in the beginning of March, and the shoot generally makes its appearance in about forty days. If reared by grafts, the process is performed when the plant is five years old: the head being cut off horizontally, at a convenient height, is partially slit or opened in its circumference, and the scions are inserted into the slits without any binding; but clay mortar, worked up with rice husks, is put round it, and kept from being washed away by being enveloped in broad slips of birch bark.

In Kashmir the walnut tree begins to fruit ordinarily when seven years old, but two or three years more elapse before it is in full bearing. This is conceived to be the case, when on a single tree the averaged annual number of nuts brought to maturity amounts to about twenty-five thousand. It has been

observed, that after a few seasons of full bearing, walnut trees fall off in producing fruit, and run with great luxuriance to leaf and branch. To this latter condition the Kashmiris apply the appellation of *must*, and to remedy it, cut down all the small branches, bringing the tree to the state of a pollard. During the year following shoots and leaves alone are produced, which are succeeded by a crop of fruit, in that ensuing, so abundant, as to compensate for the absence of nuts in the preceding season. The cut ends of the branches swell into knots, or knobs, which are somewhat unsightly, and of which the structure has not been accurately examined.

The walnuts which fall whilst green furnish the material for a colour of this tint, which, however, is not permanent; but the husks of the ripe fruit are sold to the dyers, as a basis for a fixed black. When ripe, the fruit of the wantu walnut is retailed in the city for eating, at the rate of a hundred for two pice, or about a penny; the nuts of the dunu in the same number, for three pice, and of the kaghazi for four pice, or two pence.

The country people break the walnuts at home, and carry the kernel alone to market, where it is sold to oil-pressers, at the average of seven rupees per kharwar, or ass load. Each ass load of kernel yields eight paji of oil, each weighing six ser, or forty-eight sers in the whole. The paji sells from a rupee to a rupee and a half, and the kajji, or oil cake, produced in equal weight, or eight paji, is worth eight anas in spring, or one rupee per kharwar, and double this price in winter, for feeding cows. In the latter season, a kharwar of oil cake is exchanged for the same quantity of coarse rice in the husk, or the price of the latter in the market. About twelve thousand ass loads of walnut kernels are annually appropriated to the oil-press in Kashmir, producing, in the gross return of oil and of oil cake, one hundred and thirteen thousand rupees, independently of the quantity of nuts eaten by man. Walnut oil is preferred to linseed oil for all the uses to which the latter is applied, and in Kashmir, as on the continent of Europe, it is employed in cookery, and also for burning in lamps, neither much clogging the wick, nor yielding

much smoke: it is, however, inferior, both for cooking and for burning to the oil of til (Sesamum). This oil possesses such qualities as fairly entitle it to introduction into Europe, and if divested of its mucilage, it might, perhaps, compete with oil of olives, at least for medicinal purposes, and could be raised in any quantity in the British Indian provinces. It is sufficiently free from smell to admit of being made the medium for extracting the perfume of the jasmin (Yasmin), the tuberose (Zambak), narcissus (Nerghiz), chamomile (Babena), and of the yellow rose (Zeba). The process is managed by adding one weight of flowers to three weights of oil in a bottle, which being corked, is exposed to the rays of the sun for forty days, when the oil is supposed to be sufficiently impregnated for use. Walnut oil is exported to Tibet, and brings a considerable profit. By ancient custom the crop of nuts was equally divided between the Government and the owner of the tree, but at present the former takes three-fourths, leaving but one-fourth to remunerate the farmer; yet under this oppression the cultivation of the walnut is extended, and

Kashmir, in proportion to its surface, produces a much larger quantity of nuts than any portion of Europe.

There are said to be eighteen or twenty varieties of grapes in Kashmir, of which four only are of foreign introduction. These are the Sahibi, of an oblong shape and red colour; the Maska, round, and yellowish-white; the Hoseini, of the same colour, but long; and the Kishmish, yellowish-white or green, round, and seedless: this last is small, but the other three are large, the Sahibi sometimes measuring four inches in its largest circumference: they are all thin-skinned, and grow in considerable bunches; those of the Maska are not unfrequently of the weight of five or six pounds. The Sahibi and Maska are both fine table grapes: wine and raisins might be made from the other two. These sorts are usually cultivated on high horizontal trellises of wood.

The indigenous vines are generally planted at the foot of a poplar, and run up to the height of fifty or sixty feet, bearing abundance of fruit. The grapes are commonly thick-skinned, and rather rough and astrin-

gent, but juicy. They are gathered about October, and are kept through the winter in shallow earthen vessels till the spring, when they are applied to the fabrication of wine, vinegar, and brandy. The making of wine was discountenanced under the Afghan government, but has revived under that of the Sikhs. The manufacture is ill conducted, and the liquor is kept in bottles, which are stopped only with plugs of wood, or twisted bark, or paper. No wonder, therefore, that the beverage is indifferent; but such as it is, it is sufficiently good to show, that with proper treatment and care, the wines of Kashmir might be made to rival many of those of Europe.

The Sanjit, which has been noticed as growing in Ladakh, is still more plentiful in Kashmir. The tree has a beautiful appearance; its flowers are exquisitely sweet, and its fruit by distillation yields a beverage which the Chinese hold to be not inferior to that of the grape. The horse-chesnut is wild in the forests, and has not been reclaimed. The hazel is abundant, but it is so luxuriant in the production of wood and leaf, that the

nuts, scarcely of the size of peas, do not come to perfection. The alder is of rapid growth, and the shoots, when the head happens to be destroyed, are straight, tall, and free from knots. The most valuable tree of Kashmir is, however, the Deodar, a variety of cedar, the timber of which is extensively employed in the construction of houses, temples, and bridges: pieces of it from the Zein-ul-kadal bridge were found little decayed, although exposed to the action of water for four hundred years.

The crocus of Kashmir has long been celebrated for the excellence of its saffron. It produces freely the third year after being planted: the greater part is exported to Hindustan. Amongst other useful plants occur the Alisma plantago, and the Carthamus tinctorius.

The animals and birds of Kashmir are much the same as those of Hindustan. The horses are small and indifferent; sheep are plentiful, and the mutton is well flavoured; the fat is particularly white. Whether this is owing to any peculiarity in their feed, I shall not undertake to determine; but

although it would be very possible to prepare an ample sufficiency of hay for winter fodder, the preference is given to the leaves of certain trees,—as the walnut, willow, mulberry, elm, and several others, which are considered much more warming and nutritious than hay, especially for sheep. Small branches after having been cut when in full leaf are immediately so disposed within the first forks of the tree to which they belong, as to be thereby retained; and although loosely piled, yet in consequence of being entangled amongst themselves, are not detached by the wind; neither do they lose their leaves, nor are the latter in any respect injured. This forage is reserved for the severe part of the winter, when the cattle are driven under the trees in which the store is suspended, and the dry branches being pulled down, the leaves are eaten by them with great avidity.

When grass is stored for winter fodder, it is twisted into thick ropes immediately after having been cut, and in this state hung across the upper branches of trees, without other preparation, for hay; it thus keeps free from rottenness, and generally even from mouldi-

ness, notwithstanding the great quantity of rain and snow that falls. Grass thus dried is generally given to the cattle in the morning, and leaves in the afternoon and evening: oil cake made of linseed, walnut kernels, mustard seed, along with the seed of cotton, are given to fatten cattle, as are flags or the leaves of sedge. The prangos, which likewise grows in Kashmir, is also largely used as winter fodder.

The cotton plant grows in Kashmir in every variety of situation: it is seldom much above two feet high, and if taller, is said to yield an inferior article. It is sown in May, and the cotton is gathered in September and October. The cloths made from it are in general coarse and flimsy; but one kind, called kadak, is of a texture particularly close, though not fine, and of exceeding durability. The manufacture of cotton cloths, however, is not very extensively prosecuted in Kashmir, and the cultivation of the plant is consequently not much attended to. An attempt was made to introduce the nankin or brown cotton from Yarkand into Kashmir, but it was said that although the first growth was of as deep a

tint as that of the Yarkand plant, yet the produce of the third sowing was white.

It was mentioned that silk was extensively raised in Khoten, and it appears that it extends from thence through Yarkand and Balti to Kashmir. In this latter country the fabric languishes, and the quantity produced is insufficient for domestic consumption. It might with due encouragement be carried to any extent.

About a thousand ass loads of the root of the kuth, or costus, collected in the mountains of Kashmir, are annually exported to Amritser, whence the drug is sent to Calcutta for export to China. For what purpose the Chinese use it is not known; but in the north of Hindustan it is celebrated as a vermifuge, being administered to children in an infusion of the powdered root: it is also used as a topical application in chronic rheumatism.

An interesting subject in the rural economy of Kashmir is the management of Bees.

Every farmer in the district of Lar, and I have since found the practice general throughout the whole country, in the eastern part of Kashmir, has several hives in his house, and

in some houses I have counted as many as ten.

A provision for hives is made in building the house, by leaving appropriate cavities in the walls. These somewhat differ in size, but agree in their general form, each being cylindrical, and extending quite through the wall. This tube is lined by a plastering of clay-mortar, about an inch in thickness, and the mortar is worked up with the chaff or husk of rice, or with the down of thistles, which latter is employed also for clay-mortar in general, being the first application of this substance to the use of man I have yet witnessed.

The dimensions of a hive are, on an average, about fourteen inches in diameter, and, when closed at both ends, about twenty or twenty-two inches in length. The walls of farm-houses and cottages differ in respect to their materials, but are commonly constructed of rough stones, or bricks, and of clay or lime-mortar along with a large admixture of wood, in the district just mentioned. That end of the cylinder nearest to the apartment is closed by a round platter of red pottery ware, a little

convex in the middle, but the edges are made flush with the wall by a luting of clay-mortar, and the other extremity is shut by a similar dish, having a circular hole, about a third of an inch in diameter, in its centre.

It does not appear that there is any particular rule for the height of the hives from the ground, they sometimes being confined to the walls of the lower or basement story, generally appropriated to cattle in the farm-houses of Kashmir, at others are inserted into those of the first-floor, but are frequently seen in both situations in the same house, as well as in the walls of its out-buildings. So little of difference exists betwixt the practices ordinarily pursued in Kashmir and in Europe, in respect to hiving new swarms, as not to call for notice; but that adopted in the former country, for preserving the old swarm when the honey is taken, well deserves imitation by the bee-farmer in the latter country. The process by which this is, as I witnessed it, effected, is the following:—Having in readiness a wisp of dry rice-straw, and a small quantity of burning charcoal in an earthen dish, the master of the house, with a few

strokes of the point of a short sickle, disengages the inner platter of the tube, bringing into view the combs suspended from the roof of the hive, and almost wholly covered with bees, none of which, however, offer to resent the aggression, or to enter the room. Having placed the straw upon the charcoal, and holding the dish close to the mouth of the hive, he blew the smoke strongly against the combs, but removed the straw the instant it took fire, to prevent it burning the bees, and quenched the flame before he employed it again.

Almost stifled by the smoke, the bees hurried through the outer door with such rapidity that the hive was cleared of its inhabitants within a few minutes, when the farmer introducing the sickle, cut down the combs nearest to him, which were received into a dish previously slidden underneath them, and left undisturbed about one-third of the combs, which were almost close to the outer door. He then replaced the inner platter, and brushing off hastily a few bees which clung to the combs, though apparently in a state of stupefaction, threw them out of the house. Observing many other bees lying motionless on the floor of the hive,

I inquired whether they were dead, or only stupified, and was answered, that they would recover: however, I was not wholly satisfied that this recovery would take place; but preparations for continuing my journey at a very early hour on the following morning unluckily prevented me from ascertaining the fact.

But neither the fate of these, nor of those left senseless in the hive, excited any interest in the owner, as enough remained to carry on the business of the hive, into which the expelled bees returned as soon as its cavity was freed from smoke, without stinging a single individual. The whole business was completed within ten minutes, and it was asserted that not above one-hundredth part of the community is destroyed by this method. The farmers here are well acquainted with the existence of the queen bee; but give themselves little trouble about the internal economy of the hive. Accounts differed as to the weight of the annual yield of a hive, and to the relative proportions of honey and of wax, and that now taken afforded no evidence on these points, as its combs had been removed,

in part only, two months before. Altogether, however, it seemed to me probable that the produce was less than the ordinary yield of a good swarm in England, making allowance also for the portion left for the winter support of the bees. The honey was light-coloured, and of a taste as pure and as sweet as that of Narbonne. It possessed less of the cloying quality generally attending this substance than any other I recollect to have met with, and I could not learn that the farmers had any suspicion of their honey ever being intoxicating or poisonous, as has been noticed as the case occasionally with that made by the Bhoura of Garwahl. I was directed more particularly to inquiry upon this subject by having observed monk's-hood in flower in the valley of Ranga, a few miles to the eastward of the bee-district, and think it probable that it extends to these mountains. Perhaps, however, the range of the flight of the domesticated bee, through the abundance of food, may be limited to the cultivated surface immediately in the vicinity of the house; whereas the Bhoura is compelled to take a more extensive range, and in the scarcity of food,

during the short summer, to be less select in regard to its quality. The peasantry of Kashmir are unacquainted with the employment of honey as the basis of a fermented liquor, but eat it raw, or mixed with various articles of common food, whilst the most wealthy substitute it for sugar in preserving fruits. It is customary to take the hive every year, and the end of September, or beginning of October, is found the best season for this operation, a little time still remaining for the bees to add to the portion left for their support during five months. This amounts to about a third of the whole produce, and would appear to suffice, as swarms seldom die, and the Kashmirians substitute no other material as food. It is stated that an old swarm yields more honey than a young one, and that families seldom die except of old age. I was informed, that it was no uncommon circumstance to preserve the same community for ten, or even for fifteen years; and some instances were quoted of a family having been retained for twenty years; but this was held to be of very rare occurrence.

In consequence of the bees being thus literally domiciliated, they acquire a mildness of conduct far more decided than those of Europe, by which the lives of many of these insects are saved annually; and the confidence gained subduing their natural irascibility, may generate an increase of industry, or at least an increase of produce, in relation to the number, and to the size of the individuals of each community. And it is clear that the situation of the hive keeps many of the natural enemies of the bee at a distance. The bee of Kashmir is a little smaller than that of Europe, though a little larger than the domesticated bee of Kamaon and of Garwhal. Honey sells at about threepence British a pound, but wax is considerably dearer.

The mineral productions of Kashmir have been too little investigated to admit of very exact specification. Iron is found in considerable quantity; but that used for the fabric of gun-barrels is said to be imported from the Panjab—a circumstance rather questionable. Copper-mines are said to exist, but their existence is kept secret, lest they should become

to the government an additional subject of exaction: the copper used is British or Russian, imported from Lahore or Yarkand. No lead-mines are worked, if they exist. Sulphur is an article of import from the Panjab.

CHAPTER III.

Arts and Manufactures of Kashmir—Shawl Manufacture—Wool—Carriage—Mode of Sale—Prices of Wool—Sorting—Cleaning—Phiri, or Seconds Wool—Spinning—Yarn—Prices—Assortment according to Pattern—Dyeing—Apportioning—Dressing—Silk used for Borders—Drawing—Weaving—Rates of Work—Loom—Pattern—Needles—Shawl-Cloth—Cleaning Shawls—Darning—Stamping—Valuation—Washing—Drying—Packing—Articles of Shawl-Stuff—Worked Shawls—List of Articles and Prices—Total annual Value of Manufacture—Gun-barrels—Yerak Leather—Pen-cases—Paintings—Paper.

The manufacture for which Kashmir is celebrated throughout the world, is that of the light, warm, and elegant article of dress which, from its native appellation, is known as shawl. Conceiving that it would be possible for Great Britain to partake more largely in the trade in shawl-goods, a very valuable portion of which is carried on through Bokhara and Yarkand with Russia, or even that it would be practicable to introduce the manufacture

itself into my native country, I devoted much of my time and thoughts, whilst in Kashmir, to the acquisition of authentic information on every detail connected with the subject*. The chief results of my inquiries I shall proceed to describe.

The wool that is employed in this manufacture is of two kinds—the fleece of the domestic goat, called Pashm Shal (or shawl-wool), and that of the wild goat, wild sheep, and other animals named Asali Tus. The wool of sheep is not regularly, but is sometimes clandestinely imported, being loaded with the same heavy duties as that of the goat.

The quantity of shawl-wool annually imported varies between five hundred and one thousand horse-loads, each of which is equal to nearly 300lbs.: the whole quantity of the

* The creation of the manufacture of British shawls is no doubt to be ascribed, in a great degree, if not solely, to Mr. Moorcroft. From the period of his first journey to the Hiundes he was at great pains in sending home the shawl-wool, and in his present journey he sent to England patterns of shawls, and information regarding their manufacture, which, though addressed mostly to his private friends, found their way silently to persons engaged in similar manufactures, and enabled them to imitate successfully the shawls of Kashmir.—ED.

Asali Tus does not exceed 1200 lbs. The wool was formerly supplied almost exclusively by the western provinces of Lassa and by Ladakh; but of late considerable quantities have been procured from the neighbourhood of Yarkand, from Khoten, and the families of the Great Kirghis horde. It is brought chiefly by Mogol merchants, who exchange it for manufactured shawl-goods in Kashmir, which they dispose of advantageously in Russia.

The expense of transport from Lé to Kashmir is, per horse-load, thirty-three rupees; the duties collected at various places, both in Ladakh and Kashmir, amount to ninety-five rupees. A deduction is made for the admixture of dark-coloured wool, which every load contains usually in the proportion of one-third, although the custom-house calculation is but one-fifth. Dark wool pays about half the duty charged on white wool. Asali Tus pays double.

In the first disposal of the article the parties engaged are the Bakál, or merchant importer, the Pashm farosh, or wool-retailer, and a Mokim, or broker. In Kashmir all commercial contracts of importance are discussed at din-

ner, and accordingly, when the merchant receives a cargo of wool, he invites a retail dealer and his broker to a feast. The latter mediates between the parties, and receives a commission of three anas per tarak. From each horse-load of the wool three and three-quarter sers are deducted for the weight of the bales, &c. Payment is immediate, or at one or two months' credit, according to the state of the market, but in no case is it delayed beyond that term. At the time of payment the purchaser withholds two anas per tarak, as a fund for an entertainment to be given to the merchant, and for gratuities to his servants.

The price of shawl-wool has for some time past been upon the advance: the following were the average prices at different periods:

1794 to 1807,	per Tarak,	8	Kashmir Rupees.
1807 „ 1813,	„	16 to 20	„
1813 „ 1817,	„	22	„
1817	„	25	„

It had latterly been as high as forty rupees per tarak, owing partly to the ravages made by an epidemic disease amongst the cattle, and partly to the new demand arising for wool from the British possessions in India.

This enhanced price, however, can be but of temporary duration, new sources of supply being opened, the consumption of the raw material diminishing under the exactions of the Sikh government, and the value of the manufactured article in foreign markets declining.

The price of dark-coloured wool is about one-third, or a half less than that of white wool.

The wool exposed for retail by the purchaser is bought by women for the purpose of spinning it into yarn. A pal of white wool sells for six tangas, or about as many pence. The profit of the retailer is about twelve per cent.

The first task of the spinner is to separate the different materials of which the fleece consists, usually in about the following proportions:—

Coarse Hair . .	$1\frac{1}{2}$ Sers.
Seconds, or Phiri . .	$0\frac{3}{8}$
Dust and Foreign Substances	$2\frac{1}{8}$
Fine Wool . .	2
	6 Sers, or 1 Tarak.

Much attention is required to free the wool from the hair, and the process is a tedious one.

The next step is cleaning and separating

the wool. A quantity of husked rice is steeped in clean cold water, for a day and a night, or longer, until it becomes soft, when it is ground or bruised upon a stone slab to fine flour. Thin layers of this and of the picked wool are laid alternately, and squeezed with the hand until they are completely intermixed. A little water may be occasionally sprinkled over the heap, if the weather is hot and dry, else it is not necessary. Soap is never used, as it makes the wool harsh; and its employment in Hindustan being communicated to the Kashmirians, induced them to boast that in this matter, at least, they were more knowing than Europeans. After being thus treated for about an hour, the flour is shaken out, the wool opened and torn to pieces, chiefly by the nails, and made into somewhat square, thin, elastic pads, called Tumbu. In this process the Phiri, or seconds-wool, is extricated. Though too coarse for fine shawls, it is used in the manufacture of those of inferior quality, and of a strong shawl-cloth called *Patu*. The tumbu is then worked out into a thin flat roving, about half a yard long, which is called a Málá. The málá is folded up to the

size of the tumbu, and deposited in a deep pot of red earthenware, called a Taskas, to be out of the way of dust or accident, till required for the spinning-wheel.

The wheel is constructed on the same principle as that used in Hindustan, but varying in neatness of form and finish, according to its price; the rudest, the Takhtidar, or Pachimdar, costs a half-rupee, the Katzker, which is the most serviceable, three or four rupees, and the Pakhchedar, which is used by those who spin for amusement only, costs from six to sixteen rupees. The iron spindle is enclosed in a cylindrical tube of straw or reed-grass, and runs through two elastic twists of grass, and instead of one line of radii or spokes, supporting a continued circular wooden rim, there are two circular and parallel walls of flat spokes in contact at their edges, leaving between them, at their outer circumference, an empty space. A hair cord, fastened to the loose end of one of the spokes, is carried across the space or trough, to the end of the next spoke but one on the opposite side, and having been passed round, it returns to a spoke on the side from which it began. By a

continuation of this process a rim is formed of a surface of hair-cord, over which runs a small band that is said seldom to be cut by the friction to which it is exposed. The principle kept in view by this arrangement of spindle and of rim, is to produce a continuance of soft elastic movements without jerk or stiffness, to prevent the yarn breaking on the occurrence of any slight interruption in drawing it out.

Women begin to work at daybreak, continue with little interruption the whole day, if not taken off by other domestic affairs, and extend their labour until very late in the night, spinning by moonlight, when available, and when they cannot afford to purchase oil for a lamp. The fine wool is spun commonly into about seven hundred gaz, each gaz consisting of sixteen girahs, about equal to nails. This yarn is doubled and formed into twist, which is cut into two hundred lengths, each length of three gaz and a half, this measure being suited to the length of the warp for a shawl. From the phiri, or seconds-wool, about one hundred gaz of yarn are also pro-

duced. The yarn of the fine wool is sold sometimes by measure and sometimes by weight. A hundred lengths of yarn of fine wool doubled, and each three gaz and a half, bring ordinarily seven tangas, or about sevenpence. But if the same kind of yarn be sold without being doubled and twisted, the price is regulated by weight, a pal bringing from twelve anas to one rupee four anas, according to the demands of the market. The yarn from phiri, or seconds-wool, is sold only by measure, but the gaz employed consists of no more than twelve girah, or nails, that is, of four girahs less than the gaz in ordinary use. A hundred yards of phiri twist, and each of two short gaz, or of twenty-four girah, sell for one and a half tanga three pice, or about three-halfpence. Although calculations upon this matter can be little more than approximations, yet threepence or threepence-halfpenny a day, or from three rupees to three rupees eight anas, or from six to seven shillings a month, may be taken as the *general* earnings of an industrious and expert spinner in Kashmir, out of which, however, must be subtracted

the price of the wool *, leaving only one rupee eight anas for her labour.

If shawl-wool be furnished to a spinner to clean and to spin, eight anas are paid for spinning one pal, or three and one-third rupees' weight of yarn of the requisite quality for shawls. Sheep's wool, spun by contract, is paid for by the pao, or quarter of a ser, at the rate of from two tangas, or four pice, to twelve anas per pao, according to the fineness of the yarn; and the spinning of this quantity into yarn suited for shawls will occupy a woman for eight days. There are several varieties of thread, distinguished by different degrees of fineness. From one pal of clean fine shawl-wool a spinner will draw from a hundred to a thousand threads of three and a half gaz each. There is not such a difference between the price of coarse and of fine yarn as might be expected, owing to the greater expenditure on the former of a material that is dear, and on the latter, of labour that is cheap. Shawl-wool is sometimes spun by men with a loose spindle like that used in Ladakh. These men are called Trakhans, and the yarn thus

* Thirty-two Tangas or Anas equal two Rupees.

spun is the finest; but very little of it is now made. Girls begin to spin at the age of ten, and a hundred thousand females are employed in this occupation in Kashmir. About one-tenth of this number are supposed to spin for the purpose of obtaining shawls for themselves, or for other members of their families, and nine-tenths to earn their livelihood.

The Puimangu keeps a shop for the purchase of yarn, but also sends people to collect it from the houses of the spinners, who give notice of their approach by ringing a bell. The yarn is sold to the weavers at a profit of from one pice to a tanga in the rupee. As a large stamp-duty is levied on shawl-goods when finished, the exportation of the yarn is forbidden, and the prohibition is enforced by heavy fine and imprisonment. Much of it is, nevertheless, exported to those places in the Panjab where the expatriated weavers have settled.

Having ascertained the kind of pattern most likely to suit the market, the weaver applies to persons whose business it is to apportion the yarn according to the colours required; and when this is settled, he takes it to ano-

ther, whose function it is to divide the yarn into skeins accordingly, and each skein is delivered to the rang rez, or dyer. When the body of the cloth is to be left plain, the phiri, or seconds-yarn, is alone given to be dyed. This is generally about the thickness of common cotton sewing-thread, is loosely twisted, of a coarser quality than the yarn used for the cloth, and is preferred for employment in flowers, or other ornaments, from its standing higher, and being, as it were, embossed upon the ground.

The dyer prepares the yarn by steeping in clean cold water. He professes to be able to give it sixty-four tints, most of which are permanent. Each has a separate denomination; as for instance, the crimson is termed Gulanar (pomegranate-flower); the best kind is derived from cochineal, imported from Hindustan; inferior tints are from Lacand Kirmis (Chermes), distinguished as Kirmisi, Kirmdana, and Kirmisi lac, or cochineal and lac chermes; logwood is used for other red dyes; blues and greens are dyed with indigo, or colouring matter extracted by boiling from European broad-cloth. Logwood is imported

from Multan, and indigo from India. Carthamus and saffron, growing in the province, furnish means of various tints of orange, yellow, &c. The occupation of a dyer is invariably hereditary. The whiter and finer the fibre of the wool, and the finer the yarn into which it is made, the more capable it is said to be of receiving a brilliant dye; and this is one reason why the fine white wool of the goat is preferred to that of the sheep.

The Nakatu adjusts the yarn for the warp and for the weft. That intended for the former is double, and is cut into lengths of three gaz and a half, anything short of that measure being considered fraudulent. The number of these lengths varies from two thousand to three thousand, according to the closeness or openness of texture proposed, and the fineness or coarseness of the yarn.

The weft is made of yarn which is single, but a little thicker than the double yarn or twist of the warp. The weight of the weft is estimated at a half more than that of the warp. The nakatu receives the yarn in hanks, but returns it in balls: he can prepare in one day the warp and weft for two shawls.

The Pennakam guru, or warp-dresser, takes from the weaver the yarn which has been cut and reeled, and stretching the lengths by means of sticks into a band, of which the threads are slightly separate, dresses the whole by dipping it into thick-boiled rice-water. After this the skein is slightly squeezed, and again stretched into a band, which is brushed and suffered to dry: by this process each length becomes stiffened, and set apart from the rest.

Silk is generally used for the warp on the border of the shawl, and has the advantage of showing the darker colours of the dyed wool more prominently than a warp of yarn, as well as hardening and strengthening, and giving more body to the edge of the cloth. When the border is very narrow it is woven with the body of the shawl; but when broader, it is worked on a different loom, and afterwards sewn on the edge of the shawl by the rafugar, or fine-drawer, with such nicety, that the union can scarcely be detected. The silk is twisted for the border warp by the tabgar. The warp differs in breadth, the narrowest consisting of twenty, and the

broadest of a hundred threads. From the tabgar the silk is handed to the alakaband, who reels it, and cuts it into the proper lengths.

The operation of drawing, or of passing the yarns of the warp through the heddles, is performed precisely in the same way as in Europe, and the warp is then taken by the shal-baf, or weaver, to the loom. The weavers are all males, commencing to learn the art at the age of ten years. In all transactions there are two parties, the master, or ustád, and the scholar, or shahgird, the former being the capitalist, the latter the mechanic. Work is executed under four different conditions. First, for wages, when it almost always happens that a system of advances has occurred, by which the workman is so deeply indebted to his employer that he may, in some sort, be considered as his bond-slave. Secondly, upon contract, of which the common term is, that one pice is paid for every hundred needles carrying coloured yarn that shall have been each once passed round as many yarns of the warp. Third, a sort of partnership, in which the ustád finds

all the materials, and the workmen give their labour. When a shawl is sold the outlay of the ustád is deducted from the price, and the remainder is divided into five shares, of which one goes to the master, and the other four to the workmen. The fourth mode is an equal division of the proceeds; in which case the master not only finds the materials, but feeds the workmen. Three men are employed upon an embroidered shawl of an ordinary pattern for three months, but a very rich pair will occupy a shop for eighteen months.

The loom differs not in principle from that of Europe, but is of inferior workmanship. An ustád has from three to three hundred in his establishment, and they are generally crowded together in long low apartments. When the warp is fixed in the loom the nakash, or pattern-drawer, and the tarah-gurú, and talim-guru, or persons who determine the proportion of yarn of different colours to be employed, are again consulted. The first brings the drawing of the pattern in black and white. The tarah-guru, having well considered it, points out

the disposition of the colours, beginning at the foot of the pattern, and calling out the colour, the number of threads to which it is to extend, that by which it is to be followed, and so on in succession, until the whole pattern has been described. From his dictation the talim-guru writes down the particulars in a kind of character or shorthand, and delivers a copy of the document to the weavers.

The workmen prepare the tujis, or needles, by arming each with coloured yarn of the weight of about four grains. These needles, without eyes, are made of light, smooth wood, and have both their sharp ends slightly charred, to prevent their becoming rough or jagged through working. Under the superintendence of the tarah-guru, the weavers knot the yarn of the tuji to the warp. The face, or right side of the cloth, is placed next to the ground, the work being carried on at the back or reverse, on which hang the needles in a row, and differing in number from four hundred to fifteen hundred, according to the lightness or heaviness of the embroidery. As soon as the ustád is

satisfied that the work of one line or woof is completed, the comb is brought down upon it with a vigour and repetition, apparently very disproportionate to the delicacy of the materials.

The cloth of shawls, generally, is of two kinds, one plain, or of two threads, one twilled, or of four. The former was, in past times, wrought to a great degree of fineness, but it has been, of late, less in demand. The various twilled cloths are usually from five to twelve girehs, or nails, wide. Shawls are twilled, and are commonly about twenty-four nails broad, and differ in their extent of field. Two persons are employed in weaving a cloth of this breadth. One throws the shuttle from the edge as far as he can across the warp, which is usually about half way. It is there seized by the second weaver, who throws it onwards to the opposite edge, and then returns it to his companion, who, in his turn, introducing his fingers into the warp, forwards the shuttle to the edge whence it started, and then recommences the operation. The cloth thus made is frequently irregular, the threads of some parts of the woof being

driven up tightly, and in others left open, from which results a succession of bands, sufficiently distinguishable whilst without colour, but still more obvious when dyed. The open texture is, in a degree, remediable by the introduction of fresh threads; but there is no sufficient cure for that which has been much compacted. One might be led to suspect that there existed some radical defectiveness in the principle of this mode of weaving not readily mastered, were not pieces of cloth found occasionally of an almost perfect regularity of texture. But the greatest irregularity is discoverable in those shawls which have the deepest and heaviest borders, and a further examination compels me to retract an observation somewhere made of the artist being so much engrossed by attention to the work of the pattern as to neglect the structure of the field. The edge of the warp in the loom is filled with the heavy thread of the phiri, or seconds-yarn, charged also with colour, so that in a few lines the front of the worked part advances beyond that of the plain part or field, and an endeavour to equalize this be-

trays the weaver into a work which proves fruitless; and, in general, the heavier the embroidery on the border, and, of course, the higher the price of the shawl, the less regular is the structure of the cloth. Such, indeed, in some instances, is the degradation of the cloth in the field, as to induce some foreign merchants to cause it to be removed, and another piece to be engrafted within the edge of the border. But in this case there is no other remedy than in a judicious selection of a sheet of the same breadth and fineness; for, although two breadths of the narrow cloth might fit the vacant space, yet these must be joined by the rafugar in the middle; and although this can be so done that the band differs not in thickness from the rest of the cloth, yet the joint is discernible when held between the eye and the light, from the threads in the joined breadth being not continuous in the same line; whereas any irregularity of this nature is drowned in the edge of the border. The best practice to ensure a good field seems to consist in weaving the border, in every case, separately, and inserting the field by the rafugar.

When finished, the shawls are submitted to the purusgar, or cleaner, whose business it is to free the shawl from discoloured hairs or yarn, and from ends or knots: he either pulls them out severally with a pair of tweezers, or shaves the reverse face of the cloth with a sharp knife: any defects arising from either operation are immediately repaired by the rafugar. At this stage of the manufacture the shawls are sent to the collector of the stamp-duties, by whom an ad valorem duty of twenty-six per cent. is levied, and each piece is then stamped and registered.

The goods are now handed over to the wafarosh, or person who has advanced money on them to the manufacturer, and to the mohkim, or broker, and these two settle the price, and effect the sale to the merchant; the former charges interest on his advances, the latter a commission, varying from two to five per cent. The purchaser takes the goods unwashed, and often in pieces, and the finedrawer and washerman have still to do their part.

When partly washed the dhobi brings the shawls to the merchant, that they may be ex-

amined for any holes or imperfections: should such occur, they are remedied at the expense of the seller: if there are none, the washing is completed. This is done with clear cold water, using soap very cautiously to white parts alone, and never to embroidery: coloured shawls are dried in the shade; white ones are bleached in the open air, and their colour is improved by exposure to fumes of sulphur. After being washed, the shawls are stretched in a manner which answers in some degree to calendering: a wooden cylinder in two parts is employed for this purpose, round which the shawl, folded so as not to be quite as broad as the cylinder is long, is carefully wrapped, being occasionally damped to make it fold tighter; the end is sewn down: two wedges are then gradually driven between the two parts of the cylinder at the open extremities, so as to force them asunder, and the surrounding folds of the shawl are thus stretched to as great an extent as is consistent with its texture. The piece remains in this state for two days, when it is removed to be packed. The packages are of various dimensions, but they are formed on one prin-

ciple: the shawls are separated by sheets of smooth, glazed, and coloured paper, and they are placed between two smooth planks of wood, with exterior transverse bars, which projecting beyond the planks, offer a purchase for cords to tie them together: the whole is then placed in a press, or under heavy weights for some days, when the planks are withdrawn, and the bale is sewed up in strong cloth: over this a cover of tús, or of birch bark is laid, and an envelope of wax-cloth is added, and the whole is sewed up as smoothly and lightly as possible in a raw hide, which contracting in drying, gives to the contents of the package a remarkable degree of compactness and protection.

An immense variety of articles of shawl stuff are manufactured in Kashmir, besides the shawls themselves: of them also there are two chief varieties, those made in the manner described, and the worked shawl (doshali amli), in which the whole of the embroidery is worked on the cloth, with needles having eyes, and with a particular kind of woollen thread, instead of the silk employed in the usual embroidered work. In the amli shawl

the pattern, which is in every case delineated, but which at the loom is read off in certain technical terms from a book, is covered with transparent paper, upon which the outlines of the composition are slightly traced with a charcoal twig, and the traced lines are permanently defined by being pricked through with a small needle. The cloth intended to receive the pattern is rubbed strongly upon a smooth plank, with a piece of highly-polished agate or cornelian, until it is perfectly even and regular. The pricked pattern is then stretched upon the cloth, and some fine coloured powder, charcoal, or chalk, is passed slightly over the paper, which penetrating through the holes, transfers the outline to the cloth underneath. This is next more accurately delineated with some coloured powder, rendered tenacious by mucilage of gum arabic, which, when the work is completed, is readily detached in dust by the hand.

The use of patterns by the chain-stitch embroiderer, and the carpet weaver of Kashmir, is more restricted to a confined number of forms, by being transferred from a wooden

block to the cloth, in regard to the former, and to paper in respect to the latter.

The following are the chief articles of this manufacture, with their usual prices.

Shawls in pairs form the principal article of this manufacture, and have different names, according to their nature and quality, as plain white, coloured, embroidered in the loom, or by the hand with the needle: viz.:—

Patu Pashmini, sometimes made of Asal tús, but more frequently of the coarse kinds of shawl-wool, is in length four gaz, and in breadth one and a half gaz. This is thick, and used as a blanket, or for outer clothing. Price from 5 to 6 rupees per gaz.

Shala Phiri, as its name denotes, is made of phiri, or of seconds-wool. Its length is from three and a half to four gaz, and breadth one and a half gaz. Price from 20 to 30 rupees per piece.

Halwan, or plain white cloth, of fine shawl-wool, without flower, border, or other ornament, differs in length, but is twelve giras in breadth, and is used for turbans and for dyeing. Price from 3 to 6 rupees per gaz.

Jowhar Shala Sadu, or shawl with a narrow edging of coloure yarn, is from three and a half to three and three-quarters gaz in length, and one and a half in breadth. Price from 50 to 60 rupees per piece.

As all the following shawls are of the same dimensions, viz., three and a half gaz in length, and one and a half gaz in breadth, it is un-

necessary to affix the measures to their several names.

Shala Hashiadar, is edged by a single border. 60 to 70 rupees.

Shala Dohashiadar, has a double border. 40 to 70 rupees.

Shala Chahar Hashiadar, has four borders. 60 to 70 rupees.

Hashiadar Khosar, or Khalil khani, has two borders and two tanga, sometimes with, at others without a flower in the corners. 40 to 50 rupees.

Hashiadar Kiungridar. This has a border of the usual form with another withinside, or nearer to the middle, resembling the crest of the wall of Asiatic forts, furnished with narrow niches or embrasures for wall pieces, or matchlocks, whence its name. 100 to 150 rupees.

Dhourdar, has an ornament running all round the shawl, between the border and the field. 200 to 2200 rupees per pair.

Mathandar, has flowers or decorations in the middle of the field. 300 to 1800 rupees per pair.

Chand'dar, has a circular ornament or moon in the centre of the field. 500 to 1500 rupees per pair.

Choutahidar, has four half-moons. 300 to 1500 rupees per pair.

Kunjbuthadar, has a group of flowers at each corner. 200 to 900 rupees per pair.

Alifdar, has green sprigs without any other colour, on a white ground or field. 120 to 1150 rupees per pair.

Kaddar, has large groups of flowers somewhat in the form of the cone of a pine, with the ends or points straight, or curved downwards.

Dokaddar, has two heights of such groups; Sekaddar three rows; and so on to five and upwards: in the latter case, however, the cones are somewhat small. 100 to 800 rupees per pair.

The ornaments of shawls are distinguished by different names, as Pala, Hashia, Zangir, Dhour, &c., and these are divided into different parts. By the term *Pala* is meant the whole of the embroidery at the two ends, or, as they are technically called, the heads of the shawl.

The Hashia, or border, is disposed commonly one at each side in the whole length, and if double or triple, gives particular denominations to the shawl.

The Zanjir, or chain, runs above and also below the principal mass of the Pala, and as it were confines it.

The Dhour, or running ornament, is situated to the inside in regard to the Hashia and the Zanjir, enveloping immediately the whole of the field.

The Kunjbutha, is a corner ornament, or clustering of flowers.

The Mattan, is the decorated part of the field or ground.

Butha, is the generic term for flower, but is specifically applied, when used alone, to the large cone-like ornament which forms the most prominent feature of the Pala. Sometimes there is only one line of these ornaments, extending from the lower Zanjir to the upper one. When there is a double row, one above the other, the Butha is called Dokad, Sehkad, up to five, after which it takes the name of Tukaddar.

Each Butha consists of three parts; viz., the Pai, or foot or pediment of leaves generally; the Shikam, or belly, and the Sir, or head. The head is either erect, or straight, or curved, or inclined. If the Butha slope generally, it is named Butha kaj. The Thal, or net, is the work which separates the different Buthas, but sometimes the interstice is without ornament.

Jamawar, signifies literally a gown-piece. The length of this cloth is three and three-quarter gaz, and the breadth one and a half gaz.

This article branches into many varieties, as Khirkhabutha—large compound flowers, consisting of groups of smaller ones. This is used by the Persians and Affghans.

	Rupees per piece.	
Rezabutha, small flowers thickly set,	200 to	700
Thaldar, net-work, . .	500	1700
Islîmî . . .	250	400
Mehramat . .	150	300
Khatherast . .	150	750
Marpèch . . .	200	350
Kalmkar . .	300	1000
Zakhè Angur . .	300	500
Chaporast . .	300	7000
Dogul, Seh gul, Chahar gul, &c.	500	1000
Barghe bed . . .	250	400
Gulisant . .	200	900
Duazdeh khat . .	700	1500
Duazdeh rang . .	800	1400
Gule parwane . .	300	450
Kaddhar . .	300	2000
Kayhamu, Sabzkar, Safed .	120	130

These are made by the shawl weaver alone, and go largely into Hindustan, where they are dyed, the small green flowers being previously tied up in hard small knots, so as to be protected from the action of the dye, and are, of course, when untied, each surrounded by a small white field. Small eyes of spots of yel-

low, red, and of other colours, are supposed to harmonize with the green flowers and the new ground, and these are added by embroiderers or Chikkandoz.

Kasabeh, or Rumal—Women's Veils—Square Shawls. These are from one and a half to two and a half gaz square, and are called,

Khathdar. 300 to 500 rupees.

Mehramat. 150 to 300 ditto.

Islîmî, with the thirteen other patterns of the Jamawars; and in addition there are

Chaharbagh. 300 to 350 rupees.

Hashia. 100 to 175 ditto.

Chand. 50 to 200 ditto.

Chautahi. 150 to 400 ditto.

Shash Mantahi. 250 to 200 ditto.

Feringi. 100 to 500 ditto. Exported chiefly to Russia.

Tara Armeni. 100 to 250 ditto. Ditto to Armenia and Persia.

Tara Rumi. 120 to 300 ditto. Ditto to Turkey.

Sada. 12 to 15 ditto, for domestic use.

Shamlas, or girdles for the waist, worn by the Asiatics, are eight gaz in length, and one and a half gaz broad, and of various colours and patterns, and vary from 50 to 2000 rupees a-piece, according to the richness of the work.

Doshala, or shawls, which contain three palas instead of two, go only to Tibet, and sell for 100 to 150 rupees.

Goshpech, or Patka, or turbans, are in length from eight to ten gaz, breadth one gaz, and of all colours. One variety has two palas, two zanjirs, and two hashias. 150 to 800 rupees.

Mandila, another variety, sometimes has a zanjir, and sometimes is without this ornament. This latter is from eight to ten gaz in length, and about twelve giras broad. 45 to 70 rupees.

Khalin Pashmina, shawl-carpets. This is sold at 20 to 40 rupees the square gaz of only three-quarters, and is made of any size in a single piece.

Nakash, trowsers. Some are with, others without seams. The former are made of two pieces, which are sown together by the rafugar, the latter by the jarab saz, or stocking-maker. 200 to 500 rupees a pair.

Chaharkhana, netted cloth. Length indefinite, breadth one and a half gaz, used by women. 5 to 10 rupees per gaz.

Gulbadan. Length indefinite, breadth from fourteen giras to one gaz. 5 to 6 rupees per gaz.

Lungi, girdles. Length three and a half gaz, breadth one and a half gaz. These differ from Shamlas by being in narrow check, and bordered by lines of different colours. 50 to 70 rupees.

Takhin, caps. 8 anas 4 rupees.

Jaráb, short stockings. Guldar and Mehramat, flowered and striped. 1 to 5 rupees.

Moze Pashmina, long stockings. 5 to 25 rupees.

Sakkab Posh, canopies. 300 to 1500 rupees.

Darparda, curtains for doors and windows. Same price as Jamawar, by measure.

Kajjari Asp, saddle-cloths. Ditto.

Kajjari Fil, elephants' housing. Ditto.

Balaposh, or Palang Posh, quilt or coverlet. 300 to 1000 rupees.

Galaband, cravat. 12 to 300 rupees.

Pistan band, neckerchief. 5 to 15 rupees.

Langota, waistbelts. 15 to 30 rupees.

Postin, cloths left long in the nap to line pelisses. 500 to 1000 rupees.

Paipech, leggings. Length two gaz, breadth one gira, of all colours. 2 to 10 rupees.

Yezar, or Izar band, waist-strings. 1 to 15 rupees.

Takkia, pillow-bier. Same price as Jamawar.

Khalita, bags or purses. 8 anas to 2 rupees.

Kabbar Posh, shrouds or covers for tomb-stones. Same price as Jamawar.

Takposh, covers or hangings in front of recesses or cupboards. Ditto.

And Khwanposh, dish-covers or napkins, of various qualities and patterns, from 30 to 500 rupees a piece.

The whole value of shawl-goods manufactured in Kashmir may be estimated at about thirty-five lacs of rupees per annum, or say, three hundred thousand pounds. It had, however, latterly, much declined, and it was expected that in the year 1822-3 the value would scarcely exceed half the above sum. Kashmir was formerly resorted to for shawl-goods by merchants from Turkey, both in Asia and Europe, by Armenians, Persians, Afghans, Uzbeks, and by traders from Hindustan and from Chinese Turkistan. Political events had largely reduced the trade with Persia, Turkey, and the Panjab, and that with Hindustan had sustained much de-

triment from the prevalence of British rule, and the loss of wealth by the Native courts, in which costly shawls were formerly a principal article of attire. The trade with Turkistan was on the increase, in consequence of the extending demands of Russia.

The manufacture of shawls, however important to the population of Kashmir, is not the only mechanical process to which their industry is directed, and their workmen have considerable reputation for the fabrication of gun and pistol barrels. It seems likely that upon the introduction of the use of fire-arms, the methods long, and perhaps exclusively known to the Asiatics, of manufacturing sword blades of peculiar excellence, was transferred, with some modification, to that of gun-barrels, and are still in use for that purpose. In Persia, Kabul, the Panjab, and Sindh, the same general principles prevail, but the matchlocks of the last are held deservedly in highest estimation. In some parts of India the workmen prefer for the material of their barrels the iron of old sugar-boilers, from some such notions, perhaps, as recommend horse-shoe nails in England; but where this

is not to be had, they employ the spongy, cavernous, and crude mass, which has been first reduced from the ore: the fuel used is wood-charcoal only. The forge is employed for no other sort of work, and is usually established at the mouth of an oblong chamber, raised within the gunsmith's shop. The platform of this chamber is lower than the general level of the floor of the shop, by a few inches only at the mouth, but deepens by a regular slope to the farther end, making about a foot in difference between the front and the back. The sides and the end are closed by a straight, upright walling, and the top by a vaulted roof, pierced by a vent-hole for the smoke, which is diffused through the upper part of the shop, and escapes by the roof and windows. The roof is generally horizontal, but sometimes slopes from the mouth to the end, like the upper leather of a shoe, from the instep to the toe. This forge differs in dimensions, but in the clear, from the mouth to the end, is frequently about three feet six inches, in the height of the wall inside, four feet, and the breadth about eighteen inches.

The tew-hole, or space for the nozzle of the

bellows, is invariably in the left-hand wall, on a level with the platform of the general floor of the shop, and about six inches from the mouth of the forge, which is open from the floor to the roof. The whole is built of brick, plastered both within and without with clay mortar. There is no metallic *back*, and the tew-hole is in general metallic only in part, consisting of a narrow slip of iron, about ten inches in length, worked at one end into a broad tongue, of which the edges are bent upwards, turned over, and form the circle, or end of a tube, the rest being made merely of clay; and the narrow end of the slip running through the wall, and being worked into it, keeps the whole in place. The circle of iron is covered with a coating of clay, and the opening has a direction somewhat more downwards than horizontal, so that the stream of air from the bellows strikes more directly upon the metal exposed to its action than that of an European forge. The bellows are double, as is the case through India generally. Each pair consists of a goat skin untanned, but made pliable by being rubbed between the hands, and the hair side is left outwards

For this appropriation the body of the animal is extracted by an incision, continued from the middle of the hinder part of one thigh to the same point in the other.

A cylindrical tube of iron, or of wood, is inserted into, and tied tight in the neck, as the nozzle of the bellows, and the skin of the legs is also tied at the knees. But the edges of the incision, by which, as before observed, the body was extracted, are stiffened, and kept apart by a long piece of wood sewn to each side; and these are connected with each other by thongs of white leather. These thongs, in the form of loops, admit the fingers and thumb of the operator, who, with each hand, works each pair of bellows inserted into the tew-hole by their nozzles, side by side, by opening and shutting the mouth of each alternately, and pressing the air contained in their cavities forwards and downwards. By this simple apparatus the air is thrown upon the work in a continued stream, and a welding heat is soon got up. The whole forge is a parallelogram of such a length, as is nearly capable of receiving half the whole length of the longest barrel made, and the bottom of

the platform is covered with light ashes. A brick laid on its edge from the side-wall just beyond the tew-hole projects into, and partly across the forge, and is met by another at right angles, placed in the length, from which results a space about eight inches in length, and six in breadth, bounded on one side by the wall, by the longitudinal brick on the other, and open to the mouth of the forge, having the tew-hole in the middle on the wall side. In this space is placed the charcoal, of which the consumption is small, and little of the heat is lost, through the fire being thus confined by the bricks, and by the layer of ashes, whilst the artist is capable of limiting the action of the heat to as small a surface of the work as he may desire. The whole expense of a forge of this kind constructed for myself, along with the bellows, did not exceed five shillings, although the work was paid for more largely than if it had been executed for a native.

The iron here employed is that of Bajour, as it comes from the smelting furnace, after, whilst hot, receiving a few blows, which condense it into a rude kind of pig, of

which the weight differs from five to eight sers (Kashmir), and which sells as high as four pence per pound. The first process consists in cutting the pig, when heated, into narrow strips with a cold chisel, and in this operation the iron loses one-fourth of its gross weight, from which some idea may be formed of the large proportion of unmetallic matter contained in it. Each of these strips, separately, is brought to a welding heat, and worked smartly under the hammers of two men, on a block of compact limestone, which, fixed in the ground, serves as an anvil. When the slag is expelled by this operation, each strip is drawn out under the hammer into a strap about two feet in length, an inch and a fifth in breadth, and one-fifth of an inch in thickness. One of these straps has its ends so brought together as to form a parallelogram, generally about five and a half inches long, and sufficiently broad to contain twenty lengths of the other straps cut up for the purpose. Some of these are wedged in upon their edge, their faces standing parallel to each other, and to the long sides of the belting strap, of which the ends have been pre-

viously welded together. The *pie* is then turned to its opposite face, and other pieces of strap are driven between the lengths, which were inserted on the opposite side, so as to make the whole tight; and this object is further aided by its being put into the fire, lightly heated, and receiving a few blows upon both faces as well as upon the edges. It is next smeared over with a paste of clay and water, placed near the fire, and when dried, a light welding heat being taken at it, the whole is struck up into a tolerably compact mass by smart, but rather light hammering. Exposed now to a stronger heat, the mass is vigorously and quickly hammered, and beaten out into four-sided bars, about a foot long, and a finger's thickness. These are each heated again separately, and drawn out into square rods, about a quarter of an inch broad on each face. One of these rods, neatly squared and free from scale, is pushed into the forge fire, so that the loose end penetrates under the cross firebrick into the bed of ashes, and the middle only is exposed to the fire. When it has got a red heat nearly verging upon white, it is withdrawn, and the loose

end being quickly engaged in a small square staple projecting from the surface of a log of wood close to the mouth of the forge, so as to be held fast, the fireman having previously secured the opposite end between the jaws of a small pair of tongs with a slide on the stems, begins to twist the rod on its axis from right to left, or in the contrary direction. The hottest part, or that fit for receiving a close twist, is ordinarily from two to three inches in length; and an assistant sitting close to the rod with a small pot containing cold water, and having a spout projecting from its side, pours a stream upon the part between the hot and the black portion of the bar at one end, and then quickly at the other, to prevent these portions receiving an imperfect twist; and by the same means he cools the part twisted, as soon as it has acquired the proper screw. By one complete revolution of the rod, four winds are generated from the four angles of the square, and by the repetition of the process, through a succession of heats, the whole rod is converted into a fine screw, the workmen endeavouring to render it as even as possible. Each heat furnishes about

two or three inches of twist, according as the workmen are more or less expert; and a considerable quickness, both in eye and in hand, is required on the part of the cooler to prevent the occurrence of twist in a portion of the rod not possessing a sufficient degree of heat to admit of it twisting kindly. Barrels are called plain, pechdar, or simply twisted, or jouhardar, or damasked. For the latter, which are especially the subject of this paper, the rods are disposed according to the kind of brilliant or damasked lines intended to be produced, and which are distinguished by names taken from the country in which each variety is most affected, or from the nature, or figure, in which the lines are disposed,—as Irani, or Persian, belonging to the former class, and Pigeon's Eye, Lover's Knot, Chain, &c., appertaining to the latter.

To make an Irani barrel six or eight rods are required. In regard to the latter number four are employed of those twisted from right to left, and the same number of such as have received the opposite twist, or from left to right. Every rod, after having been slightly heated, is lightly hammered on its two oppo-

site sides equally: thus a rod has four distinct portions in its circumference, of which two have the threads beaten down, and are somewhat flattened, whilst the two others have the threads standing, and retain their original roundness. The rods are now, or were previously to being flattened, lengthened by being welded end to end, and care is taken that each rod is made up of lengths of the same direction of twist, with as little disturbance to the thread at the joints as practicable. They are next laid parallel to each other, their flat sides being in contact: rods of opposite twist being disposed in alternate succession; as, first, one twisted from left to right, next, one twisted from right to left, and so on. This done, the extremities of the rods are brought into close contact, and welded together, each end of the general bar presenting a wedge of about an inch and a half in length, flat on the upper and lower surfaces, and narrow on the sides or edges, the middle rod forming the point of the wedge. In the whole extent of the bar the rods remain merely in contact, the welding being confined to its extremities

alone. The band, or *skelp*, is now ready for being formed into a hollow cylinder, through being bent or twisted in a spiral line upon itself, which process is begun at the thicker end, and continued to the thinner or muzzle, the lower extremity, or that intended for the breeching, being struck vigorously and perpendicularly down upon the stone anvil between the hammerings of every twist, for the purpose of jumping up the edges, and bringing them into close contact. When the twisting is so far completed that the edges of all the twists stand even, and touch each other, and the cylinder is nearly equal throughout its length, it is coated with a thin paste of clay and water, and is then ready for being welded. A welding heat is first taken in the middle of the cylinder, and the edges of the twists thus heated are brought into intimate contact by being jumped up, as before noticed. On this being done, the cylinder is returned to the fire, and, when the heat is well on, the twist that was jumped up is smartly hammered, so that one round is ordinarily welded at a heat. At the coming on of the second welding heat the jumping

up is repeated, followed by the welding when the heat has been regained, and so on successively until the barrel has been welded up to the muzzle. The welding is recommenced from the middle of the barrel, and, with a jumping intermediate between every two weldings, the process is continued to the breeching. This is repeated by commencing at the middle, and welding to the breeching, and afterwards proceeding from the middle to the muzzle, during which an iron rod is introduced at each end, and used as a mandril: a third heat, but merely red, is now taken at the whole surface of the barrel, which is smartly hammered, and rendered regular and level. The barrel is then fixed horizontally through a hole in an upright post, and bored, after which its surface is filed, polished, and prepared for bringing out the brilliant, or damasked lines.

The jouhar, or damask, is brought out through biting the whole surface with kassís, or sulphate of iron. The barrel is completely freed from grease or oil by being well rubbed with dry ashes and a clean rag. About three pice and one-third, or one pal,

or about three drachmas, of sulphate of iron, in powder, is mixed with as much water as is sufficient to bring it to the consistence of thick paste, which is smeared equally over the whole surface of the barrel, a stick being first introduced tightly into the muzzle to prevent any of the corrosive mixture acting upon the inside; and a like precaution is taken in respect to the breeching and the touch-hole. As soon as, by removing a little of the paste, it is seen that the metal has assumed a blackish colour, and which ordinarily happens in about two hours after it has been applied, the coating is rubbed off, and the barrel thoroughly cleaned with dry ashes and a soft rag. The same quantity of sulphate of iron as before mentioned is mixed with about four ounces of water, with which the barrel is smeared, and at the expiration of four hours is cleaned, as before mentioned, after which it is again coated with the solution, and hung up in the well. Every gunsmith, for the purpose of corroding or damasking barrels, has a well in the floor of his shop, about two yards in depth, a yard in diameter at the bottom, and diminishing gra-

dually to a span's breadth at the top, of which the mouth is crossed by a stick, and closed by a small wooden trap-door. The bottom of the well is covered with a coating of fresh horse-dung, half a yard in thickness. Suspended by a string from the cross stick, the barrel, which has been covered with the mixture of the sulphate of iron, is taken out, scrupulously, every morning, cleaned with dry ashes and a cloth, as before stated, again smeared with the solution, and hung up for twenty-four hours. If the mixture be suffered to remain on the barrel longer than this period, rusting takes place, which acts as well upon the lines expected to be brought out as upon the other parts, and defeats the object of the operation. But if the process be regularly repeated every morning, as mentioned above, prominent lines will be discovered on the surface of the barrel, separated from each other more or less by other depressed lines, or grooves, and the former will be found to have the same direction with that of the threads in the twisted rods. The prominent lines when rubbed are bright, and of a colour somewhat approaching to that of silver,

whilst the depressed lines are dark. The former are obviously the outer circumference or edge of the thread of the screw, more or less condensed and flattened by the hammer, and the latter the spaces betwixt the threads. Whether this difference in effect arise solely from a difference in hardness between the periphery of the thread produced by the twisting, or from some other circumstance, is left to the decision of others, it being the intention of the writer to confine his observations to facts, leaving deductions to future examination, when there is doubt or obscureness in the subject.

The process is generally continued for twenty days, or a month, according to the degree of prominence required in the brilliant lines; is hastened by a high temperature, and delayed by a low one, but as yet has been subjected to variations, not governed by any other rule than the result of common experience.

The principal character of difference between the Zanjir and Persian damask consists in the introduction into the former of a band of prominent and brilliant lines, dis-

posed in a manner somewhat resembling the links of a chain between parallel plain lines of damask, ultimately bounded by two twisted rods on each side of the whole; and the barrel is made up of a repetition of this pattern, by a single band being wound upon its axis in a spiral line, as in the Persian damask. The processes of cutting up the pig, and of reducing the strips into straps, are the same in both the Persian and the chain damask, but the subsequent management differs materially. In this latter the ghilaf, or pie, is made up of eighteen lengths, wedged into the belt, and treated for the manufacture of the rods, as before mentioned; but the pie for the chain contains only eight lengths, which altogether weigh little more than a pound and a quarter. This pie, when welded, is drawn out into straps, about half an inch in breadth, and one-sixth of an inch in thickness. One of these straps, being heated, is bent backwards and forwards upon itself in eight continued folds or loops, each an inch in length, and, being brought to a welding heat, is knocked up, and worked into a strap only one-third of an inch broad,

and one-tenth of an inch in thickness. Three of this kind of strap are required in this pattern, viz., one for the chain, and two for the lines before noticed. The face of the iron anvil of a gunsmith has, at one edge, a perpendicular hollow about a quarter of an inch deep, and about one-third of an inch in its opposite diameters. Across this groove one end of the strap is laid, whilst cold, and driven down into it by a small chisel and a hammer, by which the strap receives a bend or angle. Its opposite face is then placed across the die or groove, within a short distance from the acute elbow made by the chisel, and, in like manner, wedged into the former, after which the operation is reversed, and so on in succession on the opposite sides, until the whole band is converted into a frill of loops. This frill is then heated, and the operator, holding one end with a small pair of tongs, and, seizing the opposite sides of the middle of two loops of the heated extremity with the small and sharp jaws of another pair, brings them into contact, leaving the ends open. The opposite sides of the strap betwixt the two next loops is treated in

the same way, and so on till the frill is much reduced in length, through the loops of the strap standing right across its general direction, in which position they present the appearance of the links of a chain, each much drawn in at the middle. Different lengths of frill are welded together, so as to form a riband six spans long, confined laterally by being in contact with two plain straps set on edge, and bounded externally by four rods, two on each side, lying parallel and in contact, and of which latter one is twisted from left to right, and its immediate neighbour from right to left. The extremities of the general band of these seven straps and rods are welded up into a wedge, and the band being extended along the surface, a plain strap of equal breadth and length is welded upon it, afterwards hammered out and twisted, and in all other respects treated as was the band for the Persian damask. The chain damask is, in general, preferred to all other varieties yet invented, excepting the silver twist, of which I cannot speak much further than as having seen it when completed, and as this affects merely the

appearance of the barrel, and contributes not to its strength, an acquaintance with the process is rather a matter of curiosity, or of luxury, than of use. It is said that the jowhar, or damask, is imitated in Hindustan by lines being traced in a coating of wax laid over the metal, and the barrel being exposed to the action of the sulphate of iron, and a similar effect is stated to be produced by waxed threads being twisted into certain forms, and caused to adhere to the surface of a polished plain barrel; the interstices, in this case, undergoing a slight degree of corrosion, through being treated by this sulphate.

The fabrication of damasked sword-blades is no longer practised in Kashmir, but I employed some of the smiths to make some upon the principles above described, and the result of their workmanship was sent home.

A fabric of much greater importance to Great Britain than that of damasked sword-blades, is that of Yirak leather, or leather suited for saddlery. Such pieces of this as came in our way were usually old narrow slips employed as reins and head-stalls; but the leather

was strong, solid, heavy, and pliable, without any disposition to crack. Some of the pieces had been in use eighteen or twenty years, and were none the worse for constant wear. The price was four times that of other leather made in Kashmir. The skins intended for this leather, after being well cleaned, are placed in a vat of clean water, with a layer of pounded galls between every two skins; a man is employed to tread them down daily from morning to night, for twenty-five days, fresh galls being added every fifth day. They are then hung to dry; but before they are dry the grain side is well rubbed with a paste of Armenian bole. When dry the flesh side is lightly scraped, and mutton-suet is rubbed in until the leather is saturated: the rubbing is performed in the sunshine, and the skin is left for several days exposed to the sun. It is then put into water again, and trodden and rubbed until all greasiness disappears, when it is polished by being well rubbed with a blunt iron instrument.

A branch of manufacture for which Kashmir has long been celebrated, is that of ornamented pen-cases made of paper. They are

of several varieties, classed under two heads —Masnadi, or royal, and Farsi, or Persian:— the former are articles of table-furniture, more or less bulky; the latter are portable. They are usually long, shallow boxes, rounded at the ends, with a sliding convex cover, and the masnadi have sometimes trays or stands, or are fitted with feet. Part of the interior is separated to hold an inkstand. They are remarkable for the variety and elegance of the patterns with which they are painted, most generally of flowers, for the brilliancy of their colours, and the beauty of the varnish. They are most commonly made of paper, which has been written upon, but sometimes of light wood. The ground of the colouring is commonly metallic, of gold or of tin, and the pigments employed are cochineal, or the kirmis insect, ultra-marine from Yarkand, white-lead from Russia, as well as verdigris from Surat, and possibly from Britain. Other colouring drugs are found in the country, or imported from Hindustan. Varnishes are obtained from the resin of the aloe or the storax; but the best is that of the Kahruba, which is usually regarded as amber, but is by some

said to be copal. Its abundance and cheapness in Kashmir certainly indicate its being the produce of some living plant. The brushes are made of the hair of the shawl-wool goat, and the pencils from the hairs in the fur of the cat. The painting is of two kinds, raised and flat, and the former admits of several diversities, according to the greater or less relief given to the performance. The elevation of the ornamented or embossed parts is given by forming the ground of the ornaments with white-lead, mixed with a solution of glue. The surface is spotted with dots of white paint, which are left to dry, and are then trimmed with a knife; they are then covered with a surface of glue, and upon that the colour of the ornament is laid. Birds and butterflies are sometimes represented in this manner, amongst flowers and foliage, on the flat surface.

A similar style of painting is sometimes applied to palankins, elephant houdas, and even to the walls and ceilings of rooms. The painters of Kashmir are an ingenious race, and have talents which, under a fostering government and competent instruction, might

be applied with success to loftier objects than articles of furniture or decorated pen-cases.

Paper is made in Kashmir in considerable quantity, from old cloth of the san-hemp, and from cotton rags.

CHAPTER IV.

Excursion to the Deodar Forest—Kashmir Boats—Vitastha—Shadehpur—Sambhalpur—Manas Lake—River Navigation—Villages—Entrance to the Wular Lake—Lanka Island—Zein-ul-ab-addin—Shape and Character of the Lake—Shooting—Sinhára nut—Fishing—Mountains—Supur—Lalakoal River—Valley—Scenery—Peasantry—Uttar District—Dardus—Ziarat of Ghyber Shah—Darvesh—Village deserted—Segam—Deodar Forests—Return.

SHORTLY after we were domesticated in Kashmir we undertook a short excursion * to the northern parts of the valley, partly for the general purpose of exploring the country, and partly to procure the seeds of the Deodar pine, which in that situation attains its greatest size. Although some objections were started to the journey, yet these were overcome, and the necessary permission was granted. Surat Sinh and Maha Sinh were appointed ostensibly as our Mehmandars, with the additional duty, no doubt, of watch-

* These excursions in Kashmir are from the Journals of Mr. Trebeck.—ED.

ing our proceedings and checking our inquisitiveness. Part of our route was to be performed by water, along the Wular Lake, and for this purpose we had four boats, long narrow vessels of the canoe-build, with mat awnings, and two smaller ones, with Shikaris, or professional hunters. We started on the afternoon of the 15th of December, from the vicinity of Dilawar Khan's garden, a little above the bridge called Fateh kadal, and proceeded along the Vitastha to the west. The houses were on either bank close to the water's edge, and we passed under several bridges. In about half an hour we came to the confluence of the Dudh Ganga, a small stream which joins the Vitastha near the limits of the city. The river was at first about forty yards broad, but latterly double that breadth, and flowed at the rate of half a knot an hour; the water was of a greenish colour, but tolerably clear and deep, with a hard and sound bottom. We stopped just before dark at the hamlet of Palapura, on the right bank *. On the opposite was the village of Shalating.

* The Phalapura of the Chronicles, founded by Lalitaditya in the eighth century.—ED.

On the 16th we proceeded in a direction mostly to the north-west; but the course of the river was occasionally tortuous; the banks were in general low, and as regular as if they were the borders of a canal; the depth of the water was from one to three fathoms; and about a fathom higher was the greatest height to which it attained. We passed several villages: one of these, said to be, by land, seven kos from the city, Shadehpur, on the left bank, was of some extent, and the site of a market for grain. Immediately opposite to it was the conflux of the Sindh with the Behut. The former enters the latter by two channels, separated by a space of about four hundred yards. The banks are low; the river is navigable to within a short distance of Guzar Gandarbal. At two kos from Shadehpur we came to Sambhalpur, a village in two divisions, separated by the river, but connected by a fine bridge of considerable size. It rested on four piers, constructed in the river, forming five water-ways, and was, at least, a hundred yards long. On the north-east, a low ridge stretched from the mountains, and terminated within eight hundred yards of the

channel of the river. After quitting Sambhalpur, we came to the mouth of a small stream that looked like a canal. It was, however, an outlet from the lake of Manasbal, which was about three miles to the north *. This is above two miles and a half in circumference, but very deep, and, according to some reports, unfathomable. A tradition prevails, that a holy man devoted many years to the preparation of a line long enough to reach the bottom; but finding his labour vain, he at last threw himself in despair into the lake. The lake is supplied entirely by internal springs. On its north bank is the village of Safapur, where the emperor Akbar had a garden. On the southern bank is another village, that of Ahatingo; limestone is found in the neighbourhood, and is burnt there. We stopped for the night at the village of Hasim. We encountered a number of boats on this day's voyage. Some of them were passage-boats like our own. Others might more properly be denominated barges, as they were of considerable size, carrying wood and provisions to the

* This is what Jacquemont calls "le plus lac des lacs de Cachemyr, car il est le seul profond." He does not name it.—Ed.

extent, perhaps, of one hundred and fifty tons. They were flat-bottomed, slightly curved at either extremity, and drew little water. A cabin of mats, thatched, accommodated the waterman and his family. When going with the current, they were commonly pushed on by long poles: occasionally they were paddled. There was no contrivance for steering. Against the stream they were towed, twelve or fifteen men being put upon the towing-line, and with all their efforts making a progress most tediously slow. The Behut is admirably fitted for this canal-like navigation, from the level direction of its banks, and their great firmness and unbroken regularity. They were clothed with grass to the edge of the water. The bottom of the river was of stiff clay without a weed; and although the water was not exactly the liquid crystal of an alpine rill, yet it had lost little of its primitive clearness, and was rarely discoloured by soil.

Much rain had fallen during the day, and the mountain barriers of the valley had been completely hidden, so that the view from the boat resembled that which is commonly presented by the rivers of Hindustan, except that

instead of the mud or mat cottages peeping from amidst tufts of bambus, or clumps of the verdant mango or pipal, the no less rudely-constructed log-hut appeared amidst clusters of tall trees, stript of their foliage by the blasts of winter. The villages were also thinly scattered along the banks and adjacent plain, and they were in general in a ruinous and half-deserted condition. Everything wore a decidedly wintry aspect, and we felt ourselves in the climate of the north of Europe. The flocks of wild ducks and geese that had deserted the frozen lakes to seek food on the river surpassed in numbers and in clamour anything of the kind we had hitherto encountered.

On the morning of the 17th we left Hasim, and in something less than two hours came to a division of the river into two channels, leading to the lake. We followed the smaller, which was on the right, and in a quarter of an hour entered the Ular, or Wular Lake: opposite to the entrance was a small island not more than three hundred yards in circumference, on which we landed. There were two ruined buildings upon it; one of stone, at

its eastern extremity, was evidently of Hindu construction: several polygonal massive columns were strewed about, but there was no sculpture nor inscription. The other building, more to the left, was merely an oblong house with pitched roof and plastered wall, on which latter were fragments of a blue enamel. A stone with a Persian inscription was brought to us, which intimated that a mosque had been erected here by Zein-ul-ab-addin, the sovereign of Kashmir, between the Hejira years 827 and 878. The islet, which is the only one in the lake, is called Lanka, and is the subject of several traditions. According to one of these, the lake, about the time just mentioned, extended to the vicinity of Sumbhalpur, and the extent therefore to be traversed exposed the boats to sudden gales of wind, and occasioned frequent loss of lives. To prevent such accidents, Zein-ul-ab-addin determined to form a half-way landing-place, and accordingly had ordered an immense pile of stones and rubbish, derived from the Hindu temples which he had demolished, to be thrown into the water, and thus formed the substratum of the island, to which, in ridicule

of Hindu tradition, he gave the name of Lanka. Another story is, that the capital of Kashmir formerly occupied the site now covered by the lake, but that it suddenly sunk, and was submerged by some great convulsion of nature: Zein ul abaddin, it is added, caused the lake to be explored for some relics of the catastrophe, and the buildings now on Lanka were constructed by his orders, of fragments recovered from the water. The celebrated Mirza Hyder extols Lanka as a delightful spot for a party of pleasure: at present it offers nothing calculated to give a zest to recreation, containing only a few wretched huts, inhabited by tenants miserably poor, and abominably dirty: a party of women welcomed us with a song, and it was hard to say whether their squalid persons or discordant voices were most repulsive. A water line was noticed on the bank of the island, at least forty feet above the surface of the lake. We started from Lanka at half-past one, and in something less than an hour arrived at the northern edge of the lake, where we stopped for the night.

The Lake of Ular is of an oblong shape;

its northern bank is skirted by the mountains, which terminate the valley so closely, as scarcely in some parts to leave a footpath between them and the water: more to the westward they again recede, leaving an open space of perhaps a mile. The outline of the lake is very regular, and its general appearance is picturesque and pleasing: we saw it under unfavourable circumstances; in summer it would, no doubt, afford a resemblance to some of the lakes of Westmoreland or Scotland. At the season we visited it, the water being low, left a line of swamp between it and the shore: the hills beyond the level rose to one thousand or one thousand two hundred feet, and were thickly clothed with pine forests, and similar mountains shut in the view to the east and west, beyond the low and richly-wooded lands of the valley. The bottom of the lake was of soft mud, and the depth, where we sounded, varied from less than one fathom to two fathoms or something more. At the place where we rested were many boats and barges taking in rice in the husk, brought down to the water-side by the villagers, who were a stout, athletic race.

Thousands of water-fowl were sporting on the lake, but they were very shy, and it was difficult to approach near enough for sport. In shooting them, the Kashmirian sportsman employs a matchlock, the barrel of which is at least ten feet long. When rowed near to the game, he and the single boatman who accompanies him, lie down in the boat so as to be seen as little of as possible by the birds, and then with small paddles and their hands over the sides, gently push the boat onwards until within range: two or three birds generally fall at each discharge. The Kashmirians have very exaggerated ideas of the extent of this lake, and one of them gravely asked me if it was not as large as the sea. A number of boats on the lake were employed in raking up the sinhara, or water-nut: for this purpose a long stake is stuck in the muddy bottom, and a small boat with three or four men lashed to it: the men are furnished with a pole, at one end of which a flat board is fastened, and with this they rake the bottom, dragging up the plants; these at first are much entangled by their long fibrous stems, but they are unravelled by suspension for some time in the

water. The government, it is said, receives annually ninety-six thousand kharwars or ass loads of the nut. There were also boats engaged in fishing; two moderately heavy boats and two light skiffs usually act together for this object: in each of the former are two men, one rowing, the other managing the net; the latter is paddled by one man seated at the head. The net is of the shape of a cone, but of a considerable size; the mouth is stretched on a wooden frame, in the form of a parabola of nearly a fathom area, a pole extending from the base to the summit, intended both to give support to a rod which reaches to the end of the bag, keeping it stretched, and to be of use in raising the net, which is too heavy to be wholly managed by a single person. When all is ready, the sterns of the two larger boats are brought so near together, that the space between them may be wholly occupied by the nets lowered on their sides; the skiffs then go a-head, and wheeling round, make between the two larger boats, striking the water smartly; the net is drawn as they approach, and each man in the skiff assists the one in the large boat to

raise it. A single jerk empties the net of its contents, and it is again lowered; the skiffs then proceed, and turning round their companions, again row a-head, and the operation is repeated. The rapidity and regularity with which these manœuvres are repeated render the fishing on Lake Ular an amusing and interesting spectacle. The fish caught are in general small, but a variety of trout is sometimes taken ten or twelve pounds weight. The fishermen sometimes use grains for striking them.

On the morning of the 18th we proceeded towards the south-western extremity of the lake; on our right, at the horizontal distance of not more than eight hundred paces, was a small house surrounded by trees, on the top of a small hill; this is the garden of a Kashmirian saint, named Shukar-uddin: beyond this the mountains run off to the west, and the shore of the lake lies low. The crown of the range of mountains running across the valley parallel with the shore was about two miles horizontally distant from the latter: at the south-western extremity, distant about three miles

from the opposite shore, we re-entered the channel of the river, here about one hundred and fifty yards broad, and stopped early in the afternoon at Supur, a town on both sides of the stream, connected by a bridge of three piers, between eighty and a hundred yards long. At Supur was a bazar for provisions, and for the Bajauri or Peshawari iron, which passes through this on its way from the west to Srinagar. The streets were narrow, crooked, and in wet weather are very dirty, and the houses presented the same characteristic deformities as those of the capital. A small brick fort stood on the right bank of the river, at the northern end of the bridge; the walls were lofty, but not very substantial. Passing below the bridge, we found our horses and servants who had been sent to meet us. The latter had taken up their quarters in an empty house, one of the best mansions in the town, but without owner or tenant, and accessible to any one that pleased to enter. Surat Sinh and Ganes Pandit, the farmer of the revenue of the district, were at Supur with a party of Sikh soldiers, levying taxes: the

latter was a tall, thin young man, heavy in conversation, and said to bear a very indifferent character.

On the 19th of December we commenced our land journey, proceeding in a north-westerly direction from Supur. The road at some short distance skirted the northern edge of the small river Lala-koal, which joined the Behut near the village of Dabu: the breadth of the valley was about two miles. On this side of Poru, five kos from Supur, the surface was irregular; but from thence a small, but beautiful plain lay before us. At two miles further on we came to the hamlet of Chogul, where a party of Sikhs were stationed. We halted a little in advance at Nulu Nupu, where the valley was not more than eight hundred paces broad, with the Lala-koal curling sluggishly along its centre. The country along the whole of the route was very beautiful. On quitting Supur we traversed a broad, flat surface, with the mountains on either hand too remote to display their features in detail. From the top of the high bank whence Chogul was first beheld the scene was somewhat changed.

Before us was a plain nearly circular, bounded to westward by long swelling ridges, bearing broken forests of pine, interspersed with tracts of soil of evident fertility: beyond them were lofty mountains in their winter garb. Later in the day their snowy summits blended with the hazy sky, and formed an admirable background to the frowning forests and the smiling plain; the latter, studded with orchards and hamlets, which lay nearest to the spectator. The beauty of the scenery, however, ill harmonised with the appearance of the peasantry. Their huts were inferior in comfort to an English cow-house, and their clothes were insufficient to defend them from the cold of the season. Not one-twentieth part of the arable land was in cultivation, and a number of half-choked canals attested once careful, and now neglected irrigation. We were lodged in a miserable hut, which scarcely afforded as good a shelter as might have been attained underneath some trees in the neighbourhood, especially as their boughs were covered with long thick ropes of grass, hung there as a supply of winter forage. Maha Sinh and his Sikhs seemed to be practising

the usual system of violence and extortion, as far as we might judge from the clamorous remonstrances of the villagers.

The valley on the following day was much contracted: the hills on either side were low, and generally covered with pine forest; the lower part of the valley was fertile, and was mostly cultivated; amongst the trees we noticed the apple, the trela a delicious crab, the vine, the walnut, and the peach. The Lala-koal divided into two branches; one to the right, called the Lolab, was that which we followed, the other, the Poru, rises in the district of Uttar, at about eight kos distance to the westward. The district of Uttar is formed chiefly of a fine valley, partially cultivated, bounded on each side by snow-topped mountains; these approach towards its end, and beyond it we were told lay the Bamba country of Karnao. After pursuing the line of the stream for some way, we crossed it, and changed our direction from north-west to north-east, proceeding up a narrow valley. On the opposite of the hills on our north we were told was the country called Drao. It is nearly covered with forest, and is rarely

visited, except by cow-keepers, owing in some measure to the incursions of the Dardus, the last of which took place twenty years ago. The country of these latter was pointed out in the same direction, or rather at north-west, and was said to be nine days' journey distant; but on this head accounts were very contradictory, some stating the distance to be a journey of a month, and others of only four days.

At about four miles on the road we came to a holy shrine, called the Ziarat of Ghyber Shah, where two huts were erected for the accommodation of travellers; they were in the charge of an old Darwesh, who has inherited the office from his ancestors, and has been here since infancy. He pretended to be ninety years old. He could give us no account of the saint, nor seemed to understand the prayers which he muttered with considerable fluency in Arabic; part of his duty was to keep up a fire from morning till night. The surface of the valley from hence was somewhat uneven, and was in part covered by thin patches of snow: the river flowed gently along within bowshot of our right. We halted at

the village of Tsira-koth, where the valley was about eight hundred paces broad. The hills on our right were not above seven hundred feet high; those on the left were rather loftier, and in the distance were seen others of very considerable elevation; the ridge rising two thousand feet above our level, and being entirely covered with snow. The hardy pine, however, ascended nearly to its summit. The village where we stopped was half deserted, and the few inhabitants that remained wore the semblance of extreme wretchedness: without some relief or change of system, it seems probable that this part of the country will soon be without inhabitants. Yet the soil seemed favourable for rice cultivation, and the crop appeared to have been a good one. The poor people, however, were likely to reap little advantage from their labours, for a troop of tax-gatherers were in the village, who had sequestered nine-tenths of the grain for their employer, Jawahir Mal, the farmer of the revenue. The soil was rich, and the remains of watercourses showed that it had once been made productive: we rode also over lines of deserted orchards, which

must, at one period, have formed a forest of fruit-trees. The direction of our route must have taken us round the northern end of the Ular Lake, and there was a road on our right which led direct over the hills to the district of Kuhiama, on its borders. We might, therefore, have come hither in much less time, but it seemed to be part of our guide's policy to take us by the most circuitous route.

From Tsira-koth we proceeded to the village of Sogam, along a valley which runs first to the south-east and then east by south. On our way we again crossed the Lolab, which rises on this side the pass leading to Hasora and Little Tibet, about eleven miles off. The mountains seemed to increase but little in height: those on our left were the loftiest, but by no means of impracticable ascent, whilst those on our right were low, and were covered with the Deodar forest, which we had come to visit. We were too late, however, for seed, by three months. The cones had all fallen, and several young shoots had risen two or three inches above the ground. The snow was a foot deep in many places. The valley was much the

same as that of the preceding day, presenting an undulating surface, and thickly overspread with orchards of the walnut, apple, trela, or crab, and pear, intermixed with firs and cedars.

The people of Sogam were almost in a savage state. The men were, in general, tall and robust; the women haggard and ill-looking. The houses were mostly constructed of small trees, coarsely dovetailed together, and coated with rough plaster inside. A flat planking was laid over the top, resting on the walls, and above that a sloping roof was constructed, open at the ends, the space being either filled with dry grass, or serving to give shelter to the poultry. The interior was divided by partitions of wicker-work, plastered, into three or four small, dark, and dirty apartments. In summer-time the scenery here must be very lovely.

Having thus accomplished one of our purposes, at least, we set out on our homeward march on the 22nd, and reached Supur on the same day after dark. We there em-

barked, and, after crossing the lake, were towed up the river. We arrived at Dilawar Khan's garden late on the 24th of December.

CHAPTER V.

Visit to the Sources of the Behut—Canals—Dal Lake—Ruined Temple—Ancient Pillar — Small Stream—Pampur—Saffron—Sulphur Spring—Ruined Temple of the Pandus—Wantipur—Ruins—Tral—Vijipara — Garden of Dara Shekoh—Branches of the Behut—Islamabad—Vir-nag River — Shahabad—Remains of Palace of Jehangir—Springs—Visit to the Cave of Munda—Ruined Temples at Karewe Matan—Sacred Pools at Bhuvan—Return.

On the 6th of May we set out from Kashmir on a visit to the sources of the Behut and the eastern divisions of the country, attended by a Sikh escort under command of Surat Sinh.

On quitting our house we proceeded towards the river, and then, turning to the left, passed through a narrow, irregular, and dirty street parallel with it. A few yards beyond the Haba Kadal, which is the loftiest bridge

except one in the city, we again turned to the left, and at a distance of about a mile reached the winding canal of Drogjan, planted on each side with tall poplars, round which vines were twining, sometimes as high as their middle branches. We were now beyond the limits of the city. The canal receives the water of the celebrated little Dal, or lake, which is supplied principally by a stream flowing from behind the garden of Shahlimar, and pours it into the Behut, opposite to the south-east curtain of Shir Gerh. Its connexion with the lake, when the contents of the latter are much diminished, is cut off by a strong folding gate, shutting below a bridge, which we presently crossed. After passing over it we came near to the foot of the hill on which stands the Takhti Suliman, and continued along its base for more than a mile. From thence we came again to the river, which in this part winds very considerably. Hills were close upon our left. In the middle of a small, but deep tank stood a small dilapidated temple, evidently Hindu, and said to be as old as the commencement of the Christian era. The

side of the hill above it was covered with fragments of stone, on some of which figures were sculptured, and on others ornamental carving was noticed. One large stone of a conical shape had the appearance of a lingam, but the peasants said it was a mark for the ball used in playing at chaugan, employed by a race of giants who formerly dwelt here. Another was pointed out as the goal, but proved to be the upper part and capital of a huge polygonal pillar, the shaft of which was seven yards in circumference. Traces of figures sculptured on its upper part were indistinctly perceptible. This fragment lay upon the top of a small mound, entirely alone, and no other remains of sculpture or building were discoverable in its immediate vicinity. Beyond this was the commencement of the village of Pankchok, on the right bank of the Behut, and opposite was the hamlet of Lajien, where a large quantity of mats are annually manufactured.

The road continued along the river, but the hills on the left had receded to the distance of nearly two miles. The surface of the valley was much broken by swamps, but

the level was much the same throughout, and the river flowed sluggishly along the middle of it. Carved stones, the remains both of Hindu and Mohammedan architecture, were scattered about in great numbers. We met with but one inscription, and that was only the name of the Emperor Jehangir. A small rivulet, crossed on our way, was said to rise about five miles off, by two branches, near the second of which is a village called Jwalamukhi, where there is a spring considered holy by the Hindus. After crossing the stream we came to the town of Pampur, in the Pargana of Vehu. This place is celebrated for its saffron, which grows in the neighbourhood on the driest spots in great abundance. It has a bazar and two ziarats, or tombs of holy men, Sheikh Baba and Khaja Maksud. These are small low structures, chiefly of wood, with a sort of wooden spire, capped with brass. We stopped here: our baggage was conveyed hither in boats, which arrived soon after we did, and afforded us shelter for the night.

The hills again approached the river, along which we proceeded. After passing

Latapur we came to a sulphurous spring, called Kshir Nag. There was nothing remarkable in the appearance or taste of the water: it was tepid, and emitted a strong odour of sulphur. A low, and nearly perpendicular cliff on the left was pointed out as a remarkable object. Zein ul abaddin, having been defeated, it is said, and, flying from the field, was hard pressed by his pursuers, whom he escaped by urging his horse up the steep face of this rock. Two marks on the rock are shown as the impressions of the horse's hoofs, and no Kashmirian passes without making them a salam. About half a mile further on we came to an interesting ruin on our right. Like others of the same kind, it is called by the peasants a building of the Pandus, the heroic princes of Hindu epic verse, but believed here to have been giants. The edifice must have been a square temple, with four doors, approached by broad and spacious porches, and enclosed by a wall with four gates opposite to the doors of the central structure. A part of one of these was still standing, but of the walls the foundations alone remain, and the temple itself is a

confused mass of ruins. The most remarkable feature of these remains was their magnitude. All the blocks were of immense size, and many of them could not have weighed less than ten tons. Many of them also presented traces of most elaborate sculpture*. At the adjacent village of Wantipur† we found similar remains, and here also one of the gateways was nearly entire. This was much richer than in the first edifice, and was covered with ornaments, scrolls, and figures. Two masses of stone on each side of the entrance, and each supported by a single pillar, were of an extraordinary size. The shape of the temple was undefined, and the principal part of its fragments seemed to be carved cornices or portions of the roof. The stone of which these buildings were constructed is a limestone, which is susceptible of a high polish, and might be termed grey marble. It is seen at Shahlimar, and other places about the city, where the surface still

* Some drawings of these were made by Mr. Trebeck.—ED.

† The Avantipur of the Chronicles of Kashmir, founded by Avanti Varma, king of Kashmir in 876, who is recorded to have built many temples and palaces.—ED.

continues smooth and perfect. Here, however, from long exposure, the surface has become decomposed, so that the carving is nearly or wholly effaced. It is scarcely possible, however, to imagine that the state of ruin to which they have been reduced has been the work of time or even of man, as their solidity is fully equal to that of the most massive monuments of Egypt: earthquakes must have been the chief agents in their overthrow.

Beyond Wantipur we crossed the river of Tral, as the district commencing at that village is called, and shortly afterwards a second stream: both these come from the north-east, and fall into the Behut. On our right, at a distance of about fifteen miles, the lofty crest of the Pir Panchal pass was visible, but the breadth of the valley continued much the same, several ranges of low hills intervening between it and Pir Panchal. The hills on our left, about eighteen hundred feet high, were covered with snow. A considerable stream, the Arabal, descends from Pir Panchal, and joins the Behut by two branches. At the village of Wagahama we

entered the district of Dakhinpara, and passed the Liddir, a stream which comes from near the Ladakh pass of Zwaje La, or, at least, from the snows which supply the rivulet that enters the valley of Sonamurgh from the south. Further on we crossed the Behut by a sanga of some extent, but much decayed, where on either bank of the river stood the town of Vijipara, or Bijbiara. During the latter part of this day's journey the soil, a stiff clay, was generally in cultivation, and much less of it was covered by pools and swamps than in the neighbourhood of the capital.

Opposite to the town of Vijipara stood what was once the garden of Dara Shekoh. It had been laid out in the same manner as the gardens of Shahlimar, Nishat, and others in Kashmir, and consisted of little more than a number of cross avenues or walks. Some of the trees were still standing, and the chenar trees especially were of stately size and magnificent foliage. Along the centre was a line of tanks, connected by a canal, and there were also the remains of a small brick palace or lodge.

About two miles farther on we came to the junction of the two main branches of the Behut, one coming from the north-west, and the other from the south-east. The former has several heads: the chief lies in the snows at a place called Koka-náth in the district of Brang, and about eight kos distant. It divides soon after its commencement into two branches, forming an island between them of some extent. The northern branch receives a small river that rises in the mountains of Koharpara more to the west. The southern is joined by the eastern branch, the Shahabad, or Vir-nag river, and the united stream meets with the northern branches a little to the north-east of Islamabad. The valley here is about seven miles broad, and begins to rise.

The town of Islamabad is built upon the extremity of a long, low spur from the mountains to the east. At the foot of the slope is a reservoir of a triangular form, in one corner of which is a copious spring, yielding, perhaps, as much as two hundred gallons per minute of a slightly sulphurous water: it was cool and quite clear, though much gas es-

caped from it. On the side of the hill were several tanks, supplied by a similar spring. There were many fish in them, which are fed, and were quite tame: they are considered sacred, and never caught.

At Islamabad are three hundred shops of shawl-weavers, and a coarse kind of chintz, and a considerable number of gabbas, or flowered patchwork cloths of the coloured woollens of the country, are fabricated. It was as filthy a place as can well be imagined, and swarmed with beggars, some of whom were idle vagabonds, but the greater number were in real distress.

On quitting Islamabad we crossed the several eastern branches of the Behut, and proceeded along the right bank of the Viranag river, at a short distance from it, to where the valley contracted to a breadth not exceeding a thousand paces, where stood the village or town of Shahabad. This is the residence of a Malik or chief, whose ancestors were persons of some consideration, being charged with the military protection of the road to Hindustan, by the pass of Bannahal, until they incurred the displeasure of their Durani

governors, and were reduced to comparative insignificance. The superintendence of the police, however, and the collection of the revenue, are still held by the present Malik, and he is said to exercise his authority more for his own benefit than that of the district. We were lodged in one of his houses; the upper part was enclosed by a lattice-work, the interstices of which scarcely admitted a finger, and which, whilst allowing access to light and air, effectually screened the rooms from inspection from without. Shahabad had a bazar and a few shops, at which provisions, coarse cloth, and remarkably fine honey, were the chief articles for sale.

We found a Sikh sirdar and some armed men here, who had come to enforce the payment of arrears of revenue due by the Malik. It was supposed that he would evade present payment by bribing the Sikh. Shahabad is said to be twenty-three kos from the capital.

On the 10th of May we crossed the Vira-nag, and following its left bank beyond where it was divided into two branches, came at about a mile and a half to the village and spring, called also Vira Nága. The valley, in our

approach to this reputed source of the Hydaspes, retained its breadth, and extended some way before us, when it appeared to terminate in a narrow defile, beneath mountains streaked with snow, and covered with dark forests of fir. Passing through the village to the foot of the western ridge, we arrived at a spring which was at the foot of a hill covered with low herbage and brushwood. After riding along the edge of a rice-field, we came to a large stream or brook, and some thick banks, which were, in fact, the remains of the wall of an extensive building. A little plat of grass to the right was pointed out as the site of that portion of the palace where the Emperor Jehangir used to show himself to his courtiers. Some yards beyond this a large body of water was found gushing up close to the path. This communicated by a subterranean drain with a spring higher up. The main stream ran within five or six paces of it, and was here edged by the foundation and bases of arches, near which it was said were the apartments of the celebrated Nur Jehan. On turning to the right we came to a watercourse of masonry much dilapidated, conducting the main

stream from the enclosure in which the spring was situated. Round this an octagonal reservoir of stone has been constructed, nineteen fathoms broad, and said to be twenty yards deep in the centre. It was full of clear still water, the surplus of which passed off by the aqueduct above noticed in a stream three yards broad, and above two feet deep. Along the side was a causeway, or walk, six feet broad, on the outer edge of which were twenty-one small arched alcoves, about twelve feet wide, and six deep, and sufficiently high for a tall man to stand upright in them. Above them appeared a mass of substantial brick-work, now overgrown with grass, so that they, no doubt, formed the basement-story of some edifice: the whole was formerly faced with stone, but the stones have been removed. One over the entrance bears the name of Jehangir, and the date of the construction of this palace. As a summer residence the site was well chosen. The mountains on either side are low, verdant, and well wooded, and are neither tame nor rugged. The valley has here a gentle slope, and rises sufficiently for this spot to command an extensive prospect

of the whole plain of Kashmir, watered by the Behut, and bounded by the blue mountains beyond the Wular lake.

Although the spring of Vira-nag is considered sometimes as the source of the Behut, yet that character appears to belong more properly to the eastern branch, which, rising by two heads, comes from the mountains in the direction of east half-south, ten kos distant. At Shahabad we were told of a wonderful cave in the hills to the west, at the bottom of which flowed a rill, forming some way within the cave a bath in a reservoir constructed of stone. In the winter the ice that was here formed was changed, it was said, to solid crystal on being brought into the air. The origin of this last story was, no doubt, the formation of stalactites; the rest of the account we undertook to verify, and on our return proceeded to ascend the face of the mountains on our left.

On the way we crossed a considerable rivulet coming from the hills. Bannahal, across the same ridge, was about seven kos distant by a crooked path. This place is included in the Subah of Kashmir, but seems rather to

belong to the hill districts, as no pass of consequence separates it from the Panjab. Farther on we passed three springs, supplying a small brook, a feeder of the Behut, and crossing this, we ascended the lower slope of the hills, continuing for some way on the Bannahal road. Here we found the prangos growing abundantly, but the peasants were ignorant of its value as winter provender for their cattle: they applied it, however, to other purposes of more equivocal benefit. Water, in which the plant had been steeped, they asserted destroyed snails, and the root rubbed on the skin was a cure for the itch. Continuing to ascend the hills, we managed, although the ground was rough and broken, to ride to within four hundred feet of the top. There we alighted, and crossing a thick bed of snow, came to the entrance of the cave of Munda. The opening was only high enough to admit a man on his hands and knees, and a stream flowed from it sufficient to turn a mill. Taking torches with us, we crawled into it, and at about five yards came to a part sufficiently lofty to allow us to stand. Our attempt to advance was, however, frustrated,

by the bottom being entirely filled with water more than mid-deep, the depth of which, as ascertained by a stick, increased as it receded. As far as we could discern, the passage continued for above twenty yards, with a height of from six to eight feet. How much farther it penetrated the mountain we could not ascertain, but it seemed likely that it was nothing more than a natural drain for the waters of the mountain. These had now accumulated in larger quantity than usual, as the mouth of the cave had been blocked up with snow. It had been partially cleared away for our visit by order of the Malik, but the quantity was too considerable to be wholly removed, unless after some days' labour. Leaving Munda we descended to Shahabad.

On the following day we rode to Islamabad, and on this occasion visited some remarkable remains in its vicinity, on the top of the low ridge or platform formerly noticed, and which is called Karawe Matan. The summit of this was for the most part perfectly level, and commonly a mile in breadth, and according to the report of the people of the country, was formerly the site of a large city, the ca-

pital of Kashmir. Scattered over the ground, indeed, we found fragments of mortar and bricks, but no relics of any note till we came to the end of the mound, where, at a distance of about two miles from Islamabad, stood the ruins we were in quest of. These from their elevated situation were widely conspicuous, and were of very remarkable extent and character. Like most of the architectural remains in Kashmir, they are termed Khana Panduwa, a house or palace of the Pandus. They consisted of a main building in the centre of an open space, surrounded by a wall. The central structure was composed of a body and two small wings, the former about fifty-six feet long by twenty-six wide, running east and west, and twenty-eight feet high, was divided into two chambers of different dimensions; the western face comprised a large, lofty, arched portal, with four carved pilasters, two on each side; the eastern front had a wide recess, occupied by a false doorway, with an ornamental arch, and on the sides of which were pilasters; similar recesses decorated the northern and southern ends: opposite to these extremities also were the two wings

or chambers, connected formerly by a colonnade with the centre. They were built with massive walls, but the interior was not above six feet square. On the inside of the enclosing wall formerly extended a series of columns, forming a sort of portico all round, and a series of small chambers or cells ran along its outer face. The whole was constructed of stones of immense size and weight, embellished with elaborate sculpture. The roofs had generally fallen in, but where remaining, were of large flat slabs of stone. The walls were for the most part entire, their massiveness having resisted not only time and earthquakes, but the assaults of man: one of the rulers of Kashmir, Sultan Hamadan, is said to have attempted in vain to undermine the edifice, or to destroy it by fire. It is fortunate he was not acquainted with the use of gunpowder. In its present condition the palace of the Pandus is a precious specimen of ancient art, and deserves a foremost place amongst the remains of Hindu antiquity*.

From the Khana Panduwa we proceeded to Bhuvan, a village about half a mile to the

* There are some drawings of this building also.—Ed.

north-west, where two reservoirs are situated, which are considered holy by the Hindus. They appeared to have belonged to a palace, the ruins of which were near them*: they were from six to eight feet deep, filled with beautifully clear water, and swarmed with tame fish. They were surrounded by a rude dharm sala, or building for the accommodation of travellers, erected recently, and tenanted by some Brahmins. From hence we proceeded to our boats, and floated with the current: above the bridge the passage was difficult, and we were often aground, but below it all was easy. We anchored at Wantipur after midnight on the 14th. On the 15th we repeated our visit to the ruins we had first observed: their effect was somewhat impaired by the greater majesty of those at Karawe Matan, but they were in the same style, and the work evidently of the same period. We arrived at Pandenthan at three in the afternoon, and as no other means of getting at the interior of the building in the tank were available, Mr. Trebeck

* More probably of a temple of Siva, who, as Tribhuvaneswara, was at different periods prior to the twelfth century worshipped in Kashmir.—Ed.

swam to it, in order to ascertain the nature of the inscription which it was said to contain. Nothing of the kind, not a single letter did it present; the interior was quite plain, with the exception of a large lotus sculptured on the roof. Nothing else occurring to delay our return, we reached Dilawar Khan's garden before sunset.

CHAPTER VI.

Countries in the neighbourhood of Ladakh and Kashmir—Amaranath—Little Tibet—Balti—Skardo—Steppe of Deosu—Shigar—Shingo—Tsungaru—Kafalun—Kartakshe—Nagar—Hounz—Gilgit—Chilas—Lower Chitral—Upper Chitral—Wakkan—Road to Yarkand—Kara-kol Lake—Kirghiz of Pamer—Siri-kol—Tagarma.

ALTHOUGH unable to visit the countries which intervene on the north and north-west, between Ladakh and Kashmir on the south, and the Karakoram mountains and Badakhshan on the north, we had frequent opportunities of communicating with the natives of those regions, and gained from them various notices, which, though not as particular, nor, perhaps, as accurate as could be wished, yet may not be unacceptable in the absence of more authentic information.

Before, however, passing to those districts, it may be as well to advert to a place which

ought, perhaps, to be considered as included in Kashmir, and which lies in an angle between it and Ladakh, south of the pass of Zwaje Lá. This is the cave of Amaranath, a place of reputed sanctity and pilgrimage. The road to this cave proceeds from Bhuvan, along the valley of the Lidder to Ganes Bal, so called, it is said, from a rude stone figure, which is supposed to represent the Hindu divinity, Ganesa. It then continues to Pahalgam in Dakshinpara, and thence to the Pesh-bal pass; the latter part of the route is uninhabited. Beyond the pass is the lake of Sesh-nag, nine miles in circumference, and giving rise to a number of rivulets which form the Panch-tarang, or five-stream river; another pass in the mountains, the Neza-bal, lies beyond this, from which rises the Bhagavati river, flowing into the Panch-tarang. Near this is situated the cave of Amaranath, of which the entrance is said to be one hundred yards broad, and thirty high; the depth of the cave is five hundred yards. There are no inscriptions in it, nor any sculpture; but in the most remote part of the cave, there is said to be the figure of a Gosein, seated on a

pedestal, which figure increases and decreases in size with the increasing and waning moon, and at the conjunction entirely vanishes. It is customary, therefore, to visit the cave only about the full moon. The course of the Panch-tarang is not exactly known, but it is believed to pass into Ladakh, near Kartse. Persons in the cave of Amaranath assert that they can hear the barking of the dogs in Tibet.

To proceed, however, with the countries on the north, it appears that those which lie along the foot of the Karakoram mountains, and which are included in Tibet, are Kartakshe, Kafalun, Kiris, Kardo, Shigar, Rundu, Hasora, Níl or Nagar, and Hounz: of these, all except the two last, which are independent, are properly part of the principality of Balti, or Baltistan. They have, however, chiefs of their own, whose subordination to the prince of Kardo, or Iskardo, which is usually regarded as the capital of Balti, depends upon his ability to enforce their allegiance.

The capital of Balti, or Baltistan, commonly termed Skardo, Iskardo, or Kardo, is more usually called in the country Sargarkhoad. There are some vague traditions also

of its being named Iskandaria, and that it was one of the cities founded by Alexander. In the course of my correspondence with Ahmed Shah, the ruler of Balti, I inquired if any vestiges of Greek colonists were to be met with, but it did not appear that any were discoverable. Skardo is situated on the left bank of the Indus, and consists of a fort, and about one hundred and fifty houses, scattered over a considerable tract on the south of the river. The fort stands on the top of a high rock, washed by the river, and is accessible on one face only. The river is about three hundred yards broad, and very deep, running with considerable velocity. The valley is about two miles broad, and is more fertile than any part of Ladakh. It is well supplied with wood, and orchards are abundant: grapes, melons, plums, apples, pears, mulberries, flourish, and the apricots, as already observed, are of peculiar excellence, and when dried are exported. The grains cultivated are wheat and barley. Horses and ponies of a serviceable description are bred. The people are industrious and hardy, and the Raja enjoys more political power than any of

the chiefs of Little Tibet. The people of Balti are all Shiah Mohammedans.

The main roads from Ladakh and Kashmir to Skardo, lead over an extensive and elevated steppe, or plain, called by the Kashmirians, Deosu, the plain of the gods. It is bare of trees, but covered with coarse grass and Tartaric furze. It is surrounded by mountains, or rather appears to be a sunken table-land, uniting the different ranges from which various streams are formed, and cross the plain in different directions. One as large as the Dras river runs to the north-west, and joins the Indus on the west of Kardo, and another flows westward, into the river of Hasora. Two others, the Marpo and Nakpo, or red and black rivers, flow to the south-east, and meet to form the Shingo river, which falls into the Dras river, shortly before the latter enters the Indus. These streams are partly fed by the plain itself, as snow lies upon it the greater part of the year, melting entirely not more than two months at the end of the summer.

Upon the eastern edge of the Deosu are the villages of Shigar and Shingo, subject to

Kardo, and comprehending not more than thirty-five or forty houses. There is another Shigar, a fort, and large village in a different position, lying, it is said, ten kos north-west from Kardo. On the western border of the steppe lies Tsungaru, or Hasora, the country of which is contiguous to Garets, a district sometimes comprehended in Kashmir. The town of Hasora consists of about three hundred houses, defended by a fort, and stands in the middle of a plain. The country, though mountainous, is fertile, and the grapes are celebrated. Some trade from Gilgit and Yarkand passes through Hasora, and many Kashmiri weavers have settled there and manufacture coarse shawls and shawl-cloth. The people are Shiahs, but are Tibetans, and speak the language of Tibet. The Raja is nominally subject to Ahmed Shah, and assisted him, not long before, to repel a predatory attack of the Afghans. A river rising on the edge of the Deosu runs past Hasora, and then turns south to join that of Muzeffarabad. The united stream flows into the Behut.

Kafalun is a province west of Nobra, on the left bank of the Shayuk: it formerly be-

longed to Ladakh, but was taken possession of by Ahmed Shah. The same was the case with Kartakshe immediately south of Kafalun, along the northward arm of the Sinh-kha-bab. This is also called Kara-tag, Black-mountain, from the dark colour of its hills. The chief village consists of about a hundred houses, and a fort situated on a conical rock close to the right bank of the river, which is crossed by a swinging bridge. Kiris is a small state on the road between Kafalun and Balti, on the right bank of the Shayuk river.

Nagar, or Burshal, is a small state lying on the road from Skardo to Gilgit, and consists chiefly of a valley of about three days' journey in length, and six or eight miles broad. It is watered by a river which joins the river of Gilgit, and on the banks of which stands the town, with a fort as usual upon a hill. Much snow falls and fuel is scarce. The grains reared are wheat and barley; grapes and melons are plentiful and excellent. Gold is found in the river. The people are called Dungars, and the Raja is independent. Beyond Nagar, and nearer to the Pamer mountains, is the district of Hounz, also inhabited

by Dungars. Kanjut is the name of the capital, which is the residence of Selim Shah. From this province a difficult pass leads across the mountains to Badakhshan.

Proceeding to the westward, we come to the district of Gilgit, inhabited by Dardus *. The chief town is situated on a plain, three or four kos broad, and eleven or twelve long. It is bounded by mountains of moderate elevation, well wooded, on which snow rarely lies. The chief town is washed by a river which rises in the Pamer mountains, and after receiving the river of Hounz, falls into the Indus. The town stands on the right bank, and consists of about three hundred houses. The people speak a peculiar language, and are of the Shiah persuasion, mixing the Mohammedan creed with many local superstitions. According to their notions, the races of men, of all at least that they have any knowledge of,—the Tibetans, the Kashmirians, the people to the north-west of Gilgit, and the Dards,—are de-

* Few people can be traced through so long a period in the same place as these, as they are evidently the Dáradas of Sanscrit Geography, and Daradæ, or Daradræ of Strabo. They are also, no doubt, the Kafers of the Mohammedans, although they have of late been nominally converted to Islam.—Ed.

scended from four angels, named Makhpun, Shameru, Khyrullah, and Malika. On his death a Dard goes to heaven; but as the gate is guarded by a Kashmirian, who would probably refuse to admit him, the corpse is provided with a bow and arrows, with which, if necessary, he may fight for entrance. A Dard who can afford it does little bodily labour, but employs for the purpose slaves who have been carried off in some inroads on their neighbours. The chief cultivation is of rice, under the management of Kashmirians. Cotton and silk are reared for domestic use; and a substantial cloth is manufactured, of which the warp is of silk, and the woof of cotton, of wool, or of tus. Shawl-wool comes from Pamer and Yarkand, and tus is obtained in the country. Gold is found in the sands of the river, and gold-dust forms the only currency. The Raja receives a small sum from every one who searches for gold, one-twentieth of the rice-crop, and a present from every man who marries, or who has a child. Grapes are abundant and excellent, and wine is drunk in considerable quantity. There is abundance

of fruit, especially of mulberries, figs, pomegranates, walnuts, and melons.

The same race of people, the Dards, occupy the country to the south-west of Gilgit, or Chilas, also called Dardu Chilas. This is situated in the valley watered by the Gilgit river, and the town stands on the left bank. It consists of about a thousand houses, and contains four forts, each tenanted by a separate chief, who, although absolute over his own personal retainers, is associated with the other three in the government of the state. They pay a nominal obedience to the chief of Gilgit, sending there an annual present. The language and costume are the same as at that place, but Pushtu is generally understood. The Dards were originally Kafers, or infidels, but have latterly professed Mohammedanism: they are, however, but indifferent Mohammedans. The hills that skirt the valley are low and well wooded. The main crop is wheat, rice is not grown. Cotton and silk are reared for home consumption.

Westward from Gilgit is the country of

Chitral, distinguished as Upper and Lower. The latter, which is nearest to the Hindu Kosh, is situated on a river flowing from a lake called Hanu-sar, and ultimately falling into the river of Kabul. The country is rough and difficult. The Mastuch, as the capital is termed in the language of the country, is situated on the left bank of the river. It contains a bazar, with some Hindu shopkeepers, and is as large as Mozeffarabad, containing between four and five hundred houses: slavery prevails here. The people are Dardus and Dungars, and profess the Shiah faith. The Raja, who is a Suni, is known to the Afghans as the Raja of Kator.

The Mastuch, or capital of Upper Chitral, is situated in the same valley as that of Lower Chitral, at about three days' march, and about thirty miles north-west from Gilgit. It stands upon a river, and consists of about four hundred houses, with a fort, on a moderately extensive plain, from whence roads lead to Peshawar, Badakhshan, and Yarkand. The mountains in the neighbourhood are bare, and much snow falls: the

climate, however, upon the whole, is temperate. Some traffic takes place with Badakhshan and Yarkand, whence pearls, coral, cotton baftas, and chintzes, boots and shoes, and metals are imported: horses are also brought, and tea, but the latter is not much in use. The chief return is in slaves, kidnapped from the adjacent districts, or, when not so procurable, the Raja seizes and sells his own subjects. Soliman Shah, the Raja, resides chiefly at Yasin, which is not so large as the capital, but is better situated for the command of the country. He is of the Suni sect, but the people are mostly Shiahs. They are Dungars, and speak the Dardu language, but Persian, Turkish, and Pushtu are generally understood. The men are a tall, athletic race, but exceedingly cowardly. The women are coarse, and by no means reserved in their conduct, to which the men are indifferent. The heads of the Dungars are, in general, of a conical form, it being usual to tie a strong band round the head of an infant soon after birth. West from Yasin is the Darband, or fortified pass, of Chitral. The grains cultivated are wheat and barley. Fruit

is abundant, especially grapes, from which much wine is manufactured. According to tradition Chitral was the Sharáb-khana, or wine-cellar of Afrasiab.

On ascending the Belut Tag mountains towards Badakhshan, the first place of note is Panja, the capital of Wahkam, a district partly subject to Badakhshan, partly to Yarkand. It is situated on the Panj river, the main branch of the Oxus, which rises by two heads, one in the Pamer mountains, and one from the direction of Mastuch. The houses are built of stone, and the town is defended by a stone fort, which successfully resisted an attack of the Chinese. Yaks are common here, as is a race of hardy ponies. The revenue of the chief is principally derived from slaves, who are sold from his own people at his pleasure.

The road to Yarkand proceeds along the Panj river to a large lake, from which it rises. A projecting mountain separates this from the Kara-kol, or black water lake, which is about the size of the Dal of Kashmir, and gives rise to a river that passes by Siri-kol, and joins that of Yarkand. In the

lake is a small islet, on which stands a house decorated after the Tibetan fashion, with yaks' heads and tails on poles, and with flags. According to the belief of the people this islet is the resort of Jins and Peris. Lamps are seen burning upon it, horses are heard to neigh, and the sounds of music are distinguished as from a naubet khana. At times it is dangerous to approach the edge of the lake, as it is displeasing to the mysterious frequenters of the island. Confiding in this superstition the Khaja of Kashkar, retreating from the Chinese, is said to have deposited his treasures in the islet, and they remain there inviolate.

The Kirghiz, who inhabit the Pamer mountains, are a simple and superstitious race. They profess Mohammedanism, but practise few of its precepts. They live in felt tents, and have large flocks of the large-tailed sheep, goats, and yaks, hardy, though small horses, and some camels. Gillim Bai, one of their chiefs, was said to possess from thirty to forty thousand sheep and goats, five hundred yaks, and between two and three hundred camels. He resided in a house sur-

rounded by one hundred cottages of his dependants. The people are easily gratified, and a present of a small quantity of tobacco will readily procure supplies of milk, meat, kaimak, a sort of cream, and felts of their own fabrication. The country abounds with wild goats and deer, the horns of which are turned to various useful purposes.

Sir-i-kol, or the district at the head of a lake, is also the name of a town of about three hundred houses, chiefly inhabited by Tajiks. It is situated on a plain, along which flows the river, with mountains beyond it. On one of these are the remains of a building, said to have been a fort in the days of Afrasiab. The chief town of the district of Sir-i-kol is Tagarma, which, as well as the preceding, is under the authority of the Chinese*.

* Some further information respecting Balti and the adjacent countries has been recently collected by Capt. Wade.—*Journ. As. Society of Bengal*, Nov. 1835; also by Mr. Vigne, who has lately visited Iskardo. See the same Journal for Feb. 1836.—ED.

CHAPTER VII.

First departure from Kashmir—Patan—Ruins—Wular Lake—Explosions—Tomb of Shukar-ad-din—Baramula—Bamba and Khaka Country—Gilgil—Party detained—Return—Second departure—Remains at Khampur—Shupien—Tomb of Shah Hamadan—Pir Panchal Pass—Ridge of Ratan Panchal—Rajaor—Bimber—Jelum—Fort of Rotas—Manikyala—Rawal Pindi—Garden of Wah—Hasan Abdal—Tomb of Baba Wali—Plain of Chach—Indus—Attok—Khairabad—Akoṛa—Duties demanded—Attempt to detain the party—Its failure—Abbas khan of Akora—Battle of Noushehra—Peshawar—Hospitable reception—Mischief done by the Sikhs—Navigation of the Indus—Political Difficulties and Dissensions—Offer of Allegiance—Visit to the Waziris.

AFTER many vexatious delays we accomplished all that was requisite for our further progress, and on the 31st of July we quitted our residence in Kashmir for the purpose of travelling to Bokhara. Our party had been considerably augmented, for besides an addition to our escort, making it thirty in number, we were accompanied by our Ladakh friend, Shah Nyaz Khan, and by Mirza Jawad, a Persian envoy of the King of Ferghana. We were to proceed by water to Baramula, and our flotilla consisted of fourteen boats; our

party comprehended, possibly, the greatest variety of nations that ever marched together, enrolling English, Hindustanis, Gorkhas, Tibetans, Afghans, Persians, Kashmiris, Kurds, and Turks, in its ranks.

The afternoon was far advanced before we started. We passed along the Dragjan canal, and entered the Behut, opposite the north-east angle of the fort of Sher-gerh. As we passed, the fort had as imposing an appearance as possible given to it. The Dewan and his court were in one of the most conspicuous apartments, and sentinels were stationed at most of the windows; the bridges were covered with spectators, and our course was retarded by boats with beggars coming to pray for our welfare, and to solicit a reward for their benedictions. We reached Chatan-bal, just beyond the town, shortly before sunset.

On the 1st of August, leaving the boats to proceed to the village of Patan, we mounted our horses to ride to that point. We had not gone far beyond the position of Shala-ting before our road passed the edge of a swamp, along a narrow ridge of turf, which trembled under the horses' tread; the marsh, however,

had a firm clay bottom, and was the work of a small river, the Haratirth, which must have overflowed its banks higher up in its course, and laid the lower fields under water: a few drains would soon have restored the soil to cultivation, of which we were informed it was once the site. The Haratirth is navigable. We continued close to it till we were on a line, passing between the villages of Shadehpur and Sumbhelpur, when we crossed it by a sanga. About a mile further on we crossed a second stream, and came to Hanjiwar, a large village on its right bank, not far from the edge of the plain. From hence we reached Patan by a rather circuitous route early in the afternoon: we passed on our way a couple of ancient Hindu buildings, similar in style to the remains at Matan, though something ruder, smaller, and much less entire.

A low ridge or platform extends from the south-west of the valley close to Patan. The summit of the platform was a plain which had once been cultivated, as was evident by the remains of canals for irrigation. It was now bare and unproductive. From the top

an extensive and beautiful view was commanded of the valley.

We started in our boats on the morning of the 2nd, after having been tormented through the night by musquitoes, and after passing along the track of the Nambal for about an hour, came upon the line of the Hiratirth river, after it had been joined by the Hanjiwar rivulet: it then takes the name of the Takwala-bal, from a small village of that name. According to the information there received, the river rises about ten miles off, from a spring called Sukh-nag, situated on the southern edge of the valley, in the pergana of Birual. Following the direction of the river, we arrived early at a village and shrine, called Naid Khai, standing amidst much swampy ground, and from hence the same surface continued until we were actually in the Wular Lake, at a part of it called Tsako. The surface of the water was like a green field, with the sinhara plant, and occasionally a few lotuses.

As it was commonly asserted that loud explosions were frequently heard from the hill

on which stood the Ziarat of Shukar-ad-din, we determined to land and visit it. It was with some reluctance that our boatmen consented to row for this point, asserting their apprehension of violent gusts of wind, which, certainly, we were not in trim to encounter. On ascending to the summit of the hill we passed through a ruined door-way to a level platform, on which stood three ill-constructed buildings of wood recently set up. From this a few steps led to the Ziarat of the saint, a small confined chamber, with a tomb covered by wooden lattice-work. Close without, to the westward, were two hovels, one said to have been an ancient mosque, and the other covering a trench, sunk into the rock, just large enough for a man to lie down in. Shukar-ad-din, it is reported, spent twelve years in this hole. A brass-headed pike, said to have been his walking-staff, his koran, and his chaplet of beads of clay, brought from Kerbela, are shown to the people who visit the place of his interment, and who not only press them to their lips with pious fervour, but besmear their faces with sand adhering to a pair of old clogs

which Shukar-ad-din is said to have worn, exclaiming " La Allah il Allah,"—there is no God but God.

There was nothing on the hill that looked like a crater; but the people on the spot asserted their recollection of sudden explosions, in one of which, not very long ago, the door of the Ziarat and one of the windows were torn off. The noise was sudden, but as loud as the report of a cannon, and alarmed the whole neighbourhood. According to the superstitious notions of the Kashmirians, these noises precede and announce some political change. The hill commanded a fine view of the lake and plain of Zeinnagar: a storm had come on, but by keeping within the line of the Sinhara, we rowed along the edge of the Wular without being incommoded, and arrived at Supur in safety a few minutes after sunset.

Having halted during the 3rd at Supur, we proceeded on the next day to Baramula. The channel of the river was winding, but less so than in the higher parts of its course. Above the village of Daba it was joined by the Lalakoal, or Pohru river. Below Baramula, where we anchored, we found ourselves once more

amongst mountains. The distance from hill to hill was not more than three hundred and fifty yards, of which the Behut occupied about seventy. Baramula is situated on the right bank of the Behut, and consists of about two hundred houses, with a bazar and a custom-station: a wooden bridge is laid across the river, but when we saw it one of the piers had been removed, and the communication with the left bank was cut off. Below the town the whole space between the river and the mountains is closed by a wooden rampart and folding gates. In the time of the Afghans a strong guard was posted at this place, and the gateway was kept in good repair. It was now ruinous, but about five hundred Sikh soldiers were quartered in a Dharmasala, an old Ziarat, or Mohammedan shrine, and in a small fort on the left bank of the river, at the head of the bridge. On the same side of the river is another village, that of Jambaspur, where numbers of Hindus come to bathe in the collected waters of the sacred streams of Kashmir. There is little land about the place fit for cultivation, and the hills, although covered with brushwood, bear no trees.

We were detained several days at Baramula in collecting provisions for our route, as a letter from Zabardast Khan, the chief of Muzeffarabad, addressed to Surat Sinh, intimated no disposition to give any orders for our accommodation. The tone, indeed, was so hostile to the Sikhs, that it was evident the Sinh's company could be of no use to us, and might expose him to insult or danger: we therefore dispensed with his attendance, a measure in which he cheerfully concurred, and determined to trust for security to our own character and conduct.

On the 10th of August we resumed our march, proceeding to the south-west along the bed of the river, the current of which became not only much more rapid than on the table-land, but more troubled and impetuous, lamenting, according to the Kashmirians, in foam and clamour, its departure from their beautiful valley. Across it, and close upon our left, a chain of low, but steep hills, running towards the east, left the Behut, skirting a fine plain, bounded by ridges of low hills covered with wood. The scenery was very beautiful, and of the character of that of many

parts of Wales. A village, and the small fort of Fattihgerh, were observable on the plain, at the distance of about a mile and a half. The plain is bounded on the south by hills which approach close to the river, beyond which are the fragments of a ruined wall and gateway. These mark the limits of Kashmir; and the country on the right bank of the river thence belongs to the Bambas, and that on their left to another highland clan, the Khakas. As we proceeded, the valley became more confined, and the thicket which covered the hills descended close to the path: the wild vine, pomegranate, pear, mulberry, raspberry, and blackberry, were in abundance the whole way. There did not appear to be much land in cultivation, and the chief crop seemed to be rice: grass was scarce. We encamped in the shade of some fine elms, near a small village called Paruna, the residence of a Pirzada and his followers.

Early on the 11th we passed the house of Ghulam Ali Khan, the chief of the Khakas, but at that time a prisoner at Lahore. It stood on the left bank of the river, within an enclosure surrounded by a wall and bastions, with

loop-holes for musketry. It was of no great strength. The valley was of irregular width, but in general narrow. In some places the hills approached so near as to give the idea of a passage through a door. The path lay upon a ledge of the mountain, rising perpendicularly from the river, which at some distance below was rushing along with increased and increasing impetuosity. The mountains were granite; they were covered with forests, and several considerable rivulets rushed from their sides into the river. Near the end of the day's route, which terminated at the Manzil Khana of Gilgil, a station where travellers may purchase provisions, we crossed a rivulet coming from the west and north. Not far from its conflux with the Behut it was formed of two branches, the larger and more northerly of which was said to proceed from a large spring which gives rise to two other streams, one taking the direction of the Lala-koal, and the other that of Kathae. The spring is known by the name of Nil-nag, and is held sacred by the Kashmirians. It was said to be twenty kos distant; but the road is circuitous, and the horizontal distance cannot be much more

than eight miles from where we encamped. The chief of the Bambas, Muzeffar Khan, had a house, called Nun Khoa, a short way up the rivulet on its left bank.

Whilst on our march, during the 11th, we observed several small parties of armed men near our road, but had not taken particular notice of them. On arriving at our station, however, we found a considerable number, above a hundred, assembled, whose appearance was not of the most friendly character. From amongst these a person of the name of Nidan Pandit, the agent of the Sultan, came to us, and announced the approach of the Sultan's son, who shortly after came. He was a lad of about twelve or fourteen. In the conversation that ensued, his attendants professed entire allegiance to Ranjit Sinh, and their consequent readiness to promote our objects. They held themselves in some degree responsible for our safety, and could not, therefore, consistently with duty, advise our further progress, as Zabardast Khan, of Muzeffarabad, was in open insurrection, and would, no doubt, offer us some violence. Thanking them for their counsel, we acquitted them of

all responsibility, but announced our determination to proceed. It was then intimated that we must remain where we were until orders could be received from the Khan, who was in the hills; but with this we declined compliance, as expedition was an object of importance, and we saw no necessity for waiting for instructions, which it was evident must already have been received. One of the most important of the persons present, Shir Mahmud, then remarked, that we must pay duty on our goods; with which we professed our willingness to comply to any reasonable extent, and there the discussion rested for the night.

On the following day Shir Mahmud appeared to claim the duties, and for a long time hesitated to state any fixed amount; at last he had the modesty to make a demand of fifteen thousand rupees, as being likely to effect a clearance, and hinted that a refusal to pay the money would be followed by the plunder of our baggage. To resist this our party was drawn up under arms, and an offer of five hundred rupees was made, with a declaration, that if this was not accepted, we should imme-

diately return to Kashmir, as, whilst we admitted we had no right to traverse the district in defiance of the authorities, we stated that we were resolved not to submit to imposition, nor to suffer aggression. Matters remained thus in suspense, the Bambas showing no disposition to accept our terms, nor to proceed to extremities; and it appeared probable that, as they professed to acknowledge the authority of the Sikhs, the interposition of the Dewan of Kashmir might not be without weight. Accordingly the Mirza and Mr. Trebeck mounted their horses and rode off to Kashmir, to apply for the aid of Moti lal, expecting to reach the city by the following evening. At Baramula, however, they were met by Surat Sinh, who had been reprimanded by the Dewan for leaving us, and had been sent after us with all possible expedition, and with orders to accompany us to Muzeffarabad. With him, then, we returned to Tatthamula, the place where our party had remained. Surat Sinh went on to Gilgil. In the evening a letter came to him from Muzeffar Khan, giving up all claim to duties on our merchandise, but refusing to extend the same indul-

gence to the persons who were with us, none of whom, however, had any property subject to duty except, perhaps, Mirza Jawad; and to judge from the bulk of his baggage he could have had nothing of consequence. The general tone of the letter was decidedly unfriendly.

On the 14th Surat Sinh returned, and, from what had occurred, was by no means disposed to augur favourably of the result. The Sultan was almost in a state of rebellion, and Zabardast Khan was declaredly so. He had recently beheaded his wazir, a Sikh who he suspected was in the interest of Ranjit Sinh, had collected about two thousand armed men at Muzeffarabad, and had broken down the bridges on the road. Muzeffar Khan had also about one thousand armed men, and it would have been idle to have attempted to force our way; we therefore decided on returning, and despatched Surat Sinh with a letter to the Dewan, to apprize him of our determination. Our envoy, however, soon surprised us by his reappearance: at Baramula he had been met by two Kasids from Moti Ram, urging us strenuously to come back immediately, and

expressing great alarm at the danger to which we had been exposed. With his injunctions, therefore, we immediately complied, and on the 15th of August arrived at Baramula, on our way back to Kashmir.

In resuming the purpose of departure from Kashmir we had the choice of two routes—one by Prúnch, the other by Rajaor. The former was the more difficult and circuitous, and the country was in an unsettled state, and we therefore made choice of the latter. We awaited, however, the close of the rains, which are very heavy on the borders of the Panjab, and did not, consequently, set out again until the 17th of September: our party was much the same as before.

After crossing the river and passing by Shergerh, we came immediately to the Dudh Ganga, running parallel to the Behut. It then comes from the south, and our road continued at no great distance from its right bank. Our day's march terminated at about four miles from the city, at the ruined Serai of Ali

Maidan Khan, called Kampur or Kanikpur *. The building resembles those of a similar kind in Hindustan, but is very substantially constructed, and although it was now in ruins, it could afford shelter to more than a hundred people.

The adjacent country is one of those elevated platforms or tables which protrude at various places from the bases of the bordering mountains into the valley. These elevations have now the inconvenience of being scantily supplied with water; but this was not the case in the better days of Kashmir, as they were then intersected by canals, of which the remains are still observable. The people in the neighbourhood of the serai were miserably poor, and could furnish us with nothing but fuel. The crops of rice looked well, and were ready to be cut, but none of it could be reaped before the permission of the government was granted, and this was not expected to be given until all the grain of the preceding year, which had been distrained for revenue, had been

* A very ancient city according to the Chronicles of Kashmir. Kanishkapur, founded by Kanishka, a king of the country, four or five centuries before Christ.—Ed.

disposed of at an arbitrary and extravagant price. The effect of these exactions is not only the impoverishment of the people, but their banishment from the country, and they were every day emigrating in considerable numbers. A party of five hundred was to accompany us across the Pir Panchal.

Another short day's march, continuing on the same platform, brought us to another ruined serai, that of Shahji Marg. The inner court of this had been converted by the peasants into a kitchen-garden; but we found protection from the rain in some of the chambers. The situation of the serai was well chosen, and commanded a prospect rarely more pleasing, perhaps, than at the present season; the broad band of rice in the valley below was tinged with yellow, and was agreeably contrasted with the dark green of the groups of trees that concealed the wretchedness of the village.

On the 26th we made a short march to the town of Shupien, where we halted to purchase provisions. In the time of the Afghans it was said to contain above two hundred houses, besides one hundred petty shops. Upon

hearing of the defeat of the Duranis by the Sikhs, the inhabitants fled, and many never returned, so that the place is not half inhabited. It was formerly the residence of three brothers, of the family of the Malik, each of whom received from the governor five hundred loads of paddy annually, and was authorised to levy a tax of one rupee per maund on common merchandise, and two rupees on shawl-goods. One of the brothers, Mahmud Ali, discontented with his situation, materially facilitated the entrance of the Sikhs into Kashmir. If he expected increased power and profit by so doing, he was deservedly disappointed, for the management of the town and district was conferred upon a Sikh who contracted for the revenue: he falling into arrears, was imprisoned and beaten so unmercifully, that he died, and the district is unlet. In the mean time a thannadar and a hundred men are stationed at Shupien.

Having remained a day at Shupien, we proceeded on our journey, and at a short distance came to the Ziarat of Shah Hamadan, remarkable for a large flat stone which it contains, and which is an object of profound ve-

neration to devout Musselmans. It is said that when the saint had arrived on the crest of Pir Panchal, on his way to Kashmir, his horse was too much fatigued to proceed, and the Shah was at a loss what to do. In this dilemma a piece of the rock volunteered to convey him to the plain, and this stone is the carriage that presented itself. Part of it, supposed to be the impression of his foot, has been completely polished by the contact of thousands of the hands and lips of the faithful. Beyond this the road became uneven, and at times difficult, passing between the low hills forming the commencement of the pass. Close below flowed the river of Shoingulu, or Shupien, which rising on the northern slope of the boundary mountains by different rivulets, crossed our path repeatedly, and proceeds from hence through the perganas of Batu, Suprasaman, and Shakuru, to the Behut near Viranag. It was near this place that Jabar Khan, the Afghan general, was posted, with a detachment of horse to oppose the Sikhs. Instead of waiting for their attack he crossed the rivulet, and ascended the heights beyond it to meet them, where his cavalry could not

charge, and were driven back with loss by the fire of the enemy. Farther on we passed through the small and dirty village of Hirapur, where is a custom-house. The path alternated with descents and ascents, but was upon the whole ascending, and along a narrow valley, bounded by steep mountains. We halted at Dubjan, on a level with some recently fallen snow, and on an elevation commanding a view of the valley of Kashmir. Hirapur was the place where the Malik Mahmud Ali was stationed with his soldiers, with whom, instead of resisting, he joined the Sikhs, and acted as their guide. The number of Kashmirians who were to accompany us over the mountains proved here to be no exaggeration, and their appearance, half-naked and miserably emaciated, presented a ghastly picture of poverty and starvation. Yet, wretched as they were, the relentless Sikhs would have levied a pice a head for permission to pass the post, had we not interfered. The Sikhs seem to look upon the Kashmirians as little better than cattle. The murder of a native by a Sikh is punished by a fine to the government, of from sixteen to twenty

rupees, of which four rupees are paid to the family of the deceased if a Hindu, and two rupees if he was a Mohammedan. The body of a stout young man, whose throat had been cut, was lying close to the road on one part of this day's journey, and the only notice taken of it was by Mardan Ali, the Malik, who ordered it to be covered with grass, that our porters might not be frightened at the sight. Three other bodies were met with on the route; these were some of the followers of Jawahir Mal, who, to the number of forty-five, it was asserted, had perished in crossing the pass lately, in rough and cold weather, against which they were ill defended by clothing or shelter. Some of the people accompanying us were seized by our Sikhs as unpaid porters, and were not only driven along the road by a cord tying them together by the arms, but their legs were bound with ropes at night to prevent their escape. At Dubjan, Ata Mohammed Khan, governor of Kashmir, encountered the Afghan Wazir, Fateh Khan, and was defeated.

On the following day the road commenced on the slope of a grassy hill, five or six

hundred feet above the rivulet: on our left were two small towers erected as defences by Ata Mohammed; they were named Kamil Koth. Other towers were afterwards passed, all erected by the same person. They were all of a polygonal shape, built of stone, cemented with mud, and faced with mortar, and pierced with loop-holes for musketry. At the close a path of masonry, with a wall on its outer edge, led up the almost perpendicular face of the mountain, called Lala Ghulam, from a slave, whom Ali Mardan is said to have sacrificed here, and interred under the pavement: beyond this we halted, at a serai, less dilapidated than usual, called Aliabad.

About two miles of moderately ascending and winding road brought us, on the 30th, to the crest of the Pir Panchal pass, after leaving, about eight hundred yards below, the most southerly sources of the Shupien river. On the top of the ascent we found a tower and some other small buildings, and poles with votive offerings to the mountain spirits: amongst them were two shawls presented by the Diwan Moti Ram, when he had ascended

the pass on his way to the conquest of Kashmir.

The view from hence to the eastward, or towards Kashmir, was very circumscribed; but in the contrary direction was extensive and beautiful. The atmosphere in the distance was rather heavy, or we might have distinguished the plains of the Panjab over an immense surface, and the windings of the Jelum. A party of Sikhs was stationed in the tower, who ordinarily levy an unauthorised capitation from every person leaving Kashmir, besides plundering him of fuel and provisions.

On the descent the face of the mountain was exceedingly steep and difficult, and except in the line of the path, was often impracticable. After crossing a rivulet we ascended the slope of an inferior ridge, and continued about half way between their base and summit to the village of Poshana, a place consisting of about fifty flat-roofed cottages of wood and mortar, and situated on terraces, closely though irregularly connected with each other. The breadth of the valley from the summit of one ridge to that of the other was not above

a mile. Pir Panchal and the succeeding ridges appear to be granite.

From Poshana the road continued of a similar description, and for part of the way passed through a defile, varying from twenty to thirty yards in breadth: at the end a few cottages constituted the village of Doguren. Above it is a low pointed hill, called Sheikh Kamal, which was crowned by a pile of sticks and rags. Less than a mile beyond this we arrived at the hamlet of Behram Gala, where a Thanna was stationed as a check upon a freebooter in this neighbourhood; in a recent fray with whom the Thannahdar had been severely wounded. A toll is here levied on salt in transport to the northward, at the rate of one rupee for a man's load: the annual produce of this duty is said to amount to two thousand rupees. The rivulet that had been met with on descending the pass here runs off to the west, and after passing the towns of Paunch and Mirpur, enters the Jelum.

Our road on the 2nd of October lay over the ridge of Ratan Panchal, to the south of west from Pir Panchal. The country between these two chains belongs properly to Prunch, or as

the Kashmirians pronounce the name, Pruntz. South of the pass commences the district of Rajaor, a part of which, called Durhal, extends on the east nearly to Pir Panchal. The ascent was easy, and passed through woods of elms, yews, horse-chesnuts, &c.; the view to the south was extensive and rich, presenting a succession of low hills and cultivated valleys: descending the mountains, we entered the district of Thanna, which was well cultivated with crops of rice and maize. The valley is celebrated also for its breed of buffaloes. The people seemed to be better off than the Kashmiris, and in manners and speech belonged to the Panjab: a very large proportion of them spoke the Kashmiri dialect, and it seems not unlikely that they are originally from thence. Kashmirian is the language of the mountaineers of the two Panchals.

The town of Rajaor formed the limit of our next day's march; there was nothing on the road particularly worthy of note. From some spots the whole range of the Ratan Panchal was in sight, and the peaks to the eastward, where they seemed to unite with those of the

Pir Panchal, were much loftier than those near where we had crossed, and were tipped with snow. At Rajaor we were detained four days by Mr. Trebeck labouring under indisposition, which confined him to the house. We were lodged in the Raja's dwelling, a substantial stone edifice, the interior of which had been stripped of everything valuable by the Sikhs. They had also demolished the old wall of the city, which appeared to have been of great solidity. The town stands upon the side of a hill, and along the east runs a small stream, called here the Malkani Tihoï *: on the opposite side was a garden laid out in imitation of Shahlimar, but it had been demolished by the Sikhs. The bazar is small, but clean and well supplied.

The present Raja of Rajaor, Rahim Ullah Khan, was the half brother of the preceding Raja, Agar Ullah, who was now a prisoner at Lahore. Ranjit Sinh had compelled him to join his forces in his first and unsuccessful attack upon Kashmir, the failure of which he ascribed to Agar Ullah's treachery. Ac-

* This is called Makkali in the latest map of this part of the Panjab by M. Court. (*Jour. Asiat. Soc. of Bengal*, Aug., 1836.) In general, however, the map agrees with our text.—ED.

cordingly, in revenge, he sent an overpowering force against Rajaor; took, and partly destroyed it, and, having captured the Raja, threw him into confinement, and placed his half brother in the Raj. Rahim Ullah was a mild, good-humoured man, and treated us with much kindness.

The country, though fertile, is unhealthy, and fevers are very common: goître and leprosy are also frequent. The staple cultivation is rice.

We quitted Rajaor on the 8th, and proceeded on that and the two following days along the course of the Tihoï. On the 10th we passed the serai of Naushehra, an extensive building of brick, faced at the gateways with stone, and constructed so as to answer the double purpose of a serai and a fort. It was built by the Emperor Akbar, as an inscription on the gateway records, but was now in ruins. Shortly afterwards the Tihoï left us, turning off to the south-south-east, towards the town of Manávar, beyond which, at a distance of four or five kos, it falls into the Chinab.

On the 11th we crossed a ridge of low hills, overspread with jungle amidst which

fir trees were numerous, called the Kaman Ghosha, or, in a place more to the south, the Shamshir-dhar, from the sharpness of the summit compared to the edge of a sword. The ascent was rough and laborious, but not seriously difficult. After descending from this line of hills we came, on the 12th, to a similar range, called the Ali Dhak, or Katse-dhar hills. From hence a third low chain was visible, of a height not sufficient to intercept the boundless plain which lay beyond it, and afforded us the interesting prospect of the wide and fertile level of Hindustan, the termination of which seemed lost in the misty atmosphere, which hung as a pale dull curtain in the horizon. Descending the Katse-dhar we crossed a sandy plain to the town of Bimber.

The town of Bimber may be considered as the head of a small Raj of that name, which extends some distance beyond Naushehra Serai. Its whole length does not exceed twenty-five kos. It is bordered to the north and north-east by Rajaor, to the east by the district of Pauni Bharák, to the south by Kotta and Jelálpur, and to the west by the

petty chiefship of Khari Khariali. It contains three towns, Bimber, Samani, and Mangal-devi. The latter lies eight kos east of Naushehra, and is the station of a strong Sikh Thanna. The people of the country are called Chibs, and were formerly Hindus, but now mostly profess Mohammedanism: those who are Hindus intermarry with the Mohammedans. The ruler, Sultan Khan, was a faithful adherent of the Afghans, and when Ranjit first attempted the invasion of Kashmir he met with a spirited resistance from the Bimber chief, and sustained a considerable loss before his superior strength effected the subjection of the district, and the capture of its ruler. After a short interval Ranjit set Sultan Khan at liberty, and restored to him the town of Samani; but he was again induced to join the Afghans, and, being unsupported by them, again became the prisoner of the Sikhs. Ranjit Sinh, however, persisted in his liberal policy, and, after detaining him some time at Lahore, gave his prisoner liberty, and replaced him in possession of a moiety of his domains. Sultan Khan has since continued obedient to his victor. He

lives near Samani, and enjoys a revenue of sixty thousand rupees. The ancient town was at the foot of a low hill, to the northward of the present. It was deserted soon after the reign of Mohammed Shah, and the remains of its buildings are distinctly traceable. The present town contains about one thousand houses, low, and flat-roofed: about one hundred and fifty are shops, but the bazar is of no great importance. A rivulet runs past the town, and falls into the Jelum about four or five kos lower down.

The Raj presents a considerable extent of flat, uncultivated land, rich in grass fit for the scythe: no use, however, is made of it. The spring crop is of wheat and barley, that of autumn of maize and millet; but the cultivation is scanty, as the country is thinly peopled. Hawking is a favourite amusement both here and at Rajaor, and game of every kind is abundant. This might be expected from the face of the country, which consists of low hills overrun with jungle. From the same cause malaria prevails, and fevers of every type are common, affecting even animals, if current report can be believed.

We quitted Bimber on the 15th, and proceeded over a level country, dry and sandy, or, in those parts which were cultivated, a mixture of clay and sand. The crops were bajra and cotton, with a small quantity of maize and pulse. Water is almost entirely raised from wells by a clumsily-constructed Persian wheel. The people of the country were Mohammedans, but at the village of Bhalani, where we halted, they were Hindu Rajputs, and were idle, inhospitable, and arrogant.

On the following day, October 16th, we marched to the left bank of the Jelum, Behut, or Hydaspes. Where we crossed it it was about one hundred and fifty yards broad, but a few paces both above and below the ghât its width was at least six hundred. In the rains it spreads over a much more considerable expanse. It was flowing at the rate of a mile an hour, and its water, though slightly turbid, was cool and well tasted, and it contains a quantity of fish, the Masahar, Rohu, and others common in Hindustan: it is haunted, also, by alligators. The Jelum is navigable from hence to the Indus. We found several boats

at the river-side large enough to carry across five or six horses with their loads at a trip, but ill provided with oars, and sails seem to be unknown. The soundings where we crossed were from two to two fathoms and a half. After crossing the river, and traversing a dry, sandy channel, filled by it in the rainy season, we came to the town of Jelum; a town something larger than Bimber, but worse provided with a market and accommodation. The only good workmen are boat-builders, who fit the planks together with great nicety. A small mud fort near the town is the station of a Sikh Thana.

At the time of our arrival at Jelum, Ranjit Sinh was in the field preparing to march, it was said, towards the Indus. Surat Sinh, who had accompanied us, went off to procure the requisite passports, and several days elapsed before he returned. We were then delayed by difficulties in procuring cattle and carriage, and it was not till the 13th of November that we were able to resume our journey.

The Jelum is navigated upwards to Oin, in the direction of Muzeffarabad, which is

said to be eighty kos distant; from thence to Baramula, where it leaves Kashmir, its course is about thirty more. Oin is a village on the left bank, forty-three kos from Jelum, to which boatmen repair from the latter place to procure timber, especially that of the Deodar, brought down by the current from Kashmir. The trunks of the trees are formed first into small, and, as they descend, into larger rafts, guided by poles and paddles. A practicable road runs along both sides of the river, although, in some places, it runs between steep hills. Dan Gali, twenty-four kos from Jelum, on the right bank, was the capital of the Ghikar chief, who protected Humayun Shah in his flight to Persia from the pursuit of his victorious rival, Shir Shah. The site of the ancient town is designated by extensive ruins, but, apparently, none of any architectural merit. The present residence of the chief of the Ghikars is Khanpur, about thirty kos south-west from Muzeffarabad. The latter is forty kos from Baramula, and is situated on an eminence about two kos to the north of the Behut, and east of the Muzeffarabad or Hasora river, which falls into

the former near this place. It is little inferior in size to the Behut at their point of junction. It is called in our maps the Kishen Ganga, but I could not learn that it was known by this appellation in the countries through which it flows, where it is commonly termed the Hasora, or Muzeffarabad river. It was formerly crossed by a substantial sanga, but this has been destroyed, and a bridge of ropes substituted; but inflated skins form a much more convenient and safe mode of effecting a passage. The town of Muzeffarabad consists of above three thousand houses, built in the same fashion as those of Kashmir, and by Kashmirian artists. The streets are narrow and dirty, but the bazar is well supplied. The town is defended by a fort, one angle of which abuts upon the left bank of a curve of the river, but it is situated low, and commanded by neighbouring heights. Lofty mountains rise not far from the town to the northward, and the snowy summits of the Pir Panchal range, and of the most elevated parts of Karnao are in sight. The boundary of the Muzeffarabad country is between that town and Gerhi Sadet Khan,

five kos to the west, which belongs to Damtaur.

The population of Jelum is mostly Mohammedan, and the people, though much intermixed with the Kashmirians, were much darker and worse looking. Disease was extremely prevalent: fevers are common here, as in the neighbouring districts, in spring and autumn, and leprosy was very extensive. Disorders of the alimentary canal and calculus were also exceedingly common. The face of the country is much broken by ravines and irregular ridges. The soil is clay, much intermixed with sand, and the chief crops are wheat and barley: cotton is also cultivated.

Leaving Jelum on the 13th of November, we marched across a cultivated plain in a north-westerly direction, to the foot of the mound on which stands the celebrated fort of Rotas, and traversed a narrow stony defile with the fort close on the left, the base of the walls being about sixty or seventy feet higher than the pathway. The killadar refused to admit us to see the fortress; but riding along its western face, we found several practicable

breaches in the walls, by one of which we ascended and entered an abandoned outwork. The structure was found to be most massive, the walls, of stone cemented with mortar, being in some places thirty feet thick. They were crenated throughout, and provided with a double row of loop-holes. The outwork we had scaled seemed intended to protect an immense bhauli or well of masonry. Passages of great breadth wound round it to the bottom, communicating with it by arched openings into its sides, and they led to the water's edge in so many places, that from fifty to a hundred persons might draw water at once. From this spot we entered into the body of the fort, and ascended the highest part of the parapet without attracting observation. The interior of the fort extends about two miles and a half. It is of a long, narrow form, and its two sides and eastern end rest upon the edges of ravines which separate it from a table-land of equal elevation as the hill on which it stands. The western face of the hill has the Gham rivulet running along its foot, the bed of which abounds with quicksands, and must be dangerous to ford, at least in the

rains. The Sikhs have erected a small mud fort within the principal gateway. Near the fort are a serai, said to have been constructed by Aurangzeb, and a garden enclosed by a wall, attributed to Shir Shah. There was formerly a Persian inscription over one of the gateways of Rotas, recording the date of its construction by Shir Shah, and denouncing an imprecation upon any of his successors who should suffer it to fall into decay. Zeman Shah, it is reported, took offence at the tenor of the inscription, and commanded it to be effaced. The fort is said to have been erected by Shir Shah to curb the predatory incursions of the Ghikars.

Our road during the next four days lay over a rough and broken country, which may be regarded as generally a sandy plain, perpetually intersected by deep and irregular dry watercourses and ravines. Occasionally villages and cultivation were passed, but not of any great extent; the only trees visible were the mimosa and beir; but there was abundance of brushwood and jungle. On the 18th we diverged a short way from our route, in order to visit the Tope of Manikyala, which we

found to correspond with the description given by Mr. Elphinstone, except that it was much more decayed. We could gain no satisfactory information of its origin, but it has not at all the character of a Grecian edifice. It has a much greater resemblance to the monumental structures of the Tibetans. The people ascribe it to superhuman beings, and one man pointed out some large stones which he conceived could not have been raised into their actual position by merely mortal strength. They were, however, but pebbles compared with the blocks we had seen in the ruined buildings of Kashmir, and the workmanship was equally inferior.

The village of Manikyala, so named, it was said, from a prince Manik, is situated about four hundred yards to the north. The people universally asserted that this had been the site of an immense city, according to some, extending from beyond Rawal Pindi to Rotas. This, however, applied probably to the district, not to the city. They stated that old wells are often discovered over a wide surface; that fragments of old pottery are abundant; and that ancient coins are frequently

found. They brought us two small copper coins, but they had Arabic letters, too much worn to be deciphered, but sufficiently distinct to be recognised as Arabic.

Beyond Manikyala, to the north-eastward, was an old building like a fort, which was the ancient burial-place of the Ghikar chiefs. Sultan Sarang, one of their most celebrated rulers, is interred on the outside. It is a substantial edifice, surmounted by a dome, within which were the tombs of his descendants, covered by slabs of an orange-coloured marble, but almost concealed by dirt and the dung of the pigeons, martins, and swallows, that are the only frequenters of the cemetery. There are a number of graves within the inclosure, but none of note, nor were there any inscriptions. The Ghikars are not numerous now in this part of the country, though they are said to have occupied the whole tract between the Indus and the Jelum. One of their chief cities, Pharwala, was about five kos northwest from this place, on the left bank of the Sewan. Its inhabitants are but imperfectly subjected to the power of Ranjit Sinh. A vast proportion of the population of these dis-

tricts consists of emigrants from Kashmir. On the 19th we halted at the town of Rawal Pindi.

Rawal Pindi is a town of considerable size, containing a number of low mud-houses with flat roofs, and a large but irregularly-built bazar. It owes its importance to its having been selected by Shah Sujah for the residence of his family, and of Zeman Shah, whilst he engaged in the contest with Shah Mahmud for the throne of Cabul. A rather large but ill-built mansion was raised for their accommodation. It appears to be of brick without plaster, and forms a conspicuous object. From the number of persons who accompanied the family Rawal Pindi became a place of some demand for grain and merchandise, and it is now the chief mart for the trade between Amritsar and Peshawar. It is chiefly supported by its commerce, for the agriculture of the adjacent lands has been ruined by exorbitant taxation. A few years since the annual revenue raised from them was three lakhs of rupees; it is now less than one. There were a great number of Peshawaris in the town, and the general impression amongst them was

that our journey had a political bearing. It was reported that Shah Sujah had engaged to give the British government six anas in the rupee of his revenues, on their reinstating him in his kingdom. The state of affairs beyond the Indus seemed, from all accounts, to be bad enough, and not much better in Turkistan. Our information on the latter head was derived from a Hindu goldsmith of Potonhar, who had just returned from Transoxiana. It is a curious fact, that three or four hundred persons of this trade and persuasion pass backwards and forwards between the Panjab and the banks of the Oxus and Jaxartes. In the latter countries they are employed in working in the precious metals, which they manage to alloy, so as to realise a considerable profit in addition to their fair earnings. In three or four years they return to their homes with the money they have thus acquired.

Leaving Rawal Pindi on the 21st, we traversed the same description of country to which we had been accustomed, to the ascent and pass of Mar-gala—a paved road over a range of low hills covered with bushes of aca-

cia and long grass. The road through the gala or gorge is six or seven yards broad, is strongly, though not neatly paved, and at the end is cut about five feet into the rock. The latter, as well as the pavement, is a bluish or grey limestone. A strong revetment of masonry defends each side of the work, and an inscription, on a block of stone, records its completion in the Hijra year 1083. The length of the pavement is about two hundred paces less than a mile from the descent; the road crosses a small stream, the Kalapani, by a substantial stone bridge.

On the march of the 23rd our attention was attracted by a curious bhauli of singular depth. It was strongly faced with brick and mortar, and consisted of a small structure in the form of a parallelogram, serving as a vestibule to the well, having a small recess on either hand, and a flight of steps leading to a terraced roof. From this a passage led down to the well by one hundred and seventeen steps, nine feet broad, with several landing-places, the lower of which was below the level of the well, and communicated with it by an aperture six feet

high. The upper part of the well was separated from the passage by a thick wall. The well was ten feet nine inches in diameter, and thirty-six yards deep, and the passage came to within three yards of the bottom. To prevent the sides of the passage from giving way, it contained four substantial partitions resembling transoms of a gun-carriage, and consisting of a succession of arches, built one within the other; the two lowest partitions rested each upon a strong wooden beam, though they were secured by the same arrangement as the others. The well was lined by a coat of excellent plaster. Adjoining the mouth of the well, which was quite open and without any parapet, was a strong semicircular platform edged by a low wall, and intended apparently as a walk for cattle employed in drawing water from the well. It was supposed to be a work of the reign of Akbar. From hence the Hazara country was distant about twenty miles horizontally to the north-east, and farther off were mountains covered with snow. A lofty hill, about twelve miles off, north by west, was said to be the

strong hold of a tribe of Ala Zeis, called Khar-baris, whose chief, Shir Zaman, had lately provoked the resentment of Ranjit Sinh.

Advancing across a low ridge of hills, we came to a plain in which stood the village of Wah, and an extensive garden, in the usual Mohammedan style, constructed by order of the Emperor Akbar, on the site of an old serai, the beauty of which drew from the monarch the exclamation, "Wah bagh!" whence the name of the new pleasure-ground originated. It covers a space about a quarter of a mile in length, and half that in breadth, enclosed by walls partly in ruins. The gateways and turrets that were constructed along the boundary-wall are also mostly in a ruinous condition. The eastern extremity is occupied by two large stone-walled tanks; the western by parterres, and they are divided by a building which served as a pleasure-house to the Emperor and his household. It was too small for a residence, consisting of a body and two wings, the former containing three long rooms, and the latter divided into small chambers. The interior of the whole is stuccoed, and in the smaller apartments the walls are decorated

with flowers, foliage, vases, and inscriptions, in which, notwithstanding the neglected state of the building, and its antiquity, the lines of the stuccoed work are as fresh as if they had but just been completed, indicating a very superior quality in the stucco of the east over that of the west. The chambers in the southern front of the western wing, and others continued beyond it, constitute a suite of baths, including cold, hot, and medicated baths, and apartments for servants, for dressing, and reposing, heating-rooms and reservoirs: the floors of the whole have been paved with a yellow breccia, and each chamber is surmounted by a low dome with a central skylight. Fresco paintings of flowers and foliage in compartments embellish the walls, and unless injured by mechanical violence, the colouring has lost little of its original lustre. Although possessing nothing majestic or imposing, the baths at Wah bagh must have been both commodious and elegant. The water, which was supplied from the reservoirs first noticed, is clear and in great abundance. It comes from several copious springs at the base of some limestone hills in the neighbour-

hood, and, after feeding the tanks and canals of the garden, runs off with the Dhamrai river that skirts the plain on the north and west.

Between this and the Serai of Hassan Abdal the valley is somewhat contracted, although the hills are low: at the foot of one of these is the tomb of the saint from whom the place is named*, and who is also known by the more familiar denomination of Baba Wali. It is a square building, containing a tomb of marble, and standing in a walled court. The two old cypresses noticed by Mr. Elphinstone still formed its only ornaments: they were of a variety not common in this part of the country. Beyond the tomb was a spot on the edge of a rill, trickling from a block of stone, supposed to have been sanctified by a miracle wrought there by Nanak, the founder of the Sikh faith. Nanak coming to the place fatigued and thirsty, thought he had a claim upon the hospitality of his brother ascetic, and invoked the spirit of Baba Wali for a cup of water. The Moham-

* Hasan, the Mad. Abdal being the Pashtu term for mad, according to Mr. Elphinstone: the insanity intended was of a religious character.—Ed.

medan saint, indignant at the presumption of an unbeliever, replied to his application by throwing a stone at him of several tons weight. Nanak caught the missile in his hand, and then placed it on the ground, leaving the impression of his fingers upon its hard substance: at the same time he commanded water to flow from it, and this constituted the rill here observable, along which were a number of Sikh fanatics who had come in pilgrimage. This story is curious, not only as a specimen of the credulity of the people, but as the probable invention of a very recent date. A few years only have elapsed since the place was in the possession of the Afghans, whose fierce Mohammedanism would have tolerated no Sikh pilgrims nor shrines within their boundary.

After quitting the tomb of Baba Wali, the road crossed the course of the Dhamrai rivulet, and shortly afterwards that of the Haru, a stream flowing into the Indus, and formed of five smaller streams, the Kalapani, which we had before met with, joining the Dhamrai: the latter rising from the pass between Shaladatta and Khanpur, flows along the north

of the garden of Wah, and is increased by a number of small springs issuing from the garden. After it is joined by the Kalapani it receives the miraculous rivulet of Hassan Abdal, which rises at about five kos off to the east. A more considerable stream, the Nilab, rises from the hills to the northward of Khanpur, and after running for some distance, joins the main stream of the Haru, coming from the north. Their united current meets the trunk of the other three streams, opposite to the large village of Burhan, and the whole then flows westerly to the Indus, below the fort of Attok. It runs in a deep hollow with considerable impetuosity: when we forded it, it was knee deep, and above twenty yards across: in the rains it fills the hollow, of which it now only occupied a small portion.

After crossing some broken and irregular ground, with alternate hillocks and deep ravines, we came to the level plain of Chach. We passed several villages, and encamped at the small town of Hydro, or Hazro, where there was a bazar. Much cotton of a tolerably good quality is grown in the neighbourhood. There was not much land in cultiva-

tion in any part of the plain, and it was covered by a coarse grass, amidst which rat-holes were infinitely numerous. The villages were generally perched upon low mounds, and were the more conspicuous, that few trees were to be seen. At the end of the plain we skirted the base of a low rough chain of hills, and once more beheld the Indus; a very different stream from that with which we had been so well acquainted in Ladakh. It was separated by a flat, grassy island, into two large streams, the nearest of which occupied the farther part of a bed of six hundred yards in breadth, the nearest portion of which consisted of fine glistening sand. The other branch was concealed by the islet. Hardly a tree was to be seen upon the broad level along which the river flowed, and the turf of the adjacent plain had assumed a brown hue. The hills were stony, and though sprinkled with bushes of the byre, had the appearance of being entirely bare. The aspect of the gateway to Hindustan gives but little promise of the richness of the country to which it leads. We halted on the 26th at the serai of Attok, a building of considerable extent, built

of stone chiefly, with a terraced roof; the cells are more capacious than usual. A well-built mosque stands in the centre of the court, which is now used only as an additional accommodation for travellers. The serai is separated from the fort by little more than a ravine.

An order from Ranjit Sinh procured us admission into the celebrated fortress of Attok, but we were not allowed to see much of its interior. Proceeding from the serai to the gateway on the north, along a perfectly good road, unprovided with any defences, we entered into a small projecting court, about twenty yards long, in which Suja-al-mulk was confined by Jehandad Khan, after he was driven from Afghanistan. From hence we passed through another gate into the bazar, a narrow lane of shops, chiefly for the sale of provisions, and along this we were conducted to the opposite or southern gateway, which opened upon the side of the hill immediately above the ferry over the Indus. The gates of the fort are lofty and large, and the walls are of the same description as those of Rotas, thick, crenated, and pierced with loopholes:

the direction of the bazar is parallel with the river, and the bazar is four hundred paces long: between it and the river front are houses, and at the south-west angle a bastion projects into the stream: on the side of the bazar, farthest from the river, the fort contracts and extends in the form of an irregular parallelogram, about five hundred yards to the east. The interior is discernible from the right bank of the river, and the eastern end is commanded by hills of greater elevation than that on which it stands. Opposite to its southern face, and divided from it by a ravine which descends to the bank of the river, stands a petty village, on a level with the gateway. On the right bank of the river, and within musket-shot of the southern postern of the fort, is the village of Khairabad, defended on the west by a mud redoubt, and by several small stone buildings, intended as stations for infantry, erected on different points of a ridge of low hills, about a hundred yards to the westward; the most remote is within the range of artillery from the fort, and perfectly commands the latter. This is the case, however, with even the road to Peshawar, on the Khai-

rabad side, and it would not be necessary to erect batteries on the hills. The fort of Attok, however impregnable it may be to Sikhs or Afghans, could oppose no resistance whatever to European engineers.

The Indus enters the plain of Chach in a direction east by north. It is crossed both above and below the fort: at the ferry of the latter it was about a hundred yards across*; at the former it was something less. The current ran at the rate of about three miles an hour. Near the bank the soundings were two fathoms, and five near the centre. The direction of the river past the fort was south, 20 west; but six hundred yards below Attok it took a turn to the east: on the right bank, at the place where it turns, is the rock of Jelalia, and opposite to it that of Kamalia, between which is said to be a dangerous whirlpool: they offered little remarkable in their appearance, being composed, like the banks of the river and the neighbouring hills, of a

* Lieut. Burnes estimated it at one hundred and twenty yards. Mr. Elphinstone calls it two hundred and sixty. These differences are easily reconcilable with reference to the different periods of the year. Mr. Trebeck crossed in November, Lieut. Burnes in March, and Mr. Elphinstone in June.—Ed.

blue slaty rock, darkened and polished by the action of the current.

We had pitched our tents at the foot of the hills, to the west of Khairabad. These were much broken at their bases by ravines, crossed in some instances by structures, of which some broken arches remain, and which are said to be the ruins of an aqueduct, constructed by Nadir Shah, for the supply of a town which he commanded to be built on the right bank of the Indus: no other vestiges of this place, called Nadirabad, after its founder, were discovered.

On the morning of the 29th Gholam Mohammed Khan, who had been deputed to Peshawar, returned with letters from Yar Mohammed Khan, accompanied by two persons, Sheikh Mohi-ad-din and Abdul Hak Khan. The letters of the chief, and the language of his envoys, were as friendly as could have been expected, and, to judge from appearances, our journey to Peshawar had nothing in it to occasion anxiety or fear. We were given to understand, however, that a report had been spread of our having with us merchandise of immense value, and that we

were prepared to repeat the profuse liberality of the British embassy. In short, that unless very large sums were promised to Yar Mohammed and his principal courtiers, we must expect no security for our property or our persons. It was therefore necessary to be explicit, and it was only after having fully explained our situation and views to the Sheikh and his companion, and received from them the most solemn assurances of safe conduct, that we ventured to proceed towards Peshawar.

Various circumstances retarded our advance, and we quitted Khairabad only on the 6th of December. The country belonged to the Khataks, whose chief, Abbas Khan, had only recently returned from Lahore, where he had been to tender his allegiance to Ranjit Sinh. We were assailed by various reports of the predatory habits of this person and of his people, and were assured that he had been encouraged by Ranjit to oppose impediments to our journey, if not actually to plunder us. Some intimation of such a purpose showed itself in the pass of Gidar Sali, where a number of persons rolled down stones from the

tops of the hills upon our foremost cattle. A few men with muskets sent up to the summit caused them to disappear, and we met with no further obstruction until we reached Akora, the capital of the district, a town of some extent, surrounded by a mud wall, and situated on the southern bank of the river of Kabul. On our approach a large crowd was observed near the gate, leaving the way clear for us to enter; but feeling ill-assured of the prudence of trusting ourselves within the place, we made a détour round it, and encamped at some distance to the west. We were soon surrounded by a number of spectators, including many armed horsemen, who frequently gave us welcome with the cry of "Khush amdeh aid, mulk-i shuma ast," at the same time riding round us en caracole, brandishing long spears, and firing matchlocks. No Abbas Khan made his appearance, although we knew he had returned to his house. His Naib, or deputy, came in his stead, who intimated some expectation of our paying duties, or a commutation of them, to the amount of ten or twelve thousand rupees: he forbore, however, to press the subject, and after his

departure, sent to say that none would be levied; but he expressed a hope that we would remain where we were until his chief could visit us; with which we civilly declined compliance.

Upon loading our cattle on the following morning, we saw a small body of horsemen assembled on the line of our route, and a message was sent to us from the Naib, forbidding our advance, on pain of being immediately attacked. To this we determined to pay no regard; but before we moved the strength of the party had increased to about two hundred horse, and one hundred foot, whilst a mob of seven or eight hundred had issued behind us from the town. We nevertheless commenced our march, dividing our small party into two bodies, one in advance, and the other in the rear, with the camels and baggage in the centre. The road was intersected by a ravine, which about seventy or eighty of the Khatak infantry were detached to occupy; but the head of our party gained the edge of it at the same time, and threatening, if they were opposed, to open a fire upon the Khataks, from a small piece of ordnance with the

advance, they retired with great precipitation upon a body of horsemen in their rear. The Naib now joined us, and again urged our awaiting the visit of Abbas Khan; but finding us determined to proceed, he at last consented to order off his men, and to accompany us to the border, on condition of our halting there till the following morning. To this we consented, and the Khataks were withdrawn. We had scarcely marched two miles, however, before the horsemen were again in our neighbourhood; sent, the Naib protested, merely to reconnoitre, as a party of Peshawar cavalry was reported to be on the frontier. Seeing that we were rather incredulous, he left us to order his men, as he pretended, to a greater distance, and we saw no more of him or of his followers. One only of his servants attended us across the boundary, to whom, at his request, we gave a certificate addressed to Ranjit Sinh, that we had passed through the district without loss of property or reputation. A letter from Abbas Khan was received on the following day, disavowing the menacing conduct of his people, and hoping I would forgive it, as "he had well rubbed their ears."

Before dismissing Abbas Khan the opportunity may be taken of narrating some events which took place shortly after our encounter with him, and which are illustrative of the manners of him and of his countrymen. His allegiance to Ranjit Sinh was a measure distasteful to his tribe, and Khoshal Khan, the Khan of the Southern Khataks, in particular reprobated his conduct. There had been previous disagreement between the chiefs of Tiri and Akora, but it was supposed that they had been put to rest by the marriage of Khoshal Khan with the sister of Abbas Khan. Some dissensions, also, that had occurred between Khoshal Khan and his bride had been amicably adjusted, and he was invited to Akora to partake of the festivities of a hunting party. He accepted the invitation, and, with a few attendants, repaired to Akora, where he was received with great apparent cordiality. At the first hunting excursion, however, he was assailed by armed men employed by Abbas Khan, and slain. The chief of Akora marched, after one day's interval, to surprise Tiri; but the news of the murder of Khoshal

Khan preceded him, and enabled the widowed mother of the Tiri chief to close the gates of her fort against the enemy, and summon Nadir Ali Khan, the chief of the Bungush tribe, and her husband's brother, to her defence. Nadir Ali had formerly killed Arsillah Khan, the elder brother of Khoshal Khan, but his offence was seemingly forgotten in the occasion that recommended his alliance. Abbas Khan was unequal to contend with the Southern Khataks and the Bungushes, and was recalled to Akora by advice that Yar Mohammed Khan was marching against it. On his departure the mother of Khoshal Khan accused her daughter-in-law of having been a party to her son's murder, and, accordingly, put her to death. Entertaining suspicions, also, of Nadir Ali's designing to retain possession of Tiri, she had him assassinated whilst at evening prayer. Yar Mohammed Khan easily took Akora, and Abbas Khan was compelled to seek protection at the court of Ranjit Sinh *.

* Akora, which Mr. Elphinstone calls a large town, and which, from the account of our travellers, must have had a considerable population, was nearly deserted when visited by Lieut. Burnes.—Ed.

After quitting the neighbourhood of Akora our route lay along the right bank of the river of Kabul for some distance, approaching the angle of its course, in which was situated the village of Noushehra, remarkable as the site of the recent engagement, the result of which had placed Peshawar at the mercy of the Sikhs. The success of Ranjit Sinh on this occasion was owing not so much to his superior conduct and the gallantry of his troops, as to the unseasonable parsimony and unaccountable inertness of the Afghan ruler, Mohammed Azim Khan. Twenty thousand mountaineers had been levied by the influence of their Pir-zadas, and were encamped on the left bank of the river, whilst Azim Khan, with the regular Afghan army, was stationed on the right bank. Leaving a few men to keep this force in check, Ranjit Sinh crossed the river, and, with his main strength, fell upon the Ghazis, as they were termed, volunteers in holy warfare. Although defrauded of their promised pay, and left without supplies of provision, the Ghazis met the attack with extreme bravery, and would have probably won the

day had not the Sikh's disciplined regiments stood firm, or had Azim Khan acted vigorously in their support. Notwithstanding they were defeated with great slaughter, their leader, Pir-zada Mohammed Akbar, proposed to renew the conflict on the following day; but Mohammed Azim broke up his camp in the night, and fell back upon Peshawar. The Ghazis then reluctantly dispersed *.

From the neighbourhood of the scene of this action the road turned off to the south, to the village of Pir Piai, where we were received with much cordiality by Nur Mohammed Khan, the manager, a grandson of the celebrated Jehan Khan, the general of Ahmed Shah. He accompanied us on the rest of the way to Peshawar, and amused himself and his companions by reciting Persian verses. An aged Mohammedan of our party was somewhat scandalised by finding some liquor stronger than water in a vessel from which the Khan had just allayed

* Further particulars of this battle may be found in Conolly's *Journey Overland to India*, and Prinsep's *Life of Ranjit Sinh.*—Ed.

his thirst. The road to the city passed over a tolerably level and cultivated plain. Towards the end of the march we passed the remains of the wall of the ancient city of Shahabad upon our right, and encamped, on the evening of the 8th, at the village of Jehangirabad. The plain bore many marks of the devastations committed by the Sikhs in their late operations against Peshawar. On the morning of the 9th we advanced to the city, being met on the way by Pir Mohammed Khan, the younger brother of Yar Mohammed. We were conducted to him by Abdul Hak, and found him on foot at the end of a lane formed by a body of above three hundred horsemen, on the right and left of the road. Having alighted and saluted him, the whole remounted, and advanced together. A party of foot, armed with heavy matchlocks, and dressed in green caps, orange jackets, and black trowsers, preceded us. The cavalry followed: they were variously accoutred and armed, but, for the most part, well mounted. Whilst yet at some distance from the city the crowd of spectators was very considerable, but when

we came near it was almost impossible to make way, and the tops of houses and walls, and all the trees, were covered with people. At last we were relieved from this scene of dust and confusion by arriving at the house destined for our reception, the residence of the late Akram Khan. The floor of the principal apartment was covered with a rich Persian carpet, and felts were arranged round the room; trays of sweetmeats were handed to us, and Mohammed Khan took leave. At night a plentiful dinner was sent to us, and a breakfast the next morning, and several days elapsed before we could excuse ourselves from receiving such marks of hospitality. Our reception by the Duranis formed a striking contrast with that we had experienced from the Sikhs, who, whilst professing equal cordiality, omitted no opportunity of annoying us, and perpetually gave occasion to sentiments of suspicion and mistrust.

The city of Peshawar, and plain in which it is situated, have been so fully and accurately described by Mr. Elphinstone, that it is not necessary to attempt any detailed account of either. Both, however, had much

fallen off since his visit, in consequence of civil dissensions and hostilities with Ranjit Sinh. Many of the houses of the city were untenanted and in ruins, and in the plain very many of the villages were deserted, and extensive tracts of rich land were uncultivated. In the immediate vicinity of the town the Sikhs had inflicted more mischief than many years' labour could remedy, by destroying gardens and orchards, and demolishing the wells and channels of irrigation. The Bala Hisar, which, at the time of the British embassy, was the occasional residence of the king, and in which their audience took place, was now a heap of rubbish, and the only use made of it by the rulers of Peshawar was as a quarry from whence to procure materials for dwellings of their own erection. Even Kashmir, miserable as it was, was not so desolate as the vicinity of Peshawar, not because it was better governed, but because the people had less facility of escaping from the rapacity of their rulers, and because it was less exposed to the evils of war.

In times of tranquillity, and under an en-

lightened government, Peshawar is admirably situated for an *entrepôt* of commerce between the British settlements of India and the countries north of the Hindu Kosh. From British India it is accessible not only by land but by the Indus, the navigation of which, although little known to Europeans, as it has not been attempted by them since the days of Nearchus, is perfectly practicable for boats of considerable burden. From the sea to Attok there is no obstruction of any importance, and the water-carriage continues not only along the main stream some way above that fort, but, by means of the river of Kabul, to within five kos of the city of Peshawar, at a place called Sahiba Patar, where Afghans going on pilgrimage to Mecca usually embark. They reach Karachi Bandar in a month. The advantageous position of Peshawar for the commerce of Khorasan and Peshawar has been noticed by others, but the availability of the upper part of the Indus for this object has been unknown or overlooked, and it seemed, therefore, of importance to ascertain the fact *. As affecting

* Mr. Moorcroft furnishes many details, and he is entitled to

the character of Peshawar as a commercial station, it may be right to observe that the objections founded on the extent and influence of the swampy ground in its neighbourhood have been unnecessarily strong. We saw no swamp which might not be easily drained, and of which the recovery would not amply remunerate the cost.

The aggressions of a foreign enemy were not the only source of suffering to the people, but the dissensions of their rulers aggravated the disorder of the country. Mutual jealousies and disputes for authority estranged the numerous members of the Barikzye family from each other, and weakened the power which they had usurped on the downfal of the descendants of the Abdali. Besides those who were engaged in contending for supremacy at Kabul, or in its dependencies, there were at Peshawar four of the brotherhood, Yar Mohammed, Sultan Mohammed, Syed Mohammed, and Pir Mohammed, who shared amongst

the merit of having first suggested the use that might be made of the Indus as a channel for British commerce. It is unnecessary, however, to transcribe his information, as the voyage of Lieut. Burnes up the Indus, and the inquiries of that officer and others have fully determined the question.—ED.

them the administration of Peshawar and the adjacent districts, but who were united only by their mutual fears and weakness. So convinced were they of their perilous situation, that at a formal interview we were most earnestly entreated to become the channel of a negotiation for placing the whole country under British rule. So urgent, and apparently sincere were their representations, that I was obliged to acquiesce so far as to promise to forward a memorial from them to Calcutta, stating distinctly that it was to be considered as the mere act of a private individual, without any authority to advocate their cause, and without any means of offering even a conjecture as to the result of the application *.

These dissensions, and the disturbed state of the country in consequence, rendered it unsafe for us to move as early as we wished,

* These negotiations probably gave rise to the story told by Ghulam Hyder, that the brothers offered to give the country to Mr. Moorcroft upon payment to them of three lacs of rupees a year, and that upon his declining the offer, an engagement was entered into with Mr. Trebeck for one lac a year for three years, after which he was to pay the stipend first stipulated. The bargain was not effected, because Yar Mohammed began to suspect it was the purpose of the Europeans to bring back the King Suja al Mulk. *As. J.*, v. xix. p. 38.—Ed.

and we were detained at Peshawar until the beginning of May. In the interval I accomplished a visit to the country of the Waziris, in order to ascertain the quality of their breed of horses. The journey was performed under the care of Mir Kamar-ad-din, a Pirzada of great repute. The first part of the route was that pursued by Mr. Elphinstone, as far as Kobat, but it then led to Tiri, the capital of the southern Khataks, thence across the Salt hills into the country of the Barak Khataks, and then into the oasis of Banu, in the middle of a desert sixty or seventy miles long, and nearly of equal breadth, the western extremity of which is frequented in spring by the nomadic Waziris with their cattle. At the time of our visit in March, the desert was covered with a rich carpet of variegated colours, from the purple flowers of the wild sanfoin, and the yellow flowers of the marigold and bugloss. Its most valuable product, however, is the ashkar, a succulent shrub from which potash is largely prepared. The people were everywhere most hospitable and kind, laying aside their marauding propensities in favour of the solitary stranger and his holy guide. Even

amongst these barbarian tribes, however, it was not unusual to hear expressions of a wish to be protected from the Sikh and their own rulers by a British government. The Waziri tribe are said to comprehend from eighty to ninety thousand families; but they are torn to pieces by intestine feuds, village being armed against village, and man against man; and there is no one to enforce order and repress violence. The tract of Banu owes its fertility to its being more thoroughly irrigated, by canals cut from the river Kurma, and produces most luxuriant crops of barley and wheat. The Waziris are all nomadic. Their horses appear to consist of two breeds; one called Khazar-wal, from a person of the name of Khazar, who it is said introduced it; the other Dagla-gala, or 'thieves' brood,' from the parent having been stolen. My visit was late in the season, most of the families having moved to the mountains, and Banu had been recently swept by the Sikh army. Colts were therefore scarce, and I purchased but two, one at one hundred and fifty-five the other at two hundred rupees: the former, though not handsome in figure, was invaluable in work;

the latter was in appearance precisely like an Arab, and would have sold in Calcutta, as an Arab, for one thousand rupees. However serviceable for ordinary purposes the Waziri horse is not adapted for cavalry, seldom much exceeding fourteen hands.

PART IV.

JOURNEY TO KABUL AND BOKHARA.

CHAPTER I.

Departure from Peshawar—Jamrud—Khyber country—Thieves—Pass—Topes—Afghan troops—Insolence and Credulity of the Khyberis—Shenwar Khybers—Kafir castle—Hot winds—Mountains—Caves in the rocks—Kama river—Jelalabad—District—Town—Surkh-rud river—Chahar-bagh—Sultanpur—Orchards—Wandering Giljis—Bala-bagh—Congress—Topes of Amara-khel—Ancient Coins—Lamghan—Kaferistan—Bimba—District of Gandamak—Bridge over the Surkhab—Pass of Jagdelak—of Katalang—Storm—Heft Kotel—Kabul.

In the beginning of 1824 the political disputes of the Barikzyes had come to a crisis. The persons chiefly interested in the contest were Dost Mohammed Khan and his nephew, Habib Ullah, and the main object of their disagreement was the possession of Kabul. This city had been the portion of Mohammed Azim Khan, the elder brother of Dost Mohammed. Mohammed Azim Khan died shortly after the

battle of Noushehra, and his son, Habib Ullah, claimed the succession to the government of Kabul, which was disputed by his uncle. Habib Ullah was a weak profligate young man, and by no means a match for Dost Mohammed; but the reputation of his father, and his own supposed wealth, procured him partisans, and enabled him, on more than one occasion, to defeat his uncle's attacks upon him. Hostilities, however, continued between them, and subjects of grievance between Habib Ullah and some of his other uncles had occurred. It was thought advisable, therefore, by the brothers at Peshawar to interpose, and, if possible, effect an accommodation. With this view Yar Mohammed Khan left Peshawar and repaired to Kabul, and after a short interval summoned Pir Mohammed and Sultan Mohammed to join him.

We had arranged for our onward journey through the country of the Momands, but Sultan Mohammed strongly urged us to take advantage of his and his brother Pir Mohammed's march with a body of troops to Kabul, and to accompany his detachment. He pressed this with so much earnestness, giving us pri-

vately intimation that we had little security even from his brothers, except in his support; and as we had always found reason to rely upon his friendship and sincerity, we acquiesced in his recommendation. Accordingly we quitted Peshawar on the evening of the 24th of May, and bivouacked at midnight on the plain, about four or five miles from the city, at a short distance from the prince's encampment.

Early on the morning of the 30th the Afghans were in motion, collecting in troops under several leaders, each distinguished by a triangular pennon. The march lay over the western part of the plain of Peshawar; the ground was uncultivated and plentifully strewn with small stones, with patches of good pasturage. That it had been once under tillage was evident from numerous traces of water-courses and ruined villages. The plain terminated at Jamrud, at the foot of the Khyber range. It appeared to have been formerly a place of importance, from the number of broken stone walls scattered about, and some large tanks, one of which was sixty yards square. It now contained but a few houses of

stone, and some mat hovels, occupied by Khyberis, a race of notorious thieves. Their Kazi, a very Jewish-looking person, had visited us along with a number of his clansmen at Peshawar, and had been very importunate for money to purchase his protection. He made his appearance again at Jamrud, and renewed his suit, and, after some discussion, it was settled that he should attend us to the borders of the Momand country for twenty-five rupees. Notwithstanding this, we received intimation that the Khyberis had plotted to plunder us during the night, and we were therefore obliged to be upon our guard, and had little rest. The day had been intensely hot, and the wind was as scorching as if it had been blown from a blacksmith's forge.

The road on the next day passed along the course of the Shora rivulet and through narrow defiles amongst the mountains to the pass of Ali Masjid, which is considered as one of the most dangerous places in the country, both from its narrowness and difficulty, and from its being the boundary between the two clans of Koki Khail and Zaka Khail. The mountains on either hand of the defile are about one thou-

sand three hundred feet high, slaty, bare, and, to all appearance, inaccessible. On the left, between the main ridge and the pass, of which it forms one side, is a conical hill of about six hundred feet high, on the summit of which the remains of stone walls may be discerned, the relics of a fortress by which the pass was formerly commanded. A tall beetling crag rises on the right of the defile, which is nowhere above twenty-five paces broad, and in some is not more than six or seven. The length of the pass is nearly a mile. It was not without much labour and delay that Sultan Mohammed managed to get his three cannon through the pass.

After clearing the defile the mountains receded and gave us a fine view of a reach of the valley, in which our attention was caught by a structure of the character of the tope of Manikyala, standing strongly in relief against a clear sky; and rendered more conspicuous by its situation on an isolated craggy mound. When we arrived at the spot we found that the northern side of the structure had fallen in, but its southern face was tolerably perfect. The dome was more dilapidated than that of

Manikyala, and showed that the structure was solid. The building rested on a square platform of masonry, from which rose a second tier or platform divided into compartments, and ornamented with four pilasters, each a foot and a half broad. Above this was the rotunda, one hundred and ten paces in circumference, and about fifty feet in height. It was without any architectural ornament, except two cornices which encircled it, but its facing of masonry was curiously constructed of square stones on edge, divided horizontally by piles of slate of a few inches breadth, and separated into tiers by flat slabs. On the northern side a flight of steps had led apparently to the base of the rotunda, but the top of them was in ruins. Amongst the rubbish were masses of mortar and unbaked bricks. By some its erection was ascribed to the Mogul emperors of Hindustan, but others asserted that it contained the ashes of some wealthy Hindu, whose body had been burnt here. It is most probably a Hindu structure, though for what purpose is doubtful. It is evidently of great antiquity, and of the same period as the tope of Manikyala. At the foot

of the hill, to the northward, we observed different piles which were apparently structures of the same description, more or less in ruins. We encamped near a small fort, called the Gerhi, or fort of Lala Beg.

On this day's journey the Duranis observed a less straggling march than they had hitherto done. The whole force consisted of one thousand two hundred horse, exclusive of camp followers, who were comparatively few. They moved in three bodies, Pir Mohammed commanding the van, Shah Aghasi the centre, and Sultan Mohammed the rear. Though not moving at any uniform pace, they travelled generally at a quick walk of about four and a half miles an hour, and were not delayed by their baggage, as it was placed on mules or stout galloways, and the servants rode on the top of the load. These animals keep up very well with the cavalry, and when the camp is formed, are sent out to fetch provender. The troopers were variously mounted, but most of them had strong active horses, and those about the sirdars handsome chargers. They were but indifferently armed. Some had swords and spear-heads without shafts;

some had bad pistols stuck in their kamarbands; some had matchlocks with the eimak or crooked stock; and some had similar weapons with musket locks. Few of the men had ammunition enough to keep up a fire of ten minutes. The cannon were about four or five pounders, tolerably well cast, but vilely mounted on crazy carriages, and drawn by wholly untrained horses. Of the Khyberis we saw but few: they expostulated, it is said, with Sultan Mohammed for taking us with him through their district free of toll; but he maintained his right to do so, as we were his allies; and when they argued that we were too few to be of any real use, he assured them that we were possessed of such *hikmat* that we could with ease bring their largest mountains about their ears. He even offered them a specimen of our powers if they wished; but this they declined in great alarm. However credulous in this respect, they did not believe that we could not be robbed, and we were therefore obliged to keep up a vigilant watch at night.

The Khyber valley is of an irregular form, but the average breadth is about fifteen hun-

dred paces: the hills which border it may be about seven hundred feet high. In the valley we saw but few villages, and those were of no great extent. Each house was enclosed by a high wall, in some part of which was a tower for look out and defence. The Khyberis are said to be a numerous clan, the principal population being in the hills. They are tall for mountaineers, and of a singularly Jewish cast of features: some of the young women had an arch, lively look, but we saw none that could be regarded as pretty. The men were dressed in long cotton tunics of a kind of plaid, in which blue was the prevailing colour: the women wore an imitation of chintz. The leaders of the Khyberis are their Mullahs, who are said to amount to three thousand. We occasionally saw them in groups of fifty or sixty, but whether numerous or few, they were impudently urgent in their demands for "sheep," by which they intended money. We were glad to give them a trifle in general to be rid of them, but on one or two occasions were obliged to reject their demands, even at the risk of an affray.

After crossing the valley we again came to

a narrow defile, the road occasionally being cut on the side of the rock leading to Landi Khana, in the country of the Shenwari Khybers, a race even more infamous for their robberies than the Afridi Khybers. On the top of a lofty insulated crag we observed the remains of a stone fortress, called by some the Kafir Kila, the castle of the infidels; others asserted that it dated since the introduction of Islam: beyond this we passed a place called the Heft Chah, or seven wells, from there being that number in the neighbourhood: the valley opened into the valley of the Kabul river, and we encamped on its right bank, at the village of Dhaka. On the other bank, at some distance to the north-east, was Lalpura, the chief town of the Mamands, defended by a mud wall and towers.

The heat of the sun, and still more of the wind, was excessively distressing, and such were the fatigue and thirst of the people, that had the river been but a little more distant, many must have dropped. As it was we had to regret the loss of a favourite spaniel and a fine pointer; our other dogs were barely saved. We had heard of the fatal effects of the Si-

mum between Peshawar and Jelalabad, and can easily conceive its distressing influence; for notwithstanding the scorching blast we now encountered, the people agree in asserting that the hot winds had not yet set in. Several of the soldiers of Mohammed Azim Khan's army perished last year on his retreat from Peshawar. It is remarkable that the hot wind is most intense along the course of the river. It blew with less steadiness than in Hindustan, coming in puffs, alternating with a cold blast, apparently from the snows of the Safed Koh.

Our march now continued along the valley of the Kabul river, over a tolerably level and extensive plain, on which several villages were situated, all of them protected by mud walls and bastions from sudden incursions. On the left the plain was bounded by the Safed Koh range, at a distance of about nine miles; with a glass, forests, apparently of pines, clothing its summits, were descried. The mountain, especially termed the Safed Koh, lies at the head of the Mamand Dhara, a valley belonging to the Shenwaris, celebrated for its vineyards: more to the west is

another fertile valley, called Mangastura. These also rear most of the pomegranates imported into Hindustan. Across the river ran a chain of barren hills, called, from their sterility, Kohi Bedaulet. In some of them we could distinguish lines of cavern mouths; but whether these excavations were ancient or modern, we were not near enough to determine. Many of the Afghan tribes form domiciles in the rocks, and we had noticed several cave-dwellings in the Khyber country. Beyond the mountains, skirting the river on the north, part of the snowy peaks of the heights bounding Kaferistan were visible.

On the 3rd of June orders were given to make a night march, and we accordingly started at ten P.M. We moved over a dry sandy plain for some distance, and then reached broken ground, near which was a walled enclosure, called Surkh Diwar, or red wall: the spot is notorious as that whence the Simum is said to originate, and as being the haunt of Shenwari and Waziri freebooters. From thence we descended, and came again upon the bank of the river, from which we had previously made a considerable detour.

Near this it was joined by the river of Kunar, called by Macartney the Kama: it is of no great size, and rises most probably from the snows of the Himalaya. There were several villages on the left bank, Besud and others, inhabited by a people who pretend to be descended from the Arabs. We passed through the bazar of Jelalabad, which seemed worse supplied than many a village bazar in Hindustan, and encamped without the town, above a thousand paces from the river.

We remained at Jelalabad on the 5th. It rained during the preceding night and great part of the day, and the Duranis, who had pitched their tents near to the river, were obliged to strike them precipitately to get out of the way of the water. They marched off in the evening to Bala Bagh, but it was too late for us to follow. Jelalabad is said to owe its origin to the emperor Akber, styled also Jelal-ad-din, and to have been a place of considerable importance, as the capital of a province. Even at a recent period the latter had yielded a revenue of six hundred and fifty-two thousand rupees. It was raised from the fol-

lowing places, the list of which will also point out the extent of the province.

Southern Division.	Rupees.
Dhaka and Girdi	2,000
Hazar Nau	10,000
Bishbulak	10,000
Koth	40,000
Hisarak	50,000
Chaparyar	30,000
Khogiani	60,000
Gandumak	3,000
Ishpan	2,000
Chakar	,000
Hisarak of Nurkhan	8,000
	218,000
Town of Jelalabad	3,000
	221,000

Northern Division.	Rupees.
Lalpur	3,000
Goshta and Khazai	8,000
Kama	60,000
Kunar, containing six large valleys	100,000
Shiwaikiktik	30,000
Arabi and Zakhet	15,000
Lamghan	150,000
Bala Bagh	15,000
Surkhrud	60,000
	431,000

The town is advantageously situated for commerce, as besides being on the high road from Peshawar to Kabul, roads lead from it to Darband, Kashmir, Ghizni, Bamian, and through Lamghan to Badakhshan and Kashkar. At present the only traffic that subsists is the export of fruit, pomegranates chiefly, and timber from the pine forests of Komner to Peshawar. The whole number of houses at present is said not to exceed three hundred, and the aspect of the place is more ruinous than any through which we have passed in Afghanistan. The

district extends about fifty kos in length, by about thirty in breadth, and was at present under the administration of Mohammed Zeman Khan, a son of Asal Khan, the elder brother of Fatteh Khan, and consequently the cousin of Habib Ullah. The latter, however, was attempting to dispossess him in favour of his own brother, Akram Khan. The distracted state of the government was the constant theme of complaint with the Mullahs, and respectable natives who came to visit us.

We resumed our march on the 6th, having the river on the right, and across it, a range of low hills, at the distance of twelve or fifteen hundred paces, beyond which were the summits of the Hindu Kosh: on the left was a sandy plain, bounded by the Safed Koh mountains, distant about twelve miles. The river was joined by the Surkh Rud, or red river, running past Bala Bagh, then turned more to the north, being lost amongst the hills. Beyond the junction we passed the garden of Chahar Bagh, an enclosure about two hundred yards square, with one or two small buildings: the wall was broken down in many places, and the place was utterly neglected.

It was said to have been originally the work of Baber, but was latterly repaired by Zeman Shah. Hence the road proceeded along the edge of a cultivated strip of land, in which many walled gardens, containing mulberry, apricot, apple, and plum trees were observable. We encamped between two villages, to each of which the name of Sultanpur is applicable: they are distinguished as lower and upper (pain and bala), also by the epithets Safla and Galia. At the former the houses were generally situated in orchards of apricots, mulberries, quinces, and plums; the latter of a particular kind, called gurdalu, or kidney-plum: it was yet green, and its character as a fruit, therefore, could not be ascertained. At Sultanpur Galia, the malik and chief people were Tajiks, who claimed to be descended from a colony of Persians, settled here before the time of Mahmud of Ghizni. They paid me a visit, and brought presents of sugar-cane, melons, apricots, and cucumbers. On this day's march we first met with parties of wandering Ghiljis: their tents were nothing more than flimsy black blankets, stretched over forked sticks about four feet high; within,

they had some more blankets, sacks, and pack-saddles, and without, a few loads of mats, ropes, and netting, for the formation of their packages: both men and women were robust, with strongly marked features. On the 7th we advanced to the garden of Bala Bagh, within which the whole of the Durani force had taken up its position. We encamped on its outside, and whilst unloading our baggage had a specimen of the activity of the thieves of the neighbourhood: taking advantage of the confusion occasioned by unloading, and the intrusion of a number of spectators from the Afghan camp, they contrived to take a pistol from the holster of one of our men who had dismounted, even whilst holding his horse, and a sword and belt of one of the Sipahis. The Duranis had just before lost several stands of arms in a similar way.

The principal persons assembled at Bala Bagh, besides those of our party and Mohammed Zeman Khan, were Shakur Khan, and Mihr Dil Khan, brothers of Dost Mohammed, and Wali Mir Akhor, the envoy of Habib Ullah. These formed a sort of congress for determining, if possible, the family dissen-

sions, and several days were spent in discussion. As we were considered part of the expedition from Peshawar, we were obliged to await the result of the negotiations. At length it was settled that Sultan Mohammed Khan should proceed to Kabul, and we marched in his suite on the 14th of June.

Whilst we were encamped near Sultanpur we heard that there were at the foot of the Hindu Kosh range, in the district of Amara Khel, a number of burjas, or towers, which, according to the description given of them, were of the same character as that we had seen in the Khyber country, and we availed ourselves of our detention at Bala Bagh to pay them a visit. Our road lay between Sultanpur and the Surkhab, and across the latter, which we forded. The stream was so deep and rapid that it would not have been possible to have crossed it on foot, and the water was quite red from the quantity of red earth washed down by the current. Having thence ridden over some fields belonging to a walled hamlet, and over a piece of clayey land, much broken by water-courses, we reached a narrow gravelly slope, joining at a few hun-

dred yards to the left the base of the mountains bounding this side of the valley. Here we found a burj, but were much disappointed by its appearance. It differed considerably from the structure we had before seen, and, though evidently ancient, was much less substantially built, its exterior being formed for the most part of small irregular pieces of slate piled together without cement. We did not pause long to examine this, as nine others were in sight, one of which, more to the westward, appeared to be larger than the rest. We therefore proceeded to it, and found that it was situated on a stony eminence at the base of the hills, on the opposite side of which lies the main source of the Kabul river, and nearly in a line with the garden of Chahar Bagh. It was of the same style and form as the others, but was larger and more entire. It rose from a square platform, about seventy-six feet on each side, ornamented with pilasters, with simple bases but rather curious capitals: were it a tomb, it might be imagined that the centre of the latter represented rudely a skull, supported by two bones placed upright, and side by side, or by a bolster or half-

cylinder, with its lower part divided into two. On each side of this were two large pointed leaves; and the whole supported two slabs, of which the lower was smaller than the upper one. A singular feature in this decoration was its being composed of small pieces of thin slate, cleverly joined together. A flight of steps had formerly led up the southern side of the platform, but nothing remained of them except a projecting pile of ruins. On the centre of the platform stood the building, called by the people the burj. The lower half rose by perpendicular sides, and was surmounted by a cornice, whilst its centre was marked by a semicircular moulding, and the space between the moulding and the cornice was ornamented by a band of superficial niches, like false windows in miniature, arched at the top, and separated by small pilasters. The upper half of the building was smaller in diameter than the lower, and of a conical outline, but much of the top had fallen down. Intermixed with the brown slate of which it was chiefly constructed were pieces of quartz, or of some white stone, which at a distance gave to the exterior the effect of being che-

quered, or of a chess-board. This, although the largest edifice on the spot, was smaller than the tope of Manikyala, although evidently of the same character. Many of the smaller topes seemed to have been simply cylindrical towers surmounted by a dome. The greater part of them were in a very ruinous condition.

What might be the nature of these structures was an object of much speculation. The inhabitants of the village of Amerakhel declared that they had learnt from tradition that there had once been an extensive city on the spot, extending beyond the Kabul river, across which they pointed to some excavations, which they said had been included in the limits of the city. The usual appellations for them were Burjai Kafir, towers of the Kafirs; and the Tajiks who accompanied us said that their traditions had always so distinguished them. The people of the village also said that they had heard that the topes were erected by a Raja named Udi, and that the valley was inhabited by Hindus, who, upon some persecution, fled across the mountains, and were now the people of Kaferistan.

It was also mentioned that coins were often found in the neighbourhood, but not being current they were of no value, and were exchanged by the finders for common pyce at the nearest shopkeeper's. Accordingly we sent persons to the adjacent villages and to Jelalabad, to endeavour to procure some of these coins. From the latter our agent brought us two Russian copeks; from the villages we obtained between thirty and forty curious medals, having on one or both faces human figures, frequently in combination with those of the elephant or the bull, indicating their having been struck by order of a prince who was either a Buddhist or a Hindu. The variety was considerable, and two or three appeared to be Grecian, particularly one that had on one side the right arm raised and projecting, as if in an attitude of command *. On others, of a larger size, was on one face the profile figure of a man in a close vest, with a cap on his head, facing to his own right, his right hand apparently placing some-

* These notices identify the coins with others so abundantly found in the same locality by Mr. Masson and Dr. Honigberger, since the visit of our travellers.—Ed.

thing on a pile which might be meant for an altar, his left resting on his hip. The other face represented a figure wholly or partly naked, standing by the side of the Indian bull. On one was a figure riding on an elephant; on another a figure seated on a lotus. The rust upon them, and the decayed state of their surfaces, proved these coins not to be of recent fabric. Most of the coins bore inscriptions, but they were mostly indistinct, and the characters were not known. In some of the larger pieces they were more legible, and would, perhaps, be readily deciphered by persons acquainted with the alphabets of India. With regard to the buildings, it seems most likely that they were Hindu, and either monuments of Satis, or Buddhists, and tombs of the ashes of Lamas or of persons of rank. The latter is the most likely, for the general form of the edifice strongly resembles that of the Mani-pani appropriated to the ashes of the Rajas of Ladakh and the principal Lamas.

The day before we quitted our camp we were visited by Shanawaz Khan, one of the heads of the Tajiks of Lamghan, a district

which lies behind the first ridge of the Hindu Kosh. He was much the most intelligent man we met with in this part of Asia. Speaking of the topes, he stated that in two of them which had been pulled down, a kind of urn or vase of pottery had been found, similar in form to the ovens used by bakers in Peshawar, and that they were filled with ashes and fragments of burnt bones. He spoke in high terms of his country, and the high state of cultivation of the lower valleys. He also showed us some small garnets, or coarse rubies, found amongst his mountains in such profusion that the common people use them as shot in shooting small birds. Speaking of the people of Kaferistan, he stated that he had never heard of any history of the people, but that, according to their own traditions, they descended from that part of the Arab tribe of Koresh which, refusing to acknowledge the divine mission of Mohammed, were expelled from their country, and driven from place to place until they found an asylum in these mountains. Nevertheless, he admitted that the language of the people of Kaferistan was totally different from the Arabic, except in a

very few words, and that they were without any literature. He doubted if they had any knowledge of written characters. They occupy a barren and inclement region, and their country consists of a few narrow valleys, amidst mountains tipped with perpetual snow.

At Nimba, a village enclosed by a mud wall, is another royal garden, which was formerly regarded as superior to any other in this part of the country. It is a square, each side of which is three hundred and fifty yards, surrounded by a high mud wall. The area is laid out in cross avenues of chenar, or plane trees, some of which rise to the height of eighty feet, and are from ten to twelve feet in girth. A shallow canal of brick and mortar, eleven feet broad, formerly conveyed a stream of water down the principal walk. Summer-houses and chabutras or raised mounds, shaded by the cypress and plane, were scattered about the garden. Most of these are now decayed, and many of the trees have been injured or destroyed. The garden is ascribed to the Emperor Baber, but the site is memorable in modern times for the defeat and death of Akram Khan,

the Vazir of Shah Sujah, which was followed by the flight of that monarch from Kabul, and the loss of his crown.

Beyond Nimba we entered the district of Gandamuk, which is famous for its wheat, and crossed a rivulet of some size by a bridge of two arches, erected, as an inscription on it records, in the reign of the Emperor Shah Jehan. It was said that snow falls only to the west of this bridge. After crossing the rivulet we entered the district of Ishpan, and encamped near another garden, larger than that of Nimba, but of a similar description. The wheat in the neighbourhood was ready for the sickle, and many families of the Ghiljis had assembled to assist in reaping it. They are paid for their labour by one sheaf in every twenty. We were obliged to dislodge one family from a spot of ground under a tree, where they had halted. They readily moved, soon loading two asses and a camel with their effects, and unceremoniously rolling up two young children of a twelvemonth and two years old in a blanket, and tying them on the top of the camel's load. The children were evidently

accustomed to the conveyance, as they uttered no complaint, and lay perfectly quiet.

On the 16th our march led across the Surkhab, over a bridge built by Ali Mardan Khan, in the reign of Shah Jehan, in A.D. 1606, but recently repaired by Akram Khan. The bridge was one hundred and seventy yards long, and eighteen feet broad, with a single arch: it was flat at top, with a low parapet on each side. The river, which comes from the south-west, about twenty miles off, was flowing in a rocky bed with much rapidity. Below the bridge were two small butts on either side of the river, about two hundred yards apart, erected, it was said, to commemorate a well-aimed bowshot of Ahmed Shah, the founder of the Afghan sovereignty. Beyond the river the road ascended, and crossed the low line of hills continuous with the Safed Koh range at the pass of Jigdalik, from the summit of which an extensive prospect of both chains and the intermediate valley was enjoyed. Both ranges were tipped with snow, and ran nearly at an equal elevation, but the Hindu Kosh presented, occasionally, much

2 B 2

the loftier peaks. The valley contained little cultivated land, and was sprinkled with bushes or low trees of the Belut or dwarf prickly oak, interspersed with bushes of the white-flowered Daphne, and a variety of Alpine plants. The temperature of the air was very different from that to which we had been accustomed, and the change, however agreeable, was, in consequence of its suddenness, the cause of fever in several of my people. According to our Ghilji guide the valley is, for nine months in the year, the pasturage of large flocks of the broad-tailed sheep and of goats, which, during the other three months, graze in the mountains. The road descended to the village of Jigdalik, so named from the former abundance of the Jigde, or Sanjid (*Elæagnus*), of which not a tree is now to be found here, but of which the absence is compensated by a grove of mulberries. As our companions had appropriated all the supplies procurable at this mean place, we moved on two kos, and encamped on the bank of a watercourse.

On the next march we crossed another pass, the Kata Lang, from whence the de-

scent was rapid to the stream of the Barikab. The road then alternately ascended and descended to the narrow valley of Tizen, which was in cultivation with wheat and rye, both still green. A rough estimate of our elevation, by boiling water, made it about six thousand feet: here we halted. During the night the wind was so violent that it snapped the pole of my tent, and the canvas fell upon my bed. On putting up my hand to remove the pressure I received a smart shock of electricity, and, passing my fingers along the cloth, they were followed by streaks of light. The phenomenon occurred repeatedly, until the electrical matter was exhausted; but it was again excited by the flapping of the tent against the bedstead, which was of iron. After the moon rose we resumed our march. The valley narrowed to a defile between lofty mountains, not more than twenty to thirty yards in breadth, and about a mile long. Our advance was much delayed by the precautions we had to take against depredators, and it was day when we reached the foot of the Heft Kotel, where the wind was piercingly cold. From this the road be-

gan to descend, and passed by the ruins of several villages, to one of which the name of Khurd (Little) Kabul was attached. The modern village, so called, is on the plain, and it is also applied to a district. Our march had been long, and we were glad to halt near the walled village of Bhút Khad, within view of the city of Kabul. Sultan Mohammed had gone on to meet his nephew nearer the city.

During the night some thieves took advantage of the remissness of the sentries to penetrate into several of our tents, and carried off sundry articles of wearing apparel, Mr. Trebeck's cloak, blanket, pistol, and, what was a severe loss, his compass, one made with sights. The alarm was given by Mr. Trebeck, who, putting his hand under his pillow, missed the pistol, which was usually deposited there. The thieves, however, had escaped, and the property was never restored, although I offered a liberal reward for its recovery.

From Bhut Khad we proceeded, on the 20th of June, to the capital, passing along a narrow and ill-constructed causeway, over a

plain, which is occasionally flooded, from a river that runs from the south-west, and is subject to sudden swells. It was crossed by a small bridge, from the end of which the road ascended to an eminence, whence the plain of Kabul, on the edge of which stands the city, came in view. Here we were met by a party of horse, under whose escort we entered Kabul by the gate of Lahore. The concourse of spectators was considerable, but less so than at Peshawar. We were led from the gate through a narrow street, which skirted the walls, and then through open and covered bazars, to the residence of Sultan Mohammed, who had caused his haram-serai to be appropriated to our accommodation. We were comfortably lodged, with the convenience of a garden, surrounded by a high wall. Sultan Mohammed sent us also a dinner and a dessert. The fruit consisted of cherries, a small morella, and mulberries, the latter called Ibrahim Khani, a black species, remarkably fine.

CHAPTER II.

Departure from Kabul—Alarm of the Followers, and Desertion—Fort of Allahdad Khan—Threshing Corn—Thieves—Mydan—Sir-cheshme—Trout—Winter Forage—Forts—Helmand River—Pass of Hajikak—Hazaras—Bamian—Figures—Paintings—Caves—Origin—Sykan—Afghan Extortion—Assafœtida—Slaves—Khurm—Aibek—Apricots—The Wali—Takhti Rustam—Caves—Hill.

THE account of Kabul, published by Mr. Elphinstone, precludes the necessity of our entering upon any particulars, and the period of our stay was one of continual bustle and alarm. The disputes between Habib Ullah and his uncle, Dost Mohammed, agitated the city, and at last came to an actual encounter, in which the latter acquired the ascendancy, which he has since maintained. Various attempts were made by Habib Ullah to extort money from us, but we succeeded, with the support of our Peshawar friends, in resisting them. Their protection, however,

was not wholly disinterested, and, under the name of a loan, I was obliged to raise money to a considerable amount by bills upon Calcutta for the use of Sultan Mohammed Khan. It was, therefore, with no slight satisfaction that we got away from both friends and foes, and, after the middle of August departed from Kabul.

Our baggage was sent off on the evening of the 16th to Deh Mazan, a village about a kos and a half to the west of Kabul, across a rivulet, and near the foot of the gorge, which affords a road through the mountains. We followed on the ensuing day, but were delayed by several vexatious occurrences, so that we did not move from thence until the 19th. The worst feature in the events alluded to was the feeling of alarm and despondency that pervaded many of our party. At the last moment all the servants I had engaged in Kashmir refused to proceed, and my Munshi also insisted on his dismissal. On the next day four of my Gorkha soldiers deserted: they had become Mohammedans, and were but indifferent characters: but I had a severe loss in the Naik, who also dis-

appeared, and who had always been a steady and active adherent. Even Mir Izzet Ullah partook of the panic, and, although he determined to accompany me himself, and share my fortunes, he deemed it prudent to send his son back to Hindustan, that, in case of any calamity, his family might not be left without a head. Replacing the defaulters with Afghans as well as the time permitted, and encouraging those who remained to think lightly of the dangers of the journey, we resumed our road, resolved that no groundless apprehensions, at least, should prevent our arrival at Bokhara.

The road on the 19th continued to the west, skirting the hills on our right. Several forts were observable on either hand. The path was tolerably level, over a sandy soil, abounding, where not under the plough, with camels' thorn. The wheat had been gathered, and the crop still remaining was that of the carthamus, or safflower, the flower of which is a more vivid red and is richer in colouring matter than the safflower of Hindustan, to which it is exported. On the spot it sells at two and a half to five rupees a ser.

This part of the plain would be almost unproductive were it not for the melting of the snow, which is rendered subservient to irrigation by stone watercourses and canals, led from the slopes of the hills. In many places the land is hollowed into lines of deep ravines, with steep banks, in the beds of which a series of wells, twenty or thirty feet apart, and lined with stone, is constructed. Indian corn is cultivated, and, though it seldom exceeds three feet in height, yields a return of forty to sixty for one. The sanjid tree, in tolerably good years, yields, per tree, from eight to ten sers of dried fruit. At Khush Khak, where stood a fort of Allahdad Khan, a friend of Dost Mohammed, we halted for the night. On his corn floors I saw a considerable quantity of wheat, which women with heavy sticks were employed in threshing: another mode was by piling it in a heap about twenty feet high, and thirty or forty in diameter, from the top of which a quantity was successively thrown down under the feet of a couple of heavy bullocks, dragging after them a heart-shaped frame of willow branches

stuffed with straw. By this brush, and the feet of the oxen, the grain is detached from the ear, but the operation is tedious and imperfect: much of the grain remains mixed with the chaff: it is not lost, however, as this chaff is given to the horses. The feed of horses is here most economically practised; the allowance for twenty-four hours for a working horse being six pounds of barley and ten of dry straw; yet I never saw horses in better condition, or more free from disease. Allahdad Khan had a large vineyard, in which some of the vines were in trellis, and others in stocks, three feet high. The latter broke out into sideshoots, which ran along the ground, and were little productive. Notwithstanding the proximity of the fort, and the presence of an escort of fifteen horsemen, belonging to Sultan Mohammed Khan, we were disturbed during the night by thieves. They were seen, however, and fired upon by the sentinels we had taken the precaution to place. The attempt took place during Mr. Trebeck's watch, who, riding up on the report of the piece, was mistaken by one of the

sentinels for an Afghan: he fired, and brought down the horse: luckily Mr. Trebeck escaped unhurt.

From Khush Khak we marched on the 20th to the district of Mydan, following a direction generally west by north, over a stony and irregular plain, leading to the ascent and pass of Safed Khak. Beneath this spread the valley of Mydan, studded with forts; the land was worse than the east of the pass, and fruit trees were giving place to the willow and poplar. The road continued along the valley, on this and the following day, to the village of Takina, on the road to Bamian, where we encamped. The wheat and barley had been cut, but we saw crops of horse beans and other pulse, and some rice, but it was low, and appeared backward. In the vicinity of the village I found the prangos growing, though but a span high; it was here called kamai, and used for winter forage for cattle and horses: five pounds of it ground to coarse powder, and mixed with double the quantity of wheat or barley-chaff, is an allowance for a horse for a day and night, and is said to fatten him more readily than any other kind

of food. On the following day we made a short move to Sir-Cheshme (the head of the springs), the head of the long valley up which we have marched, where we were to lay in a stock of barley for our horses, as the crops in advance were yet green. On my way to the fort of Aziz Khan, the Hazara manager of the district for Dost Mohammed, I passed a small pond, filled by a stream from a holy spring, which was so full of trout as to baffle description or credibility. They were held sacred, and were exceedingly tame. On the 21st of March, to a day, according to the report of the people, the fish desert the pond for the rivulet that waters the valley. It is then lawful to catch them. Besides this spring, there are others in the same locality, the waters of which unite, and the rivulet resulting from their confluence is the head of the Jui Shir, running past Kabul.

The valley of Mydan contains about thirty-five thousand inhabitants, Tajiks and Hazaras; they are both cultivators, and the latter are also soldiers and marauders. The revenue is said to be ten thousand rupees in specie, and eight thousand in grain. The district

had been taken from Habib Ullah by Dost Mohammed, who had made it over to Amir Mohammed Khan; he again had granted it to Zulficar Khan, with a portion of the revenue, on condition of his furnishing, when required, an armed force of one hundred footmen and twelve horsemen. At Lower Tahina I saw some shaftal, or clover, cut for seed, and never saw ground so covered with hay of any kind. After the seed is trodden out, the chaff, mixed with wheat and barley-chaff, is given to horses as winter forage. Almost all the troop horses of Kabul are wintered at Mydan, on this food and lucerne, at the cost of two or two and a half rupees a-head, and come out of this feed in the spring in excellent condition.

The first part of the march on the 24th was along a narrow defile, of an irregular, but in the main, ascending elevation. It then descended into a ravine, and crossed the upper or main branch of the Helmand river. It was here knee-deep, and about ten yards across, and was said to come from a portion of the Hindu Kosh, behind the district of

Pagman, three days' journey distant. Beyond this the road opened into a valley, in which stood the village of Gardan Diwar, where we encamped. Many forts were passed in the early part of the march, with patches of cultivation, chiefly of shaftal; towards the end of it we saw the naked barley of Tibet, called here kal jao, and some wheat. Numerous parties of Ghiljis were encountered, who were descending from their mountains into milder regions for the winter. They had with them numerous droves of camels, sheep, and goats; many of the former were young ones, and were covered with a blanket, with a hole for the hump. The furniture and tents of the people were carried on the camels, as were their children, and the lambs and sheep when infirm. The Hunai pass divides Afghanistan from the country of the Hazaras.

From hence the road proceeded up a zigzag defile, with a branch of the Helmand, generally to the right, but frequently crossing the path; on the left, at no great distance, was the Kohi Baba range of hills. The road continued to ascend somewhat steeply to the

pass of Hajikak*; the total ascent during the day was about three thousand feet. The pass is dangerous and difficult in winter, as it is exposed to snow drifts from every quarter. From its summit the road descends into the district of Kalu, between a ridge of high hills on the right, and a rough, irregular valley on the left, extending to the foot of the Kohi Baba mountains. From the latter a rapid rivulet descended, which, we were told, passes by Ghori to the Oxus; beyond it, on some level eminences, were the forts of Kalu, belonging to the Darghun tribe of the Hazaras. The parent clan, who spread from near Herat, and from Sykan, on the borders of Turkistan, to the frontiers of Afghanistan, are said to be descended from a portion of the Mongols, left here by Holaku Khan. Their physiognomy, however, indicates a very different origin, and from the formation of their heads, and features of their faces, I should be disposed to class them with the Tibetans, the Nepalese, and the Mugs: a connexion with the same races seems to be indicated also by the traces

* It is twelve thousand four hundred feet above the sea. Burnes, i. 181.—Ed.

of a common religion, afforded by the topes of Amarakhel and Jelalabad, and the figures and devices on the coins found in the same situations. The character of the country through which we had latterly passed reminded us strongly of Ladakh; the vegetable productions were greatly similar; we had the naked barley and the prangos smaller, but abundant, and the rhubarb with circular unbroken leaves was in great profusion. Its medicinal virtues are unknown, but it is extensively used, both raw and dressed, as a fruit and a vegetable; the leaves are also collected, and piled up in dry places as winter fodder for cows.

The 25th brought us to Bamian. In the first part of the journey the road was very rough, and irregular along the sides of the hills, ascending to the pass of Kalu, which was still more elevated than that of Hajikak. It then descended to the valley of Bamian, passing by the small fort of Topchu. Farther on we crossed the Bamian river, which running westward, is joined by that of Kalu. The valley then became level and grassy, and, as it approached Bamian, widened to about

one thousand two hundred yards across. We encamped between two channels of the river, in front of the fort of the deputy-governor of the district. Upon our left, and in front, rose the perpendicular rock, in which are the two celebrated idols, and the whole face of which was honeycombed with caves.

Bamian has usually attached to it the designation of Bhut, or Idol-Bamian, from two remarkable statues carved on the face of the rock in its vicinity. The ancient city, called Gulgula, stood on and around a detached conical hill, which is covered with extensive ruins, and remains of buildings are strewn all over the valley, showing it to have been formerly the site of a numerous population. Utensils of copper and brass, and coins are frequently found, and writings, said to be in Persian and Arabic, as well as some unknown language, are sometimes discovered. According to the Mohammedan traditions, Gulgula was built by Jelal-ud-din, King of Khwarism; but it seems probable, that although it may have been enlarged and improved by him, it may boast of much higher antiquity. The hill had been fortified, and its interior was

pierced with caves, communicating with the surface, and containing the remains of reservoirs, no doubt of water, for the use of the garrison.

Of the two colossal idols cut out of the rock, opposite to the hill on which stood the city, one larger than the other is called Sang-sal, or Rang-sal, and is said to represent a male; the smaller, called Shah-muma, is considered to be a female; but the general appearance and costume of both are essentially the same, and indicate no difference of sex. On either side of the figures are numerous caves excavated in the rock, usually with vaulted roofs, which were sometimes carved with flowers. The figures stand in porches or recesses cut out of the rock, the upper part of which is arched, so as to form an alcove or vaulted canopy over the head of the figure; the sides advance so as to form wings, in which are staircases ascending to a gallery behind the neck of the statue, whilst other galleries run off from their sides, right and left, into the rock. The flights of steps of the larger image were so much decayed as to be inaccessible, but one of those on the side of the smaller

was tolerably entire, and led to the head of the figure. Both figures have been mutilated, by order, it is said, of Aurangzeb. The faces and fore arms of both were knocked off, and a thigh of the larger was broken. They are both clad in long loose robes, descending below the knee. The height of the smaller figure was one hundred and seventeen feet; that of the larger we could not measure, but it must have been about one-third more. The inside of the alcove, or top of the porch, was covered with fresco paintings of flying figures, and a border contained various half-length figures, whose heads were invested with a halo. Paintings of this kind had descended to within thirty feet of the ground, but the plaster had, for the most part, peeled off. An embellishment of the ground, a white ball with a pyramid rising from it, a common ornament of sculpture in Tibet, was frequent here. Four figures under the spring of the arch of the alcove were of very beautiful delineation, and painted with much delicacy of colouring; below them was the head of a male figure, which resembled in expression the divinity called, by the Tibetans, Cham-ba.

At the western end of the range which we ascended we found a number of caves, one of which, of a quadrangular form, displayed considerable architectural decoration. The front had fallen in, but the sides were made up of fluted and square pillars, with and without capitals, at intervals not greater than the breadth of a pillar. The roof was carved so as to represent tiers of beams crossing each other at angles, and diminishing their distance as they ascended, until they left an octangular space of about twenty inches only, imitating the roof of a log-house in Tibet and Kashmir. The pillared cells communicated by a gallery with a large vault, and beyond that with a chamber fifty-three feet long, thirty-eight broad, and forty high, along the sides of which were a number of small arched recesses, in which the vestiges of fresco paintings might be discovered, although impaired by time and blackened by smoke. At the end, opposite to the entrance, a large recess indicated the site of a statue, and a small portion of frieze at the angle of the arch showed the perfection to which the art of sculpture had been brought at the period when the

chamber was constructed. This was about two feet and a half long, and eighteen inches broad, divided, as to its subject, into three compartments: a superior and inferior fillet contained representations of pheasants in high relief; the middle band consisted of foliage; and the whole was executed with singular truth and spirit.

The origin and use of these excavations are matters of speculation. According to an account given us by an old and intelligent native of Bamian, dead bodies have been occasionally found in subterranean chambers in considerable numbers, and which have fallen to dust upon being exposed to the air. It is not impossible, therefore, that part of these excavations may have served as catacombs; but I have no doubt that they were also, as indeed they still are to a certain extent, habitations of the living. My own conviction, from the character of the buildings, of the caves, paintings, and sculptures, is, that Bamian, whatever its ancient appellation, was the residence of a great Lama, bearing the same relation to the Lamaism of the west, as Lhassa does now to that of the east. The name of the smaller

idol, Shah-muma, is evidently only a corruption of Shak-muni; but this is evidence of minor importance. From a somewhat intimate acquaintance, however, with the structures used as monasteries in Ladakh and Chanthan, I am legitimately empowered to say that those excavations which were connected by means of galleries and staircases constituted the accommodations of the higher orders of the Lama clergy, and that the insulated cells and caves were the dwelling-places of the lower classes of the monastic society, as gelums and anis, monks and nuns, and as serais or hostels for visitors. The laity inhabited the adjoining city *.

At a comparatively modern period the destruction of Gulgula is attributed to Jangez Khan, who, from some cause not now remembered, being highly exasperated with the

* Bamian has since been visited by Captain Burnes (*Travels to Bokhara*, vol. i.) and Mr. Masson (*Journal Asiatic Society of Bengal, Nov.* 1836). Their accounts generally agree with those of our text, except that they have a lower estimate of the height of the two principal images, which they suppose to be severally one hundred and twenty and seventy feet. In one of the caves, Mr. Masson writes, he saw " the names of W. Moorcroft, G. Trebeck, and W. Guthrie, written with charcoal."—ED.

people, came upon them suddenly, put them without mercy to the sword, and overturned and demolished the place. It was said that at a day's journey from Bamian, to the south-west, were the remains of an extensive fortress, called Bandeh Berber, erected near a large lake.

We were detained two days at Bamian, in consequence of the reported dangers of the road; a chief, named Ali Gohar, a dependant upon the government of Bamian, being in rebellion, and plundering the caravans. A letter from Allahdad Khan was addressed to Mohammed Ali Beg, at Sykan, to request his protection of us through his country; and he shortly sent word that he awaited us at the pass of Ak-robat, with two hundred horse, which he would double should there be any appearance of danger. We therefore started on the 28th. The road was rough and irregular, ascending to the fort of Ak-robat, a small mud-fortress with a round tower: a further ascent led to the summit of the pass of the same name, which is about the elevation of those of Hajikak and Kalu. To our north the mountains were much less lofty than those we

had crossed, and were all bare. We here entered Sykan, and were met by Ali Beg, a Tajik, who was the chief of the district. We accordingly took leave of Allahdad Khan and Zulficar Khan, with our Afghan escort, after a discussion in which the former attempted to extort from me a most exorbitant remuneration for his attendance. He had received from me four hundred rupees, and I offered him three hundred more, which, as the maintenance of the party had fallen on me, amounted to above one thousand one hundred. He however rated his services at a much higher value, and asserted that it was for my credit and name to pay at least some three or four thousand rupees, and that Sultan Mohammed Khan had desired him to receive no less. Satisfied that this was as false as the demand was unreasonable, I persisted in my first offer, and the Khan was at last compelled to be contented with what he could get. Notwithstanding my confidence in the friendship of Sultan Mohammed Khan, I felt as if a load was taken off my breast on quitting the Afghan territory, such were the intrigue and villany I had witnessed, and the perilous situ-

ations from which I had with difficulty, but I trust with honour, emerged. We encamped on the 29th near the village of Sykan.

The chief article of the commerce of this place is assafœtida, of which about two hundred maunds are gathered annually from plants that grow wild upon the mountains. In the spring the earth is partly removed from about the root, and the stem and leaves cut off close to the ground; a juice exudes from the surface, which, when dried, is scooped off; a slice is then cut from the root, and the juice exudes again from the fresh surface; this is repeated a third and a fourth time. A root of a good size yields about half a pound of the dried juice. Another article of commerce is slaves; Mohammed Ali Beg, in conformity with the practices of his neighbours, and, as he professes, only in the way of retaliation, making incursions upon the Uzbeks and Hazaras, and carrying off their population for sale. He was an officer of Mir Kalich Ali, of Khurm, and since his death has raised himself to importance. He has twenty-five forts in Sykan and the vicinity, and is extending his power. He was very urgent with us to stay

with him and aid him in an attack upon Khulm, which he was confident of mastering with our assistance.

On the two following days we left the Sykan territory by the pass of Bala-farash, and proceeded along the valley of Kamur, the chief of which was a feudatory of Murad Beg, of Kunduz; thence we proceeded over alternations of hill and valley to the fort of Doaba, surrounded by black tents of felt, and a few stone houses, the residence of an Uzbek population, under a Malik of the same nation. The valley continued to Rohu, where the people, who were Hazaras, called themselves Habsh, pretending to be of Arabian origin. They were rich in cattle, having about three hundred brood mares, and many black cattle and sheep: the former were of an indifferent kind; the latter were broad-tailed. Hitherto all the sheep we had seen had been brown-legged and brown-headed; many at this place had white heads, and some were wholly white or black. They were long in the body and very fat, and the mutton was excellent. The wool was coarse, and the price varied from two to four rupees a sheep.

Our next halting place was Khurm, where we arrived on the 3rd of September. It is a long narrow town, on the banks of a rivulet, which had accompanied the road from the valley of Doaba. The houses were rudely built of lumps of limestone, with flat roofs of clay; many were unoccupied, their tenants quitting them at this season to take their flocks to distant pastures, and residing in felt tents. Even about the town the tents were pitched in the orchards for the summer habitation, where the members of each family were engaged in weaving cloth, made of the wool of their own sheep, or watching their crops, chiefly of panic, kangni, and fern, growing under the fruit trees. Wheat and barley are also grown. The management of orchards in this country is carried to a great extent. It seems to matter little what the nature of the soil may be, as long as there is abundance of water. Apples, pears, peaches, plums, walnuts, are all cultivated; but the apricot is the staple of the district, and the people of Khurm assert that theirs is the best in Turkistan,—a claim contested only by the apricots of Aibek. The vines were of several

kinds, and were trained over the top of the likhe, or white thorn. The willow, poplar, and aspen, along the river attained a great size, and the Sanjid was beautifully loaded with fruit. We were rather too early for the fruit season. The whole course of the river was richly fringed with orchards. In some places on the road we noticed an ingenious adaptation of a natural process to the construction of solid dykes: the neighbouring mountains are of limestone, and the water, though beautifully clear, was fully charged with that earth. It therefore deposited a quantity of tufa or stalactite as it rolled somewhat sluggishly along, on any stones placed to intercept or confine its stream, and thus cemented them in a short time into a substantial wall. In one part of our route, at a place called Ghazi Mir, the level of the river was higher than the road, but it was prevented from overflowing by a walled bank of this construction.

The inhabitants of Khurm seem to be in more comfortable circumstances than any we have met with for some time. They call themselves Tajiks, but have no tradition of

their origin. They are evidently a mixed race, some of them with remarkably large heads and features, some with small heads and sharp lineaments. The complexion of the men was dark, but that of the girls and young women fair, although they had all black hair and eyebrows, the latter as regularly arched as if they had been pencilled; they were generally pretty, almost handsome. Persons of both sexes, and of all conditions, crowded into my tent, but they were remarkably good-humoured and civil, and their Mullahs apologized for their intrusion, by representing that they had never seen a European before. I could not learn that any remains of antiquity were known to them, except the ruins of a mud fort which we had passed on our road, and which they said had been constructed by the Kafirs before the time of the Mohammedans.

A continuation of the same valley led to Jas-bagh, a place of a similar character as Khurm, but less extensive, and thence to Aibek, the residence of Mohammed Ahmed Beg, the second son of the late Mir Kalich Ali, who had assumed the title of

Wali, or Protector of Balkh. On hearing of the demise of his father, who, in reply to my letters from Kashmir, had promised me his protection on visiting his country, as I proposed, I wrote to him letters of condolence from Jas-bagh, and intimated my purpose of waiting upon him. His authority over Aibek was that of a feudatory to Murad Beg, the Khattagan Chief of Kunduz, who, upon the death of Kalich Ali, had taken advantage of disputes amongst the three elder sons of that chief to extend his own possessions. In this he was assisted by Baba Beg, the second son, through whose treachery the elder brother and heir was removed by poison; in reward for which he had been invested with the government of Khurm. The third son, our new acquaintance, had endeavoured to assert his independence, and occupied Aibek. He was unable, however, to cope with the superior power of Murad Beg, and was compelled to acknowledge him as his superior for that district. Balkh he held of the King of Bokhara. Report spoke favourably of the young man's abilities and general conduct, and I indulged a hope that he would extend to me

the friendship of which his father had made several demonstrations. The first view of Aibek was rather imposing, presenting a castle on an insulated eminence, surrounded by houses with cupola roofs, with a projecting chimney in the centre. On a nearer approach it was found that many of the houses were tenantless and in ruins; the people, however, seemed busy in preparations for their repair. Aibek is famous for its apricots, which, when dried, are largely exported to Bokhara and Astrakhan. When dried with the stone they are sold at two Kabul sers for a rupee: they are also split and strung with other kinds, in which form they are called khista, and are sold at one ser for a rupee. The chief cultivation round Aibek was millet, of which three sorts were reared: it grew to the height of three feet, and yielded double the weight of wheat on the same soil. On approaching Aibek, the mountains on either hand receded, the climate had become much warmer, and the fruit had been some time gathered.

Shortly after we had encamped the Wali came to visit us: he was about twenty-four, with Uzbek features, but not unpleasing ex-

pression: he was very civil, and assured us that he looked upon us as old friends, in consequence of our intercourse with his late father. He stated that the ancient name of Aibek was Simingan, and that it was the residence of the father of Rudaba, the wife of the hero Rustam; that at the time when it was destroyed by Jangez Khan, the buildings extended to the foot of the Yetimtal mountains, nearly a day's march in advance of us. According to tradition there were seven thousand Hindu families in the town, most of whom were exterminated by the conqueror. At present there were scarcely any Hindus in the country, and those were merely temporary sojourners, who had no families. To my inquiry after ancient remains, he indicated a place in the vicinity, dignified with the title of Takhti Rustam, to which he accompanied us on the following day.

About a mile to the west of the fort we found an isolated hill in which were a number of excavations; one of these, called the apartment of Rudaba, consisted of a square vestibule, and a circular chamber with a cupola ceiling: the former was now open at top,

but appeared to have had a roof formerly: the latter was thirty-two feet in diameter, and twenty-six feet high, with an opening in the roof, at the part farthest from the entrance, to admit light and let out smoke.

In the centre of the dome was a large medallion, much defaced, but from the circumference of it were distinctly seen large leaves like those of the calyx of the lotus, spreading towards the lower edge of the dome, at the meeting of which with the walls, a broad cornice extended round the room. From this chamber an inner corridor, following the face of the wall, one hundred and thirty-two feet long, by sixteen and a half feet broad, led to another circular and vaulted chamber, of about thirty-seven feet in diameter, but much blocked up by rubbish. The room was of a similar character with the first, but the style of decoration was widely different. There were several other excavations, but these were the most worthy of notice *.

On the shoulder of a ridge of hills facing the west, a few hundred yards from the exca-

* The manuscript refers to a drawing, which has not been received.

vated hill, was situated the throne of Rustam. This consisted of a small and insignificant square edifice, remarkable chiefly from its site. It stood upon a conical mound with a tabular summit, which had been cut off from the rest of the mountain by a deep trench all round it. The trench was cut into an inclined plane, and opened by a vaulted passage through the surrounding belt of rock into the valley. The building proved to have been part of the original rock; the interior consisted of a conical cell, entered by a vaulted passage, of a man's height, whilst on the top of it, which was level and solid, was a sort of basin or well. On the western front, beyond the trench, were several platforms on a kind of rampart, which had been scarped in front, and within which was a spacious vaulted chamber, part of the front of which had fallen into the fosse. Several small cells were observed in the sides of the ditch. There were no traces of steps from the bottom of the ditch to the top of the mound, but the fallen fragments now afforded means of ascending. From some niches in its edge, corresponding with similar ones in the side of the rampart on the original

hill, it should seem that a sort of drawbridge formerly connected them. The height of the mound was seventy-four feet; the circumference of the top we omitted to measure, but the house was twenty feet square; the cell within it was about seven feet in diameter; the passage about eight feet long by nearly six feet high and four broad. It gave a loud echo to sounds uttered in the cell. Tradition, as the name imports, assigns this structure to Rustam, and he is said to have drank wine from the basin in the upper platform; but a more inconvenient position for the consequences of strong potations can scarcely be conceived, and we cannot accede, therefore, to the notion that Rustam made merry in such a situation. It is difficult, however, to conjecture with any confidence, what could have been the object of the structure. The excavations in the mountains, in connexion with those in Afghanistan, at Bamian, and others observed on the whole road hither, and with the topes of the Panjab, and the figures at Bamian, would seem to intimate its being the work of a Buddhist people. It differs, however, so much from anything we saw in Tibet, that I cannot

acquiesce in such an appropriation. It has much more the character of an altar, and might be thought to have been a fire-altar of the ancient Guebers of Bactria, the first seat of the religion of Zerdusht. There was no appearance, however, of discoloration, such as might have been expected from the action of fire, and this conjecture, therefore, must be abandoned. That it was an altar, however, derived some confirmation from a number of deep notches in the edges of the basin on the upper platform, evidently made with a sharp cutting instrument, the axe or knife, perhaps, used in slaying the victims sacrificed. Were the altars erected by Alexander sacrificial or commemorative? If the former, may not this mound have been either his work, or that of some of the Greek princes of Bactria, within which kingdom Aibek must have been comprised? I could find no traces of inscriptions nor any coins; and the origin of the mound of Aibek, the throne of Rustam, must be left to the determination of those better qualified and more favourably circumstanced for the prosecution of the inquiry.

The rock in which these works were discovered was limestone, and the sides exposed large masses of organic substances, nearly as hard as quartz, semitransparent, and resembling madrepore.

CHAPTER III.

Return of Messengers to Kunduz—Unfavourable Reports—Advance—Excavations of Bazar Súm—Horses—Houses—Tangi—Khulm or Tash Kurghan—Baba Beg—Visit to Kunduz—Yang Arekh—Reservoirs—Pass of Arganna—Plain of Kunduz Ghori river—Town and Fort—Atma Ram—Audience of Murad Beg—Suspicions of the Chief—Difficulties—Enemies—Persian cannon—Return to Khulm—Delays—Exorbitant Duties—Departure of Mir Izzet Ullah—Summons to Kunduz—Detention Charge of being a Spy—Removal of Goods to Kunduz—Izzet Ullah's return—Audience—Military expedition of Murad Beg.

On the 7th of September, Mir Fazl Hak and Mir Wazir Ahmed arrived at Aibek. They had crossed the Hindu Kosh and visited Kunduz, where they had delivered my letters to the chief, but unfortunately the Dewan Begi, Atma Ram, was absent in a distant part of the country, and my letter and presents to him were not delivered. Some evil disposed persons, it appeared, had been endeavouring to prejudice Murad Beg against us. The English, they said, never entered

into any part of Asia but for interested purposes, and ultimately became its masters. It was asserted that our party was strong in soldiers and cannon, and that in consequence of our interference in the affairs of Kabul, a large portion of the fine intended to be levied on Mir Mohammed Ali had been remitted, whilst the money with which we had supplied Sultan Mohammed had enabled him to make himself governor of the city. These imputations had been warmly refuted by Mir Wazir Ahmed, and the result of the discussion was, in his opinion, entirely favourable to us. We therefore resumed our journey, in the hope that no difficulties or dangers were before us, although the character of Murad Beg, the Kattaghan chief of Khulm, Kunduz, Talikan, Inderab, Badakhshan, and Hazrat Imam, forbad our feeling entirely secure. We left Aibek on the 8th; the baggage followed the direct road, but we kept more to the left, in order to visit some excavations to which the Wali had directed us.

At about twelve miles from Aibek, where the cultivated ground of the valley terminated in bare and rugged swells, leading to a range

of low hills, we found a set of caves, called the Hazar Súm, or thousand houses, excavated in the face of a platform of stalactite deposit. They were in two tiers, built in arches, generally from twelve to twenty feet broad, and the same height, but partly choked with dust and rubbish and animal excrement. Niches were worked in the walls, and one was larger than the rest, as if for the reception of an image. In one of them I observed marks of vermilion, and traces of letters which, though mutilated, resembled strongly the common or vulgar character of Tibet. The largest apartments had been plastered, and washed either white or black. The lower range of apartments communicated with the upper by passages, but they were in total darkness, and not having torches with us, we were unable to explore them. Coins and ornaments, it is said, are sometimes found; but we did not meet with any remains, except some fragments of a cream-coloured pottery. These caves are the reputed haunts of wild beasts and of robbers, and it was unsafe to linger in their neighbourhood.

From Aibek to the foot of the mountains

was about eight miles. There were several towns in ruins, having been destroyed by Murad Beg, who had made slaves of their inhabitants. There still remained a number of inhabited villages, and the land, where cultivated, was well tilled and watered. Every village had large droves of brood mares, and they were more numerous than cows: they were generally about fourteen hands high, something too long in their bodies, but in other respects well formed. They would have been well worth from two hundred and fifty to three hundred rupees in Hindustan: here they were purchaseable for a toman, or a toman and a half, or from twenty to thirty rupees. The country is said to abound in deer and other game, and a part of the mountains to the right has the appellation of Kani Kansa (Bear-mine). All the houses were built with domes. There is little timber in the country, except that of the fruit trees; and the scarcity of this article, which probably drove the ancient inhabitants to live in caves, has occasioned the adoption of vaulted roofs. Each chamber in a house has its own dome, with a square opening in the roof for

light and ventilation. The walls are built of stiff clay with pebbles, the roofs of sun-dried bricks, coated with a luting of clay and chopped straw. A family house consists of three chambers, and is enclosed by a clay wall, and costs about thirty or forty rupees. These houses are very comfortable, and are well suited to a climate where the snow of winter seldom falls heavily or lies long, and where the rain that falls in spring and autumn is never violent.

The road to Ghizni Yek continued over rough and uneven ground, and along a narrow and ill cultivated valley, in which scarcely any tree but the tamarisk presented itself. It then narrowed to a pass between a small stream and a ridge of rocks, called Tangi. The strait continued more or less contracted, till, at about twelve miles from that village, it passed through a narrow gorge for a few hundred paces, and then opened upon a view of Khulm. Crossing a rivulet, we began to march over a hard gravelly plain. The mountains receded on either hand, and the plain in prospect was, in appearance, as flat and unbroken as that of India on emerging

from the Himalaya. The change from the arid and rocky defiles we had traversed to the orchards and domed houses of Khulm, or Tash Kurghan, was highly grateful.

We had been met on our way from Ghizni Yek by a Hindu custom officer, named Bysakhi Ram, whose business it was to count our packages, and report to his superiors. He was also sent to act as our guide, and led us to the skirts of the town, where we encamped. We were soon visited by crowds of Uzbeks and by a number of Hindus, settled in the town as merchants and traders. The latter, by their conversation and familiarity, mixed with much respect, claimed us as old acquaintances, and were evidently glad to meet with persons whom, notwithstanding the difference of creed and complexion, they had learnt to look upon as friends and protectors. The Uzbeks were very civil, but exceedingly curious.

Baba Beg, the ruler of Tash Kurghan, as before noticed, was absent on our arrival. His return was scarcely announced to us when it was reported that he was entering the gateway of the enclosure in which we

were encamped. I left my seat to meet him, and had scarcely advanced twenty paces when I saw a short, thick-set person, about thirty-five, clothed in an outer vest of flame-coloured silk, with an inner dress of black satin. On my approach to embrace him in the usual manner, he somewhat repelled me, and I merely, therefore, took his hand, and led him into the building I had occupied, and seated him on a chair. He then coldly bade me welcome, and inquired the object of my visit. To my account of my being a merchant he observed this was a bad country for trade. Turning to one of my people, he inquired of him if he was a Mohammedan, and, being answered in the affirmative, he asked the man if he could find no other service than that of Kafirs (Infidels)? On this I remarked that his father would not have asked such a question, and that the man, being no subject of his, was not accountable to him for his conduct. This somewhat checked him, and, after a time, he became rather more polite. He informed us that he had been commanded by his chief to send us on to Kunduz, and to furnish an escort for our

journey, and with this, however inconvenient and undesirable, I was ultimately obliged to comply. Taking with me Mir Izzet Ullah, and a handsome present for Mir Murad Beg, of English broadcloth, chintzes, muslin, silk, a double-barrelled gun, and double-barrelled pistol, we departed for Kunduz on the 16th of September.

On setting out we crossed a ledge of the mountains which are in the immediate neighbourhood of the town, and had then on our right, or to the south, those mountains, running east and west. On the east the horizon was bounded by a chain of mountains, crossing from north to south. Before us to the north was an extensive plain, which, with exception of the ruins of ancient Khulm, and the remains of its orchards, was a desert, bearing little else than camel's thorn. Traces of former cultivation were, however, discoverable. At the distance of about nine miles we came to the town of Yang Arekh (New River) founded by Abdulla Khan, who governed this country in the reign of Akbar Shah, and who induced many Hindus to settle here, whose descendants still exist. The

town has been much reduced of late in extent and population, but it may contain about one thousand houses. It is supported chiefly by its filatures of raw silk. This is of two kinds, white and yellow, and is exported to Kabul and Peshawar. It is worthy of note that the pans in which the water is heated are of cast-iron, manufactured in Russia. The water of the Khulm river reaches little beyond Yang Arekh, and the plain remains sterile through want of irrigation: this, however, might be easily managed under a steady government, as the level is rather below that of the Oxus, and the whole distance from the river to the mountains to the south is not above two miles. We halted at Yang Arekh.

At about seven miles on the road on the following day we crossed the hills coming from the north, at the pass of Shaibaghli, neither very lofty nor very difficult. The descent led to another plain of a similar character to that which we had crossed: it was enlivened, however, by the occasional encampments of shepherds and flocks of sheep. These seemed to be in good condition, but

the wool was coarse: they are an article of export to Yarkand. Neat cattle of an inferior sort were also grazing on the plain in considerable numbers. We were obliged to make a long march on this day, as no water was found at the abdan, or reservoir, where it had been intended to halt: we had, therefore, to continue our march to the foot of a range of low hills, in which another reservoir, the third on the road, was situated. These reservoirs are constructed of brick, covered over by a dome, and were formerly fed by a canal from Yang Arekh: they seem now to derive their supply from the rain alone, and the water in them was yellow and fetid. There was, however, a sufficiency in the third, or Abdan Bash, and we were not fastidious as to its quality. At this place the sides of the hills were plentifully peopled by the bushy-tailed rat, the *Mus Hamster* of Pallas. A large spotted lizard was also frequent, burrowing in holes in the ground.

I had scarcely laid down to rest when Izzet Ullah came to inform me that a portion of our escort had received orders from Kunduz to return to Tash Kurghan on the following

morning, and bring from thence the whole of our party. Looking upon this as of evil augury, I determined to send back the men of my own whom I had brought with me, and wrote to Mr. Trebeck to desire him to avoid moving, if possible; hoping that I might be able to prevail upon Murad Beg to retract his orders.

We were early on horseback on the 18th, and ascended the pass of Arganna, whence the plain of Kunduz came in view, level and broad like the others, but bounded everywhere, except to the north, by mountains, of which those of Badakshan, to the south-east, were covered with snow. In the early part of our march we passed the village of Akserai, a few houses on a rivulet, which we crossed by a temporary bridge. Farther on we were entangled amongst swamps, thickly overgrown with rushes, amidst which the paths occasionally united in one narrow track, scarcely broad enough for a single horseman. These terminated on the left bank of the Ghori river, which was about fifty yards across. One of its heads, as has been observed, was the water of Doaba, and

at about a day's journey to the north it falls, along with six other streams, into the Oxus at Killa Zal.

At three miles from this, to the north, we reached Kunduz, and after passing through a mean bazar, were conducted into the old fort, part of which was in a ruinous condition. In an angle of the fort, in a wooden porch, we found the minister, Atma Ram, attended by a number of followers. Seats were given us, and a conversation ensued, in which a sort of apology was offered for the message requiring the presence of our whole party; the Mir, it was said, being anxious to see us all. Tea was served, and a matted chamber was assigned to me for my accommodation. In the evening our conductor, the Dewan Begi of Baba Beg, came to me with an air of concern, and apprized me that some persons had been telling strange stories of us to the Mir; amongst other things, that we had a fortress concealed in our packages, with artillery which went off of its own accord, and had the power of discriminating friends from foes. The chief of Doaba had come to report that we had ninety parcels, some of which had discharged

their contents, as he had in some degree witnessed. Other accounts stated that some of our chests were full of gold and jewels; and these various reports had so stimulated the curiosity and cupidity of the Mir, that he was resolved to inspect the whole of our bales and chests in person. To this I contented myself with replying, that I had come into the country upon the Mir's own assurances of security and protection; that I was in his hands, and he might use his power; but that I would not consent to have my merchandise brought to Kunduz. That with regard to the examination of the packages, the officers of Baba Beg at Tash Kurghan might select any three or four and open them, and compare them with our lists; when, if they were found to correspond, it was hoped that the whole might be passed in the usual manner. The Dewan Begi said he should report what I stated, but he repeated his story so often, that I began to suspect he was under the influence of a beverage, to which the Mir himself is said to be addicted, a strong spirit obtained from camel's milk by fermentation.

On the following morning I had a long con-

versation with Atma Ram upon our affairs: he seemed to be a reasonable man, and willing to accede to my proposals, but had no independent authority. He conducted me to his master, who, it was announced, expected us. We left the fort for a new edifice of clay, surrounded by a moat, which was crossed by a bridge. The gateway opened into a court, from the opposite front of which a covered passage led to a second court of considerable extent. On the right was an area, of which three sides were flanked by a broad veranda with a flat roof, supported by wooden pillars; the floor was raised above the level of the court about three feet. In this, on our left, was seated Mir Mohammed Murad Beg, in the centre of a line of some thirty or forty courtiers, who were seated on their knees, with their feet to the wall, their bodies inclined forwards, and their looks directed to the ground. On the floor of the area stood a long line of attendants in front of the chief, some with white wands, and all bending their bodies slightly forward, and declining their heads. Between them and the veranda, im-

mediately opposite the chief, sat the Arż Begi, or presenter of petitions. The whole was orderly and respectful: not a sound was heard, nor did a limb move, when Izzet Ullah and myself advanced and saluted the chief with the usual Salám Ali-kum. We were desired to take our places in the next veranda, where a carpet had been spread for us. A prayer was then said, after which all present stroked their beards with the most profound gravity. The courtiers wore large turbans, and long loose tunics, either of striped chintz or shot silk. The Mir sat upon a cushion of China damask, which raised him above his courtiers. His tunic was of blue silk, with a sash of the same, but he wore over it an open coat, apparently of wool, of an almond colour: he had on long brown boots, with high iron-tipped heels. He appeared to be about forty-five, and was of a dark complexion, with decided Uzbek features, and eyes so small, that when he smiled, which he did frequently, they were scarcely visible. The attendants were all very smartly clad in dresses of Bokhara silks, and the whole had a more uniform and re-

spectable character than any Asiatic court at which I was ever present: not a single person wore any offensive weapons.

The chief, after a short while, said he had sent for us to satisfy his curiosity and converse with us. My presents were laid before him by one of my servants, of whom he inquired if he was a Musselman. Prepared for this question by what had occurred with Baba Beg, the man replied that he was, and that hundreds of thousands of Mohammedans were the servants of the English, whom they found kind and good masters. The Mir made no comment, but cast his eyes over the presents, and seemed satisfied with them. He then commenced a series of questions regarding the extent of the British possessions in Hindustan, the name of the Governor-General, the amount of the revenue of India in former times and at present, the nature of our relations with Ranjit Sinh, and why we were not at war with him. He asked my name, my age, my place of residence, and the objects of my journey. Speaking of horses, he inquired if I was fond of them, and being answered in the affirmative, ordered some of his to be

passed before me, desiring me to point out those of which I most approved; and, on my so doing, asked particularly on what points my opinion of the goodness of a horse was formed. When this was explained to him, he observed, that I should not find such horses as I looked for in his country; his horses were active and capable of fatigue, more so than the Turkman, but that I should meet with good horses at Shehr Sabz and Bokhara.

After some further questions, which he appeared to put after much reflection, frequently pushing up his turban, and passing his hand across his forehead, he asked if I ate the food of Musselmans, and being answered that I did, ordered some bread and slices of melon to be placed before me; some pears and pomegranates were presented to him, and he distributed them amongst his courtiers: a plate of them was also handed to us. We were dismissed with civility, and in the evening the chief sent me a fat sheep, with rice and fruit.

On the evening of the following day Murad Beg sent for Izzet Ullah, and conversed with him till late at night. According to the Mir's

report, the conversation turned upon the British power in India, and our military discipline and resources. He inquired also minutely into the state of parties in Afghanistan, indicating a strong disposition to take advantage of its distracted condition. He also asked many questions concerning the political institutions and power of England, and made a number of just and pertinent remarks on the difference between them and those of Turkistan. With regard to myself, the chief remarked that he had been informed it was the practice of Europeans to send spies and secret emissaries into foreign countries, preparatory to their subjugation, and that he had been informed such was my real character. To this the Mir replied, that had I been a spy, I should have come in disguise, not avowedly as an Englishman, and that I had no other object than the establishment of a commercial intercourse, which would be as beneficial to Turkistan as to India. Murad Beg said this might be, but many were attempting to deceive him in regard to us, and he was determined to judge for himself. Our chests, he had been informed, contained an immense

treasure in gold and jewels. This was of course denied, and he was assured that our chests contained only such articles as had been offered to him, of which he might easily be satisfied, by having some of them opened by his officers at Tash Kurghan; that great inconvenience and expense would be incurred by removing the whole to Kunduz, and that I had come into his country in full reliance upon his good faith and entire confidence in the contents of his letter. After much hesitation Murad Beg at last acceded to the arrangement, and the Dewan Begi was ordered to accompany us to Tash Kurghan.

I may here remark, that the absurdly exaggerated accounts of the value of my goods might be traced to the ingratitude and treachery of some of my own people. At Kabul, the rapacity of Habib Ullah was excited by the reports of an Englishman, a deserter, of the name of Lyons, whom I had found in Kashmir in a state of great destitution, and had brought with me to Kabul. This man assured the Afghan he could point out chests filled with jewels and gold. Similar stories had been circulated on my subsequent march

by Khyum Khaja, a native of Hissar, whom I had been prevailed upon, against my own judgment, to take into my service at Kashmir. He became so obnoxious to all the people by his dishonesty, meanness, and quarrelsomeness, that I was obliged to discharge him from my service, but in compassion permitted him to accompany our caravan, as he would otherwise have run a risk of being taken and made a slave of on the road to his own home. At several places on our route we detected him in exciting suspicion of our objects, and spreading exaggerated reports of our wealth, and he was now one of those who had lab ured, with a malevolence scarcely conceivable, to prejudice the mind of Murad Beg against us.

Khyum Khaja was corroborated in his calumnies by a physician of Kabul, settled at Tash Kurghan, who had endeavoured to force himself into my employ, and being disappointed, repaired to Murad Beg with a tissue of falsehoods, relating both to Izzet Ullah and myself. A third enemy was a man who had been a servant of Mr. Elphinstone, whom he accompanied to Calcutta. There he became a professed convert to Christianity, but had

returned to Turkistan and to his former faith. This man, after an audience with Murad Beg, publicly boasted that he had done for the Europeans, and had prevailed upon the chief to put them to death and seize their property. These two, however, unlike the preceding, added not ingratitude to malevolence. Another person from whom I experienced a similar return for kindness was an Armenian, but he was the least culpable of the three. The best servants I have met with in my journeys are Hindustanis, engaged in their own country. Those picked up on the road are less entitled to confidence, but even they are preferable to natives of any other part of Asia.

A dispatch from Mr. Trebeck, brought by a courier in nine hours, informed me he had been much pressed to move with all our baggage to Kunduz, but had hitherto persisted in awaiting fresh instructions from me. He also expressed himself anxious to join me, as the idea of his being in safety, whilst I was exposed to danger, was intolerable, and he was satisfied that the owners of the goods in our charge would never place their preservation in comparison with my personal security. Baba

Beg had been very earnest with Mr. Trebeck to quit Tash Kurghan, assuming a friendly tone, and warning him against his superior, who, he said, was a cruel tyrant that would not scruple to attain his ends by violence. At the same time he offered to take, privately, charge of any gold or jewels we might have, and be responsible for their safe redelivery. He was thanked for his offers, but was told that we had nothing to conceal—a reply that evidently afforded him but little satisfaction.

Before setting out on my return I inspected, at the desire of the chief, a piece of ordnance in his possession. It was a brass cannon of considerable size, cast, as a Persian inscription denoted, by Yakub Firingi, for the Persian king, Shah Tamasp; the vent had been spiked, and though this might have been remedied, there was no artificer in Kunduz who could repair it. The gun had been dragged hither from Balkh by fifteen pair of oxen.

It had been settled that we should depart on the 22nd; but it had occurred to the chief that his minister might take the opportunity of conducting from two to three thousand sheep to Tash Kurghan, to be sold there in-

stead of being forwarded to Yarkand, as the season was far advanced. The passage of these occupied so long, that our journey was deferred till the following day. I took the lead, in the hope of meeting with game, and roused some pheasants, of which I killed one. The sedgy land in the neighbourhood of Kunduz abounds with game,—partridges, pheasants, the yellow grouse, and hares. In the desert plain, between this and the left bank of the Amu or Oxus, deer, foxes, wolves, hogs, and lions, are numerous; the latter resemble those in the vicinity of Hariana. We reached Tash Kurghan on the afternoon of the 24th.

On the third day after our return the Dewan Begi, with his deputy, Bysakhi Ram, took from our books the account and particulars of our merchandise; and we also apprized the Dewan, privately, that we had a small quantity of pearls and coral, which we did not wish to produce in public, as their value might be exaggerated by common report. The Dewan acquiesced in the prudence of not publicly noting these articles. He inspected some of our chests, which he admitted contained articles of necessity, not of merchan-

dise. We invited him to open any of the bales, but this he postponed, and seemed to think the business would be easily and speedily adjusted. Some days, however, elapsed, and no further communication was received; at last, after several applications to the Dewan Begi, Bysakhi appeared and said that all the bales must be opened. That with regard to chintzes, a horse-load was valued at one hundred and forty pieces, which was here sold for sixty tilas, of which two were deducted for duty. Now the fact was, that the usual duty was one in forty, not in thirty; but this was not worth disputing. Broad-cloths, he said, were never before brought, and their value could be only decided by actual inspection. To this I objected as injurious to the articles, and contrary to the arrangement authorised by the chief at Kunduz. These fresh delays appeared to me to be an excuse for extorting money. Bysakhi Ram had said, on the morning of the inspection, he was an umedwar (an expectant), and was answered, that his meaning was understood. He wished to receive a bribe; but concession in this respect would have been criminal and degrading.

We had professed our readiness to conform to the usages of the country, and even to go further, in submitting to have our bales opened in the manner I proposed—a thing never done with native merchants. I foresaw a scheme, either to extort money by bribe, or by exorbitant duty, or to force a sale at Tash Kurghan, in order that the Hindus might reap the profit of a resale at Bokhara. However, I was resolved not to offer any bribe.

Our prospects continued without improvement, and repeated efforts to obtain a specific demand from the Dewan Begi were fruitless. At last, through the intervention of a Hindu trader, it was communicated to us, that nothing less than a payment of twenty thousand rupees would be received in lieu of duties, as our merchandise was estimated at eight lakhs of rupees. As this demand was wholly disproportionate to the expected out-turn of the goods, we declared it impossible that we could accede to it, and offered instead the following alternatives;—to pay one in forty upon a lakh and a half of rupees; to sell our goods to the Dewan for a lakh and a half; or to allow him to open the bales and take one article in each

forty. To anything beyond this it could not in justice be expected we should agree. These proposals, however, were disregarded, and the demand for twenty thousand rupees was reiterated.

As the case seemed to be hopeless, it became necessary to make the best terms we could for our deliverance from actual durance, for as matters stood, no Kafila Bashi would venture to furnish means of transport for our goods, and the Mir came forward to do what I had before urged, but what, from feelings which I could not satisfactorily develope, he had hitherto evaded, visit the Dewan Begi, and learn his final determination. He found the Dewan full of professions, but declaring his inability to act from himself. It was finally settled, however, that we should be let off on payment of the following sums:—Duty, three thousand seven hundred and fifty rupees; Dewan Begi, one thousand two hundred; Bysakhi, three hundred; which, with the value of the presents to Murad Beg and his servants, made a total disbursement of nearly seven thousand rupees.

After the payment of this sum it was pre-

sumed that we might at once prosecute our journey, but an order was issued by the governor of Tash Kurghan, prohibiting any persons from leaving the place, as Murad Beg had marched on some expedition, and did not wish information of his departure from Kunduz to be spread abroad. The Dewan assured us that he had dispatched a message to his master to announce that all things were arranged with us, and that we should soon have permission to depart. Nine days passed without news. The Dewan Begi then went to meet the Mir at Kamand, but on the road was ordered to dispossess the governor of Ghori, and take his place. No tidings were received from him up to the 21st of October, although Bysakhi pretended to expect a letter from him from day to day.

In the mean time our party sustained some serious losses by defection and disease. Mir Izzet Ullah Khan, as I have before observed, had long entertained but indifferent hopes of the successful prosecution of our journey, and the transactions at Kunduz were ill calculated to inspirit his expectations. He looked upon us as little better than prisoners, with a

very remote prospect of escape; and, to increase his alarm, he was taken ill with the bilious remittent fever, which prevails in the country about Kunduz, and despaired of recovering, a Turkestani, a servant of his, and another person, a traveller, having recently died of the complaint. The Mir recovered, but insisted upon it that he should die if he remained longer in the country, and, however reluctant to quit us, he could not resign himself to the prospect of never seeing his country or his family again. I at first withheld my consent, but his distress was so great that it excited Mr. Trebeck's compassion as well as my own, and I gave my permission to his departure, furnishing him with a letter of recommendation to the Governor General's agent at Delhi. On the 19th he departed, having asked me for the service of Askar Ali Khan, a friend of his, whom he had introduced to me, and who was to return. I directed him to endeavour to come back to me by way of Bajaor, Chitral, and Badakhshan, so as to ascertain the practicability of avoiding Afghanistan. My writer of accounts, Mir Mahmud, also took his departure.

On the 22nd of October a message arrived from the Mir to Baba Beg, ordering him to send the Europeans to Kunduz. Some of the people of Murad Beg had been severely wounded in his attack upon the Hazaras of Kamand, and he required our surgical assistance. He also desired we would bring some of our men, that he might inspect their military exercise. Although apprehensive that this was a mere pretext for separating and weakening us, it was of no avail to resist, and on the 23rd, therefore, accompanied by Mr. Guthrie and ten of our escort, I retraced my steps to Kunduz. On our march, when near the middle reservoir, we were overtaken by a sudden storm of wind, which brought with it such a cloud of dust that it was utterly impossible to distinguish objects a few feet distant, and the whole of the surrounding atmosphere was darkened. This happened at night, but the obscurity continued for several hours after sun-rise, and we were obliged to halt the whole time, in the fear of missing our road. The wind did not abate until the afternoon. When we arrived the apartment I had formerly occupied was in the possession

of some Turkman horse dealers, and no other accommodation was provided. The Dewan Begi was reported to be in consultation with the chief, and we were glad to lie down on the floor of a small open chamber, where, notwithstanding my fatigue, the restless activity of the fleas precluded all chance of repose. Nothing was heard of the Dewan Begi till the afternoon of the next day, when he appeared with Mirza Rahmat, a secretary of the chief. The countenance of the former seemed stiffened into a singular hardness of expression, and he began his discourse by observing that reports had reached the chief of his having accepted a bribe of four thousand tilas, or twenty-four thousand rupees, to conclude the arrangement he had made with us regarding the duties; that he had informed the Mir of his having, almost by force, obtained from us first one sum and then another, in which, by the way, I observed he said nothing of the one thousand two hundred rupees he had himself received, and that it was unlikely he should have endangered all that he owed to his master's bounty to serve a person whom he had never seen

before, and might never see again: the Mir, he said, had been, in some degree, pacified by his representations, but it seemed as if much depended upon my reply, and that the secretary was there to witness it. Although I had no great reason to be satisfied with Atma Ram's conduct, I could not be accessary to his degradation, or, perhaps, his murder, and I, therefore, at once observed that, having actually paid more than the usual rate of one in forty, it would have been monstrously absurd in me to have given to any one four thousand tilas, four hundred, or even forty. My answer produced an instant relaxation of his features, and, after observing that Europeans were superior to deceit, he departed, stating the Mir would see me on the following morning. Accordingly I waited on the chief, and made a present to him of one of the beautiful guns made by Mr. Donnithorne. He was highly pleased with it, and asked if I could make such? When told that I could not, he repeated the question to Gholam Hyder Khan, who was with me, and received a similar reply. In the course of conversation he said he had heard that I had

been shooting near Kunduz, and that I was very welcome to pursue the sport wherever I pleased. I replied that my game lay near Bokhara, to which I was anxious to proceed as soon as he would release me. The answer did not exactly please him, and I was desired to withdraw, but, after the Durbar, many persons congratulated me on my reply, the question being considered as a trap to discover if I was desirous of an opportunity of making myself acquainted with the country.

On the following day the secretary assisted me in the composition of a memorial, which, on the next morning, I presented to the Mir, who said he would inquire into the contents, it having been represented to him that my journey was a mere pretence, and that I had other objects than merchandize or horses. I had been privately informed by Atma Ram that the Turkistani above referred to was the chief author of these calumnies, and I desired the Mir to confront me with any person who would prefer such false accusations. This, he said, was not possible. I then asked him how he proposed to inquire. He said he

would write to the Hakm of Kabul, and Dost Mohammed Khan. I reminded him that I had brought a letter from that chief, and that further reference to him was unnecessary. As he seemed bent upon some such application, I referred him to the Sahebzanda, Mir Fazl Hak, who had gone on to Bokhara, and whose testimony he admitted would be decisive. He desired me not to be impatient, as the delay of two or three weeks would be of no importance; but I hesitated not to express my sense of his treatment, and told him he might as well take off my head at once, as cause the ruin of my property. This, he said, should be perfectly secure, and, for that purpose, should be conveyed to Kunduz, where I must remain: it should not be touched if the bales were filled with gold. I was then dismissed, with the conviction that my goods were actually on the road; and accordingly on the following day they arrived, with Mr. Trebeck and the rest of my party. In the evening also, Mir Izzet Ullah joined us: he had been stopped by order of Murad Beg, at Ghori, where he had had a relapse, and, notwithstanding his illness, was compelled to return

to the unhealthy situation of Kunduz. He brought with him a letter from the Kohistanis to Murad Beg, proposing to him to join them in a descent upon Kabul, in which they engaged to establish his authority. The Mir had also engaged to advocate their application, an undertaking of which I could not but disapprove, and I enjoined him, at any rate, not to implicate us in the negotiation.

It occurred to me, upon consideration, that I had with me vouchers of which Murad Beg could scarcely refuse to admit the authority, in letters from Mahmud Shah, when king of Kabul; from Fatteh Khan, the Wazir; from Nand Ram, the Dewan; and from Mir Kalich Ali Khan, the late Atalik of Khulm. They were of old date, having been written in answer to my application when, twelve years before, I was projecting a journey to Turkistan; but they were all couched in a friendly tone, encouraging me to pay them a visit, and would afford undeniable testimony to my character. I showed them to the Dewan Begi, and to the Yesawal of Baba Beg, who had been formerly in the service of Kalich Ali, and recognised his signet. They were both

of opinion that they should be submitted to the chief, and accompanied me to him for that purpose. We found him seated on the floor of the area, in the veranda of which he usually gave audience; some strangers were seated on felts, about twelve yards before him. In front of him stood the secretary, and Mirza Yakub, the governor of Kunduz, sat on his right hand. When we were seated at a similar distance as the other strangers, I explained the object of my waiting upon him, and delivered to him the letters above mentioned. The secretary read each of them aloud; but when he had half-perused that of Kalich Ali, the patience of Murad Beg was exhausted, and he broke out into a volley of abuse against the writers, calling Mahmud Shah an opium eater, Fatteh Khan a bhang-drinker, and Kalich Ali by some equally abusive epithet, whilst he addressed me by the appellation of Kafir. The letters, he said, were twenty-four years old, and, therefore, of no value. I observed that he had made a mistake of twelve years, and that if the weight of the document depended upon its date, I could produce one not twelve months old, a letter of Mir Mo-

hammed Murad Beg, which invited me into his country, under assurances that I should experience the same treatment as other foreign merchants. As I uttered this with some warmth, it increased the irritation of the chief, who talked with a volubility and indistinctness which rendered it impossible for me to comprehend more than the expressions infidel, and armed men. An individual present, who I understood was the Governor of Hazrat Imam, joined the chief in inveighing against us; but before he had finished his oration Murad Beg jumped up from his cushion, and retired hastily into his apartments, on which the assembly broke up. I remained for a short time to collect my papers, and, somewhat unluckily, dropped the chief's letter, of which, however, I had a copy. The result of this conference had not tended to brighten our prospects, but it seemed that it had not the effect of rendering them darker, for on the following morning Mirza Yakub came to me for the purpose of allaying any apprehensions I might entertain in consequence of our interview, and assured me from the chief, that nothing wrong was intended. A similar

message was repeated on the following day by a Khajeh Zada, of Balkh. There was no alternative but patience; but, apprehensive that we might be detained under the pretence that the messenger to Fazl Hakh had not returned, I dispatched to Bokhara a servant of my own, with letters to the Pir Zada, and to Mir Wazir Ahmed, to apprise them of all that had occurred.

Whilst we were thus detained, a confederacy was formed against Murad Beg by the neighbouring chiefs, amongst whom were the Wali of Aibek; Zulfakar Sher, of Siripol; Ishan Khan, of Balkh; the chief of Mazar, and others; who had raised a force of eight thousand men, better equipped and mounted than those of Murad Beg. He had, however, increased his force to twenty thousand, by levies of militia, who held lands on condition of military service.

CHAPTER IV.

Favourable testimonials—Return of Wazir Ahmed—Extortion of Murad Beg—Departure to Khulm—Izzet Ullah's final departure—Absence of Mr. Guthrie—Tash Kurghan—Old Khulm—Renewed summons to Kunduz—Charges by Mohammed Amin—Flight of Mr. Moorcroft to Talikan—Appeal to Kasim Ján, the spiritual guide of Murad Beg—He takes Mr. Moorcroft under his protection—Interviews with Baba Beg and Khan Jan—Confronted with Mohammed Amin—The latter dismissed—Private fepresentations of the Pir Zada—Arrival of Murad Beg—Final adjustment.

During the absence of the chief, couriers arrived both from Bokhara and Kabul, in reply to his letters, bearing testimony to our inoffensive character, and our being what we represented ourselves, merchants. The son of the Mir who had been left in the fort assured us that his father was satisfied that we had been misrepresented, and that in a few days we should be at liberty to proceed: days passed on, however, and no such liberty was given; and even after Murad Beg's return no

notice was taken of us. The child of his eldest son, Khan Jan, being taken ill, Mr. Guthrie was ordered to go to Talikan, about forty miles from Kunduz, where the prince resided, to prescribe for it. Luckily the complaint was not serious, and was subdued without his interference. The father of the infant generously presented him with a coarse striped cotton gown, worth about three rupees, as a remuneration for his journey.

Mir Wazir Ahmed, who had gone on our behalf to Bokhara, and had found in the king a disposition favourable to our visit to that city, learning our embarrassments at Kunduz, came to us to endeavour to effect our extrication. He had been the agent through whose means the permission of Murad Beg for our coming had been obtained, and he now adjured him, if he had any regard to his character, not to violate the pledge of safe conduct which he had given. Murad Beg replied to his remonstrances, "What have I, what has an Uzbek to do with character? Do I not sit here to plunder the faithful, and shall I withhold my hands from an infidel?" The Mirza then said that he would bring disgrace

upon his Pir Zada, or spiritual guide, Mir Fazl Hak, by disregarding his intercession, and this so far weighed with the robber that he said, as the holy man took an interest in us, he would let us off for fifty thousand rupees, otherwise we must have a taste of the summer of Kunduz. "Tell them," he concluded, "what I say, and let us hear their reply." My answer was, that I had no money, and he might do his pleasure. The Dewan Begi was then sent to us to endeavour to make some settlement, and after much discussion it was agreed that we should be suffered to depart on payment of ten thousand rupees to the Mir, and two thousand to Atma Ram. This being determined, we had an audience of the Beg, who affected to receive us as friends, and talked to me of his ailments, and asked me to prescribe for him; his civility was evidently inspired by the complacency he felt at having so successfully concluded his machinations against us.

On the 17th of December we once more began our march to Tash Kurghan. Izzet Ullah had departed the day preceding to Hindustan, and Mir Wazir Ahmed succeeded

to his situation. Heavy rain fell, and the river of Ghori was so much swollen as to be forded with difficulty. One of the camels, carrying a kojama in which were a servant of Mr. Trebeck, and an old cook, Ismail, fell, and the two men were thrown into the water. The cook, who was paralytic, would have been drowned, but was saved by Mr. Trebeck; the other man made his way out, but a valuable compass, entrusted to his charge, was lost, and we had none left but such as were of an inferior description. We reached Tash Kurghan without further mischances, and were welcomed by Baba Beg with apparent, and by many of the townspeople with unaffected cordiality. I found on my arrival a Kasid from Kabul, who brought me a certificate that I was, as I pretended to be, a merchant, bearing the seals of fifty of the principal merchants and bankers of Kabul, who had, unsolicited, prepared and forwarded this voucher when they heard of our detention, and the reason assigned for it. The man had been here a fortnight, having been prevented, on various pretexts, from proceeding to Kunduz.

However anxious to get clear of the terri-

tory of Murad Beg, we were obliged to remain some time, in the hope of being joined by Mr. Guthrie, who had been desired by the chief to proceed to Hazrat Imam, to visit a sick person there. A week having elapsed, we began to apprehend that some new design was on foot to delay our advance, and resolved to wait no longer, being assured that Mr. Guthrie should be forwarded to us with a suitable escort. I also wrote to that gentleman to explain the necessity of no longer awaiting his return, and directing him what measures to adopt, fully expecting that he would overtake us at Balkh, where we should have to halt for three or four days.

Tash Kurghan is about three miles in circumference, and may comprise about twenty thousand houses. They are built of clay and sun-dried bricks, of one story, with domes in the usual fashion of the country, and each stands by itself in a walled enclosure, often containing fruit-trees. The streets are straight, of a moderate breadth, intersecting each other at right angles, and have commonly a stream of water running through them. A branch of the river of Doaba, increased by many rivulets,

passes through the town, but it is absorbed by the soil soon after it has passed old Khulm. Nothing can be more cheerless than the streets of Tash Kurghan, formed as they are of lines of bare walls, and very little frequented, except on bazar days. It is rare to meet with five or six men in the line of a long street; and if a woman be seen, she is so muffled up that it is impossible to form any notion of her person. The inhabitants are chiefly Tajiks and Kabulis, with a sprinkling of Uzbeks. They are all, rich or poor, dressed much alike, in long gowns of striped cotton ginghams. Bazars are held every Monday and Thursday, when horses, asses, mules, camels, cows, sheep, and goats, are brought to their respective markets. The horses were numerous in the time of Kalich Ali, but are now few: a sheep sells at from two to four rupees; they are of the large-tail variety, and the fat of the tail and along the back is commonly one-third of the weight of the sheep, inclusive of the bones. Cotton cloths, cotton in the pod, tanned leather, raw hides, fuel, grapes, raisins, pistachio nuts, pomegranates, dried plums, fossil salt, brown leather boots with iron-shod heels, dyes, as

the pomegranate bark, madder (indigenous), and indigo, from Hindùstan, are exposed for sale, along with blankets of fine wool from Chitral, and raw wool from thence and Badahksha. Printed chintzes, quilts, and turbans are also brought from India. Coarse saddlery is much in request. There is one market entirely for melons, which are raised in this neighbourhood in great quantities.

The shops for dyes and drugs are usually kept by Hindus, who also act, in a small way, as bankers. The vendors of dried fruits are mostly from Kabul. The number of the Kabulis increased considerably even during our detention, in consequence of the disturbances in Afghanistan. The Uzbeks engage little in traffic. The trade with Yarkand is almost monopolised by Atma Ram. He buys up the sheep and furs of Kunduz, which are exchanged at Yarkand for tea, disposed of in Turkistan at an advance of six hundred per cent. The following were the prices of different articles at the time of our visit :—

Mutton, four to five pysa per charah, or two pounds and a half.
Beef, three pysa, do.

Sheeptail fat, eight pysa per charah.
Sheep butter, twenty-four do.
Cow butter, twenty do.
Wheat-flour, seven do. for four do.
Bread, four or five loaves for four pysa.
Oil, sixteen pysa a charah.
Rice, four do. do.
Barley, about one maund and a half for a rupee.

The pysa is the fiftieth part of a Mahmud Shahi rupee.

The workmen in wood, leather, and metal were very indifferent, but demanded high wages, half to three quarters of a rupee per day. Most of them, in fact, had lands, and were, in some degree, independent of labour.

There were four tolerably good serais for travellers. The town was guarded by two forts, one on an eminence on the right bank of the river, to the south-east, the other on the left bank, and on the plain: both are of earth, and of no strength.

The town is surrounded by a wall of earth, with wooden gates, a sufficient protection against sudden incursions of horsemen, but none against artillery. The people of Tash Kurghan had been threatened the year before with a compulsory removal to Kunduz, to which Murad Beg occasionally transplants

whole villages or towns. Last year he had carried thither the population of Sar-bagh and Khulm, and that of Tash Kurghan escaped only by largely bribing his officers. The havock made by the fever of Kunduz would soon depopulate the valley, if it was not thus despotically and cruelly maintained.

Old Khulm is situated about four miles from Tash Kurghan. It was a place of importance in the time of Kalich Ali, but its situation on the plain exposed it to the predatory incursions of the Khattaghans beyond the mountains, whilst, on this side, the Hazaras dammed up or diverted the course of the river, upon which the fertilization of its soil depended. The chief, therefore, removed his capital to Tash Kurghan, much to the regret of the people of Khulm, whose orchards had been celebrated throughout the East for the quantity and quality of their produce.

The consequences which we apprehended from the delay of our departure did not fail to occur, and we were soon made to feel that we were not yet out of the clutches of the Khattaghan robber. The camels were assembled close to our encampment, the packages

were corded, and the Kafila Bashi was distributing them amongst the drivers, when we were astounded by the news that a message had arrived from Kunduz to direct that our baggage should be detained, and that I should be sent back. The message was brought by Torab Beg, the principal Yesawal, with instructions to compel obedience, if necessary, and he was accompanied by a strong party of horse, who were posted round our camp. The Yesawal reported that Mulla Mohammed Amin, the person spoken of as formerly in Mr. Elphinstone's service, as soon as the news of our liberation reached him had hastened to Kunduz, and had thrown his turban at the feet of the chief, pledging himself to prove me to be a person of great importance, engaged as a spy, preparatory to the invasion of Turkistan, which would most certainly fall into the hands of the infidels, unless Murad Beg baffled their designs by putting me and my whole party to death. The chief, on this representation, announced his resolve that, unless I paid two lakhs of rupees, I should pass the summer at Kunduz, calculating, no doubt, upon my

death or destruction, and that of my principal followers, when he would sell the survivors as slaves, and seize upon our property. Convinced that nothing but evil was designed, I declared my unwillingness to go to Kunduz, when it was proposed that Mr. Trebeck should go instead. To this I refused assent, as, if there was the personal danger which we apprehended, it was for me to encounter it. The Yesawal then said, unless one of us consented to accompany him he must use force, rather than afford a pretext for which, I submitted. I declared, however, that I would not depart that evening, as he wished me to do, but would be ready to accompany him early the next morning. He had been all the previous night upon the road, and was not sorry, apparently, to have a reasonable excuse for repose: he, therefore, agreed to allow me to remain over the night, and this, at least, gave us an opportunity of considering what was to be done.

The detachment which had attended the Yesawal, amounting to about two hundred horse, were posted for the night in two divisions, one in our front at about one hundred

paces, the other in our rear rather more distant. My young friend proposed that we should divide our party into two bodies, and fall upon the Uzbeks in the night, disperse them, seize their horses, and make a forced march out of the territory of the Kattaghan chief. The plan was feasible, for, although inferior in number, we were better appointed and disciplined, and our men, holding the Uzbeks very cheap, were quite prepared, and indeed anxious for a trial of strength. I entertained little doubt of our success, but it could only be effected by loss of life on either side, and, although we might escape, the vengeance of Murad Beg would be wreaked upon Mr. Guthrie and his servants. Upon full consideration, and in concert with a native friend, who was attached to our interests, I determined to try a different scheme; to leave my tents privately during the night, and repair to Kasim Jan, Khaja of Talikan, the Pir, or spiritual guide and father-in-law of Murad Beg, and implore his intercession.

In order to elude the vigilance of the Yesawal and his detachment, it was agreed that three of my horses should be led into the

town, as if to be in readiness for the morning's journey, that after nightfall they should be conducted to a burying-ground at some distance, by a couple of trusty persons, who were to act as my guides to Talikan, and that I should endeavour to join them as soon and as secretly as practicable. The horses were sent off. As the evening advanced the guard was reinforced, and horsemen from the town were continually approaching and parading round my tent. No time was to be lost: going forth in my usual attire, and inspecting my sentinels, I returned, and in a few minutes threw an Uzbek silk dress over my own, with an upper woollen mantle commonly worn, put a sheepskin cap upon my head, enfolded at bottom by a lungi or turban, one end of which hung loose, and the other was brought across my mouth and chin, so as to conceal my face and want of beard; and thus equipped, I sallied forth on foot, directing my path towards an unfrequented part of the mountains, concealing my person as much as possible, by descending into ravines and hollows. The moon was young, but rain fell, and the clouds augmented the obscurity of the night. Hav-

ing walked about half a mile, I with some difficulty made out the place where I was to meet my guides, and at last found them at their posts, with one of my own people, and our three horses. We mounted and galloped to the south, until we reached the foot of the mountain, when, skirting the adjacent portion of the town, we followed the foot of the range for some miles, finding our way with difficulty. The path we had taken was little frequented, and as the badness of the night was unfavourable to travelling, we met with no one upon the road. At Yang Arekh we were embarrassed amongst the ruins, but at last cleared them, and passed close to the fort without being observed. Beyond this place the plain, without tree or shrub, was fetlock deep in water, and our horses had great difficulty in making way over the clayey soil. At Bash Abdan we were nearly detected, for my guides having imprudently entered to light a pipe, found there a party of Hindus, the servants of the Dewan Begi. Luckily I remained without awaiting their return. At the pass of Shahbagli some uncertainty prevailed as to our proper road, and my guides, after some

time, found themselves at the bottom of a ravine, where it became necessary to dismount and wait the break of day. However, on the rain diminishing and the atmosphere clearing a little, we resumed confidence, and discovered a path by which we crossed the mountain, just as the day was beginning to dawn. Providential it was that we had not traversed the mountain in the night by the usual road, for in the grey of the morning we discerned, at the eastern foot of the pass, the fires of a party which must have been one of alemans, or banditti, as travellers never halt in such a situation. We continued our advance on the direct road, as if we had not noticed them; but as soon as we had got behind a rising ground, which screened us from view, we turned off to the north, and galloped hard until we thought ourselves out of danger of pursuit. Proceeding on the same line, we came to an abdan, or a path which led to the Oxus, and then returned to the direction of Kunduz. Leaving it a short distance to our left, we rode to the east and south, traversing a large extent of barren plain. After many deviations, which made me apprehend the competency of my

guides, we observed some Uzbeks fording the Ghori river, and followed their direction. The river was about a hundred yards broad, and the current was rapid. We then rode on till it was dark, when we came upon an Uzbek encampment, where it was thought we might venture to stop and give our horses a feed of barley, which we had brought in our saddle-bags. The animals had been without food for twenty-four hours. One of my men, who spoke Turki like an Uzbek, went amongst their tents to purchase some milk and salted tea, whilst I lay down upon a felt, and the other guide who remained with me replied to those who inquired who I was, that I was his fellow traveller, and was very ill with fever. Milk was not procurable, but we obtained a little tea. I was then anxious to depart, but my guides were overcome with fatigue, and I was obliged to consent to their taking about an hour's rest. We then remounted and rode on. The night was dark, and the path was indistinct, and when it wanted about three hours of day my guides declared they could not venture to proceed, as they were uncertain of the road. We were

therefore obliged to halt till towards dawn, when we were joined by another benighted traveller, from whose information it was ascertained that we had lost our way. It was with great difficulty that we recovered it, and the morning had fairly broke, when it was discovered that we had considerably retrograded, and were not above four kos in advance from Kunduz, on a track abounding with water and mud, frequently up to the horses' knees. At eight o'clock we were opposite to Khanahabad, about seven kos from Kunduz. It seemed to be a large town on the right bank of the Furkhan river, with a fort of some extent, but not in good repair. We pushed on as fast as we could, and avoiding the main road, which was somewhat circuitous, forded the river and crossed a rice level. Whilst yet far distant from Talikan, a person was met who reported that Baba Beg was on his way to the same place, at some distance in our rear. We had not proceeded much farther when we had the mortification of descrying Baba Beg with a numerous party, advancing at a round pace and gaining upon us rapidly. We, however, cleared the pass that leads to

the plain of Talikan, and encountered a cavalcade, both of horse and foot, going out to meet the governor of Tash Kurghan, who was accompanied by Khan Jan, the eldest son of Murad Beg. The interchange of civilities, indispensable on such occasions, would, we hoped, delay the approach of our pursuers, if such they were, and give us time to reach the residence of the Pir. Unfortunately, this was at some distance beyond the town, and we thought it expedient to make a circuit across a ridge of mountains, in preference to traversing the town. I was here obliged to change horses with one of my guides, as my own was unable to get beyond a walk, a failure which, considering his steadiness, I ascribed to his being galled by my English saddle.

On clearing the hills we descried from an eminence an orchard within low walls, in which were a number of circular felt and matted tents, and this we were informed by an Uzbek was the residence of the Khaja. In half an hour more, and between three and four in the afternoon, we arrived at the dwelling, when I alighted, and sending in one of my guides with a letter to the Pir Zada from

Mirza Wazir Ahmed, awaited the result. In about half an hour my messenger returned, and said the Khaja would see me. I passed through a low porch formed of mats, and entered a circular chamber, on one side of which, close to the door, the saint was seated. I made the customary salutation, which was returned with courtesy. I then stooped, and taking hold of the skirt of his vest, which lay on the ground, I stated that I had a request to make, apologizing for my imperfect use of the Persian language, and any mistake or impropriety which I might in consequence commit. I stated that I was in some embarrassment as to what I had to state, as it concerned a person with whom he was closely connected. The Khaja desired me to speak freely. I accordingly entered into a full detail of the vexatious detention and extortion to which I had been subjected by Murad Beg, after having been encouraged by him to enter his dominions, and threw myself upon the equity and commiseration of the Khaja.

The Pir Zada listened very attentively to my address, and asked me one or two questions, with the replies to which he appeared to be

satisfied. When I had concluded he assured me of his good offices as far as they might avail me, and that he was willing to hope that he could secure both my property and person from any further aggression. This was a duty, he said, which he owed to a stranger who had thrown himself upon his protection, and had become his guest. It was a duty he owed to God, and from these motives alone he discharged it, not with the view or hope of any remuneration. This he said in allusion to a pair of handsome shawls and two dresses of broad cloth, which I had tendered to him according to the custom of the country. He accepted what was offered, he added, but having done so, it became him to give it back again, that it might not be reported that his interposition was interested. It was in vain that I urged his acceptance: he persisted in declining it, not through any disrespect for me, he assured me, but regard to his own reputation. After I had withdrawn to a chamber assigned for my accommodation, I was visited by Izzet Bai, a respectable merchant of Yarkand, who had been present at my interview with the Pir Zada, and who confirmed my re-

liance upon his protection. Izzet Bai was at Yarkand when Mir Izzet Ullah arrived there from Ladakh, and while he did justice to the abilities and exertions of my agent, he expressed his regret that I had not gone at once there myself, instead of sending an agent before me. The Ak-sikels, literally white wands or elders of the merchants of Badakhshan, Indijan, and Kashmir, were quite disposed to have facilitated my intercourse, but my sending a representative inspired the authorities with doubts, of which the Kashmirian, Nakaju, took advantage. This account agreed with what I had heard from other quarters, and inspired the greatest regret that I had suffered myself to be biassed against my own impression by the opinions of others.

On the following morning Baba Beg paid his respects to the Pirzada, and I was summoned to the audience: the former admitted that I had been in correspondence with his father, but said he had been directed by his superior to remove to Kunduz with my party, to await further information respecting my being a merchant. To this I replied, that

sufficient testimony had been already furnished, and that unless the Pirzada withdrew the protection he had promised, I would not leave his dwelling. After I had withdrawn I was again sent for by Baba Beg, and found him standing without the gate, whilst the Pirzada was within the court. The former said he wished to have some private conversation with me, to which I replied I was ready, but that I would not cross the threshold unless the khaja pledged his word for my safe return. The khaja smiled, and said I might go in safety. The precaution I used was quite necessary; for, agreeably to the Uzbek notions of sanctuary, it would have been no discredit to the Pirzada had I been carried off forcibly, after going forth from his house without his express sanction. When I had accompanied Baba Beg out of the house, he said I had taken the only steps that could have saved us, and advised me on no account to leave my present abode till the business was settled, and a person deputed on the part of the Pirzada to escort us to Tash Kurghan. I really believe that this individual, however

he might have been disposed to despoil us himself, would not be sorry to see us disappoint the avarice of his superior.

On the next day the Pirzada was visited by Khan Jan, and I was again sent for and interrogated, particularly on the very delicate subject of my religion. I evaded all controversy by stating, that as a merchant I pretended to no theological knowledge, that I followed the faith of my fathers, and that in my country every man was allowed full liberty of conscience. Khan Jan desired me to pronounce some of the common Arabic prayers, to which I pleaded ignorance, beyond such a formula as I had read in Persian books, and I repeated the sentence, Bismillah arrahman arrahim, to the great delight of my auditors. I took this opportunity of repeating a declaration I had made in the presence of Baba Beg, that no Uzbek had taken the slightest share in my evasion from Tash Kurghan. Khan Jan repeated the attempt of Baba Beg to decoy me forth under the pretext that he wished me to look at some of his horses. In the evening one of my servants came from Kunduz, to which place all my people and

baggage had been conveyed, with a letter from Mr. Trebeck. He informed me that my evasion, when discovered, had created the greatest consternation amongst the Uzbeks, and both Torab Beg, the Yasawal, and Baba Beg, made up their minds to suffer death from the rage and disappointment of their superiors. My servant was accompanied by Mullah Sangin, whom Mirza Wazir Ahmed had dispatched to my aid, with a letter from himself to the Pirzada, in which he alluded to the efforts made by Mohammed Amin for our destruction. I was thereupon sent for and desired to state what I knew of that person, and I gave that account of him which has been mentioned above. With regard to his apostacy from Mohammedanism, I spoke guardedly, as, although I had the fact from unquestionable authority, it was not one of which I had personal knowledge. I could see, however, that it made a deep impression upon the assembly.

Whilst walking in the outer court on the following day several persons passed me, amongst whom I observed Mullah Mohammed Amin, and a haji of Kunduz, whom

Murad Beg had sent to prejudice the Pirzada against me. My friend, Mullah Sangin, followed them to the audience-chamber, and, after a time, returned with information that they had preferred such accusations against me, and had so strenuously urged the dangerous consequences of admitting my party into Turkistan, as to have evidently alarmed the chief and many of his attendants, who were well disposed towards me. On hearing this I sent the Mullah to request that I also might be admitted to an audience, and permission was obtained. After the usual compliments, I informed the Pirzada that I had heard that persons had come to his house with charges against me, and solicited him to allow me to hear their accusations from their own mouths, questioning them myself as to what they knew against me, but engaging to press no questions which the Pirzada might think improper. The khaja acquiesced, and pointed out my adversary, a man of low stature, in attire somewhat mean and neglected, with a long beard, and a countenance sharp and intelligent, but strongly expressive of malevolence. He said to me, in

Hindustani,—"Speak in Hindustani;" but I took advantage of this to apprize the Pirzada that he wished our conversation to be carried on in a language which few present understood, and appealed to him if this was allowable?—although it was true that I could but imperfectly express myself in that more generally known. He replied, "Speak in Persian, you will be understood." I then asked Mohammed Amin to say who I was? He replied, "A general." "My name?" "Metcalfe." "What was the duty of a general?"—which he explained in a manner that showed him well acquainted with the constitution of the Company's army. I here begged that our dialogue might be taken down in writing, to which the Mullah vehemently objected: the Pirzada ordered it to be done. I then questioned him as to the strength of the Company's army, which he stated to be a lakh and thirty thousand, of which I was the chief commander. The length of time I had been travelling?—he said, "Eight years." I then addressed the Pirzada, and pointed out the errors the Mullah had committed as to my name and

the period of my travels, and submitted the impossibility of an army such as had been described subsisting in a state of discipline during so protracted an abscncc of its commander; it being well known to all present how entirely the organisation of an armed body of men depended upon the efficiency and activity of its head. It was also absurdly improbable that an individual of the high station and command which he had assigned to me should submit to the degradation and danger which the office of a spy involved. But, besides arguments drawn from these considerations, I could produce undeniable evidence of my mercantile character, not from one or two questionable witnesses, but fifty, respectable merchants of Kabul, headed by the Sheikh ul Islam, or head of the religion, by the chief Mufti, and by the Kazi of the same city, to whom I was well known. Here the Mullah lost his temper, and inveighed against the persons I had referred to, but was checked by a reprimand from the Pirzada. Restraining his vehemence, he said he would prove me to be a spy, or submit to any punishment that might

be imposed. "This man," continued he, "wherever he goes, takes the likenesses of the mountains, rivers, towns, forts, and orchards, and has already painted, n red, and green, and yellow, every object between Sykan and Tash Kurghan." He then asserted that the English government kept up an extensive establishment of spies at every principal city between India and Turkistan, and named several individuals whom he knew to act in that capacity, they being, in fact, the news-writers of the government. These declarations made some impression upon the assembly, but I hastened to dispel them by showing the impossibility of our taking the likenesses he spoke of, as our marches were those usually performed, and we tarried nowhere on the road, unless, as in the present case, compulsorily delayed. I admitted that I made notes of many things that I witnessed in agriculture and the arts, in the hope that the information thus acquired would enable me to benefit my own country or that which I visited, and I appealed to all present if such was not a common practice with travellers in foreign coun-

tries. With regard to the agents employed by the British government I explained their originating in the necessity of counteracting the designs of the King of the French, who had declared his intention of marching to invade British India, which made it incumbent on the government of that country to procure news of his approach. The Pirzada observed this was nothing more than prudent. The Mullah then inveighed against the British power. He declared that I alone had conquered the whole of Tibet, that I had nearly taken possession of Kashmir, and that I should certainly be the means of conquering Turkistan; that Ranjit Sinh only escaped destruction by paying, annually, to us twelve lakhs of rupees, and that the disturbances in Afghanistan were entirely owing to our policy and our gold. I had had the address, he observed, to turn the tables against him, and persuade those present that I was an inoffensive person, but that he should find more reliance placed upon his evidence at Kunduz, where he would repair, and leave nothing undone to effect my destruction. If foiled in

this, he would meet me on every stage between this place and Bokhara, and, if necessary, finally appeal to the king of that city. "If you will not plunder and slay him," exclaimed he at the top of his voice, and with a most satanic expression of countenance, "send him back to his own country. Go back," he called out to me. "Why wast thou not satisfied with Tibet?—why didst thou not go to Yarkand? Go back, and leave this country, at least, in peace." He spoke with so much volubility and violence, that it was some time before I could reply, when I denied his assertions respecting myself, and the interference of my government with any of their neighbours, and expressed my astonishment at the malignity of an individual whom I had never injured, concluding by expressing my entire reliance on the wisdom and compassion of the Pirzada. The intemperance of my accuser, and the answers I had given to his accusations, had secured the judgment of the audience, and the Pirzada, turning to the Mullah, said, "The European has spoken truth—thou falsehood,—

get thee hence." He accordingly slunk away, and soon after mounted his horse for Kunduz. I withdrew to my apartment.

Shortly afterwards the Pirzada came himself to me, and said I must be aware that he was only a Fakir, and that my enemy was a powerful chief, with whom he could but be supposed ill qualified to contend: he, therefore, wished for my advice. I told him that, as the head of the religion in the country, and the spiritual guide of Murad Beg, the latter was his inferior. It was true, he replied, that, if he exercised his authority, the chief must obey, but the exercise of that authority would dissolve the union which had hitherto subsisted between them, and would create him many enemies: he wished, therefore, so to arrange the business as to secure me without incensing the chief: he would see my friend, the Sahebzada, Mir Wazir Ahmed, and discuss with him what plan it would be most prudent to adopt. Accordingly, Wazir Ahmed was sent for, and, after several interviews with the Pirzada, it was thought that a further pecuniary sacrifice might conciliate Murad Beg, and render him

less indignant at our escape. The sum first proposed was six thousand rupees, but the Pirzada reduced it to two thousand, and a messenger was sent to Kunduz to make the offer.

Soon after his departure the appearance of Mohammed Murad Beg himself at Talikan was announced; he arrived late in the afternoon, and encamped about two miles from the town. No communication took place between him and his father-in-law that evening, but it was reported to the latter that he had received the letter of the Pirzada on the road, and expressed the highest dissatisfaction at its purport, and that a durbar was held by him, at which it had been determined that the Pirzada should be compelled to abandon our cause, and that nothing less than two lakhs of rupees should purchase our liberation. The Pirzada was overwhelmed with consternation at the intelligence, and retired to his private apartments. At an unusually early hour in the morning he paid a visit to Murad Beg, which was, after a short interval, returned by the chief. What passed at the first interview I was not exactly apprized, but in the second

the Pirzada warmly advocated my cause. He had heard my accusers, he said, and was satisfied that they uttered calumnies and falsehoods; that I was no spy, but a peaceable merchant, who had come into the country upon the faith of the chief's own seal, and that I was entitled to protection; instead of which I had suffered heavy loss and delay. Now I had sought his assistance, which he had promised, and that he now considered my person and property as his own, which could not be molested without injury to his reputation. Out of consideration for the interests of the chief he had advised me to agree to a further payment of two thousand rupees, and a duty of three rupees on every horse on my return, to which I had acceded, on his pledging himself for my safety; he expected, therefore, if the chief had any respect for him, that he would be satisfied with the conditions and suffer me to depart. After some hesitation, Murad Beg acquiesced, stipulating only that my chests should be opened and examined at Kunduz. He then retired. The Pirzada accompanied him part of the way, and then came to me to tell me what had been determined.

The arrangement was satisfactory in every respect but the last, for the Pirzada, supposing all our goods to be packed in chests, had assented to the examination of all our packages. I represented to him that our bales could not be opened without injury to their contents, and he was much concerned at his mistake. It was then settled that they should not be opened, but a slit made in the envelopes on one side, so as to exhibit their contents; and a messenger was sent off to apprize the Mir of the alteration. Three days afterwards I had the satisfaction to learn that Murad Beg had refused to have the bales cut open, out of respect, as he professed, to the Pirzada.

I had hoped that on payment of the two thousand rupees we should be allowed to proceed, but Murad Beg was going out on a marauding excursion towards Mazar and Balkh, and would allow of no travelling, lest his movements should be made known. It was proposed by a messenger on his part that I should wait his return at Kunduz; but I deemed it more prudent to remain where I was, for which I readily obtained the Pirzada's permission.

CHAPTER V.

Notice of Kasim Jan—Translations from Gibbon—Lodging—Food—Prince of Badakhshan—Talikan — Khyrabad — Departure from Talikan—Kunduz—Interview with the Mir—Shah-bagli pass—Fossil Shells—Tash Kurghan—Mazar—Deh dada—Orchards—Greyhounds—Balkh—Ruined Bazar— Storm — Plain of the Oxus—Akberabad—Farakhabad—Khaja Saleh—Oxus—Ferry-boats—Kazak encampment—Optical illusion—Karshi—Visit to the Prince—Departure—Arrival at Bokhara.

KASIM JAN, khaja of Talikan, was a person of about forty, of a fair complexion and pleasing features for an Uzbek. Notwithstanding his saintly character, he was a dealer in merchandise, and especially in slaves, of whom a portion taken in his forays were usually presented to his Pirzada by Murad Beg. I saw a number of Badakhshani boys and girls detained until an opportunity offered of sending them for sale to Yarkand. Their price is from two hundred to five hundred rupees. The amount is brought back in tea, china, satin, and porcelain, which is sold in the neighbour-

ing countries. Besides the profits of trade, the Pirzada derives some advantage from his cattle, as he has one hundred brood mares, and several very large flocks of sheep ; but he is not wealthy, as he is obliged to keep open house for all comers, and accumulation would be incompatible with his religious character. Although not a man of much learning, he was intelligent and curious of information. Whilst under his protection, I attempted to render into Persian, for his use, the chapters of Gibbon which treat of Jangez Khan and Timur, in which the khaja took much interest, and corrected the style of the translation. He was much surprised that a European should have known so much of the history of the Moguls, and admitted that many of the facts were new to him, although he did not doubt their correctness. The subject was frequently spoken of by him to his attendants and visitors.

After my first interview with the Pirzada I was first lodged in a khirgah, or circular tent, the only furniture of which was a few mats, and a clay stand for a lamp ; but as this filled with travellers I was removed to a clay-walled room, with a door, and a small window with

shutters. The roof was supported by beams resting at one end on the walls, and at the other on four pillars of fir, in the centre of the apartment. Within their area was a circular clay fire-place, and over it was a small opening in the roof for the issue of the smoke. At about ten in the morning I was served with salted tea and a cake of wheaten bread, and about one with a dish of boiled rice and pulse, in the middle of which above a pint of kurut, or dried curd, brought into the consistence of cream, was poured, and over it about two ounces of melted fat from the tail of the Dumba sheep. In the evening tea was again brought me, and about ten o'clock, broth and bread, with mutton or beef, or, upon one or two occasions, with what I suspected to be horse-flesh. I had also sometimes a pilau of plain rice and mutton, dressed with Dumba fat. This fat is admirably suited for the purpose of cooking, and might recommend to epicures in England the introduction of the Dumba sheep. The cookery of the Pirzada household was performed by Badakhshani women.

Amongst the protégées of the Pirzada was Mir Mohammed Reza Beg, the fugitive bro-

ther of the last prince of Badakhshan. On questioning him regarding the descent of his family from Alexander, he stated this was impossible, as they had been settled in the country little more than a century. The Shah of Darwaz he believed to be so descended, and to possess a genealogical record of his lineage: he thought that a copy of the document might be readily obtained; but the passes were blocked up with snow whilst I was at Talikan. Neither the mines of rubies or lapis lazuli were worked; but this was not owing to their unproductiveness, but to the distracted state of the country. Iron is cast at Fyzabad, and pots and pans are supplied to the markets of Hissar and Bokhara. I had before me an iron lamp of flower and open work, which indicated that the metal must have been brought into the most complete fluidity.

Talikan is a town of considerable extent, but of a fluctuating population, as the Uzbeks migrate in the summer to the neighbouring highlands with their flocks, leaving only the Tajik cultivators and traders. The number of mud-houses of one story may amount to about fifteen hundred; but in the winter nu-

merous huts of mats and reeds, and khirgahs of lattice-work and felts, are added to the fixed habitations. There are very near to Talikan several considerable villages, and the whole population of the district must be large. The flocks and herds of sheep, goats, cows, asses, horses, and camels, were exceedingly numerous. The fleece of the sheep is good, and is mixed with a fine wool, nearly approaching in quality to shawl-wool. The fleece of the goat yields also at its roots wool of a similar description. The chief of Kunduz is said to receive annually from this district thirty-five thousand sheep, at the rate of one per cent. The fort of Talikan is a quadrangular building, with conical towers at the angles, and is of no importance. About half way between Talikan and Kunduz is the town of Khyrabad, on the right bank of the Farkham river, with a fort similar to that of Talikan. The situation is said to be healthy, in which it presents a remarkable contrast to Kunduz. The road between these places is much intersected by watercourses, and there is much sedgy land, frequented in the winter season by immense flocks of wild ducks. Ta-

likan may be about forty miles from Kunduz, but from the many detours and deviations made in my journey thither, I must have traversed between it and Khulm at least one hundred and fifty miles.

After a detention of some days we received at last the permission to proceed; but after the arrival of the messenger who brought this intimation, the Pirzada wished me to remain a day, until an auspicious moment for my departure should occur. When it arrived, and I took leave of him, he embraced me; a mark of favour I had never seen him confer upon any one before. He then blessed me, and I took my leave, sincerely grateful to him for an interposition which alone could have preserved us from destruction, and which had been exercised throughout the whole affair in a manner uniformly kind, benevolent, and, though gentle, yet resolute. Izzet Bai brought from him a present of two pieces of green China silk, and one of crimson satin brocade, with flowers of gold, the latter of which he hoped I would wear in remembrance of him. He had persisted in declining any presents of value from me, but I prevailed upon him

to accept some articles of cutlery, razors, and scissors, and a small quantity of genuine atar of roses, and of unadulterated musk. I also shortly before quitting him induced him to accept a telescope and a gold repeater, which had excited the wonder and admiration of himself, and of all his attendants.

I arrived at Kunduz on the same day, and on the following morning prepared to march, but was told that the chief wished to see me. He inquired after my health, and said he had meant to do me no harm, but only wished to ascertain who I was: he asked me what I had got for him, to which I replied by inquiring what he wished, and I found that my chair had taken his fancy. I told him if he would send a man for it it should be his. He then desired me to visit Mirza Abdul Tusah, who was ill, and had been attended by Mr. Guthrie. I met Murad Beg again at his house: some medicines had been prepared for the patient, emetics and purgatives, which were to be left with him, but Murad Beg laid his hands upon them, saying, I will take these, you can have others prepared for the Mirza.

I was seated close to Murad Beg, and scarcely ever beheld a more forbidding countenance. His excessively high-cheek bones gave the appearance to the skin of the face of its being unnaturally stretched, whilst the narrowness of the lower jaw left scarcely room for the teeth, which were standing in all directions: he was extremely near-sighted. He wanted to persuade me to leave Mr. Guthrie behind; but to this of course I would not consent. When we took leave, Abdul Tusah, who is the Mutawali, or manager of the religious establishment at Hazrat Imam, prayed for our welfare, and the hypocritical Beg held up his hands as if joining in the prayer. I then repaired to my party, and we got clear of the town before dark, encamping on the snow.

It is not worth while to record some further delays and extortions to which we were subjected on our march to Tash Kurghan, and which originated, perhaps, rather with the petty rapacity and vindictiveness of Atma Ram, than the more daring dishonesty of his master. We had to pay more than the usual duties levied on merchandise going for sale to

and from Kunduz, although our transport of goods was unconnected with traffic, and was altogether compulsory.

On descending the western face of the Sháh-bagli pass, having strayed a little from the usual line of road, I observed what appeared to be a bivalve shell, and alighting from my horse, found such numbers as to give rise to a suspicion that I was standing upon an ante-diluvian oyster bed. They were in general separated and defaced. I had not time to look for perfect specimens, but procured two which were entire. I also picked up some pebbles which looked like cats' eyes, or moon stones, along with agates in lumps, and in flat pieces with opals, also a small fragment of topaz. The face of the rock here forms part of a basin, and fronts to the east. It seems composed in a great measure of fossile shells and siliceous stones.

It was our wish to have passed through Tash Kurghan without stopping, but pecuniary arrangements detained us till nightfall. Anxious to quit a territory where we had suffered so much, we moved out and bivouacked in the snow. At midnight we recommenced

our march, accompanied by many more camels than belonged to us. Had we delayed a few hours, two hundred more would have been sent in reliance on our protection. After travelling about four hours over a plain strongly frozen, we reached the foot of the pass of Mazar.

For some time past I had lost count of the course of time, and am unable to specify the dates of my adventures at Talikan. It was on the 1st of February that we came to the borders of the district of Mazar, crossing over a low ridge of hills by a pass which is frequently the scene of an attack upon caravans. We encountered no robbers. The whole length of the pass may be about a kos: from the western face a view of Mazar opens, and at a greater distance, of buildings, said to be in the vicinity of Balkh. The country on the approach to Mazar was flat, and the soil rich, being watered by a large nala or canal, proceeding from the main trunk, called Band-amir.

At about a mile from the town we were met by a party deputed by the chief, Shujá ud Din Khan, to welcome us, and we entered

Mazar under their guidance. The snow had melted, and the water mixing with the loam rendered the streets so plashy, that our horses were sometimes up to their knees in mud. Mazar is inclosed by a mud-wall, and seems to be larger than Tash Kurghan. The houses are of clay, of one story, with either domed or flat roofs, surrounded by a court, but less separated by orchards than at Tash Kurghan. It takes its name from a tomb (Mazar), supposed to contain some of the bones of Ali. There is another mausoleum which has been of some importance, but is now in a state of dilapidation. It nevertheless preserves its sanctity, and in its neighbourhood, at a place which is marked by a pole, every mounted passenger is expected to alight and walk reverentially by. We found a house assigned for our accommodation, and the chief sent us a present of two sheep.

On the following morning we waited on the Khan, and were introduced to him in the fort, in a long, low, and narrow apartment, which seemed to have been intended for a stable: he was seated with many of his people on felts ranged along the wall, and rose and em-

braced me; he welcomed me to Mazar, and assured me of his friendship. We were then joined by the Wali of Balkh, who evinced much satisfaction at seeing me again, and both he and the Khan inveighed against the conduct of Murad Beg, as bringing shame upon all Turkistan. We then took our leave, but the badness of the weather, and the state of the roads, detained us two days at Mazar. The Khan returned our visit, and displayed the greatest kindness, promising us every assistance in his power, and giving us unsolicited letters of recommendation to the Governor of Balkh, and to the Hakim Bè, or chief minister of Bokhara. The Khan was an uncle of the Wali by the mother's side: he seemed to be about forty-five years of age, and was of middle stature, with plain, unaffected manners, and more like a Tajik than an Uzbek. He is the Mutawali, or person in charge of the Ziarat Gah, or shrine of Ali.

At the request of the Khan I visited a friend of his, who had received a sword wound a year before, and which was not yet healed. He resided at Deh Dadeh, a walled town about six miles west from Mazar: a very large

body of water, the great canal of Mazar, flowed by it, and was seen to come from a gorge in the hills at some distance. The orchards of Deh Dadeh are famous for pomegranates and plums. There are two kinds of the latter; one a large black plum or gage, the other, called Kara Alu, the damson of England. This is preserved in an intermediate state between dry and fresh, so perfectly, that the skin can be readily separated from the pulp: at the time I had an opportunity of tasting it, the beginning of February, it was infinitely preferable to the best French prune. The plums are gathered with their footstalks, and tied with thread to a willow twig so that they do not touch; they are then hung up to dry. Deh Dadeh is also celebrated for its breed of greyhounds, and for brown or Nankin cotton, called there the Mullah's cotton; vestments made of it unbleached being worn almost exclusively by that class of persons, many of whom reside at Mazar.

After clearing the dirty lanes and suburbs of Mazar, we passed upon the left the fort and village of Shirabad, the residence of the brother of the Mutawali, and beyond this Deh

Dadeh. We then passed a break in a ridge of hills to our left, whence issued the main stream of the water of Balkh, or the eighteen canal river, from its feeding formerly that number of watercourses; the greater part had been choked, but some had been recently cleared by order of the Governor of Balkh. One large branch is that which supplies Mazar. A short distance in advance brought us to the ruins of some buildings, said to have been the elephant stables of the kings of Turkistan: similar remains accompanied the road to the wall of the modern town, which we entered by a mean gateway, the folding-doors of which were off their hinges and lying in the mud, no insignificant type of neglect and decay. The same prevailed in the streets, along which we made our way with difficulty over heaps of rubbish and broken bricks, and between long lines of clay walls in a crumbling and ruinous condition. Passing by the face of an unfinished college we entered a narrow bazar, covered in some places by a coarse and imperfect roof of wood, and in others by a half-destroyed roofing of brick; it was about six or seven hundred yards long,

and was almost the only inhabited remains of the once-celebrated capital of Bactria: issuing by the gate at the end of the bazar, we halted close to the walls of an extensive, but seemingly scantily inhabited fort, the residence of the governor, Ishán Khaja.

Some indecision was shown in assigning a place for our stay, and at last we were directed to a mulberry ground, the soil of which was a perfect quagmire. We had scarcely pitched our tents when a strong wind blew, and heavy rain and snow falling, made our position uncomfortable in the extreme. On the day after our arrival the snow prevented our going out, but on the next day we waited on the governor, who received us kindly: he expressed himself highly indignant at the conduct of Murad Beg, and disposed to forward our journey by any means in his power. He was a man of about forty, of a dark complexion, and disfigured by the loss of his nose from disease, a deformity which I observed very common at Talikan, Mazar, and Balkh, in young persons of both sexes. The whole circumference of Balkh, including the Bala Hissar, or fort, may be between four or five

miles, marked by the remains of an irregular and indifferently constructed brick and mud wall; the number of inhabited houses is inconsiderable. There are no relics of antiquity, nor of any buildings of note, except the mausoleum of the Khwaja Parsi, which has been elegantly fronted with enamelled tiles. The population exceeds not a thousand families, with a few Hindus and Jews: the former are shopkeepers, the latter shopkeepers and mechanics. They are subject to the Jezia, a capitation tax on infidels; the Hindus are known by a painted mark on the forehead, the Jews by wearing a black sheep-skin cap: commerce seemed to be at a low ebb, and nothing of material value was exhibited in the bazar.

We left Balkh about noon on the 8th of February, and marching over a continuation of the plain, arrived at day-break at Tule Yek, a village contiguous on the east to another called Karshi Yek, or Little Karshi, containing together about six hundred houses, and defended by two redoubts of clay. These villages are situated on the edge of the desert plain that leads to the Amu, and are famous

for their melons, which are said to be the finest in Turkistan. Broken walls and heaps of rubbish show the neighbourhood to have been at one time thickly inhabited, and in every direction are seen large mounds, which, though now coated with earth, consist probably of architectural remains. The orchards of this place are fertilized by the Balkh river, none of the waters of which reach the Oxus, being wholly absorbed in the process of irrigation.

Akberabad is a walled village of some size, with very extensive ruins. The houses, though of but one story, are capacious, some of them having half a dozen good-sized chambers. They were built of clay and pebbles, or of sun-dried bricks, surmounted by domes. These buildings, with occasional repair, were said to last a very long time, although there is no scarcity of rain or snow.

At a place called Panjal, a village of four or five hundred houses, I was informed that large silver coins, with legends in an unknown character, are sometimes found, and that not long since a number of gold coins, with the figure of a man, were discovered. They had all, however, been consigned to the crucible.

A few kos from Akberabad we came to Farakhabad, a place where there were extensive ruins, but merely of earth or sun-dried bricks. Contiguous to them are the remains of a pleasure-ground, with a square building, called Takhti Khan. The edifice must once have been very elegant, having been constructed of white marble, embellished with enamelled tiles of the colour of the turquoise and lapis lazuli. It consists of one central and several lateral chambers, surmounted by domes, but having a flat platform at their bases. The interior walls of the apartment are lined half way with the coloured bricks, and are painted with white flowers on a blue ground; some of the tiles and the cornices have been inlaid with gold. Two causeways skirting a canal have formerly led to the principal entrances.

Sirdaba, about two kos from Takhti Khan, is a large reservoir, supplied by rain and melted snow. It has been constructed in the centre of a natural basin, formed by the slope of the ground about it. There had been a serai adjoining it, but it was entirely destroyed. Both were the work of Abdullah Khan, who

was the great benefactor of all this part of Turkistan.

Khwaja Salah owes its origin and its name, it is said, to a saint so called, who, being detained on the bank of the river at this place, founded a village. It is usually a place of some population; but whilst we were at Tash Kurghan it was surprised by a party of marauders, who put all the men to the sword, and carried off the women and children as slaves. We found it without inhabitants. The assailants were, it was uniformly reported, Turkmans from Urganj; but it was difficult to suppose they could have been Urganjis, as in that case they must have been fully twenty days upon the road. Mymana is three days' ordinary marching, and travellers state that Urganj is from fifteen to twenty days beyond it, many of which lie across a desert. The ferry of Khwaja Salah had three boats, each capable of containing twenty horses, for the passage of each of which, and for each camel, the charge was one tanga.

The Oxus, at the ferry of Khwaja Salah, appeared to be about as broad as the Thames opposite the Temple gardens; but we found,

upon trial, that a rifle, and even a carbine, carried a ball to the opposite bank: higher up it was much broader, and was divided into two streams by an island, and the breadth of the sandy bed on the right bank, now dry, was about one thousand five hundred paces broad. When full, the river may be about two thousand two hundred paces in breadth. The current was less rapid than I expected to have found it, not exceeding two miles an hour; the depth nowhere exceeded five fathoms. The banks were low, and the soil loose, like those of the Ganges, and the water was similarly discoloured by sand.

This river begins to rise in April, and remains full till July, when it again falls. When at its height it inundates the plain on either side, but especially on the right bank. The extent of its inundation is marked by a belt of sedge and weeds, and then by a thick jangal of dwarf trees and brushwood. Of the former the principal is called Patta, and is of great service to the people, as the boats are constructed of its timber. The Oxus is said to be navigable from Syah to Urganj, the distance between which two points is five hun-

dred kos. No use of it, however, is made for commerce, and the only boats upon it are ferry-boats. These are made of the entire trunks of the Patta-tree, used as planks simply squared and fastened together by clamps of iron. The oars are two crooked pieces of timber, not in the least trimmed, whilst a third serves the purpose of a rudder: these are sufficient in calm weather, and when the current is moderate. At other periods a different mode of crossing is had recourse to.

We arrived at the river on the morning of the 11th, but the wind was too violent to permit our making the passage. After several boats had crossed the wind increased, on which the boatmen adopted the novel plan of employing horses to tow the boats over the river. Two horses were fastened, one behind the other, to each boat, on the side next the current; two locks of the mane were tied together to form a noose, through which a halter was passed and fastened to a stout bight in the bow; a bridle was put into the horse's mouth, and that of the leader was secured to a stout staff held by a man opposite his head: the bridle of the rear horse was held by a man

in the boat, the object being not only to guide the horses, but to keep their heads above water. A second man, attached to each horse, prevented him from being carried under the boat, either with his leg over the side or with a pole. The horses were taken indiscriminately from our train, and although at first somewhat frightened, yet soon overcame their fear, and worked with good will, carrying the boats across in about ten or fifteen minutes. We encamped on the right bank close to the water. On the following day we passed through an owal, or station of Khirgahs and Kappahs, or circular huts of mats and reeds, with a conical top. Horses stood saddled at the doors of the tents, and mares and foals, and many camels, were grazing in the adjoining jangal. The cows were stabled in holes made in the ground, roofed with branches of trees and grass, and covered with sand and bushes. The dogs were of middle size, of a foxy colour, but strong and courageous. There were also many good-looking greyhounds. The people were Kazaks. We met here some Turkman women, some riding on camels, some on horseback behind men; they had

turbans on their heads, with a yellow silk veil, which some of them dropped over their faces, whilst others indulged their curiosity freely. The faces we saw were broad and plump, of the true Uzbek character.

On this day's march I was the subject of an optical illusion of a very striking description. At about two hours after daylight I had ridden away from the caravan to examine some ruins to the north, and was contemplating the hills beyond Khilef, when my attention was suddenly arrested by a large isolated building on the plain to the north-west, apparently about four or five miles distant. The morning was frosty but clear. I was in perfect health and self-possession, and looked repeatedly at the edifice, which, though low, appeared to be extensive. As I galloped towards it to take a nearer view, it became more distinct, and shone in the sun, the rays of which now fell upon it as if it were of marble. Although I held on my route, my attention was for a moment diverted by beholding my friend Trebeck gaining upon a flock of bustards, and driving them across my track, and on again turning my eyes towards the sup-

posed palace, it had vanished. I saw merely the range of rocks on which stands the fort of Khilef. I was the only one of the party whose eyes had thus been deceived.

On this and the two following marches the road continued across a desert plain, in which not a tree was discernible, and where, in summer, water is scarce, and of brackish quality. At the time we traversed the plain heavy rain and snow fell, and the soil was everywhere soft and miry, occasioning great distress to our cattle, as well as discomfort to ourselves. We arrived at Karshi on the 16th.

Karshi is a town that is considered second in importance only to Bokhara. It is situated in an oasis, in the midst of the arid tract that separates that city from the Oxus, and which owes its fertility to the waters of a river from the mountains to the eastward of Shahr Sabz, a place three marches distant, usually subject to Bokhara, but at present in a state of revolt. Karshi did not appear, however, to be of great extent. The houses were generally of mud, and flat-roofed, standing in the midst of orchards, except in the

case of the shops in the bazar. The population is fluctuating, as the nomadic tribes come in with their families during winter, and go out again in summer. The resident population, consisting in the largest proportion of Tajiks, amounts to about twenty thousand families: in the winter the number may be doubled, when the Uzbeks predominate. The plain around Karshi is irrigated by cuts from the river, the water of which is expended a little further to the westward. Besides the orchards, which are numerous and highly productive, wheat and barley are cultivated, and the bread made from the former is remarkably light and well tasted. The following were the prices of various articles of provision at the time of our arrival, converted into English denominations. Barley about twelve pounds for sixpence. Broken straw from eightpence to one shilling for a horse-load. Fuel was scarce and dear; a camel load of the plant resembling broom, gathered green, and emitting more smoke than heat, and packed so loosely that the load could be easily carried by a horse, was about a rupee. Ghee, or clarified butter,

three pounds for a rupee. Sheeptail butter, five pounds for the same. Wheat flour, a penny a pound. Rice, eight pounds for eighteenpence. Grape syrup, which is used throughout these countries as a substitute for sugar, threepence a pound. Mutton, about fourpence a pound; but it was the least good of any we had eaten since leaving Hindustan. A cake of wheaten bread, two of which were a good meal for a man, cost about a pyce of Hindustan, or less than a halfpenny. Unseasonable cold had damaged the blossoms of the apricots, and the fruit was unusually dear.

It had been intimated to us that on the third day after our arrival we were expected to wait upon the Prince, Tora Bahadar, who was the governor of Karshi, a lad of about sixteen, the son of the king by a bondmaid, and, accordingly, on the 19th, at an early hour, we were summoned to an audience, and desired to bring our soldiers with their arms. As we passed along the streets we found them knee-deep in mud, under which the surface, which it concealed, was broken into ruts and holes which rendered it danger-

ous to proceed. I had seen bad roads in other countries, and particularly the cross roads of some parts of Normandy in a wet winter, but they were absolutely good in comparison with the streets of the second city of the kingdom of Bokhara. We managed, however, to make way without any serious mishap, until we were desired to stop in an open area, fronted by three large brick and mortar colleges of two stories, of which the iron latticed windows gave them the aspect of prisons rather than of seminaries of learning. We halted here for about a quarter of an hour, during which several Uzbeks, whose clothing bespoke them of a respectable class of the community, passed us, as if on their way to the court. From hence we proceeded to a gate-house, where we were desired to dismount. Within the gateway was a raised apartment on either hand, open to the front, in which a number of persons were seated. On entering an interior road, walled on each side, with a seat of earth the whole length, we saw other persons, of whom the principal was a fair, stout, short, good-humoured looking personage, in a dress of

China gold-flowered brocade; this was the master of the ceremonies. He was attended by his deputy, who was dressed in a coat of purple broad cloth, and held a painted and gilded stick. After instructing us in the manner of paying our respects, which consists in crossing the arms upon the breast, and bowing the head, these officers conducted us to a large court, opposite to the gateway of which was a line of men with white wands. When arrived at the middle of the area, the sides of which were lined by well-dressed persons, we saw the Prince sitting on the floor, in the opening of a small door opposite. After making our obeisance, we were desired to sit, or rather kneel, and then, in imitation of the master of the ceremonies, raised our hands, open, with the palms inwards, to a level with our faces, whilst our prompter recited the usual prayer. At the conclusion we stroked our beards, rose, sat down again, repeated our salutation, and once more stood up, when we were told we might depart.

The Prince was a ruddy, well-looking youth, whose face was in a constant smile

whilst we were in his presence, which scarcely exceeded three minutes. The master of the ceremonies attended us to the court-door, when his deputy conducted us to seats in the passage, and we stopped about ten minutes longer, during which many of those who had had an audience came forth. It was then signified that the ceremonial was over, and that we might depart on the morrow. The manner in which we had been received was, according to Uzbek etiquette, highly respectful, and augured well for our reception at Bokhara. The conduct of the people was also very civil, and although their curiosity was somewhat troublesome, it was never rude. They pressed upon us in great numbers both in the streets and at our tents, but when they crowded too much about us the Yasawal rushed amongst them, and with a long and thick stick distributed blows at random, which speedily cleared the ground. The more respectable who were allowed to approach repeatedly said that we were objects of great interest to them, as they had never seen any of our countrymen. The questions they asked us were very much alike, and were not very

sapient. It was a remark which frequently occurred to us, on our journey in Turkistan, that a singularly uniform mediocrity of intellect prevailed amongst even the best informed of the Uzbek population. It was rare indeed to find an individual shrewd or sagacious beyond his fellows.

We left Karshi on the 21st of February, and resumed our journey to Bokhara. The country we traversed resembled that we had passed between Karshi and the Oxus: after quitting the confines of the strip of cultivated ground on which that city stands, we again came to a sandy and steril tract, less undulating than that nearer the river, but equally unproductive. It was with no slender satisfaction that on the morning of the 25th of February, 1825, we found ourselves at the end of our protracted pilgrimage, at the gates of that city which had for five years been the object of our wanderings, privations, and perils.

THE END.